.NET DEVELOPER'S GUIDE

murach's C#

Joel Murach
Doug Lowe

MIKE MURACH & ASSOCIATES, INC

3484 W. Gettysburg Ave., Suite 101 • Fresno, CA 93722-7801
www.murach.com • murachbooks@murach.com

Authors: Doug Lowe
Joel Murach

Editor: Anne Prince

Cover Design: Zylka Design

Production: Tom Murach
Karen Schletewitz

Other books for .NET programmers

Murach's ASP.NET 2.0 Upgrader's Guide: C# Edition

Murach's ASP.NET 2.0 Upgrader's Guide: VB Edition

Murach's ASP.NET Web Programming with VB.NET

Murach's Beginning Visual Basic .NET

Murach's VB.NET Database Programming with ADO.NET

Murach's SQL for SQL Server

Two books for Java programmers

Murach's Beginning Java 2, JDK 5.0

Murach's Java Servlets and JSP

Four books for IBM mainframe programmers

Murach's Mainframe COBOL

Murach's CICS for the COBOL Programmer

Murach's OS/390 and z/OS JCL

DB2 for the COBOL Programmer, Part 1

Printed in the United States of America

10 9 8 7 6 5 4 3 2
ISBN: 1-890774-22-7

Contents

Expanded contents

Section 1 Introduction to C# programming

Chapter 6 How to code methods and event handlers

Chapter 7 How to handle exceptions and validate data

Chapter 8 How to use arrays and collections

Chapter 14 How to work with inheritance

Chapter 15 How to work with interfaces, structures, and class libraries

Section 4 Database programming with C#

Chapter 16 An introduction to database programming

Chapter 17 How to develop a simple database application

Section 5 Specialized skills for C# developers

Chapter 21 How to work with text and binary files

Chapter 22 How to work with XML

Chapter 23 How to enhance the user interface

Introduction

Visual C# is quickly becoming the programming language of choice for Microsoft's .NET Framework. C# is an elegant, object-oriented language that uses syntax that's similar to C++ and Java. As a result, it provides an easy migration path for C++ and Java developers who want to leverage the power of the .NET Framework. In addition, C# provides an opportunity for Visual Basic developers to learn a new language that's in the C++ family without leaving the comfort of Microsoft's development environment, Visual Studio.

Who this book is for

This book is for anyone who wants to learn how to use C# for developing professional Windows applications using Visual Studio and the .NET Framework. That includes the entire range from beginning programmers to experienced Java, C++, and Visual Basic programmers.

To be able to work equally well for beginners, experts, and everyone in between, this book uses a unique, modular instructional method that allows you to set your own pace through the material. For example, section 1 expertly guides you through the basics of using the Visual Studio IDE and the .NET Framework. Whether you are a Java or C++ programmer or a complete beginner, you can get up to speed quickly with this development environment by reading this section and doing the exercises at the end of each chapter. On the other hand, if you're a Visual Basic programmer who is already comfortable with this IDE and Framework, you can skip or skim this section.

Sections 2 and 3 use the same modular, self-paced approach to methodically teach the coding skills that you need to become productive with the C# language. If you're already familiar with another language in the C++ family, such as Java, you should be able to move through this section quickly, focusing on the classes and methods that are available from the .NET Framework. Conversely, if you're already familiar with .NET, you can focus on the details of the C# syntax. Either way, you're going to learn C#, and you're going to learn it at a pace that's right for you.

Once you complete the first three sections of this book, section 4 shows how to use ADO.NET to develop database applications with C#. Unlike most other C# books that only have one introductory chapter on ADO.NET, though, this book has *five* chapters! And these five chapters show how to develop ADO.NET applications the way they're developed by the best professionals. In fact, we think you're going to find that this is really two books in one: a C# book and an ADO.NET book.

What software this book works with

This book is designed specifically for version 7.1 of C#, the version that's supplied with Visual Studio 2003 or the less-expensive (about $99) Visual C# Standard Edition 2003. However, it will also work if you're using version 7.0, the version that comes with Visual Studio 2002 or Visual C# Standard Edition 2002.

Although the C# language itself is the same for versions 7.0 and 7.1, there are a few minor differences in the .NET Framework classes used by each version. There are also minor differences in the development environments for the 2002 and 2003 versions. Still, you should have no trouble using this book with either version.

When you get to the database section of this book, you'll need to have a database server available if you want to create and test your own database applications. You can use any database server that works with the .NET Framework for this purpose. However, this book is designed to work with Microsoft SQL Server 2000. Fortunately, you don't have to install SQL Server 2000 to create and test SQL Server applications. Instead, you can download and install the free desktop version of SQL Server, called MSDE, from Microsoft's web site. You'll find more information about installing Visual Studio and MSDE in appendix A.

What this book does

- Section 1 tours the .NET Framework and teaches the basics of working with Microsoft's development environment, Visual Studio .NET. In this section, you'll learn how to develop a simple Windows application. To do that, you'll use the Forms Designer to design a Windows form, and you'll use the Code Editor to add and edit the code for the form.
- Section 2 presents the data types, control structures, and other essential elements of the C# language as well as the core .NET classes you'll use to develop basic Windows applications. Along the way, you'll also learn how to handle the tasks that are required in most business apps. In chapter 7, for example, you'll learn professional data validation techniques that we haven't seen presented in any competing book, even though data validation is an essential part of every business application.
- Section 3 teaches the powerful object-oriented programming features of the C# language. You'll learn how to create and use your own custom business objects, and you'll learn how to use database classes to populate those objects with data from files or a database. That, of course, is how applications work in the real world, even though most C# books don't show you that. In this section, you'll also learn how to use inheritance, polymorphism, interfaces, and much more. Even if you're an experienced programmer, we think you'll find that this book brings a new clarity to all of these subjects.

- Section 4 teaches you how to use ADO.NET to develop database applications because these applications account for most of the applications in the business world. Here, you'll start by learning how to use a wizard to create the ADO.NET database objects and how to work with typed datasets that use bound and unbound controls. But then, you'll also learn how to use untyped datasets and data commands to create database classes that work with the three-tiered architecture that's commonly used by object-oriented applications.
- Section 5 shows how to work with text files, binary files, and XML. You'll also learn how to enhance a Windows interface with a Multi-Document Interface (MDI), menus, toolbars, and help, all finishing touches that make your applications thoroughly professional.

Why you'll learn faster and better with this book

Like all our books, this one has features that you won't find in competing books. That's why we believe that you'll learn faster and better with our book than with any other. Here are five of those features.

- Unlike other C# books, this book shows you how to get the most from Visual Studio as you develop your applications. Many C# books ignore Visual Studio or don't get to it until late in the book. However, using the features of this IDE is one of the keys to development productivity. So we incorporate Visual Studio throughout the entire book.
- The exercises at the end of each chapter give you a chance to apply what you've learned and gain valuable, hands-on experience. These exercises expertly guide you through the development of some of the book's applications, and they challenge you to apply what you've learned in new ways. Because we provide the starting points for the exercises from our web site, you get the maximum amount of practice in a minimum of time.
- Unlike most other C# books, all of the examples presented in this book are drawn from real-life business applications. This difference becomes especially apparent in the object-oriented programming section, where most C# books resort to silly metaphors rather than realistic examples. For example, many books illustrate objects by creating animal classes such as mammals, cats, and dogs. Other books use vehicle classes such as trucks, cars, and motorcycles. Then they leave it up to you to figure out how to transfer these concepts to business applications. In contrast, we present realistic business objects such as customers, invoices, and products so you can see how object-oriented programming is used in the real world.
- To help you develop applications at a professional level, this book presents 12 complete, non-trivial applications. For example, chapter 20 presents an Order Entry database application that uses business classes, database classes, and transactions. You won't find sophisticated business applications like this in other C# books, even though studying these types of applications is the best way to master C# development.

- All of the information in this book is presented in our unique paired-page format with the essential syntax, guidelines, and examples on the right page and the perspective and extra explanation on the left page. Programmers tell us that they love this format because they can learn new skills whenever they have a few minutes and because they can quickly get the information that they need when they use our books for reference.

Downloadable files that can help you learn

If you go to our web site at www.murach.com, you can download the files that you need for doing the exercises in this book. These files include:

- the starting points for the exercises throughout the book
- the database for the exercises in section 4
- the text, binary, and XML files for the exercises in section 5

In addition, you can download some of the applications that are described in the book so you can view the complete source code and run them on your own PC.

Support materials for trainers and instructors

If you're a trainer or instructor who would like to use this book for a course, we offer an Instructor's CD that includes everything that you need for an effective course. This CD includes solutions to the exercises, a complete set of PowerPoint slides, multiple-choice tests, student projects, and solutions to the projects.

To download a sample of this Instructor's Guide and to find out how to get the complete Guide, please visit our web site at www.murach.com and click on the Instructors link. Or, if you prefer, call Kelly at 1-800-221-5528 or send an email to kelly@murach.com.

Please let us know how this book works for you

When we started working with C#, we found that it presented many complexities that weren't adequately treated by the documentation or the available books. So our goal in writing this book has been to make it the book we wish we'd had when we were learning. Now that we're done, we hope that the months of effort we put into its development will help you become a proficient C# programmer in just a few weeks.

So if you have any comments about this book, we would appreciate hearing from you. And good luck with your C# programming.

Doug Lowe, Author
doug@murach.com

Joel Murach, Author
joelmurach@yahoo.com

Section 1

Introduction to C# programming

This section gets you started right by giving you a solid introduction to C# programming. After chapter 1 introduces you to Visual Studio and the .NET development environment, chapter 2 shows you how to use Visual Studio to design a form for a Windows application. Then, chapter 3 shows you how enter and edit the code that determines how the form works.

When you complete this section, you should have a general understanding of what you do when you develop a Windows application with Visual Studio .NET and C#. You should also have the skills that you need for designing a Windows form and entering the code for it. Then, the next section of this book will teach you the essentials of the C# language.

Introduction to Visual Studio .NET

Before you can learn how to develop applications with the C# language, you need to become familiar with the .NET Framework and Visual Studio .NET. So that's what you'll be introduced to in this chapter. Along the way, you'll learn some basic concepts and skills for working with the .NET Framework and Visual Studio .NET.

An introduction to the .NET Framework and Visual Studio .NET

The *.NET Framework* (pronounced "dot net framework") defines the environment that you use to execute Visual C# .NET applications and the services you can use within those applications. One of the main goals of this framework is to make it easier to develop applications that run over the Internet. However, this framework can also be used to develop traditional business applications that run on the Windows desktop.

To develop a .NET application, you use a product called *Visual Studio .NET* (pronounced "Visual Studio dot net"). This is actually a suite of products that includes the four programming languages described in figure 1-1. In this book, of course, you'll learn how to use *Visual C# .NET* (pronounced "Visual C sharp dot net"), which we'll refer to as simply C#.

The three other languages that come with Visual Studio .NET are Visual Basic, C++, and J#. Visual Basic .NET uses some of the same syntax as Microsoft Visual Basic 6, but it has been completely redesigned to work with the .NET Framework. Visual C++ .NET is Microsoft's version of the C++ language. And Visual J# .NET is Microsoft's version of the Java language.

To develop applications in any of these languages, you use a component of Visual Studio .NET called the *Integrated Development Environment* (*IDE*). The IDE lets you design and code C# applications as well as manage the files they contain. You'll learn how to work with the IDE throughout this book.

In this figure, you can see that Visual Studio .NET can be used on any PC that runs Windows 2000 or later. You can also see that the applications that are developed with Visual Studio .NET can be run on any PC that runs Windows 98 or later, depending on which .NET components are used by the application. From a practical point of view, though, you can assume that the applications that you develop with C# will be run on PCs that are using Windows 2000 or later.

This figure also shows that Visual Studio .NET comes in an inexpensive Standard Edition that includes only the C# language. All of the C# features presented in this book work with the Standard Edition as well as the full Visual Studio .NET.

Although the four languages shown in this figure are the only four programming languages that come with Visual Studio .NET, other vendors are free to develop languages for the .NET Framework. For example, Fujitsu has already developed a version of COBOL for the .NET Framework.

Programming languages supported by Visual Studio .NET

Language	Description
Visual Basic .NET	Designed for rapid application development
Visual C# .NET	A new language that combines the features of Java and C++ and is suitable for rapid application development
Visual C++ .NET	Microsoft's version of C++ that can be used for developing high-performance applications
Visual J# .NET	Microsoft's version of Java that can be used for developing high-performance applications

Platforms that can run Visual Studio .NET

- Windows 2000 and later releases of Windows

Platforms that can run Visual Studio .NET applications

- Windows 98 and later releases of Windows, depending on which .NET components the application uses

Visual C# .NET Standard Edition

- An inexpensive alternative to the complete Visual Studio .NET package that supports a limited version of Visual C# .NET as its only programming language

Description

- The *.NET Framework* defines the environment that you use for executing C# applications.
- *Visual Studio .NET* is a suite of products that includes all four of the programming languages listed above. These languages run within the .NET Framework.
- To develop applications in Visual Studio .NET, you use its *Integrated Development Environment* (*IDE*). You can use this IDE with any of the four supported languages.
- You can develop business applications using either *C#* or Visual Basic .NET. Because these languages are integrated with the development environment, the development techniques are similar. However, the language details vary.
- Besides the programming languages listed above, third-party vendors can develop languages for the .NET Framework.
- Microsoft also provides a desktop version of their SQL Server database management system, called the *Microsoft SQL Server 2000 Desktop Engine* (*MSDE*), that you can use to develop database applications from Visual Studio .NET. You can download MSDE from the Microsoft web site free of charge. For details, see appendix A.

Figure 1-1 Visual Studio .NET and the .NET Framework

Windows Forms and Web Forms applications

You can use C# for developing the two types of applications shown in figure 1-2. A *Windows Forms application* is a typical Windows application that runs on the user's PC. Each *Windows form* (or just *form*) in the application provides a user interface that lets the user interact with the application. In the example in this figure, the application consists of a single form that lets the user perform either of two calculations: a future value or a monthly investment calculation. Many applications, though, require more than one form.

As part of the user interface, a Windows Forms application uses *Windows Forms controls*. For instance, the form in this figure uses radio buttons, labels, text boxes, and buttons. In the next chapter, you'll start learning how to develop Windows Forms applications.

The other type of application that you can develop with C# is a *Web Forms application*. Like a Windows Forms application, a Web Forms application consists of one or more *web forms* that can contain controls. Unlike Windows forms, web forms are accessed by and displayed in a *web browser*. For instance, the web form in this figure is displayed in Microsoft's web browser, which is called the Internet Explorer.

As part of the user interface, a web form uses *Web Forms controls*. These controls are similar to the Windows Forms controls, but they work only with web forms.

In contrast to a Windows Forms application, which runs on the user's PC, the code for a Web Forms application runs on a web server. As this code is executed, it passes the visual portion of the application to the browser running on the client in the form of HTML (Hypertext Markup Language). The browser then interprets the HTML and displays the form.

A Windows Forms application running on the Windows desktop

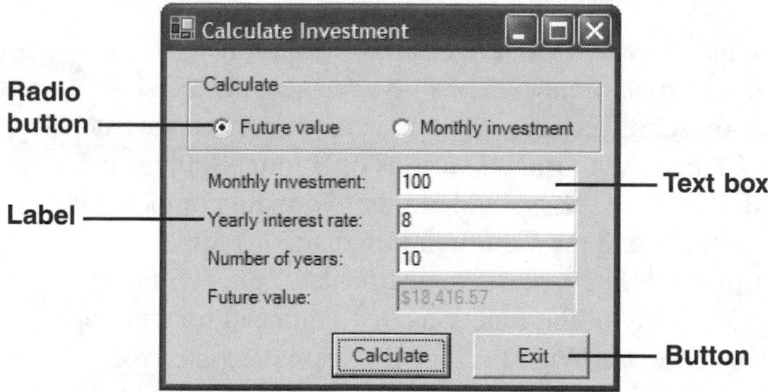

A Web Forms application running in a Web browser

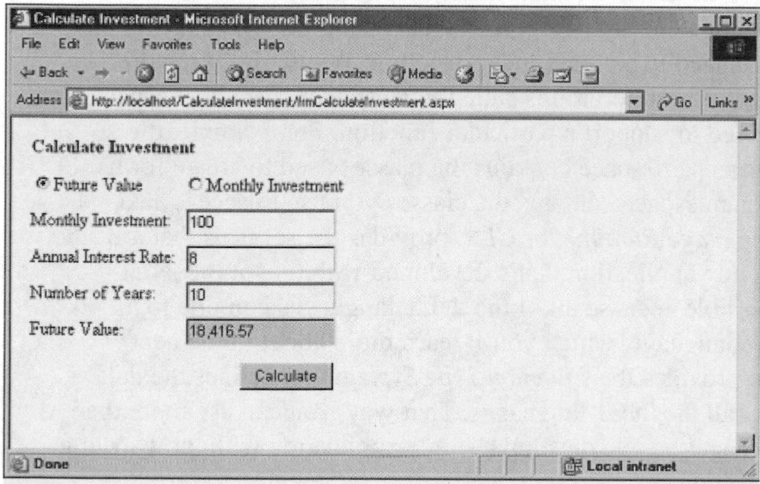

Description

- A *Windows Forms application* runs in its own window and can consist of one or more *Windows forms* that provide the graphical user interface (GUI) for the application.
- Each Windows form can contain *Windows Forms controls* like labels, text boxes, buttons, and radio buttons. These controls let the user interact with the application.
- A *Web Forms application* runs on a web server, but its user interface is displayed in a *web browser* on the client machine. A Web Forms application consists of one or more *web forms* that provide the user interface for the application.
- Each web form can contain *Web Forms controls* like labels, text boxes, buttons, and radio buttons.

Figure 1-2 Windows Forms and Web Forms applications

The components of the .NET Framework

To give you a more detailed view of the .NET Framework, figure 1-3 presents the main components of this framework. As you can see, the .NET Framework provides a common set of services that application programs written in a .NET language such as C# can use to run on various operating systems and hardware platforms. The .NET Framework is divided into two main components: the .NET Framework Class Library and the Common Language Runtime.

The *.NET Framework Class Library* consists of segments of pre-written code called *classes* that provide many of the functions that you need for developing .NET applications. For instance, the Windows Forms classes are used for developing Windows Forms applications. The ASP.NET classes are used for developing Web Forms applications. And other classes let you work with databases, manage security, access files, and perform many other functions.

Although it's not apparent in this figure, the classes in the .NET Framework Class Library are organized in a hierarchical structure. Within this structure, related classes are organized into groups called *namespaces*. Each namespace contains the classes used to support a particular function. For example, the System.Windows.Forms namespace contains the classes used to create forms and the System.Data namespace contains the classes you use to access data.

The *Common Language Runtime*, or *CLR*, provides the services that are needed for executing any application that's developed with one of the .NET languages. This is possible because all of the .NET languages compile to a common intermediate language, which you'll learn more about in the next figure. The CLR also provides the *Common Type System* that defines the data types that are used by all the .NET languages. That way, you can use more than one of the .NET languages as you develop a single application without worrying about incompatible data types.

If you're new to programming, you might not understand this diagram completely, but that's all right. For now, all you need to understand is the general structure of the .NET Framework and the terms that have been presented so far. As you progress through this book, this diagram will begin to make more sense, and you will become more familiar with each of the terms.

The .NET Framework

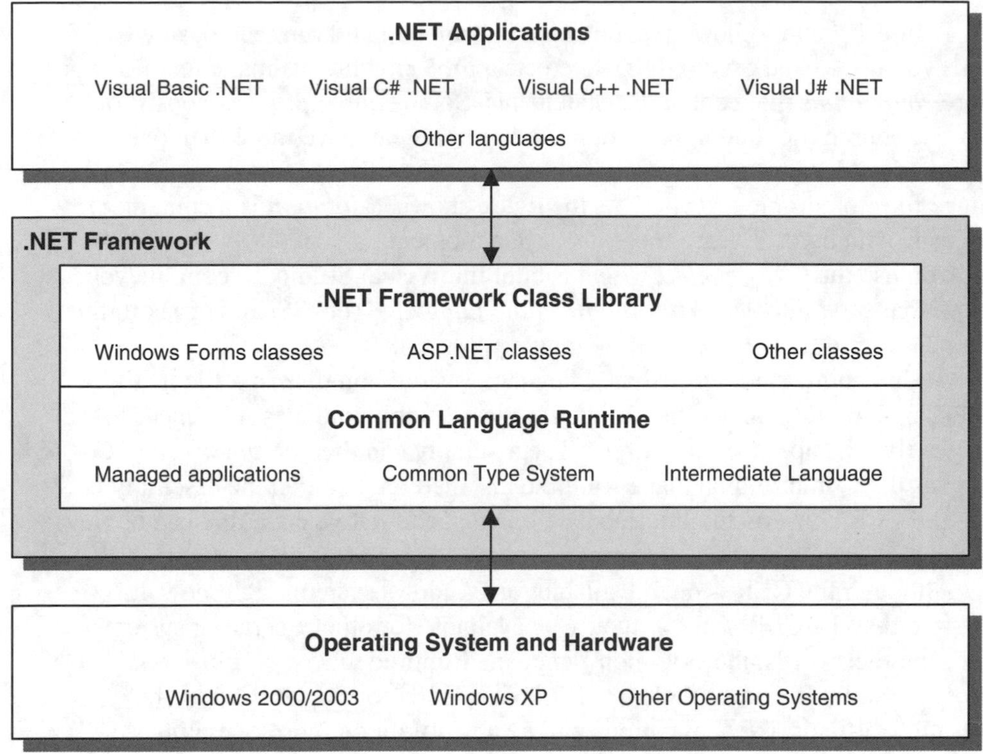

Description

- .NET applications do not access the operating system or computer hardware directly. Instead, they use services of the .NET Framework, which in turn access the operating system and hardware.
- The .NET Framework consists of two main components: the .NET Framework Class Library and the Common Language Runtime.
- The *.NET Framework Class Library* provides pre-written code in the form of *classes* that are available to all of the .NET programming languages. This class library consists of hundreds of classes, but you can create simple .NET applications once you learn how to use just a few of them.
- The *Common Language Runtime*, or *CLR*, is the foundation of the .NET Framework. It manages the execution of .NET programs by coordinating essential functions such as memory management, code execution, security, and other services. Because .NET applications are managed by the CLR, they are called *managed applications*.
- The *Common Type System* is a component of the CLR that ensures that all .NET applications use the same basic data types regardless of what programming languages were used to develop the applications.

Figure 1-3 The components of the .NET Framework

How a C# application is compiled and run

Figure 1-4 shows how an application is compiled and run when using C#. To start, you use Visual Studio .NET to create a *project,* which is made up of one or more *source files* that contain C# statements. Some simple projects consist of just one source file, but more complicated projects can have more than one source file. A project may also contain other types of files, such as sound files, image files, or simple text files. As the figure shows, a *solution* is a container for projects, which you'll learn more about in a moment.

You use the C# *compiler*, which is built into Visual Studio, to compile your C# source code into *Microsoft Intermediate Language* (or *MSIL*). For short, this can be referred to as *Intermediate Language* (or *IL*).

At this point, the Intermediate Language is stored on disk in a file that's called an *assembly*. In addition to the IL, the assembly includes references to the classes that the application requires. The assembly can then be run on any PC that has the Common Language Runtime installed on it. When the assembly is run, the CLR converts the Intermediate Language to native code that can be run by the Windows operating system.

Although the CLR is only available for Windows systems right now, it is possible that the CLR will eventually be available for other operating systems as well. In other words, the Common Language Runtime makes *platform independence* possible. If, for example, a CLR is developed for the Unix and Linux operating systems, C# applications will be able to run on those operating systems as well as Windows operating systems. Whether this will happen and how well it will work remains to be seen.

How C# differs from the other .NET languages

C# uses the same .NET Framework classes as all of the other .NET programming languages. These classes affect almost every aspect of programming, including creating and working with forms and controls, using databases, and even working with basic language features such as arrays and strings. In addition, C# works with the same Visual Studio .NET development environment as the other .NET languages. As a result, C# has many similarities to the other .NET languages. The main difference is the syntax of the language.

How C# differs from Java

The C# language uses a syntax that's similar to the syntax for the Java language. However, Java relies on a different framework of supporting classes, and the development environments for working with Java are different than Visual Studio .NET. As a result, if you have experience with Java, it should be easy for you to learn the C# language. However, if Visual Studio .NET and the .NET Framework classes are new to you, it may take some time for you to learn how they work.

How a C# application is compiled and run

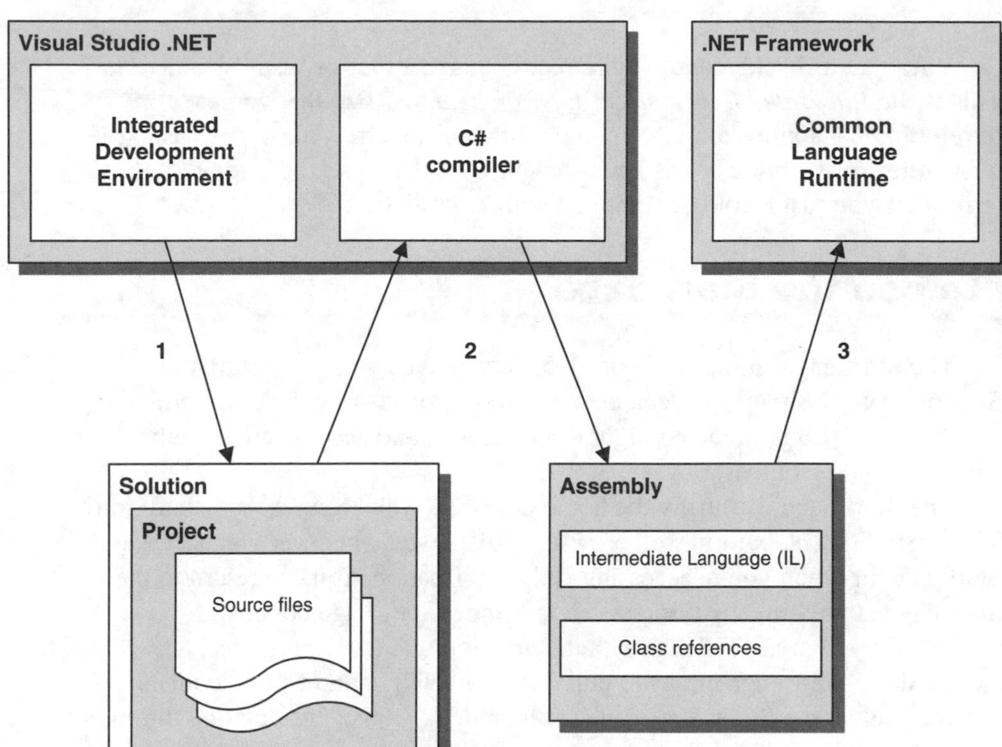

Description

1. The programmer uses Visual Studio's Integrated Development Environment to create a *project*, which includes one or more C# *source files*. In some cases, a project may contain other types of files, such as graphic image files or sound files.

   A *solution* is a container that holds projects. Although a solution can contain more than one project, the solution for most simple applications contains just one project. So you can think of the solution and the project as essentially the same thing.

2. The C# *compiler* translates or *builds* the source code into *Microsoft Intermediate Language* (*MSIL*), or just *Intermediate Language* (*IL*). This language is stored on disk in an *assembly* that also contains references to the classes that the application requires. An assembly is simply an executable file that has an *.exe* or *.dll* extension.

3. The assembly is then run by the .NET Framework's Common Language Runtime. The CLR manages all aspects of how the assembly is run, including converting the Intermediate Language to native code that can be run by the operating system, managing memory for the assembly, enforcing security, and so on.

Figure 1-4 How a C# application is compiled and run

A tour of Visual Studio

With that as background, you're ready to take a tour of Visual Studio .NET. This is the *Integrated Development Environment*, or *IDE*, that you use for developing C# applications. Along the tour, you'll learn some of the basic techniques for working in this environment. You'll also see how some of the terms that you just learned are applied within the IDE.

How to use the Start page

The Start page, shown in figure 1-5, is displayed when you start Visual Studio. From this page, you can open existing projects or create new projects, change your Visual Studio configuration settings, and access various online Visual Studio resources.

The Start page is actually the home page of a web browser that's built into Visual Studio. The built-in web browser is displayed whenever you access the Start page or when you're accessing Help information. You can return to the Start page at any time by using the Help→Show Start Page command.

In case you aren't familiar with the notation that this figure uses, Help→Show Start Page means to pull down the Help menu from the menu bar and then select the Show Start Page command. We'll use this notation throughout this book because it makes it easier to find the command that you need. Usually, you only need to pull down one menu and select a command. But sometimes, you need to go from a menu to one or more submenus and then to the command.

By default, the Projects tab of the Start page is usually displayed. This tab lets you open existing projects and start new projects. However, the first time you start Visual Studio, the My Profile tab may be displayed. This tab lets you customize your Visual Studio settings as shown in the next figure. And finally, the Online Resources tab lets you access other Visual Studio resources, including online communities and download libraries.

The Projects tab of the Start page

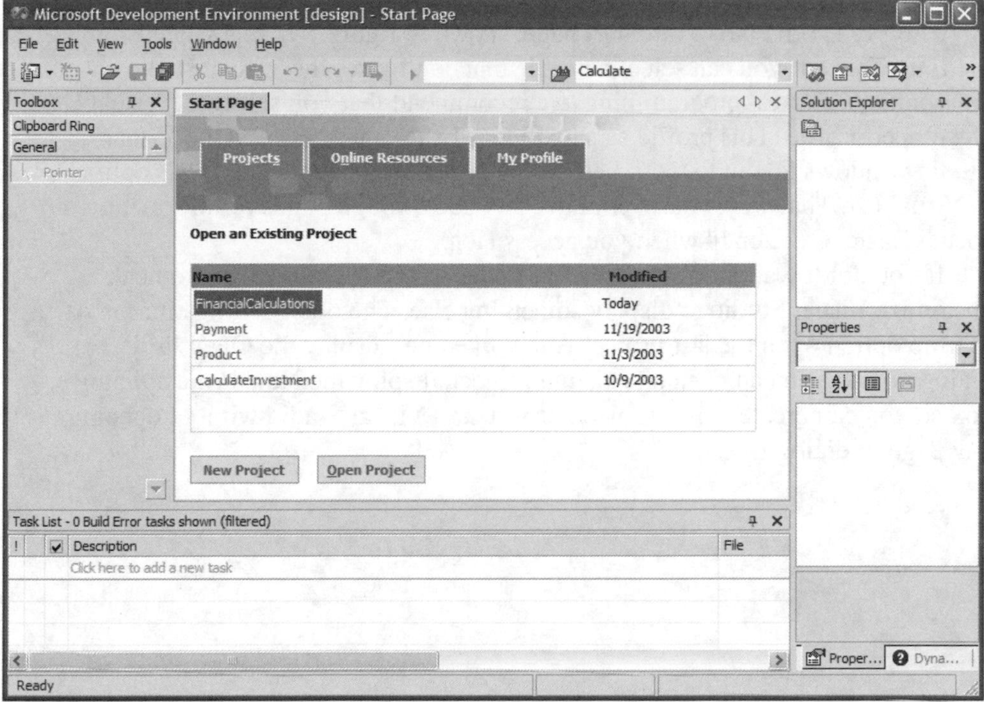

Description

- When you develop applications with Visual Studio, you use its Integrated Development Environment (IDE). The IDE contains all of the tools you need to develop .NET programs using Visual Basic, C#, C++, or J#.
- To start the Visual Studio IDE, open the Windows Start menu, then locate and select the Microsoft Visual Studio .NET 2003 program.
- The Start page is displayed by default when you start Visual Studio. It contains three tabs that let you work with projects, access online resources, and customize your Visual Studio settings (see figure 1-6).
- You can use the Projects tab to open an existing project or to start a new project. By default, the Projects page is displayed at startup, and it lists the four most recent projects so you can open them with a single click.
- As you work with Visual Studio, the Start page will be obscured by other information. But you can return to the Start page at any time by clicking the Start Page tab that's located in the upper left portion of the window, just below the toolbars, or by choosing the Help→Show Start Page command.

Figure 1-5 How to use the Start page

How to customize Visual Studio for use with C#

The My Profile tab of the Start page, shown in figure 1-6, lets you customize the IDE. To start, you can select a profile that configures the Visual Studio environment. For C# programming, we recommend that you select the Visual C# Developer profile. This profile sets up the keyboard shortcuts and the Visual Studio windows layout to work best with C#. And it sets the Help Filter option to Visual C#. That way, you won't have to wade through pages of information on Visual Basic, C++, or J# when you access Help.

If you don't want to display the Start page as the opening page, you can customize Visual Studio to display something else. The other settings for the At Startup option open the last project you worked on, display the Open Project dialog box so you can open an existing project, display the New Project dialog box so you can create a new project, or just start Visual Studio without opening any page or dialog box.

The My Profile tab of the Start page

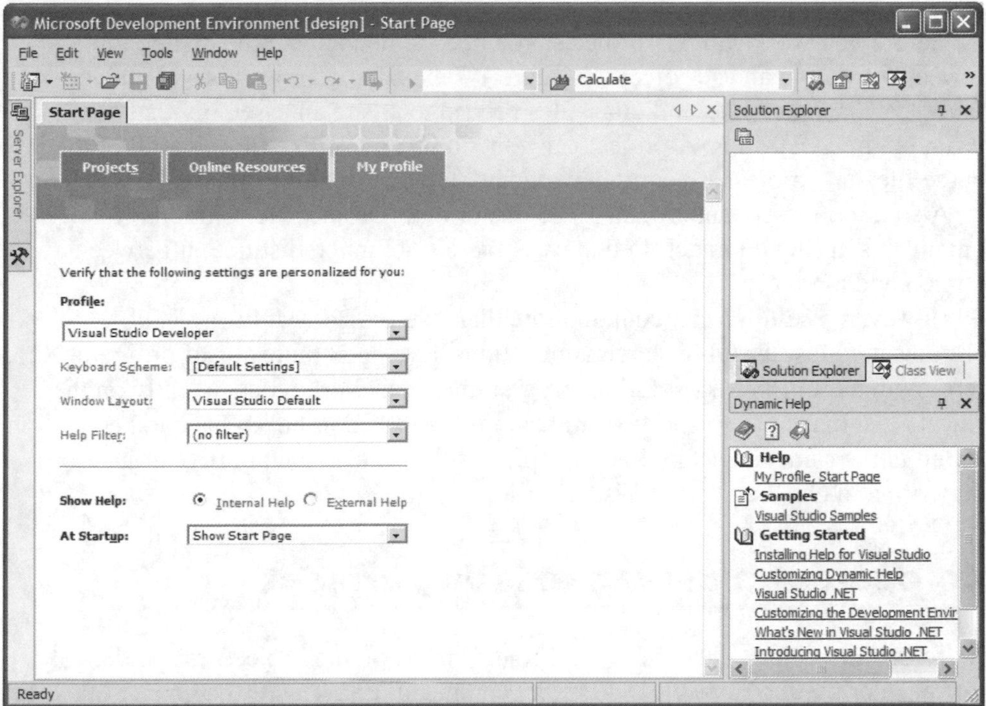

Description

- The My Profile tab of the Start page lets you configure Visual Studio to work the way you want.
- To customize Visual Studio for use with C#, select Visual C# Developer for the Profile setting. You'll see the effects of these changes in later figures.
- If you want to filter the help information so that only information related to C# is displayed, select the Visual C# option for the Help Filter setting. You can also change the filter as you use the Help feature.
- By default, help information is displayed as part of the Visual Studio IDE. To display it separately from the IDE, select the External Help option for the Show Help setting.
- To display something other than the Start page when you start Visual Studio, select a different option for the At Startup setting. The other options let you load and display the last solution you worked on, display the dialog box for opening an existing project or for starting a new project, or display an empty environment.

Figure 1-6 How to customize Visual Studio for use with C#

Solutions and projects

Before you work with C# projects, you need to understand the distinction between a solution and a project. As figure 1-7 explains, a project is a container that holds C# source files and other files needed to create an assembly that can be run by the .NET CLR. A project can contain several source files, but all of the source files in a project are compiled together to create a single assembly.

A solution is a container than holds one or more projects. A solution often contains just a single project. In that case, there's not much distinction between a solution and a project.

However, a solution can contain more than one project. Multi-project solutions are most useful for large applications developed by teams of programmers. With a multi-project solution, programmers can work independently on the projects that make up the solution. In fact, the projects don't even have to be written in the same language. For example, a solution can contain two projects, one written in C#, the other in Visual Basic.

How to open or close an existing project

To open a project, click the Open Project button on the Projects tab of the Start page or use the File→Open→Project command. Either way, the Open Project dialog box shown in figure 1-7 is displayed. From this dialog box, you can locate and open your C# projects.

You can also open a project you've recently worked on directly from the Projects tab of the Start page. To do that, just click the project name in the list of projects that's displayed (see figure 1-5). You can also open a recently used project by choosing the project from the Recent Projects submenu of the File menu.

At this point, you might wonder whether you should open projects or solutions. Both are shown in the Open Project dialog box. In figure 1-7, FinancialCalculations.sln is a solution and FinancialCalculations.csproj is a C# project.

In most cases, it doesn't matter whether you open the solution or the project. Each way, both the solution and the project files will be opened. If you open the project, Visual Studio automatically opens the solution that contains it. And if you open the solution, Visual Studio automatically opens all of the solution's projects.

In contrast, you can't close a project. Instead, you have to close the solution that contains it. To do that, you use the Close Solution command in the File menu.

The Open Project dialog box

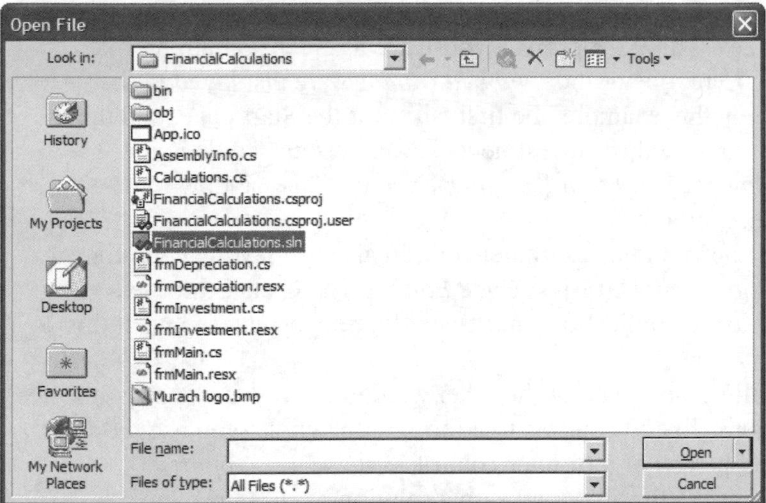

Project and solution concepts

- Every C# project has a *project file* with an extension of *csproj* that keeps track of the files that make up the project and records various settings for the project. In this figure, the project file is just above the highlighted file.
- Likewise, every solution has a *solution file* with an extension of *sln* that keeps track of the projects that make up the solution. In this figure, the solution file is highlighted.
- When you open the project file, Visual Studio automatically opens the solution that contains the project. And when you open a solution file, Visual Studio automatically opens the projects contained in the solution. So in most cases, it doesn't matter whether you open the project or the solution. Either way, both are opened.
- Visual Studio uses a file with an extension of *csproj.user* to store the user options for the project.

How to open a project

- To open an existing project, use the Open Project dialog box. To access this dialog box, click the Projects tab in the Visual Studio Start page, then click the Open Project button. Or, use the File→Open→Project command.
- Use the controls in the Open Project dialog box to locate and select the project or solution you want to open.
- After you've worked on one or more projects, the names of those projects will be listed in the Projects tab of the Start page and in the File→Recent Projects submenu. Then, you can click a project name to open the project.

How to close a project

- Use the File→Close Solution command.

Figure 1-7 How to open or close an existing project

How to work with the IDE

When you open an existing C# project, you'll see a screen something like the one in figure 1-8. Here, one or more *tabbed windows* are displayed in the main part of the IDE. In this example, the first tab is for the Start page, and the second tab is for a form named frmInvestment.cs, which is displayed in the *Form Designer window* (or just *Form Designer*). You use this window to develop the user interface for a form.

Although it isn't shown in this example, you can also display the code for a form in the *Code Editor window* (or just *Code Editor*). The Code Editor lets you develop the C# code for an application. In the next figure, you can see what this window looks like.

This figure also illustrates some of the other windows that you use as you develop C# applications. To add controls to a form, for example, you use the *Toolbox*. To set the properties of a form or control, you use the *Properties window*. And to manage the files that make up a solution, you can use the *Solution Explorer window* (or just *Solution Explorer)*. If all three of these windows aren't shown when you open a project, you can use the techniques in figure 1-11 to open and arrange them.

This figure also points out two of the toolbars that are available in the IDE. You can use these toolbars to perform a variety of operations, and the toolbars change depending on what you're doing. Of course, you can also perform any operation by using the menus at the top of the IDE. And you can perform some operations using the context-sensitive shortcut menu that's displayed when you right-click anywhere in the IDE.

The Visual Studio IDE with a Form Designer window displayed

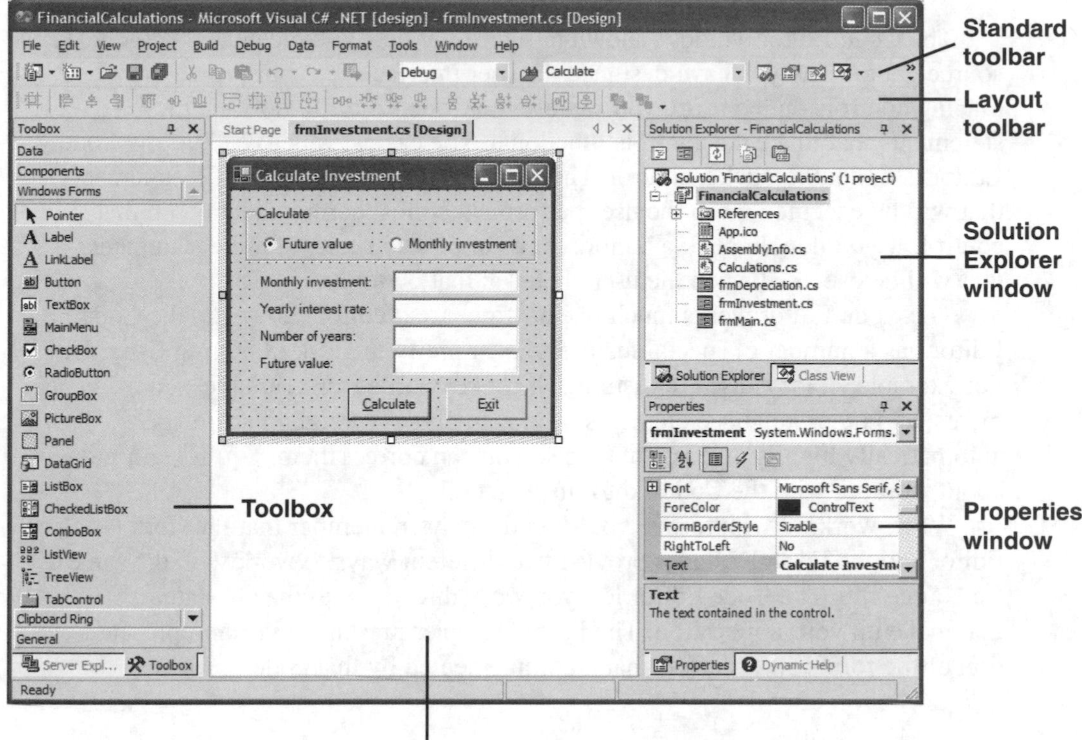

Description

- The main part of the Visual Studio IDE contains one or more *tabbed windows*. To develop a form, you use the *Form Designer window*. And to develop code, you use the *Code Editor window* that's described in figure 1-9.
- To add controls and other items to a form, you use the *Toolbox*. The Toolbox contains a variety of items organized into categories such as Data, Components, Windows Forms, and so on. The items you'll use most are the controls in the Windows Forms category.
- To change the way a form or control looks or operates, you use the *Properties window*. This window displays the properties of the item that's selected in the Form Designer window.
- You use the *Solution Explorer window* to manage project files. You'll learn more about the Solution Explorer in figure 1-10.
- At the top of the Visual Studio window are several toolbars. The Standard toolbar includes standard Windows toolbar buttons such as Open, Save, Cut, Copy, and Paste. On the right side of the Standard toolbar, you'll find several buttons that summon other windows in the IDE. As you work with Visual Studio, you'll find that additional toolbars are occasionally displayed, depending on the function you're performing.

Figure 1-8 How to work with the IDE

How to use the Code Editor

The Code Editor window, shown in figure 1-9, lets you create and edit C# source code. After you have designed the user interface for your project by placing controls on the form, you can use the Code Editor to develop the C# statements that make the controls functional. The easiest way to call up the Code Editor is to double-click a control. Then, you can begin typing the C# statements that will be executed when the user performs the most common action on that control. If you double-click a button, for example, you can enter the statements that will be executed when the user clicks on that button.

The Code Editor works much like any other text editor. However, the Code Editor has a number of special features that simplify the task of editing C# code. For example, color is used to distinguish C# keywords from variables, comments, and other language elements. And many types of coding errors are automatically highlighted as you type so you can correct them. You'll learn more about working with the Code Editor in chapter 3.

When working with forms, you should always remember that the Code Editor and the Form Designer provide two different ways to work with the same C# source file. The Code Editor lets you work directly with the C# statements that make up your application. The Form Designer presents a visual representation of the forms and controls that are implemented by that code.

A project with a Code Editor window displayed

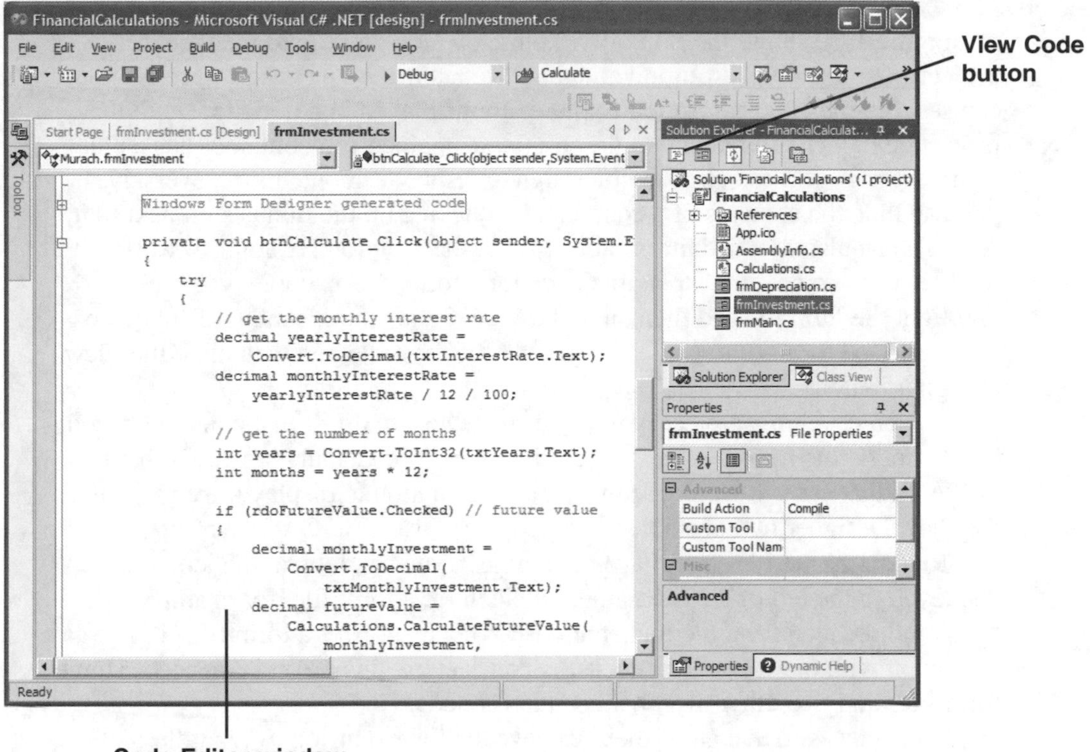

Description

- The Code Editor window is where you create and edit the C# code that your application requires. The Code Editor works much like any other text editor you have used, so you shouldn't have much trouble learning how to use it.
- You can display the Code Editor by double-clicking the form or one of the controls in the Form Designer window. Or, you can click the View Code button in the Solution Explorer.
- Once you've opened the Code Editor, you can return to the Form Designer by clicking the [Design] tab for that window or the View Designer button in the Solution Explorer (to the right of the View Code button). You can also move among these windows by pressing Ctrl+Tab or Shift+Ctrl+Tab.
- It's important to realize that the Form Designer and the Code Editor do not represent two different files. Instead, they provide you with two views of the same C# source file. The Form Designer gives you a visual representation of the form that is implemented by your C# code. The Code Editor lets you edit the code for the form.

Figure 1-9 How to use the Code Editor

How to use the Solution Explorer

Figure 1-10 shows the Solution Explorer, which you use to manage the projects that make up a solution and the files that make up each project. As you can see, the files in the Solution Explorer are displayed in a tree view with the project container subordinate to the solution container. If a container has a plus sign next to it, you can click the plus sign to display its contents. Conversely, you can hide the contents of a container by clicking on the minus sign next to it.

You can also use the buttons at the top of the Solution Explorer to work with the files in a project. To display the code for a form, for example, you can highlight the *form file* and then click the View Code button. And to display the user interface for a form, you can highlight the form file and then click the View Designer button.

As you develop a project, you can also create *class files* that contain C# code but do not define forms. In this figure, the file named Calculations.cs is that type of file. In that case, you can use the View Code button to display the code, but the View Designer button isn't shown.

To identify the files that make up a project, you can look at the icon that's displayed to the left of the file name. The icon for a form file, for example, is a form, and the icon for a file that contains C# code but isn't a form file is a document with the # character on it. As you can see, this project consists of three form files and two other files that contain C# code.

Note, however, that all of the files have the file extension *cs* regardless of their contents. Because of that, we recommend that you give your files names that identify their contents. For example, we add the prefix *frm* to the names of our form files. That way, it's easy to identify the form files when you work with them outside of the Solution Explorer.

The last four files shown in this figure are custom files that we developed for this project. In contrast, the AssemblyInfo.cs file was added automatically when this project was created. This file receives information whenever the project is compiled into an assembly.

The App.ico file was also added to the project automatically. This file contains an icon that you can customize for use with your applications when you deploy them.

This project also includes a folder named References. This folder contains references to the assemblies that contain the namespaces that are available to the project. Remember that the namespaces contain the classes that the application requires. In this case, all of the assemblies were added to the project automatically when this project was created.

This should give you some idea of how complicated the file structure for a single project can be. For this relatively simple application, three form files and one code file were created by the developer. And five namespaces, an assembly file, and an icon file were added to the project automatically. Although you can't see it here, each C# program you develop also has access to the Microsoft.CSharp namespace. This namespace contains the classes that support compilation and code generation using the C# language.

The Solution Explorer

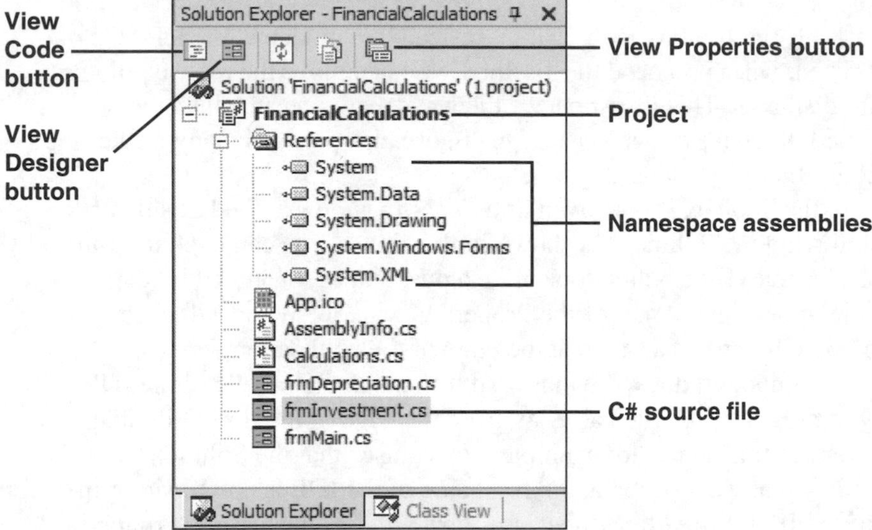

Description

- You use the Solution Explorer to manage and display the files and projects in a solution. The Solution Explorer lists all of the projects for the current solution, as well as all of the files that make up each project.
- Plus (+) and minus (-) signs in the Solution Explorer indicate groups of files. You can click these signs to expand and collapse the groups.
- You can perform most of the functions you need using the buttons at the top of the Solution Explorer window. The buttons you'll use most are the View Code and View Designer buttons, which open the Code Editor and Form Designer windows.

Project files

- C# source files are stored with the file extension *.cs*. Each form you create for a project will have its own *form file*. You can also create *class files* that contain C# code but do not define forms. The Solution Explorer uses different icons to distinguish between form files and class files.
- The App.ico file is created automatically when the project is created. It is an icon file that you can customize and use when you deploy your applications.
- The AssemblyInfo.cs file is created automatically when the project is created. It contains information about the assembly that's created when you compile the project.
- The References folder contains references to the assemblies for the namespaces that the application can use. These namespaces contain the classes that the project requires. In most cases, all the assemblies that you need are included when the project is created.

Figure 1-10 How to use the Solution Explorer

How to work with the windows in the IDE

In figure 1-11, the Toolbox isn't visible. Instead, it's hidden at the left side of the window. Then, when you need the Toolbox, you can move the mouse pointer over its tab to display it. This is just one of the ways that you can adjust the windows in the IDE so it's easier to use. This figure also presents many of the other techniques that you can use.

By default, the Toolbox is displayed as a *docked window* at the left side of the application window. To hide it as shown in this figure, you can click its Auto Hide button. The Auto Hide button looks like a pushpin, as illustrated by the button near the upper right corner of the Properties window. When a docked window is hidden, it appears as a tab at the edge of the application window.

You can also undock a docked window so it floats in the middle of the IDE. To do that, you drag it by its title bar away from the edge of the IDE or double-click its title bar. In this figure, for example, you can see that the Solution Explorer window that was docked at the right side of the IDE is now floating in the middle of the IDE. In addition, the Class View window, which was grouped with the Solution Explorer window as a tabbed window, has been separated from the Solution Explorer window. Although we don't recommend this arrangement of windows, it should give you a good idea of the many ways you can arrange them.

As you review the information in this figure, notice that you can't hide, separate, or undock the windows in the main area of the IDE. For the most part, you'll just move between these windows by clicking on their tabs or by using one of the other techniques.

If you experiment with these techniques for a few minutes, you'll see that they're easy to master. Then, as you get more comfortable with Visual Studio, you can adjust the windows so they work best for you.

The IDE with two floating windows and a hidden window

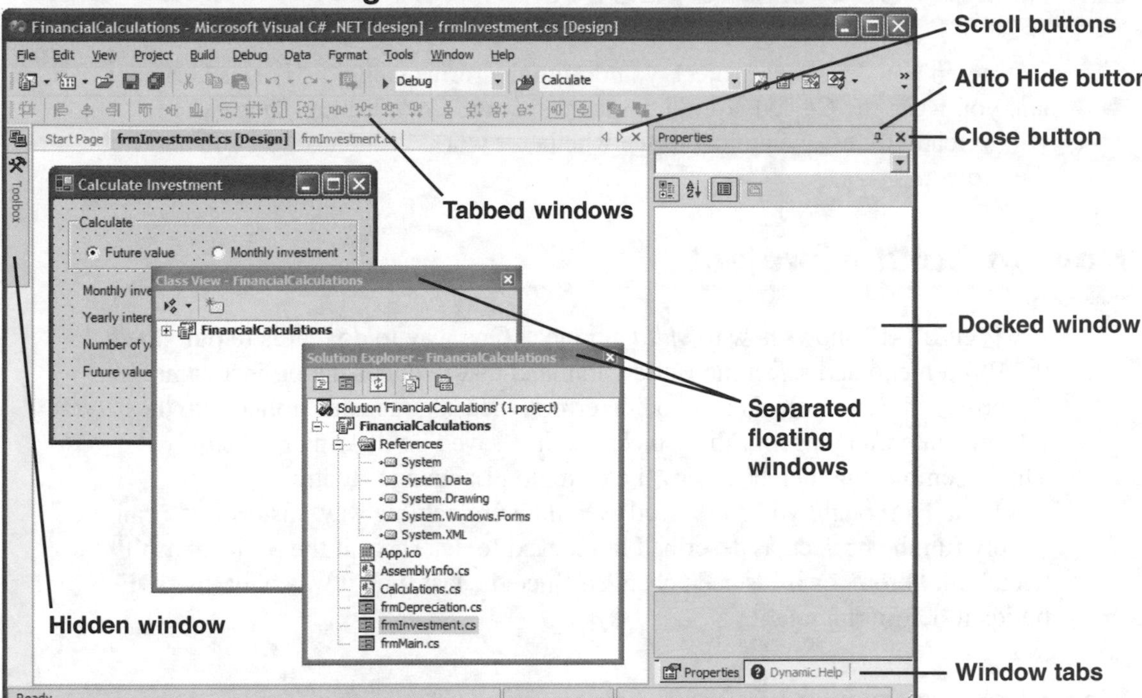

How to rearrange windows

- To close a window, click its Close button. To redisplay it, click its button in the Standard toolbar (if one is available) or select it from the View menu.
- To undock a *docked window* so it floats on the screen, drag it by its title bar away from the edge of the application window or double-click its title bar. To dock a floating window, drag it by its title bar to the edge of the application window or double-click its title bar to return it to its default location.
- To hide a docked window, click its Auto Hide button. Then, the window is displayed as a tab at the edge of the screen, and you can display it by placing the mouse pointer over the tab. To change it back, display it and then click the Auto Hide button again.
- To size a window, place the mouse pointer over an edge or a corner of the window, and then drag it.
- If two or more windows are grouped into tabbed windows, you can display any window in the group by clicking on its tab. If you dock, undock, hide, or unhide a tabbed window, all the windows in the group are docked, undocked, hidden, or unhidden.
- To reset the windows to their default arrangement, you can use the Environment/General settings category of the Tools→Options command.

Warning

- Be careful when modifying the window layout. It's easy to lose track of your windows and to move or close a window and not know how to get it back.

Figure 1-11 How to work with the windows in the IDE

How to test a project

When you develop a project, you design the forms using the Forms Designer and you write the C# code for the project using the Code Editor. Then, when you're ready to test the project to see whether it works, you need to build and run the project.

How to build a project

Figure 1-12 shows how to *build* a project. One way to do that is to pull down the Build menu and select the Build command that includes the project name. If the project doesn't contain any coding errors, the C# code is compiled into the Intermediate Language for the project and it is saved on disk in an assembly. This assembly can then be run by the Common Language Runtime.

Usually, though, you don't need to build a project this way. Instead, you can simply run the project, as described in the next topic. Then, if the project hasn't been built before, or if it's been changed since the last time it was built, the IDE builds it before running it.

How to run a project

The easiest way to *run* a project is to click the Start button that's identified in figure 1-12. Then, the project is built if necessary, the Intermediate Language is executed by the Common Language Runtime, and the first (or only) form of the project is displayed. In this figure, for example, you can see the first form that's displayed when the Financial Calculations project is run. This form contains two buttons that let you display the other forms of the project.

To test the project, you try everything that the application is intended to do. When data entries are required, you try ranges of data that test the limits of the application. When you're satisfied that the application works under all conditions, you can exit from it by clicking on the Close button in the upper right corner of the form or on a button control that has been designed for that purpose. If the application doesn't work, of course, you need to fix it, but you'll learn more about that in chapter 3.

The form that's displayed when the Financial Calculations project is run

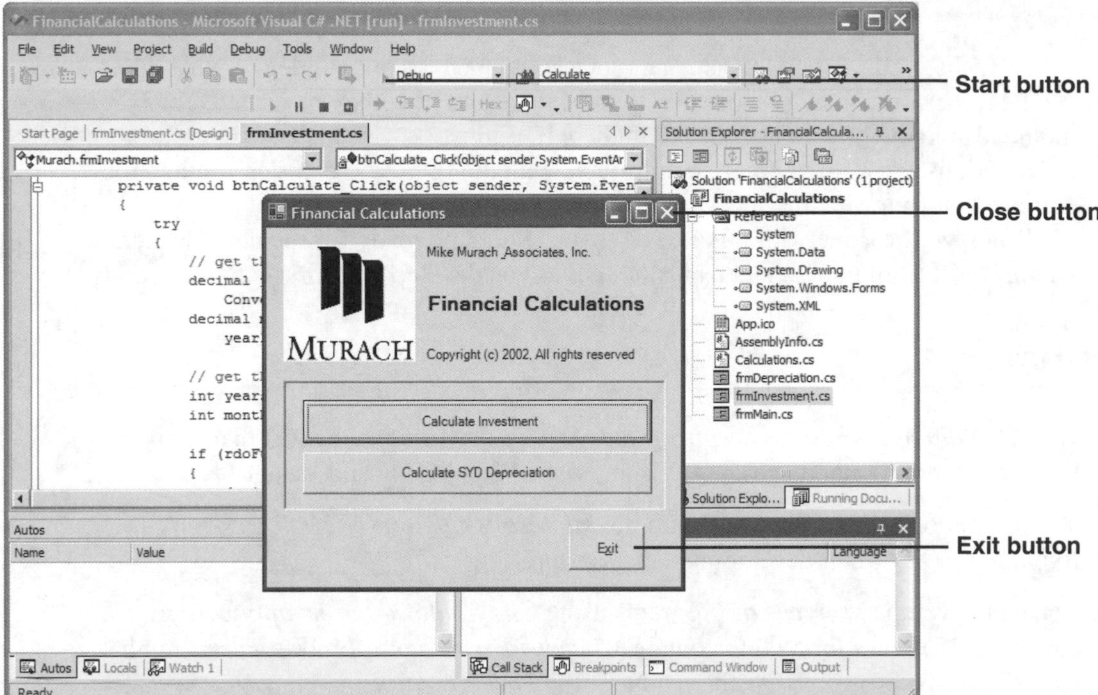

How to build a project without running it

- Use the Build→Build *project name* command. Or, right-click the project in the Solution Explorer and select the Build command from the shortcut menu. This *builds* the Intermediate Language for the project and saves it in an assembly.

How to run a project

- You can run a project from the IDE by clicking on the Start button in the Standard toolbar or by pressing F5. Then, the program's startup form is displayed on top of the Visual Studio window.
- If the project hasn't already been built, the project is first built and then run. As a result, it isn't necessary to use the Build command before you run the program.

Two ways to exit from a project that is running

- Click the Close button in the upper right corner of the startup form.
- Click the button control that's designed for exiting from the application. This is typically a button that is labeled Exit, Close, or Cancel.

Figure 1-12 How to build and run a project

Perspective

Now that you've read this chapter, you should have a general idea of what the .NET Framework, Visual Studio .NET, and C# are and how they're related. You should also know how to use Visual Studio's IDE to work with the files in projects and solutions. Now, to get more comfortable with the IDE, you can step through the exercise that follows.

When you're done with this exercise, you should be ready for the next chapter. There, you'll learn more about using the IDE as you develop your first C# application.

Summary

- *Visual Studio .NET 2003* is an *Integrated Develop Environment* (*IDE*) that supports four programming languages: *C#*, Visual Basic, Visual C++, and Visual J#.
- Visual Studio .NET can be used with the *Microsoft SQL Server 2000 Desktop Engine (MSDE)* when developing database applications.
- You can develop two types of programs using C#. *Windows Forms applications* consist of *Windows forms* that contain *Windows Forms controls*. *Web Forms applications* consist of *web forms* that contain *Web Forms controls*.
- The primary components of the *.NET Framework* are the .NET Framework Class Library and the Common Language Runtime. The *.NET Framework Class Library* provides pre-written code that makes it easier to develop applications, and the *Common Language Runtime* (*CLR*) supports the excution of any application written in a .NET language.
- The Class Library is organized into *namespaces* that contain the classes you need for developing applications.
- When you develop a C# application, the *source code* is *compiled* into *Intermediate Language* (*IL*) that's saved in an *assembly*. Then, the assembly can be run by the Common Language Runtime.
- You develop C# applications from within Visual Studio .NET. You use the *Form Designer* to design the user interface for a form, and you use the *Code Editor* to enter the C# code for the form.
- A *solution* consists of one or more projects, and a *project* consists of one or more files. To work with the files in a project, you use the *Solution Explorer*.
- To *build* a project, you use the Build command in the Build menu. To *run* a project, you click the Start button in the Standard toolbar. And to end a project that's running, you can click the built-in Close button or on a button control that's provided by the application.

Terms

.NET Framework
Visual Studio .NET
C#
Microsoft SQL Server 2000 Desktop Engine (MSDE)
Windows Forms application
Windows form
form
Windows Forms control
Web Forms application
web form
web browser
Web Forms control
.NET Framework Class Library
class
Common Language Runtime (CLR)
managed applications
Common Type System
namespace
project
source file
solution
compiler
Microsoft Intermediate Language (MSIL)
Intermediate Language (IL)
assembly
platform independence
Integrated Development Environment (IDE)
project file
solution file
tabbed window
Form Designer window
Form Designer
Code Editor window
Code Editor
Toolbox
Properties window
Solution Explorer window
Solution Explorer
form file
class file
docked window
build a project
run a project

Objectives

- List the four languages that are supported by Visual Studio .NET.
- Describe the main difference between a Windows Forms application and a Web Forms application.
- Describe the two main components of the .NET Framework.
- Describe the use of Microsoft Intermediate Language and the Common Language Runtime.
- Describe the use of each of these windows in the Visual Studio IDE: Form Designer, Code Designer, and Solution Explorer.
- Customize the Visual Studio environment for use with C#.
- Use Visual Studio .NET to do any of these operations: (1) Open an existing C# project or solution; (2) Display the designer for each of the forms in a project; (3) Display the code for each of the forms and classes in a project; (4) Open, hide, and adjust the windows for a project; (5) Build the project; (6) Run the project; or (7) Close the project.

Before you do the exercises in this book

Before you do any of the exercises in this book, you need to download the folders and files for this book from our web site (www.murach.com) and install them on your C drive starting with C:\C#.NET. For complete instructions, please refer to appendix A.

Exercise 1-1 Tour the Visual Studio IDE

This exercise guides you through the process of customizing Visual Studio for use with C#, opening an existing C# project, working with the windows in the IDE, and building and running a project. When you're done, you should have a better feel for the some of the techniques that you will use as you develop C# applications.

Start Visual Studio and customize it for use with C#

1. Start Visual Studio and click the My Profile tab on the Start page.
2. Select the Visual C# Developer option from the combo box at the top of the page. For now, leave the other options the way they are. If you want to, you can come back and change them later.

Open an existing project

3. Click the Projects tab to display a screen like the one in figure 1-5. Then, click the Open Project button to display the Open Project dialog box, shown in figure 1-7.
4. Use the drop-down list at the top of the dialog box to locate the project file named FinancialCalculations.csproj in the C:\C#.NET\Chapter 01\ FinancialCalculations folder. Then, double-click the file to open the project.

Experiment with the IDE

5. If the Form Designer window for the Calculate Investment form isn't displayed as shown in figure 1-8, highlight the file that contains this form in the Solution Explorer and click the View Designer button at the top of this window.
6. Highlight the file for the Calculate Investment form (frmInvestment.cs) in the Solution Explorer and click the View Code button. A Code Editor window like the one shown in figure 1-9 should be displayed.
7. Click the tab for the Form Designer window to display it. Then, press Ctrl+Tab to move back to the Code Editor window.
8. If the Toolbox is displayed, locate the pushpin near its upper right corner and click it. The Toolbox should now be displayed as a tab along the left side of the window. Place the mouse pointer over the tab to display the Toolbox, and then move the pointer outside the Toolbox to see that it's hidden again.

9. Undock the Solution Explorer window by dragging its title bar to the center of the screen. Notice that the Properties window expands to fill the space that was occupied by the docked Solution Explorer window. Double-click the title bar of the Solution Explorer window to return the window to its docked position.
10. Click the plus sign next to the References folder in the Solution Explorer window to see the namespaces that are included in the project. When you're done, click the minus sign next to the References folder to close it.

Close and reopen the solution

11. Select the File→Close Solution command to close the solution that contains the project. If a dialog box is displayed that asks whether you want to save changes, click the No button.
12. Reopen the solution by selecting the File→Open Solution command and then locating and selecting the solution file from the dialog box that's displayed.

Build and run the application

13. Build the project by pulling down the Build menu and selecting the Build Financial Calculations command. This assembles the project into Intermediate Language. It also opens another window, but you don't need to be concerned with that until the next chapter.
14. Run the application by clicking on the Start button in the Standard toolbar. When the first form is displayed, click the Calculate Investment button to go to the next form. Then, experiment with this form until you understand what it does. When you're through experimenting, click this form's Exit button to return to the first form.
15. Click the Calculate SYD Depreciation button to go to another form. Then, experiment with that form to see what it does. When you exit from it, you will return to the first form.
16. Exit from the first form by clicking on either the Close button or the Exit button.

Close the project and exit from Visual Studio

17. Close the project the way you did in step 11.
18. Exit from Visual Studio by clicking on the Close button in the Visual Studio window.

2

How to design a Windows Forms application

In the last chapter, you learned the basic skills for working with Visual Studio, you toured a Windows Forms application, and you tested an application with three Windows forms. Now, in this chapter, you'll learn how to use Visual Studio to design a Windows Forms application.

How to create a new project

When you create a new C# project, you use the New Project dialog box to set the basic options for the project, such as the project's name and location. In addition, you can use the Options dialog box to set some options that affect how Visual Studio handles projects and solutions.

How to use the New Project dialog box to start a new project

To create a new project and set the basic options for that project, you use the New Project dialog box shown in figure 2-1. This dialog box lets you select the type of project you want to create by choosing one of several *templates*. To create a Windows Forms application, for example, you select the Windows Application template. Among other things, this template includes references to all of the assemblies that contain the namespaces you're most likely to use as you develop a Windows application.

The New Project dialog box also lets you specify the name for the project, and it lets you identify the folder in which it will be stored. By default, projects are stored in the Visual Studio Projects folder under the My Documents folder. However, as you'll soon learn, you can change this default. You can also click the Browse button to select a different location; you can display the drop-down list to select a location you've used recently; or you can type a path directly. If you specify a path that doesn't exist, Visual Studio will create the necessary folders for you.

When you click the OK button, Visual Studio automatically creates a new folder for the project, using the project name you specify. In the dialog box in this figure, for example, InvoiceTotal is the project name and C:\C#.NET\Chapter 02 is the location. As a result, Visual Studio will create a folder named InvoiceTotal in the Chapter 02 folder. You can see the complete path for the new project near the bottom of the New Project dialog box.

When you create a new project, Visual Studio also creates a new solution to hold the project. By default, the solution is given the same name as the project and is stored in the same folder. If that's not what you want, you can click the More button in the New Project dialog box. This displays additional options that let you create a solution folder above the project folder and provide a separate name for the solution.

Incidentally, the terms *folder* and *directory* are used as synonyms throughout this book. With the introduction of Windows 95, Microsoft started referring to *directories* as *folders*. But most of the Visual Studio documentation still uses the term *directory*. That's why this book uses whichever term seems more appropriate at the time.

The New Project dialog box

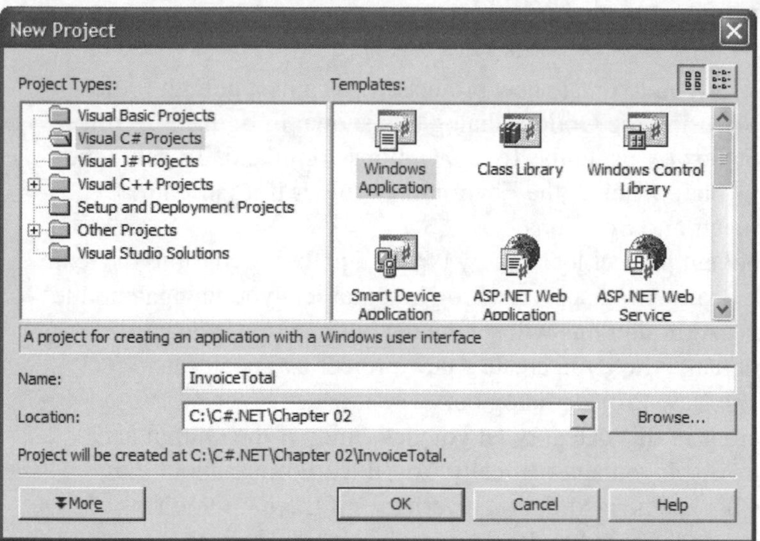

How to create a new project

1. Click the New Project button on the Projects tab of the Start page. Or use the File→New→Project command. Either way, the New Project dialog box is displayed.
2. Highlight the Visual C# Projects folder in the Project Types list to display the templates that are available for C#. Then, highlight the template you want to use. For a Windows Forms application, you highlight the Windows Application template.
3. Enter a name for the project and select the location for the project. A folder with the same name as the project is automatically added to the location you specify.
4. Click the OK button to start the new project.

Description

- The project *template* that you select determines the initial files, assembly references, code, and property settings that are added to the project.
- By default, Visual Studio creates a new solution with the same name as the project and stores the solution file in the same folder as the project. If you prefer, you can click the More button to create a separate folder for the solution file and give the solution file a different name.

Figure 2-1 How to use the New Project dialog box

How to use the Options dialog box to set the options for projects and solutions

To make it easier for you to create new projects, you can set default project and solution options by using the Options dialog box shown in figure 2-2. You can display this dialog box by using the Tools→Options command. To get to the Projects and Solutions options, click the Environment folder if it isn't already open. Then, click Projects and Solutions.

You can set the default project location by typing a path directly into the text box, or you can click Browse to display a dialog box that lets you navigate to the folder you want to use. Although this will set the default location, you can always override the default when you create a new project by specifying a different location in the New Project dialog box.

The next two options in this category let you determine if the Output and Task List windows are displayed automatically. You'll learn more about these windows later in this book. The next option determines if the item you're currently working on is highlighted in the Solution Explorer. Then, the last group of options determines whether or not Visual Studio saves changes to the files when you build and run a project.

As you can see in this figure, you can set a variety of options in addition to the ones described here. You'll learn about some of these options later in this book, and you'll have a chance to experiment with some of them in the exercise at the end of this chapter.

The Options dialog box for setting the project options

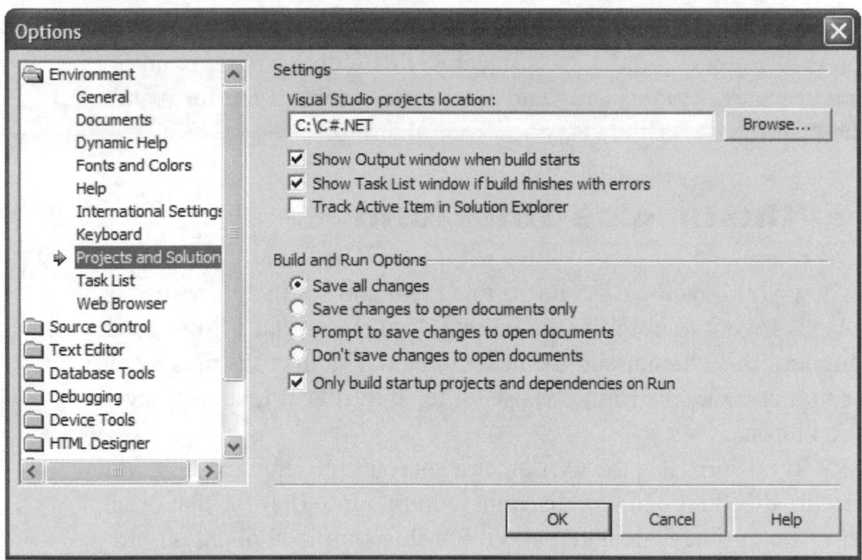

How to use the Options dialog box

- To display the Options dialog box, select the Tools→Options command. The Environment folder is open by default, and the General category is displayed.
- To display another category of options, click on that category. To display the categories in another folder, click on that folder to open it.
- Although most of the options should be set the way you want them, you may want to familiarize yourself with the options in each category so you know what's available.
- To set the default location for all projects you start from Visual Studio, you can change the Visual Studio projccts location shown above.
- To control the windows that are shown when you're working with Visual Studio, you can change the Show Output window and Show Task List window options in the Settings group.
- If you want Visual Studio to highlight the item you're currently working on in a designer or editor in the Solution Explorer, select the Track Active Item in Solution Explorer option.
- To control how changes are saved when you build and run a project, you can change the options in the Build and Run Options group.

Figure 2-2 How to use the Options dialog box

How to design a form

When you create a new project, the project begins with a single, blank form. You can then add controls to this form and set the properties of the form and controls so they look and work the way you want them to.

The design of the Invoice Total form

Before I show you how to add controls to a form and set the properties of the form and controls, I want to describe the Invoice Total form that I'll use as an example throughout this chapter and the next chapter. This form is presented in figure 2-3. As you can see, the form consists of ten controls: a text box, seven labels, and two buttons.

The Invoice Total form lets the user enter a subtotal into the text box, and then calculates the discount percent, discount amount, and total for that order when the user clicks on the Calculate button. For this simple application, the discount percent is based upon the amount of the subtotal, and the results of the calculation are displayed in label controls.

After the results of the calculation are displayed, the user can enter a different subtotal and click the Calculate button again to perform another calculation. This cycle continues until the user clicks on the Close button in the upper right corner of the form or clicks on the Exit button. Then, the form is closed and the application ends.

This application also provides keystroke options for users who prefer using the keyboard to the mouse. In particular, the user can activate the Calculate button by pressing the Enter key and the Exit button by pressing the Esc key. The user can also activate the Calculate button by pressing Alt+C and the Exit button by pressing Alt+X.

In the early days of computing, it was a common practice to sketch the user interface for an application on paper before developing the application. That's because a programmer had to enter the code that defined the user interface, and the task of writing this code would have been error prone if the interface wasn't planned out first. As you'll see in this chapter, however, the Form Designer makes it easy to create Visual Studio's implementation of a user interface, called a form. Because of that, you usually don't need to sketch the layout of a form before you design it in Visual Studio.

Note that as you use the Form Designer, Visual Studio automatically generates the code that's needed to define the form and its controls. Then, all you have to do is write the code that gives the form its functionality. You'll learn how to do that in the next chapter.

The Invoice Total form

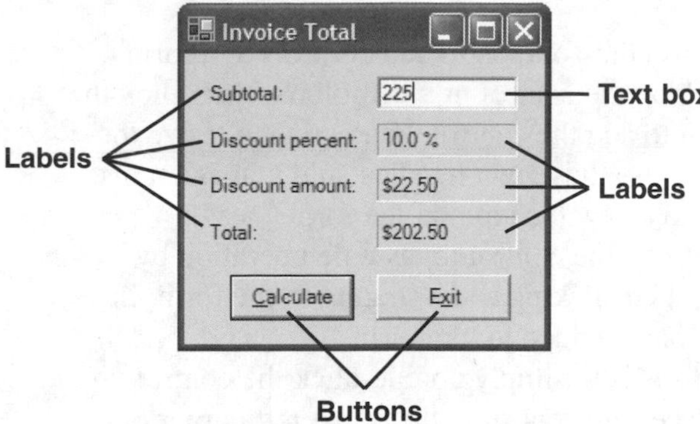

Description

- The user enters the subtotal into a text box, and the discount percent, discount amount, and total are displayed in label controls. Label controls are also used to identify the amounts that are displayed on the form.
- After entering a subtotal, the user can click the Calculate button to calculate the discount percent, discount amount, and the total. Alternatively, the user can press the Enter key to perform the calculation.
- To calculate another invoice total, the user can enter another subtotal and then click the Calculate button or press the Enter key again.
- To close the form and end the application, the user can click the Close button in the upper right corner of the form or on the Exit button. Alternatively, the user can press the Esc key to exit from the form.
- The user can press Alt+C to access the Calculate button or Alt+X to access the Exit button. On some systems, the letters that provide the access to these buttons aren't underlined until the user presses the Alt key.

Three types of controls

- A *label* displays text on a form.
- A *text box* lets the user enter text on a form.
- A *button* initiates form processing when clicked.

Figure 2-3 The design of the Invoice Total form

How to add controls to a form

Figure 2-4 shows how you can use the Toolbox to add controls to a form. The easiest way to do that is to click on the control in the Toolbox, then click the form at the location where you want to add the control. You can then resize the control by dragging one of the control's adjustment handles, and you can move the control by dragging the control to a new location on the form.

If you prefer, you can place and size the control in a single operation by clicking the control in the Toolbox, then clicking and dragging in the form. In this figure, for example, a button is being added to the form.

A third method for adding controls is to simply double-click the control you want to add in the Toolbox. This places the control in the upper left corner of the form. You can then move and resize the control.

A fourth way to add a control is to drag the control from the Toolbox to the form. The control is placed wherever you drop it. You can then resize the control.

If the AutoHide feature is activated for the Toolbox and you move the mouse pointer over the Toolbox tab to display it, the display frequently obscures some or all of the form. This makes it difficult to add controls. As a result, it's a good idea to turn off the AutoHide feature when you're adding controls. To do that, just click the pushpin button in the upper right corner of the Toolbox.

After you have added controls to the form, you can work with several controls at once. For example, let's say that you have four text box controls on your form and you want to make them all the same size with the same alignment. To do that, first select all four controls by holding down the Ctrl or Shift key as you click on them or by using the mouse pointer to drag around the controls. Then, use the commands in the Format menu or the buttons in the Layout toolbar to move, size, and align the first three controls relative to the fourth control (the *primary control*). To format the controls relative to a control other than the last one you selected, click on that control to make it the primary control. (The primary control will have different color handles so you can identify it.)

Although these techniques may be hard to visualize as you read about them, you'll find that they're relatively easy to use. All you need is a little practice, which you'll get in the first exercise for this chapter.

A form after some controls have been added to it

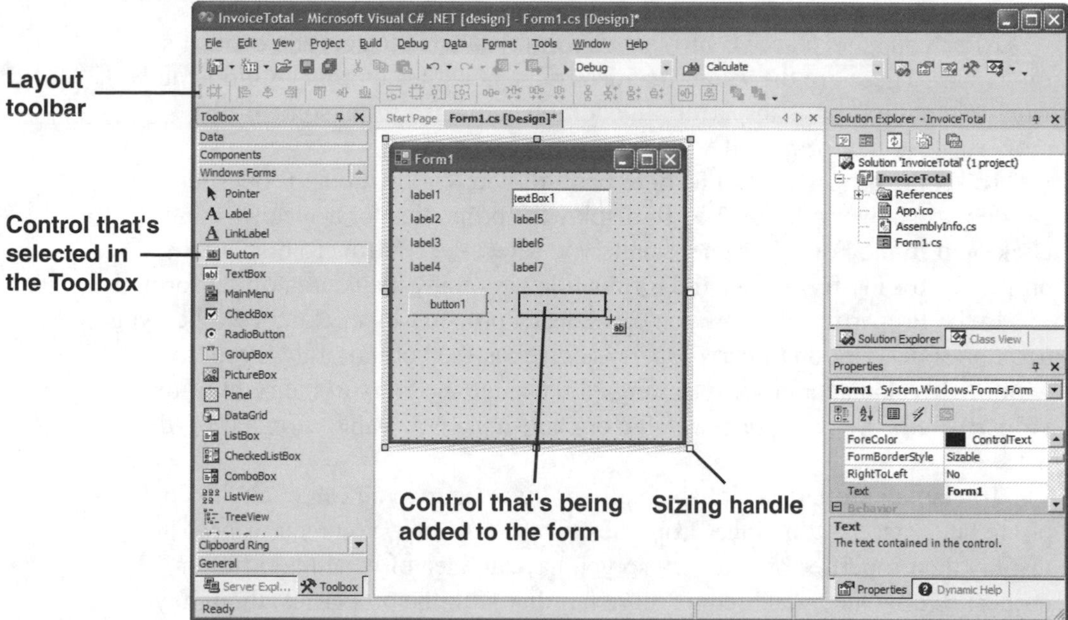

How to add a control

- To add a control to a form, select the control in the Toolbox. Then, click in the form where you want to place the control and drag the pointer on the form to size the control.
- You can also add a control by double-clicking it or by dragging and dropping it onto the form. If you double-click on it, the control is placed in the upper left corner of the form. If you drag it, it's placed wherever you drop it. Then, you can move and size the control.

How to select and work with controls

- To select a control on the form, click on it. To move a control, drag it. To size a selected control, drag one of its handles.
- To select more than one control, hold down the Shift or Ctrl key as you click on each control. You can also select a group of controls by clicking on a blank spot in the form and then dragging around the controls.
- To align, size, or space a group of selected controls, click on a control to make it the *primary control*. (By default, the last control you select is the primary control.) Then, use the commands in the Format menu or the buttons on the Layout toolbar to align, size, or space the controls relative to the primary control.
- You can also size all of the controls in a group by sizing the primary control in the group. And you can drag any of the selected controls to move all the controls.
- To change the size of a form to accommodate the controls, click on the form and then drag it by one of its handles.

Figure 2-4 How to add controls to a form

How to set properties

After you have placed controls on a form, you need to set each control's *properties*. These are the values that determine how the controls will look and work when the form is displayed. In addition, you need to set some of the properties for the form itself.

To set the properties of a form or control, you work with the Properties window as shown in figure 2-5. To display the properties for a specific control, click on it in the Form Designer window to select the control. To display the properties for the form, click the form's title bar or any blank area of the form.

In the Properties window, you can select a property by clicking it. When you do, a brief description of that property is given at the bottom of the Properties window. To change a property setting, you change the entry to the right of the property name by typing a new value or choosing a new value from a drop-down list.

To display properties alphabetically or by category, you can click the appropriate button at the top of the Properties window. At first, you may want to display the properties by category so you have an idea of what the different properties do. Once you become more familiar with the properties, though, you may be able to find the ones you're looking for faster if you display them alphabetically.

As you work with properties, you'll find that most are set the way you want them by default. In addition, some properties such as Height and Width are set interactively as you size and position the form and its controls in the Form Designer window. As a result, you usually only need to change a few properties for each object.

A form after the properties have been set

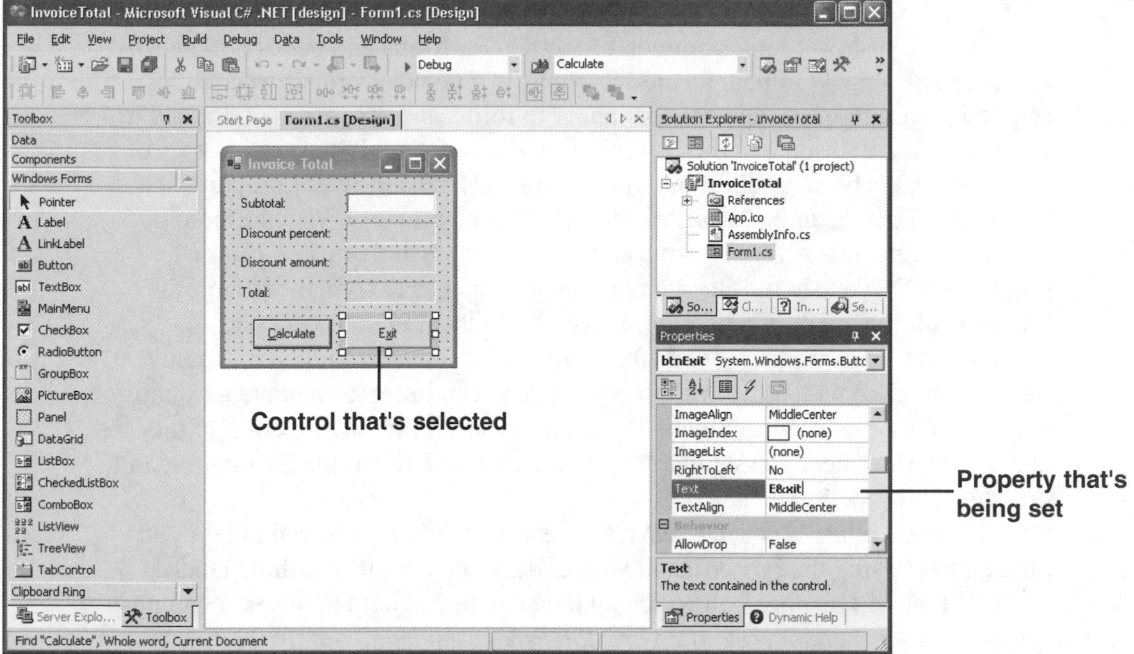

Description

- The Properties window displays the *properties* for the object that's currently selected in the Form Designer window. To display the properties for another object, click on that object or select the object from the drop-down list at the top of the Properties window.
- To change a property, enter a value into the text box or select a value from its drop-down list if it has one. If a button with an ellipsis (...) appears at the right side of a property's text box, you can click on the ellipsis to display a dialog box that lets you set options for the property.
- To change the properties for two or more controls at the same time, select the controls. Then, the common properties of the controls are displayed in the Properties window.
- When you click on a property in the Properties window, a brief explanation of the property appears in a pane at the bottom of the window. For more information, press F1 to display the help information for the property.
- You can use the first two buttons at the top of the Properties window to sort the properties by category or alphabetically.
- You can use the plus and minus signs displayed to the left of some of the properties and categories in the Properties window to expand and collapse the list of properties.

Note

- If a description isn't displayed when you click on a property in the Properties window, right-click on the window and select Description from the shortcut menu.

Figure 2-5 How to set properties

Common properties for forms and controls

Figure 2-6 shows some common properties for forms and controls. The first two properties apply to both forms and controls. The other properties are presented in two groups: properties that apply to forms and properties that apply to controls. Note that some of the control properties only apply to certain types of controls. That's because different types of controls have different properties.

Since all forms and controls must have a Name property, Visual Studio creates generic names for all forms and controls, such as Form1 or Button1. Often, though, you should change these generic names to something more meaningful, especially if you're going to refer to them in your C# code.

To make your program's code easier to read and understand, you should begin each name with a two- or three-letter prefix in lowercase letters to identify the control's type. Then, complete the name by describing the function of the control. For instance, you should use a name like *btnExit* for the Exit button and *txtSubtotal* for the Subtotal text box.

For label controls, you can leave the generic names unchanged unless you plan on modifying the properties in your code. For example, the three label controls that will display the invoice total calculation should be given meaningful names such as *lblDiscountPercent*, *lblDiscountAmount,* and *lblTotal*. But there's no reason to change the names for the other four label controls, which display text that won't be changed by the program.

Forms and most controls also have a Text property that is visible when the form is displayed. A form's Text property is displayed in the form's title bar. For a control, the Text property is displayed somewhere within the control. The Text property of a button, for example, is displayed on the button, and the Text property of a text box is displayed in the text box.

As you work with properties, you'll find that you can set some of them by selecting a value from a drop-down list. For example, you can select a True or False value for the TabStop property of a control. For other properties, you have to enter a number or text value. And for some properties, a button with an ellipsis (...) is displayed. Then, when you click this button, a dialog box appears that lets you set the property.

The Name property

- Sets the name you use to identify a form or control in your C# code.
- Should only be changed if you intend to refer to the form or control in your code. For label controls whose values won't change during your program's execution, you can leave the name set to the default value.
- Use a three-letter prefix to indicate whether the name refers to a form (*frm*), button (*btn*), label (*lbl*), or text box (*txt*).

The Text property

- Sets the text that's displayed on the form or control. The default value is the generic form or control name that's generated by Visual Studio, which you'll almost always want to change.
- For a form, the Text value is displayed in the title bar. For controls, the Text value is displayed directly on the control.
- For a text box, the Text value changes when the user types text into the control. As a result, you can use the Text property to access the information entered by the user.
- If you want a text box to be initially blank, be sure to clear its Text property.

Other properties for forms

Property	Description
AcceptButton	Identifies the button that will be activated when the user presses the Enter key.
CancelButton	Identifies the button that will be activated when the user presses the Esc key.
ControlBox	Determines whether a control box will be displayed in the upper left corner of the form.
FormBorderStyle	Sets the border style for the form.
MaximizeBox	Determines whether a Maximize button will be displayed on the form.
MinimizeBox	Determines whether a Minimize button will be displayed on the form.
StartPosition	Sets the position at which the form is displayed. To center the form, set this property to CenterScreen.

Other properties for controls

Property	Description
BorderStyle	Sets the border style for controls.
Enabled	Determines whether the control will be enabled or disabled.
ReadOnly	Determines whether the text in some controls like text boxes can be edited.
TabIndex	Indicates the control's position in the tab order, which determines the order in which the controls will receive the focus when the user presses the Tab key.
TabStop	Determines whether the control will accept the focus when the user presses the Tab key to move from one control to another. Some controls, like labels, don't have the TabStop property because they can't receive the focus.
TextAlign	Sets the alignment for the text displayed on a control.

Figure 2-6 Common properties for forms and controls

How to add navigation features

Windows forms have features that make it easier for users to move around in the forms without using the mouse. These navigation features are described in figure 2-7.

The *tab order* is the order in which the controls on a form receive the *focus* when the user presses the Tab key. The tab order should usually be set so the focus moves left-to-right and top-to-bottom, beginning at the top left of the form and ending at the bottom right. However, in some cases you'll want to deviate from that order. For example, if you have controls arranged in columns, you may want the tab order to move down each column.

The tab order is initially set based on the order in which you add controls to the form. So if you add the controls in the right order, you won't need to alter the tab order. But if you do need to change the tab order, you can do so by adjusting the TabIndex property settings. The TabIndex property is simply a number that represents the control's position in the tab order, beginning with zero. So, the first control in the tab order has a TabIndex of 0, the second control's TabIndex is 1, and so on.

Access keys are shortcut keys that let the user move directly to a control. You set a control's access key by using the Text property. Just precede the letter in the Text property value with an ampersand (&). Then, the user can activate the control by pressing Alt plus the access key.

If you assign an access key to a control that can't receive the focus, such as a label control, pressing the access key causes the focus to move to the next control in the tab order. As a result, you can use an access key with a label control to create a shortcut for a text box control, which can't have an access key.

Finally, you should usually set the AcceptButton and CancelButton form properties. These properties specify the buttons that are activated when the user presses the Enter and Esc keys. That can make it easier for a user to work with a form. If, for example, the AcceptButton property of the Invoice Total form in figure 2-3 is set to the Calculate button, the user can press the Enter key after entering a subtotal instead of using the mouse to click the Calculate button.

Incidentally, chapter 10 will show you another way to set the tab order of the controls for a form. You can do that by using Tab Order view. When a form consists of more than a few controls, it is easier to use this view than to set the tab order for one control at a time.

How to adjust the tab order

- *Tab order* refers to the sequence in which the controls receive the *focus* when the user presses the Tab key. You should adjust the tab order so the Tab key moves the focus from one control to the next in a logical sequence.
- Each control has a TabIndex property that indicates the control's position in the tab order. You can change this property to change a control's tab order position.
- If you don't want a control to receive the focus when the user presses the Tab key, change that control's TabStop property to False.
- Label controls don't have a TabStop property so they can't receive the focus.

How to set access keys

- *Access keys* are shortcut keys that the user can use in combination with the Alt key to quickly move to individual controls on the form.
- You use the Text property to set the access key for a control by placing an ampersand immediately before the letter you want to use for the access key. For example, &Invoice sets the access key to *I*, but I&nvoice sets the access key to *n*.
- Since the access keys aren't case sensitive, &N and &n set the same access key.
- When you set access keys, make sure to use a unique letter for each control. If you don't, the user may have to press the access key two or more times to select a control.
- You can't set the access key for a text box. However, if you set an access key for a label that immediately precedes the text box in the tab order, the access key will take the user to the text box.

How to set the Enter and Esc keys

- The AcceptButton property of the form sets the button that will be activated if the user presses the Enter key.
- The CancelButton property of the form sets the button that will be activated if the user presses the Esc key. This property should usually be set to the Exit button.
- You set the AcceptButton or CancelButton values by choosing the button from a drop-down list that shows all of the buttons on the form. So be sure to create and name the buttons you want to use before you attempt to set these values.

Another way to set the tab order

- In chapter 10, you'll learn how to use Tab Order view to set the tab order of the controls on the form. If the form consists of more than a few controls, that is the best way to set that order.

Figure 2-7 How to add navigation features

The property settings for the Invoice Total form

Figure 2-8 shows the property settings for the Invoice Total form. As you can see, you don't need to change many properties to finish the design of this form. You only need to set three properties for the form, and you only use five properties (Name, Text, TextAlign, BorderStyle, and TabIndex) to set the properties for the controls. Depending on the order in which you create the controls, though, you may not need to change the TabIndex settings.

Notice that the three labels that display the form's calculation have their BorderStyle property set to Fixed3D. This setting gives the labels a recessed and boxed appearance, as you saw in figure 2-3. Incidentally, you can also use text boxes instead of labels to display the calculation. Then, to prevent the user from entering data into the text boxes, you could change the Enabled property to False. The resulting form would look similar.

Finally, the settings for the TabIndex properties of the text box and the two buttons are 1, 2, and 3, while the settings for all of the label controls are zero. Since the label controls can't receive the focus, this is just one way these properties could be set. If, for example, the TabIndex properties for the 8 controls were set from 0 through 7, from top to bottom in this summary, the tab order would work the same.

The property settings for the form

Default name	Property	Setting
Form1	Text	Invoice Total
	AcceptButton	btnCalculate
	CancelButton	btnExit

The property settings for the controls

Default name	Property	Setting
Label1	Text	Subtotal:
	TextAlign	MiddleLeft
Label2	Text	Discount percent:
	TextAlign	MiddleLeft
Label3	Text	Discount amount:
	TextAlign	MiddleLeft
Label4	Text	Total:
	TextAlign	MiddleLeft
TextBox1	Name	txtSubtotal
	Text	(empty)
	TabIndex	1
Label5	Name	lblDiscountPercent
	Text	(empty)
	TextAlign	MiddleLeft
	BorderStyle	Fixed3D
Label6	Name	lblDiscountAmount
	Text	(empty)
	TextAlign	MiddleLeft
	BorderStyle	Fixed3D
Label7	Name	lblTotal
	Text	(empty)
	TextAlign	MiddleLeft
	BorderStyle	Fixed3D
Button1	Name	btnCalculate
	Text	&Calculate
	TabIndex	2
Button2	Name	btnExit
	Text	E&xit
	TabIndex	3

Note

- Because label controls can't receive the focus, you can leave the TabIndex properties for these controls at their default values.

Figure 2-8 The property settings for the Invoice Total form

How to name and save the files of a project

When you're working on a project, you may want to change the names of some of the files from their defaults. Then, you'll want to save the files with their new names. You'll learn how to do that in the two topics that follow.

How to name the files of a project

You may have noticed throughout this chapter that I didn't change the default name of the form (Form1.cs) that was added to the Invoice Total project when the project was created. If you'd like, you can change the name of this form so that it's more descriptive. For example, this figure shows how to change the name of the form to frmInvoiceTotal.cs.

You may also want to change the name of the project or solution. For example, if you accepted the default project name when you started the project (WindowsApplication1.proj), you many want to change it to something more meaningful. Or, you may want to change the name of the solution so it's different from the project name. The techniques for doing that are presented in figure 2-9.

How to save the files of a project

Figure 2-9 also describes how to save the files of a project. Because C# saves any changes you make to the files in a project when you build the project, you won't usually need to save them explicitly. However, it's easy to do if you need to.

Notice in this figure that two factors determine which files are saved: what's selected in the Solution Explorer and the command you use to perform the save operation. If, for example, a single file is selected, you can use the Save command to save just that file, and you can use the Save All command to save the file along with the project and solution that contain the file. In contrast, if a project is selected in the Solution Explorer, the Save command causes the entire project to be saved, and the Save All command causes the entire solution to be saved.

The Properties window for a form file

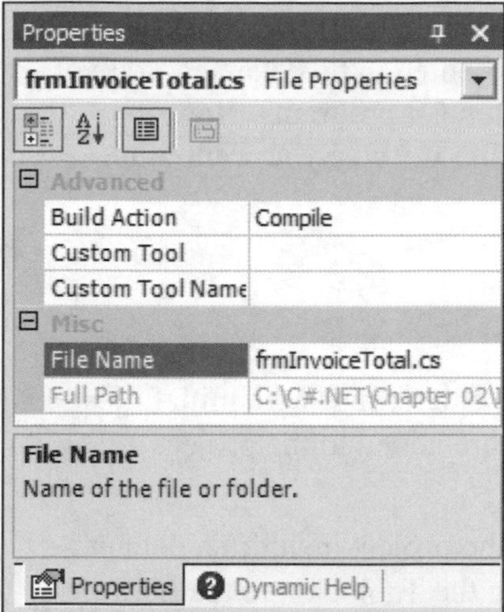

How to rename a file, project, or solution

- To rename a file, highlight it in the Solution Explorer window to display its properties and then change the File Name property.
- Be sure not to change or omit the file extension when you rename a file. Remember too that using a three-letter prefix to indicate the contents of the file (like *frm* for a form file) makes it easier to tell what each file represents.
- To change the name of the project, highlight it in the Solution Explorer and then change the Project File property. To change the name of the solution, highlight it in the Solution Explorer and then change the Name property.
- You can also rename a file, project, or solution by right-clicking on it in the Solution Explorer and then selecting the Rename command from the shortcut menu that's displayed.

How to save a file, project, or solution

- You can use the Save All button in the Standard toolbar or the Save All command in the File menu to save all files and projects in the solution.
- You can use the Save button in the Standard toolbar or the Save command in the File menu to save a file, project, or solution. The files that are saved depend on what's selected in the Solution Explorer window. If a single file is selected, just that file is saved. If a project is selected, the entire project and its solution are saved. And if a solution is selected, the entire solution and all its projects are saved.
- If you try to close a solution that contains modified files, a dialog box is displayed that asks you if you want to save those files.

Figure 2-9 How to name and save the files of a project

Perspective

If you can design the Invoice Total form that's presented in this chapter, you've taken a critical first step toward learning how to develop C# programs. Now, the next step is to add the code that makes the form function the way you want it to. That's what you'll learn to do in the next chapter.

Summary

- When you create a C# project, the *template* you choose determines the initial files, assembly references, code, and property settings that are added to the project by default.
- When you start a new Windows Application project, the project includes a default form. Then, you can add controls to the form by using the Toolbox and the Form Designer window, and you can set the *properties* of the form and controls by using the Properties window.
- You can align, size, and space a group of selected controls on a form relative to the *primary control*. You can also move and size all the controls in a group by moving or sizing the primary control.
- In most cases, you'll want to change the name of the default form file so it's more descriptive. You can also change the name of the project file or the solution file if necessary.

Terms

template
label
text box
button
primary control
property
tab order
focus
access key

Objectives

- Given the form design and property settings for a simple application, use the Form Designer to design the form.
- When necessary, rename the form, project, and solution files for an application.

Exercise 2-1 Design the Invoice Total form

This exercise will guide you through the process of starting a new project and developing the user interface for the Invoice Total form shown in this chapter.

Start the project

1. Start Visual Studio. If the Start page isn't displayed, select the Help→Show Start Page command to display it.
2. Click the New Project button to display the New Project dialog box. Note the path that's specified for the new project in the Location box. Then, close this dialog box without starting a new project.
3. Select the Tools→Options command to display the Options dialog box. Highlight the Projects and Solutions category in the Environment folder, and then change the Visual Studio projects location setting to C:\C#.NET.
4. If you're interested, take a few minutes to review the other options that are available in this dialog box. Then, close the dialog box.
5. Open the New Project dialog box again and notice that the new project location has changed to the location you specified in the Options dialog box.
6. If necessary, highlight the Visual C# Projects folder in the Project Types list and then highlight the Windows Application template. Next, enter InvoiceTotal for the name of the project, and add \Chapter 02 to the end of the location path. Finally, click the OK button to start the new project.

Add controls to the new form

7. Use the techniques in figure 2-4 to add the controls to the form with approximately the same sizes and locations as in that figure.
8. Use the buttons in the Layout toolbar to size and align the controls. Then, size the form so it looks like this, but without the text on the form and its controls:

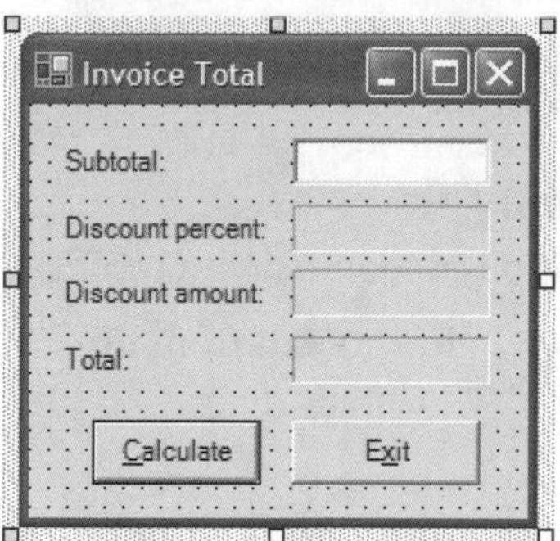

9. Use the Properties window to set the properties for the form and its controls so it looks like the form shown above. These properties are summarized in figure 2-8.

Test the user interface

10. Click the Start button in the Standard toolbar or press F5 to build and run the project. That will display this form:

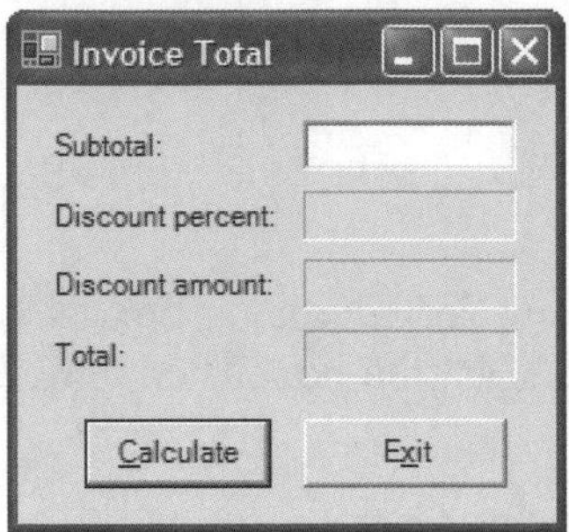

11. Experiment with the form to see what it can do. When you press the Tab key, notice how the focus moves from one control to the other. When you click a button, notice how it indents and then pops back out just like any other Windows button control. However, nothing happens in response to these button clicks because you haven't written the code for the button yet.

    Notice that the Calculate button has a dark outline around it to indicate that its function will be executed if you press the Enter key. (If it doesn't have a dark outline, you haven't set the AcceptButton property of the form to the button.)

    Notice that an underline appears under the first *c* in *Calculate* and the *x* in *Exit* to indicate that you can use an access key to activate these buttons. (If underlines don't appear, you may need to press the Alt key, or you may need to set the Text properties of these buttons properly.)

12. If you notice that some of the properties are set incorrectly, click the Close button in the upper right corner of the form to close the form. Then, make the necessary changes and run the project again. When you're satisfied that the form is working right, close the form to return to the Form Designer window.

13. Use one of the techniques presented in figure 2-9 to change the name of the form file from Form1.cs to frmInvoiceTotal.cs.

Save the project and exit from Visual Studio

14. Save the project by clicking the Save All button in the Standard toolbar.

15. Click the Close button for the Visual Studio window to exit from this application.

3

How to code and test a Windows Forms application

In the last chapter, you learned how to design a form for a Windows Forms application. Now, in this chapter, you'll learn how to code and test a Windows Forms application. When you're done, you'll be able to develop simple applications of your own.

An introduction to coding

Before you learn the mechanics of adding code to a form, it's important to understand some of the concepts behind object-oriented programming.

Introduction to object-oriented programming

Whether you know it or not, you are using *object-oriented programming* as you design a Windows form with the Visual Studio IDE. That's because each control on a form is an object, and the form itself is an object. These objects are derived from classes that are part of the .NET Class Library.

When you start a new project from the Windows Application template, you are actually creating a new *class* that inherits the characteristics of the Form class that's part of the .NET Class Library. Later, when you run the form, you are actually creating an *instance* of your form class, and this instance is known as an *object*.

Similarly, when you add a control to a form, you are actually adding a control object to the form. Each control is an instance of a specific class. For example, a text box control is an object that is an instance of the TextBox class. Similarly, a label control is an object that is an instance of the Label class. This process of creating an object from a class can be called *instantiation*.

As you progress through this book, you will learn much more about classes and objects because C# is an *object-oriented language*. In chapter 12, for example, you'll learn how to use the C# language to create your own classes. At that point, you'll start to understand what's actually happening as you work with classes and objects. For now, though, you just need to get comfortable with the terms and accept the fact that a lot is going on behind the scenes as you design a form and its controls.

Figure 3-1 summarizes what I've just said about classes and objects. It also introduces you to the properties, methods, and events that are defined by classes and used by objects. As you've already seen, the *properties* of an object define the object's characteristics and data. For instance, the Name property gives a name to a control, and the Text property determines the text that is displayed within the control.

In contrast, the *methods* of an object determine the operations that can be performed by the object. An object's *events* are signals sent by the object to your application that something has happened that can be responded to. For example, a Button control object generates an event called Click if the user clicks the button. Then, your application can respond by running a C# method to handle the Click event.

By the way, the properties, methods, and events of an object or class are called the *members* of the object or class. You'll learn more about properties, methods, and events in the next three figures.

A form object and its ten control objects

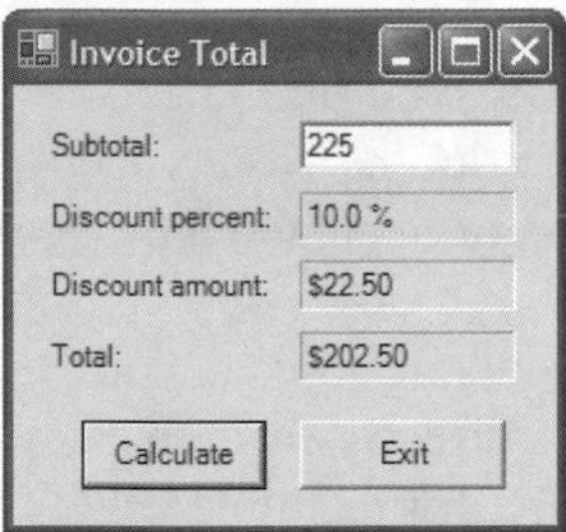

Class and object concepts

- An *object* is a self-contained unit that combines code and data. Two examples of objects you have already worked with are forms and controls.
- A *class* is the code that defines the characteristics of an object. You can think of a class as a template for an object.
- An object is an *instance* of a class, and the process of creating an object from a class is called *instantiation*.
- More than one object instance can be created from a single class. For example, a form can have several button objects, all instantiated from the same Button class. Each is a separate object, but all share the characteristics of the Button class.
- A class can be based on an existing class. In that case, the existing class is referred to as the *base class*, and the new class inherits the characteristics of the base class.

Property, method, and event concepts

- *Properties* define the characteristics of an object and the data associated with an object.
- *Methods* are the operations that an object can perform.
- *Events* are signals sent by an object to the application telling it that something has happened that can be responded to.
- Properties, methods, and events can be referred to as *members* of an object.
- If you instantiate two or more instances of the same class, all of the objects have the same properties, methods, and events. However, the values assigned to the properties can vary from one instance to another.

Objects and forms

- When you use the IDE to design a form, the IDE automatically generates C# code that creates a new class based on the Form class. Then, when you run the project, a form object is instantiated from the new class.
- When you add a control to a form, the IDE automatically generates C# code in the Form class that instantiates a control object from the appropriate class and sets the control's default properties. When you move and size a control, the IDE automatically sets the properties that specify the location and size of the control.

Figure 3-1 Introduction to object-oriented programming

How to refer to properties, methods, and events

As you enter the code for a form in the Code Editor window, you often need to refer to the properties, methods, and events of its objects. To do that, you type the name of the object, a period (also known as a *dot operator*, or *dot*), and the name of the member. This is summarized in figure 3-2.

In addition to referring to the properties, methods, and events of objects, you can also refer to some of the properties and methods of a class directly from that class. The code shown in the Code Editor window in this figure, for example, refers to the ToDecimal method of the Convert class. A property or method that you can refer to directly from a class like this is called a *static member*. You'll learn more about static members in chapter 4. For now, you just need to realize that you can refer to static properties and methods using the same techniques that you use to refer to the properties and methods of an object.

To make it easier for you to refer to the members of an object or class, Visual Studio provides the Auto List Members feature shown in this figure. This is part of the Intellisense feature provided by Visual Studio. After you type a class or object name and a period, this feature displays a list of the members that are available for that class or object. Then, you can highlight the entry you want by clicking on it, typing the first few letters of its name, or using the arrow keys to scroll through the list. In most cases, you can then complete the entry by pressing the Tab key.

To give you an idea of how properties, methods, and events are used in code, this figure shows examples of each. In the first example for properties, code is used to set the value that's displayed for a text box to 10. In the second example, code is used to set a text box's ReadOnly property to True. Although you can also use the Properties window to set these values, that just sets the properties at the start of the application. By using code, you can change the properties as an application is running.

In the first example for methods, the Focus method of a text box is used to move the focus to that text box. In the second example, the Close method of a form is used to close the active form. Notice in this example that the keyword *this* is used instead of the name of the form. In this case, *this* refers to the current instance of the active Invoice Total form. Also, notice that the name of the method is followed by a set of parentheses. As you progress through this book, you'll learn how to use the methods for many types of objects. For now, though, just try to understand the concept.

Although you'll frequently refer to properties and methods as you code an application, you'll rarely need to refer to an event. That's because Visual Studio automatically generates the code for working with events, as you'll see later in this chapter. To help you understand the code that Visual Studio generates, however, the last example in this figure shows how you refer to an event. In this case, the code refers to the Click event of a button named btnExit.

A member list that's displayed in the Code Editor window

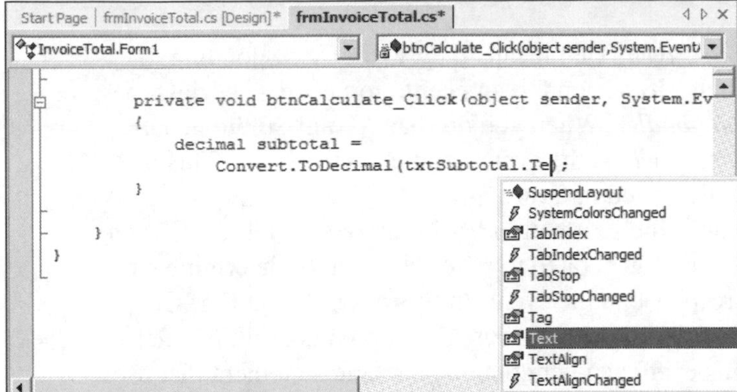

The syntax for referring to a member of a class or object

```
ClassName.MemberName
objectName.MemberName
```

Statements that refer to properties

`txtTotal.Text = "10";`	Assigns a string holding the number 10 to the Text property of the text box named txtTotal.
`txtTotal.ReadOnly = true;`	Assigns the true value to the ReadOnly property of the text box named txtTotal so the user can't change its contents.

Statements that refer to methods

`txtMonthlyInvestment.Focus();`	Uses the Focus method to move the focus to the text box named txtMonthlyInvestment.
`this.Close();`	Uses the Close method to close the form that contains the statement. In this example, *this* is a keyword that is used to refer to the current instance of the class.

Code that refers to an event

`btnExit.Click`	Refers to the Click event of a button named btnExit.

How to enter member names when working in the Code Editor window

- To display a list of the available members for a class or an object, type the class or object name followed by a period (called a *dot operator*, or just *dot*). Then, you can type the first few letters of the member name, and the Code Editor will select the first entry in the list that matches those letters. Or you can scroll down the list to select the member you want. Once it's selected, press the Tab key to insert the member into your code.
- If a member list isn't displayed, select the Tools→Options command to display the Options dialog box. Then, click on the Text Editor folder, select the C# category, and check the Auto list members and Parameters information boxes.

Figure 3-2 How to refer to properties, methods, and events

How an application responds to events

C# applications are *event-driven*. That means they work by responding to the events that occur on objects. To respond to an event, you code a special type of method known as an *event handler*. When you do that, Visual Studio generates a statement that connects, or *wires*, the event handler to the event. This is called *event wiring*, and it's illustrated in figure 3-3.

In this figure, the user clicks the Exit button on the Invoice Total form. Then, Visual Studio uses the statement it generated to wire the event to determine what event handler to execute in response to the event. In this case, the btnExit.Click event is wired to the event handler named btnExit_Click, so this event handler is executed. As you can see, this event handler contains a single statement that uses the Close method to close the form.

This figure also lists some common events for controls and forms. One control event you'll respond to frequently is the Click event. This event occurs when the user clicks an object with the mouse. Similarly, the DoubleClick event occurs when the user double-clicks an object.

Although the Click and DoubleClick events are started by user actions, that's not always the case. For instance, the Enter and Leave events can occur when the user moves the focus to or from a control, but they can also occur when the C# code moves the focus to or from a control. Similarly, the Load event of a form occurs when an application first starts. And the Closed event occurs after the Close method is executed for a form.

In addition to the events shown here, most objects have many more events that the application can respond to. For example, events occur when the user positions the mouse over an object or when the user presses or releases a key. However, you don't typically respond to those events.

Event: The user clicks the Exit button

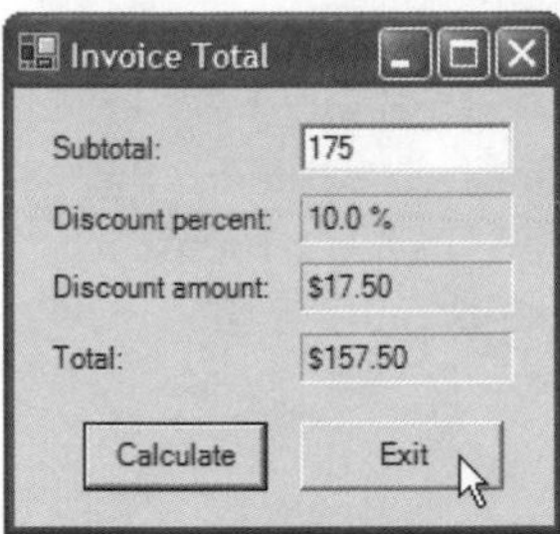

Wiring: The application determines what method to execute

```
this.btnExit.Click += new System.EventHandler(this.btnExit_Click);
```

Response: The method for the Click event of the Exit button is executed

```
private void btnExit_Click(object sender, System.EventArgs e)
{
    this.Close();
}
```

Common control events

Event	Occurs when...
Click	...the user clicks the control.
DoubleClick	...the user double-clicks the control.
Enter	...the focus is moved to the control.
Leave	...the focus is moved from the control.

Common form events

Event	Occurs when...
Load	...the form is loaded into memory.
Activated	...the form becomes the active form.
Closing	...the form is closing.
Closed	...the form is closed.

Concepts

- Windows applications work by responding to events that occur on objects.
- To indicate how an application should respond to an event, you code a method that handles the event, called an *event handler*.
- To connect the event handler to the event, Visual Studio automatically generates a statement that wires the event to the event handler. This is known as *event wiring*.
- An event can be an action that's initiated by the user like the Click event, or it can be an action initiated by program code like the Closed event.

Figure 3-3 How an application responds to events

How to add code to a form

Now that you understand some of the concepts behind object-oriented coding, you're ready to learn how to add code to a form. Because you'll learn the essentials of the C# language in the chapters that follow, though, I won't focus on the coding details right now. Instead, I'll focus on the concepts behind the code and the mechanics of adding the code to a form.

How to create an event handler for the default event of a form or control

Although you can create an event handler for any event of any object, you're most likely to create event handlers for the default event of a form or control. So that's what you'll learn to do in this chapter. Then, in chapter 6, you'll learn how to create event handlers for other events.

To create an event handler for the default event of a form or control, you double-click the object in the Form Designer window. Then, Visual Studio opens the Code Editor window, generates a *method declaration* for the default event of the object, and places the insertion point on a blank line between the opening and closing braces of that declaration. As a result, you can immediately start typing the C# statements that you want to include in the body of the method.

To illustrate, figure 3-4 shows the code that was generated when I double-clicked the Calculate button on the Invoice Total form. Notice that the name of the method is the name of the object (btnCalculate), an underline, and the name of the event (Click). Also notice that you can't see the statement that wires the Click event of this button to this event handler because it's stored in a hidden region of code. Later in this chapter, you'll learn how to view that hidden region.

Before you start an event handler for a control, you should set the Name property of the control as described in chapter 2. That way, this name will be reflected in the name of the event handler as shown in this figure. If you change the control name after starting an event handler for it, Visual Studio will change the name of the object in the event wiring, but it won't change the name of the object in the name of the event handler. And that can be confusing when you're first learning C#.

You should also avoid modifying the method declaration that's generated for you when you create an event handler. In chapter 6, you'll learn how to modify the method declaration. But for now, you should leave the method declaration alone and focus on adding code within the body of the method.

The method that handles the Click event of the Calculate button

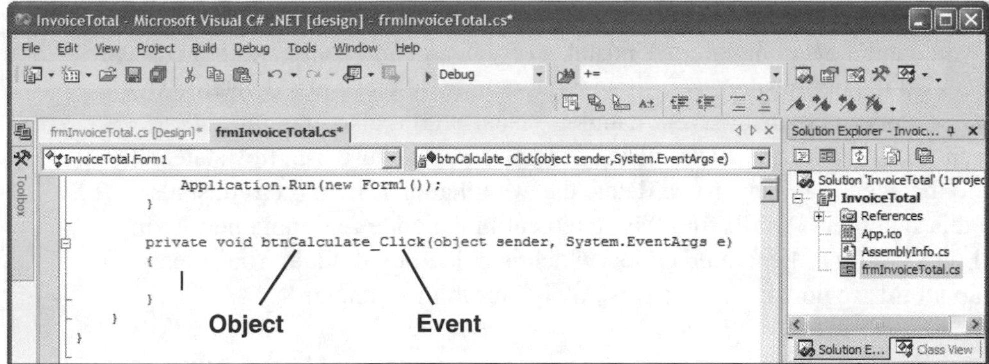

How to handle the Click event of a button

1. In the Form Designer, double-click the control. This opens the Code Editor window, generates the declaration for the method that handles the event, and places the cursor within this declaration.
2. Type the C# code between the opening brace ({) and the closing brace (}) of the method declaration.
3. When you are finished writing code, you can return to the Form Designer by clicking the View Designer button in the Solution Explorer window.

How to handle the Load event for a form

- Follow the procedure shown above, but double-click the form itself.

How to handle the default event for any control

- Follow the procedure shown above, substituting any control for the button.

Description

- The method declaration that's generated when you double-click a control or the form includes the name of the object and the event that the method handles. The method name that's generated consists of the object name, an underscore, and the event name. Thus, btnCalculate_Click is the name of the procedure that handles the Click event of the btnCalculate button.
- The statement that wires the event to the event handler is stored in a hidden region. As a result, it isn't shown in this figure.

Notes

- For now, you'll work only with the default events of controls. In chapter 6, you'll learn how to handle other events that aren't the default event.

Figure 3-4 How to create an event handler for the default event of a form or control

How to delete an event handler

If you add an event handler by mistake, or you add an event handler and then later decided it's not needed, you should know that you can't just delete it. That's because when you create an event handler, Visual Studio also generates a statement that handles the event wiring. As you saw in figure 3-3, this statement refers to the event handler. If you delete the event handler, then, you must also delete this statement. You'll find this statement in the code region named "Windows Form Designer generated code," which is hidden by default. You'll learn more about this region and how to display it later in this chapter.

The event handlers for the Invoice Total form

Figure 3-5 presents the two event handlers for the Invoice Total form. The code that's shaded in this example is the code that's generated when you double-click the Calculate and Exit buttons in the Form Designer. You have to enter the rest of the code yourself.

I'll describe this code briefly here so you have a general idea of how it works. If you're new to programming, however, you may not understand the code completely until after you read the next two chapters. The event handler for the Click event of the Calculate button calculates the discount percent, discount amount, and invoice total based on the subtotal entered by the user. Then, it displays those calculations in the appropriate label controls. For example, if the user enters a subtotal of $1000, the discount percent will be 20%, the discount amount will be $200, and the invoice total will be $800. The event handler for the Click event of the Exit button contains just one statement that executes the Close method of the form. So when the user clicks this button, the form is closed, and the application ends.

In addition to the code that's generated when you double-click the Calculate and Exit buttons, Visual Studio generates other code that's hidden in the "Windows Form Designer generated code" region. When the application is run, this is the code that implements the form and controls that you designed in the Form Designer. For now, you can accept that all of this generated code should work the way you want it to. By the time you finish this book, though, you'll understand all of this code.

When you enter C# code, you must be aware of the coding rules summarized in this figure. In particular, you should notice that each method contains a *block* of code that's enclosed in braces. As you'll see throughout this book, braces are used frequently in C# to identify blocks of code.

You should also realize that C# is a case-sensitive language. As a result, you must use exact capitalization for all C# keywords, class names, object names, variable names, and so on. If you enter the name of a control without using the correct capitalization, for example, the Code Editor won't recognize the control. Similarly, if you enter the name of a variable without using the same capitalization that you used when you declared it, the Code Editor won't recognize it.

The event handlers for the Invoice Total form

```
private void btnCalculate_Click(object sender, System.EventArgs e)
{
    decimal subtotal = Convert.ToDecimal(txtSubtotal.Text);
    decimal discountPercent = 0m;
    if (subtotal >= 500)
        discountPercent = .2m;
    else if (subtotal >= 250 && subtotal < 500)
        discountPercent = .15m;
    else if (subtotal >= 100 && subtotal < 250)
        discountPercent = .1m;

    decimal discountAmount = subtotal * discountPercent;
    decimal invoiceTotal = subtotal - discountAmount;

    lblDiscountPercent.Text = discountPercent.ToString("p1");
    lblDiscountAmount.Text = discountAmount.ToString("c");
    lblTotal.Text = invoiceTotal.ToString("c");
    txtSubtotal.Focus();
}

private void btnExit_Click(object sender, System.EventArgs e)
{
    this.Close();
}
```

Coding rules

- Use spaces to separate the words in each statement.
- Use exact capitalization for all keywords, class names, object names, variable names, etc.
- End each *statement* with a semicolon.
- Each *block* of code must be enclosed in braces ({}). That includes the block of code that defines the body of a method.

Description

- When you use the Form Designer to create a form, it creates a class that defines the form, and it generates most of the code for the form. This code isn't shown in the figure above, and you don't need to understand or modify this code for now.
- When you double-click the Calculate and Exit buttons in the Form Designer, it generates the shaded code shown above. Then, you can enter the remaining code within the event handler.
- The first event handler for the Invoice Total form is executed when the user clicks the Calculate button. This method calculates the discount percent, discount amount, and total based on the subtotal entered by the user.
- The second event handler for the Invoice Total form is executed when the user clicks the Exit button. This method closes the form, which ends the application.

Figure 3-5 The event handlers for the Invoice Total form

How to detect and correct syntax errors

As you enter code, Visual Studio checks the syntax of each statement. If a *syntax error*, or *build error*, is detected, Visual Studio displays a wavy line under the code in the Code Editor window. In the Code Editor window in figure 3-6, for example, you can see the lines under the reference to two controls named txtDiscountPercent and txtDiscountAmount.

If you place the mouse pointer over the code in error, a brief description of the error is displayed. In this case, the error message indicates that the control could not be found. That's because the prefix for the names of these controls is *lbl*, not *txt*. To correct these errors, you just correct the names in the Code Editor window.

If the *Task List window* is open as shown in this figure, any errors that Visual Studio detects will also be displayed in that window. When you build an application, the Task List window is displayed automatically. But you can also display this window before building an application as described in this figure. Then, you can jump to the error by double-clicking on it in the Task List window. This can be useful when you're working with an application that has more code than can be displayed on the screen at one time.

By the way, Visual Studio isn't able to detect all syntax errors as you enter code. Instead, some syntax errors aren't detected until the project is built. You'll learn more about building projects later in this chapter.

The Code Editor and Task List windows with syntax errors displayed

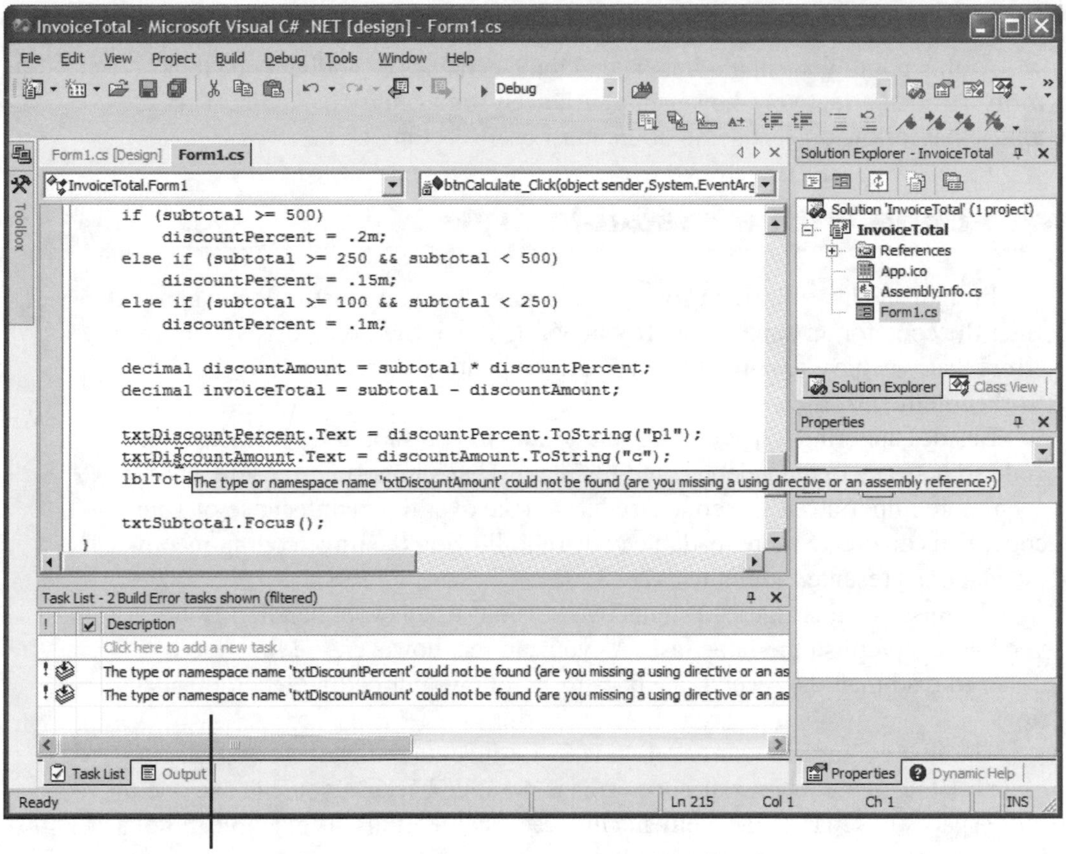

Task List window

Description

- Visual Studio checks the syntax of C# code as you enter it. If a syntax error is detected, it's highlighted with a wavy underline in the Code Editor window, and you can place the mouse pointer over it to display a description of the error.
- If the *Task List window* is open, all of the *syntax errors* (or *build errors*) are listed in that window. Then, you can double-click on any error in the list to take you to its location in the Code Editor window. When you correct the error, it's removed from the *task list*.
- By default, the Task List window is displayed when you build an application that contains a syntax error. To open this window and display the syntax errors before building the application, use the View→Other Windows→Task List command and click the Task List tab.
- Visual Studio doesn't detect some syntax errors until the project is built. As a result, you may encounter more syntax errors when you build and run the project. See figure 3-11 for more information.

More coding skills

At this point, you should understand the mechanics of adding code to a form. To code effectively, however, you'll need some additional skills. The topics that follow present some of the most useful coding skills.

How to code with a readable style

In figure 3-5, you learned some coding rules that you must follow when you enter the code for an application. If you don't, Visual Studio reports syntax errors that you have to correct before you can continue. You saw how that worked in the last figure.

Besides adhering to the coding rules, though, you should try to write your code so it's easy to read, debug, and maintain. That's important for you, but it's even more important if someone else has to take over the maintenance of your code. You can create more readable code by following the three coding recommendations presented in figure 3-7.

To illustrate, this figure presents two versions of an event handler. Both versions accomplish the same task. As you can see, however, the first one is easier to read than the second one because it follows our coding recommendations.

The first coding recommendation is to use indentation and extra spaces to align related elements in your code. This is possible because you can use one or more spaces to separate the elements in a C# statement. In this example, all of the statements within the event handler are indented. In addition, the if-else statements are indented and aligned so you can easily identify the parts of this statement.

The second recommendation is to separate the words, values, and operators in each statement with spaces. In the unreadable code in this figure, for example, you can see that each line of code except for the method declaration includes at least one operator. Because the operators aren't separated from the word or value on each side of the operator, the code is difficult to read. In contrast, the readable code includes a space on both sides of each operator.

The third recommendation is to use blank lines before and after groups of related statements to set them off from the rest of the code. This too is illustrated by the first method in this figure. Here, the code is separated into five groups of statements. In a short method like this one, this isn't too important, but it can make a long method much easier to follow.

Throughout this chapter and book, you'll see code that illustrates the use of these recommendations. You will also receive other coding recommendations that will help you write code that is easy to read, debug, and maintain.

As you enter code, the Code Editor will automatically assist you in formatting your code. When you press the Enter key at the end of a statement, for example, the Editor will indent the next statement to the same level.

A method written in a readable style

```
private void btnCalculate_Click(object sender, System.EventArgs e)
{
    decimal subtotal = Convert.ToDecimal(txtSubtotal.Text);

    decimal discountPercent = 0m;
    if (subtotal >= 500)
        discountPercent = .2m;
    else if (subtotal >= 250 && subtotal < 500)
        discountPercent = .15m;
    else if (subtotal >= 100 && subtotal < 250)
        discountPercent = .1m;

    decimal discountAmount = subtotal * discountPercent;
    decimal invoiceTotal = subtotal - discountAmount;

    lblDiscountPercent.Text = discountPercent.ToString("p1");
    lblDiscountAmount.Text = discountAmount.ToString("c");
    lblTotal.Text = invoiceTotal.ToString("c");

    txtSubtotal.Focus();
}
```

A method written in an unreadable style

```
private void btnCalculate_Click(object sender, System.EventArgs e){
decimal subtotal=Convert.ToDecimal(txtSubtotal.Text);
decimal discountPercent=0m;
if (subtotal>=500) discountPercent=.2m;
else if (subtotal>=250&&subtotal<500) discountPercent=.15m;
else if (subtotal>=100&&subtotal<250) discountPercent=.1m;
decimal discountAmount=subtotal*discountPercent;
decimal invoiceTotal=subtotal-discountAmount;
lblDiscountPercent.Text=discountPercent.ToString("p1");
lblDiscountAmount.Text=discountAmount.ToString("c");
lblTotal.Text=invoiceTotal.ToString("c");txtSubtotal.Focus();}
```

Coding recommendations

- Use indentation and extra spaces to align statements and blocks of code so they reflect the structure of the program.
- Use spaces to separate the words, operators, and values in each statement.
- Use blank lines before and after groups of related statements.

Note

- As you enter code in the Code Editor window, Visual Studio may adjust its alignment.

Figure 3-7 How to code with a readable style

How to code comments

Comments are used to document what the program does and what specific blocks and lines of code do. Since the C# compiler ignores comments, you can include them anywhere in a program without affecting your code. Figure 3-8 shows you how to code two types of comments.

The first example in this program shows a *delimited comment* at the start of a method. This type of comment is typically used to document information that applies to the entire method or to any other large block of code. You can include any useful or helpful information in a delimited comment such as a general description of the block, the author's name, the completion date, the files used by the block, and so on.

To document the purpose of a single line of code, you can use *single-line comments*. Once the compiler reads the slashes (//) that start this type of comment, it ignores all characters until the end of the current line. In this figure, single-line comments have been used to describe each group of statements. In addition, single-line comments have been used at the end of some lines of code to clarify the code.

Although many programmers sprinkle their code with comments, that shouldn't be necessary if you write your code so it's easy to read and understand. Instead, you should use comments only to clarify code that's difficult to understand. The trick, of course, is to provide comments for the code that needs explanation without cluttering the code with unnecessary comments. An experienced C# programmer wouldn't need any of the comments shown in this figure, for example.

One problem with comments is that they may not accurately represent what the code does. This often happens when a programmer changes the code, but doesn't change the comments that go along with it. Then it's even harder to understand the code, because the comments are misleading. So if you change the code that you've written comments for, be sure to change the comments too.

Incidentally, all comments are displayed in the Code Editor window in a different color from the words in the C# statements. By default, the C# code is blue and black (blue for C# keywords and black for the rest of the code), while the comments are green. That makes it easy to identify the comments.

A method with comments

```
private void btnCalculate_Click(object sender, System.EventArgs e)
{
    /****************************************
    * this method calculates the total
    * for an invoice depending on a
    * discount that's based on the subtotal
    ****************************************/

    // get the subtotal amount from the Subtotal text box
    decimal subtotal = Convert.ToDecimal(txtSubtotal.Text);

    // set the discountPercent variable based
    // on the value of the subtotal variable
    decimal discountPercent = 0m;          // the m indicates a decimal value
    if (subtotal >= 500)
        discountPercent = .2m;
    else if (subtotal >= 250 && subtotal < 500)
        discountPercent = .15m;
    else if (subtotal >= 100 && subtotal < 250)
        discountPercent = .1m;

    // calculate and assign the values for the
    // discountAmount and invoiceTotal variables
    decimal discountAmount = subtotal * discountPercent;
    decimal invoiceTotal = subtotal - discountAmount;

    // format the values and display them in their labels
    lblDiscountPercent.Text =              // percent format
        discountPercent.ToString("p1");    // with 1 decimal place
    lblDiscountAmount.Text =
        discountAmount.ToString("c");      // currency format
    lblTotal.Text =
        invoiceTotal.ToString("c");

    // move the focus to the Subtotal text box
    txtSubtotal.Focus();
}
```

Description

- *Comments* are used to help document what a program does and what the code within it does.
- To code a *single-line comment*, type // before the comment. You can use this technique to add a comment on its own line or to add a comment at the end of a line.
- To code a *delimited comment*, type /* at the start of the comment and */ at the end. You can also code asterisks to identify the lines in the comment, but that isn't necessary.

Recommendation

- Use comments only for portions of code that are difficult to understand. Then, make sure that the comments are correct and up-to-date.

Figure 3-8 How to code comments

How to work with the Text Editor toolbar

Figure 3-9 shows how you can use the Text Editor toolbar to work with code. If you experiment with this toolbar, you'll find that its buttons provide some useful functions for working with comments and indentation and for moving from one place to another.

In particular, you can use the Text Editor toolbar to modify several lines of code at once. For example, during testing, you can use this toolbar to *comment out* several lines of code by selecting the lines of code and then clicking on the Comment Out button. Then, you can test the program without those lines of code. If necessary, you can use the Uncomment button to restore those lines of code. Similarly, you can use the Increase Indent and Decrease Indent buttons to adjust the indentation for selected lines of code.

You can also use the Text Editor toolbar to work with *bookmarks*. After you use the Toggle Bookmark button to mark lines of code, you can easily move between the marked lines of code by using the Next and Previous Bookmark buttons. Although you usually don't need bookmarks when you're working with simple applications like the one shown here, bookmarks can be helpful when you're working with applications that contain more than a few pages of code.

If you experiment with the other buttons on the Text Editor toolbar, you'll find that they provide Intellisense features like the ones you learned about earlier in this chapter for referring to properties, methods, and events. Since most of these features are on by default, though, you'll only need to use these buttons if you turn the associated feature off.

How to expand and collapse blocks of code

As you write the code for an application, you may want to *collapse* and *expand* some of the regions, comments, and methods to make it easier to scroll through the code and locate specific sections of code. To do that, you can use the techniques described in figure 3-9. In the Code Editor window in this figure, for example, the Main method has been collapsed so that all you can see is its method declaration.

You may also want to collapse and expand code before you print it. Then, only the expanded code, in other words, the code that appears in the Code Editor window, is printed. The collapsed code is not. To print the code, you can use the Print command in the File menu.

The Code Editor window and the Text Editor toolbar

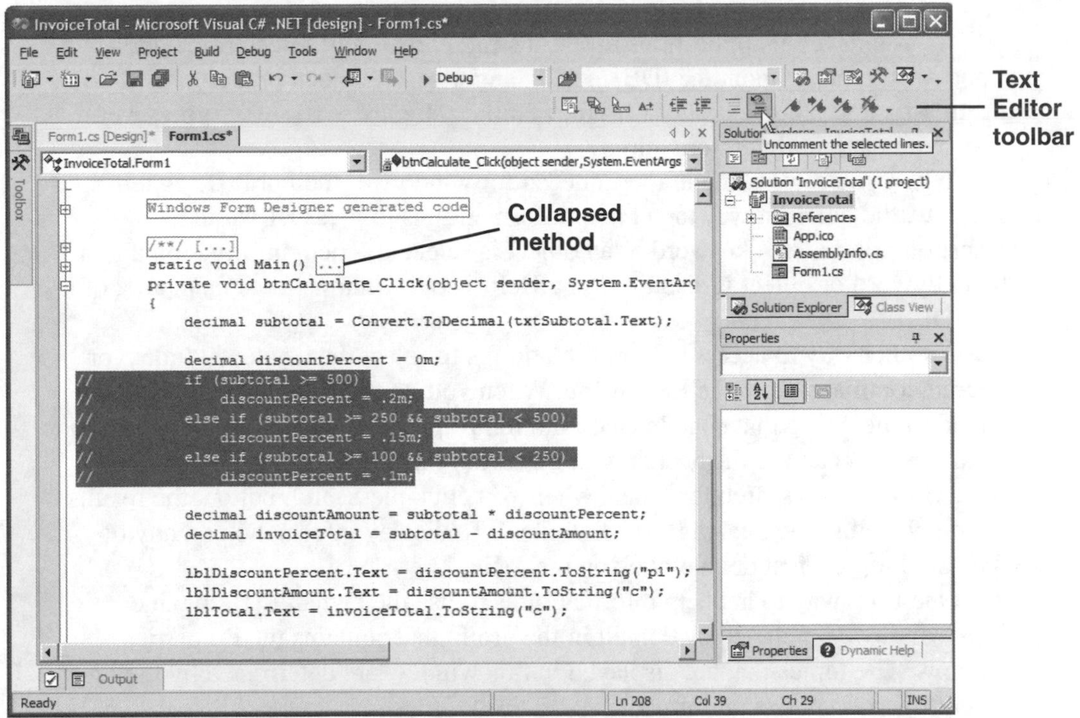

How to use the buttons of the Text Editor toolbar

- To display or hide the Text Editor toolbar, right-click in the toolbar area and choose Text Editor from the shortcut menu.
- To comment out or uncomment several lines of code at once, select the lines and click the Comment or Uncomment button. During testing, you can *comment out* a line of code. That way, you can test a new statement without deleting the old statement.
- To increase or decrease the indentation of several lines of code at once, select the lines and click the Increase Indent or Decrease Indent button.
- To move quickly between lines of code, you can use the last four buttons on the Text Editor toolbar to set and move between *bookmarks*.

How to collapse and expand the source code

- If a procedure appears in the Code Editor window with a minus sign (-) next to it, you can click the minus sign to *collapse* the method so just the first statement is displayed.
- If a procedure appears in the Code Editor window with a plus sign (+) next to it, you can click the plus sign to *expand* the method so you can see all of it.
- You can also view the code that's generated automatically as you design a form by clicking on the plus sign next to the block of code that's labeled "Windows Form Designer generated code," but you shouldn't edit this code.

Figure 3-9 How to use the Text Editor toolbar and collapse and expand source code

How to get help information

As you develop applications in C#, it's likely that you'll need some additional information about the IDE, the C# language, an object, property, method, event, or some other aspect of C# programming. Figure 3-10 shows you several ways you can get that information.

When you're working in the Code Editor window or the Form Designer window, the quickest way to get help information is to press F1 while the insertion point is in a keyword or an object is selected. Then, information about that keyword or object is displayed in a Help Topic window in the main area of the IDE.

Another way to access help information is to select the Contents, Index, or Search command from the Help menu. When you do that, a tabbed window is added to the group that contains the Solution Explorer window. In this figure, for example, you can see the Search window. From this window, you can enter a word or phrase to search for. Then, when you click the Search button, the results are displayed in the Search Results window. To display information on any of the listed topics, just double-click on the topic.

One final way to get help information is to use the Dynamic Help window. This window is included by default in the group that contains the Properties window. The topics that are displayed in this window are determined by the most recent operations you performed.

When you display information in the Help Topic window, you should realize that you're actually using a web browser that's built into Visual Studio. To work with this browser, you can use the buttons in the Web toolbar that appears when a help topic is displayed. This toolbar includes buttons that lets you go to the previous or next page or go to the MSDN home page. If you've worked with a web browser such as Internet Explorer before, you shouldn't have any trouble using this built-in browser.

Help information for using the Solution Explorer

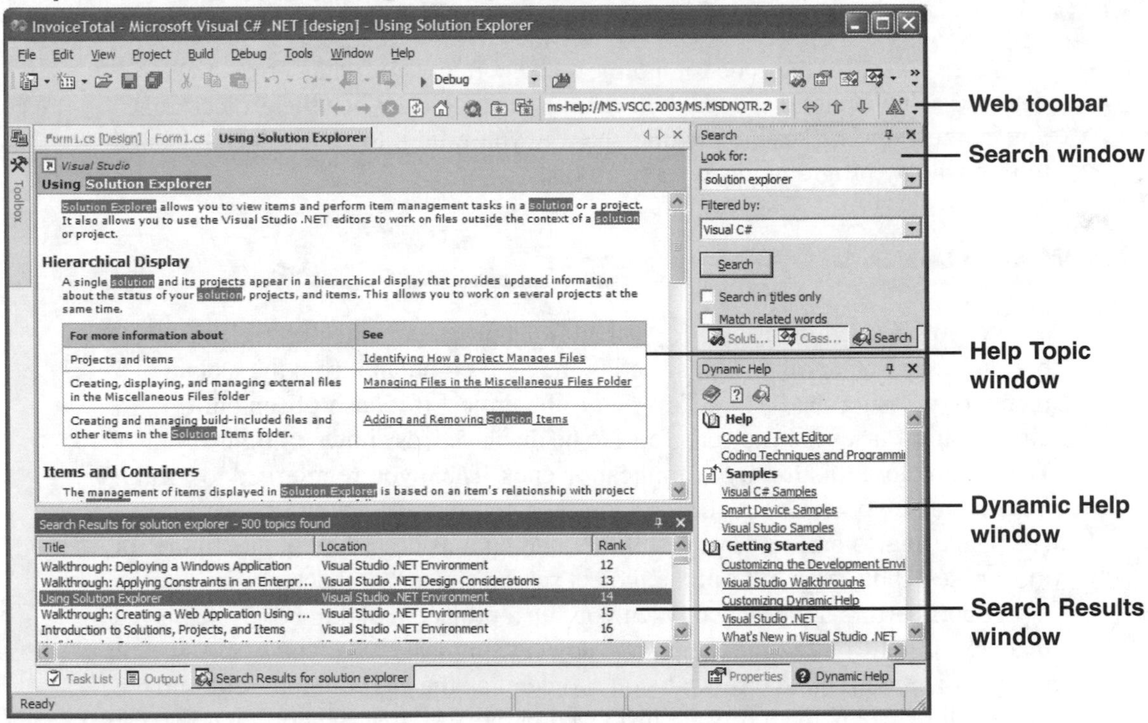

Description

- To display context-sensitive help information, select an object in the Form Designer window or position the insertion point in a keyword in the Code Editor window. Then, press F1. If the Help feature recognizes the object or keyword, information is displayed in the Help Topic window.
- You can also get help information by selecting the Contents, Index, or Search command from the Help menu. Then, a tabbed window is combined with the Solution Explorer window, and you can use that window to select the appropriate topic.
- The Contents window lets you select a topic from the table of contents, and the Index window lets you select an entry in the index. When you select a topic or index entry, it's displayed in the Help Topic window.
- The Search window lets you search for information based on keywords you enter. The results of the search are displayed in the Search Results window at the bottom of the screen. Then, you can double-click on an entry to display the related topic.
- The Dynamic Help window provides context-sensitive help depending on the operations you performed most recently. To display one of the listed topics, just click on it.
- Online help is implemented using a built-in web browser. To work with this browser, you can use the buttons in the Web toolbar that's displayed when you select a help topic.

Figure 3-10 How to get help information

How to run, test, and debug a project

After you enter the code for a project and correct any syntax errors that are detected as you enter this code, you can run the project. When the project runs, you can test it to make sure it works the way you want it to, and you can debug it to remove any programming errors you find.

How to run a project

As you learned in chapter 1, you can *run* a project by clicking the Start button in the Standard toolbar, selecting the Start command from the Debug menu, or pressing the F5 key. This *builds* the project if it hasn't been built already and causes the project's form to be displayed, as shown in figure 3-11. When you close this form, the application ends. Then, you're returned to Visual Studio where you can continue working on your program.

You can also build a project without running it as described in this figure. In most cases, though, you'll run the project so you can test and debug it.

If build errors are detected when you run a project, a dialog box is displayed that asks if you want to run the project anyway. In most cases, you won't want to run a project with build errors, so you should click the No button to return to the Code Editor. Then, the errors are displayed in the Task List window, and you can use this window to identify and correct the errors. When you do that, you should realize that the errors will still be listed in the Task List window and highlighted in the Code Editor window even after you've corrected them. The errors aren't cleared until you build the project again.

The form displayed when you run the Invoice Total project

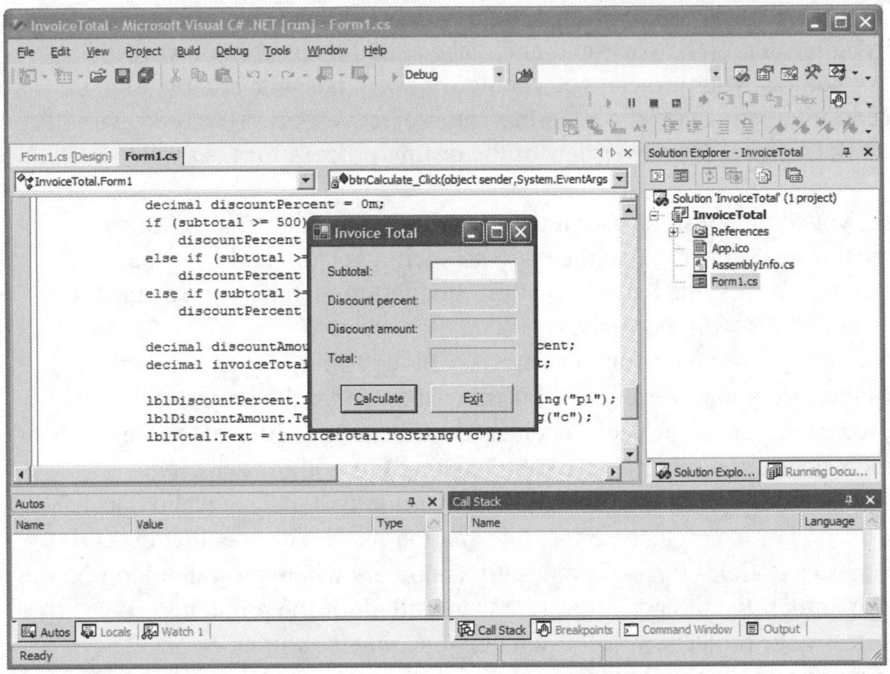

Description

- To *run* a project, click the Start button located in the Standard toolbar, select the Debug→Start menu command, or press the F5 key. This causes Visual Studio to *build* the project and create an assembly. Then, assuming that there are no build errors, the assembly is run so the project's form is displayed over the IDE as shown above.
- If syntax errors are detected when a project is built, they're listed in the Task List window and a dialog box asks whether you want to run the project even though there were build errors. Click No to return to the Code Editor.
- To locate a statement in error, you can double-click on the error description in the Task List window. After you've corrected all the errors, run the project again to rebuild it and clear the errors.
- If you prefer, you can build a project without actually running it by selecting the Build→Build *project name* command.
- When you build a project for the first time, all of the components of the project are built. After that, only the components that have changed are rebuilt. To rebuild all components whether or not they've changed, use the Build→Rebuild *projectname* command.
- If a solution consists of two or more projects, you can build all of the projects at once by using the Build→Build Solution command. To rebuild all the projects in a solution, use the Build→Rebuild Solution command.

How to test a project

When you *test* a project, you run it and make sure the application works correctly. As you test your project, you should try every possible combination of input data and interactions to be certain that the project works correctly in every case. Figure 3-12 provides an overview of the testing process for C# applications.

To start, you should test the user interface. Make sure that each control is sized and positioned properly, that there are no spelling errors in any of the controls or in the form's title bar, and that the navigation features such as the tab order and access keys work properly.

Next, subject your application to a carefully thought-out sequence of valid test data. Make sure you test every combination of data that the project will handle. If, for example, the project calculates the discount at different values based on the value of the subtotal, use subtotals that fall within each range.

Finally, test the program to make sure that it properly handles invalid data entered by users. For example, type text information into text boxes that expect numeric data. Leave fields blank. Use negative numbers where they shouldn't be allowed. Remember that the goal of testing is to find all of the problems.

As you test your projects, you'll eventually encounter *runtime errors*. These errors, also known as *exceptions*, occur when C# encounters a problem that prevents a statement from being executed. If, for example, a user enters "ABC" into the Subtotal text box on the Invoice Total form, a runtime error will occur when the program tries to assign that value to a decimal variable.

When a runtime error occurs, a dialog box like the one in this figure is displayed. This dialog box lets you break into the debugger (Break) so you can debug the error or end the application (Continue). When you break into the debugger, you can use the debugging tools that you'll be introduced to in the next figure.

Runtime errors, though, should only occur when you're testing a program. Before an application is put into production, it should be coded and tested so all runtime errors are caught by the application and appropriate messages are displayed to the user. You'll learn how to do that in chapter 7 of this book.

The dialog box that's displayed when a runtime error occurs

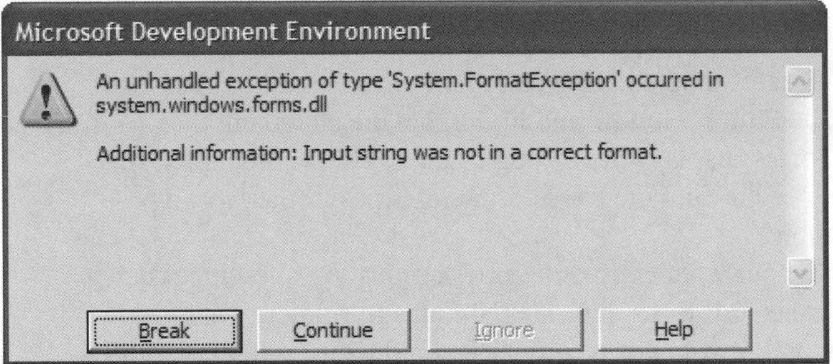

How to test a project

- Begin by testing the user interface. Visually check all the controls to make sure they are displayed properly with the correct text. Use the Tab key to make sure the tab order is set correctly, verify that the access keys work right, and see if both the Esc key and the Exit button properly close the application.
- Continue by testing the application with valid input data. For the Invoice Total application, you should enter a variety of subtotal amounts to make sure the discount percent, discount amount, and invoice totals are always calculated properly. For applications with more input controls, you need to test all possible combinations of valid input data.
- Complete your testing by making sure the project properly handles invalid or unexpected data or user actions. For example, leave required fields blank, enter text data into numeric input fields, and use negative numbers where they are not appropriate. Try everything you can think of to make the program fail.
- If a statement in your application can't be executed, a *runtime error*, or *exception*, occurs. Then, if the exception isn't handled by your application, a dialog box like the one above is displayed. At that point, you need to debug the application as explained in the next figure.

Description

- To *test* a project, you run the project to make sure it works properly no matter what combinations of valid or invalid data you enter or what sequence of controls you use.
- Because an application should never end with a runtime error, one of your goals in testing is to force runtime errors. For now, you can identify runtime errors, but you don't know enough C# programming to prevent them from occurring. In chapter 7, you'll learn how to write code that prevents runtime errors.

Figure 3-12 How to test a project

How to debug runtime errors

When a runtime error occurs and you click the Break button in the dialog box that's displayed, Visual Studio enters *break mode*. In that mode, Visual Studio displays the Code Editor window and highlights the statement that couldn't be executed. It also displays the Debug toolbar. This is illustrated in figure 3-13. Then, you need to find the cause of the exception (the *bug*) by *debugging* the application.

Often, you can figure out what caused the problem just by knowing what statement couldn't be executed. But sometimes, it helps to find out what the current values in some of the variables or properties in the program are. To do that, you place the mouse pointer over a variable or property in the code so a *data tip* is displayed. This tip displays the current value of the variable or property.

In the example in this figure, the current value of the Text property of the txtSubtotal control is "ABC", which isn't numeric data. Since the variable named subtotal requires numeric data, the highlighted statement can't be executed.

Once you find the cause of a bug, you can correct it. But first, you must exit from break mode. To do that, you can click the Stop Debugging button in the Debug toolbar. Then, you can correct the problem in the Code Editor window and test the application again.

The last of the three debugging techniques that are summarized in this figure lets you stop a program that you can't stop any other way. To do that, you can click the Break All button in the Debug toolbar. Although you shouldn't need to do that when working with a simple program like the one in this chapter, it can come in handy when you're working with programs that perform loops, which you'll learn about in chapter 5.

How a project looks in break mode

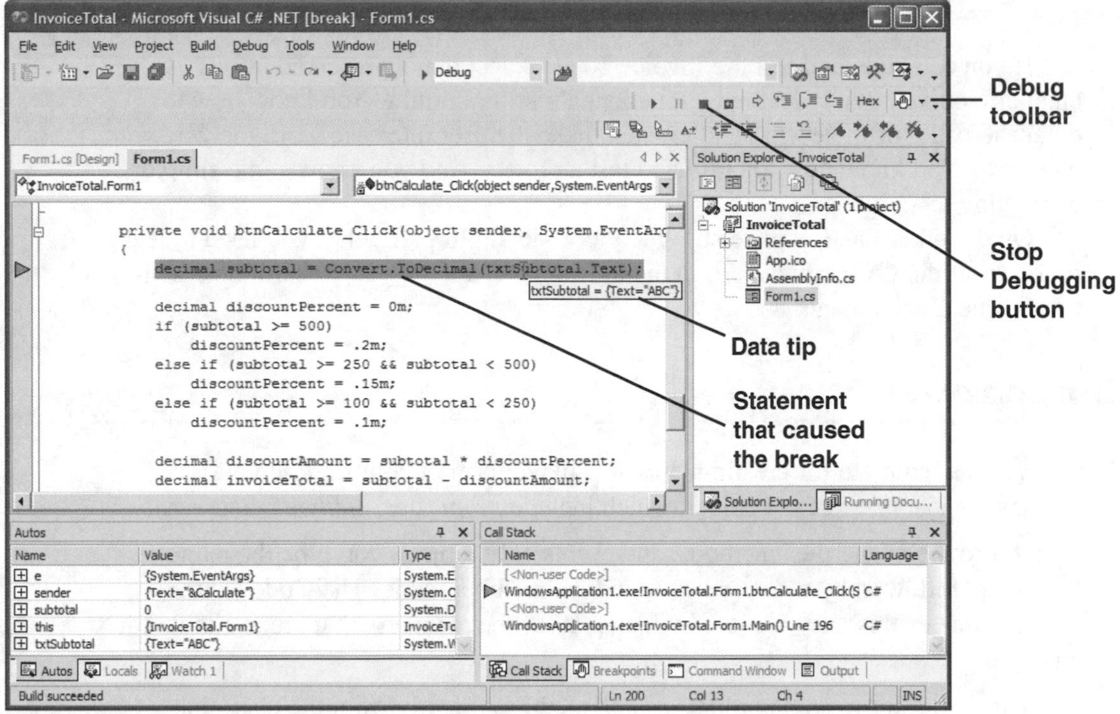

Description

- When an application ends with a runtime error, you need to fix the error. This is commonly referred to as *debugging*, and the error is commonly referred to as a *bug*.
- If you click the Break button in the dialog box for a runtime error, Visual Studio displays the Code Editor window and highlights the statement that caused the exception.
- When a program enters break mode, the debugging windows and the Debug and Debug Location toolbars are displayed.

Debugging techniques for simple applications

- In *break mode*, you can display the value of a variable or property in a *data tip* by positioning the mouse pointer over it.
- To exit break mode and end the application, click the Stop Debugging button in the Debug toolbar.
- To enter break mode any time that an application is running, click the Break All button in the Debug toolbar. This is useful if you need to stop a program that's caught in a loop.

Figure 3-13 How to debug runtime errors

Perspective

If you can code and test the Invoice Total project that's presented in this chapter, you've already learned a lot about C# programming. You know how to enter the code for the event handlers that make the user interface work the way you want it to. You know how to build and test a project. And you know some simple debugging techniques.

On the other hand, you've still got a lot to learn. In particular, you need to learn more about the C# language. So in the next eight chapters, you'll learn the essentials of the C# language.

Summary

- A *class* is a template for creating an *object* like a form or control. Each class defines the *members* of the object, which include *properties*, *methods*, and *events*.
- To refer to the properties, methods, and events of an object, you type the name of the object followed by a *dot operator* and the member name. The Code Editor window makes this easy for you by listing all of the members that are available for an object.
- You can also refer to some properties and methods directly from the class that defines them. These properties and methods are called *static members*.
- Windows applications work by responding to the events that occur on objects. To respond to an event, you code an *event handler*. To generate the *method declaration* for an event handler, you can double-click the form or one of its controls in the Form Designer window.
- C# is a case-sensitive language, which means that you must use exact capitalization when entering keywords and names. You must also end each statement with a semicolon, and you must enclose each block of code in braces.
- As you enter code, the Visual Studio checks for *syntax errors*. It highlights any errors it finds in the Code Editor window and lists them in the *Task List window* so you can locate and correct them.
- In the Code Editor window, you can *collapse* or *expand* blocks of code by clicking the minus and plus signs that are displayed on the left side of the window.
- You can use *comments* to document what a program does. You can also *comment out* a line of code for testing purposes.
- You can get context-sensitive help for an object in the Form Designer window or for a keyword in the Code Editor window. You can also use the Contents, Index, and Search commands in the Help menu to get information.
- When you *run* a project, Visual Studio first *builds* the project to create an assembly. Then, if no syntax errors are detected, the project's form is displayed.

- You should *test* a project thoroughly to make sure it properly handles all combinations of input, including incorrect or missing data.
- If a statement in the application can't be executed, a *runtime error* (or *exception*) occurs. Then, you must *debug* the application.

Terms

object-oriented programming
object-oriented language
object
class
instance
instantiation
base class
property
method
event
member
dot operator
dot
static member
event-driven application
event handler
event wiring
method declaration
statement
block of code
syntax error
build error
Task List window
task list
comment
single-line comment
delimited comment
comment out a line
bookmark
collapse
expand
build a project
run a project
test a project
runtime error
exception
bug
debug
break mode
data tip

Objectives

- Given the code for a simple application, use the skills presented in this chapter to add the code and test the application.
- Given the code for an application and a description of what it does, use indentation and blank lines to make the code easy to read, and use comments to document the purpose of the program.
- Use any of the help features presented in this chapter to display help information on a given topic.
- Explain how an application responds to events.
- Distinguish between a syntax (or build) error and a runtime error.
- Distinguish between testing and debugging.
- Describe how to debug a runtime error.

Exercise 3-1 Code and test the Invoice Total form

In this exercise, you'll add code to the Invoice Total form that you designed in exercise 2-1. Then, you'll build and test the project to be sure it works correctly. You'll also experiment with debugging and review some help information.

Copy and open the Invoice Total application

1. Use the Windows Explorer to copy the Invoice Total project that you created for chapter 2 from the C:\C#.NET\Chapter 02 directory to the C:\C#.NET\Chapter 03 directory.
2. Open the Invoice Total project (InvoiceTotal.csproj) that's now in the C:\C#.NET\Chapter 03\InvoiceTotal directory.

Add code to the form and correct syntax errors

3. Display the Invoice Total form in the Form Designer window. Then, double-click the Calculate button to open the Code Editor window and generate the method declaration for the Click event of this object. Enter the code for this method as shown in figure 3-5.
4. Return to the Form Designer, and double-click the Exit button to generate the method declaration for the Click event of this object. Enter the statement shown in figure 3-5 for this event handler.
5. Open the Task List window as described in figure 3-6. If any syntax errors are listed in this window, double-click on the error to move to the error in the Code Editor window. Then, correct the error. Repeat this for any other errors listed in the Task List window.

Test the application

6. Click the Start button in the Standard toolbar to build and run the project. If you corrected all the syntax errors in step 5, the build should succeed and the Invoice Total form should appear. If not, you'll need to correct the errors and click the Start button again.
7. Enter a valid numeric value in the first text box and click the Calculate button or press the Enter key to activate this button. Assuming that the calculation works, click the Exit button or press the Esc key to end the application. If either of these methods doesn't work right, of course, you need to debug the problems and test the application again.

Enter invalid data and display data tips in break mode

8. Start the application again. This time, enter xx for the subtotal. Then, click the Calculate button. This will cause a runtime error and display a dialog box. (Note: Be sure to click the Calculate button instead of pressing the Enter key. If you press the Enter key instead, the correct statement won't be highlighted in the next step. This is probably a bug in Visual Studio.)

9. Click the Break button to enter break mode, and note the highlighted statement. Then, move the mouse pointer over the variable and property in this statement to display their data tips. This shows that the code for this application needs to be enhanced so it checks for invalid data. You'll learn how to do that in chapter 7. For now, though, click the Stop Debugging button in Debug toolbar to end the application.

Create syntax errors and see how they affect the IDE

10. When you return to the Code Editor window, display the Task List window and then close it by clicking on the Close button in its upper right corner. Next, change the name of one of the labels that are referred to in the code so it's incorrect.
11. Start the application without correcting the error. A dialog box will be displayed indicating that there are build errors. Click the No button in this dialog box to end the application and return to the Code Editor window.
12. Notice that the Task List window is displayed again, and it lists the build error that was detected. Double-click on this error and it will be highlighted in the Code Editor window. Correct the error. Then, run the application and close the form.

Generate and delete an event handler

13. Display the Form Designer for the Invoice Total form and double-click the title bar for the form. This should generate an event handler for the Load event of the form.
14. Delete the event handler for the Load event of the form. Then, run the application. When you do, you'll get a build error that indicates that the form does not contain a definition for this event handler.
15. Double-click on the error to jump to the statement that wires the event handler. Because this statement is in the region that contains the generated code for the form, this region will be expanded. Delete this statement to correct the error.

Collapse and expand blocks of code

16. Click the minus sign to the left of the btnCalculate_Click method to collapse its code. Then, click its plus sign to expand it again.
17. Scroll up through the code until you see the region named "Windows Form Designer generated code." Then, review the code that's generated for this simple form. When you're done, click the minus sign to the left of the region name to collapse this region.

Experiment with the Help feature

18. To see how context-sensitive help works, place the insertion point in the Focus method in the last statement of the first event handler and press F1. This should open a Help Topic window that tells you more about this method.

19. Select the Index command from the Help menu to display the Index window. Type "focus" into the Look for box in this window to see the entries that are listed under this topic. Next, if the Visual C# item isn't selected in the Filter by drop-down list, select this item to show just the topics related to C#. Then, click on one or more topics to display them in the Help Topic window.
20. Continue experimenting with the Index feature until you're comfortable with it. Then, experiment with the Contents and Search commands in the Help menu to see how they work, and try using some of the buttons in the Web toolbar to see how they work.

Exit from Visual Studio

21. Click the Close button for the Visual Studio window to exit from this application. If you did everything and got your application to work right, you've come a long way!

Section 2

The C# language essentials

In section 1, you were introduced to C# programming. In particular, you learned how to use Visual Studio to design a Windows form, how to enter the code for that form, and how to test that code. However, you didn't actually learn the details for coding C# statements.

Now, in this section, you'll learn the C# language essentials. In chapter 4, for example, you'll learn how to code arithmetic operations. In chapter 5, you'll learn how to code selection and iteration statements. In chapter 6, you'll learn how to code your own methods. And in chapter 7, you'll learn how to check the user's entries to make sure they're valid. This gets you off to a great start.

Then, chapter 8 shows you how to use arrays and collections, chapter 9 shows you how to work with dates and strings, and chapter 10 shows you how to work with other types of controls and with applications that require two or more forms. To conclude your mastery of these essentials, chapter 11 presents more of the Visual Studio features for debugging.

How to work with numeric and string data

To start your mastery of the C# language, this chapter shows you how to work with the various types of data that C# offers. In particular, you'll learn how to perform arithmetic operations on numeric data, how to work with string data, and how to convert one type of data to another.

How to work with the built-in value types

To start, this chapter shows you how to work with the *built-in value types* that the C# language provides. Then, later on in this chapter, you'll be introduced to the *reference types* that C# provides. Together, they make up the C# *data types*.

The built-in value types

Figure 4-1 summarizes the built-in value types that C# provides. To refer to each of these data types, C# provides a keyword. You can use the first eleven data types to store numbers, and you can use the last two data types to store characters and true or false values.

The first eight data types are used to store *integers*, which are numbers that don't contain decimal places (whole numbers). When you use one of the integer types, you should select an appropriate size. Most of the time, you can use the *int* type. However, you may need to use the *long* type if the value is too large for the int type. On the other hand, if you're working with smaller numbers and you need to save system resources, you can use the *short* or *byte* type. If you're working with positive numbers, you can also use the unsigned versions of these types.

You can use the next three data types to store numbers that contain decimal places. Since the *decimal* type is more accurate than the *double* and *float* types, it's commonly used for monetary values. If you need to save system resources, however, the double and float types are adequate for most situations.

You can use the *char* type to store a single character. Since C# supports the two-byte *Unicode character set*, it can store practically any character from any language around the world. As a result, you can use C# to create programs that read and print Greek or Chinese characters. In practice, though, you'll usually work with the characters that are stored in the older one-byte *ASCII character set*. These characters are the first 256 characters of the Unicode character set.

Last, you can use the *bool* type to store a true value or false value. This type of value is known as a *Boolean value*.

The built-in value types

C# Keyword	Bytes	.NET type	Description
byte	1	Byte	A positive integer value from 0 to 255
sbyte	1	SByte	A signed integer value from -128 to 127
short	2	Int16	An integer from –32,768 to +32,767
ushort	2	UInt16	An unsigned integer from 0 to 65,535
int	4	Int32	An integer from –2,147,483,648 to +2,147,483,647
uint	4	UInt32	An unsigned integer from 0 to 4,294,967,295
long	8	Int64	An integer from –9,223,372,036,854,775,808 to +9,223,372,036,854,775,807
ulong	8	UInt64	An unsigned integer from 0 to +18,446,744,073,709,551,615
float	4	Single	A non-integer number with approximately 7 significant digits
double	8	Double	A non-integer number with approximately 14 significant digits
decimal	16	Decimal	A non-integer number with up to 28 significant digits (integer and fraction) that can represent values up to 79,228 x 10^{24}
char	2	Char	A single Unicode character
bool	1	Boolean	A true or false value

Description

- The *built-in data types* are actually aliases for the data types defined by the Common Type System of the .NET Framework.
- All of the data types shown in this figure are *value types*, which means that they store their own data. In contrast, *reference types* store a reference to the area of memory where the data is stored. See figure 4-10 for more information on value types and reference types.
- A *bit* is a binary digit that can have a value of one or zero. A *byte* is a group of eight bits. As a result, the number of bits for each data type is the number of bytes multiplied by 8.
- *Integers* are whole numbers, and the first eight data types above provide for signed and unsigned integers of various sizes.
- Since the decimal type is the most accurate non-integer data type, it's typically used to store monetary values.
- The *Unicode character set* provides for over 65,000 characters, with two bytes used for each character. Each character maps to an integer value.
- The older *ASCII character set* that's used by most operating systems provides for 256 characters with one byte used for each character. In the Unicode character set, the first 256 characters correspond to the 256 ASCII characters.
- A *bool* data type stores a *Boolean value* that's either true or false.

Figure 4-1 The built-in value types

How to declare and initialize variables

A *variable* stores a value that can change as the program executes. Before you can use a variable, you must declare its data type and name and then initialize it by assigning a value to it. Figure 4-2 shows two ways you can do that.

First, you can use separate statements to *declare* and *initialize* the variable as shown in the first example in this figure. Second, you can use a single statement that declares the variable and assigns a value to it. This figure presents several examples that use this technique. Notice that the last example declares and initializes two variables with the same data type.

Although you can declare a variable without assigning a value to it, you must assign a value to the variable before you can use it in your code. Otherwise, you'll get a build error when you try to run the project. As a result, it's a good coding practice to declare and initialize a variable in one statement or to assign a value to a variable immediately after you declare it.

You should also notice in the examples in this figure that the first word of each variable name starts with a lowercase letter, and the remaining words start with an uppercase letter. This is known as *camel notation*, and it's a common coding convention in C#.

When you work with variables, you can assign a *literal value,* or *literal*, to the variable. For example, you can assign a literal value of 1 to an int variable. When you code a number that has a decimal point, such as 8.125, the C# compiler assumes that you want that literal value to be a double value. As a result, if you want it to be interpreted as a decimal value, you need to code the letter *m* or *M* after the value (think *m* for *money*). Similarly, for a float type, you code the letter *f* or *F* after the value. If you omit the letter, you'll get a build error when you try to run the project.

You can use *scientific notation* to express the value of extremely large or small non-integer numbers. To use this notation, you code the letter *e* or *E* followed by a power of 10. For instance, 3.65e+9 is equal to 3.65 times 10^9 (or 3,650,000,000), and 3.65e-9 is equal to 3.65 times 10^{-9} (or .00000000365). If you have a scientific or mathematical background, you're already familiar with this notation. If you don't have that background, you probably won't ever use this notation.

You can also assign a literal value to a variable with the char data type. To do that, you enclose the value in single quotes. To assign a literal value to a variable with the bool type, you can use the *true* and *false* keywords.

How to declare and initialize constants

A *constant* stores a value that can't be changed as the program executes. Many of the skills for declaring and initializing variables also apply to declaring and initializing constants. However, you always use a single statement to declare and initialize a constant, and that statement must begin with the *const* keyword. In addition, it's a common coding convention to capitalize the first letter in each word of a constant, including the first word.

How to declare and initialize a variable in two statements

Syntax

```
type variableName;
variableName = value;
```

Example

```
int counter;                        // declaration statement
counter = 1;                        // assignment statement
```

How to declare and initialize a variable in one statement

Syntax

```
type variableName = value;
```

Examples

```
int counter = 1;
long numberOfBytes = 20000;
float interestRate = 8.125f;        // f or F indicates a float value
double price = 14.95;
decimal total = 24218.1928m;        // m or M indicates a decimal value
double starCount = 3.65e+9;         // scientific notation
char letter = 'A';                  // enclose a character value in single quotes
bool valid = false;
int x = 0, y = 0;                   // initialize 2 variables with 1 statement
```

How to declare and initialize a constant

Syntax

```
const type ConstantName = value;
```

Examples

```
const int DaysInNovember = 30;
const decimal SalesTax = .075m;
```

Description

- A *variable* stores a value that can change as a program executes, while a *constant* stores a value that can't be changed. Before you can use a variable or constant, you must declare its type and assign an initial value to it.
- Common initial values are 0 for variables that store integer values, 0.0 for variables that store decimal values, and false for variables that store Boolean values.
- To declare or initialize more than one variable for a single data type in a single statement, use commas to separate the variable names or assignments.
- To identify *literal values* as float values, you must type the letter *f* or *F* after the number. To identify decimal values, you must type the letter *m* or *M* after the number.
- The keywords for data types must be coded with all lowercase letters.

Naming conventions

- Start the names of variables with a lowercase letter, and capitalize the first letter of each word after the first word. This is known as *camel notation*.
- Capitalize the first letter of each word of a constant name.

Figure 4-2 How to declare and initialize variables and constants

How to code arithmetic expressions

Figure 4-3 shows how to code *arithmetic expressions*. To create an arithmetic expression, you use the *arithmetic operators* to indicate what operations are to be performed on the *operands* in the expression. An operand can be a literal or a variable.

The first five operators listed in this figure work on two operands. As a result, they're referred to as *binary operators*. For example, when you use the subtraction operator (-), you subtract one operand from the other. In contrast, the last four operators work on one operand. As a result, they're referred to as *unary operators*. For example, you can code the negative sign operator (-) in front of an operand to reverse the value of the operand. You can also code a positive sign operator (+) in front of an operand to return the value of the operand. Since that doesn't change the value of the operand, however, the positive sign is rarely used as a unary operator.

While the addition (+), subtraction (-), and multiplication (*) operators are self-explanatory, the division (/) and modulus (%) operators require some additional explanation. If you're working with integer data types, the division operator returns an integer value that represents the number of times the left operand goes into the right operand. Then, the modulus operator returns an integer value that represents the remainder (which is the amount that's left over after dividing the right operand by the left operand). If you're working with non-integer data types, the division operator returns a value that uses decimal places to indicate the result of the division, which is usually what you want.

When you code an increment (++) or decrement (--) operator, you can *prefix* the operand by coding the operator before the operand. This is illustrated by the last two examples in the first two groups. Then, the operand is incremented or decremented before the result is assigned.

You should realize, though, that you can also *postfix* the operand by coding the operator after the operand. Then, the result is assigned before the operand is incremented or decremented. When an entire statement does nothing more than increment a variable, as in

```
counter++;
```

both the prefix and postfix forms yield the same result.

Since each char variable holds a Unicode character that maps to an integer, you can perform some integer operations on char variables. For instance, this figure shows an example of how you can use the increment operator to change the numeric value of a char variable from 67 to 68. This changes the character from the letter *C* to the letter *D*.

Arithmetic operators

Operator	Name	Description
+	Addition	Adds two operands.
-	Subtraction	Subtracts the right operand from the left operand.
*	Multiplication	Multiplies the right operand and the left operand.
/	Division	Divides the right operand into the left operand. If both operands are integers, then the result is an integer.
%	Modulus	Returns the value that is left over after dividing the right operand into the left operand.
+	Positive sign	Returns the value of the operand.
-	Negative sign	Changes a positive value to negative, and vice versa.
++	Increment	Adds 1 to the operand (x = x + 1).
--	Decrement	Subtracts 1 from the operand (x = x - 1).

Examples of arithmetic expressions

```
// integer arithmetic
int x = 14;
int y = 8;
int result1 = x + y;          // result1 = 22
int result2 = x - y;          // result2 = 6
int result3 = x * y;          // result3 = 112
int result4 = x / y;          // result4 = 1
int result5 = x % y;          // result5 = 6
int result6 = -y + x;         // result6 = 6
int result7 = --y;            // result7 = 7
int result8 = ++x;            // result8 = 15, x = 15

// decimal arithmetic
decimal a = 8.5m;
decimal b = 3.4m;
decimal result11 = a + b;       // result11 = 11.9
decimal result12 = a - b;       // result12 = 5.1
decimal result13 = a / b;       // result13 = 2.5
decimal result14 = a * b;       // result14 = 28.90
decimal result15 = a % b;       // result15 = 1.7
decimal result16 = -a;          // result16 = -8.5
decimal result17 = --a;         // result17 = 7.5
decimal result18 = ++b;         // result18 = 4.4

// character arithmetic
char letter1 = 'C';             // letter1 = 'C'  Unicode integer is 67
char letter2 = ++letter1;       // letter2 = 'D'  Unicode integer is 68
```

Description

- An *arithmetic expression* consists of one or more *operands* and *arithmetic operators*.
- The first five operators above are called *binary operators* because they operate on two operands. The next four are called *unary operators* because they operate on just one operand.

How to code assignment statements

Figure 4-4 shows how you can code an *assignment statement* to assign a new value to a variable. In a simple assignment statement, you code the variable name, an equals sign, and an expression. This is illustrated by the first group of assignment statements in this figure. Notice that the expression can be a literal value, the name of another variable, or any other type of expression, such as an arithmetic expression. After the expression is evaluated, the result is assigned to the variable.

When you code assignment statements, it's common to code the same variable on both sides of the equals sign as shown in the second group of statements. That way, you can use the current value of the variable in an expression and then update the variable by assigning the result of the expression to it. For example, you can easily add 100 to the value of a variable and store the new value in the same variable.

Since it's common to use a variable on both sides of an assignment statement, C# provides the five shorthand *assignment operators* shown in this figure. These operators are illustrated in the third group of statements. Notice that these statements perform the same functions as the second group of statements. However, the statements that use the shorthand operators are more compact.

If you need to increment or decrement a variable by a value of 1, you can use the increment or decrement operator instead of an assignment statement. For example:

```
month = month + 1;
```

is equivalent to

```
month += 1;
```

which is equivalent to

```
month++;
```

The technique you use is mostly a matter of preference.

Assignment operators

Operator	Name	Description
=	Assignment	Assigns a new value to the variable.
+=	Addition	Adds the right operand to the value stored in the variable and assigns the result to the variable.
-=	Subtraction	Subtracts the right operand from the value stored in the variable and assigns the result to the variable.
*=	Multiplication	Multiplies the variable by the right operand and assigns the result to the variable.
/=	Division	Divides the variable by the right operand and assigns the result to the variable. If the variable and the operand are both integers, then the result is an integer.
%=	Modulus	Divides the variable by the right operand and assigns the remainder to the variable.

The syntax for a simple assignment statement

```
variableName = expression;
```

Typical assignment statements

```
counter = 7;
newCounter = counter;
discountAmount = subtotal * .2m;
total = subtotal - discountAmount;
```

Statements that use the same variable on both sides of the equals sign

```
total = total + 100m;
total = total - 100m;
price = price * .8m;
```

Statements that use the shortcut assignment operators

```
total += 100m;
total -= 100m;
price *= .8m;
```

Description

- A simple *assignment statement* consists of a variable, an equals sign, and an expression. When the assignment statement is executed, the expression is evaluated and the result is stored in the variable.
- Besides the equals sign, C# provides the five other *assignment operators* shown above. These operators provide a shorthand way to code common assignment operations.

How to work with the order of precedence

Figure 4-5 gives more information for coding arithmetic expressions. Specifically, it gives the *order of precedence* of the arithmetic operations. This means that all of the prefixed increment and decrement operations in an expression are done first, followed by all of the positive and negative operations, and so on. If there are two or more operations at each order of precedence, the operations are done from left to right.

Because this sequence of operations doesn't always work the way you want it to, you may need to override the sequence by using parentheses. Then, the expressions in the innermost sets of parentheses are done first, followed by the expressions in the next sets of parentheses, and so on. Within each set of parentheses, though, the operations are done from left to right in the order of precedence.

The need for parentheses is illustrated by the two examples in this figure. Because parentheses aren't used in the first example, the multiplication operation is done before the subtraction operation, which gives an incorrect result. In contrast, because the subtraction operation is enclosed in parentheses in the second example, this operation is performed before the multiplication operation, which gives a correct result.

In practice, you should use parentheses to dictate the sequence of operations whenever there's any doubt about it. That way, you don't have to worry about the order of precedence.

This figure also summarizes the information on prefixed and postfixed increment and decrement operations that I mentioned earlier, and the last set of examples shows the differences in these operations. Because this can get confusing, it's best to limit these operators to simple expressions and to use the prefix form whenever there's any doubt about how an expression will be evaluated.

The order of precedence for arithmetic operations

1. Increment and decrement
2. Positive and negative
3. Multiplication, division, and remainder
4. Addition and subtraction

A calculation that uses the default order of precedence

```
decimal discountPercent = .2m;          // 20% discount
decimal price = 100m;                   // $100 price
price = price * 1 - discountPercent;    // price = $99.8
```

A calculation that uses parentheses to specify the order of precedence

```
decimal discountPercent = .2m;          // 20% discount
decimal price = 100m;                   // $100 price
price = price * (1 - discountPercent);  // price = $80
```

The use of prefixed and postfixed increment and decrement operators

```
int a = 5;
int b = 5
int y = ++a;          // a = 6, y = 6
int z = b++;          // b = 6, z = 5
```

Description

- Unless parentheses are used, the operations in an expression take place from left to right in the *order of precedence*.
- To specify the sequence of operations, you can use parentheses. Then, the operations in the innermost sets of parentheses are done first, followed by the operations in the next sets, and so on.
- When you use an increment or decrement operator as a *prefix* to a variable, the variable is incremented or decremented and then the result is assigned. But when you use an increment or decrement operator as a *postfix* to a variable, the result is assigned and then the variable is incremented or decremented.

Figure 4-5 How to work with the order of precedence

How to work with casting

As you develop C# programs, you'll frequently need to convert data from one data type to another. To do that, you can sometimes use a technique called *casting*. Figure 4-6 illustrates how casting works.

As you can see, C# provides for two types of casting. *Implicit casts* are performed automatically and can be used to convert data with a less precise type to a more precise type. This is called a *widening conversion* because the resulting value is always wider than the original value. The first statement in this figure, for example, causes an int value to be converted to a double value. Similarly, the second statement causes a char value to be converted to an int value.

C# will also perform an implicit cast on the values in an arithmetic expression if some of the values have more precise data types than other values. This is illustrated by the next three statements in this figure. Here, the variables a, b, and c are used in an arithmetic expression. Notice that a is declared with the double data type, while b and c are declared with the int data type. Because of that, both b and c will be converted to double values when this expression is evaluated.

A *narrowing conversion* is one that casts data from a more precise data type to a less precise data type. With this type of conversion, the less precise data type may not be wide enough to hold the original value. Because C# uses *strict type semantics*, you must use an *explicit cast* to perform narrowing conversions.

To perform an explicit cast, you code the data type in parentheses before the variable that you want to convert. When you do this, you should realize that you may lose some information. This is illustrated by the first example in this figure that performs an explicit cast. Here, a double value of 93.75 is cast to an int value of 93. An explicit cast is required in this example because C# won't automatically cast a double value to an integer value since an integer value is less precise. Notice here that the double value is truncated rather than rounded.

When you use explicit casting in an arithmetic expression, the casting is done before the arithmetic operations. This is illustrated by the last two examples of explicit casts. In the last example, two integer types are cast to decimal types before the division is done so the result will have decimal places if they are needed. Without explicit casting, the expression would return an integer value that would then be cast to a decimal.

When you code an explicit cast, an exception may occur at runtime if the new data type isn't wide enough to hold the result of the expression. As a result, you should use an explicit cast only when you're sure that the new data type can hold the value.

Although you typically cast between numeric data types, you should know that you can also cast between the int and char types. That's because every char type corresponds to an int value that identifies it in the Unicode character set.

How implicit casting works

Casting from less precise to more precise data types

byte→short→int→long→float→double→decimal
char→int

Example

```
double grade = 93;                 // convert int to double

int letter = 'A';                  // convert char to int

double a = 95.0;
int b = 86, c = 91;
double average = (a+b+c)/3;        // convert b and c to double values
                                   // (average = 90.666666...)
```

How to code an explicit cast

The syntax for coding an explicit cast

```
(type) expression
```

Examples

```
int grade = (int) 93.75;           // convert double to int (grade = 93)

char letter = (char) 65;           // convert int to char (letter = 'A')

double a = 95.0;
int b = 86, c = 91;
int average = ((int)a+b+c)/3;      // convert a to int value (average = 90)

decimal result = (decimal) b / (decimal) c;     // result has decimal places
```

Description

- If you code an assignment statement that assigns a value with a less precise data type to a variable with a more precise data type, C# automatically converts the less precise data type to the more precise data type. This can be referred to as an *implicit cast* or a *widening conversion.*
- When you code an arithmetic expression, C# implicitly casts operands with less precise data types to the most precise data type used in the expression.
- To code an assignment statement that assigns a value with a more precise data type to a variable with a less precise data type, you must code the less precise data type in parentheses preceding the value to be assigned. This can be referred to as an *explicit cast* or a *narrowing conversion.*
- You can also use an explicit cast in an arithmetic expression. Then, the casting is done before the arithmetic operations.

Figure 4-6 How to work with casting

How to use the Math class

Figure 4-7 presents five methods of the Math class that you can use to work with numeric data. Although this class provides a variety of methods for performing mathematical operations, these are the ones you're most likely to use. Note in the syntax summaries that square brackets indicate that a clause is optional, braces indicate a choice between two or more elements, and bold type indicates language elements that must be entered exactly as shown.

The five methods shown in this figure are *static methods*. As a result, you can call these methods directly from the Math class by coding the name of the class, a dot, the name of the method, and one or more *arguments* enclosed in parentheses. For example, the Round method requires at least one argument that represents the value to be rounded, plus an optional second argument. The Sqrt method requires just one argument. And the Pow, Min, and Max methods require two arguments.

You use the Round method to round a decimal, double, or float value to a specified number of decimal digits, called the *precision*. For instance, the first statement in this figure rounds the value in the shipWeight variable to a whole number, because that's the default. In contrast, the second statement specifies two decimal places.

You use the Pow method to raise a number to the specified power. The third statement in this figure, for example, raises the variable named radius to the second power. In other words, it calculates the square of this variable, which is used to calculate the area of a circle. Note that C# doesn't provide an arithmetic operator for raising a number to a power like some other languages do. Because of that, you'll want to use the Pow method any time you need to perform this operation.

This figure also presents three other static methods of the Math class: Sqrt, Min, and Max. The Sqrt method calculates the square root of a number. The Min and Max methods return the minimum or maximum of two numeric values that you specify. These three methods can be used with any of the numeric data types. However, when you use the Min or Max method, the two values you specify must be of the same type.

Four static methods of the Math class

The syntax of the Round method

```
Math.Round(decimalNumber [, precision])
```

The syntax of the Pow method

```
Math.Pow(number, power)
```

The syntax of the Sqrt method

```
Math.Sqrt(number)
```

The syntax of the Min and Max methods

```
Math.{Min|Max}(number1, number2)
```

Statements that use static methods of the Math class

```
int shipWeight = Math.Round(shipWeightDouble);  // round to a whole number
double orderTotal = Math.Round(orderTotal, 2);  // round to 2 decimal places
double area = Math.Pow(radius, 2) * 3.1416
double sqrtX = Math.Sqrt(x);
double maxSales = Math.Max(lastYearSales, thisYearSales);
int minQty = Math.Min(lastYearQty, thisYearQty);
```

Results from static methods of the Math class

Statement	Result
Math.Round(23.75)	24
Math.Round(23.754, 2)	23.75
Math.Round(23.755, 2)	23.76
Math.Pow(5, 2)	25
Math.Sqrt(20.25)	4.5
Math.Max(23.75, 20.25)	23.75
Math.Min(23.75, 20.25)	20.25

Description

- To use one of the *static methods* of the Math class, code the class name, a dot, the method name, and one or more *arguments* in parentheses. The arguments provide the values that are used by the method.
- The Round method rounds a decimal or double argument to the specified *precision*, which is the number of significant decimal digits. If the precision is omitted, the number is rounded to the nearest whole number.
- The Pow method raises the first argument to the power of the second argument. Both arguments must have the double data type.
- The Sqrt method returns the square root of the specified argument, which can have any numeric data type.
- The Min and Max methods return the minimum and maximum of two numeric arguments. The two arguments must have the same data type.

Figure 4-7 How to use the Math class

How to work with strings

In the topics that follow, you'll learn some basic skills for working the string data type. These skills should be all you need for many of your applications. Then, in chapter 9, you'll learn the skills you need for advanced string operations.

Basic skills for working with strings

A *string* can consist of any letters, numbers, and characters. Figure 4-8 summarizes the techniques that you can use to work with string variables. To start, you use the string keyword to declare a string. Then, you can assign a *literal string* to a string by enclosing the characters within double quotes.

To assign an *empty string* to a variable, you can code a set of double quotes with nothing between them. You do that when you want the string to have a value, but you don't want it to contain any characters. A third alternative is to assign a *null value* to a string by using the null keyword, which usually indicates that the value of the string is unknown.

If you want to join, or *concatenate*, two or more strings into one string, you use the + operator as shown in the second example in this figure. Here, two string variables are concatenated with a string literal. The result is then stored in another string variable.

You can also join a string with a value data type. This is illustrated in the third example in this figure. Here, a variable that's defined with the double data type is appended to a string. When you use this technique, C# automatically converts the value to a string.

You can also use the + and += operators to *append* a string to the value of a string variable. This is illustrated in the last two examples in this figure. Notice that when you use the + operator, you include the string variable in the expression that you're assigning to this variable. In contrast, when you use the += operator, you can omit the string variable from the expression. Because of that, it's common to use this operator to simplify your code.

How to declare and initialize a string

```
string message1 = "Invalid data entry.";
string message2 = "";
string message3 = null;
```

How to join strings

```
string firstName = "Bob";                       //firstName is "Bob"
string lastName = "Smith";                      //lastName is "Smith"
string name = firstName + " " + lastName;       //name is "Bob Smith"
```

How to join a string and a number

```
double price = 14.95;
String priceString = "Price: " + price;
```

How to append one string to another string

```
string firstName = "Bob";                       //firstName is "Bob"
string lastName = "Smith";                      //lastName is "Smith"
string name = firstName + " ";                  //name is "Bob "
name = name + lastName;                         //name is "Bob Smith"
```

How to append one string to another with the += operator

```
string firstName = "Bob";                       //firstName is "Bob"
string lastName = "Smith";                      //lastName is "Smith"
string name = firstName + " ";                  //name is "Bob "
name += lastName;                               //name is "Bob Smith"
```

Description

- A *string* can consist of any characters in the character set including letters, numbers, and special characters like *, &, and #.
- To specify the value of a string, you can enclose text in double quotes. This is known as a *string literal.*
- To assign a *null value* to a string, you can use the *null* keyword. This means that the value of the string is unknown.
- To assign an *empty string* to a string, you can code a set of double quotes with nothing between them. This usually indicates that the value of the string is known, but the string doesn't contain any characters.
- To join, or *concatenate*, a string with another string or a value data type, use a plus sign. If you concatenate a value data type to a string, C# will automatically convert the value to a string so it can be used as part of the string.
- When you *append* one string to another, you add one string to the end of another. To do that, you can use assignment statements.
- The += operator is a shortcut for appending a string expression to a string variable.

Figure 4-8 Basic skills for working with strings

How to include special characters in strings

Figure 4-9 shows two techniques that you can use to include certain types of special characters within a string. In particular, this figure shows how to include backslashes, quotation marks, and control characters such as new lines, tabs, and returns.

One technique you can use to include these characters in a string is to use the *escape sequences* shown in this figure. Although these escape sequences are the ones you'll use most often, C# provides other escape sequences for hexadecimal and Unicode characters.

If you're assigning a string literal to a string, you may prefer to use a *verbatim string literal* instead of escape sequences. To use a verbatim string literal, you code an @ sign before the opening quote for the string. Then, you can enter backslashes, tabs, and new line characters between the opening and closing quotes. For example, you can press the Enter key to enter new line characters. Then, the verbatim string literal will span two or more lines.

Although verbatim string literals work well for literals that include backslashes and single quotes, a complication occurs when you need to include a double quote in the literal. That's because double quotes are used to indicate the beginning and end of the literal. To include a double quote in a verbatim string literal, then, you must enter two double quotes.

At this point, you may be wondering when you should use escape sequences to include special characters in a string and when you should use verbatim string literals. The answer is that each technique is appropriate for certain types of coding situations. For example, verbatim string literals work well for coding file locations. On the other hand, it's often easier to use escape sequences to include new line characters and tabs in a string. Because of that, you'll want to become familiar with both techniques. Then, you can decide which technique works best for a given situation.

Common escape sequences

Key	Description
`\n`	New line
`\t`	Tab
`\r`	Return
`\\`	Backslash
`\"`	Quotation

Examples that use escape sequences

Code	Result

`string code = "JSPS";`
`decimal price = 49.50m;`
`string result =`
`    "Code: " + code + "\n" +`
`    "Price: $" + price + "\n";`
	`Code: JSPS`
	`Price: $49.50`

`string names =` `    "Joe\tSmith\rKate\tLewis\r";`	`Joe     Smith` `Kate    Lewis`
`string path = "c:\\c#.net\\files";`	`c:\c#.net\files`
`string message =` `    "Type \"x\" to exit";`	`Type "x" to exit`

Examples that use verbatim string literals

Code	Result
`string names = @"Joe     Smith` `Kate    Lewis";`	`Joe     Smith` `Kate    Lewis`
`string path = @"c:\c#.net\files";`	`c:\c#.net\files`
`string message =` `    @"Type ""x"" to exit";`	`Type "x" to exit`

Description

- Within a string, you can use *escape sequences* to include certain types of special characters.
- To code a *verbatim string literal*, you can code an @ sign, followed by an opening double quote, followed by the string, followed by a closing double quote. Within the string, you can enter backslashes, tabs, new line characters, and other special characters without using escape sequences. However, to enter a double quote within a verbatim string literal, you must enter two double quotes.

Figure 4-9 How to include special characters in strings

How to convert data types

In chapter 3, you were introduced to the use of classes, which provide properties and methods for the objects that are instantiated from the classes. Now, you'll be introduced to *structures*, which are similar to classes. Then, you'll learn how you can use these structures and classes to convert data from one type to another.

The .NET structures and classes that define data types

Figure 4-10 summarizes the structures and classes that define the C# data types, along with the C# keywords that you can use to work with these structures. To work with the Decimal structure, for example, you use the decimal keyword. To work with the Int32 structure, you use the int keyword. And to work with the String class, you use the string keyword.

When you declare a variable as one of the data types that's supported by a structure, that variable is a *value type*. That means that the variable stores its own data. If, for example, you declare a variable as a decimal type, that variable stores the decimal value. In addition, if you assign that variable to another decimal variable, the new variable will store a separate copy of the value.

In contrast, when you declare a variable as one of the data types that's supported by a class, an object is created from the class. Then, the variable stores a reference to the object, not the object itself. Because of that, object data types are called *reference types*.

The two reference types defined by the .NET Framework are string and object. So when you declare a variable as a string, that variable holds a reference to a String object, which contains the data for the string. As a result, it's possible for two or more variables to refer to the same String object.

In addition to the String class, the .NET Framework also provides a generic Object class. You can use a variable created from this class to hold a reference to any type of object. You'll learn more about working with the Object class in chapter 13.

Common .NET structures that define value types

Structure	C# keyword	What the value type holds
Byte	byte	An 8-bit unsigned integer
Int16	short	A 16-bit signed integer
Int32	int	A 32-bit signed integer
Int64	long	A 64-bit signed integer
Single	float	A single-precision floating-point number
Double	double	A double-precision floating-point number
Decimal	decimal	A 96-bit decimal value
Boolean	bool	A true or false value
Char	char	A single character

.NET classes that define reference types

Class name	C# keyword	What the reference type holds
String	string	A reference to a String object
Object	object	A reference to any type of object

Description

- Each built-in data type is supported by a structure or a class within the .NET Framework. When you use a C# keyword to refer to a data type, you're actually using an alias for the associated structure or class.
- A *structure* defines a *value type*, which stores its own data.
- A class defines a *reference type*. A reference type doesn't store the data itself. Instead, it stores a reference to the area of memory where the data is stored.
- All of the structures and classes shown in this figure are in the System namespace of the .NET Framework.

Note

- The .NET Framework also provides structures for the other built-in data types that were listed in figure 4-1.

Figure 4-10 The .NET structures and classes that define data types

How to use methods to convert data types

Figure 4-11 presents two ways you can use methods to convert data from one type to another. First, you can use the ToString and Parse methods, which are available from any of the data structures defined by the .NET Framework. Second, you can use the static methods of the Convert class to convert a value to any of the data structures defined by the .NET Framework.

The ToString method lets you convert any value to a string. In the first group of statements in this figure, for example, the ToString method is used to convert a decimal value to a string value. Notice in this example that no arguments are provided on the ToString method. In the next figure, you'll learn how to code an argument that formats the resulting string.

Before I go on, you should realize that C# calls the ToString method implicitly in certain situations. You learned about one of those situations earlier in this chapter, and that example is repeated here. In this case, a double value is automatically converted to a string when it's joined with another string.

The Parse method is a static method that performs the reverse operation of the ToString method. In other words, it converts a string value to another data type. In last statement in the first group of statements, for example, the Parse method of the Decimal structure is used to convert the value of a string variable to a decimal value. Note that this method only recognizes standard numeric characters. As a result, an exception will occur if you try to convert a string that includes characters such as a dollar sign, a percent sign, or a letter.

The Convert class also provides static methods that you can use to convert a value with any data type to any other data type. This is illustrated by the last group of statements in this figure. Here, the first statement uses the ToDecimal method to convert a string that's entered in a text box to a decimal value. The second statement uses the ToInt32 method to convert a string that's entered in a text box to an integer value. The third statement uses the ToString method to convert a decimal value to a string value. And the fourth statement uses the ToInt32 method to convert a decimal value to an integer value.

When you use the Convert class, you should realize that the results of the conversion will vary depending on the type of conversion that you perform. If, for example, you convert a decimal to an integer as illustrated in the last statement in this figure, the conversion will round the decimal digits. In other cases, C# won't be able to perform the conversion, and an exception will occur.

Common methods for data conversion

Method	Description
ToString([format])	A method that converts the value to its equivalent string representation using the specified format. If the format is omitted, the value isn't formatted.
Parse(string)	A static method that converts the specified string to an equivalent data value.

Some of the static methods of the Convert class

Method	Description
ToDecimal(value)	Converts the value to the decimal data type.
ToDouble(value)	Converts the value to the double data type.
ToInt32(value)	Converts the value to the int data type.
ToChar(value)	Converts the value to the char data type.
ToBool(value)	Converts the value to the bool data type.
ToString(value)	Converts the value to the string data type.

Conversion statements that use the ToString and Parse methods

```
decimal sales = 2574.98m;
string salesString = sales.ToString();      // decimal to string
sales = Decimal.Parse(salesString);         // string to decimal
```

An implicit call of the ToString method

```
decimal price = 49.50;
string priceString = "Price: $" + price;    // automatic ToString call
```

Conversion statements that use the Convert class

```
decimal subtotal = Convert.ToDecimal(txtSubtotal.Text); // string to decimal
int years = Convert.ToInt32(txtYears.Text);             // string to int
txtSubtotal.Text = Convert.ToString(subtotal);          // decimal to string
int subtotalInt = Convert.ToInt32(subtotal);            // decimal to int
```

Description

- The ToString and Parse methods are included in all of the data structures.
- In some situations where a string is expected, the compiler will automatically call the ToString method.
- The Convert class contains static methods for converting all of the built-in types. To see all of the methods of this class, you can use the Visual Studio's online help to look up the Convert class.

Figure 4-11 How to use methods to convert data types

How to convert numbers to formatted strings

Figure 4-12 shows the standard codes that you can use to format a number when you convert it to a string. To use any of these codes with the ToString method, you simply code it as an argument of this method as illustrated in the first group of statements in this figure. Notice in these examples that the formatting code must be enclosed in double quotes.

You can also include an integer after any of the numeric formatting codes. In most cases, this integer indicates the number of decimal places in the resulting string. For example, if you specify the code "c0" for the value 19.95, that number will be converted to $20. Note that if you don't specify the number of decimal places, two decimal places are assumed.

If you specify a number on the D or d formatting code, it indicates the minimum number of digits in the result. Since these formatting codes are used with integers, that means that the value is padded on the left with zeroes if the number you specify is greater than the number of digits in the integer. If you specify the code "d3" for the number 28, for example, it will be converted to 028.

Another way to format numbers is to use the Format method of the String class. Since this is a static method, you access it directly from the String class rather than from an instance of this class. You must also provide two arguments.

The first argument is a string literal that contains the format specification for the value to be formatted, and the second argument is the value to be formatted. The syntax for the format specification is shown in this figure. Here, the index indicates the value to be formatted, and the format code specifies how the value is to be formatted. Although you can format up to three values using the Format method, you'll typically use it to format a single value. In that case, the index value will be 0. In chapter 9, you'll learn how to use this method to format two or three values.

The second group of statements in this figure shows how to use the Format method. As you can see, these statements perform the same functions as the statements that use the ToString method. In this case, though, these statements use literal values so you can see what the values look like before they're formatted. Notice in these statements that the format specification is enclosed in braces. In addition, the entire argument is enclosed in double quotes.

Standard numeric formatting codes

Code	Format	Description
C or c	Currency	Formats the number as currency with the specified number of decimal places.
P or p	Percent	Formats the number as a percent with the specified number of decimal places.
N or n	Number	Formats the number with thousands separators and the specified number of decimal places.
F or f	Float	Formats the number as a decimal with the specified number of decimal places.
D or d	Digits	Formats an integer with the specified number of digits.
E or e	Exponential	Formats the number in scientific (exponential) notation with the specified number of decimal places.
G or g	General	Formats the number as a decimal or in scientific notation depending on which is more compact.

How to use the ToString method to format a number

Statement	Example
`string monthlyAmount = amount.ToString("c");`	`$1,547.20`
`string interestRate = interest.ToString("p1");`	`2.3%`
`string quantityString = quantity.ToString("n0");`	`15,000`
`string paymentString = payment.ToString("f3");`	`432.818`

How to use the Format method of the String class to format a number

Statement	Result
`string monthlyAmount = String.Format("{0:c}", 1547.2m);`	`$1,547.20`
`string interestRate = String.Format("{0:p1}", .023m);`	`2.3%`
`string quantityString = String.Format("{0:n0}", 15000);`	`15,000`
`string paymentString = String.Format("{0:f3}", 432.8175);`	`432.818`

The syntax of the format specification used by the Format method

```
{index:formatCode}
```

Description

- You can include a number after some of the numeric formatting codes to specify the number of decimal places in the result. If the numeric value contains more decimal places than are specified, the result will be rounded. If you don't specify the number of decimal places, the default is 2.
- You can include a number after the D or d formatting code to specify the minimum number of digits in the result. If the integer has fewer digits than are specified, zeroes are added to the beginning of the integer.
- You can use the Format method of the String class to format up to three values. For more information, see chapter 9.

Figure 4-12 How to convert numbers to formatted strings

Two other skills for working with data

To complete the subject of working with data, the next two topics present two more useful skills: how to work with scope and how to work with enumerations.

How to work with scope

When you work with C#, the *scope* of a variable is determined by where you declare it, and the scope determines what code can access the variable. If, for example, you declare a variable within an event handler, the variable has *method scope* because an event handler is a method. In that case, the variable can only be referred to by statements within that method.

Often, though, you want all of the methods of a form to have access to a variable. Then, you must declare the variable within the class for the form, but outside all of the methods. In that case, the variable has *class scope* and can be called a *class variable*.

This is illustrated and summarized in figure 4-13. Here, you can see that two variables are declared after the last of the generated code for the form class, but before the first event handler for the form. As a result, these variables have class scope. In contrast, the four variables that are declared at the start of the first event handler have method scope. Note that the variables with class scope are used by both of the event handlers in this example, which is one reason for using class scope.

The other reason for using variables with class scope is to retain data after a method finishes executing. This has to do with the *lifetime* of a variable. In particular, a method variable is available only while the method is executing. When the event handler finishes, the variable is no longer available and the data is lost. Then, when the event handler is executed the next time, the method variables are declared and initialized again.

In contrast, a class variable lasts until the instance of the form class is terminated. That happens when you exit from a form and the form is closed. As a result, class variables can be used for accumulating values like invoice totals. You'll see this illustrated by the last application in this chapter.

Code that declares and uses variables with class scope

```
static void Main()
{
    Application.Run(new Form1());
}
```
The last generated method

```
decimal numberOfInvoices = 0m;
decimal totalOfInvoices = 0m;
```
Class scope

```
private void btnCalculate_Click(object sender, System.EventArgs e)
{
    decimal subtotal = Convert.ToDecimal(txtSubtotal.Text);
    decimal discountPercent = .2m;
    decimal discountAmount = subtotal * discountPercent;
    decimal invoiceTotal = subtotal - discountAmount;

    numberOfInvoices++;
    totalOfInvoices += invoiceTotal;

    // the rest of the code for the method
}

private void btnClearTotals_Click(object sender, System.EventArgs e)
{
    numberOfInvoices = 0m;
    totalOfInvoices = 0m;
}
```
Method scope

Description

- The *scope* of a variable determines what code has access to it. If you try to refer to a variable outside of its scope, it will cause a build error.
- The scope of a variable is determined by where you declare it. If you declare a variable within a method, it has *method scope*. If you declare a variable within a class but not within a method, it has *class scope*.
- A variable with method scope can only be referred to by statements within that method. A variable with class scope can be referred to by all of the methods in a class.
- The *lifetime* of a variable is the period of time that it's available for use. A variable with method scope is only available while the method is executing. A variable with class scope is available while the class is instantiated.
- You can declare *class variables* right after the code that is generated for a form.

Figure 4-13 How to work with scope

How to declare and use enumerations

An enumeration is a set of related constants that define a value type. The enumerations provided by the .NET Framework are generally used to set object properties and to specify the values that are passed to methods. For example, the FormBorderStyle enumeration includes a group of constants that you can use to specify the settings for the FormBorderStyle property of a form.

The first example in figure 4-14 summarizes three of the constants within the FormBorderStyle enumeration, and the first example shows how you can use code to set this form property. Normally, though, you'll use the Properties window to choose the constant from the enumeration for this form property.

To define your own enumerations, you use the syntax shown in this figure. After you provide a name for an enumeration, you code the constant names within braces. In the first example, the enumeration is named Terms, and the constants are named Net30Days, Net60Days, and Net90Days. In this case, because values aren't provided for these constants, the default values of 0, 1, and 2 are assigned to the constants.

If you want to assign other values to the constants, you can provide a value for each constant as shown in the second example. Here, the values 30, 60, and 90 are assigned to the constants for the TermValues enumeration. In this case, these values are stored as short data types because a colon and the data type are coded after the enumeration name. If the data type is omitted, the constant values are stored as integers.

To refer to a constant value in an enumeration, you code the name of the enumeration followed by a dot and the name of the constant. This is illustrated by the first two statements in the third group of examples. And if you want to refer the name of the constant instead of its value, you can use the ToString method as in the last example in this group.

Incidentally, when you code an enumeration, you normally want it to have class scope so it can be used by all of the methods in the class. As a result, you code the enumeration after the generated code for a class as shown in the previous figure.

Some of the constants in the FormBorderStyle enumeration

Constant	Description
FormBorderStyle.FixedDialog	A fixed, thick border typically used for dialog boxes.
FormBorder.Style.FixedSingle	A single-line border that isn't resizable.
FormBorderStyle.Sizable	A resizable border

A statement that uses the FormBorderStyle enumeration

```
this.FormBorderStyle = FormBorderStyle.FixedSingle;
```

The syntax for declaring an enumeration

```
enum EnumerationName [: type]
{
    ConstantName1 [= value] [,
    ConstantName2] [= value]...
}
```

An enumeration that sets the constant values to 0, 1, and 2

```
enum Terms
{
    Net30Days,
    Net60Days,
    Net90Days
}
```

An enumeration that sets the constant values to 30, 60, and 90

```
enum TermValues : short
{
    Net30Days = 30,
    Net60Days = 60,
    Net90Days = 90
}
```

Statements that use the constants in these enumerations

```
int i = (int) Terms.Net30Days;              // i is 0
int i = (int) TermValues.Net60Days;         // i is 60
string s = Terms.Net30Days.ToString();      // s is Net30Days
```

Description

- An *enumeration* defines a set of related constants. Each constant is known as a *member* of the enumeration.
- By default, an enumeration uses the int type and sets the first constant to 0, the second to 1, and so on.
- To use one of the other integer data types, you can code a colon after the enumeration name followed by the data type.
- To specify other values for the constants, you can code an equals sign after the constant name followed by the integer value.
- When you declare an enumeration, you usually give it class scope so all of the methods have access to it.

Figure 4-14 How to declare and use enumerations

Two versions of the Invoice Total application

To give you a better idea of how you can use data, arithmetic, data conversion, and scope, this chapter concludes by presenting two illustrative applications.

The basic Invoice Total application

Figure 4-15 presents a simple version of the Invoice Total application that you developed for chapter 3. Now that you have learned how to work with data, you should be able to understand all of the code in the application.

To start, this figure shows the user interface for this application, which is the same as it was in the last chapter. Then, this figure lists the six controls that the code refers to so you can see how the code relates to those controls.

This figure also presents the code for the two event handlers of the Invoice Total application. If you study the code for the Click event of the Calculate button, you'll see that it begins by converting the string value that's entered by the user to a decimal value. Then, it sets the discount percent to .25, or 25%. This percent is then used to calculate the discount for the invoice, and the discount is subtracted from the subtotal to get the invoice total. Finally, the calculated values are formatted and displayed on the form.

If rounding is necessary when the values are displayed, the formatting statements in this application will do the rounding. Note, however, that the values stored in discountAmount and invoiceTotal aren't rounded. To round these values, you would need to use the Round method of the Math class. You often need to do that when you work with values that are going to be stored in a file or database.

You also should realize that this application will work only if the user enters a numeric value into the Subtotal text box. If the user enters any non-numeric characters, an exception will occur when the application tries to convert that value to a decimal. In chapter 7, you'll learn how to prevent this type of error.

The Invoice Total form

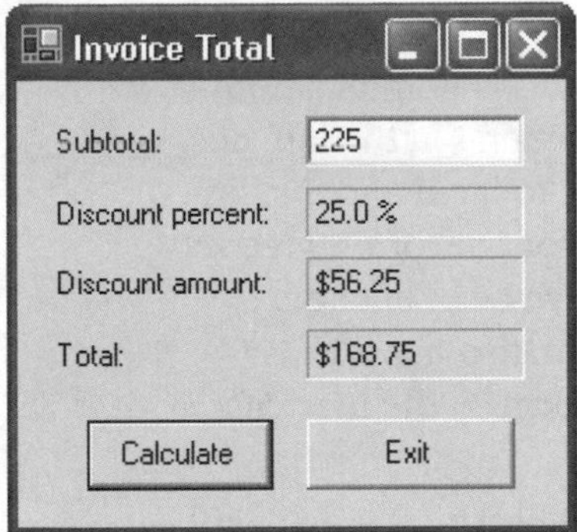

The controls that are referred to in the code

Object type	Name	Description
TextBox	txtSubtotal	Accepts a subtotal amount
Label	lblDiscountPercent	Displays the discount percent
Label	lblDiscountAmount	Displays the discount amount
Label	lblTotal	Displays the invoice total
Button	btnCalculate	Calculates the discount amount and invoice total when clicked
Button	btnExit	Closes the form when clicked

The event handlers for the Invoice Total form

```
private void btnCalculate_Click(object sender, System.EventArgs e)
{
    decimal subtotal = Convert.ToDecimal(txtSubtotal.Text);
    decimal discountPercent = .25m;
    decimal discountAmount = subtotal * discountPercent;
    decimal invoiceTotal = subtotal - discountAmount;

    lblDiscountPercent.Text = discountPercent.ToString("p1");
    lblDiscountAmount.Text = discountAmount.ToString("c");
    lblTotal.Text = invoiceTotal.ToString("c");

    txtSubtotal.Focus();
}

private void btnExit_Click(object sender, System.EventArgs e)
{
    this.Close();
}
```

Figure 4-15 The basic Invoice Total application

The enhanced Invoice Total application

Figure 4-16 presents an enhanced version of the Invoice Total application that illustrates some of the other skills presented in this chapter. On the left side of the form, two labels have been added below the text box to label and display the last subtotal that the user has entered. On the right side of the form, three sets of labels are used to display the number of invoices that have been entered, a total of the invoice totals, and the invoice average. The form also has a Clear Totals button that clears the totals on the right side of the form so the user can enter another batch of invoices.

The controls that have been added to this form are named with our standard naming conventions, which are based on the names that are used to identify text boxes and labels. For instance, lblSubtotal is used for the label that displays the last subtotal that the user has entered, lblNumberOfInvoices is used for the label that displays the number of invoices, lblTotalOfInvoices is used for the label that displays the total of the invoice totals, and btnClearTotals is used for the Clear Totals button.

In the code for this form, the enhancements are shaded so they're easy to review. This code starts with the declarations of the three class variables: numberOfInvoices, totalOfInvoices, and invoiceAverage. These are the variables whose values need to be retained from one execution of an event handler to another. They are initialized with zero values.

In the event handler for the Click event of the Calculate button, the first shaded line adds rounding to the calculation for the discount amount. That's necessary so only the exact amount of the invoice is added to the total for the invoices. Then, the next shaded statement moves the user's entry to the subtotal label. That way, all of the data for the last invoice is shown in the labels on the left side of the form while the user enters the subtotal for the next invoice.

The next set of shaded statements shows how the class variables are used after each subtotal entry has been processed. The first three statements add 1 to the number of invoices, add the invoice total to the total of invoices, and calculate the invoice average. Then, the next three shaded lines assign the new values of the class variables to the labels that will display them. The last shaded line in this event handler assigns an empty string to the subtotal text box so the user can enter the subtotal for the next invoice.

In the event handler for the Click event of the Clear Totals button, the first three statements reset the class variables to zeros so the user can enter the subtotals for another batch of invoices. Then, the next three statements set the labels that display these variables to spaces. The last statement moves the focus to the subtotal text box so the user can start the first entry of another batch of invoices.

The enhanced Invoice Total form

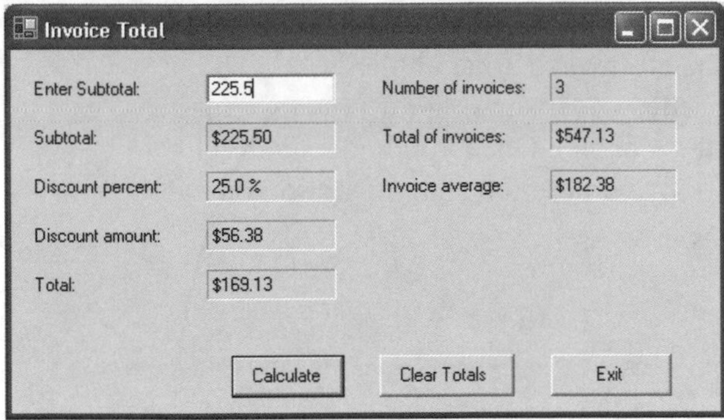

The code for the class variables and two event handlers

```
int numberOfInvoices = 0;
decimal totalOfInvoices = 0m;
decimal invoiceAverage = 0m;

private void btnCalculate_Click(object sender, System.EventArgs e)
{
    decimal subtotal = Convert.ToDecimal(txtSubtotal.Text);
    decimal discountPercent = .25m;
    decimal discountAmount = Math.Round(subtotal * discountPercent, 2);
    decimal invoiceTotal = subtotal - discountAmount;
    lblSubtotal.Text = subtotal.ToString("c");
    lblDiscountPercent.Text = discountPercent.ToString("p1");
    lblDiscountAmount.Text = discountAmount.ToString("c");
    lblTotal.Text = invoiceTotal.ToString("c");

    numberOfInvoices++;
    totalOfInvoices += invoiceTotal;
    invoiceAverage = totalOfInvoices / numberOfInvoices;
    lblNumberOfInvoices.Text = numberOfInvoices.ToString();
    lblTotalOfInvoices.Text = totalOfInvoices.ToString("c");
    lblInvoiceAverage.Text = invoiceAverage.ToString("c");

    txtSubtotal.Text = "";
    txtSubtotal.Focus();
}

private void btnClearTotals_Click(object sender, System.EventArgs e)
{
    numberOfInvoices = 0;
    totalOfInvoices = 0m;
    invoiceAverage = 0m;

    lblNumberOfInvoices.Text = "";
    lblTotalOfInvoices.Text = "";
    lblInvoiceAverage.Text = "";
    txtSubtotal.Focus();
}
```

Figure 4-16 The enhanced Invoice Total application

Perspective

If you understand the code in the enhanced Invoice Total application, you've come a long way. If not, you should get a better understanding for how this application works when you do the exercises for this chapter. Once you understand it, you'll be ready to learn how to code selection and iteration statements so you can add logical operations to your applications.

Summary

- C# provides *data types* to store numbers, Boolean values, characters, and strings.
- *Variables* store the values that change as an application runs. Before you can refer to variables in your code, you must declare and initialize them.
- A *constant* provides a value that doesn't change as an application runs.
- You can use the *arithmetic operators* to form *arithmetic expressions* that calculate values that can be assigned to numeric variables.
- You can use the *assignment operators* to assign the value of a variable, a *literal value*, or an expression to a variable.
- Whenever necessary, you can use parentheses to override the *order of precedence* for arithmetic operations.
- C# can *implicitly cast* data from a less precise data type to a more precise data type. C# also lets you *explicitly cast* a more precise data type to a less precise data type.
- When calling a method, you can code one or more *arguments* within the parentheses for the method. Then, those arguments are passed to the method.
- A *string* consists of any of the characters in the character set including letters, numbers, and special characters. You can use the plus sign to *concatenate* strings.
- You can use the backslash character to code *escape sequences* that can be used within strings. You can also include special characters within a string by creating a *verbatim string literal*.
- The C# data types are based on the structures and classes of the .NET Framework. A *structure* defines a *value type*, which stores its own data, while a class defines a *reference type*, which stores a reference to an object.
- You can use the ToString and Parse methods of the data structures or the static methods of the Convert class to convert a value from one data type to another.
- The *scope* of a variable determines where it can be accessed from as well as its lifetime. A variable with *class scope* can be accessed from any of the methods in a class. A variable with *method scope* can be accessed only from the statements within that method.
- An *enumeration* defines a set of related constants that are its *members*.

Terms

built-in data type
bit
byte
integer
Unicode character set
ASCII character set
Boolean value
variable
constant
declare
initialize
camel notation
literal
scientific notation
arithmetic expression
arithmetic operator
operand
binary operator
unary operator
prefix an operand
postfix an operand
assignment operator
order of precedence
casting
implicit cast
widening conversion
explicit cast
narrowing conversion
strict type semantics
static method
argument
precision
string
string literal
null value
empty string
concatenate
append
escape sequence
verbatim string literal
structure
value type
reference type
scope
class scope
class variable
method scope
lifetime
enumeration
member

Objectives

- Given the form design and specifications for an application that requires any of the language elements presented in this chapter, write the code for the application.
- Distinguish between a variable and a constant.
- Describe any of the built-in data types.
- Describe the difference between integer and non-integer numbers.
- Describe what is stored in Boolean and string variables.
- Describe the difference between a value type variable and a reference type variable.
- Describe the differences between class scope and method scope, and describe two reasons for using class scope.
- Describe an enumeration and the code for referring to one of its members.

Exercise 4-1 Modify the Invoice Total application

In this exercise, you'll modify the Invoice Total application that you developed in chapter 3.

Open the Invoice Total application

1. Open the Invoice Total application that's in the C:\C#.NET\Chapter 04\InvoiceTotal directory. This is the application that's presented in figure 4-15.

Modify and test the code for the Invoice Total application

2. Build and run the application, and enter a valid subtotal to verify that the correct discount is being taken. Then, enter a valid subtotal like 225.50 that will yield a discount amount that has more than two decimal places, and make sure that only two decimal places are displayed for the discount amount and total.
3. Enter "$1000" for the subtotal and click the Calculate button (don't press the Enter key to activate the Calculate button). This time, an exception should occur and a dialog box should be displayed. Click the Break button in this dialog box to enter break mode.
4. Note the highlighted statement. This shows that the assignment statement can't convert a non-numeric value to the decimal data type. Then, click the Stop Debugging button in the Debug toolbar to end the application.

Experiment with the code

5. Modify the first statement in the btnCalculate_Click procedure so it uses the Parse method of the Decimal class instead of the ToDecimal method of the Convert class. Then, test the application to verify that it works the same as it did before.
6. Round the values that are stored in the discountAmount and invoiceTotal variables to two decimal places, and delete the formatting codes for the statements that convert these variables to strings. Then, test the application to make sure that only two decimal places are displayed for the discount amount and total.

Save and close the project

7. Save the solution and close it.

Exercise 4-2 Enhance the Invoice Total application

This exercise will guide you through the process of enhancing the Invoice Total application of exercise 4-1 so it works like the application in figure 4-16. This will give you more practice in developing forms and working with data.

Open the Invoice Total application and enhance the form

1. Open the enhanced Invoice Total application that's in the C:\C#.NET\Chapter 04\EnhancedInvoiceTotal directory. This is a copy of the application that's in figure 4-15.
2. Use the techniques that you learned in chapter 2 to enlarge the form and to add the new controls that are shown in figure 4-16 to the form.
3. Set the properties for each of the controls. You should be able to do this without any guidance, but try to name each control that's going to be referred to by code with the proper prefix followed by the name that identifies it in the form (like lblNumberOfInvoices).

Add the code for the enhancements

4. Switch to the Code Editor, find the end of the generated code, and enter the three instance variables in figure 4-16. These are the variables that will accumulate the data for all the invoices.
5. Enhance the code for the Click event of the Calculate button so it calculates and displays the new data. Try to do this without referring to figure 4-16.
6. Use the techniques you learned in chapter 3 to start the event handler for the Click event of the Clear Totals button. Then, add the code for this event. Here again, try to do this without referring to the code in figure 4-16.
7. Test the application and fix any errors until the application works properly. Be sure that it restarts properly when you click the Clear Totals button and enter another batch of invoices.

Add more labels and code

8. Add six more labels below the two columns of labels on the right side of the form. The three labels on the left should say "Largest invoice", "Smallest invoice", and "Mid point". The three labels to the right of these labels should display the values for the largest invoice amount, the smallest invoice amount, and the invoice total that's halfway between these amounts.
9. Add the code for making this work. If you're new to programming, this may challenge you. (Hint: To display the correct value for the smallest invoice after the first invoice is entered, you can initialize the class variable that stores the smallest invoice total to a large number.)
10. Test the application and fix any errors until the application works properly. Then, close the project.

Project 4-1 Calculate area and perimeter

At this point, you should be able to develop projects like this one from scratch. In fact, you should be able to design and develop projects of your own.

The form

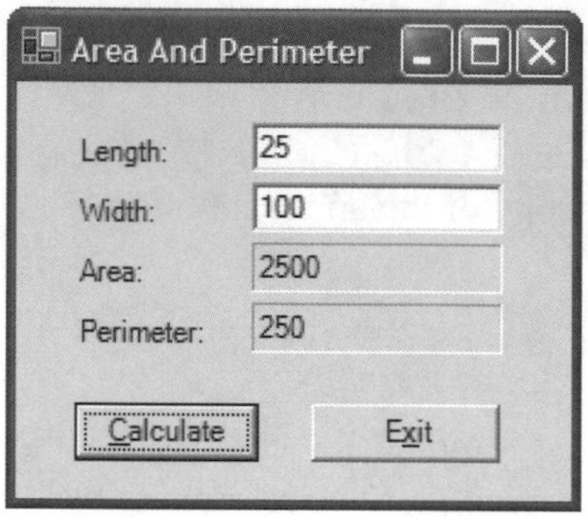

Operation

- The user enters values for the length and width of a rectangle and clicks on the Calculate button or presses the Enter key to activate that button.
- The application then displays the area and perimeter of the rectangle in the third and fourth labels on the right side of the form.

Specifications

- The formula for calculating the area is width * length.
- The formula for calculating the perimeter is 2 * width + 2 * length.
- The application should accept fractional decimal entries like 10.5 and 20.65.
- Assume that the user will enter valid numeric data for the length and the width.

Enhancements

- After you read chapter 6, add an event handler that will clear the data that's displayed in the area and perimeter labels if you change the value in either of the text boxes.
- After you read chapter 7, add exception handling and data validation.

5

How to code control structures

In the last chapter, you learned how to write code that works with the most common data types. Now, you'll learn how to code the three types of control structures that are common to all modern programming languages: the selection, case, and iteration structures. When you finish this chapter, you'll be able to write applications that perform a wide range of logical operations.

How to code Boolean expressions

When you code an expression that evaluates to a true or false value, that expression can be called a *Boolean expression*. Because you use Boolean expressions within the control structures you code, you need to learn how to code Boolean expressions before you learn how to code control structures.

How to use the relational operators

Figure 5-1 shows how to use six *relational operators* to code a Boolean expression. These operators let you compare two operands, as illustrated by the examples in this figure. Notice in these examples that an operand can be any expression, including a variable, a literal, an arithmetic expression, or a keyword such as null, true, or false.

The first six expressions in this figure use the equality operator (==) to test if the two operands are equal. To use this operator, you must code two equals signs instead of one. That's because a single equals sign is used for assignment statements. As a result, if you try to code a Boolean expression with a single equals sign, your code won't compile.

The next expression uses the inequality operator (!=) to test if a variable is not equal to a string literal. The two expressions after that use the greater than operator (>) to test if a variable is greater than a numeric literal and the less than operator (<) to test if one variable is less than another. The last two expressions are similar, except they use the greater than or equal operator (>=) and less than or equal operator (<=) to compare operands.

If you want to include a Boolean variable in an expression, you often don't need to include the == or != operator. That's because a Boolean variable evaluates to a Boolean value by definition. So if isValid is Boolean variable,

```
isValid
```

works the same as

```
isValid == true
```

and

```
!isValid
```

works the same as

```
isValid != true   or   isValid == false
```

When comparing numeric values, you usually compare values with the same data type. However, if you compare different types of numeric values, C# will automatically cast the value with the less precise type to the more precise type. For example, if you compare an int value to a decimal value, the int value will be cast to a decimal value before the comparison is performed.

If you're coming from another programming language such as Java, you may be surprised to find that you can also use some of these operators on strings, which are actually String objects. This is possible because the C# language allows classes and structures to define operators. In this case, since the String class defines the == and != operators, you can use those operators on strings.

Relational operators

Operator	Name	Description
`==`	Equality	Returns a true value if the left and right operands are equal.
`!=`	Inequality	Returns a true value if the left and right operands are not equal.
`>`	Greater than	Returns a true value if the left operand is greater than the right operand.
`<`	Less than	Returns a true value if the left operand is less than the right operand.
`>=`	Greater than or equal	Returns a true value if the left operand is greater than or equal to the right operand.
`<=`	Less than or equal	Returns a true value if the left operand is less than or equal to the right operand.

Examples

```
firstName == "Frank"        // equal to a string literal
txtYears.Text == ""         // equal to an empty string
message == null             // equal to a null value
discountPercent == 2.3      // equal to a numeric literal
isValid == false            // equal to the false value
code == productCode         // equal to another variable

lastName != "Jones"         // not equal to a string literal

years > 0                   // greater than a numeric literal
i < months                  // less than a variable

subtotal >= 500             // greater than or equal to a literal value
quantity <= reorderPoint    // less than or equal to a variable
```

Description

- You can use the *relational operators* to create a *Boolean expression* that compares two operands and returns a Boolean value.
- To compare two operands for equality, make sure you use two equals signs. If you use a single equals sign, the compiler will interpret it as an assignment statement, and your code won't compile.
- You can only use the equality and inequality operators to compare strings.
- If you compare two numeric operands with different data types, C# will cast the less precise operand to the type of the more precise operand.

Figure 5-1 How to use the relational operators

How to use the logical operators

Figure 5-2 shows how to use the *logical operators* to code a Boolean expression that consists of two or more Boolean expressions. For example, the first expression in this figure uses the && operator. As a result, it evaluates to true if both the first operand *and* the second operand evaluate to true. Conversely, the second expression uses the || operator. As a result, it evaluates to a true value if either the first operand *or* the second operand evaluates to true.

When you use the && and || operators, the second expression is only evaluated if necessary. Because of that, these operators are sometimes referred to as the *short-circuit operators*. To illustrate, suppose that the value of subtotal in the first example is less than 250. Then, the first expression evaluates to false. That means that the entire expression evaluates to false regardless of the value of the second expression. As a result, the second expression isn't evaluated. Since this is more efficient than always evaluating both operands, you'll want to use these operators most of the time.

However, there may be times when you want to evaluate the second expression regardless of the value that's returned by the first expression. For example, the second expression may increment a variable, as illustrated by the third an fourth examples in this figure. In these cases, you can use the & and | operators to make sure that the second expression is evaluated.

You can also use two or more logical operators in the same expression, as illustrated by the fifth and sixth examples. When you do, you should know that And operations are performed before Or operations. In addition, both arithmetic and relational operations are performed before logical operations. If you need to change this sequence or if there's any doubt about how an expression will be evaluated, you can use parentheses to control or clarify the sequence.

If necessary, you can use the Not operator (!) to reverse the value of an expression as illustrated by the last example in this figure. Because this can create code that's difficult to read, however, you should avoid using this operator whenever possible. For example, instead of coding

```
!(subtotal < 100)
```

you can code

```
subtotal >= 100
```

Although both expressions return the same result, the second expression is easier to read.

Logical operators

Operator	Name	Description
`&&`	Conditional-And	Returns a true value if both expressions are true. This operator only evaluates the second expression if necessary.
`||`	Conditional-Or	Returns a true value if either expression is true. This operator only evaluates the second expression if necessary.
`&`	And	Returns a true value if both expressions are true. This operator always evaluates both expressions.
`|`	Or	Returns a true value if either expression is true. This operator always evaluates both expressions.
`!`	Not	Reverses the value of the expression.

Examples

```
subtotal >= 250 && subtotal < 500
timeInService <= 4 || timeInService >= 12

isValid == true & counter++ < years
isValid == true | counter++ < years

date > startDate && date < expirationDate || isValid == true
((thisYTD > lastYTD) || empType=="Part time") && startYear < currentYear

!(counter++ >= years)
```

Description

- You can use the *logical operators* to create a Boolean expression that combines two or more Boolean expressions.
- Since the && and || operators only evaluate the second expression if necessary, they're sometimes referred to as *short-circuit operators*. These operators are slightly more efficient than the & and | operators.
- By default, Not operations are performed first, followed by And operations, and then Or operations. These operations are performed after arithmetic operations and relational operations.
- You can use parentheses to change the sequence in which the operations will be performed or to clarify the sequence of operations.

Figure 5-2 How to use the logical operators

How to code conditional statements

Now that you know how to code Boolean expressions, you're ready to learn how to code conditional statements. These statements include the if-else statement and the switch statement.

How to code if-else statements

Figure 5-3 shows how to use the *if-else statement* (or just *if statement*) to control the logic of your programs. This type of statement is the primary logical statement of all programming languages. It is the C# implementation of a control structure know as the *selection structure* because it lets you select different actions based on the results of Boolean expressions.

In the syntax summary in this figure, the brackets [ ] indicate that a clause is optional, and the ellipsis (...) indicates that the preceding element can be repeated as many times as needed. In other words, this syntax shows that you can code an *if* clause with or without *else if* clauses or an *else* clause. It also shows that you can code as many else if clauses as you need.

When an if statement is executed, C# begins by evaluating the Boolean expression in the if clause. If it's true, the statements within this clause are executed and the rest of the if-else statement is skipped. If it's false, C# evaluates the first else if clause (if there is one). If its Boolean expression is true, the statements within this else if clause are executed and the rest of the if-else statement is skipped. Otherwise, C# evaluates the next else if clause. This continues with any remaining else if clauses. Finally, if none of the clauses contains a Boolean expression that evaluates to true, C# executes the statements in the else clause. If the if statement doesn't include an else clause, C# doesn't execute any statements.

If a clause within an if-else statement contains a single statement, you don't need to enclose that statement in braces. This is illustrated by the first example in this figure. If you need to include two or more statements within a clause, however, you'll need to enclose the statements in braces as illustrated by the second example. The braces identify the block of statements that's executed for the clause.

Note that if you declare a variable within a block, that variable is available only to the other statements in the block. This can be referred to as *block scope*. As a result, if you need to access a variable outside of the block, you should declare it before the if statement.

When coding if statements, it's a common practice to code one if statement within another if statement. This type of statement is known as a *nested if statement*. When you code nested if statements, it's a good practice to indent the nested statements and their clauses. This makes the code easier to read by making it easy to identify where the nested statement begins and ends. In the last example in this figure, you can see that C# will execute the nested if statement only if the customer type is "R". Otherwise, it executes the statements in the outer else clause.

The syntax of the if-else statement

```
if (booleanExpression) { statements }
[else if (booleanExpression) { statements }] ...
[else { statements }]
```

If statements without else if or else clauses

With a single statement

```
if (subtotal >= 100)
   discountPercent = .2m;
```

With a block of statements

```
if (subtotal >= 100)
{
   discountPercent = .2m;
   status = "Bulk rate";
}
```

An if statement with an else clause

```
if (subtotal >= 100)
   discountPercent = .2m;
else
   discountPercent = .1m;
```

An if statement with else if and else clauses

```
if (subtotal >= 100 && subtotal < 200)
   discountPercent = .2m;
else if (subtotal >= 200 && subtotal < 300)
   discountPercent = .3m;
else if (subtotal >= 300)
   discountPercent = .4m;
else
   discountPercent = .1m;
```

Nested if statements

```
if (customerType == "R")
{
   if (subtotal >= 100)
      discountPercent = .2m;
   else
      discountPercent = .1m;
}
else    // customerType isn't "R"
   discountPercent = .4m;
```

Description

- An *if-else statement*, or just *if statement*, always contains an *if* clause. In addition, it can contain one or more *else if* clauses and a final *else* clause.
- If a clause requires just one statement, you don't have to enclose the statement in braces. You can just end the clause with a semicolon.
- If a clause requires more than one statement, you enclose the block of statements in braces. Then, any variables or constants that are declared in the block have *block scope* so they can only be accessed by statements in the block.

Figure 5-3 How to code if-else statements

How to code switch statements

Figure 5-4 shows how to use the *switch statement*. This is the C# implementation of a control structure known as the *case structure*, which lets you code different actions for different *cases*. The switch statement can sometimes be used in place of an if statement with else if clauses.

To code a switch statement, you start by coding the switch keyword followed by a switch expression. Note that this expression must evaluate to one of the data types listed in this figure. After the switch expression, you can code one or more *case labels* that represent the possible values of the switch expression. Then, when the switch expression matches the value specified by a case label, the statements that follow the label are executed. A switch statement can also contain a *default label* that identifies the statements that are executed if none of the values specified by the case labels match the switch expression. All of these labels are coded within braces.

When you code a case label or a default label, you must be sure to code a colon after it. Then, if the label contains one or more statements, you must code a *break statement* after those statements to exit from the switch statement. That's because C# doesn't allow execution to *fall through* to the next label. This is know as the *no fall through rule*. The only exception to this rule is a case label that doesn't contain any statements. In that case, the statements within the following label are executed.

The first example in this figure shows how to code a switch statement that sets the discount percent based on the values in a string variable named customerType. If the customer type is "R", the discount percent is sent to .1 If the customer type is "C", the discount percent is set to .2. And otherwise, the discount percent is set to the default value of 0.

Please note in this example that even though the default label is the last label, it must still end with a *break statement*. You should also realize that you can code the case and default labels in any sequence. However, it's a common practice to code the default label last.

The second example is similar but it doesn't include a default label. Because of that, no code will be executed if none of the values in the case labels match the switch expression. The other difference is that the first case label doesn't include any statements. Because of that, if the customer type is "R", execution with fall through to the next case label. That means that the discount percent will be set to .2 if the customer type is either "R" or "C".

When you use a switch statement, you can code if statements within the cases of the statement. You can also code switch statements within the cases of another switch statement. That can make switch statements more useful. In general, though, most programmers prefer to use if-else statements instead of switch statements because if-else statements aren't as limited.

The syntax of the switch statement

```
switch (switchExpression)
{
    case constantExpression:
        statements
        break;
    [case constantExpression:
        statements
        break;]...
    [default:
        statements
        break;]
}
```

A switch statement with a default label

```
switch (customerType)
{
    case "R":
        discountPercent = .1m;
        break;
    case "C":
        discountPercent = .2m;
        break;
    default:
        discountPercent = .0m;
        break;
}
```

A switch statement that falls through the first case label

```
switch (customerType)
{
    case "R":
    case "C":
        discountPercent = .2m;
        break;
    case "T":
        discountPercent = .4m;
        break;
}
```

Description

- A *switch statement* begins by evaluating its switch expression. This expression must evaluate to a string, char, long, sbyte, byte, short, ushort, int, uint, long, or ulong type.
- After evaluating the switch expression, the switch statement transfers control to the appropriate *case label*. If control isn't transferred to one of the case labels, the optional *default label* is executed.
- The *break statement* exits the switch statement. If a label contains one or more statements, the label must end with a break statement.
- If a label doesn't contain any statements, code execution will *fall through* to the next label. That means that the statements contained by the next label will be executed.

Figure 5-4 How to code switch statements

An enhanced version of the Invoice Total application

To give you a better idea of how if-else statements can be used, figure 5-5 presents an enhanced version of the Invoice Total application that you developed for chapter 3. This time, the form for the application provides for two user entries: customer type and subtotal.

If you look at the event handler in this figure, you can see that the discount percent is determined by nested if statements. If, for example, the customer type is "R" and the subtotal is greater than or equal to 250, the discount percent is .25. Or, if the customer type is "C" and the subtotal is less than 250, the discount percent is .2.

When you code if statements like this, it's a good practice to code the conditions in a logical order. For instance, the expressions in the nested if statement for customer type "R", go from a subtotal that's less than 100, to a subtotal that's greater than or equal to 100 and less than 250, to a subtotal that's greater than or equal to 250. That covers all of the possible subtotals from the smallest to the largest. Although you could code these conditions in other sequences, that would make it harder to tell whether all possibilities have been covered.

For efficiency, it's also good to code the conditions from the one that occurs the most to the one that occurs the least. If, for example, most customers are type "R", that condition should be treated first so it will be processed first. In some cases, though, the most efficient sequence isn't logical so you have to decide whether it's worth sacrificing the readability of the code for efficiency.

If you prefer, you can use a switch statement that contains if statements to get the same result as the nested if statements in this figure. That might even make the code easier to read. On the other hand, if you use indentation properly, an extensive series of nested if statements should be easy to read and understand.

The enhanced Invoice Total form

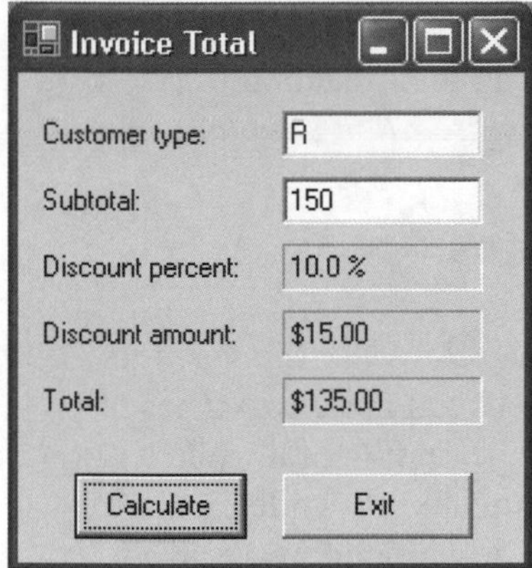

The event handler for the click event of the Calculate button

```
private void btnCalculate_Click(object sender, System.EventArgs e)
{
    string customerType = txtCustomerType.Text;
    decimal subtotal = Convert.ToDecimal(txtSubtotal.Text);
    decimal discountPercent = .0m;

    if (customerType == "R")
    {
        if (subtotal < 100)
            discountPercent = .0m;
        else if (subtotal >= 100 && subtotal < 250)
            discountPercent = .1m;
        else if (subtotal >= 250)
            discountPercent =.25;
    }
    else if (customerType == "C")
    {
        if (subtotal < 250)
            discountPercent = .2m;
        else
            discountPercent = .3m;
    }
    else
        discountPercent = .4m;

    decimal discountAmount = subtotal * discountPercent;
    decimal invoiceTotal = subtotal - discountAmount;

    lblDiscountPercent.Text = discountPercent.ToString("p1");
    lblDiscountAmount.Text = discountAmount.ToString("c");
    lblTotal.Text = invoiceTotal.ToString("c");

    txtCustomerType.Focus();
}
```

Figure 5-5 An enhanced version of the Invoice Total application

How to code loops

C# provides three different statements for controlling the execution of *loops*. These statements provide the C# implementations of the *iteration structure*.

How to code while and do-while loops

Figure 5-6 shows how to use the *while statement* and *do-while statement* to code *while loops* and *do-while loops*. The difference between these two types of loops is that the Boolean expression is evaluated at the beginning of a while loop and at the end of a do-while loop. As a result, the statements in a while loop are executed zero or more times, while the statements in a do-while loop are always executed at least once.

When coding while loops, it's common to use a counter variable to execute the statements in a loop a certain number of times. This is illustrated in the first example in this figure. Here, the counter variable is an int type named i, and this counter is initialized to 1. Notice that the last statement in the loop increments the counter with each iteration of the loop. As a result, the first statement in this loop will be executed as long as the counter variable is less than 5. Incidentally, it is a common coding practice to name counter variables with single letters like *i, j,* and *k.*

Most of the time, you can use either of these two types of loops to accomplish the same task. For instance, the second example in this figure uses a while loop to calculate the future value of a series of monthly payments at a specified interest rate, and the third example uses a do-while loop to perform the same calculation.

When you code loops, it's important to remember that any variables that you declare within the loop have block scope so they can't be used outside of the loop. That's why all of the variables used in the loops shown here have been declared outside of the loops. That way, you can use these variables after the loops have finished executing.

When you code loops, it's possible to code an *infinite loop*, which is a loop that never ends. That can happen, for example, if you forget to code a statement that increments the counter variable so the condition in the while or do-while loop never becomes false. Then, you can use the Break All command in the Debug menu or toolbar to enter break mode and debug the program as shown later in this chapter. Alternatively, you can use the Stop Debugging command to end the application.

The syntax of the while statement

```
while (booleanExpression)
{
   statements
}
```

A while loop that adds the numbers 1 through 4

```
int i = 1, sum = 0;
while (i < 5)
{
    sum += i;
    i++;
}
```

A while loop that calculates a future value

```
int i = 1;
while (i <= months)
{
    futureValue = (futureValue + monthlyPayment) *
        (1 + monthlyInterestRate);
    i++;
}
```

The syntax of the do-while statement

```
do
{
   statements
}
while (booleanExpression);
```

A do-while loop that calculates a future value

```
int i = 1;
do
{
    futureValue = (futureValue + monthlyPayment) *
        (1 + monthlyInterestRate);
    i++;
}
while (i <= months);
```

Description

- When you use a *while statement*, the condition is tested before the *while loop* is executed. When you use a *do-while statement*, the condition is tested after the *do-while loop* is executed.
- A while or do-while loop executes the block of statements within its braces as long as its Boolean expression is true.
- If a loop requires more than one statement, you must enclose the statements in braces. Then, any variables or constants that are declared in the block have block scope. If a loop requires just one statement, you don't have to enclose the statement in braces.
- If the conditional expression never becomes false, the statement never ends. Then, the program goes into an *infinite loop* that you can cancel by using the Break All or Stop Debugging commands from the Debug menu or toolbar.

Figure 5-6 How to code while and do-while loops

How to code for loops

Figure 5-7 shows how to use a *for statement* to code a *for loop*. This type of loop is useful when you need to increment or decrement a counter variable that determines how many times the loop is going to be executed.

To code a for loop, you start by coding the *for* keyword followed by three expressions enclosed in parentheses and separated by semicolons. The first expression is an initialization expression that assigns a starting value to the counter variable. This expression can also declare the counter variable, if necessary. The second expression is a Boolean expression that specifies the condition under which the loop executes. And the third expression is an increment expression that determines how the counter variable is incremented or decremented each time the loop is executed.

The first example in this figure illustrates how to use these expressions. Here, the initialization expression declares a counter variable named i with the int type and assigns an initial value of 0 to it. Next, the Boolean expression specifies that the loop will be repeated as long as the counter is less than 5. Then, the increment expression adds 1 to the counter at the end of each repetition of the loop. When this loop is executed, the numbers 0 through 4 will be stored as a string variable like this:

```
0
1
2
3
4
```

Notice that you can code this loop using a single statement or a block of statements. If you use a block of statements, you must enclose the statements in braces.

The next example calculates the sum of the numbers 8, 6, 4, and 2. In this example, the sum variable is declared before the loop so it will be available outside the block of statements that are executed by the loop. Then, the initialization expression initializes the counter variable to 8, the Boolean expression specifies that the loop will execute as long as the counter is greater than zero, and the increment expression uses an assignment operator to subtract 2 from the counter variable with each repetition of the loop. Within the loop, the value of the counter variable is added to the value that's already stored in the sum variable. As a result, the final value for the sum variable is 20.

The last example shows how to code a loop that calculates the future value of a series of monthly payments. Here, the loop executes one time for each month. If you compare this example with the last example in figure 5-6, you can see how a for loop improves upon a while loop when a counter variable is required.

The syntax of the for statement

```
for(initializationExpression; booleanExpression; incrementExpression)
{
   statements
}
```

A for loop that stores the numbers 0 through 4 in a string

With a single statement

```
string numbers = null;
for (int i = 0; i < 5; i++)
    numbers += i + "\n";
```

With a block of statements

```
string numbers = null;
for (int i = 0; i < 5; i++)
{
    numbers += i;
    numbers += "\n";
}
```

A for loop that adds the numbers 8, 6, 4, and 2

```
int sum = 0;
for (int j = 8; j > 0; j-=2)
{
   sum += j;
}
```

A for loop that calculates a future value

```
for (int i = 1; i <= months; i++)
{
    futureValue = (futureValue + monthlyPayment) *
        (1 + monthlyInterestRate);
}
```

Description

- The *for statement* is useful when you need to increment or decrement a counter that determines how many times the *for loop* is executed.
- Within the parentheses of a for loop, you code an initialization expression that assigns a starting value to the counter variable, a Boolean expression that specifies the condition under which the loop executes, and an increment expression that indicates how the counter variable should be incremented or decremented each time the loop is executed.
- If necessary, you can declare the counter variable before the for loop. Then, this variable can be accessed outside the loop.

Figure 5-7 How to code for loops

Loops that use break and continue statements

In most cases, the statements within the loop are executed in the order that they're coded, and the loop ends when the Boolean expression for the loop evaluates to false. However, for some loops, you may need to use *jump statements* to control the order in which the statements are executed. Figure 5-8 presents two of those statements. You can use the break statement to jump to the end of a loop, and you can use the *continue statement* to jump to the start of a loop.

The first example in this figure shows how the break statement works. Here, a while loop calculates a future value as described in figure 5-6. If the future value becomes greater than 100,000, however, this loop assigns a string literal to the message variable, and it executes a break statement to end the loop.

The second example shows how to use the continue statement to jump to the beginning of a loop. When control is transferred to the beginning of the loop, the expressions that control the loop's operation are executed again. As a result, this will cause the counter variable to be incremented, and it will cause the Boolean expression to be evaluated again.

In addition to the break and continue statements, C# provides other jump statements you can code within loops. You'll learn about most of these statements as you progress through this book. One statement you won't learn about, however, is the *goto* statement. That's because goto statements often result in code that's difficult to read and maintain. As a result, it's a good coding practice to avoid using them.

A loop with a break statement

```
string message = null;
int i = 1;
while (i <= months)
{
    futureValue = (futureValue + monthlyPayment) *
        (1 + monthlyInterestRate);
    if (futureValue > 100000)
    {
        message = "Future value is too large.";
        break;
    }
    i++;
}
```

A loop with a continue statement

```
string numbers = null;
for (int i = 1; i < 6; i++)
{
    numbers += i;
    numbers += "\n";
    if (i < 4)
        continue;
    numbers += "Big\n";
}
```

The result of the previous loop

```
1
2
3
4
Big
5
Big
```

Description

- You code a *break statement* to jump out of a loop.
- You can code a *continue statement* to jump to the start of a loop.

Figure 5-8 Loops that use break and continue statements

Debugging techniques for programs with loops

When you code programs that use loops, debugging often becomes more difficult because it's hard to tell how the loop is operating. As a result, you may want to use the debugging techniques that are summarized in figure 5-9. These techniques let you stop the execution of a program and enter break mode when a loop starts. Then, you can observe the operation of the loop one statement at a time.

To stop the execution of a program and enter break mode, you set a *breakpoint*. To do that, you can click the *margin indicator bar* at the left-hand side of the Code Editor window. The breakpoint is then marked by a red dot. Later, when the application is run, execution will stop just prior to the statement at the breakpoint.

Once in break mode, a yellow arrowhead marks the next statement that will be executed, which is called the *execution point*. In addition, several windows are automatically opened, one of which is the *Autos window*. This window displays the current values of the variables used by the current statement and the previous statement. Then, you can see how those variables change each time through the loop.

While in break mode, you can also *step through* the statements in the loop one statement at a time. To do that, you repeatedly press the F11 key or click the Step Into button on the Debugging toolbar. This lets you observe exactly how and when the variable values change as the loop executes. Once you understand how the loop works, you can remove the breakpoint and press the F5 key to continue normal execution.

Of course, these techniques are also useful for debugging problems that don't involve loops. If, for example, you can't figure out what's wrong with a complex set of nested if statements, you can set a breakpoint at the start of the statement. Then, when the program enters break mode, you can step through the clauses in the statement to see exactly how the expressions are being evaluated.

A for loop with a breakpoint and an execution point

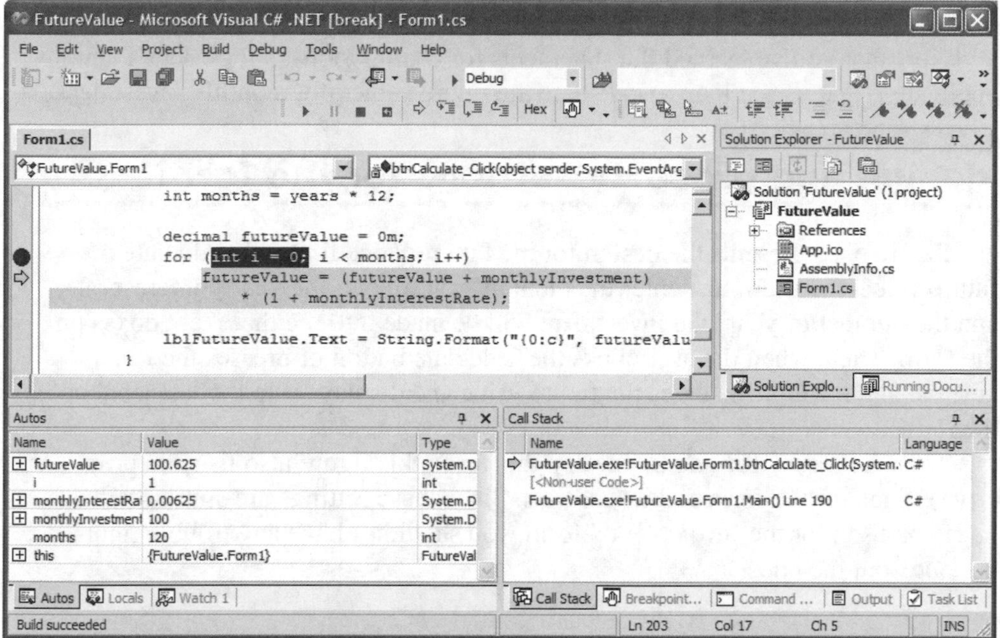

How to set and clear breakpoints

- To set a breakpoint, click in the *margin indicator bar* to the left of a statement. Or, press the F9 key to set a breakpoint at the cursor insertion point. Then, a red dot will mark the breakpoint.
- To remove a breakpoint, use either technique for setting a breakpoint. To remove all breakpoints at once, use the Clear All Breakpoints command in the Debug menu.

How to work in break mode

- In break mode, a yellow arrowhead marks the current *execution point*, which points to the next statement that will be executed.
- To *step through* your code one statement at a time, press the F11 key or click the Step Into button on the Debugging toolbar.
- To continue normal processing until the next breakpoint is reached, press the F5 key.

Description

- When you set a *breakpoint* at a specific statement, the program stops before executing that statement and enters break mode. Then, you can step through the execution of the program one statement at a time.
- In break mode, the *Autos window* displays the current values of the variables in the current statement and the previous statement.

Figure 5-9 Debugging techniques for programs with loops

The Future Value application

Now that you've learned the statements for coding loops, I'll present a new application that uses a loop to calculate the future value of a monthly investment.

The design and property settings for the form

Figure 5-10 presents the design for the Future Value form. To calculate a future value, the user must enter the monthly investment, the yearly interest rate, and the number of years the investment will be made into the three text boxes on the form. Then, when the user clicks the Calculate button or presses the Enter key, the application calculates the future value and displays it in the last label on the form.

To make it easy for you to develop this form, this figure also lists the property settings for the form and its controls. Since these settings are similar to the ones you used for the Invoice Total form, you shouldn't have any trouble figuring out what they do.

The Future Value form

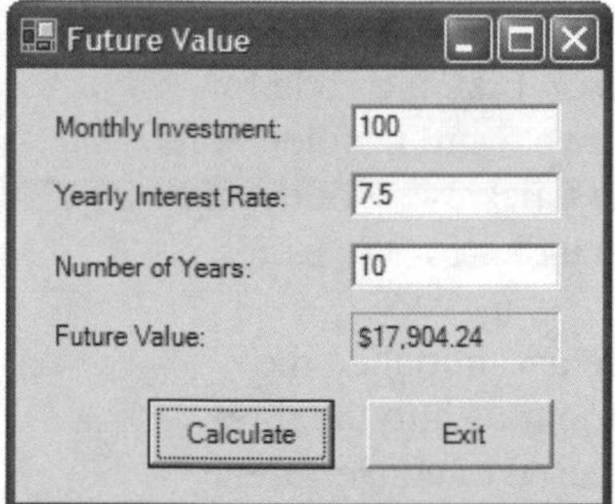

The property settings for the form

Default name	Property	Setting
Form1	Text	Future Value
	AcceptButton	btnCalculate
	CancelButton	btnExit

The property settings for the controls

Default name	Property	Setting
Label1	Text	Monthly Investment:
Label2	Text	Yearly Interest Rate:
Label3	Text	Number of Years:
Label4	Text	Future Value:
Text1	Name	txtMonthlyInvestment
Text2	Name	txtInterestRate
Text3	Name	txtYears
Label 5	BorderStyle Name	Fixed3D lblFutureValue
Button1	Name Text	btnCalculate &Calculate
Button2	Name Text	btnExit E&xit

Additional property settings

- The TextAlign property of each of the five labels is set to MiddleLeft.
- The Text property of each text box and the fifth label is cleared so the controls are empty when the form is first displayed.
- The TabIndex properties of the controls are set so the focus moves from top to bottom and left to right.

Figure 5-10 The form design and property settings for the Future Value application

The code for the form

Figure 5-11 presents the code for the Future Value form. Like the code for the Invoice Total form, the code for this form consists of two event handlers: one for the Click event of the Calculate button and one for the Click event of the Exit button. Here, most of the processing occurs in the event handler for the Click event of the Calculate button.

The first three statements in this event handler declare and initialize the variables that will be used to store the values that the user enters into the three text boxes. Here, the To methods of the Convert class are used to convert the string values that are returned from the Text property of the text boxes to the appropriate numeric data types.

The next two statements perform calculations that convert the yearly values entered by the user to monthly values. That way, all of the variables used in the future value calculation will be in terms of months. The first statement converts the number of years to months by multiplying the years by 12. The second statement divides the yearly interest rate by 12 to get a monthly interest rate, and then divides that result by 100 to convert the number to a percentage.

The next group of statements uses a for loop to calculate a new future value for each month of the investment. Here, the variable that stores the future value is declared before the loop so it can be used after the loop finishes its processing. Then, within the loop, the single assignment statement that calculates the future value is executed once for each month. Since this loop contains a single statement, it doesn't require braces.

Within the loop, the arithmetic expression adds the monthly investment amount to the future value, which has an initial value of zero. Then, the expression multiplies that sum by 1 plus the monthly interest rate. If, for example, the monthly investment amount is $100 and the monthly interest rate is 1% (or .01), future value is $101 after the expression is executed the first time through the loop:

```
(0 + 100) * (1 +.01) = 100 * 1.01 = 101
```

And future value is $203.01 after the expression is executed the second time:

```
(101 + 100) * (1 + .01) = 201 * 1.01 = 203.01
```

Continue this process for as many months as the user indicates, and future value will contain the correct result for a series of equal monthly investments.

After the loop ends, the last statement formats the future value and displays it on the form. To do that, the ToString method converts a decimal value to a string that uses the currency format. Then, this string value is assigned to the Text property of the Future Value label.

To keep this program simple, it doesn't validate the data that's entered by the user. As a result, an exception will occur if the user enters nonnumeric data in one of the text boxes. In the next chapter, you'll learn how to add data validation to this program to prevent exceptions like this.

The code for the Future Value application

```
private void btnCalculate_Click(object sender, System.EventArgs e)
{
    decimal monthlyInvestment = Convert.ToDecimal(txtMonthlyInvestment.Text);
    decimal yearlyInterestRate = Convert.ToDecimal(txtInterestRate.Text);
    int years = Convert.ToInt32(txtYears.Text);

    int months = years * 12;
    decimal monthlyInterestRate = yearlyInterestRate / 12 / 100;

    decimal futureValue = 0m;
    for (int i = 0; i < months; i++)
        futureValue = (futureValue + monthlyInvestment)
                    * (1 + monthlyInterestRate);

    lblFutureValue.Text = futureValue.ToString("c");
}

private void btnExit_Click(object sender, System.EventArgs e)
{
    this.Close();
}
```

Description

- This application uses a for loop to calculate the future value of a monthly investment amount. For this calculation to work correctly, all of the variables that it uses must be converted to the same time period. In this case, that time period is months.
- Each time through the for loop, the assignment statement adds the monthly investment amount to the future value, which starts at zero. Then, this sum is multiplied by 1 plus the monthly interest rate. The result is stored in the futureValue variable so it can be used the next time through the loop.
- Since this application doesn't provide data validation, the user will be able to enter invalid data, which will cause an exception to occur.

Figure 5-11 The code for the Future Value application

Perspective

If this chapter has succeeded, you now know how to code if statements, switch statements, while statements, do-while statements, and for statements. These are the C# statements that implement the selection, case, and iteration structures, and they provide the logic of an application. Once you master them, you'll be able to develop significant C# applications.

Summary

- You can use the *relational operators* to create a *Boolean expression* that compares two operands and returns a true or false value.
- You can use the *logical operators* to connect two or more Boolean expressions.
- You can use *if-else statements* and *switch statements* to control the logic of a program. You can also code *nested if statements* by coding one if statement within another.
- You can use *while*, *do-while*, and *for loops* to execute one or more statements until a Boolean expression evaluates to false.
- You can use the *break statement* to jump to the end of a loop, and you can use the *continue statement* to jump to the beginning of a loop.
- To debug a program that contains a loop, you can set a *breakpoint* and *step through* the statements in the loop. As you do that, you can use the *Autos window* to observe the changes in the variables that are used.

Terms

Boolean expression
relational operator
logical operator
short-circuit operator
block scope
if-else statement
if statement
selection structure
nested if statement
switch statement
case structure
case label
default label
break statement
fall through
no fall through rule
loop
iteration structure
while statement
while loop
do-while statement
do-while loop
infinite loop
for statement
for loop
jump statement
continue statement
breakpoint
margin indicator bar
execution point
Autos window
step through

Objectives

- Given the form design and specifications for an application that requires any of the language elements presented in this chapter, write the code for the application.
- Explain how you can use breakpoints, the Autos window, and the step-through technique to debug errors within loops.
- Compare the if-else and switch statements.
- Describe the differences between while, do-while, and for loops.
- Explain how the break and continue statements work when used within a loop.

Exercise 5-1 Enhance the Invoice Total application

In this exercise, you'll use if-else statement to determine the discount percent for the Invoice Total application that's in figure 5-5.

Open the application and change the if-else statement

1. Open the Invoice Total application that's in the C:\C#.NET\Chapter 05 directory.
2. Change the if-else statement so customers of type "R" with a subtotal that is greater than or equal to $250 but less than $500 get a 25% discount and those with a subtotal of $500 or more get a 30% discount. Next, change the if-else statement so customers of type "C" always get a 20% discount. Then, test the application to make sure this works.
3. Add another customer type to the if-else statement so customers of type "T" get a 40% discount for subtotals of less than $500, and a 50% discount for subtotals of $500 or more. Also, make sure that customer types that aren't "R", "C", or "T" get a 10% discount. Then, test the application.

Use a switch statement with if-else statements to get the same results

4. Comment out the entire if-else statement for this application. To do that, select all of the lines in the statement and click the Comment out button in the Text Editor toolbar.
5. After the commented out if-else statement, code a switch statement that handles the three cases for customer types, and use if-else statements within these cases whenever necessary to provide for the discounts that are based on subtotal variations. Then, test this coding alternative. Is this code easier to read and understand?
6. When you're through experimenting, close the application.

Exercise 5-2 Develop the Future Value application

In this exercise, you'll develop and test the Future Value application that was presented in this chapter. You'll also step through its loop.

Develop the form, write the code, and test the application

1. Open the New Project dialog box by selecting the File→New→Project command. Then, enter "FutureValue" for the name of the project, enter "C:\C#.NET\Chapter 05" for the location, and click the OK button.
2. Add the controls to the form and set the properties of the form and its controls as shown in figure 5-10. Then, generate the event handlers for the two Click events, and add the code for these handlers. If necessary, you can refer to the code in figure 5-11, but try to write the code without doing that.
3. Test the application by entering valid data in each of the three text boxes. To start, enter simple values like 100 for the monthly investment, 12% for the yearly interest rate (which is 1% per month), and 1 for the number of years. (The result should be $1,280.93).
4. After you're sure that the application works for valid data, test it with nonnumeric entries and with large values like 100 for the interest rate and 1000 for the number of years. In either case, the application will end with a runtime error. In chapter 7, you'll learn how to prevent errors like this.

Set breakpoints and step through the loop

5. In the Code Editor window, set a breakpoint at the for statement by clicking in the Margin Indicator Bar to the left of the statement as shown in figure 5-9. A red dot will indicate that you have set the breakpoint.
6. Run the application, and enter 100 as the monthly investment, 12 as the yearly interest rate, and 1 as the number of years. Then, click the Calculate button. This will cause the program to enter break mode.
7. Press F11 repeatedly to step through the loop. As you do this, the Autos window will display the values for i, futureValue, monthlyInvestment, and monthlyInterestRate. That way, you'll be able to see exactly how these values change as the loop is executed.
8. Press F11 to continue stepping through the application or press F5 to run the application until another breakpoint is reached.
9. Remove the old breakpoint and set a new breakpoint on the statement within the for loop. Then, run the application and note that the new breakpoint causes the application to enter break mode for each iteration of the loop. As a result, you can press F5 to move from one iteration to the next.
10. When you're through experimenting, remove the breakpoint and close the project.

6

How to code methods and event handlers

To this point, you've been writing methods called event handlers for the Click events of button controls. Now, in this chapter, you'll learn how to code methods that can be called from other methods. That will help you logically divide the code for an application into manageable parts. You'll also learn how to code event handlers for events other than the Click event.

How to code and call methods

In chapter 3, you learned how to code methods that are executed automatically when a Click event occurs. Now, you'll learn how to code methods that you call explicitly from other methods in the application. That can lead to code that's easier to read and maintain.

How to code methods

Figure 6-1 shows how to code a *method*. To start, you code an *access modifier* that indicates whether or not the method can be called from other classes. In most cases, you'll use the *private* access modifier so that the method can only be called from within the class where it's coded. If you need to call the method from another class, however, you can use the *public* access modifier.

After the access modifier, you code the return type for the method, which identifies the type of data that the method returns. To specify a return type, you can use the keyword for any of the built-in data types, or you can specify the name of any class, structure, or enumeration. Then, within the method, you must code a *return statement* that identifies the value to be returned. This value must correspond to the data type that's specified as the return type.

If the method doesn't return any data, though, you code the *void* keyword as the return type. Then, you don't code a return statement.

After the return type, you code the name of the method. In most cases, you'll give the method a name that indicates the action it performs. A common coding convention is to start each method name with a verb followed by a noun or by an adjective and a noun. This convention is used in the names for the methods in this figure: DisableButtons, GetDiscountPercent, and CalculateFutureValue.

After the method name, you code a set of parentheses. Within the parentheses, you declare the *parameters* that are required by the method. Later on, when you call the method, you pass arguments that correspond to these parameters. You'll learn more about that in the next figure.

If a method doesn't require any parameters, you can code an empty set of parentheses as shown in the first example in this figure. Here, a method named DisableButtons simply assigns a false value to the Enabled properties of two buttons. The second example shows a method that uses a single parameter. This method calculates and returns a discount percent based on a subtotal that's passed to it. The third example shows a method that uses three parameters. This method calculates and returns a future value based on a monthly investment, a monthly interest rate, and a number of months.

When you code the name and parameter list of a method, you form the *signature* of the method. Later in this book, you'll learn how to code two or more methods with the same name but with different parameters. This is known as *overloading* a method.

The basic syntax for coding a method

```
{public|private} returnType MethodName([parameterList])
{
    statements
}
```

A method with no parameters and no return type

```
private void DisableButtons()
{
    btnCalculate.Enabled = false;
    btnExit.Enabled = false;
}
```

A method with one parameter that returns a decimal value

```
private decimal GetDiscountPercent(decimal subtotal)
{
    decimal discountPercent = 0m;
    if (subtotal >= 500)
        discountPercent = .2m;
    else
        discountPercent = .1m;
    return discountPercent;
}
```

A method with three parameters that returns a decimal value

```
private decimal CalculateFutureValue(decimal monthlyInvestment,
    decimal monthlyInterestRate, int months)
{
    decimal futureValue = 0m;
    for (int i = 0; i < months; i++)
        futureValue = (futureValue + monthlyInvestment)
                    * (1 + monthlyInterestRate);

    return futureValue;
}
```

Description

- To allow other classes to access a *method*, use the *public* access modifier. To prevent other classes from accessing a method, use the *private* modifier.
- To code a method that doesn't return data, use the *void* keyword for the return type. To code a method that returns data, code a return type in the method declaration and code a *return statement* in the body of the method. The return statement ends the execution of the current method and returns the specified value to the calling method.
- It's a common coding practice to start the name of a method with a verb that indicates what the method does.
- Within the parentheses of a method, you can code an optional *parameter list* that contains one or more *parameters*, with the parameters separated by commas. When you code a parameter, you must code a data type and you must provide a name for the parameter.
- The name of a method along with its parameter list form the *signature* of the method, which must be unique.

Figure 6-1 How to code methods

How to call methods

Figure 6-2 shows how to *call* a method that's coded within a form class. By now, you should be familiar with the basic syntax for calling a method, so most of this figure should be review. To start, you can type the optional this keyword to specify the current form, followed by the dot operator and the method name. Otherwise, you just code the method name. Then, if the method requires *arguments*, you code the *argument list* within parentheses. Otherwise, you code an empty set of parentheses.

Before I go on, you should realize that the terms *parameter* and *argument* are often used interchangeably. In this book, however, we'll use the term parameter to refer to the variables of a method declaration, and we'll use the term argument to refer to the values that are passed to a method.

The three examples in this figure show how you would call the three methods you saw in figure 6-1. The first example calls the DisableButtons method, which has no parameters. Because of that, the statement call doesn't include any arguments. In addition, the method doesn't return any data, so the statement simply calls the method.

The second example calls the GetDiscountPercent method. Since this method is defined with one parameter, the statement that calls it passes one argument. In this case, the argument is a variable named subtotal. However, you could also code the argument as a literal value, such as 49.50m. In addition, because this method returns a value, the method call is coded as part of an assignment statement. When this statement is executed, the return value from the method, which is declared with the decimal type, is assigned to the discountPercent variable, which is also declared as a decimal.

The third example shows how to call a method that requires three arguments. When you call a method like this, you must be sure to pass the correct number of arguments with the correct data types. In addition, you must be sure to pass the arguments in the same order that the corresponding parameters are declared in the method. If you don't, your code won't compile. However, the names of the arguments don't have to be the same as the names of the parameters.

When you call a method that returns a value, you can assign that value to a variable as shown in the second and third examples in this figure. However, you can also code a method call within an expression. For example, you could use the GetDiscountPercent method in an expression like this:

```
total = subtotal * (1 - this.GetDiscountPercent(subtotal));
```

In this case, the decimal value that's returned by the method will be used to perform a calculation.

The syntax for calling a method

```
[this.]MethodName([argumentList])
```

A statement that calls a method that has no parameters

```
this.DisableButtons();
```

A statement that passes one argument

```
decimal discountPercent = this.GetDiscountPercent(subtotal);
```

A statement that passes three arguments

```
decimal futureValue = CalculateFutureValue(
    monthlyInvestment, monthlyInterestRate, months);
```

The IntelliSense feature for calling methods

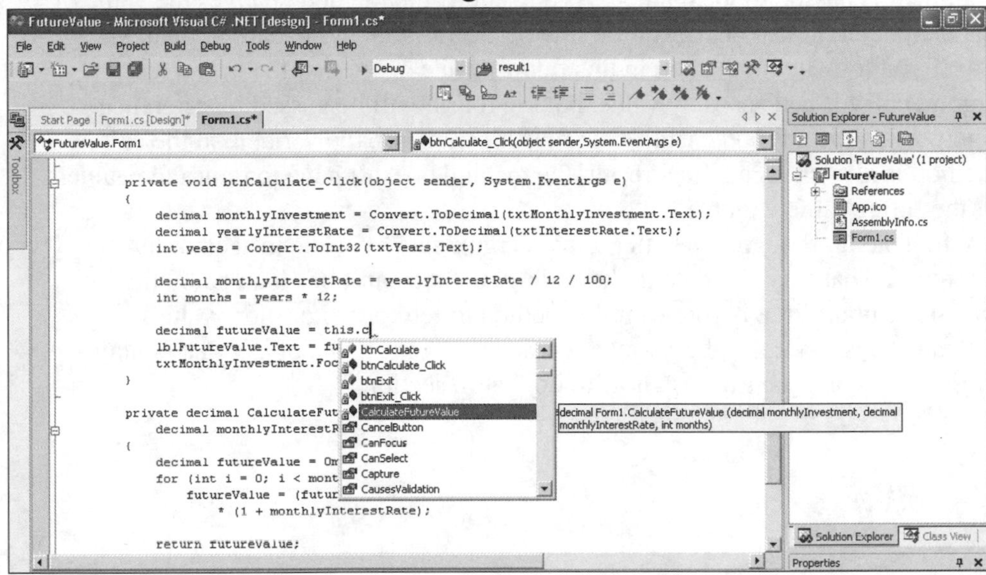

Description

- When you *call* a method, the *arguments* that you code in the *argument list* that's passed to the method must be in the same order as the parameters in the parameter list defined by the method, and they must have compatible data types. However, the names of the arguments and the parameters don't need to be the same.
- When you call a method in the current form class, using the this keyword allows you to use Visual Studio's IntelliSense feature to select the method you want from a list.

Figure 6-2 How to call methods

When and how to pass arguments by reference and by value

By default, the arguments that are passed to a method are passed *by value*. That means that the value of each passed variable is assigned to the corresponding parameter in the method. Because of that, the method can change the value of the parameter without affecting the value of the variable in the calling method.

In some cases, though, you'll want to be able to change the value of the variable in the calling method from the called method. To do that, you can pass the argument *by reference* as shown in figure 6-3 by coding the *ref* keyword before the argument and before the parameter declaration. Then, when you call the method, a reference to the variable that you specify for the corresponding argument is passed to the method. As a result, if the method changes the value of the parameter, it also changes the value of the variable in the calling method.

If you look at the method in this figure, you can see that the first three arguments will be passed by value, but the fourth will be passed by reference. Then, when the method changes the fourth parameter, the variable in the calling method is also changed. As a result, the method doesn't have to return the value of the futureValue variable.

In general, though, it's better to pass arguments by value instead of by reference. That way, the data in the calling method can't be changed by the called method. What if you want the method to return two or more values instead of just one? The best way to do that is to return one object that contains those values, and you'll learn how to do that in section 3.

The syntax of the parameters in a parameter list

```
[ref] dataType variablename
```

A method named CalculateFutureValue that requires four parameters

```
private void CalculateFutureValue(decimal monthlyInvestment,
    decimal monthlyInterestRate, int months, ref decimal futureValue)
{
    for (int i = 0; i < months; i++)
        futureValue = (futureValue + monthlyInvestment)
            * (1 + monthlyInterestRate);
}
```

Three statements that work with the CalculateFutureValue method

```
decimal futureValue = 0m;
this.CalculateFutureValue(monthlyInvestment,
    monthlyInterestRate, months, ref futureValue);
lblFutureValue.Text = String.Format("{0:c}", futureValue);
```

Description

- When you call a method, each argument can be passed to the method *by value* or *by reference*.
- If you pass an argument by value, the value of the variable in the calling method can't be changed by the called method. That's because the value of the variable is passed, not the variable itself.
- If you pass an argument by reference and the called method changes the value of the corresponding parameter, the value of the variable in the calling method is changed. That's because the passed argument provides a reference that points to the variable in the calling method.
- By default, arguments are passed by value. To pass an argument by reference, you use the *ref* keyword as shown above.
- When you pass an argument by reference and update the argument in the called method, you don't have to use the return statement to return the value of the argument.

Figure 6-3 When and how to pass arguments by reference and by value

How to work with events and delegates

In chapter 3, you learned how to generate the event handler for the default event of a control by double-clicking on the control in the Form Designer. Now, you'll learn how to create an event handler for any form or control event. In addition, you'll learn more about how event wiring works, and you'll learn how to handle two or more events with the same event handler.

How to generate an event handler for any event

Figure 6-4 shows how to generate an event handler for any event of a form or control. To do that, you select the form or control in the Form Designer and then click the Events button in the Properties window. When you do, a list of events for that form or control is displayed. In this figure, for example, you can see a list of the events for the first text box on the Future Value form. Below the list of events, you can see a short description of the highlighted event.

To generate a handler for any of these events, you can double-click on the event in this list. Then, Visual Studio will generate the method declaration for the event along with a statement that wires the event to the event handler (as you'll see in the next figure). When you use this technique, Visual Studio will give the event handler a name that combines the name of the control and the name of the event. For example, if you double-click the Validating event for the Monthly Investment text box, Visual Studio will generate an event handler with this name:

```
txtMonthlyInvestment_Validating
```

If you want to generate an event handler with a name other than the default, you can do that by entering the name next to the event in the Properties window. Then, when you press the Enter key, Visual Studio will create an event handler with that name. In most cases, you'll use this technique only when you generate an event handler that will be used to handle more than one event. You'll learn more about that in figure 6-6.

If you look through the list of events for a form or a control, you'll see that there are many events for each one. For instance, there 54 different events for a text box and 61 different events for a form. In practice, though, you'll use just a few events for each form or control. As you go through this book, you'll be introduced to the ones that are commonly used.

The Events list for a text box control

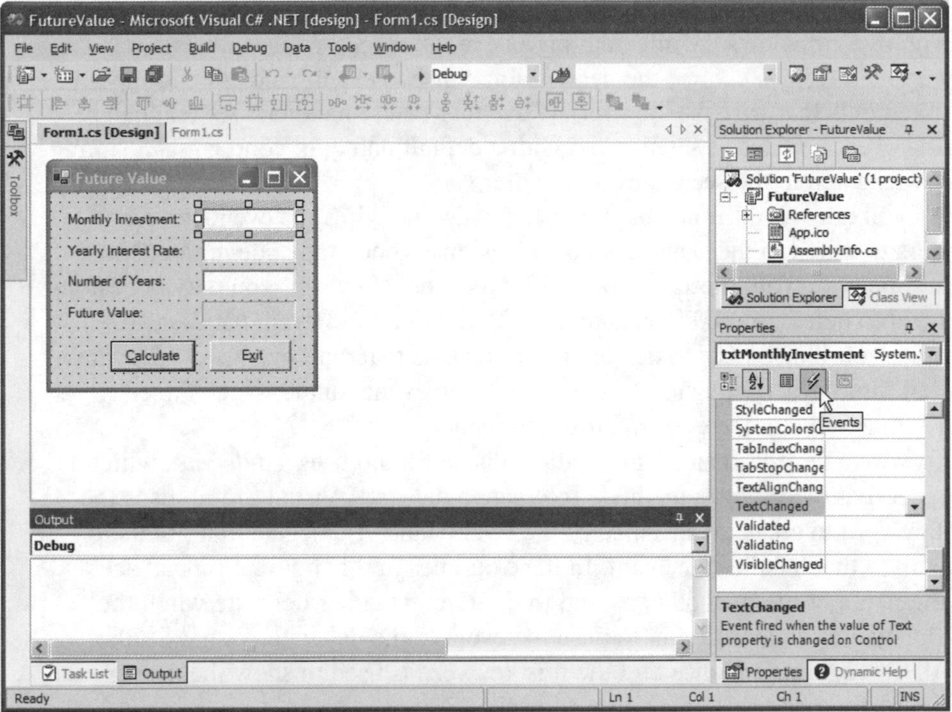

Description

- To generate the event handler for the default event of a form or control, you can double-click the form or control in the Form Designer.
- To view a list of all events for a form or control, you can select the form or control and click the Events button in the Properties window to display the Events list. Then, you can double-click on any event to generate an event handler for that event.
- By default, an event handler is given a name that consists of the form or control name, an underline, and the event name. To generate an event handler with a custom name, you can type the name of the event handler to the right of the event in the Events list and then press Enter to generate the event handler.
- When you generate an event handler for a control, Visual Studio generates the method declaration for the event handler and it connects, or *wires*, the event to the event handler as shown in the next figure.

Figure 6-4 How to generate an event handler for any event

How event wiring works

Figure 6-5 reviews the information on event wiring that was presented in chapter 3. Here, you can see the declarations for two event handlers, along with the statements that wire the appropriate events to these handlers. As you can see, the first event handler was generated with a default name. In contrast, a custom name was given to the second event handler.

As you may recall from chapter 3, the code that wires the events to event handlers is stored in the Windows Form Designer generated code region. Most of the time, you won't need to work with this code. However, you may occasionally need to delete or modify a statement. If you delete an event handler, for example, you'll also need to delete any statements that wire events to the event handler. Similarly, if you modify the name of an event handler, you'll need to modify that name in the event wiring statements too.

To wire an event to an event handler, Visual Studio uses a *delegate*, which is an object that represents a method. To create a delegate, Visual Studio uses the *new* keyword to create an instance of the EventHandler delegate that points to the method that handles the event. In the examples in this figure, you can see that the name of the method is passed to the EventHandler delegate when the new delegate is created. Then, to wire the event to the delegate, Visual Studio uses the += operator. Notice that the this keyword is used to show that the event and the method belong to the current form.

Although you can use the C# language to define your own delegates, you probably won't need to do that. As a result, you can focus on working with the delegates that are provided by the .NET Framework. In particular, you can focus on using the System.EventHandler delegate to work with code like the code in this figure.

For C# to recognize a method as an event handler, the method must include the two parameters shown in the examples, and it must include only those parameters. The first parameter is an object named *sender*. When an event handler is executed, this parameter receives the object that the event occurred on. The second parameter identifies an EventArgs object that contains information about the event. The exact content of this object depends on the event that occurred.

The default event handler for a text box

The method declaration for the event handler

```
private void txtMonthlyInvestment_TextChanged(object sender,
    System.EventArgs e)
{

}
```

The generated statement that wires the event to the event handler

```
this.txtMonthlyInvestment.TextChanged +=
    new System.EventHandler(this.txtMonthlyInvestment_TextChanged);
```

A custom event handler for a text box

The method declaration for the event handler

```
private void ClearFutureValue(object sender, System.EventArgs e)
{

}
```

The generated statement that wires the event to the event handler

```
this.txtMonthlyInvestment.TextChanged +=
    new System.EventHandler(this.ClearFutureValue);
```

Description

- When you use the Form Designer to generate an event handler, a statement is also generated in the Windows Form Designer generated code region. This statement wires the event to a delegate that points to the method for the event handler.
- A *delegate* is an object that represents a method. You can use the new keyword to create an instance of a delegate, and you can use the += operator to wire an event to the delegate.
- When Visual Studio generates the method declaration for an event handler, it includes two parameters that identify the method as an event handler. The *sender* parameter identifies the object that the event occurred on, and the *e* parameter identifies an EventArgs object that contains additional information about the event. These objects are passed to the event handler when the event occurs.

Figure 6-5 How event wiring works

How to handle multiple events with one event handler

In some cases, you'll want to use the same event handler to handle two or more events. For example, it's common to use one event handler for the TextChanged event of every text box on a form. To do that, you can use the procedure shown in figure 6-6.

To start, you must generate the event handler as described in figure 6-4. Typically, you will want to give this event handler a name that's not specific to any one control. Suppose, for example, that any time the user changes the value in any text box on the Future Value form, you want to clear the future value that's currently displayed. Then, when you create the event handler for the first text box, you might give this event handler the name ClearFutureValue.

Once you've created this event handler, it will appear in the drop-down list of event handlers that's available for each event. In this figure, for example, you can see that the ClearFutureValue event handler is included in the drop-down list for the TextChanged event of the Yearly Interest Rate text box. Then, you can select this event handler to generate a statement that wires the event to the event handler.

How to select an existing event handler for an event

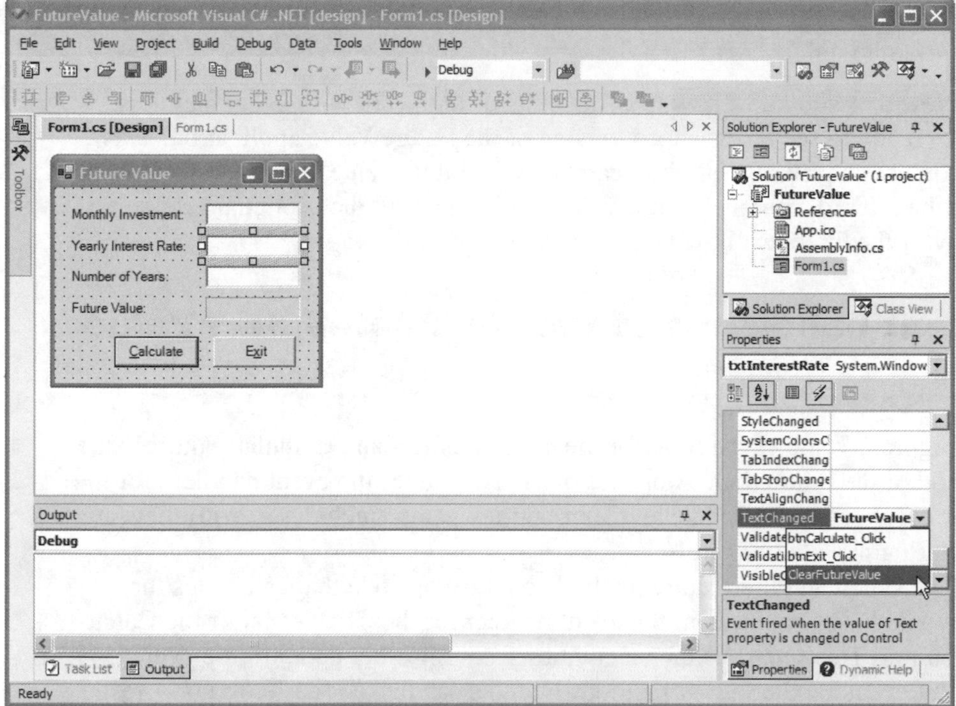

Procedure

1. Select the control in the Form Designer.
2. If necessary, click the Events button in the Properties window to display a list of the events for the control.
3. Select the event handler you want to use from the drop-down list for the event you want to handle. This list includes all of the event handlers for the current form.

Description

- When you create an event handler, that handler is included in the drop-down list of event handlers for each event of each control on the form. That way, you can wire two or more events to the same event handler.
- When you select an event handler from the drop-down list, Visual Studio generates a statement that wires the event to the event handler.

Figure 6-6 How to handle multiple events with one event handler

Another version of the Future Value application

Now that you know how to code methods and work with event handlers, you're ready to see an enhanced version of the Future Value application. This version uses a private method to calculate the future value, and it uses a single event handler to clear the Future Value label whenever the user changes the text in any of the three text boxes on the form.

The event handlers and the CalculateFutureValue method

Figure 6-7 shows the code for the event handlers and CalculateFutureValue method of the Future Value application. This includes the event handlers for the Click events of the Calculate and Exit buttons. It also includes a custom event handler named ClearFutureValue.

The CalculateFutureValue method contains the code that calculates the future value. It's called from the event handler for the Click event of the Calculate button. This separates the calculation from the other code for the event. In a lengthy event handler, using methods like this can make it easier to code, test, and debug an application. You'll see more of this in the next chapter.

The ClearFutureValue event handler contains a single statement that sets the Text property of the Future Value label to an empty string. In other words, it clears the future value that's displayed on the form. Since this event handler is wired to the TextChanged event of all three text boxes on the form, this code clears the Future Value label every time the user changes a value in any of these text boxes. Then, the future value isn't displayed until the user clicks the Calculate button again. As a result, this code prevents the future value label from displaying a value that isn't accurate for the values that are displayed in the text boxes.

The code for the methods for the Future Value application

```
private void btnCalculate_Click(object sender, System.EventArgs e)
{
    decimal monthlyInvestment = Convert.ToDecimal(txtMonthlyInvestment.Text);
    decimal yearlyInterestRate = Convert.ToDecimal(txtInterestRate.Text);
    int years = Convert.ToInt32(txtYears.Text);

    decimal monthlyInterestRate = yearlyInterestRate / 12 / 100;
    int months = years * 12;

    decimal futureValue = CalculateFutureValue(
        monthlyInvestment, monthlyInterestRate, months);
    lblFutureValue.Text = futureValue.ToString("c");
}

private decimal CalculateFutureValue(decimal monthlyInvestment,
    decimal monthlyInterestRate, int months)
{
    decimal futureValue = 0m;
    for (int i = 0; i < months; i++)
        futureValue = (futureValue + monthlyInvestment)
                    * (1 + monthlyInterestRate);

    return futureValue;
}

private void btnExit_Click(object sender, System.EventArgs e)
{
    this.Close();
}

private void ClearFutureValue(object sender, System.EventArgs e)
{
    lblFutureValue.Text = "";
}
```

Description

- The use of the CalculateFutureValue method separates the calculation from the rest of the code for the event handler for the Click event of the Calculate button. This use of methods can make an application easier to code, test, and debug.
- The TextChanged event of all three text boxes is wired to the ClearFutureValue event handler. As a result, the Future Value label will be cleared every time the user changes the data in a text box.
- Since this application doesn't provide data validation, the user will be able to enter invalid data, which will cause an exception to occur.

Figure 6-7 The event handlers and other methods of the Future Value application

Some of the generated code

Figure 6-8 shows some of the generated code for the Future Value application that you can find in the Windows Form Designer generated code region. To start, you can see the variable declarations for three of the controls on the form: the first two text boxes and the Calculate button. Then, within the InitializeComponent method, you can see the statements that create instances of the appropriate control classes and assign those instances to these variables.

Next, the InitializeComponent method includes a group of statements for each control. Most of these statements set the starting properties for these controls. The last statement in each group, however, wires an event to an event handler. Here, the TextChanged events of the two text boxes are wired to an event handler named ClearFutureValue, and the Click event of the Calculate button is wired to an event handler named btnCalculate_Click. (Although you can't see it here, the TextChanged event of the third text box on this form is also wired to the ClearFutureValue event handler.)

If you do everything right as you develop an application, you usually don't have to work with this generated code. You should nevertheless be aware that it exists and that it is essential to the proper operation of your application. You should also be prepared to delete or modify some of this code. If, for example, you start an event handler and decide to delete it, you also need to delete any statements that wire events to the event handler.

Some of the generated code for the Future Value form

```
private System.Windows.Forms.TextBox txtMonthlyInvestment;
private System.Windows.Forms.TextBox txtInterestRate;
private System.Windows.Forms.Button btnCalculate;
...
private void InitializeComponent()
{
    this.txtMonthlyInvestment = new System.Windows.Forms.TextBox();
    this.txtInterestRate = new System.Windows.Forms.TextBox();
    this.btnCalculate = new System.Windows.Forms.Button();
    ...
    //
    // txtMonthlyInvestment
    //
    this.txtMonthlyInvestment.Location = new System.Drawing.Point(133, 14);
    this.txtMonthlyInvestment.Name = "txtMonthlyInvestment";
    this.txtMonthlyInvestment.Size = new System.Drawing.Size(84, 20);
    this.txtMonthlyInvestment.TabIndex = 5;
    this.txtMonthlyInvestment.Text = "";
    this.txtMonthlyInvestment.TextChanged +=
        new System.EventHandler(this.ClearFutureValue);
    //
    // txtInterestRate
    //
    this.txtInterestRate.Location = new System.Drawing.Point(133, 42);
    this.txtInterestRate.Name = "txtInterestRate";
    this.txtInterestRate.Size = new System.Drawing.Size(84, 20);
    this.txtInterestRate.TabIndex = 6;
    this.txtInterestRate.Text = "";
    this.txtInterestRate.TextChanged +=
        new System.EventHandler(this.ClearFutureValue);
    //
    // btnCalculate
    //
    this.btnCalculate.Location = new System.Drawing.Point(53, 132);
    this.btnCalculate.Name = "btnCalculate";
    this.btnCalculate.Size = new System.Drawing.Size(74, 27);
    this.btnCalculate.TabIndex = 8;
    this.btnCalculate.Text = "&Calculate";
    this.btnCalculate.Click +=
        new System.EventHandler(this.btnCalculate_Click);
    ...
}
```

Description

- The first three statements shown above declare variables that will hold instances of three of the controls on the form.
- The InitializeComponent method starts by creating an instance of each control on the form and assigning it to the variable that's used to refer to that control. Then, it sets the properties of each control, and it wires control events to the appropriate event handlers.
- The InitializeComponent method is included in the Windows Form Designer generated code region.

Figure 6-8 Some of the generated code for the Future Value application

Perspective

If this chapter has succeeded, you should now know how to code and call methods. You should also be able to code event handlers for any event of a form or control. With those skills, you are well on your way toward developing programs at a professional level.

Summary

- To code a *method*, you declare its *return type*, name, and *parameters*. This forms the *signature* of the method.
- To *call* a method, you code the method name followed by an *argument* list. The arguments must be in the same sequence and have the same data types as the parameters in the method, but they don't need to have the same names.
- When arguments are passed to a method *by value*, they can't be changed by the called method. When they're passed *by reference*, they can be changed.
- The *wiring* for an event of an object is the code that connects the event to an event handler. To wire an event, the C# language uses a *delegate*, which is an object that stores a reference to a method.

Terms

method
access modifier
return statement
parameter
parameter list
signature
overloading a method
call a method
argument
argument list
pass by value
pass by reference
event wiring
delegate

Objectives

- Given the form design and specifications for an application that requires any of the language elements presented in this chapter, write the code for the application.
- Describe the signature of a method.
- Explain the difference between passing an argument by value and by reference.
- Describe the procedure for creating an event handler for an event other than the default event for a form or control.
- Explain how you can handle more than one event with one event handler.

Exercise 6-1 Enhance the Future Value application

In this exercise, you'll enhance the Future Value application that you created in chapter 5 so it works like the one in figure 6-7.

Open the application and add the CalculateFutureValue method

1. Open the Future Value application that's in the in the C:\C#.NET\Chapter 06 directory.
2. Add a method named CalculateFutureValue method that works like the one in figure 6-7. To do that, you can move the related code from the btnCalculate_Click method to the new method and then modify it.
3. Modify the code in the btnCalculate_Click method so it calls the CalculateFutureValue method. As you enter the call to the method, note how the IntelliSense feature helps you remember what the arguments are.
4. Test the application to make sure the new method works correctly.

Add an event handler for the TextChanged events

5. In the Form Designer, select the first text box. Then, click the Events button in the Properties Window to display the Events list for that text box. Review the events that are available.
6. Enter "ClearFutureValue" to the right of the TextChanged event and press Enter. When you do, the Code Editor will open and an event handler named ClearFutureValue will be created. Enter a statement that clears the Future Value label as shown in figure 6-7.
7. Open the Windows Form Designer generated code region, and locate the statements that set the properties of the Monthly Investment text box. At the end of those statements, you'll find a statement that wires the TextChanged event of this control to the ClearFutureValue event handler.
8. Return to the Form Designer and select the Yearly Interest Rate text box. Drop down the list for the TextChanged event of this control, and notice that the ClearFutureValue event handler is included in this list. Select this event handler to wire the event to it. Repeat this process for the Number of Years text box.
9. Run the application and perform a calculation. Then, change the value that's displayed in one of the text boxes. When you do that, the value that's displayed for the Future Value label should be cleared.
10. When you're sure the enhancements are working correctly, close the application.

Exercise 6-2 Experiment with events

This exercise will give you a chance to experiment with events and the event wiring for the Future Value application.

Generate and delete an event handler

1. Open the Future Value application that you enhanced in exercise 6-1.
2. In the Form Designer, double-click on the form to generate the handler for the default event of a form, which is the Load event. Then, delete this event handler in the Code Editor, and try to build and run the application, which will lead to one build error.
3. Double-click on the error message, which will lead you to the event wiring for the event handler. Then, delete that wiring, and try to build and run the application again. This time, it should work.

Use a form event and two more control events

4. Go to the Form Designer, select the form, click the Events button in the Properties window, and double-click on the DoubleClick event to generate its event handler. Next, write the code for this handler so all three of the text boxes and the label for future value will be reset to an empty string. Then, test the application to make sure this works.
5. In the Form Designer, select the Monthly Investment text box. Next, select the MouseHover event, read its description, drop down its list, and select the ClearFutureValue event handler so it will be executed whenever the user lets the mouse hover over this text box. Then, test the application to make sure this works.
6. In the Form Designer, select the Yearly Interest Rate text box, and double-click on the DoubleClick event to generate its event handler. Next, write the code for this handler so it sets the value in the Yearly Interest Rate text box to 12. Then, test this enhancement.
7. Use your own imagination to work with other events. When you're through experimenting with events, close the application.

7

How to handle exceptions and validate data

In the last two chapters, you learned how to code a Future Value application that calculates the future value of a series of monthly payments. However, if the user enters data that can't be handled by this application, an exception will occur and the application will crash. In this chapter, you'll learn how to prevent that from happening by handling any exceptions that occur and by validating data to prevent exceptions.

An introduction to exceptions

Before you learn how to handle exceptions, it's helpful to know more about how exceptions work. In addition, it's helpful to know how to display a dialog box that contains a message about an exception that has occurred. So that's what you'll learn in the two topics that follow.

How exceptions work

It's inevitable that your applications will encounter exceptions. For example, a user may enter data that's not appropriate for the application. Then, if the application doesn't check to be sure that the data is valid, C# will *throw an exception* when it tries to work with that data. An exception is an object that's created from the Exception class or one of its subclasses like the ones shown in figure 7-1. Exception objects represent errors that have occurred, and they contain information about those errors.

A well-coded application will *catch* any exceptions that might be thrown and handle them. This is known as *exception handling*. Exception handling can be as simple as notifying users that they must enter valid data. However, for more serious exceptions, exception handling may involve notifying users that the application is being shut down, saving as much data as possible, cleaning up resources, and exiting the application as smoothly as possible.

When you're testing an application, it's common to encounter exceptions that haven't been handled. In that case, Visual Studio will display a dialog box like the one shown in this figure that lets you enter Break mode to debug the application. As you can see, this dialog box also includes the name of the exception class and a brief message that describes the cause of the exception.

All exceptions are subclasses of the Exception class. For example, the FormatException class is a subclass of the Exception class that represents a specific type of exception that occurs when a value of one data type can't be converted to another data type. This exception can be thrown by the To methods of the Convert class or the Parse method of any class.

The ArithmeticException class is also a subclass of the Exception class. It represents an exception that occurs during an arithmetic, casting, or conversion operation. This class contains other subclasses, including the OverflowException and DivideByZeroException classes shown here. An overflow exception occurs when the result of an arithmetic, casting, or conversion operation is too large for the receiving variable. A divide-by-zero exception occurs if an application attempts to divide a number by zero.

For now, that's all you need to know about the Exception hierarchy. As you progress through this book, though, you'll learn about other types of exceptions. In section 3, for example, you'll learn how to work with the exceptions that can occur when you're working with databases. You'll also learn more about subclasses and how they work in chapter 14.

The dialog box for an unhandled exception

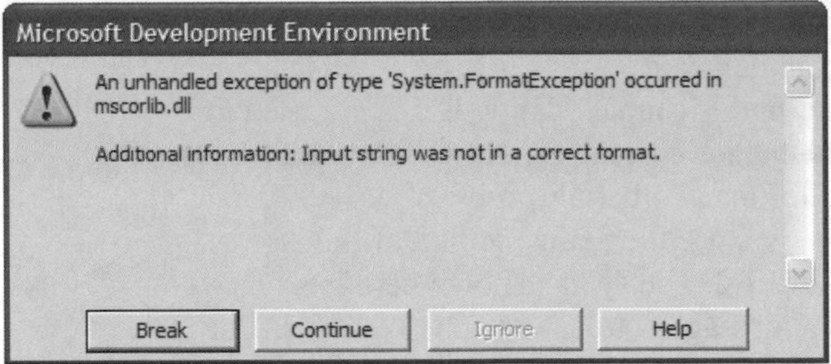

The Exception hierarchy for five common exceptions

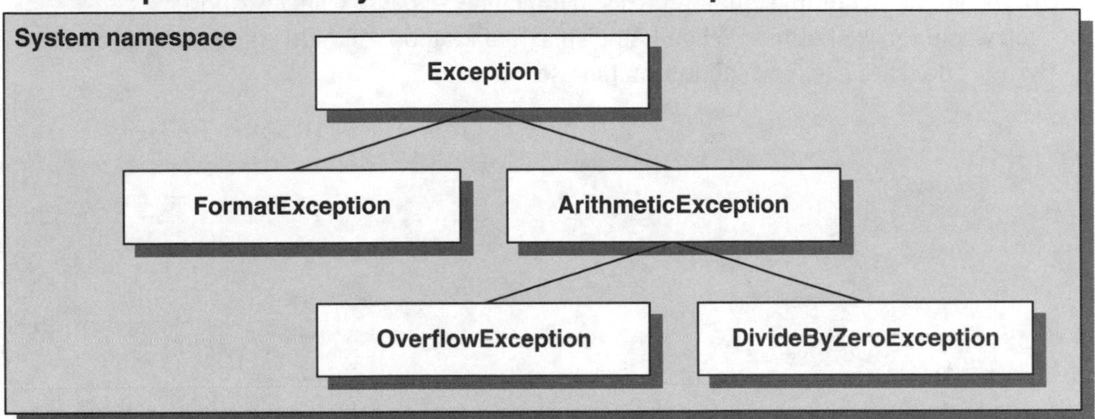

Methods that might throw exceptions

Class	Method	Exception
`Convert`	`ToDecimal(string)`	`FormatException`
`Convert`	`ToInt32(string)`	`FormatException`
`Decimal`	`Parse(string)`	`FormatException`
`DateTime`	`Parse(string)`	`FormatException`

Description

- An *exception* is an object that contains information about an error that has occurred. When an error occurs in a method, the method *throws* an exception that contains information about the error.
- If an exception is thrown when you're testing an application, Visual Studio will display a dialog box that you can use to enter break mode and debug the error.
- All exceptions are *subclasses* of the Exception class. The Exception class represents the most general type of exception. Each successive layer of subclasses represents more specific exceptions.
- If any of the To methods of the Convert class or the Parse method of any class isn't able to perform a conversion, it throws an exception of the FormatException type.

Figure 7-1 How exceptions work

How to display a dialog box

One way an application can communicate with its users is by displaying a dialog box that contains a message. In this chapter, dialog boxes are used to display messages about exceptions that have occurred. Keep in mind, however, that dialog boxes can also be used for many other purposes.

To display a simple dialog box, you use the Show method of the MessageBox class as shown in figure 7-2. The syntax shown here lets you display a dialog box that contains a message, a title, and an OK button. For now, this simple dialog box is adequate.

In chapter 10, however, you'll learn how you can use the MessageBox class to display more complex dialog boxes that include Yes, No, Cancel, Abort, Retry, and Ignore buttons. When you display a dialog box like this, you can write code that checks which button the user selected.

The syntax to display a dialog box with an OK button

```
MessageBox.Show(text[, caption]);
```

A dialog box with an OK button

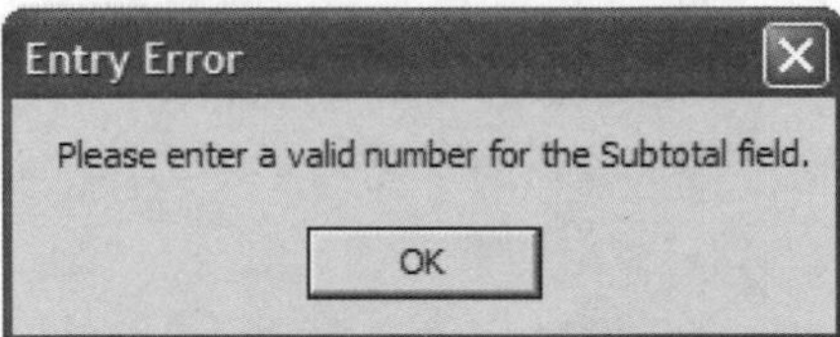

The statement that displays this dialog box

```
MessageBox.Show(
    "Please enter a valid number for the Subtotal field.",
    "Entry Error");
```

Description

- You can use the static Show method of the MessageBox class to display a dialog box. Dialog boxes are commonly used to display information about an exception to the user.
- If you omit the *caption* argument, the dialog box will be displayed without a caption in its title bar.

Note

- In chapter 10, you'll learn how to use the MessageBox class to display more complex dialog boxes that contain Yes, No, Cancel, Abort, Retry, and Ignore buttons and accept a response from the user.

Figure 7-2 How to display a dialog box

How to use structured exception handling

To prevent your applications from crashing due to runtime errors, you can write code that handles exceptions when they occur. This is known as *structured exception handling*, and it plays an important role in most applications.

How to catch an exception

Figure 7-3 shows how to use *try-catch* statements to catch and handle exceptions. First, you code a *try block* around the statement or statements that may cause an exception. Then, you code a *catch block* immediately after the try block that contains the statements that will be executed if an exception is thrown by a statement in the try block. This is known as an *exception handler*.

The try-catch statement in this figure shows how you might catch any exceptions thrown by four of the statements in the Invoice Total application. For example, if the user enters a non-numeric value into the Subtotal text box, the ToDecimal method of the Convert class will throw an exception. Then, the application will jump into the catch block, skipping all the remaining statements in the try block. In this case, the catch block simply displays a dialog box that notifies the user of the problem. Then, the user can click the OK button and enter a valid number.

The syntax for a simple try-catch statement

```
try { statements }
catch { statements }
```

A try-catch statement

```
try
{
    decimal subtotal = Convert.ToDecimal(txtSubtotal.Text);
    decimal discountPercent = .2m;
    decimal discountAmount = subtotal * discountPercent;
    decimal invoiceTotal = subtotal - discountAmount;
}
catch
{
    MessageBox.Show(
        "Please enter a valid number for the Subtotal field.",
        "Entry Error");
}
```

The dialog box that's displayed if an exception occurs

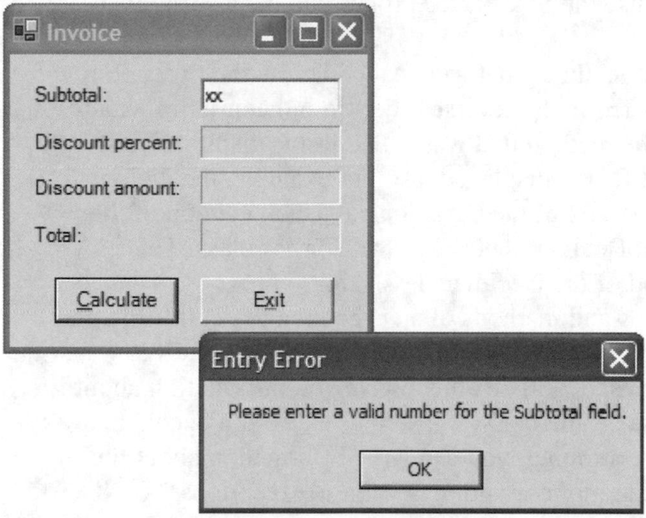

Description

- You can use a try-catch statement to code an *exception handler* that catches and handles any exceptions that are thrown.
- You can code a *try block* around any statements that may throw an exception. Then, you can code a *catch block* that contains the statements to be executed when an exception is thrown in the try block.

Figure 7-3 How to catch an exception

How to use the properties and methods of an exception

Since an exception is an object, it has properties and methods. If you want to use the properties or methods of an exception in the catch block that catches the exception, you must supply a name for the exception as shown in figure 7-4. As you can see, you code a set of parentheses after the catch keyword. Within those parentheses, you code the name of the exception class, followed by a name for the exception.

Note that if you're coding the try-catch statement within an event handler, you can't use e as the name of the exception. That's because the event handler already uses this name for one of its parameters (the EventArgs parameter). As a result, you must specify another name such as x or ex.

Once you specify a name for an exception, you can use the Message property to get a brief description of the error. You can also use the GetType method to get the type of class that was used to create the exception object. Then, to get the name of that type, you can use the ToString method as shown in the example in this figure. Finally, you can use the StackTrace property to get a string that represents the *stack trace*.

A stack trace is a list of the methods that were called before the exception occurred. These methods are listed in the reverse order from the order in which they were called. As a result, the method that was called last is displayed first, and the method that was called first is displayed last. For example, the dialog box in this figure shows that line 202 of the btnCalculate_Click method of the Invoice Total form called the ToDecimal method of the Convert class. This method called the Parse method of the Decimal class. And so on.

When you use the properties and methods of an exception to get information about the exception, you can display that information in a dialog box. That way, if an exception is thrown, your users will be able to give you information about the exception so you can fix the problem. Or, if a serious exception occurs that prevents the application from continuing, you can write information about the exception to a log file so you can monitor and review these exceptions. You'll learn how to write data to files in chapter 21.

The syntax for a try-catch statement that accesses the exception

```
try { statements }
catch(ExceptionClass exceptionName) { statements }
```

Two common properties for all exceptions

Property	Description
`Message`	Gets a message that briefly describes the current exception.
`StackTrace`	Gets a string that lists the methods that were called before the exception occurred.

A common method for all exceptions

Method	Description
`GetType()`	Gets the type of the current exception.

A try-catch statement that accesses the exception

```
try
{
    decimal subtotal = Convert.ToDecimal(txtSubtotal.Text);
}
catch(Exception ex)
{
    MessageBox.Show(
        ex.Message + "\n\n" +
        ex.GetType().ToString() + "\n" +
        ex.StackTrace,
        "Exception");
}
```

The dialog box that's displayed if an exception occurs

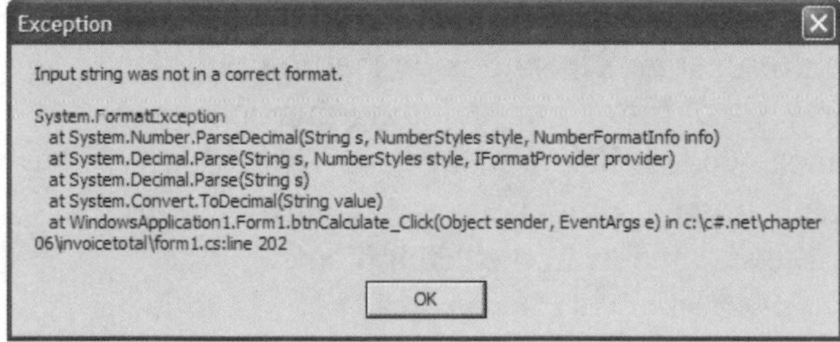

Description

- If you want to use the properties or methods of the exception in the catch block, you must supply a name for the exception.
- The *stack trace* is a list of the methods that were called before the exception occurred. The list appears in reverse order, from the last method called to the first method called.

Note

- If you're coding the try-catch statement within an event handler, you can't use e for the name of the exception because it's used as the name of a parameter for the handler.

Figure 7-4 How to use the properties and methods of an exception

How to catch specific types of exceptions

In some cases, the statements in the try block of a try-catch statement can throw more than one type of exception. Then, you may want to handle each exception differently. To do that, you can code catch blocks like the ones shown in figure 7-5. Here, the first catch block catches a format exception, the second catch block catches an overflow exception, and the third catch block catches any other exceptions.

When you catch specific exceptions, you should realize that you must code the catch blocks for the most specific exceptions in a class hierarchy first, and you must code the catch blocks for the least specific exceptions last. In this figure, for example, the FormatException type and the OverflowException type are both more specific than the Exception type. As a result, their catch blocks must be coded before the catch block for the Exception type. If they were coded after the Exception type, you would get a build error when you tried to compile the project. That's because the catch blocks are evaluated in sequence, which means that the catch block for the Exception type would catch any exception that occurred. In other words, the other catch blocks would never be executed.

Although you have to code the catch blocks for the FormatException and OverflowException types before the catch block for the Exception type, you don't have to code the catch block for the OverflowException type before the FormatException type. That's because the OverflowException class is a subclass of the ArithmeticException class, not the FormatException class. In other words, the least specific exception to most specific exception rule applies only within subclasses that are based on the same class.

When you code try-catch statements, you may find that you have some code that should run regardless of whether an exception is thrown or what type of exception is thrown. For example, if your application is using system resources such as files or fonts, it's common to perform some cleanup code that releases those resources when they're no longer needed. Instead of including this code in the try block and each catch block, you can code it in a *finally block*. Then, this code is executed after all of the statements in the try block are executed. Or, if an exception is thrown, it's executed after the statements in the catch block.

The complete syntax for the try-catch statement

```
try { statements }
[catch(MostSpecificException [exceptionName]) { statements }]...
catch([LeastSpecificException [exceptionName]]) { statements }
[finally { statements }]
```

A try-catch statement that catches two specific exceptions

```
try
{
    decimal monthlyInvestment =
        Convert.ToDecimal(txtMonthlyInvestment.Text);
    decimal yearlyInterestRate =
        Convert.ToDecimal(txtInterestRate.Text);
    int years = Convert.ToInt32(txtYears.Text);
}
catch(FormatException)   // a specific exception
{
    MessageBox.Show(
        "A format exception has occurred. Please check all entries.",
        "Entry Error");
}
catch(OverflowException) // another specific exception
{
    MessageBox.Show(
        "An overflow exception has occurred. Please enter smaller values.",
        "Entry Error");
}
catch(Exception ex)     // all other exceptions
{
    MessageBox.Show(ex.Message, ex.GetType().ToString());
}
finally        // this code runs whether or not an exception occurs
{
    PerformCleanup();
}
```

Description

- You can code one catch block for each type of exception that may occur in the try block. If you code more than one catch block, you must code the catch blocks for the most specific types of exceptions first.
- Since all exceptions are subclasses of the Exception class, a catch block for the Exception class will catch all types of exceptions.
- You can code a *finally block* after all the catch blocks. The code in this block is executed whether or not an exception occurs. It's often used to free any system resources.

How to throw an exception

Now that you've learned how to catch exceptions, you're ready to learn how to throw exceptions from the methods that you code. To do that, you can use the *throw* statement as shown in figure 7-6. As you can see, you can use this statement either to throw a new exception or to throw an existing exception.

To throw a new exception, you code the throw keyword followed by the *new* keyword and the name of the exception class you want to create the exception from. (As you'll see throughout this book, new is the keyword you use to create an instance of any class.) When you do that, you can also supply a string argument that provides a brief description of the exception. This argument is assigned to the Message property of the exception. Then, when you handle the exception, you can use the Message property to get this string.

This use of the throw statement is illustrated in the first example in this figure. Here, before performing its calculation, the CalcuateFutureValue method checks if the values used in the calculation are less than or equal to zero. If so, an exception that's created from the Exception class is thrown. Notice that each of the two throw statements shown here indicates the specific error that occurred. Then, the method that calls this procedure can catch the exception and display the error in a dialog box so the user can correct it.

Although this example shows how to throw an exception from a method, you should realize that this isn't the best way to handle this type of error. A better way would be to just return a false value to the calling procedure or to display a dialog box that indicates the type of error that occurred. In general, then, you should throw an exception only when a truly exceptional condition occurs.

You can also use the throw statement to test an exception handling routine as shown in the second example. Here, the throw statement is coded within the try block of a try-catch statement. Then, when this statement is executed, the code within the catch block is executed so you can be sure that it works properly.

The third example in this figure shows how to throw an existing exception. This technique is useful if you need to catch an exception, perform some processing that partially handles the exception, and then throw the exception again so that another exception handler can finish handling the exception. In this case, the ToDecimal method is used within a try block to convert the value the user enters into a text box to a decimal. If the user enters a value that's not a valid decimal, a format exception is thrown. Then, the catch block catches this exception, moves the focus to the text box, and rethrows the exception. That way, the calling method can also catch the exception and perform some additional processing.

The syntax for throwing a new exception

```
throw new ExceptionClass([message]);
```

The syntax for throwing an existing exception

```
throw exceptionName;
```

A method that throws an overflow exception

```
private decimal CalculateFutureValue(decimal monthlyInvestment,
    decimal interestRateMonthly, int months)
{
    if (monthlyInvestment <= 0)
       throw new Exception("Monthly Investment must be greater than 0.");
    if (interestRateMonthly <= 0)
       throw new Exception("Interest Rate must be greater than 0.");
        .
        .
}
```

Code that throws an exception for testing purposes

```
try
{
    decimal subtotal = Convert.ToDecimal(txtSubtotal.Text);
    throw new Exception("An unknown exception occurred.");
}
catch (Exception ex)
{
    MessageBox.Show(ex.Message + "\n\n"
        + ex.GetType().ToString() + "\n"
        + ex.StackTrace, "Exception");
}
```

Code that rethrows an exception

```
try
{
    Convert.ToDecimal(txtSubtotal.Text);
}
catch (FormatException fe)
{
    textBox.Focus();
    throw fe;
}
```

When to throw an exception

- When a method encounters a situation where it isn't able to complete its task.
- When you want to generate an exception to test an exception handler.
- When you want to catch the exception, perform some processing, and then throw the exception again.

Description

- You can use the throw statement to throw a new or existing exception. When you create a new exception, you can specify a string that's assigned to the Message property.

Figure 7-6 How to throw an exception

The Future Value application with exception handling

Figure 7-7 presents an improved version of the Future Value application you saw in the last chapter. As you can see, this version uses structured exception handling to catch any exceptions that might be thrown when the user clicks the Calculate button on the form.

To catch exceptions, all of the statements in the btnCalculate_Click method are coded within a try block. Then, the first catch block catches and handles any format exceptions that are thrown if the user enters data with an invalid numeric format in one of the text boxes. Next, the second catch block catches and handles any overflow exceptions that are thrown if the user enters numbers that are too large. If either of these exceptions are thrown, the code in the catch block displays a dialog box that describes the exception and indicates a corrective action that the user can take.

While the first two catch blocks catch specific exceptions, the third catch block catches all other exceptions. Since the cause of these exceptions isn't known, the application uses the properties and methods of the exception to display some information about the exception in a dialog box. In this case, the name of the exception class is displayed in the title bar of the dialog box, and a brief description of the exception is displayed in the body of the dialog box. That way, the user will be able to provide some information about the exception so you can debug the application.

Notice that if an exception occurs in the CalculateFutureValue method, the exception isn't caught by that method. Because of that, the exception is passed back to the calling method, in this case, btnCalculate_Click. Then, the appropriate catch block in that procedure catches and handles the exception.

The code for the Future Value application with exception handling

```
private void btnCalculate_Click(object sender, System.EventArgs e)
{
    try
    {
        decimal monthlyInvestment =
            Convert.ToDecimal(txtMonthlyInvestment.Text);
        decimal yearlyInterestRate =
            Convert.ToDecimal(txtInterestRate.Text);
        int years = Convert.ToInt32(txtYears.Text);

        decimal monthlyInterestRate = yearlyInterestRate / 12 / 100;
        int months = years * 12;

        decimal futureValue = this.CalculateFutureValue(
            monthlyInvestment, monthlyInterestRate, months);
        lblFutureValue.Text = futureValue.ToString("c");
    }
    catch(FormatException)
    {
        MessageBox.Show(
            "Invalid numeric formation. Please check all entries.",
            "Entry Error");
    }
    catch(OverflowException)
    {
        MessageBox.Show(
            "Overflow error. Please enter smaller values.",
            "Entry Error");
    }
    catch(Exception ex)
    {
        MessageBox.Show(
            ex.Message,
            ex.GetType().ToString());
    }
}

private decimal CalculateFutureValue(decimal monthlyInvestment,
    decimal monthlyInterestRate, int months)
{
    decimal futureValue = 0m;
    for (int i = 0; i < months; i++)
        futureValue = (futureValue + monthlyInvestment)
            * (1 + monthlyInterestRate);

    return futureValue;
}
```

Figure 7-7 The Future Value application with exception handling

How to validate data

Whenever a user enters data, that data usually needs to be checked to make sure that it's valid. This is known as *data validation*. When an entry is invalid, the application needs to display an error message and give the user another chance to enter valid data. This needs to be repeated until all the entries on the form are valid.

How to validate a single entry

When a user enters text into a text box, you may want to perform several types of data validation. In particular, it's common to perform the three types of data validation shown in figure 7-8.

First, if the application requires that the user enters a value into a text box, you can check the Text property of the text box to make sure the user has entered one or more characters. Second, if the application requires that the user enters a number in the text box, you can use the appropriate To method of the Convert class within a try-catch statement to check that the Text property of the text box can be converted to the appropriate numeric data type. Third, if the application requires that the user enters a number within a specified range, you can use if-else statements to check that the number falls within the specified range. This is known as *range checking*.

Although this figure only shows how to check data that the user has entered into a text box, the same principles apply to other types of controls. In chapter 10, you'll learn more about validating entries made in other types of controls. In addition, although this figure only shows how to check the range of a number, you can also check strings and dates to make sure that they fall within certain ranges. You'll learn more about working with dates and strings in chapter 9.

Often, the code that performs the data validation prevents exceptions from being thrown. For example, if the user doesn't enter a value in the Monthly Investment text box, the code in this figure displays a dialog box and moves the focus to the Monthly Investment text box. If you didn't include this code, an exception would occur when the application tried to convert the empty string to a numeric data type.

Since code that validates data without using exception handling runs faster than code that uses exception handling, you should avoid using exception handling to validate data whenever possible. Of course, this isn't always practical or possible. For example, it's difficult to parse a string to check whether it contains a valid numeric format without using the ToDecimal method. That's why the second example uses a try-catch statement to check whether converting a string to a decimal throws an exception. In chapter 9, though, you'll learn how to write code that performs the same function without catching an exception.

Code that checks that an entry has been made

```
if (txtMonthlyInvestment.Text == "")
{
    MessageBox.Show(
        "Monthly Investment is a required field.", Entry Error);
    txtMonthlyInvestment.Focus();
}
```

Code that checks an entry for a valid decimal format

```
try
{
    Convert.ToDecimal(txtMonthlyInvestment.Text);
}
catch (FormatException)
{
    MessageBox.Show(
        "Monthly Investment must be a numeric value.", "Entry Error");
    txtMonthlyInvestment.Focus();
}
```

Code that checks an entry for a valid range

```
decimal monthlyInvestment = Convert.ToDecimal(txtMonthlyInvestment.Text);
if (monthlyInvestment <= 0)
{
    MessageBox.Show(
        "Monthly Investment must be greater than 0.", "Entry Error");
    txtMonthlyInvestment.Focus();
}
else if (monthlyInvestment >= 1000)
{
    MessageBox.Show(
        "Monthly Investment must be less than 1,000.", "Entry Error");
    txtMonthlyInvestment.Focus();
}
```

Description

- When a user enters data, that data usually needs to be checked to make sure that it is valid. This is known as *data validation*.
- When an entry is invalid, the program needs to display an error message and give the user another chance to enter valid data.
- Three common types of validity checking are (1) to make sure that a required entry has been made, (2) to make sure that an entry has a valid numeric format, and (3) to make sure that an entry is within a valid range (known as *range checking*).
- To test whether a value has been entered into a text box, you can check whether the Text property of the box is equal to an empty string.
- To test whether a text box contains valid numeric data, you can code the statement that converts the data in a try block and use a catch block to catch a format exception.
- To test whether a value is within an acceptable range, you can use if-else statements.

Figure 7-8 How to validate a single entry

How to use generic methods to validate an entry

Since it's common to check text boxes for valid data, it often makes sense to create generic methods like the ones shown in figure 7-9 for data validation. These methods perform the same types of validation described in the previous figure, but they work for any text box instead of for a specific text box.

In this figure, the IsPresent method checks to make sure the user has entered data in a text box. This method accepts two parameters and returns a Boolean value. The first parameter is a variable that refers to the text box, and the second parameter is a string that contains a name that describes the text box. If the user hasn't entered any characters into the text box, this method displays a dialog box with a message that includes the name parameter. Then, it moves the focus to the text box. Finally, it returns a false value. However, if the user has entered one or more characters, the method returns a true value.

The IsDecimal method accepts the same parameters as the IsPresent method, but it uses a try-catch statement to check if the value entered by the user is a decimal value. If it isn't, the ToDecimal method of the Convert class will throw an exception and the statements in the catch block will be executed. These statements display a dialog box with an appropriate message, move the focus to the text box, and return a false value.

Once you understand how the IsDecimal method works, you can code methods for other numeric types. For example, you can code an IsInt32 method that uses the ToInt32 method to check if the user has entered a valid int value.

The IsWithinRange method begins with the same two parameters as the IsPresent and IsDecimal methods, but it includes two additional parameters: min and max. These parameters contain the minimum and maximum values that can be entered into the text box.

The IsWithinRange method begins by converting the value the user entered into the text box to a decimal value. Then, it uses an if statement to check if the decimal value is within the range specified by the min and max parameters. If not, this method displays a dialog box with an appropriate message, moves the focus to the text box, and returns a false value.

The code at the bottom of this figure shows how to call these three methods to make sure a valid decimal value has been entered in the Monthly Investment text box. First, this code calls the IsPresent method to make sure the user has entered one or more characters. Then, it calls the IsDecimal method to make sure the user has entered a string that can be successfully converted to a decimal value. Finally, it calls the IsWithinRange method to make sure that this decimal value is greater than 0 and less than 1000. If all three methods return a true value, this code displays a dialog box that indicates that the entry is valid.

Note that since the literal values that are passed to the min and max parameters of the IsWithinRange method don't end with the letter *m*, these values aren't interpreted as decimal values. Because the min and max parameters are declared as decimals, however, and because decimal is the widest (most accurate) data type, the C# compiler will implicitly cast all other numeric types to the decimal type.

A method that checks for a required field

```
private bool IsPresent(TextBox textBox, string name)
{
    if (textBox.Text == "")
    {
        MessageBox.Show(name + " is a required field.", "Entry Error");
        textBox.Focus();
        return false;
    }
    return true;
}
```

A method that checks for a valid numeric format

```
private bool IsDecimal(TextBox textBox, string name)
{
    try
    {
        Convert.ToDecimal(textBox.Text);
        return true;
    }
    catch(FormatException)
    {
        MessageBox.Show(name + " must be a decimal value.", "Entry Error");
        textBox.Focus();
        return false;
    }
}
```

A method that checks for a valid numeric range

```
private bool IsWithinRange(TextBox textBox, string name,
    decimal min, decimal max)
{
    decimal number = Convert.ToDecimal(textBox.Text);
    if (number <= min || number >= max)
    {
        MessageBox.Show(name + " must be between " + min.ToString()
            + " and " + max.ToString() + ".", "Entry Error");
        textBox.Focus();
        return false;
    }
    return true;
}
```

Code that uses these methods to check the validity of one entry

```
if (IsPresent(txtMonthlyInvestment, "Monthly Investment") &&
    IsDecimal(txtMonthlyInvestment, "Monthly Investment") &&
    IsWithinRange(txtMonthlyInvestment, "Monthly Investment", 0, 1000))
{
    MessageBox.Show("Monthly Investment is valid.", "Test");
}
```

Description

- Since it's common to need to check text boxes for valid data, it often makes sense to create generic methods like these for data validation.

Figure 7-9 How to use generic methods to validate an entry

How to validate multiple entries

Figure 7-10 shows two ways to code a method named IsValidData that validates multiple entries on a form. The methods shown here validate the Monthly Investment and Interest Rate text boxes on the Future Value form using the three methods you saw in figure 7-9. Although these methods only check two text boxes, you can use methods like this to check every entry on a form for validity. That way, all the data validation for the form is coded in one location, which makes the code easy to read and maintain.

The first method in this figure uses a series of if statements to check each of the three conditions. Within each if statement, the Not (!) operator is used to reverse the Boolean value that's returned by each method. For example, if an entry for the Monthly Investment text box is *not* present, the IsPresent method displays a dialog box and returns a false value. Then, the Not operator reverses this value so that the if condition is true, the IsValidData method returns a false value, and the method ends. As a result, the rest of the if statements in the method aren't executed.

The second method uses a single return statement to check all the validation conditions. To do this, it returns the result of all the validation conditions, connected with the conditional-And operator (&&). Since this operator is a short-circuit operator, the next condition is evaluated only if the previous condition returns a true value. As a result, the validation methods will only be called until the first one returns a false value. Then, that method will display the appropriate dialog box, and the entire IsValidData method will return a false value.

Note that both of these methods call the IsPresent method first, followed by the IsDecimal method, followed by the IsWithinRange method. In this case, IsDecimal must be called before IsWithinRange because IsWithinRange assumes that the text box that's being passed to it contains a valid decimal value. If you pass a text box that contains an invalid decimal value, this method will throw a format exception. If you use the IsDecimal method to check the text box for a decimal value first, however, the IsWithinRange method should never throw a format exception.

Code that uses a series of simple if statements

```
private bool IsValidData()
{
    // Validate the Monthly Investment text box
    if (!IsPresent(txtMonthlyInvestment, "Monthly Investment"))
        return false;
    if (!IsDecimal(txtMonthlyInvestment, "Monthly Investment"))
        return false;
    if (!IsWithinRange(txtMonthlyInvestment, "Monthly Investment", 0, 1000))
        return false;

    // Validate the Interest Rate text box
    if (!IsPresent(txtInterestRate, "Interest Rate"))
        return false;
    if (!IsDecimal(txtInterestRate, "Interest Rate"))
        return false;
    if (!IsWithinRange(txtInterestRate, "Interest Rate", 0, 20))
        return false;

    return true;
}
```

Code that uses compound conditions in a single return statement

```
private bool IsValidData()
{
    return

        // Validate the Monthly Investment text box
        IsPresent(txtMonthlyInvestment, "Monthly Investment") &&
        IsDecimal(txtMonthlyInvestment, "Monthly Investment") &&
        IsWithinRange(txtMonthlyInvestment, "Monthly Investment",
           0, 1000) &&

        // Validate the Interest Rate text box
        IsPresent(txtInterestRate, "Yearly Interest Rate") &&
        IsDecimal(txtInterestRate, "Yearly Interest Rate") &&
        IsWithinRange(txtInterestRate, "Yearly Interest Rate", 0, 20);

}
```

Description

- Both of these methods use the methods shown in the previous figure to check multiple entries on a form. Methods like these let you code all of the data validation for an entire form in one location.

Figure 7-10 How to validate multiple entries

The Future Value application with data validation

In figure 7-7, you saw a version of the Future Value application that used structured exception handling to catch all exceptions that might be thrown. Now, you'll see an improved version of this application that includes code that validates the user entries. This code prevents format and overflow exceptions from being thrown, and it provides more descriptive messages to the user.

The dialog boxes

Figure 7-11 shows the dialog boxes that are displayed when the user enters invalid data. For example, the first dialog box is displayed if the user doesn't enter a value for the Yearly Interest Rate text box. In contrast, the last dialog box is displayed if an exception that hasn't been anticipated is thrown. To test this dialog box, you can code a throw statement within the code for the Future Value application as shown in figure 7-6.

The code

Figure 7-12 shows the code for this version of the Future Value application. To start, the btnCalculate_Click method contains an exception handler that catches and handles any unanticipated exceptions. Within the try block, an if statement checks if the IsValidData method returns a true value. If so, the future value is calculated and displayed. Otherwise, none of the statements within the if block are executed. However, the data validation method that detected the error will display a dialog box with an appropriate message and move the focus to the appropriate text box.

The IsValidData method checks all three of the text boxes on the form to make sure that they contain valid numeric entries. Notice that a method named IsInt32 is called to check that the user entered a valid int value into the Number of Years text box. Since this method works like the IsDecimal method, you should be able to understand how it works.

When you review this code, notice how each method performs a specific task. For example, the btnCalculate_Click method gets the values from the text boxes and displays the resulting future value on the form. Then, it calls the IsValidData method to validate the data, and it calls the CalculateFutureValue method to perform a calculation. Similarly, the IsValidData method calls the IsPresent, IsDecimal, IsInt32, and IsWithinRange methods as necessary. This is a good design because it leads to code that's reusable and easy to maintain.

You should realize, however, that this code could be more efficient. For example, if the user enters a valid decimal value in the Monthly Investment text box, the ToDecimal method is called three times: once by the IsDecimal method, once by the IsWithinRange method, and once by the btnCalculate_Click method. For most applications, however, the benefits that result from being able to reuse and easily maintain this code far outweigh any performance issues.

The Future Value form with a dialog box for required fields

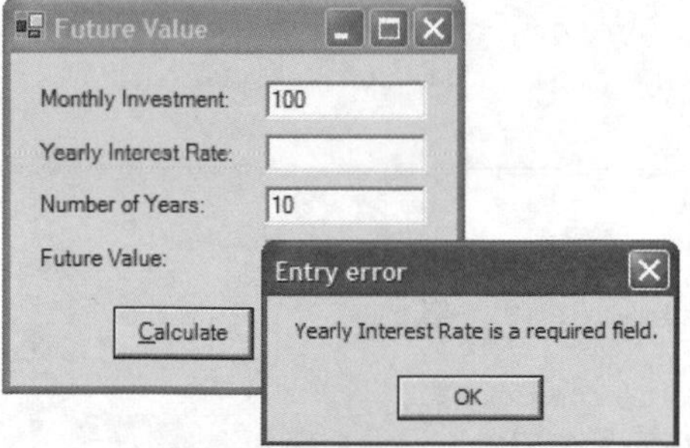

The dialog box for invalid decimals

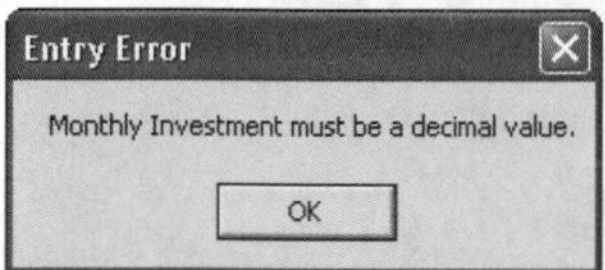

The dialog box for invalid ranges

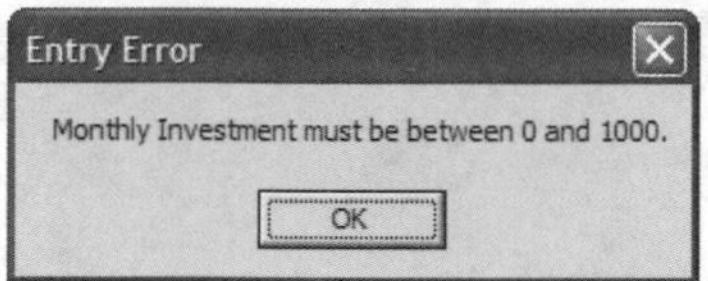

The dialog box for an unanticipated exception

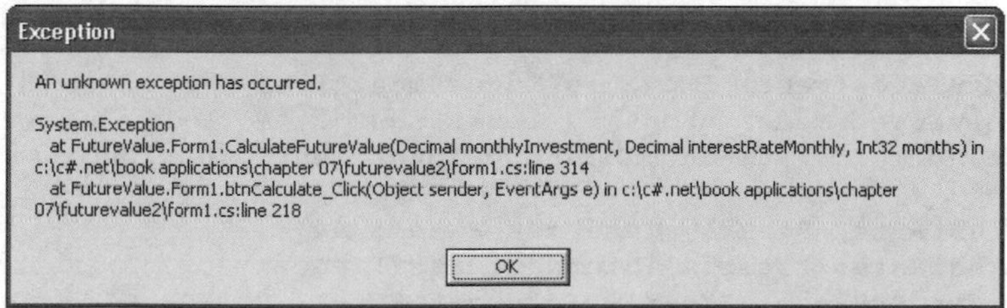

Description

- The first dialog box is displayed if the user doesn't enter a required field.
- The second dialog box is displayed if the user enters a value for the monthly investment or yearly interest rate that isn't in a valid decimal format.
- The third dialog box is displayed if the user enters a number that isn't within the range specified by the application.
- The fourth dialog box is displayed if any other type of exception occurs that hasn't been provided for in the validation code.

Figure 7-11 The dialog boxes of the Future Value application

The code for the Future Value application

```
private void btnCalculate_Click(object sender, System.EventArgs e)
{
    try
    {
        if (IsValidData())
        {
            decimal monthlyInvestment =
                Convert.ToDecimal(txtMonthlyInvestment.Text);
            decimal interestRateYearly =
                Convert.ToDecimal(txtInterestRate.Text);
            int years = Convert.ToInt32(txtYears.Text);

            int months = years * 12;
            decimal interestRateMonthly = interestRateYearly / 12 / 100;
            decimal futureValue = CalculateFutureValue(
                monthlyInvestment, interestRateMonthly, months);

            lblFutureValue.Text = futureValue.ToString("c");
        }
    }
    catch(Exception ex)
    {
        MessageBox.Show(ex.Message + "\n\n" +
            ex.GetType().ToString() + "\n" +
            ex.StackTrace, "Exception");
    }
}

private bool IsValidData()
{
    return
        IsPresent(txtMonthlyInvestment, "Monthly Investment") &&
        IsDecimal(txtMonthlyInvestment, "Monthly Investment") &&
        IsWithinRange(txtMonthlyInvestment, "Monthly Investment", 0, 1000) &&

        IsPresent(txtInterestRate, "Yearly Interest Rate") &&
        IsDecimal(txtInterestRate, "Yearly Interest Rate") &&
        IsWithinRange(txtInterestRate, "Yearly Interest Rate", 0, 20) &&

        IsPresent(txtYears, "Number of Years") &&
        IsInt32(txtYears, "Number of Years") &&
        IsWithinRange(txtYears, "Number of Years", 0, 40);
}

private bool IsPresent(TextBox textBox, string name)
{
    if (textBox.Text == "")
    {
        MessageBox.Show(name + " is a required field.", "Entry Error");
        textBox.Focus();
        return false;
    }
    return true;
}
```

Figure 7-12 The code for the Future Value application (part 1 of 2)

The code for the Future Value application

```
private bool IsDecimal(TextBox textBox, string name)
{
    try
    {
        Convert.ToDecimal(textBox.Text);
        return true;
    }
    catch(FormatException)
    {
        MessageBox.Show(name + " must be a decimal value.", "Entry Error");
        textBox.Focus();
        return false;
    }
}

private bool IsInt32(TextBox textBox, string name)
{
    try
    {
        Convert.ToInt32(textBox.Text);
        return true;
    }
    catch(FormatException)
    {
        MessageBox.Show(name + " must be an integer.", "Entry Error");
        textBox.Focus();
        return false;
    }
}

private bool IsWithinRange(TextBox textBox, string name,
    decimal min, decimal max)
{
    decimal number = Convert.ToDecimal(textBox.Text);
    if (number < min || number > max)
    {
        MessageBox.Show(name + " must be between " + min.ToString()
            + " and " + max.ToString() + ".", "Entry Error");
        textBox.Focus();
        return false;
    }
    return true;
}

private decimal CalculateFutureValue(decimal monthlyInvestment,
    decimal interestRateMonthly, int months)
{
    decimal futureValue = 0m;
    for (int i = 0; i < months; i++)
        futureValue = (futureValue + monthlyInvestment)
            * (1 + interestRateMonthly);

    return futureValue;
}
```

Figure 7-12 The code for the Future Value application (part 2 of 2)

Perspective

In this chapter, you learned how to handle exceptions and validate data. At this point, you should be able to code your applications at a professional level. But there's still a lot more for you to learn about the C# language.

In chapter 8, you'll learn how to work with arrays and collections. In chapter 9, you'll learn how to work with dates, and you'll learn more about working with strings. And in chapter 10, you'll learn how to develop forms that use other types of controls. When you finish these chapters, you'll be able to develop applications of considerable complexity.

Summary

- An *exception* is an object that's created from the Exception class or one of its subclasses. This object contains information about an error that has occurred.
- You can use the Show method of the MessageBox class to display a dialog box that contains information about an exception.
- You can code a try-catch statement to create an *exception handler* that will catch and handle any exceptions that are *thrown*. This is known as *structured exception handling*.
- To code a try-catch statement, you code a *try block* around any statements that might throw exceptions, and you code a *catch block* that contains the statements that handle the exceptions.
- You can use the properties and methods of an exception object to get information about the exception.
- The *stack trace* is a list of methods that were called before the exception occurred.
- If the statements in a try block can throw several types of exceptions, you can code one catch block for each type of exception.
- You can code a *finally block* after one or more catch blocks. The code in this block will always be executed regardless of whether an exception is thrown.
- You can use the throw statement to throw an exception that you create from the Exception class or any of its subclasses. You can also use the throw statement to throw an exception that you catch.
- *Data validation* refers to the process of checking input data to make sure that it's valid.
- *Range checking* refers to the process of checking an entry to make sure that it falls within a certain range.

Terms

exception
throw an exception
catch an exception
try-catch statement
exception handling
exception handler
structured exception handling
try block
catch block
stack trace
finally block
data validation
range checking

Objectives

- Given a form that uses text boxes to accept data from the user, write code that catches any exceptions that might occur.
- Given a form that uses text boxes to accept data and the validation specifications for that data, write code that validates the user entries.
- Describe the Exception hierarchy and name two of its subclasses.
- Explain how you use the try-catch statement to catch specific exceptions as well as all exceptions.
- Explain how you can use the properties and methods of an exception object.
- Describe the use of a finally block.
- Describe two ways that you can throw an exception, and explain when you might want to use each technique.
- Describe the three types of data validation that you're most likely to perform on a user entry.
- Explain why you might want to use generic methods for data validation.

Exercise 7-1 Enhance the Invoice Total application

This exercise guides you through the process of enhancing the Invoice Total application so it catches any runtime errors and validates the Subtotal entry.

1. Open the Invoice Total application that's in the C:\C#.NET\Chapter 07 directory. This is the version that you worked on in chapter 4.
2. Add a try-catch statement to the btnCalculate_Click method so it catches any exception that the ToDecimal method of the Convert class might throw. The catch block should display a dialog box like the one in figure 7-2. Then, test the application to make sure this works correctly.
3. Add code to the try block that checks that the user enters a value in the Subtotal text box. If a value isn't entered, a dialog box should be displayed with a message indicating that Subtotal is a required field. Then, test this enhancement.

4. Add code to the try block that range checks the user entry so it's greater than zero and less than 10,000. If it isn't, a dialog box should be displayed that specifies the acceptable range. Then, test this enhancement. When you're satisfied that the application works correctly, close it.

Exercise 7-2 Enhance the Future Value application

This exercise guides you through the process of enhancing the Future Value application that you worked on in chapter 6.

1. Use the Windows Explorer to copy the Future Value application from the C:\C#.NET\Chapter 06 folder to the Chapter 07 folder. Then, open the Future Value application in the Chapter 07 folder.
2. Add a try-catch statement to the btnCalculate_Click method that catches and handles any format or overflow exception that might occur. These catch blocks should display dialog boxes with appropriate messages. Then, test these enhancements.
3. Add another catch block to the try-catch statement that will catch any other exception that might occur. This catch block should display a dialog box that displays the message contained in the exception object, along with the exception type and the stack trace.
4. Add a throw statement to the CalculateFutureValue method that throws a new exception of the Exception class regardless of the result of the calculation. This statement will be used to test the enhancements of step 3, and it should specify a generic message that indicates an unknown error. Then, test the application by entering valid values in the three text boxes and clicking the Calculate button. If the exception is thrown and the last catch block works correctly, end the application and delete the throw statement.
5. Code four generic validation methods named IsPresent, IsDecimal, IsInt32, and IsWithinRange that test whether a text box contains an entry, a valid decimal value, a valid int value, and a value within a given range. If the validation is unsuccessful, each method should display a dialog box with a message that includes the name of the text box that's being validated. If you need help in coding these methods, you can refer to figure 7-9.
6. Code an IsValidData method that calls the four generic methods you created in step 5 to validate the data the user enters into the three text boxes. Each text box should be tested for three types of invalid data: (1) nothing entered, (2) invalid format, and (3) invalid range. You can use either of the two techniques presented in figure 7-10 to do this.
7. Modify the code in the event handler for the Calculate button so it uses the IsValidData method to validate the data before it processes it. Then, test the application to be sure it works correctly. If it does, end the application and delete the catch blocks for the format and overflow exceptions since these exceptions are now prevented by the data validation.
8. Do a final test of the application, and close it.

8

How to use arrays and collections

Arrays and collections are objects that act as containers. As you develop C# applications, you'll find many uses for arrays and collections. For example, you can use a sales array or a sales collection to hold the sales amounts for each of the 12 months of the year. Then, you can use that array or collection to perform calculations on those amounts. In this chapter, you'll learn the basic concepts and techniques for working with arrays and collections.

How to work with one-dimensional arrays

You can use an *array* to store a set of related data. Since a *one-dimensional array* is the simplest type of array, you'll start by learning how to create and use one-dimensional arrays.

How to create an array

To create a one-dimensional array, you use the syntax shown in figure 8-1. As you can see, you can create an array using either one or two statements. This is similar to the techniques you use to declare variables, except that you code square brackets after the data type to indicate that the variable refers to an array. Within the second set of brackets, you code a number that indicates the *length*, or *size*, of the array. This specifies the number of *elements* that the array can hold.

Notice that you also use the new keyword to create an array. That's because, as you'll learn later in this chapter, arrays are created from the Array class that's provided by the .NET Framework. So when you create an array, you're creating an instance of this class.

When you create an array, each element in the array is initialized to a default value. This value depends on the data type of the array as indicated by the table in this figure. Specifically, numeric types are set to zero, char types are set to the null character, Boolean types are set to false, DateTime types are set to 12:00:00 AM on January 1, 0001, and reference types are set to nulls. In the next figure, you'll learn how to assign new values to the elements of an array.

In most cases, all of the elements in an array will contain the same type of data, and you'll declare the array with that data type. However, if you don't know what type of data an array will contain, you can declare it with the object data type. Then, each element can contain data of any type.

The syntax for creating a one-dimensional array

With two statements

```
type[] arrayName;                          // declaration statement
arrayName = new type[arrayLength];         // assignment statement
```

With one statement

```
type[] arrayName = new type[arrayLength];
```

How to create an array of decimal types

With two statements

```
decimal[] totals;
totals = new decimal[4];
```

With one statement

```
decimal[] totals = new decimal[4];
```

Other examples

An array of strings

```
string[] description = new string[3];
```

Two arrays in one statement

```
const int MaxCount = 100;
decimal[] prices = new decimal[MaxCount],
          discountPercentages = new decimal[MaxCount];
```

Default values for array elements

Data type	Default value
numeric	0 (zero)
char	'\0' (the null character)
Boolean	false
DateTime	01/01/0001 00:00:00
reference types	null

Description

- An *array* can store one or more *elements*. The *length*, or *size*, of an array is the number of elements in the array.
- When you create an array, each element of the array is set to a default value. If the array contains value types, each element is set to the value shown above. If the array contains reference types, each element is set to null.

Figure 8-1 How to create an array

How to assign values to the elements of an array

Figure 8-2 shows how to assign values to the elements of an array. As the syntax at the top of this figure indicates, you refer to an element in an array by coding the array name followed by its *index* in brackets. The index that you specify must be from 0, which refers to the first element in the array, to the *upper bound* of the array, which is one less than the length of the array.

To understand how this works, take a look at the first example in this figure. This example declares an array of decimals that contains four elements. Then, it uses indexes 0 through 3 to assign values to those four elements. Here, the length of the array is 4, and the upper bound of the array is 3. Note that if you use an index that's greater than the upper bound, an IndexOutOfRangeException will be thrown.

The syntax and examples at the bottom of this figure show how to declare an array and assign values to its elements in a single statement. Here, you start the array declaration as before, but you code a list of values in braces after the declaration. Notice that when you use this technique, you can omit the new keyword and the type and length specification. Then, C# automatically sets the length of the array to the number of elements within the braces. If you include the data type and length specification, however, they must match the list of values you provide.

The three statements shown here illustrate how this works. The first statement creates the same array as the first example in this figure. Notice that this statement specifies the data type and length of the array. The second statement creates the same array, but the data type and length are omitted. Finally, the third statement creates the same array of strings that was created by the second example in this figure. Like the second statement, the data type and length are omitted from this statement.

The syntax for referring to an element of an array

```
arrayName[index]
```

Examples that assign values by accessing each element

Code that assigns values to an array of decimal types

```
decimal[] totals = new decimal[4];
totals[0] = 14.95m;
totals[1] = 12.95m;
totals[2] = 11.95m;
totals[3] = 9.95m;
//totals[4] = 8.95m;    this would throw an IndexOutOfRangeException
```

Code that assigns objects to an array of strings

```
string[] names = new string[3];
names[0] = "Ted Lewis";
names[1] = "Sue Jones";
names[2] = "Ray Thomas";
```

The syntax for creating an array and assigning values in one statement

```
type[] arrayName = [new type[length]] {value1[, value2][, value3]...};
```

Examples that create an array and assign values in one statement

```
decimal[] totals = new decimal[4] {14.95m, 12.95m, 11.95m, 9.95m};
decimal[] totals = {14.95m, 12.95m, 11.95m, 9.95m};
string[] names = {"Ted Lewis", "Sue Jones", "Ray Thomas"};
```

Description

- To refer to the elements in an array, you use an *index* where 0 is the first element, 1 is the second element, 2 is the third element, and so on. The index of the last element in an array is known as the *upper bound.*
- If you list the values to be assigned to an array without using the new keyword to create the array, an array is created with a length equal to the number of values in the list. If you use the new keyword with a list of values, the length you specify for the array must match the number of values in the list, and the values must match the type you specify.
- If you specify an index that's less than zero or greater than the upper bound of an array, an IndexOutOfRangeException will be thrown when the statement is executed.

Figure 8-2 How to assign values to the elements of an array

How to work with arrays

Now that you understand how to declare an array and assign values to its elements, you're ready to learn how to work with the values in an array. Figure 8-3 presents some of the basic techniques for doing that.

This figure starts by presenting the Length property of an array, which gets the number of elements in the array. You'll use this property frequently as you work with arrays.

The first example in this figure shows how to get the values from an array and calculate the average value of the elements. Here, the first statement declares a totals array that contains four decimal values. Then, the second statement sets the sum variable equal to the sum of the four elements in the array. Finally, the third statement computes the average value of these elements by dividing the sum by four.

The second example uses a for loop to put the numbers 0 through 9 into an array. Here, the first statement declares an array named numbers that contains 10 int values. Then, the for loop assigns the value of the loop's counter to each of the elements in the array.

The third example uses a for loop to display the elements of the numbers array in a message box. Here, the first statement declares a string variable. Then, the for loop accesses each element of the numbers array, converts it to a string, and appends the string and a space to the string variable. When the for loop finishes, the next statement displays the string that contains the numbers in a message box.

The fourth example shows how to use a loop to calculate the average value of the elements in the totals array. Here, the first statement declares the sum variable. Then, the for loop gets the value of each element of the array and adds that value to the current value of the sum variable. After the loop, the next statement uses the sum variable and the Length property of the array to calculate the average. If you compare this code to the code in the first example, you'll see that they both accomplish the same task. However, the code in this example will work equally well whether the totals array contains 4 or 400 values. As a result, it usually makes sense to use loops when working with arrays.

The last example shows how to display the elements of the totals array, along with the sum and average for the array, in a message box. Like the third example, this one uses a for loop to convert the values in the array to strings. Then, it appends each string and a new line character to a string variable. Finally, it displays the string and the sum and average values in a message box.

The syntax for using the Length property of an array

```
arrayName.Length
```

Code that computes the average of an array of totals

```
decimal[] totals = {14.95m, 12.95m, 11.95m, 9.95m};
decimal sum = totals[0] + totals[1] + totals[2] + totals[3];
decimal average = sum/4;
```

Code that puts the numbers 0 through 9 into an array

```
int[] numbers = new int[10];
for (int i = 0; i < numbers.Length; i++)
    numbers[i] = i;
```

Code that displays the numbers array in a message box

```
string numbersString = "";
for (int i = 0; i < numbers.Length; i++)
    numbersString += numbers[i].ToString() + " ";
MessageBox.Show(numbersString, "Numbers Test");
```

The message box that's displayed

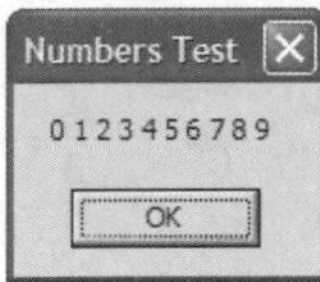

Code that uses a for loop to compute the average of the totals array

```
decimal sum = 0.0m;
for (int i = 0; i < totals.Length; i++)
    sum += totals[i];
decimal average = sum/totals.Length;
```

Code that displays the totals array in a message box

```
string totalsString = "";
for (int i = 0; i < totals.Length; i++)
    totalsString += totals[i].ToString() + "\n";
MessageBox.Show("The totals are:\n" +
    totalsString + "\n" +
    "Sum: " + sum + "\n" +
    "Average: " + average, "Totals Test");
```

The message box that's displayed

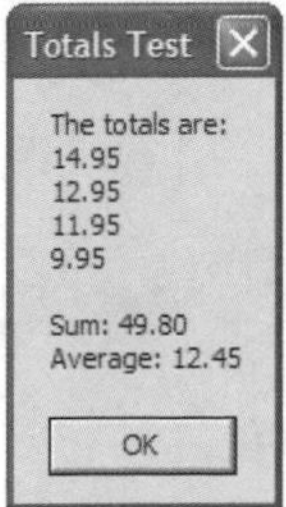

Figure 8-3 How to work with arrays

How to use foreach loops to work arrays

Although you can use for loops to work with the elements of an array, it's often easier to use a *foreach statement* to code a *foreach loop*. Figure 8-4 shows how to do that.

To code a foreach loop, you begin by coding the *foreach* keyword followed by a set of parentheses. Within the parentheses, you code the data type of the elements in the array, the name you want to use to access the elements, the *in* keyword, and the name of the array. Then, you can code one or more statements that use the element name to work with the element. If the foreach loop contains two or more statements, you must code braces around them. Otherwise, you can omit the braces.

When a foreach loop is executed, its statements are executed once for each element in the array. For example, the first example in this figure shows how you can use a foreach loop to display the elements in the numbers array that you saw in the previous figure. Similarly, the second example computes the average of the totals array, and the third example displays the elements in the totals array.

If you compare these examples to the for loop examples in the previous figure, you'll see that foreach loops are less complicated. In particular, when you use a foreach loop, you don't need to use a counter variable, and you don't need to use an index to get an element from the array. As a result, it's often easier to use a foreach loop than a for loop.

You should realize, however, that there are still times when you'll need to use a for loop to work with an array. For example, if you only want to access some of the elements in an array, you'll need to use a for loop. You'll also need to use a for loop if you want to use a counter variable to assign values to the elements of the array as shown in the second example in figure 8-3.

The syntax of a foreach loop

```
foreach (type elementName in arrayName)
{
   statements
}
```

Code that displays the numbers array in a message box

```
string numbersString = "";
foreach (int number in numbers)
{
    numbersString += number.ToString();
    numbersString += " ";
}
MessageBox.Show(numbersString, "Numbers Test");
```

The message box that's displayed

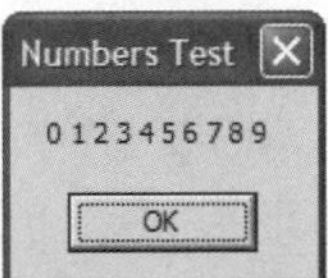

Code that computes the average of the totals array

```
decimal sum = 0.0m;
foreach (decimal total in totals)
    sum += total;
decimal average = sum/totals.Length;
```

Code that displays the totals array in a message box

```
string totalsString = "";
foreach (decimal total in totals)
    totalsString += total.ToString() + "\n";
MessageBox.Show("The totals are:\n" +
    totalsString + "\n" +
    "Sum: " + sum + "\n" +
    "Average: " + average,
    "Totals Test");
```

The message box that's displayed

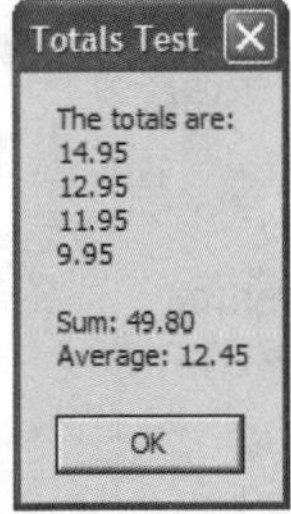

Description

- You can use a *foreach loop* to access each element of an array. You can also use foreach loops to work with collections like the ones you'll learn about later in this chapter.

Figure 8-4 How to use foreach loops to work with arrays

How to work with rectangular arrays

So far, this chapter has shown how to use an array that uses one index to store elements in a one-dimensional array. Now, you'll learn how to work with *rectangular arrays* that use two indexes. You can think of a rectangular array as a table that has rows and columns. Since rectangular arrays store data in two dimensions, they're also known as *two-dimensional arrays*.

Although it's possible to create arrays that contain more than two dimensions, that's rarely necessary. However, if you do need to use an array that has three or more dimensions, you can extend the two-dimensional techniques that you'll learn next.

How to create a rectangular array

Figure 8-5 shows how to create a rectangular array. To do that, you code a comma within the set of brackets that follows the data type declaration. This indicates that the array will have two dimensions. Then, when you use the new keyword to create the array, you specify the number of rows in the array, followed by a comma, followed by the number of columns in the array.

The first statement in this figure creates a rectangular array of integers. In this case, the array has three rows and two columns. After this statement executes, each element in the array will be assigned the default value of 0 as described in figure 8-1.

How to assign values to a rectangular array

After you create an array, you can assign values to it. To do that, you refer to each element of the array using its row and column index. This is illustrated by the table of index values shown in figure 8-5. Because this array consists of four rows and four columns, the index values range from 0,0 to 3,3.

To assign values to the elements of a rectangular array, you can code one statement for each element as shown in the first example. These statements assign values to the elements of the numbers array that was created by the first statement in this figure.

You can also assign values to a rectangular array when you declare it as illustrated by the second and third examples. Here, the second example creates the numbers array and assigns values to it by coding three sets of braces within an outer set of braces. The three inner braces represent the three rows in the array, and the values in these braces are assigned to the two columns in each row. The third example works the same except that it uses string objects instead of int values.

How to create a rectangular array

The syntax for creating a rectangular array

```
type[,] arrayName = new type[rowCount,columnCount];
```

A statement that creates a 3x2 array

```
int[,] numbers = new int[3,2];
```

How to assign values to a rectangular array

The syntax for referring to an element of a rectangular array

```
arrayName[rowIndex, columnIndex]
```

The index values for the elements of a 4x4 rectangular array

```
0,0    0,1    0,2    0,3
1,0    1,1    1,2    1,3
2,0    2,1    2,2    2,3
3,0    3,1    3,2    3,3
```

Code that assigns values to the numbers array

```
numbers[0,0] = 1;
numbers[0,1] = 2;
numbers[1,0] = 3;
numbers[1,1] = 4;
numbers[2,0] = 5;
numbers[2,1] = 6;
```

Code that creates a 3x2 array and assigns values with one statement

```
int[,] numbers = { {1,2}, {3,4}, {5,6} };
```

Code that creates and assigns values to a 3x2 array of strings

```
string[,] products = { {"BVBN", "Murach's Beginning Visual Basic .NET"},
                       {"JAVA", "Murach's Begining Java 2"},
                       {"VASP", "Murach's ASP.NET Web Programming"} };
```

Description

- A *rectangular array* uses two indexes to store data. You can think of this type of array as a table that has rows and columns. Rectangular arrays are sometimes referred to as *two-dimensional arrays.*
- Although it's rarely necessary, you can extend this two-dimensional syntax to work with arrays that have more than two dimensions.

Figure 8-5 How to create a rectangular array and assign values to its elements

How to work with rectangular arrays

Figure 8-6 presents some examples that show how to work with rectangular arrays. The first example shows how to use the GetLength method to get the number of elements in a dimension of an array. Here, the first statement gets the number of rows in the numbers array by calling the GetLength method and specifying 0 to get the length of the first dimension. Then, the second statement gets the number of columns in the array by calling the GetLength method and specifying 1 to get the length of the second dimension. Finally, the third statement uses indexes to get the values from both of the elements in the first row of the array and add them together.

The second example shows how to use nested for loops to display the elements of a rectangular array in a message box. In this case, the elements of the numbers array you saw in figure 8-5 are displayed. As you can see, the outer for loop uses a counter variable to cycle through the rows in the array. To determine the number of rows in the array, this loop uses the GetLength method. Then, the inner for loop uses another counter variable to cycle through each column of each row in the array. Just like the outer for loop, the inner for loop uses the GetLength method to determine the number of columns in the array.

To display the value of each element, the statement within the inner for loop uses both counter variables to get the value of the element and append it to a string. Each element is also separated from the next element by a space. Then, after each row is processed by the inner loop, a new line character is appended to the string so that the elements in each row will appear on a separate line. When the outer loop ends, the string is displayed in a message box as shown in this figure.

The third example is similar, except that it displays the array of products you saw in figure 8-5. If you compare this code with the code in the second example, you'll see the only difference is that the elements in the two columns are separated by tab characters so that they're aligned as shown here.

The syntax for using the GetLength method of a rectangular array

```
arrayName.GetLength(dimensionIndex)
```

Code that works with the numbers array

```
int numberOfRows = numbers.GetLength(0);
int numberOfColumns = numbers.GetLength(1);
int sumOfFirstRow = numbers[0,0] + numbers[0,1];
```

Code that displays the numbers array in a message box

```
string numbersString = "";
for (int i = 0; i < numbers.GetLength(0); i++)
{
    for (int j = 0; j < numbers.GetLength(1); j++)
        numbersString += numbers[i,j] + " ";

    numbersString += "\n";
}
MessageBox.Show(numbersString, "Numbers Test");
```

The message box that's displayed

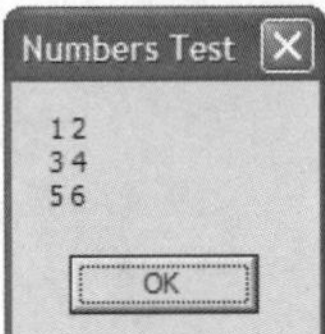

Code that displays the products array in a message box

```
string productsString = "";
for (int i = 0; i < products.GetLength(0); i++)
{
    for (int j = 0; j < products.GetLength(1); j++)
        productsString += products[i,j] + "\t";

    productsString += "\n";
}
MessageBox.Show(productsString, "Products Test");
```

The message box that's displayed

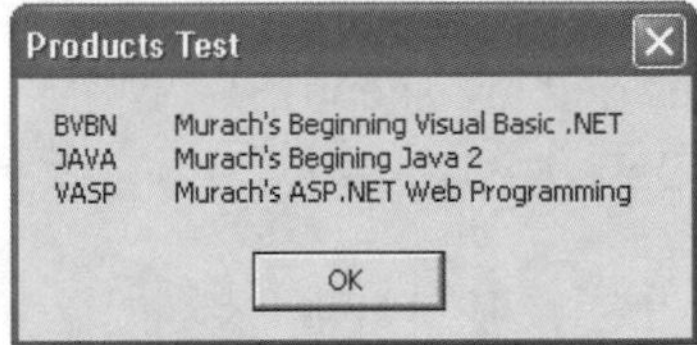

Description

- You can use the GetLength method to get the number of rows or columns in a rectangular array. To get the number of rows, specify 0 for the *dimensionIndex* argument. To get the number of columns, specify 1 for this argument.
- You can use nested for loops to iterate through the rows and columns of a rectangular array.

Figure 8-6 How to work with rectangular arrays

How to work with jagged arrays

Jagged arrays let you store data in a table that can have rows of unequal lengths. Since each row in a jagged array is stored as a separate array, a jagged array is also known as an *array of arrays*.

How to create a jagged array

Figure 8-7 shows how to create a jagged array. To start, you code the data type followed by two sets of brackets. This indicates that each row of the array will contain another array. Then, when you use the new keyword to create the jagged array, you specify the number of rows that the array will contain. For example, the first statement in the first example creates a jagged array named numbers that contains three rows. Finally, when you declare the array for each row, you specify the number of columns in that row. The first row of the numbers array, for example, has three columns, the second row has four columns, and the third row has two columns.

How to assign values to a jagged array

Once you create a jagged array, you use row and column indexes to refer to the elements in the array just as you do for a rectangular array. When you refer to an element in a jagged array, however, you code each index within a separate set of brackets as illustrated in figure 8-7. To assign values to the numbers array, for example, you can use the statements shown in the second example in this figure.

You can also create a jagged array and assign values to its elements in one statement. The third and fourth examples illustrate how this works. The third example creates the same array as the first example. Here, you can see that a set of braces is used to enclose a list of array declarations. Each declaration in this list defines an array for one row in the jagged array. Notice in this example that the declarations don't specify the number of columns in each row. Instead, the number of columns is determined by the number of values that are specified for that row. Similarly, the number of rows in the jagged array is determined by the number of arrays in the list of arrays.

The fourth example is similar, except that each array declaration specifies the number of columns in the array. In that case, the number of values in each list of values must match the numbers you specify.

How to create a jagged array

The syntax for creating a jagged array

```
type[][] arrayName = new type[rowCount][];
```

Code that creates a jagged array with three rows of different lengths

```
int[][] numbers = new int[3][];        // the number of rows
numbers[0] = new int[3];               // the number of columns for row 1
numbers[1] = new int[4];               // the number of columns for row 2
numbers[2] = new int[2];               // the number of columns for row 3
```

How to refer to the elements of a jagged array

The syntax for referring to an element of a jagged array

```
arrayName[rowIndex][columnIndex]
```

The index values for the elements of a jagged array

```
0,0    0,1    0,2
1,0    1,1    1,2    1,3
2,0    2,1
```

Code that assigns values to the numbers array

```
numbers[0][0] = 1;
numbers[0][1] = 2;
numbers[0][2] = 3;
numbers[1][0] = 4;
numbers[1][1] = 5;
numbers[1][2] = 6;
numbers[1][3] = 7;
numbers[2][0] = 8;
numbers[2][1] = 9;
```

Code that creates the numbers array with one statement

```
int[][] numbers = { new int [] {1, 2, 3},
                    new int [] {4, 5, 6, 7},
                    new int [] {8, 9} };
```

Code that creates a jagged array of strings

```
string[][] titles = {
   new string [3] {"War and Peace", "Wuthering Heights", "1984"},
   new string [4] {"Casablanca", "Wizard of Oz", "Star Wars", "Birdy"},
   new string [2] {"Blue Suede Shoes", "Yellow Submarine"} };
```

Description

- You can use a *jagged array* to store data in a table that has rows of unequal lengths. Each row in a jagged array is stored as a separate array. Because of that, a jagged array is also known as an *array of arrays*.
- If you don't assign values to the elements of a jagged array when you declare the array, the declaration statement must specify the number of rows in the array. Then, you must declare the number of columns in each row before you assign values to the elements in that row.
- To assign values to the elements of a jagged array when you declare the array, you create a list of arrays that defines one array for each row. Then, the jagged array is created with one row for each array in that list.

Figure 8-7 How to create a jagged array and assign values to its elements

How to work with jagged arrays

Figure 8-8 shows how to work with jagged arrays. Since the examples in this figure are similar to the examples for working with rectangular arrays shown in figure 8-6, you shouldn't have much trouble understanding how they work. However, you should notice two differences in these examples.

First, two sets of brackets are used within the inner for loop to refer to each element in the array. Second, the inner loop uses the Length property to get the number of columns in each row. That makes sense if you remember that each row in a jagged array is an array. You must use the Length property because each row can have a different length. As a result, you can't use the GetLength method to return the number of columns in a row as you do with rectangular arrays.

Code that displays the numbers array in a message box

```
string numbersString = "";
for (int i = 0; i < numbers.GetLength(0); i++)
{
    for (int j = 0; j < numbers[i].Length; j++)
        numbersString += numbers[i][j] + " ";

    numbersString += "\n";
}
MessageBox.Show(numbersString, "Jagged Numbers Test");
```

The message box that's displayed

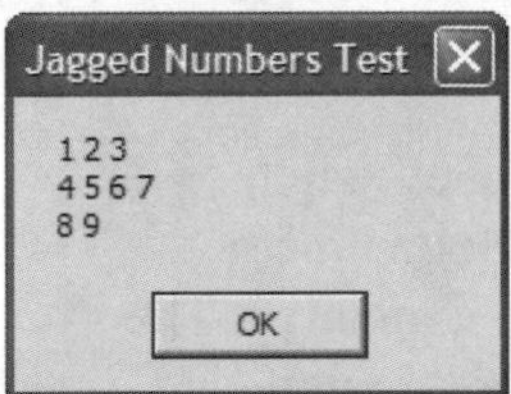

Code that displays the titles array in a message box

```
string titlesString = "";
for (int i = 0; i < titles.GetLength(0); i++)
{
    for (int j = 0; j < titles[i].Length; j++)
        titlesString += titles[i][j] + "|";

    titlesString += "\n";
}
MessageBox.Show(titlesString, "Jagged Titles Test");
```

The message box that's displayed

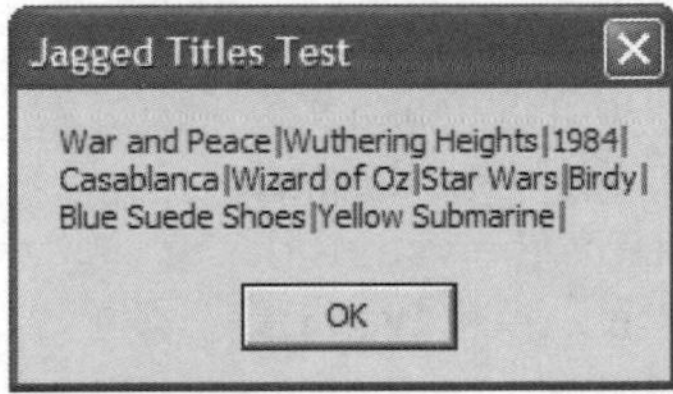

Description

- Since the number of columns in each row of a jagged array varies, you can't use the GetLength method to get the length of a row. Instead, you have to use the Length property of the array for that row.

More skills for working with arrays

Now that you know how to work with one-dimensional, rectangular, and jagged arrays, you're ready to learn some additional skills for working with arrays.

How to use the Array class

Because an array is actually an instance of the Array class, you can use the properties and methods of this class to work with your arrays. Figure 8-9 presents the properties and methods you're most likely to use.

You've already seen how to use the Length property and the GetLength method. Another property you may want to use is the GetUpperBound method, which returns the index of the last element in a given dimension of an array. The first example in this figure illustrates the difference between the GetLength and GetUpperBound methods. Here, you can see that the GetLength method returns a value of 4 for a one-dimensional array that contains four elements. In contrast, the GetUpperBound method returns a value of 3 because the four elements are referred to with the index values of 0 through 3.

Although values have been assigned to the elements of the array that's used in this example, you should realize that the GetLength and GetUpperBound methods return the same values whether or not values have been assigned to the array. In other words, these methods depend only on the number of elements that were declared for the array. That's true of the Length property as well.

The Sort method of the Array class lets you sort the elements in a one-dimensional array. This is illustrated by the second example in this figure. Here, the first statement declares an array that consists of three last names. Then, the Sort method is used to sort the names in that array. Notice that because this method is a static method, it's called from the Array class, not from the array itself. After the array is sorted, a string is created that contains the values of the elements in ascending order. Then, the string is displayed in a message box.

The third example shows how you can use the BinarySearch method to locate a value in a one-dimensional array. This code uses the BinarySearch method to get the index of the specified employee in an employees array. Then, this index is used to get the corresponding sales amount from a salesAmounts array.

For the BinarySearch method to work properly, the array must be sorted in ascending sequence. If it's not, this method usually won't be able to find the specified value, even if it exists in the array. When the BinarySearch method can't find the specified value, it returns a value of -1. Then, if you try to use this value to access an element of an array, an IndexOutOfRangeException will be thrown.

Common properties and methods of the Array class

Property	Description
`Length`	Gets the number of elements in all of the dimensions of an array.
Instance method	**Description**
`GetLength(dimension)`	Gets the number of elements in the specified dimension of an array.
`GetUpperBound(dimension)`	Gets the index of the last element in the specified dimension of an array.
Static method	**Description**
`Copy(array1, array2, length)`	Copies some or all of the values in one array to another array. For more information, see figure 8-10.
`BinarySearch(array, value)`	Searches a one-dimensional array that's in ascending order for an element with a specified value and returns the index for that element.
`Sort(array)`	Sorts the elements in a one-dimensional array into ascending order.

Code that uses the GetLength and GetUpperBound methods

```
int[] numbers = new int[4] {1, 2, 3, 4};
int length = numbers.GetLength(0);                // length = 4
int upperBound = numbers.GetUpperBound(0);        // upperBound = 3
```

Code that uses the Sort method

```
string[] lastNames = {"Prince", "Lowe", "Murach"};
Array.Sort(lastNames);
string message = "";
foreach (string lastName in lastNames)
    message += lastName + "\n";
MessageBox.Show(message, "Sorted Last Names");
```

The message box that's displayed

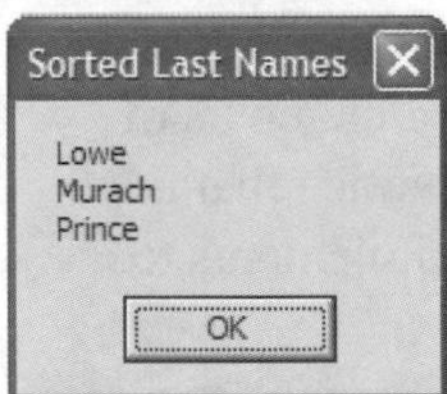

Code that uses the BinarySearch method

```
string[] employees = {"AdamsA", "FinkleP", "LewisJ", "PotterE"};
decimal[] salesAmounts = {3275.68m, 4298.55m, 5289.57m, 1933.98m};
int index = Array.BinarySearch(employees, "FinkleP");
decimal salesAmount = salesAmounts[index];        // salesAmount = 4298.55
```

Note

- The BinarySearch method only works on arrays whose elements are in ascending order. If the array isn't in ascending order, you must use the Sort method to sort the array before using the BinarySearch method.

Figure 8-9 How to use the Array class

How to refer to and copy arrays

Because arrays are created from a class, they are reference types. That means that an array variable contains a reference to an array object and not the actual values in the array. Because of that, you can use two or more variables to refer to the same array. This is illustrated in the first example in figure 8-10.

The first statement in this example declares an array variable named inches1, creates an array with three elements, and assigns values to those elements. Then, the second statement declares another array variable named inches2 and assigns the value of the inches1 variable to it. Because the inches1 variable contains a reference to the array, that means that the inches2 variable now contains a reference to the same array. As a result, if you use the inches2 variable to change any of the elements in the array as shown in the third statement, those changes will be reflected if you use the inches1 variable to refer to the array.

Once you declare the length of an array, it can't grow or shrink. In other words, arrays are *immutable*. However, you can use an existing array variable to refer to another array with a larger or smaller number of elements. To do that, you simply create the new array and assign it to the existing variable as shown in the second example in this figure. Here, an array that contains 20 elements is assigned to the inches1 variable, which originally contained only three elements. Note that when this statement is executed, the original array is discarded unless another array variable refers to it. In this case, the inches2 variable refers to the original array, so the array is maintained.

If you want to create a copy of an array, you can use the Copy method of the Array class as shown in this figure. Then, each array variable will point to its own copy of the elements of the array, and any changes that are made to one array won't affect the other array.

You can use two techniques to copy the elements of an array. First, you can copy one or more elements of the array starting with the first element by specifying the source array, the target array, and the number of elements to be copied. This is illustrated by the third example in this figure. Here, all of the elements of an array named inches are copied to an array named centimeters. Notice that the Length property of the inches array is used to specify the number of elements to be copied.

You can also copy one or more elements of an array starting with an element other than the first. To do that, you specify the index of the first element you want to copy. In addition, you specify the index of the element in the target array where you want to store the first element from the source array.

This is illustrated in the last example in this figure. Here, the first statement creates an array that contains three string values, and the second statement creates an array that can hold two string values. Then, the third statement copies the second and third strings from the first array into the second array. To do that, the first two arguments specify the source array and a starting index of 1 (the second element). Then, the next two arguments specify the target array and a starting index of 0 (the first element). Finally, the last argument specifies that two elements should be copied.

Code that creates a reference to another array

```
double[] inches1 = new double[3] {1,2,3};
double[] inches2 = inches1;
inches2[2] = 4;     // changes the third element
```

Code that reuses an array variable

```
inches1 = new double[20];  // make a new array with 20 elements
```

How to copy elements of one array to another array

The syntax for copying elements of an array

```
Array.Copy(fromArray, toArray, length);
```

Another way to copy elements from one array to another

```
Array.Copy(fromArray, fromIndex, toArray, toIndex, length);
```

Code that copies all the elements of an array

```
double[] inches = new double[3] {1,2,3};
double[] centimeters = new double[3];
Array.Copy(inches, centimeters, inches.Length);
for (int i = 0; i < centimeters.Length; i++)
    centimeters[i] *= 2.54;    // set the new values for this array
```

Code that copies some of the elements of an array

```
string[] names = {"Lowe", "Murach", "Prince"};
string[] lastTwoNames = new string[2];
Array.Copy(names, 1, lastTwoNames, 0, 2);
```

Description

- An array is a reference type, which means that an array variable contains a reference to an array object. To create another reference to an existing array, you assign the array to another array variable. Then, both array variables point to the same array in memory.
- To reuse an array variable so it refers to an array with a larger or smaller number of elements, you create a new array and assign it to that variable. When you do, the original array is discarded unless another array variable refers to it.
- To copy the elements of one array to another array, you use the Copy method of the Array class.
- To copy a specified number of elements from an array beginning with the first element, you can use the first syntax shown above. Then, you use the *length* argument to specify the number of elements to copy.
- To specify the first element in an array that you want to copy, you use the second syntax shown above. Then, the *fromIndex* argument specifies the index of the first element that's copied, the *toIndex* argument specifies the index where the first element is copied to, and the *length* argument specifies the number of elements that are copied.
- When you copy an array, the target array must be the same type as the sending array and it must be large enough to receive all of the elements that are copied to it.

Figure 8-10 How to refer to and copy arrays

How to code methods that work with arrays

Figure 8-11 presents the techniques you can use to code methods that return and accept arrays. To return an array from a method, you follow the return type for the method with brackets as shown in the first example. Then, you define an array within the code for the method and use the return statement to return that array.

To call a method that returns an array, you use the same techniques that you use for calling any other method. In this figure, the statement that calls the GetRateArray method declares an array variable and assigns the return value of the method to this variable. In this case, the method requires an argument that supplies the number of elements that the array should contain.

The second example shows how to code a method that accepts an array as an argument. To do that, you follow the data type of the parameter that accepts the argument with brackets to indicate that it's an array. Then, within the method, you can use all the techniques that you've learned for working with arrays to work with this parameter. In this case, a method named ToCentimeters is used to convert the inch measurements in an array to centimeters.

To call a method that's defined with an array parameter, you just pass an array argument as shown here. Note, however, that unlike other arguments, arrays are automatically passed by reference. As a result, any changes that you make to the values stored in the array parameter will be reflected in any array variables in the calling method that refer to the array. In this figure, for example, the values in the measurements array are updated after the ToCentimeters method is called.

The third example shows how to use the *params* keyword with an array parameter. When you use this keyword, the statement that calls the method can pass an array to the method, or it can pass a list of values. This is illustrated in the third example in this figure. Here, the statement that calls the method passes three values, which are then stored in the array parameter. Then, after these values are converted to centimeters, the array is passed back to the calling method.

Because the ToCentimeters method that uses the params keyword can accept either an array or a list of values, it's more flexible than the first ToCentimeters method. However, you should be aware of some restrictions when you use the params keyword. First, you can only use this keyword on one parameter within a method. Second, if a method is defined with two or more parameters, this keyword must be coded on the last parameter.

How to return an array from a method

The code for a method that returns an array

```
private decimal[] GetRateArray(int elementCount)
{
    decimal[] rates = new decimal[elementCount - 1];
    for (int i = 0; i < rates.Length; i++)
        rates[i] = (decimal) (i + 1) / 100;

    return rates;
}
```

A statement that calls the method

```
decimal[] rates = this.GetRateArray(4);
```

How to code a method that accepts an array argument

A method that converts inches to centimeters

```
private void ToCentimeters(double[] measurements)
{
    for (int i = 0; i < measurements.Length; i++)
        measurements[i] *= 2.54;
}
```

Statements that declare the array and call the method

```
double[] measurements = {1,2,3};
this.ToCentimeters(measurements);
```

How to code a method that uses the params keyword

A method that converts inches to centimeters

```
private double[] ToCentimeters(params double[] measurements)
{
    for (int i = 0; i < measurements.Length; i++)
        measurements[i] *= 2.54;
    return measurements;
}
```

A statement that calls the method

```
double[] measurements = this.ToCentimeters(1,2,3);
```

Description

- To return an array from a method, you code a set of brackets after the return type declaration to indicate that the return type is an array.
- To accept an array as a parameter of a method, you code a set of brackets after the parameter type to indicate that the parameter is an array. By default, arrays are passed by reference.
- If you want to pass two or more arguments that haven't been grouped in an array to a method and have the method store the values in an array, you can include the *params* keyword on the parameter declaration. You code this keyword before the array type and name, you can code it on a single parameter, and you must code it on the last parameter.

Figure 8-11 How to code methods that work with arrays

How to work with collections

A *collection* is an object that can hold one or more other objects. Unlike arrays, collections don't have a fixed size. Instead, the size of a collection is increased automatically when elements are added to it. In addition, most types of collections provide methods you can use to change the capacity of a collection. In other words, collections are *mutable*. As a result, collections are usually more appropriate and can usually manage system resources better than arrays when you need to work with a varying number of elements.

Another difference between arrays and collections is that collections aren't data typed. As a result, you can store any type of object in a collection. In fact, you can store different types of objects in the same collection, although that usually isn't a good idea.

In the topics that follow, you'll learn how to use four types of collections: array lists, sorted lists, queues, and stacks. Although the .NET Framework provides for other collections, these are the ones you'll use most often.

How to create an array list

To create an *array list*, you use the ArrayList class as shown in figure 8-12. Notice that when you create an array list, you can specify its initial capacity by coding it within parentheses after the class name as illustrated in the first statement in this figure. If you omit the initial capacity, though, it's set to 16 as illustrated by the second statement.

Properties and methods of the ArrayList class

Figure 8-12 also lists some common properties and methods of the ArrayList class. You'll see how to use some of these properties and methods in the next figure. For now, you should notice that some of these properties and methods provide functions that aren't available with arrays. For example, you can use the Insert method to insert an element into the middle of an array list, and you can use the RemoveAt method to remove an element from an array list.

You should also realize that when you use the Add or Insert method to add elements to an array list, the capacity of the array list is doubled each time its capacity is exceeded. This is illustrated by the last seven statements in this figure. Each of these statements adds another element to the lastNames array that was created with an initial capacity of three elements. Then, when the fourth element is added, the capacity is increased to six elements. Similarly, when you add the seventh element, the capacity is doubled again to 12.

A statement that creates an array list with a capacity of 3 elements

```
ArrayList lastNames = new ArrayList(3);  // Initial capacity is 3 elements
```

A statement that creates an array list with the default capacity

```
ArrayList titles = new ArrayList();      // Initial capacity is 16 elements
```

Common properties and methods of the ArrayList class

Index	Description
[index]	Gets or sets the element at the specified index. The index for the first item in an array list is 0.
Property	**Description**
Capacity	Gets or sets the number of elements the array list can hold.
Count	Gets the number of elements in the array list.
Method	**Description**
Add(object)	Adds an element to the end of an array list and returns the element's index.
Clear()	Removes all elements from the array list and sets its Count property to zero.
Contains(object)	Returns a Boolean value that indicates if the array list contains the specified object.
Insert(index, object)	Inserts an element into an array list at the specified index.
Remove(object)	Removes the first occurrence of the specified object from the array list.
RemoveAt(index)	Removes the element at the specified index of an array list.
BinarySearch(object)	Searches an array list for a specified object and returns the index for that bject.
Sort()	Sorts the elements in an array list into ascending order.

Code that causes the size of the array list of names to be increased

```
lastNames.Add("Prince");
lastNames.Add("Lowe");
lastNames.Add("Murach");
lastNames.Add("Taylor");              //Capacity is doubled to 6 elements
lastNames.Add("Menendez");
lastNames.Add("Steelman");
lastNames.Add("Schletewitz");         //Capacity is doubled to 12 elements
```

Description

- A *collection* is an object that can hold one or more other objects. An *array list* is a collection that automatically adjusts its capacity to accommodate new elements.
- The default capacity of an array list is 16 elements, but you can specify a different capacity when you create a list, and you can set the Capacity property to adjust that capacity. When the number of elements in an array list exceeds its capacity, the capacity is automatically doubled.
- The elements of an array list are automatically defined with the object data type, so each element can contain any type of data.
- The ArrayList class is part of the System.Collections namespace.

Figure 8-12 How to create an array list and use its properties and methods

How to work with an array list

Figure 8-13 shows how to use some of the methods shown in the previous figure to work with the elements in an array list. Here, the first example shows how to use the Add method within a for loop to add elements to the end of an array list. In this example, four decimal values are added to an array list named salesTotals.

Since each element of an array list is stored as an object type, any value type you store in an array list must be converted to a reference type. To do that, an object is created and then the value is stored in that object. The process of putting a value in an object is known as *boxing*, and it's done automatically whenever a value type needs to be converted to a reference type.

The second example shows how to use an index to refer to an element in an array list. The syntax for doing that is similar to the syntax for referring to an element in an array. The difference is that you must cast the object that's returned to the appropriate data type. The process of getting a value out of the object is known as *unboxing*, and you must write code like this whenever you need to unbox a value.

The third example shows how to insert and remove elements from an array list. Here, a new element with a decimal value of 2745.73 is inserted at the beginning of the salesTotals array list. As a result, the other four values in the array list are pushed down one index. Then, the second element of the array list is removed, and the other three values are moved back up one index. The final result is that the first element is replaced with a new element.

The fourth example uses a foreach loop to display the elements in the salesTotals array list in a message box. As you can see, this works the same as it does for an array.

The fifth example shows how to use the Contains method to check if the salesTotals array list contains an object. If it does, the Remove method is used to remove the object from the array list. In this case, the object contains a decimal value of 2745.73. However, this would work regardless of the data type the object contained.

The sixth example shows how you can sort and search the elements in an array list. Here, the first statement uses the Sort method to sort the elements in the salesTotals array list. Then, the second statement uses the BinarySearch method to search for an element that contains a decimal value of 4398.55.

You should notice in this example that, unlike the Sort method of the Array class, the Sort method of the ArrayList class is an instance method. Because of that, you call it from the array list object. That's true for the BinarySearch method too. Otherwise, these methods work similarly.

The syntax for retrieving a value from an array list

```
(type) arrayName[index]
```

Code that creates an array list that holds decimal values

```
decimal[] newSalesTotals = {3275.68m, 4398.55m, 5289.75m, 1933.98m};
ArrayList salesTotals = new ArrayList();
foreach (decimal d in newSalesTotals)
    salesTotals.Add(d);
```

Code that retrieves the first value from the array list

```
decimal sales1 = (decimal) salesTotals[0];  // sales1 = 3275.68
```

Code that inserts and removes an element from the array list

```
salesTotals.Insert(0, 2745.73m);             // insert a new first element
sales1 = (decimal) salesTotals[0];           // sales1 = 2745.73
decimal sales2 = (decimal) salesTotals[1];   // sales2 = 3275.68
salesTotals.RemoveAt(1);                     // remove the second element
sales2 = (decimal) salesTotals[1];           // sales2 = 4398.55
```

Code that displays the array list in a message box

```
string salesTotalsString = "";
foreach (decimal d in salesTotals)
    salesTotalsString += d.ToString() + "\n";
MessageBox.Show(salesTotalsString, "Sales Totals ArrayList");
```

The message box that's displayed

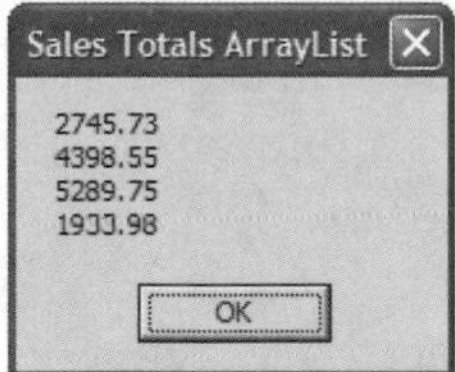

Code that checks for an element in the array list and removes it if it exists

```
decimal x = 2745.73m;
if (salesTotals.Contains(x))
    salesTotals.Remove(x);
```

Code that sorts and searches the array list

```
salesTotals.Sort();
int sales2Index = salesTotals.BinarySearch(sales2);
```

A message box that displays the results of the sort and search operation

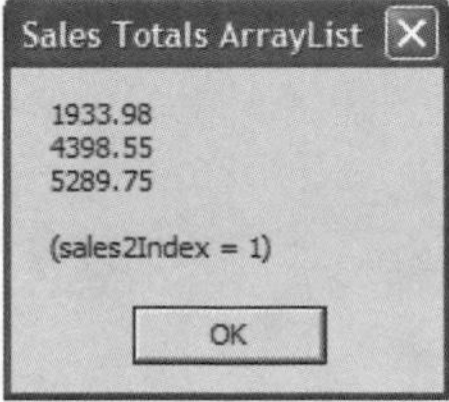

Figure 8-13 How to work with an array list

How to work with a sorted list

You can also implement a collection by using the SortedList class that's described in figure 8-14. A sorted list is useful when you need to look up values in the list based on a key value. If, for example, a sorted list consists of item numbers and unit prices, the keys are the item numbers. Then, the list can be used to look up the unit price for any item number. Each item in a sorted list is actually a DictionaryEntry structure that consists of two properties: Key and Value. Here, the Value property can store value types or reference types.

Like an array list, you can set the initial capacity of a sorted list by specifying the number of elements in parentheses when the list is created. Then, if the number of elements in the list exceeds the capacity as the program executes, the capacity is automatically doubled.

The first example in this figure shows how to create and load a sorted list. When you add an element to a sorted list, you specify the key along with the value associated with that key. In this example, the keys are the names of employees, and the values are the sales totals for those employees. Note that although the keys in this list are added in alphabetical order, a sorted list automatically sorts itself by key values regardless of the order in which the elements are added.

The second example shows how to look up a value in a sorted list based on a key. Here, a value of "LewisJ" is specified as the key for the element. As a result, this key returns an object that contains a decimal value of 5289.75. Then, the object is cast to the decimal type.

The third example creates a string that contains the keys and values in a sorted list. To start, it declares and initializes the string. Then, it uses a foreach loop to retrieve each DictionaryEntry in the sorted list. Within the foreach loop, it uses the Key and Value properties of the DictionaryEntry structure to access each element's key and value. In this example, a tab character is placed between the key and the value and a new line character is placed after the key/value pair.

Since a sorted list makes it easy to look up a key and return its corresponding value, it's the ideal collection to use when you need to do this type of lookup. It would be much more difficult to perform the same task with an array list. However, an array list works fine when you need to look up an element by an index.

Common properties and methods of the SortedList class

Index	Description
[key]	Gets or sets the value of the element with the specified key.
Property	**Description**
Capacity	Gets or sets the number of elements the list can hold.
Count	Gets the number of elements in the list.
Method	**Description**
Add(key, value)	Adds an element with the specified key and value to the sorted list.
Clear()	Removes all elements from the sorted list.
ContainsKey(key)	Returns a Boolean value that indicates whether or not the sorted list contains the specified key.
ContainsValue(value)	Returns a Boolean value that indicates whether or not the sorted list contains the specified value.
GetByIndex(index)	Gets the value of the element at the specified index. The index for the first item in the collection is 0.
GetKey(index)	Gets the key of the element at the specified index.
Remove(key)	Removes the element with the specified key from the sorted list.
RemoveAt(index)	Removes the element at the specified index from the sorted list.
SetByIndex(index, value)	Sets the element at the specified index to the specified value.

Properties of the DictionaryEntry structure

Property	Description
Key	The key for the SortedList item.
Value	The value associated with the key.

Code that creates and loads a sorted list

```
SortedList salesList = new SortedList(4);
salesList.Add("AdamsA", 3275.68m);
salesList.Add("FinkleP", 4398.55m);
salesList.Add("LewisJ", 5289.75m);
salesList.Add("PotterE", 1933.98m);
```

Code that looks up a value in the sorted list based on a key

```
string employeeKey = "LewisJ";
decimal salesTotal = (decimal) salesList[employeeKey];
```

Code that converts the sorted list to a tab-delimited string

```
string salesTableString = "";
foreach (DictionaryEntry employeeSalesEntry in salesList)
    salesTableString += employeeSalesEntry.Key + "\t"
                     + employeeSalesEntry.Value.ToString() + "\n";
MessageBox.Show(salesTableString, "Employee Sales Totals");
```

Figure 8-14 How to work with a sorted list

How to work with queues and stacks

Figure 8-15 shows the properties and methods of the Queue and Stack classes. You can use these classes to create *queues* and *stacks*. Queues and stacks are collections that have some distinct features.

Unlike other collections, queues and stacks do not use the Add method to add items or an index to retrieve items. Instead, queues use the Enqueue and Dequeue methods to add and retrieve items, and stacks use the Push and Pop methods.

You can think of a queue (pronounced *cue*) as a line of items waiting to be processed. When you use the Enqueue method to add an item to the queue, the item is placed at the end of the queue. When you use the Dequeue method to retrieve an item from the queue, the item is taken from the front of the queue. Because items are retrieved from a queue in the same order in which they were added, a queue can be referred to as a *first-in, first-out* (*FIFO*) collection.

In contrast, a stack is a *last-in, first-out* (*LIFO*) collection. When you use the Push method to place an item on a stack, that item is placed on the top of the stack. If you then push another item onto the stack, the new item is placed on the top of the stack and the item that was previously on the top of the stack moves to second from the top. In contrast, the Pop method retrieves the top item and removes it, so the item that was second from the top moves to the top position.

The two examples in this figure illustrate these differences between queues and stacks. Each example begins by defining a new queue or stack, and then adding three names. Next, a while loop is used to build a string that contains the names in the order that they are retrieved from the queue or stack, and the resulting list is displayed in a message box. If you compare the message boxes for these examples, you can see that the queue names are displayed in the same order that they were added to the queue. But in the stack example, the names are retrieved in the opposite order.

In both examples, the while loop repeats as long as the Count property is greater than zero. This works because the Dequeue and Pop methods remove the item from the queue or stack, so the Count property is automatically decreased by one each time through the loop. When all of the items have been read from the queue or stack, the Count property reaches zero and the while loop terminates.

Properties and methods of the Queue class

Property	Description
Count	Gets the number of items in the queue.
Method	**Description**
Enqueue(object)	Adds the specified object to the end of the queue.
Dequeue()	Gets the object at the front of the queue and removes it from the queue.
Clear()	Removes all items from the queue.
Peek()	Retrieves the next item in the queue without deleting it.

Code that uses a queue

```
Queue nameQueue = new Queue();
nameQueue.Enqueue("Prince");
nameQueue.Enqueue("Lowe");
nameQueue.Enqueue("Murach");
string nameQueueString = "";
while (nameQueue.Count > 0)
    nameQueueString += nameQueue.Dequeue() + "\n";
MessageBox.Show(nameQueueString, "Queue");
```

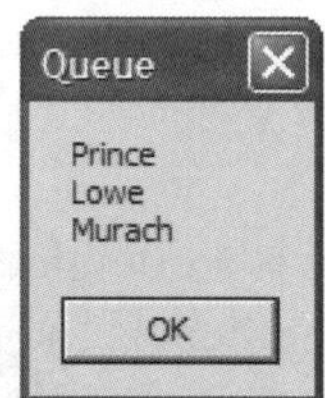

Properties and methods of the Stack class

Property	Description
Count	Gets the number of items in the stack.
Method	**Description**
Push(object)	Adds the specified object to the top of the stack.
Pop	Gets the object at the top of the stack and removes it from the stack.
Clear	Removes all items from the stack.
Peek	Retrieves the next item in the stack without deleting it.

Code that uses a stack

```
Stack nameStack = new Stack();
nameStack.Push("Prince");
nameStack.Push("Lowe");
nameStack.Push("Murach");
string nameStackString = "";
while (nameStack.Count > 0)
    nameStackString += nameStack.Pop() + "\n";
MessageBox.Show(nameStackString, "Stack");
```

Description

- *Queues* and *stacks* provide distinct features that let you process them like lists.
- A queue is sometimes called a *first-in, first-out* (*FIFO*) collection because its items are retrieved in the same order in which they were added.
- A stack is sometimes called a *last-in, first-out* (*LIFO*) collection because its items are retrieved in the reverse order from the order in which they were added.

Figure 8-15 How to work with queues and stacks

Perspective

In this chapter, you've learned how to use both arrays and collections for working with groups of related data. You've also learned that the .NET Framework provides several different classes that offer useful properties and methods for working with arrays and collections. These include the Array, ArrayList, SortedList, Queue, and Stack classes.

As you develop your own applications, you need to decide between the use of an array or collection. Then, if you decide to use a collection, you need to choose the most appropriate type of collection. If you make the right decisions, your code will be easier to write, debug, and maintain.

Summary

- An *array* is a container that can store one or more *elements*. The *length*, or *size*, of an array indicates the maximum number of elements that can be stored in the array.
- To refer to an element in an array, you use an *index* that can range from zero to the *upper bound* of the array, which is one less than the length of the array.
- A *one-dimensional array* contains data that's stored using one index, and a *two-dimensional array* contains data that's stored using two indexes.
- A *rectangular array* is a two-dimensional array that stores data in rows that have an equal number of columns. A *jagged array* is a two-dimensional array where each row can have a different length.
- You can use a for loop to work with arrays and collections. You can also use a *foreach loop* to access each element of an array or a collection.
- An array is created from the Array class. As a result, you can use the properties and methods of this class to work with arrays.
- Because an array is a reference type, two array variables can refer to the same array.
- You can use the params keyword to code a method that accepts multiple arguments of a given type and converts them to an array.
- A *collection* is an object that stores other objects.
- You can use the ArrayList and SortedList classes to create collections that automatically adjust their size whenever needed. You can use an index to return a value from an array list. You can use a key to look up and return a value from a sorted list.
- The Queue and Stack classes let you create queues and stacks. A *queue* is a *first-in, first-out* collection. A *stack* is a *last-in, first-out* collection.

Terms

array
element
length
size
one-dimensional array
index
upper bound
foreach statement
foreach loop
rectangular array
two-dimensional array
jagged array
array of arrays
immutable
collection
mutable
boxing
unboxing
queue
stack
first-in first-out
FIFO
last-in first-out
LIFO

Objectives

- Given the specifications for an application that uses a one-dimensional, rectangular, or jagged array, write the code that works with the array.
- Given the specifications for an application that uses an array list, a sorted list, a queue, or a stack, write the code that works with the collection.
- Describe the primary benefit of using an array list instead of an array.
- Describe the primary benefit of using a sorted list.
- Distinguish between a queue and a stack.

Exercise 8-1 Use an array and an array list

This exercise will guide you through the process of adding an array and an array list to the Invoice Total application that you enhanced in the last chapter.

Open the Invoice Total application

1. Open the Invoice Total application that's in the C:\C#.NET\Chapter 08\InvoiceTotal directory.

Use an array to store invoice totals

2. Declare two class variables for an array that can hold up to five invoice totals and an index that you can use to work with that array.
3. Add code that adds the invoice total to the next element in an array each time the user clicks the Calculate button.
4. Add code that displays all the invoice totals in the array in a message box when the user clicks the Exit button. To do that, use a for loop to loop through the totals, and format the message box so it looks like this:

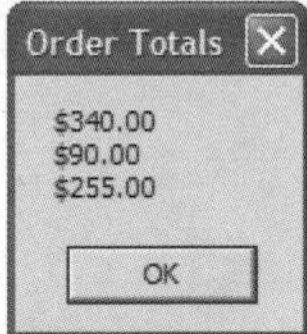

5. Test the program by entering subtotals for up to five invoices and then clicking the Exit button. (If you enter more than five invoices, an IndexOutOfRangeException will be thrown, and this exception will be caught by the catch block.)

Sort the invoice totals

6. Add code to sort the invoice totals in the array and display the sorted totals in a second message box.
7. Test the program again to be sure that the second message box displays the invoice totals in the correct sequence.

Modify the program to use an array list

8. Modify the program so it uses an array list to hold the totals and so it uses foreach loops to display the totals. Then, test the program.
9. When you've got this working right, close the solution.

Exercise 8-2 Use a rectangular array

This exercise will guide you through the process of adding a rectangular array to the Future Value application. This array will store the values for each calculation that's performed.

Open the Future Value application

1. Open the Future Value application that's in the C:\C#.NET\Chapter 08\FutureValue directory.

Use a rectangular array to store future value calculations

2. Declare class variables for a row counter and a rectangular array of strings that provides for 10 rows and 4 columns.
3. Add code that stores the values for each calculation in the next row of the array when the user clicks the Calculate button. Store the monthly investment and future value in currency format, and store the interest rate in percent format.
4. Add code to display the elements in the array in a message box when the user clicks the Exit button. Format the message box so it looks like this:

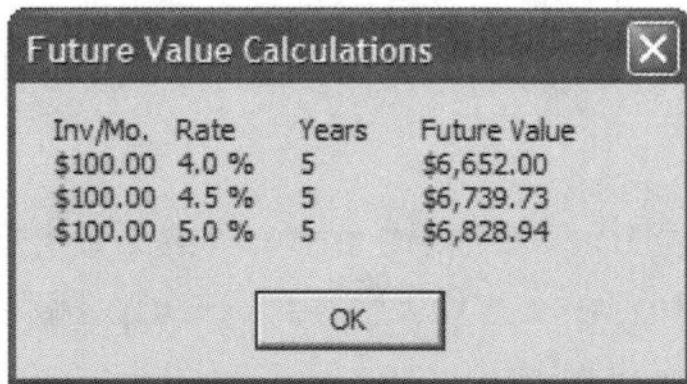

5. Test the program by making up to 10 future value calculations.
6. When you've got this working right, close the solution.

9

How to work with dates and strings

In chapter 4, you learned some basic skills for working with strings. In this chapter, you'll learn more about working with strings, and you'll learn how to work with dates. Because you'll use dates and strings in many of the applications you develop, you'll want to be sure you know how to use the skills presented in this chapter.

How to work with dates and times

To work with dates and times in C#, you use the DateTime structure. As you'll see, this structure provides a variety of properties and methods for getting information about dates and times, formatting DateTime values, and performing operations on dates and times.

How to create a DateTime value

Figure 9-1 presents two ways that you can create a DateTime value. First, you can use the new keyword to create a DateTime value from the DateTime structure. This is different from the way you create other built-in value types. That's because C# doesn't provide a keyword for working with this structure like it does for the other value types.

When you create a DateTime value using the new keyword, you must always specify the year, month, and day. In addition, you can specify the time in hours, minutes, seconds, and milliseconds. If you don't specify the time, it's set to 12:00 AM. This is illustrated by the first two statements in this figure.

You can also create a DateTime value using the static Parse method of the DateTime structure. When you use the Parse method, you specify the date and time as a string as illustrated by the third, fourth, and fifth statements in this figure. Here, the third statement specifies just a date. Because of that, the time portion of the DateTime value is set to 12:00 AM. The fourth statement specifies both a date and time. The fifth statement illustrates that you can create a DateTime value from a property or variable that contains a date/time string. In this case, a DateTime value is created from the Text property of a text box.

When you use the Parse method to create a DateTime value, the date and time you specify must be in a valid format. Some of the most common formats are listed in this figure. Later in this chapter, you'll learn more about the acceptable date and time formats.

Although the statements in this figure indicate the DateTime values that are created, you should realize that these aren't the actual values that are stored in the variables. Instead, they show what happens when a DateTime value is converted to a string. The date and time are actually stored as the number of *ticks* (100 nanosecond units) that have elapsed since 12:00:00 AM, January 1, 0001. That makes it easy to perform arithmetic operations on dates and times, as you'll see later in this chapter.

The syntax for creating a DateTime value

```
DateTime variableName = new DateTime(year, month, day
    [, hour, minute, second[, millisecond]]);
```

Another way to create a DateTime value

```
DateTime variableName = DateTime.Parse(string);
```

Statements that create DateTime values

```
DateTime startDate = new DateTime(04, 01, 30);     // 1/30/2004 12:00 AM
DateTime startDateAndTime =
    new DateTime(2004, 1, 30, 14, 15, 0);          // 1/30/2004 2:15 PM

DateTime startDate = DateTime.Parse("01/30/04");  // 1/30/2004 12:00 AM
DateTime startDateAndTime =
    DateTime.Parse("Jan 30, 2004 2:15 PM");        // 1/30/2004 2:15 PM

DateTime invoiceDate = DateTime.Parse(txtInvoiceDate.Text);
```

Valid date formats

```
01/30/2004
1/30/04
01-01-2004
1-1-04
2004-01-01
Jan 30 2004
January 30, 2004
```

Valid time formats

```
2:15 PM
14:15
02:15:30 AM
```

Description

- In C#, you can use the DateTime structure of the .NET Framework to create and work with dates and times.
- To create a DateTime value, you can use the new keyword and then specify the date and time values you want to use to create the date.
- You can also use the static Parse method of the DateTime structure to create a DateTime value from a string.
- If you omit the time specification when you create a DateTime value, the time is set to 12:00 AM. You can also omit the date specification when you create a DateTime value using the Parse method. Then, the date is set to the current date.
- If the Parse method can't parse the string you specify, a format exception occurs.
- A date is stored as a 64-bit signed integer that represents the number of *ticks* (100 nanosecond units) that have elapsed since 12:00 AM, January 1, 0001.

Figure 9-1 How to create a DateTime value

How to get the current date and time

Figure 9-2 presents two additional properties of the DateTime structure that you can use to get the current date and time. If you use the Now property, both the date and time are returned. If you use the Today property, only the date is returned, and the time is set to 12:00:00 AM. The first two statements in this figure illustrate how this works. Note that these properties are static properties.

How to format DateTime values

To format dates and times, you can use the four methods of the DateTime structure that are shown in figure 9-2. Note, however, that these formats may vary somewhat from the formats that are used on your system. The exact formats depend on your computer's regional settings. If these methods don't provide the format you need, you can use the formatting techniques you'll learn about later in this chapter to format the date and time the way you want them.

DateTime properties for getting the current date and time

Property	Description
`Now`	Returns the current date and time.
`Today`	Returns the current date.

Statements that get the current date and time

```
DateTime currentDateTime = DateTime.Now;          // 1/30/2004 4:24:59 AM
DateTime currentDate = DateTime.Today;            // 1/30/2004 12:00:00 AM
```

DateTime methods for formatting a date or time

Method	Description
`ToLongDateString()`	Converts the DateTime value to a string that includes the day of the week name, the month name, the day of the month, and the year.
`ToShortDateString()`	Converts the DateTime value to a string that includes the numeric month, day, and year.
`ToLongTimeString()`	Converts the DateTime value to a string that includes the hours, minutes, and seconds.
`ToShortTimeString()`	Converts the DateTime value to a string that includes the hours and minutes.

Statements that format dates and times

```
string longDate =
    currentDateTime.ToLongDateString();        // Friday, January 30, 2004
string shortDate =
    currentDateTime.ToShortDateString();       // 1/30/2004
string longTime =
    currentDateTime.ToLongTimeString();        // 4:24:59 AM
string ShortTime =
    currentDateTime.ToShortTimeString();       // 4:24 AM
```

Description

- The Now and Today properties are static properties of the DateTime structure.
- The format that's used for a date or time depends on your computer's regional settings.

Figure 9-2 How to get the current date and format DateTime values

How to get information about dates and times

The DateTime structure provides a variety of properties and methods for getting information about dates and times. These properties and methods are listed in figure 9-3, and the statements presented here show how to work with most of them.

The first statement uses the Now property to get the current date and time. Then, the second statement uses the Month property to get the month of that date, the third statement uses the Hour property to get the hour of that time, and the fourth statement uses the DayOfYear property to get a number between 1 and 366 that represents the day of the year.

The next two statements show how to use the two methods for getting information about a date. Since both of these methods are static, they're accessed through the DateTime structure. The first method, DaysInMonth, returns the number of days in a given month and year. In this example, since 2004 is a leap year, there are 29 days in February instead of the usual 28. The second method, IsLeapYear, returns a true or false value that indicates whether the specified year is a leap year.

The last code example in this figure shows how to use the DayOfWeek property. Note that this property returns a member of the DayOfWeek enumeration. In this case, the first statement gets the day of the week for the current date. Then, an if statement checks if the current date is a Saturday or a Sunday. If so, a string variable named message is set to "Weekend." Otherwise, it's set to "Weekday."

DateTime properties and methods for working with dates and times

Property	Description
`Date`	Returns the DateTime value with the time portion set to 12:00:00 AM.
`Month`	Returns an integer for the month portion of the DateTime value.
`Day`	Returns an integer for the day portion of the DateTime value.
`Year`	Returns an integer for the year portion of the DateTime value.
`Hour`	Returns an integer for the hour portion of the DateTime value.
`Minute`	Returns an integer for the minute portion of the DateTime value.
`Second`	Returns an integer for the second portion of the DateTime value.
`TimeOfDay`	Returns a TimeSpan value that represents the amount of time that has elapsed since 12:00:00 AM. For more information about the TimeSpan structure, see figure 9-4.
`DayOfWeek`	Returns a member of the DayOfWeek enumeration that represents the day of the week of a DateTime value.
`DayOfYear`	Returns an integer for the numeric day of the year.
Method	**Description**
`DaysInMonth(year, month)`	Returns the number of days in a specified month and year.
`IsLeapYear(year)`	Returns a Boolean value that indicates whether or not a specified year is a leap year.

Statements that get information about a date or time

```
DateTime currentDateTime = DateTime.Now;           // 1/30/2004 10:26:35 AM
int month = currentDateTime.Month;                  // 1
int hour = currentDateTime.Hour;                    // 10
int dayOfYear = currentDateTime.DayOfYear;          // 30
int daysInMonth = DateTime.DaysInMonth(2004, 2);    // 29
bool isLeapYear = DateTime.IsLeapYear(2004);        // true
```

Code that uses the DayOfWeek property and enumeration

```
DayOfWeek dayOfWeek = currentDateTime.DayOfWeek;
string message = "";
if (dayOfWeek == DayOfWeek.Saturday ||
    dayOfWeek == DayOfWeek.Sunday)
    message = "Weekend";
else
    message = "Weekday";
```

Figure 9-3 How to get information about dates and times

How to perform operations on dates and times

Figure 9-4 presents some of the methods of the DateTime structure that you can use to perform operations on dates and times. Most of these methods let you add a specific number of intervals, like hours, days, or months, to a date or time. However, you can use the Add method to add a TimeSpan value to a date, and you can use the Subtract method to determine the time span between two dates, which is often required in business applications.

Like DateTime values, TimeSpan values are based on a structure defined by the .NET Framework. TimeSpan values also hold a number of ticks, just like DateTime values. However, a TimeSpan value represents a time interval. In contrast, a DateTime value represents a specific time.

The first group of statements in this figure show how some of the Add methods work. For example, the second statement shows how to add two months to a DateTime value, and the third statement shows how to add 60 days. Similarly, the fourth statement shows how to add 30 minutes, and the fifth statement shows how to add 12 hours.

The second group of statements show how you can use a TimeSpan variable to determine the number of days between two DateTime values. Here, the first statement retrieves the current date, and the second statement assigns a date to another DateTime variable. Next, the third statement uses the Subtract method to subtract the two date values and assign the result to a TimeSpan variable, which represents the number of days, minutes, hours, and seconds between the two dates. Finally, the last statement uses the Days property of the TimeSpan structure to extract the number of days from the TimeSpan value. This is one of several properties of this structure that let you extract the data from a TimeSpan value.

In addition to the properties and methods provided by the DateTime structure for working with dates, you can use some of the standard operators to work with dates. For instance, the third example in this figure shows how to use the subtraction operator to calculate the time between two dates instead of using the Subtract method. The last example shows that you can also use DateTime values in a conditional expression. Here, the conditional expression tests if one DateTime value is greater than another.

DateTime methods for performing operations on dates and times

Method	Description
AddDays(days)	Adds the specified numbers of days to a DateTime value and returns another DateTime value.
AddMonths(months)	Adds the specified number of months to a DateTime value and returns another DateTime value.
AddYears(years)	Adds the specified number of years to a DateTime value and returns another DateTime value.
AddHours(hours)	Adds the specified number of hours to a DateTime value and returns another DateTime value.
AddMinutes(minutes)	Adds the specified number of minutes to a DateTime value and returns another DateTime value.
AddSeconds(seconds)	Adds the specified number of seconds to a DateTime value and returns another DateTime value.
Add(timespan)	Adds the specified TimeSpan value to a DateTime value and returns another DateTime value.
Subtract(datetime)	Subtracts the specified DateTime value from a DateTime value and returns a TimeSpan value.

Statements that perform operations on dates and times

```
DateTime dateTime =
    DateTime.Parse("3/1/2004 13:28");              // 3/1/2004 1:28:00 PM
DateTime dueDate = dateTime.AddMonths(2);          // 5/1/2004 1:28:00 PM
dueDate = dateTime.AddDays(60);                    // 4/30/2004 1:28:00 PM
DateTime runTime = dateTime.AddMinutes(30);        // 3/1/2004 1:58:00 PM
runTime = dateTime.AddHours(12);                   // 3/2/2004 1:28:00 AM
```

Code that results in a TimeSpan value

```
DateTime currentDate = DateTime.Today;                  // 1/30/2004
dueDate = DateTime.Parse("2/15/2004");                  // 2/15/2004
TimeSpan timeTillDue = dueDate.Subtract(currentDate);   // 16:00:00:00
int daysTillDue = timeTillDue.Days;                     // 16
```

A statement that uses the – operator to subtract two dates

```
TimeSpan timeTillDue = dueDate - currentDate;     // 16:00:00:00
```

An if statement that uses the > operator on DateTime values

```
bool pastDue = false;
if (currentDate > dueDate)
    pastDue = true;
```

Description

- A TimeSpan value represents a period of time stored as ticks. You can use the Days, Hours, Minutes, and Seconds properties of a TimeSpan value to get portions of that value.
- In addition to the DateTime methods, you can use the +, -, ==, !=, >, >=, <, and <= operators to work with DateTime values.

Figure 9-4 How to perform operations on dates and times

How to work with strings

Many types of programs require that you work with the characters within strings. If, for example, a user enters the city, state, and zip code of an address as a single entry, your program may need to divide (or *parse)* that single string into city, state, and zip code variables. Or, if a user enters a telephone number that includes parentheses and hyphens, you may need to remove those characters so the number can be stored as a 10-digit integer.

When you create a string, you are actually creating a String object from the String class. Then, you can use the properties and methods of the String class to work with the String object. Another alternative, though, is to create StringBuilder objects from the StringBuilder class so you can use the properties and methods of that class to work with strings. In the topics that follow, you'll learn both ways of working with strings.

The properties and methods of the String class

Figure 9-5 summarizes some of the properties and methods of the String class that you can use as you work with String objects. When you use these properties and methods, you often need to use an *index* to refer to a specific character within a string. To do that, you use 0 to refer to the first character, 1 to refer to the second character, and so on. Just as you do when you refer to an element of an array, you code the index for a string character within brackets.

The property and methods listed in this figure provide the operations that you'll need as you parse strings and work with them in other ways. In the next two figures, you'll see coding examples that will help you understand how to use these properties and methods.

One method that's particularly useful for parsing strings is Split. This method returns an array where each element contains a substring of the original string. The argument that you specify on this method identifies the character that's used to delimit each substring. You'll see examples of this method in figure 9-7.

Common properties and methods of the String class

Index	Description
`[index]`	Gets the character at the specified position.
Property	**Description**
`Length`	Gets the number of characters in the string.
Method	**Description**
`StartsWith``(string)`	Returns a Boolean value that indicates whether or not the string starts with the specified string.
`EndsWith``(string)`	Returns a Boolean value that indicates whether or not the string ends with the specified string.
`IndexOf``(string[, startIndex])`	Returns an integer that represents the position of the first occurrence of the specified string starting at the specified position. If the starting position isn't specified, the search starts at the beginning of the string. If the string isn't found, -1 is returned.
`LastIndexOf``(string[, startIndex])`	Returns an integer that represents the position of the last occurrence of the specified string starting at the specified position. If the starting position isn't specified, the search starts at the end of the string. If the string isn't found, -1 is returned.
`Insert``(startIndex, string)`	Returns a string with the specified string inserted beginning at the specified position.
`PadLeft``(totalWidth)`	Returns a string that's right-aligned and padded on the left with spaces so it's the specified width.
`PadRight``(totalWidth)`	Returns a string that's left-aligned and padded on the right with spaces so it's the specified width.
`Remove``(startIndex, count)`	Returns a string with the specified number of characters removed starting at the specified position.
`Replace``(oldString, newString)`	Returns a string with all occurrences of the old string replaced with the new string.
`Substring``(startIndex[, length])`	Returns the string that starts at the specified position and has the specified length. If the length isn't specified, all of the characters to the end of the string are returned.
`ToLower``()`	Returns a string in lowercase.
`ToUpper``()`	Returns a string in uppercase.
`Trim``()`	Returns a string with leading and trailing spaces removed.
`Split``(splitCharacters)`	Returns an array of strings where each element is a substring that's delimited by the specified character or characters.

Description

- You can use an *index* to access each character in a string, where 0 is the index for the first character, 1 is the index for the second character, and so on.

Figure 9-5 The properties and methods of the String class

Code examples that work with strings

Figure 9-6 shows how to use most of the properties and methods summarized in the last figure. The first example shows how you can use an index to return a character from a string. Then, the second example shows how you can use an index and the Length property in a for loop to insert a space character between each character in the string. The third example performs the same operation as the second example, but it uses a foreach loop instead of a for loop.

The fourth example shows how you can use the StartsWith and EndsWith methods. Here, the first statement checks if the chars string that was created in the first example starts with the string *abc*, and the second statement checks if this string ends with *abc*. As you can see, the result of the first statement is true, and the result of the second statement is false.

The fifth example shows how to use the IndexOf and LastIndexOf methods. Here, the first statement sets the value of the string. Then, the second and third statements use the IndexOf method to retrieve the index of the first space in the string. The fourth statement uses the same method to return the index of a string of characters. Notice that since the characters don't exist in the string, this method returns a value of -1. The last statement uses the LastIndexOf method to return the index of the last space in the string.

The sixth example shows how to use the Remove, Insert, and Replace methods to work with the string in the fifth example. Here, the first statement removes the first five characters of the string. In this statement, the first argument specifies the starting index, and the second argument specifies the number of characters to remove. In this case, the number of characters to remove is calculated by adding 1 to the index of the first space, which is 4. Then, the second statement uses the Insert method to insert ", Inc." at the end of the string. Here, the first argument uses the Length method to set the starting index at the end of the string, and the second argument specifies the string to be inserted. Finally, the third statement uses the Replace method to replace all occurrences of "and" with "And".

The seventh example shows how to use the Substring, ToUpperCase, and ToLowerCase methods to make sure a string is lowercase with an initial cap. Here, the second statement returns a substring that contains the first character in the string. To do that, the first argument specifies a starting index of 0 and the second argument specifies a length of 1. Then, to convert the returned substring to uppercase, this statement calls the ToUpperCase method. The third statement is similar, but it uses the ToLowerCase method to return the remaining characters in the string and convert them to lowercase. The last statement combines the two strings into a single string.

The eighth example shows how to use the = operator to copy one string to another string. Because a string is a reference type, you might think that the second statement would copy the reference to the string object created by the first statement to the second string variable. In this case, however, a new string object is created and the value in the original string is copied to that object. Then, a reference to the new object is assigned to the new string variable.

Code that uses an index to access a character in a string

```
string chars = "abcdefg";
char a = chars[0];                        // 'a'
char b = chars[1];                        // 'b'
```

Code that uses a for loop to access each character in the string

```
string charsAndSpaces = "";
for (int i = 0; i < chars.Length; i++)
    charsAndSpaces += chars[i] + " ";
MessageBox.Show(charsAndSpaces, "String Test");
```

The message box that's displayed

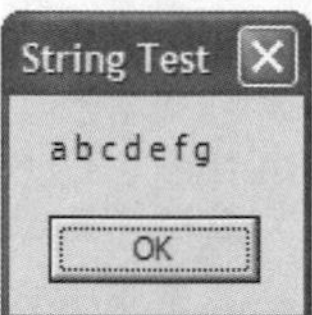

Code that uses a foreach loop to access each character in the string

```
string charsAndSpaces = "";
foreach (char c in chars)
    charsAndSpaces += c + " ";
MessageBox.Show(charsAndSpaces, "String Test");
```

Code that uses the StartsWith and EndsWith methods

```
bool startsWithABC = chars.StartsWith("abc");  // true
bool endsWithABC = chars.EndsWith("abc");      // false
```

Code that uses the IndexOf method

```
string companyName = "Mike Murach and Associates";
int index1 = companyName.IndexOf(" ");       // 4
int index2 = companyName.IndexOf(' ');       // 4
int index3 = companyName.IndexOf("Inc.");    // -1
int index4 = companyName.LastIndexOf(" ");   // 15
```

Code that uses the Remove, Insert, and Replace methods

```
companyName = companyName.Remove(0, index1 + 1);
companyName = companyName.Insert(companyName.Length, ", Inc.");
companyName
    = companyName.Replace("and", "And");     // Murach And Associates, Inc.
```

Code that uses the Substring, ToUpper, and ToLower methods

```
string firstName = "anne";
string firstLetter = firstName.Substring(0, 1).ToUpper();
string otherLetters = firstName.Substring(1).ToLower();
firstName = firstLetter + otherLetters;        // Anne
```

Code that copies one string to another string

```
string s1 = "abc";
string s2 = s1;     // this copies the value stored in s1 to s2
s2 = "def";         // this doesn't change the value stored in s1
```

Figure 9-6 Code examples that work with strings

More code examples that work with strings

Figure 9-7 presents some additional string-handling routines. The first four parse the data in strings. The fifth one adds characters to a string. And the sixth one replaces some of the characters in a string with other characters. If you can understand the code in these routines, you should be able to write your own routines whenever needed.

The first routine shows how to parse the first name from a string that contains a full name. Here, the full name is assigned to the fullName variable so you can visualize how the statements that follow work with that name. In practice, though, the name would be entered by a user or read from a file so you wouldn't know what it was.

To start, this routine uses the Trim method to remove any spaces from the beginning and end of the string that a user may have typed accidentally. Next, the IndexOf method is used to get the position of the first space in the string, which should be between the first name and the middle name or last name. If this method doesn't find a space in the string, though, it returns a -1. In that case, the if-else statement that follows assigns the entire string to the first name variable. Otherwise, it uses the Substring method to set the first name variable equal to the string that begins at the first character of the string and that has a length that's equal to the position of the first space.

The second routine in this figure shows how to parse a string that contains an address into the components of the address. In this case, a pipe character (|) separates each component of the address. In addition, the string may begin with one or more spaces followed by a pipe character, and it may end with a pipe character followed by one or more spaces.

To remove the spaces from the beginning and end of the string, this routine also uses the Trim method. Then, it uses the StartsWith and EndsWith methods to determine whether the first or last character in the string is a pipe character. If it is, the Remove method removes that character from the string.

The next three statements use the IndexOf method to determine the index values of the first character for each substring other than the first. (The first substring will start at index 0.) To do that, it determines the index of the next pipe character and then adds 1. After that, the next four statements use these index variables as arguments of the Substring method to return the street, city, state, and zip code substrings. To calculate the length of each substring, this code subtracts the starting index from the ending index and then subtracts 1 from that value. This results in the length of the substring without the pipe character.

The third and fourth routines use the Split method to perform the same operations as the first and second routines. As you can see, the Split method can simplify your code significantly, particularly if the string you're parsing consists of several elements.

The fifth and sixth routines show how to add hyphens to a phone number and change the hyphens in a date to slashes. To add hyphens, you simply use the Insert method to insert the hyphens at the appropriate index. And to change hyphens to slashes, you use the Replace method.

Code that parses a first name from a name string

```
string fullName = " Edward C Koop   ";              // " Edward C Koop   "
fullName = fullName.Trim();                         // "Edward C Koop"
int firstSpace = fullName.IndexOf(" ");             // 6
string firstName = "";
if (firstSpace == -1)
    firstName = fullName;
else
    firstName = fullName.Substring(0, firstSpace);  // Edward
```

Code that parses a string that contains an address

```
string address = " |805 Main Street|Dallas|TX|12345| ";
address = address.Trim();
if (address.StartsWith("|"))
    address = address.Remove(0, 1);
if (address.EndsWith("|"))
    address = address.Remove(address.Length - 1, 1);
int cityIndex = address.IndexOf("|") + 1;
int stateIndex = address.IndexOf("|", cityIndex) + 1;
int zipIndex = address.IndexOf("|", stateIndex) + 1;
string street = address.Substring(0, cityIndex - 1);
string city = address.Substring(cityIndex, stateIndex - cityIndex - 1);
string state = address.Substring(stateIndex, zipIndex - stateIndex - 1);
string zipCode = address.Substring(zipIndex);
```

Code that uses the Split method to parse the name string

```
string fullName = " Edward C Koop   ";
fullName = fullName.Trim();
string[] names = fullName.Split(' ');
string firstName = names[0];                        // Edward
```

Code that uses the Split method to parse the address string

```
address = address.Trim();
if (address.StartsWith("|"))
    address = address.Remove(0, 1);
string[] columns = address.Split('|');
string street = columns[0];             // 805 Main Street
string city = columns[1];               // Dallas
string state = columns[2];              // TX
string zipCode = columns[3];            // 12345
```

Code that adds hyphens to a phone number

```
string phoneNumber = "9775551212";
phoneNumber = phoneNumber.Insert(3, "-");
phoneNumber = phoneNumber.Insert(7, "-");  // 977-555-1212
```

Code that replaces the hyphens with slashes

```
string date = "12-27-2003";
date = date.Replace("-", "/");             // 12/27/2003
```

Figure 9-7 More code examples that work with strings

Two methods for validating user entries

In chapter 7, you learned how to code a data validation method named IsDecimal that checked whether a user entry contained a valid decimal value. To do that, this method used the ToDecimal method to try to convert the entry string to a decimal. Then, an exception was thrown if the user entered any non-numeric characters, including dollar signs, percent signs, and commas. Since these characters are used frequently to format numeric values, however, it makes sense to allow them in numeric entries. To do that, you can use methods like the ones shown in figure 9-8.

The first method in this figure is another version of the IsDecimal method that can be used to validate decimal entries. This method has two advantages over the IsDecimal method presented in chapter 7. First, it runs more quickly when an error is encountered because it doesn't use exception handling to catch the error. Second, it lets the user enter numeric formatting characters, including dollar signs, percentage signs, commas, and white space. As a result, the user can enter these characters and this method will still recognize the entry as a valid decimal value.

The IsDecimal method works by using a foreach loop to check each character in the entry string to be sure it contains a number from 0 through 9, a decimal point, or a valid formatting character ($, %, comma, or space). If an invalid character is encountered, a Boolean variable named validDecimal is set to false and a break statement ends the foreach loop. If all the characters are valid, however, the loop continues by checking if the character is a decimal point. If so, a variable named decimalCount is incremented by 1.

The if statement that follows the foreach loop checks that all of the characters are valid and that the entry contains no more than one decimal point. If both conditions are true, the method returns a true value to the calling method. Otherwise, it displays an error message and returns a false value.

Because the IsDecimal method allows the user to enter formatting characters, you'll need to remove these characters before attempting to convert the string to a decimal. To do that, you can use the Strip method shown in this figure. Like the IsDecimal method, this method uses a foreach loop to check each character in the entry string. Then, if a character is one of the valid formatting characters, it uses the Remove method to remove that character from the string.

The code at the bottom of this figure shows how you might call these two methods to validate the monthly investment that the user enters into the Future Value application. As you can see, the IsDecimal method is specified as the condition on an if statement. Then, if this method returns a true value, the Strip method is called to remove any formatting characters, and the resulting string is converted to a decimal.

A method that checks if a string contains a decimal value

```
public bool IsDecimal(TextBox textBox, string name)
{
    string s = textBox.Text;
    int decimalCount = 0;
    bool validDecimal = true;
    foreach (char c in s)
    {
        if (!(
            c == '0' || c == '1' || c == '2' ||  // numeric chars
            c == '3' || c == '4' || c == '5' ||
            c == '6' || c == '7' || c == '8' ||
            c == '9' || c == '.' ||
            c == '$' || c == '%' || c == ',' ||  // formatting chars
            c == ' '
            ))
        {
            validDecimal = false;
            break;
        }
        if (c == '.')
            decimalCount++;
    }
    if (validDecimal && decimalCount <= 1)
        return true;
    else
    {
        MessageBox.Show(name + " must be a decimal value.",
            "Entry Error");
        textBox.Focus();
        return false;
    }
}
```

A method that strips formatting characters from a numeric string

```
public string Strip(string s)
{
    foreach (char c in s)
    {
        if (c == '$' || c == '%' || c == ',' || c == ' ')
        {
            int i = s.IndexOf(c);
            s = s.Remove(i, 1);
        }
    }
    return s;
}
```

Code that calls the two methods shown above

```
decimal monthlyInvestment = 0;
if (IsDecimal(txtMonthlyInvestment, "Monthly Investment"))
{
    monthlyInvestment = Convert.ToDecimal(
        Strip(txtMonthlyInvestment.Text));
}
```

Figure 9-8 Two methods for validating user entries

How to use the StringBuilder class

When you use the String class to create a string, the string has a fixed length and value. In other words, the String class creates strings that are *immutable*. Then, when you assign a new value to a string variable, the original String object is deleted and it's replaced with a new String object that contains the new value.

Another way to work with strings, though, is to use the StringBuilder class. Then, you create StringBuilder objects that are *mutable* so you can add, delete, or replace characters in the objects. This makes it easier to write some types of string-handling routines, and these routines run more efficiently. As a result, you should use the StringBuilder class for string handling routines that append, insert, remove, or replace characters in strings, especially if you're working with long strings that use significant system resources.

In figure 9-9, you can see some of the most useful properties and methods for working with a string that's created from the StringBuilder class. As you can see, you can use an index to refer to a character in a StringBuilder object, and you can use the Length property to get the number of characters in a string just as you can with a String object. You can also use the Insert, Remove, and Replace methods with StringBuilder objects. Note, however, that instead of returning a new string, these methods change the existing string.

When you use the StringBuilder class, you'll want to include a *using* statement for the namespace that contains it as shown in the first example in this figure. You code this statement at the start of the class, along with the using statements that are added to the class by default. That way, you can refer to the StringBuilder class without qualifying it with the name of this namespace.

When you create a StringBuilder object, you can code one or two arguments that assign an initial value, an initial capacity, or both. The statements in the second example illustrate how this works. Here, the first statement doesn't include any arguments, so the StringBuilder object is created with a default capacity of 16 characters and an initial value of the empty string (""). The second statement creates a StringBuilder object with an initial capacity of 10. The third and fourth statements are similar, but they specify an initial value for the object.

The last example in this figure shows how you can use five methods of the StringBuilder class. Here, the first statement creates a StringBuilder object with an initial capacity of 10, and the second statement appends a 10-character phone number to the object. The third and fourth statements insert periods into the string to format the number. The fifth statement removes the area code and the period that follows it. The sixth statement replaces the remaining period with a hyphen. And, the last statement converts the characters stored in the StringBuilder object to a string.

This example also shows how a StringBuilder object automatically increases its capacity when necessary. Here, the StringBuilder object has a capacity of 10 when it's created, and this capacity remains at 10 until the first period is inserted. Then, to be able to store the 11 characters, the StringBuilder object automatically doubles its capacity to 20.

The syntax for creating a StringBuilder object

```
StringBuilder variableName = new StringBuilder([value] [,] [capacity]);
```

Common properties and methods of the StringBuilder class

Index	Description
`[index]`	Gets the character at the specified position.
Property	**Description**
`Length`	Gets the number of characters in the string.
`Capacity`	Gets or sets the number of characters the string can hold.
Method	**Description**
`Append(string)`	Adds the specified string to the end of the string.
`Insert(index, string)`	Inserts the specified string at the specified index in the string.
`Remove(startIndex, count)`	Removes the specified number of characters from the string starting at the specified index.
`Replace(oldString, newString)`	Replaces all occurrences of the old string with the new string.
`ToString()`	Converts the StringBuilder object to a string.

A statement that simplifies references to the StringBuilder class

```
using System.Text;
```

Statements that create and initialize StringBuilder objects

```
StringBuilder addresses1 = new StringBuilder();          // Capacity is 16
StringBuilder addresses2 = new StringBuilder(10);        // Capacity is 10
StringBuilder phoneNumber1 =
    new StringBuilder("9775551212");                     // Capacity is 16
StringBuilder phoneNumber2 =
    new StringBuilder("9775551212", 10);                 // Capacity is 10
```

Code that creates a phone number and inserts dashes

```
StringBuilder phoneNumber = new StringBuilder(10);       // Capacity is 10
phoneNumber.Append("9775551212");                        // Capacity is 10
phoneNumber.Insert(3, ".");                              // Capacity is 20
phoneNumber.Insert(7, ".");                              // 977.555.1212
phoneNumber.Remove(0, 4);                                // 555.1212
phoneNumber.Replace(".", "-");                           // 555-1212
lblPhoneNumber.Text = phoneNumber.ToString();            // 555-1212
```

Description

- Unlike string objects, StringBuilder objects are *mutable*, which means that they can be changed.
- To refer to the StringBuilder class, you must either qualify it with System.Text or include a *using* statement for this namespace at the start of the class that uses it.
- The capacity of a StringBuilder object is the amount of memory that's allocated to it. That capacity is increased automatically whenever necessary. If you don't set an initial capacity when you create a StringBuilder object, the default is 16 characters.

Figure 9-9 How to use the StringBuilder class

How to format numbers, dates, and times

In chapter 4, you learned how to apply standard numeric formats to numbers. Then, earlier in this chapter, you learned how to apply standard formats to dates and times. However, you can also apply custom formatting to numbers, dates, and times. To do that, you can use the skills described in the topics that follow.

How to format numbers

Figure 9-10 shows how to use the Format method of the String class to format numbers. Because this is a static method, you access it directly from the String class rather than from an instance of this class. The result of this method is a string that contains the formatted number.

As you can see in the syntax for this method, the first argument is a string. This string contains the format specifications for the value or values to be formatted. Following this string, you can specify two or more values that you want to format. In most cases, however, you'll use this method to format a single value.

For each value to be formatted, you code a format specification within the string argument. This specification is divided into three parts. The first part indicates the value to be formatted. Because the values are numbered from zero, you'll usually code a zero to indicate that the first value is to be formatted. The next part indicates the width of the formatted value along with its alignment. In most cases, you'll omit this part of the specification.

The third part of the format specification contains the actual format string. This string can contain multiple formats. If only one format is specified, it's used for all numbers. If two formats are specified, the first is used for positive numbers and zero values, and the second is used for negative values. If all three formats are specified, the first is used for positive numbers, the second is used for negative numbers, and the third is used for zero values.

Each format can consist of one of the standard numeric formatting codes listed in this figure. If, for example, you want to format a number as currency, you can code a statement like the first statement in this figure. Here, the format specification indicates that the first value (value 0) should be formatted with the currency format (c). Notice that the format specification is enclosed in braces, and the entire string argument is enclosed in quotes just like any string literal.

If the standard numeric formatting codes don't provide the format you want, you can create your own format using the custom codes presented in this figure. For instance, the second statement uses these codes to create a custom currency format. Here, the first format string indicates that positive numbers and the value 0 should be formatted with a decimal and thousands separators (if appropriate). In addition, the first digit to the left of the decimal point and the first two digits to the right of the decimal are always included, even if they're zero. The other digits are included only if they're non-zero.

The syntax of the Format method of the String class

```
Format(string, value1[, value2]...)
```

The syntax of a format specification within the string argument

```
{N[, M][:formatString]}
```

Explanation

N	An integer that indicates the value to be formatted.
M	An integer that indicates the width of the formatted value. If M is negative, the value will be left-justified. If it's positive, it will be right-justified.
formatString	A string of formatting codes.

The syntax of a format string

```
positiveformat[;negativeformat[;zeroformat]]
```

Standard numeric formatting codes

C or c	Formats the number as currency with the specified number of decimal places.
D or d	Formats an integer with the specified number of digits.
E or e	Formats the number in scientific (exponential) notation with the specified number of decimal places.
F or f	Formats the number as a decimal with the specified number of decimal places.
G or g	Formats the number as a decimal or in scientific notation depending on which is more compact.
N or n	Formats the number with thousands separators and the specified number of decimal places.
P or p	Formats the number as a percent with the specified number of decimal places.

Custom numeric formatting codes

0	Zero placeholder	,	Thousands separator
#	Digit placeholder	%	Percentage placeholder
.	Decimal point	;	Section separator

Statements that format a single number

```
string balance1 = String.Format("{0:c}", 1234.56);          // $1,234.56
string balance2 =
    String.Format("{0:$#,##0.00;($#,##0.00)}", -1234.56);  // ($1,234.56)
string balance3 =
    String.Format("{0:$#,##0.00;($#,##0.00);Zero}", 0);    // Zero
string quantity = String.Format("{0:d3}", 43);              // 043
string payment =  String.Format("{0:f2}", 432.8175);        // 432.82
```

A statement that formats two numbers

```
string totalDue =
    String.Format("Invoice total: {0:c}; Amount due: {1:c}.", 354.75, 20);
// Invoice total: $354.75; Amount due: $20.00.
```

Figure 9-10 How to format numbers

The format for negative numbers is similar. However, this format includes parentheses, which means that negative numbers will be displayed with parentheses around them as shown in the result for this statement. Notice that the parentheses aren't actually formatting codes. They're simply literal values that are included in the output string. The same is true of the dollar signs.

The third statement is similar to the second one, but it includes an additional format for zero values. In this case, a zero value is displayed as the literal "Zero" as you can see in the result for this statement.

The last two statements show how to use standard formatting codes for integers and decimals. In the first statement, an integer is formatted with three digits since the number 3 is included after the formatting code. In the second statement, a decimal is formatted with two decimal places. As you can see, if the number includes more decimal places than are specified, the number is rounded.

The example at the bottom of this figure shows how you can use the Format method to format two numbers. Notice here that the string argument includes text in addition to the format specifications for each of the two values to be formatted. In this case, the first value is formatted according to the first format specification. Similarly, the second value is formatted according to the second format specification. Notice that when you include two or more format specifications, they must be separated by a semicolon.

How to format dates and times

You can also use the Format method of the String class to format dates and times. This method works the same way that it does for numeric formatting, but you use the standard and custom formatting codes for DateTime values that are presented in figure 9-11. The examples in this figure show how this works. If you understand how to use this method to format numbers, you shouldn't have any trouble using it to format dates and times.

Standard DateTime formatting codes

Code	Description	Code	Description
d	Short date	f	Long date, short time
D	Long date	F	Long date, long time
t	Short time	g	Short date, short time
T	Long time	G	Short date, long time

Custom DateTime formatting codes

Code	Description	Code	Description
d	Day of the month without leading zeros	h	Hour without leading zeros
dd	Day of the month with leading zeros	hh	Hour with leading zeros
ddd	Abbreviated day name	H	Hour on a 24-hour clock without leading zeros
dddd	Full day name	HH	Hour on a 24-hour clock with leading zeros
M	Month without leading zeros	m	Minutes without leading zeros
MM	Month with leading zeros	mm	Minutes with leading zeros
MMM	Abbreviated month name	s	Seconds without leading zeros
MMMM	Full month name	ss	Seconds with leading zeros
y	Two-digit year without leading zero	f	Fractions of seconds (one *f* for each decimal place)
yy	Two-digit year with leading zero	t	First character of AM/PM designator
yyyy	Four-digit year	tt	Full AM/PM designator
/	Date separator	:	Time separator

Statements that format dates and times

```
DateTime currentDate = DateTime.Now;              // 1/30/2004 10:37:32 PM
String.Format("{0:d}", currentDate)               // 1/30/2004
String.Format("{0:D}", currentDate)               // Friday, January 30, 2004
String.Format("{0:t}", currentDate)               // 10:37 PM
String.Format("{0:T}", currentDate)               // 10:37:32 PM
String.Format("{0:ddd, MMM d, yyyy}",
    currentDate)                                  // Fri, Jan 30, 2004
String.Format("{0:M/d/yy}", currentDate)          // 1/30/04
String.Format("{0:HH:mm:ss}", currentDate)        // 22:37:32
```

Figure 9-11 How to format dates and times

Perspective

Now that you've completed this chapter, you should be able to use the DateTime structure to work with dates and times and the String and StringBuilder classes to work with strings. These are useful skills that you will use often as you develop C# applications. You should also be able to use the Format method of the String class to provide custom formatting for numbers, dates, and times, although most of the applications that you develop won't require custom formatting.

Summary

- You use the properties and methods of the DateTime structure to work with dates and times.
- DateTime values are stored as the number of *ticks* that have passed since 12:00 AM, January 1, 0001. A tick is 100 nanoseconds.
- You use the properties and methods of the String class to *parse* the substrings within strings and to perform other operations on the characters within strings.
- You can use an *index* to refer to each character in a string.
- Strings created from the String class are *immutable*, which means that they have a fixed length and value. So when you change the value of a string variable, the original String object is deleted and replaced with a new String object.
- You can use the properties and methods of the StringBuilder class to work with *mutable* strings that are stored in StringBuilder objects.
- You can use the Format method of the String class to format numbers, dates, and times, and you can customize those formats.

Terms

tick
parse
index
immutable
mutable

Objectives

- Given the date-handling requirements of an application, write the code that satisfies the requirements.
- Given the string-handling requirements of an application, write the code that satisfies the requirements.

- Given the formatting requirements of an application, use the Format method of the String class to provide the formatting.
- Describe the way a DateTime variable is stored.
- Explain how a String object differs from a StringBuilder object.

Exercise 9-1 Work with dates and times

In this exercise, you'll use the DateTime and TimeSpan structures. To make this easier, we have provided a form so all you have to do is add the code.

Open the application and add code to calculate the due days

1. Open the DateHandling application that's in the C:\C#.NET\Chapter 09\DateHandling folder. Within this project, you'll find a form that accepts a future date and a birth date from the user and provides buttons for performing the due days and age calculations.
2. Add code to calculate the due days when the user enters a future date and clicks the Calculate Due Days button. For simplicity, you can assume valid user entries. Then, display the results in a message box like this:

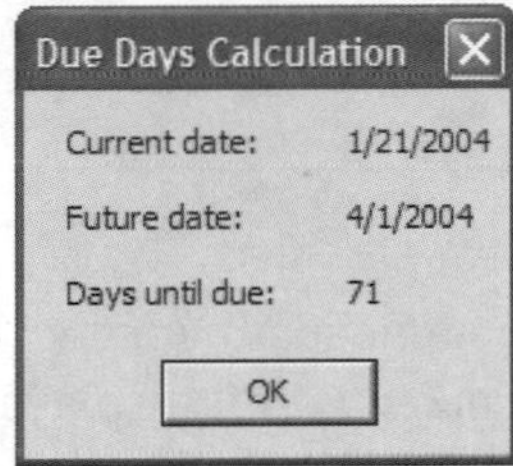

3. Test your code with a variety of date formats to see what formats can be successfully parsed. When you're done, close the form.

Add code to calculate the age

4. Add code to calculate the age when the user enters a birth date and clicks the Calculate Age button. Then, display the results in a message box like the one that follows. For simplicity, you can assume valid user entries, but be sure to take the month and day into account when calculating the age.

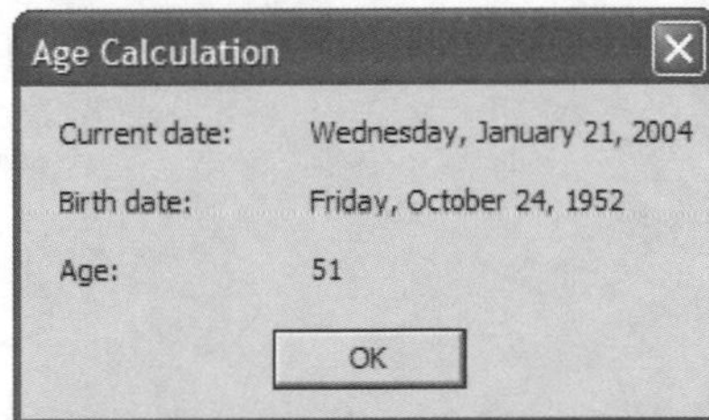

5. Run the application and test your code to make sure it works for all dates. When you're done, close the form.

Exercise 9-2 Work with strings

In this exercise, you'll use methods of the String class to work with strings. To make this easier, we have provided a form so all you have to do is add the code.

Open the application and add code to parse a name

1. Open the StringHandling application that's in the C:\C#.NET\Chapter 09\StringHandling folder. Within this project, you'll find a form that accepts a name and a phone number from the user and provides buttons for parsing the name and editing the phone number.
2. Add code to parse the name when the user enters a name and clicks the Parse Name button. This code should work whether the user enters a first, middle, and last name or just a first and last name. It should also convert the parsed name so the first letters are uppercase but the other letters are lowercase. The results should be displayed in a message box like this:

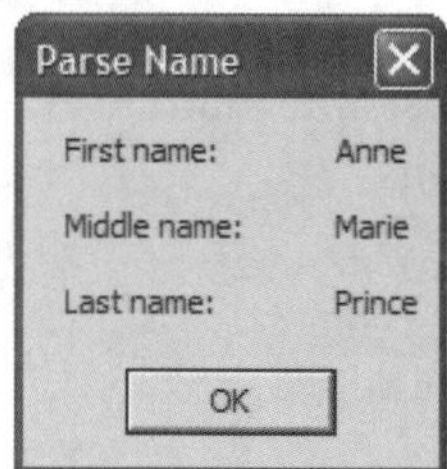

3. Test the application to see if it works. Try entering the name in all uppercase letters or all lowercase letters to make sure the parsed name is still displayed with only the first letters capitalized. When you're done, close the form.

Add code to edit a phone number

4. Add code to edit the phone number when the user enters a phone number and clicks the Edit Phone Number button. This code should remove all special characters from the user entry so the number consists of 10 digits. Then, format the phone number with hyphens. These results should be displayed in a message box like the one that follows. For simplicity, you can assume that the user enters ten digits.

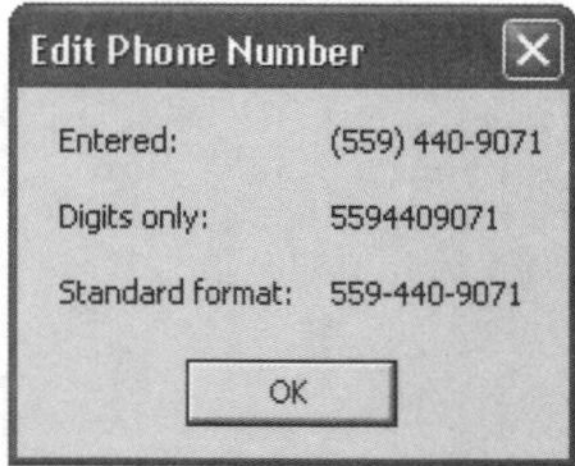

5. Test the application with a variety of entry formats to make sure it works. When you're done, close the form and then close the solution.

Exercise 9-3 Enhance the Future Value application

This exercise will guide you through the process of enhancing the Future Value application of chapter 7 so it can accept numeric entries that contain formatting characters, such as dollar signs, percent signs, commas, and spaces.

Open the Future Value application

1. Use the Windows Explorer to copy the directory for the Future Value application that you created for exercise 7-2 to the C:\C#.NET\Chapter 09 directory. Then, open the application.

Add the code that provides for formatted entries

2. Modify the IsDecimal method so it checks that the string value in a text box only contains numbers and numeric formatting characters (dollar signs, percent signs, commas, and spaces). If you need help, refer to figure 9-8.
3. Modify the IsInt32 method so it works like the IsDecimal method, but doesn't allow a decimal point.
4. Add a Strip method that strips numeric formatting characters (dollar signs, percent signs, commas, and spaces) from a string.
5. Modify the btnCalculate_Click method so it uses the Strip method to strip invalid characters from the user entries before they're converted to the appropriate numeric format.
6. Test the application by entering numeric values that contain formatting characters.
7. (Optional) Modify the IsDecimal method so it only allows one decimal point. Then, test that enhancement.

Add code to format the displayed values

8. Add statements to the btnCalculate_Click method that format the values that are displayed in each text box like this:

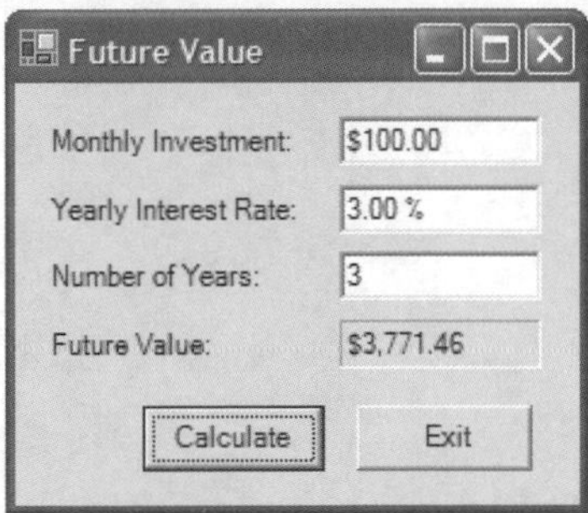

9. Test the application to make sure it works correctly. Then, close the application.

10

More skills for working with Windows forms and controls

In previous chapters, you learned how to work with a project that uses a single form that contains labels, text boxes, and buttons. In this chapter, you'll learn how to use some other commonly used controls, such as combo boxes and check boxes, and you'll learn some basic skills for working with two or more forms in the same project. When you're done, you'll be able to develop a project that contains multiple forms and uses any of the controls presented in this chapter. In addition, you'll have the background you need for learning how to use other controls on your own.

How to work with controls

Although you'll use label, text box, and button controls on almost every form you develop, their functionality is limited. As a result, you need to know how to use some of the other controls provided by the .NET Framework. In particular, you need to learn how to use the five controls presented in the topics that follow.

Five more types of controls

Figure 10-1 shows a form that contains two combo boxes, one list box, one group box, two radio buttons, and a check box. Although you've undoubtedly used these controls before when working with Windows programs, take a moment to consider these controls from a programmer's point of view.

You can use a *combo box* to let the user select one item from a list of items. That reduces the amount of typing that's required by the user, and it reduces the chance that the user will enter invalid or inaccurate data. As you'll see in the next figure, you can also create combo boxes that let the user enter text that doesn't appear in the list.

Like a combo box, a *list box* lets the user select an item from a list of items. However, the list portion of a list box is always visible. In contrast, the list portion of a combo box is typically hidden until the user clicks the arrow at the right side of the control. The user can also select two or more items from a list box, but can only select a single item from a combo box.

Radio buttons provide a way to let the user select an item from a group of items. To create a group of radio buttons, you can place two or more radio buttons within a *group box*. Then, when the user selects one radio button, all the other radio buttons in the group are automatically deselected. Since the user can only select one radio button within each group, these buttons present mutually exclusive choices.

Check boxes provide a way to present the user with choices that are not mutually exclusive. That means that if the user checks or unchecks one check box, it doesn't affect the other check boxes on the form.

A form with five more types of controls

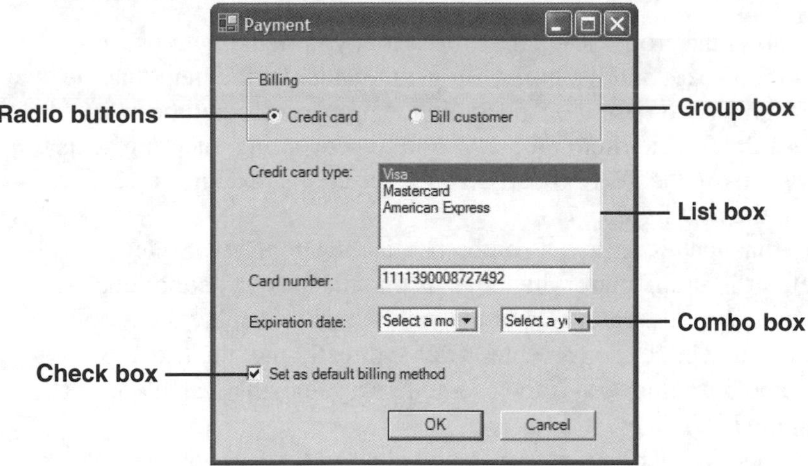

Description

- A *combo box* lets the user select one option from a drop-down list of items. A combo box can also let the user enter text into the text box portion of the combo box.
- A *list box* lets the user select one or more options from a list of items. If a list box contains more items than can be displayed at one time, a vertical scroll bar is added automatically.
- *Radio buttons* let the user select one option from a group of options.
- A *group box* can group related controls. For example, it's common to place related radio buttons within a group box. Then, the user can only select one of the radio buttons in the group.
- A *check box* lets the user select or deselect an option.

Figure 10-1 Five more types of controls

How to work with combo boxes and list boxes

Figure 10-2 shows the properties and methods that you're likely to use as you work with combo boxes and list boxes. To get the index of the item that the user selects, for example, you use the SelectedIndex property. To get the selected item itself, you use the SelectedItem property. And to get a string that represents the selected item, you use the Text property. You'll see coding examples that use these properties in the next figure.

One property that applies only to a combo box is the DropDownStyle property. The default is DropDown, which means that the user can either click on the drop-down arrow at the right side of the combo box to display the drop-down list and select an item, or he can enter a value directly into the text box portion of the combo box. Note that if the user enters a value, that value doesn't have to appear in the list.

If you want to restrict user entries to just the values in the list, you can set the DropDownStyle property to DropDownList. Then, the user can only select a value from the list or enter a value that appears in the list.

The third option for the DropDownStyle property is Simple. Like the DropDown setting, this setting lets the user enter any value into the text box portion of the control. However, instead of having to click on an arrow to display the list, the list is always visible.

One property that applies only to a list box is the SelectionMode property. The default is One, which means that the user can only select one item from the list box. However, you can let the user select multiple items by setting this property to MultiSimple or MultiExtended. If you set it to MultiSimple, the user can only select multiple entries by clicking on them. If you set it to MultiExtended, the user can hold down the Ctrl and Shift keys to select nonadjacent and adjacent items. This works just as it does for any standard Windows application. By the way, you can also set this property to None, in which case the user can't select an entry. You might use this setting if you just want to display items.

When you work with the items in a list box or combo box, you should realize that you're actually working with the items in a collection. To refer to this collection, you use the Items property of the control. Then, you can use an index to refer to any item in the collection. Or, you can use properties and methods that the .NET Framework provides for working with collections. The most common properties and methods are summarized in this figure.

The most common event for working with combo boxes and list boxes is the SelectedIndexChanged event. This event occurs when the value of the SelectedIndex property changes, which happens when the user selects a different item from the list. For a combo box, you can also use the TextChanged event to detect when the user enters a value into the text box portion of the control. Keep in mind, though, that this event will occur each time a single character is added, changed, or deleted.

Common members of list box and combo box controls

Property	Description
`SelectedIndex`	The index of the selected item. Items are numbered from 0. If no item is selected, this property has a value of -1.
`SelectedItem`	The object that contains the selected item.
`Text`	The contents of the text box portion of a combo box control.
`Sorted`	If set to true, the items in the list are sorted alphabetically.
`Items`	Provides access to the collection of items in a list box or combo box list.
`DropDownStyle`	Determines whether the user can edit the text box portion of a combo box and whether the user must click the arrow button to display the list. If this property is set to DropDown or Simple, the user can enter any value into the text box portion. If it's set to DropDownList, the user must select an item from the list or type an existing list item into the text box portion of the control. If this property is set to DropDown or DropDownList, the user must click the arrow to display the list. If it's set to Simple, the list is always visible.
`SelectionMode`	Determines whether the user can select more than one item from a list box. If this property is set to One, the user can only select one item. If it's set to MultiSimple or MultiExtended, the user can select multiple items.
Event	**Description**
`SelectedIndexChanged`	Occurs when the user selects a different item from the list.
`TextChanged`	Occurs when the user enters a value into the text box portion of a combo box.

Common members of the Items collection

Index	Description
`[index]`	Gets or sets the item at the specified index in the list.
Property	**Description**
`Count`	Gets the number of items in the list.
Method	**Description**
`Add(object)`	Adds the specified item to the list.
`Insert(index, object)`	Inserts an item into the list at the specified index.
`Remove(object)`	Removes the specified item from the list.
`RemoveAt(index)`	Removes the item at the specified index from the list.
`Clear()`	Removes all items from the list.

Description

- To work with the items in a list box or combo box list, you use the Items property of the control. To refer to any item in this collection, you can use an index.

Figure 10-2 How to work with combo boxes and list boxes

Code examples for working with combo boxes and list boxes

After you add a combo box or list box to a form and set its properties the way you want, you can use code like that shown in figure 10-3 to work with the control. Here, the first example uses a foreach loop to load the name of each month in an array into a combo box. Each time through the loop, the Add method is used to add a month name to the Items collection for this combo box.

Notice that the first item in the array that's loaded into the list indicates that the user should select a month from the list. This is a common technique that's used to provide instructions to the user. As you'll see later in this chapter, though, you'll need to include additional code when you use this technique to be sure that the user selects an item other than the one that provides instructions.

The second example is similar, but it uses a for loop to load eight integer values into a combo box. The first value is the current year, and the next values are the seven years that follow. Like the combo box that contains the names of the months, the first entry in this combo box provides instructions for the user.

The third example shows how you can load a list box like the one shown in figure 10-1. To make sure that no items have already been loaded into this list box, this example begins by calling the Clear method to clear all the items. Then, it adds three items to the list box. Finally, it sets the SelectedIndex property to 0, which causes the first item in the list to be selected.

Although it's not shown here, it's common to put code that loads a combo box or list box in the event handler for the Load event of the Form. That way, the combo box is loaded when the form is loaded. After that, the user can select an item from the combo box or list box and other methods can get information about that item.

The statements in the fourth example show four ways that you can get information from a combo or list box. The first statement uses the SelectedIndex property to get the index of the item that's currently selected in the Years combo box. The second statement shows how to get the value that's displayed in the text box portion of this combo box. The third statement shows how to get the value of the item that's currently selected in this combo box. Notice that because the SelectedItem property returns an object type, you must cast this object to the appropriate data type to get the value of the item. Finally, the fourth statement uses an index to get the second item in the Months combo box. Since the value of this item is a string, the ToString method is used to get the value of this item.

The fifth example shows how to use the Add, Insert, and RemoveAt methods to work with the items in a combo box list. This example begins with a for loop that adds three names to the list. Then, the Insert method inserts a new name at the beginning of the list, and the RemoveAt method removes the last item from the list. When you use these methods, you indicate the index where you want the item inserted or removed. Finally, the last statement shows how you can initialize a combo box so that no value is selected. To do that, you set the SelectedIndex property of the control to -1.

Code that loads the Months combo box shown in figure 10-1

```
string[] months =
    {"Select a month...",
    "January", "February", "March", "April",
    "May", "June", "July", "August",
    "September", "October", "November", "December"};

foreach (string month in months)
    cboExpirationMonth.Items.Add(month);
```

Code that loads the Years combo box shown in figure 10-1

```
int year = DateTime.Today.Year;
int endYear = year + 8;
cboExpirationYear.Items.Add("Select a year...");
while (year < endYear)
{
    cboExpirationYear.Items.Add(year);
    year++;
}
```

Code that clears and loads the list box shown in figure 10-1

```
lstCreditCardType.Items.Clear();
lstCreditCardType.Items.Add("Visa");
lstCreditCardType.Items.Add("Mastercard");
lstCreditCardType.Items.Add("American Express");
lstCreditCardType.SelectedIndex = 0;            // select the first item
```

Statements that get information from a combo box or list box

```
int expYearIndex = cboExpirationYear.SelectedIndex;
string expYearText = cboExpirationYear.Text;
int expYearValue = (int) cboExpirationYear.SelectedItem;
string expMonthValue = cboExpirationMonth.Items[1].ToString();
```

Code that works with a combo box of names

```
string[] names = {"Doug Lowe", "Anne Prince", "Ed Koop"};
foreach (string name in names)
    cboNames.Items.Add(name);
cboNames.Items.Insert(0, "Joel Murach");
cboNames.Items.RemoveAt(3);
cboNames.SelectedIndex = -1;                    // don't select an item
```

Notes

- You can also use the String Collection Editor to load items into a combo box or list box. To display this editor, select the control in the Form Designer, then click the ellipsis button (...) that appears when you select the Items property in the Properties window.
- In chapter 19, you'll learn how to load combo boxes and list boxes with data that's stored in a database.

Figure 10-3 Code examples for working with combo boxes and list boxes

How to work with check boxes and radio buttons

Figure 10-4 shows you how to work with check boxes and radio buttons. The main difference between these two types of controls is that radio buttons in a group are mutually exclusive and check boxes operate independently. In other words, if the user selects a radio button in a group, all of the other buttons are automatically turned off. In contrast, when the user selects a check box, it has no effect on the other check boxes on the form, even if they appear as a group.

To group radio buttons, you typically place them in a group box control. If you place any radio buttons outside of a group, however, all of the radio buttons on the form that aren't in a group box function as a group.

The property you're most likely to use when working with radio buttons and check boxes is the Checked property. This property can have a value of either true or false to indicate whether or not the control is checked. You can see how this property is used in the examples in this figure.

The two statements in the first example set the Checked properties of a radio button and a check box to true. Then, the if-else statement in the second example tests the Checked property of the radio button. If the value of this property is true, a method named EnableControls is executed. But if the value of this property is false, it indicates that another radio button is selected. In that case, a method named DisableControls is executed.

Notice that the if-else statement in this example is coded within the event handler for the CheckedChanged event of the control. This event occurs when you select or deselect a radio button or check box, and it's the event you're most likely to use. Also note that because the Checked property contains a Boolean value, you could code the if clause without the equality operator like this:

```
if (rdoCreditCard.Checked)
```

The third example in this figure simply retrieves the Checked property of the check box and stores it in a Boolean variable. If the user has checked this box, this variable will be set to true. Otherwise, it will be set to false.

How to work with group boxes

Figure 10-4 also illustrates how to use a group box. For example, the group box shown at the top of this figure contains two radio buttons. That makes it clear that these controls function as a group. You specify the name of the group, which is displayed in the upper left corner of the group box, by setting the Text property of the control.

When you use a group box, you should know that all the controls it contains will move with the group box when you move it in the Form Designer. You should also know that you can't add existing controls on a form to a group box by dragging the group box over them. Instead, you have to add the group box and then drag the controls into the group box.

A group box that contains two radio buttons

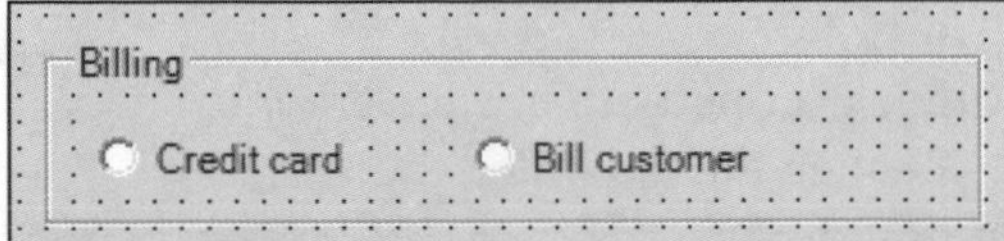

Common members of radio button and check box controls

Property	Description
`Checked`	Gets or sets a Boolean value that indicates whether the control is checked.
Event	**Description**
`CheckedChanged`	Occurs when the user checks or unchecks the control.

Code that sets the value of a radio button or check box

```
rdoCreditCard.Checked = true;
chkDefault.Checked = true;
```

Code that checks the value of a radio button

```
private void rdoCreditCard_CheckedChanged(object sender, System.EventArgs e)
{
    if (rdoCreditCard.Checked == true)
        EnableControls();
    else
        DisableControls();
}
```

Code that gets the value of a check box

```
bool isDefaultBilling = chkDefault.Checked;
```

Description

- To determine whether a radio button or check box is checked, you test its Checked property.
- You can use a group box to group controls. Group boxes are typically used to group controls like radio buttons that function as a group.
- To add controls to a group box, drag them from the Toolbox into the group box. If you've already added the controls you want to include in the group box to the form, just drag them into the group box.
- Any radio buttons that aren't placed within a group box function as a separate group.
- If you move a group box, all of the controls it contains move with it.

Figure 10-4 How to work with radio buttons, check boxes, and group boxes

How to use Tab Order view to set the tab order

In chapter 2, you learned how to use the TabIndex property to change the *tab order* of the controls on a form. An easier way to change the tab order, though, is to use Tab Order view. This view is illustrated in figure 10-5.

When you display a form in Tab Order view, an index value is displayed at the left of each control that indicates the control's position in the tab order. Notice that the index values of the two radio button controls indicate their position in the tab order relative to the group box that contains them.

To change the tab order, you click on each control in the appropriate sequence. As you click on each control, the numbers are displayed as shown in the second form in this figure. Here, I clicked on the list box, followed by the text box, followed by the two combo boxes, followed by the check box, followed by the two buttons and then the group box. That way, when the form is first displayed, the focus will be on the list box. Then, when the user presses the Tab key, the focus will move through the controls in sequence.

Notice that when I selected the group box control, the main indexes of the radio buttons within this control changed too so that they're the same as the group box. However, the sub index of each radio button didn't change. In other words, the indexes of the radio buttons relative to each other remained the same. If you wanted to change these indexes, though, you could do that by clicking on them just like any other control.

Also notice in the second form that I didn't set the tab index for any of the labels. In most cases, it's not necessary to change the tab order of controls that can't receive the focus.

One case where you will want to include a label control explicitly in the tab order is if it defines an access key. In that case, you'll want to position it in the tab order just before the control it identifies. Then, if the user presses the access key for that control, the focus will move to the control it identifies since it's next in the tab order.

A form in Tab Order view before and after the tab order is changed

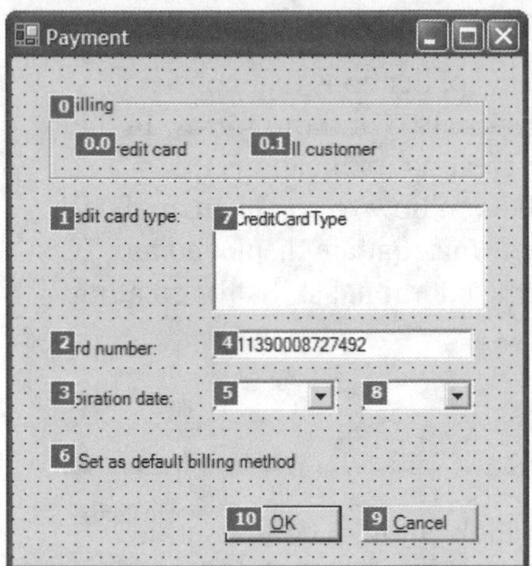

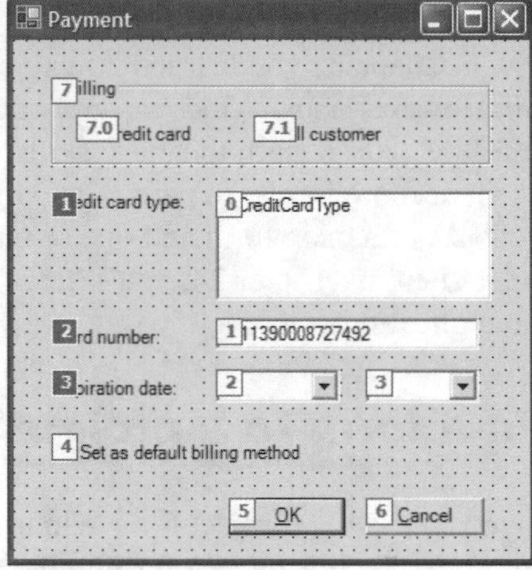

How to use Tab Order view to change the tab order

- To display a form in Tab Order view, select the form and then select the View→Tab Order command. This displays the tab index for each control as in the first form above.
- To change the tab indexes of the controls, click on the controls in the sequence you want to use. As you click, the new tab indexes appear as in the second form above.
- If a group box contains other controls, the controls in the group box are displayed with sub indexes as illustrated by the radio buttons above. Then, you can click on the group box to change its index and the main indexes of the controls it contains. To change the sub indexes of the controls in the group box, click on them individually.

Description

- The *tab order* determines the order in which controls receive the focus when the Tab key is pressed. The TabIndex property of the controls determines this order.
- By default, the value of a control's TabIndex property is determined by the sequence in which it's added to the form. The TabIndex property is set to 0 for the first control, to 1 for the second control, and so on.
- A label can't receive the focus. As a result, you typically don't need to include the labels in the tab order. However, if the label defines an access key, the TabIndex property of the label should be set to one less than its related control. That way, the related control will receive the focus when the access key for the label is activated.
- When setting the tab order, you can skip controls whose TabStop, Enabled, or Visible properties have been set to false, unless those properties will change as the form runs.

Figure 10-5 How to use Tab Order view to set the tab order

How to work with multi-form projects

In previous chapters, you learned how to create applications that consist of a single form. However, most Windows applications use two or more forms. In the topics that follow, you'll learn the basic skills for creating applications that consist of two or more forms. In particular, you'll learn how to create an application that consists of a main form and one or more forms that are displayed as dialog boxes. Then, in chapter 24, you'll learn some additional skills for creating multi-form applications.

How to add a form to a project

When you start a new project for a Windows application, it consists of a single blank form. To add another form to the project, you use the Add New Item dialog box shown in figure 10-6. From this dialog box, you select the Windows Form template and then enter the name of the new form. When you click the Open button, the new form is created with the name you specify.

You can also add an existing form to a project using the Add Existing Item dialog box. This can be useful if you want to use the same form in two different projects or if you want to create a form that's similar to an existing form. Note that when you add an existing form from another project, that form is copied into the new project. That way, you don't have to worry about changing the original form inadvertently.

The Add New Item dialog box

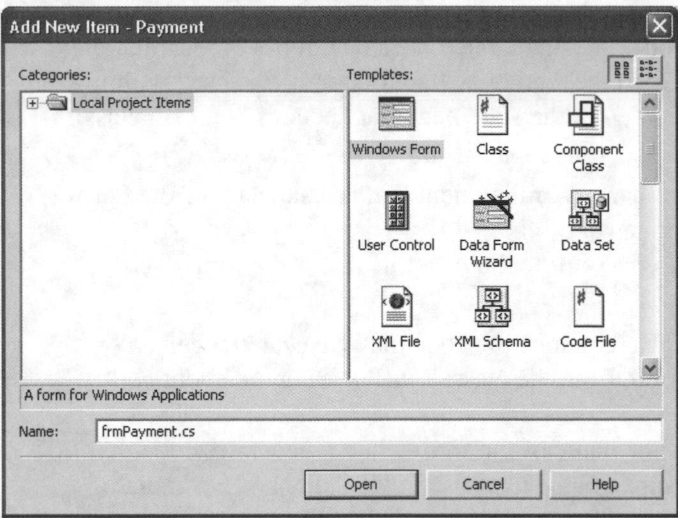

How to add a new form

- Display the Add New Item dialog box by selecting the Project→Add New Item command. Or, select the Add→Add New Item command from the shortcut menu that's displayed when you right-click on the project in the Solution Explorer.
- To add a new form, select the Windows Form template from the Add New Item dialog box, enter a name for the form, and click the Open button.

How to add an existing form

- Display the Add Existing Item dialog box by selecting the Project→Add Existing Item command. Or, select the Add→Add Existing Item command from the shortcut menu for the project.
- To add an existing form, select the cs file for the form from the Add Existing Item dialog box and then click the Open button.

Note

- When you name a form, we recommend you use the prefix *frm* so it's clear that the file contains a form.

Figure 10-6 How to add a form to a project

The code that's generated for a new form

Figure 10-7 shows the code that's generated for a new form. Notice that the name you specify for the form in the Add New Item dialog box is used within the generated code. First, it's used in the statement that declares the form class:

```
public class frmPayment : System.Windows.Forms.Form
```

This statement defines a class named frmPayment that is a subclass of the Form class defined in the .NET Framework.

The form name is also used to define the *constructor* for the form class:

```
public frmPayment(){...}
```

The constructor is a method that contains the code that's executed when an object is created, or constructed, from the class. You'll learn more about constructors in chapter 12.

Since Visual Studio uses the name of the form when it generates code, it makes sense to specify the name you want to use in the Add New Form dialog box. If you don't, however, you can modify this code by changing the name of the form. You'll learn how to do that in the next figure.

Before I go on, you should notice the lines throughout the generated code that start with three slashes (///). These lines are *documentation comments* that are used to document the contents of a class. Although you can change these comments, you're not likely to do that unless you're creating your own classes. If you rename a form, however, you may want to change the name that's included in the comment that appears just before the class declaration.

The generated code for a new form named frmPayment

```
using System;
using System.Drawing;
using System.Collections;
using System.ComponentModel;
using System.Windows.Forms;

namespace Payment
{
    /// <summary>
    /// Summary description for frmPayment.
    /// </summary>
    public class frmPayment : System.Windows.Forms.Form
    {
        /// <summary>
        /// Required designer variable.
        /// </summary>
        private System.ComponentModel.Container components = null;

        public frmPayment()
        {
            //
            // Required for Windows Form Designer support
            //
            InitializeComponent();

            //
            // TODO: Add any constructor code after InitializeComponent call
            //
        }

        /// <summary>
        /// Clean up any resources being used.
        /// </summary>
        protected override void Dispose( bool disposing )
        {
            if( disposing )
            {
                if(components != null)
                {
                    components.Dispose();
                }
            }
            base.Dispose( disposing );
        }

        #region Windows Form Designer generated code

    }
}
```

Description

- The code shown above is generated automatically by Visual Studio when you add a new form to a project.
- The name you specify for the form in the Add New Item dialog box appears several times in the generated code. Because of that, you'll need to change each occurrence of this name if you want to change the name of the form. See figure 10-8 for details.
- The form that's created by default when you start a new project also includes a Main method that starts the application. See figure 10-9 for details.

Figure 10-7 The code that's generated for a new form

How to rename a form

Figure 10-8 shows a procedure that you can use to rename a form. You're most likely to use this procedure to rename the form that's added to a project by default when you create the project. However, you can also use it to rename a form that you added using one of the techniques presented in figure 10-6.

To start, you change the name of the file that contains the code for the form. To do that, you can select the form in the Solution Explorer and then change the File Name property of the form. In the project shown in this figure, for example, I renamed the form that was originally named Form1.cs to frmCustomer.cs.

Next, you change the name of the form so it corresponds with the new file name. To do that, you select the form in the Form Designer and then change the Name property of the form. When you do, Visual Studio automatically changes the class declaration and the constructor for the form.

If you add any event handlers for form events before you rename a form, you'll also need to change the event handlers and the event wiring so they use the new name. In this figure, for example, you can see the method declaration and event wiring for the Load event of a form. Remember that the event wiring is included in the Windows Form Designer generated code region, so you'll need to display this region to locate and change the event wiring.

A project that contains two forms

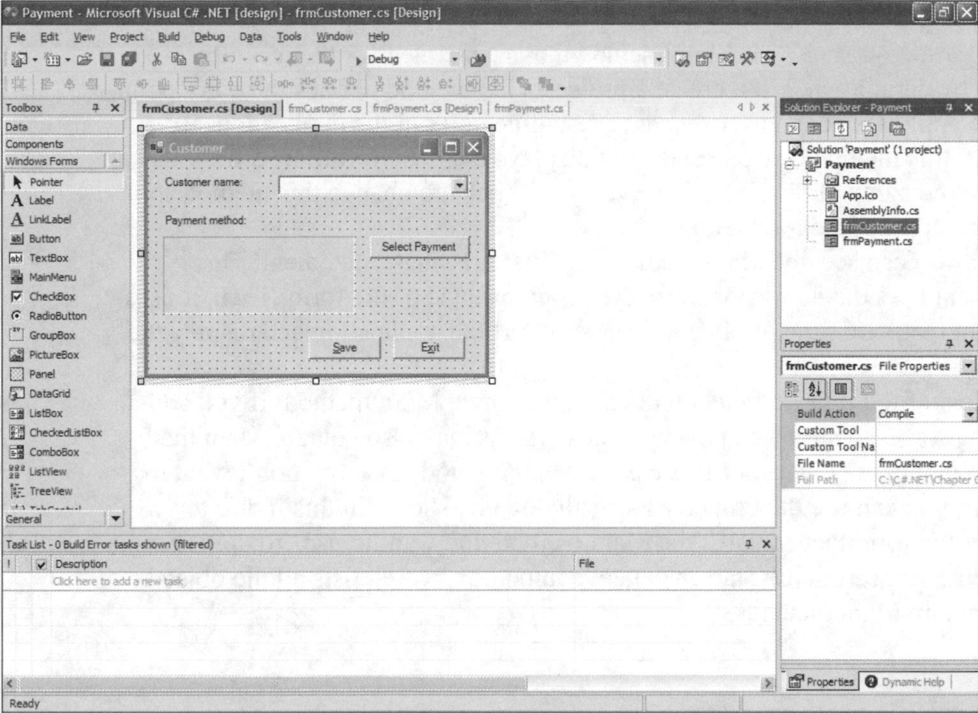

The Load event for the frmPayment form

```
private void frmPayment_Load(object sender, System.EventArgs e)
```

The wiring for the Load event handler

```
this.Load += new System.EventHandler(this.frmPayment_Load);
```

How to change the name of a form

1. Select the form in the Solution Explorer. Then, change the File Name property of the form to change the name of the form file.
2. Select the form in the Form Designer. Then, change the Name property of the form. This automatically changes the name of the form class and the name used in the constructor for the form.
3. If you've added event handlers for any form events, use the Code Editor to change the event handlers and the event wiring so they use the new name.
4. If the form is the startup object for the project, use the Code Editor to change the form name in the Main method (see figure 10-9).

Note

- Although you can change the name of a form file without changing the name of the form class, it's a good programming practice to use the same name for the file and class.

Figure 10-8 How to rename a form

How to display the first form of an application

Figure 10-9 shows the Main method that's generated for the form that's added by default when you create a project. This method defines the entry point for the application, and it's executed every time you run the application. By default, this method contains code that displays the default form (Form1). If you change the name of this form, however, you'll need to change this method so it uses the appropriate form name.

As you can see, the Main method consists of a single statement. This statement uses the new keyword to create an instance of the form. Then, it uses the Run method of the Application class to start the application and display the form.

Most of the time, a project will contain a single Main method. If you add existing forms to a project, however, those forms may also contain Main methods. In that case, you can just delete the Main methods that you don't want to use. Or, you can use the Property Pages dialog box shown in this figure to specify the form that contains the Main method you want to use. To do that, you select the form from the Startup Object combo box, which lists all the objects that contain Main methods.

Code that defines the main entry point for an application

```
/// <summary>
/// The main entry point for the application.
/// </summary>
[STAThread]
static void Main()
{
    Application.Run(new Form1());
}
```

The Property Pages dialog box

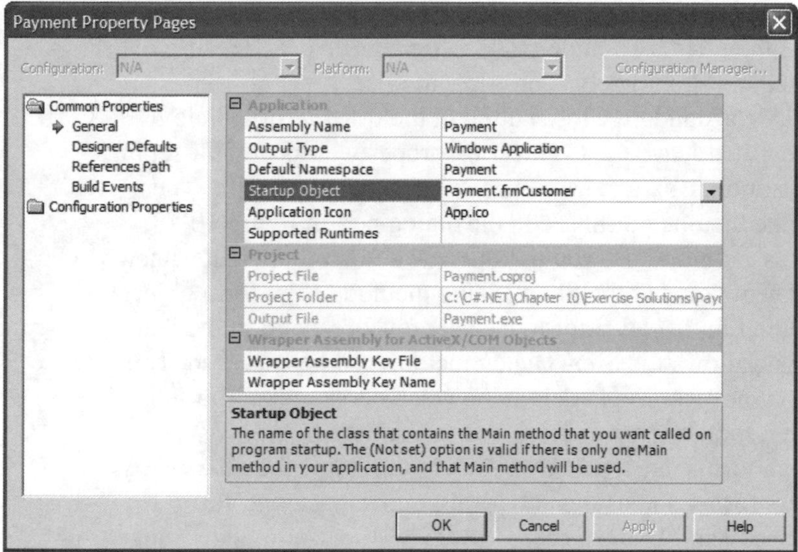

Description

- When you create a Windows application, Visual Studio automatically generates a Main method in the default form. This method defines the main entry point for the application.
- The Main method uses the Run method of the Application class to display the first form for the application. If you want to display a form other than the default form when the application starts, you can change the form name that's specified on the Run method.
- If you use the Form Designer to change the name of the form that's displayed by the Main method, Visual Studio doesn't automatically update the name in the Main method. As a result, you'll need to change this name manually.
- If you add existing forms to a project, more than one form in the project may contain a Main method. Then, you can delete the Main methods that you don't want to use. Or, you can use the Project→*ProjectName* Properties command to display the Property Pages dialog box and then select the form that you want to use from the Startup Object list.

Figure 10-9 How to display the first form of an application

How to display a form as a dialog box

When designing applications that contain two or more forms, it's common to display a form as a dialog box, also called a *modal form*. In figure 10-10, for example, you can see a Payment form that's displayed as a dialog box. This form is displayed when the user clicks the Select Payment button in the Customers form that's also shown here.

When you create a form that will be displayed as a dialog box, you typically set the form properties as shown in this figure. These property settings prevent the user from changing the size of the form or from closing the form other than by using the controls you provide on the form. Note that although setting the ControlBox property to False removes the Maximize button from a form, the user can still maximize the form by double-clicking on its title bar. Because of that, you should also set the MaximizeBox property to false.

If you want to include a standard Close button in the title bar of a dialog box, you can do that too. Just leave the ControlBox property at its default setting of True, and set the MaximizeBox and MinimizeBox properties to false. Then, the title bar will look like the one you'll see in the dialog box in figure 10-13.

To display a form as a dialog box, you use the new keyword to create a new instance of the form. Then, you call the ShowDialog method of the form object. When you use this method to display a form, the user must respond to the dialog box before the code that follows the ShowDialog method can be executed. This code typically tests the user response to determine what's done next. You'll learn more about getting the response from a dialog box in the next figure.

In addition to modal forms, an application can also contain *modeless forms*. When you use modeless forms, the user can typically move back and forth between the forms as necessary. In most cases, that gives the user a wider range of possible actions, which means that the program must include code that provides for all of those actions. While this type of form is appropriate for some applications, it can make an application more difficult to develop. So whenever possible, you should use dialog boxes to control the flow of the application and the user actions.

The Payment form displayed as a dialog box

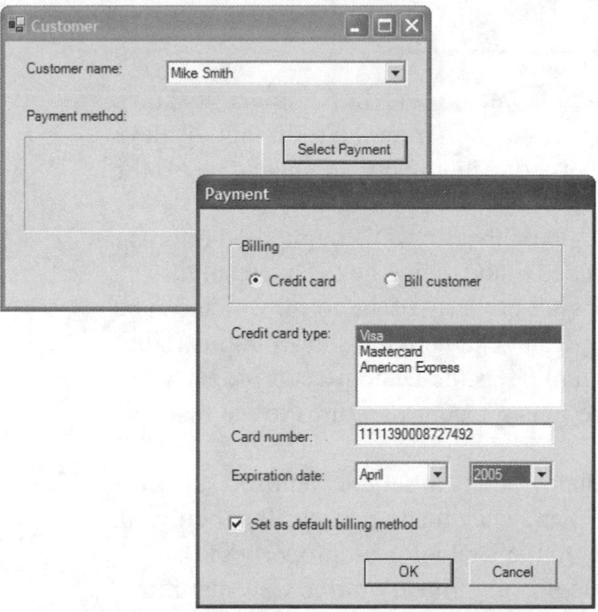

Properties for creating custom dialog boxes

Property	Description
`FormBorderStyle`	Typically set to FixedDialog to prevent the user from resizing the form by dragging its border.
`ControlBox`	Typically set to false so the control box and the Maximize, Minimize, and Close buttons don't appear in the title bar of the form.
`MaximizeBox`	Typically set to false so the user can't maximize the form by double-clicking the title bar.
`MinimizeBox`	Can be set to false to prevent the Minimize button from being displayed if the ControlBox property is set to true.

Code that creates and displays a custom dialog box

```
Form paymentForm = new frmPayment();
paymentForm.ShowDialog();
// execution continues here after the user responds to the dialog box
```

Description

- If you display a form as a dialog box, the user must respond to the form before continuing to any other forms. A form like this is sometimes referred to as a custom dialog box or a *modal form*.
- You use the ShowDialog method of a form object to display the form as a dialog box. After the user responds to the dialog box, execution continues with the statement that follows the ShowDialog method.

Figure 10-10 How to display a form as a dialog box

How to pass data between a form and a custom dialog box

Figure 10-11 shows how to pass data between forms. In particular, it shows how to get the user response to a custom dialog box from the form that displays it, and it shows how to use the Tag property of a dialog box to make data available to the form that displays it.

When you display a form as a dialog box, the ShowDialog method returns a value that indicates how the user responded to the dialog box. This result is determined by the value of the DialogResult property of the form, which can be set to any of the members of the DialogResult enumeration shown in this figure. The first statement shown here, for example, sets the DialogResult property to DialogResult.OK. As soon as this property is set, control returns to the main form.

Another way to set the result of a dialog box is to set the DialogResult property of a button in the dialog box. Then, when the user clicks that button, the DialogResult property of the form is set to the DialogResult property of the button. If, for example, you set the DialogResult property of the Cancel button on the Payment form shown in figure 10-10 to Cancel, that value is returned when the user clicks that button and the dialog box is closed. In that case, no code is required for the Click event of that button unless some additional processing is required.

You can also set the DialogResult property of a button to Cancel by setting the CancelButton property of the form. Then, the Cancel member of the DialogResult enumeration is returned when the user clicks that button. Here again, no code is required for the Click event of the button unless some additional processing is required.

After the DialogResult property is set and control returns to the form that displayed the dialog box, that form can use the DialogResult enumeration to determine how the user responded. To see how this works, take a look at the third example in this figure. Here, the first statement creates an instance of the Payment form. Then, the second statement displays that form using the ShowDialog method and stores the result of that method in a DialogResult variable named button. Next, an if statement is used to test if the result is equal to DialogResult.OK.

Another way to pass data between a dialog box and another form is to use the Tag property of the dialog box. The second statement in this figure, for example, sets the Tag property of a dialog box to a variable named msg. Note that you must set this property before control returns to the main form.

Once control returns to the main form, you can get the data that was stored in the Tag property as shown in the last statement of the example. Here, the Text property of a label is set to the value that was stored in the Tag property of the dialog box. Notice that because the Tag property holds an object type, the object must be converted to a string before it can be assigned to the Text property.

An enumeration that works with dialog boxes

Enumeration	Members
`DialogResult`	OK, Cancel, Yes, No, Abort, Retry, Ignore, None

The Tag property

Property	Description
`Tag`	Gets or sets data associated with the form or a control. The Tag property holds a reference to an object type, which means that it can hold any type of data.

A statement that sets the DialogResult property of a form

```
this.DialogResult = DialogResult.OK;
```

A statement that sets the Tag property of a form

```
this.Tag = msg;
```

Code that uses the result of a dialog box and the Tag property

```
Form paymentForm = new frmPayment();
DialogResult button = paymentForm.ShowDialog();
if (button == DialogResult.OK)
    lblPayment.Text = paymentForm.Tag.ToString();
```

How to use the DialogResult enumeration

- The DialogResult enumeration provides members that represent the values that a dialog box can return. The ShowDialog method returns a member of this enumeration.
- You specify the result value of a custom dialog box by setting its DialogResult property. Or, you can set the DialogResult property of a button in the dialog box. Then, when the user clicks that button, the DialogResult property of the form is set accordingly.
- If you set the CancelButton property of a form to a button on that form, the DialogResult property of that button is automatically set to Cancel.
- After you set the DialogResult property of a dialog box, the form is closed and control is returned to the form that displayed it. If you close a dialog box without setting the DialogResult property, a value of Cancel is returned to the main form.

How to use the Tag property

- The Tag property provides a convenient way to pass data between forms in a multi-form application. A dialog box can set its Tag property before it returns control to the main form. Then, the main form can get the data from this property and use it as necessary.
- Because the Tag property is an object type, you must explicitly cast it to the appropriate type to retrieve the data it contains. Or, you can use the ToString method to convert the data to a string.

Note

- You can also pass data between forms using a public variable.

Figure 10-11 How to pass data between a form and a custom dialog box

How to use the MessageBox class

Although you can create custom dialog boxes using the techniques you learned in the last two topics, it's also common to use the MessageBox class to display certain types of dialog boxes. In chapter 7, for example, you learned how to use the MessageBox class to display a simple dialog box with an error message and an OK button. Now, you'll learn how to use the MessageBox class to display more complex dialog boxes, and you'll learn how to get the user's response to these dialog boxes.

How to display a dialog box and get the user response

Figure 10-12 shows how to display a dialog box and get a response from a user. To display a dialog box, you use the Show method shown at the top of this figure. As you can see, you can specify up to five arguments on this method. The first argument is the text message that you want to display. Although this is the only argument that's required, you'll typically code the second argument too, which displays a caption in the title bar of the dialog box.

You can use the third argument to control the buttons that are displayed in the dialog box. You can use the fourth argument to control the icon that's displayed in the dialog box. And you can use the fifth argument to control the default button that's activated when the user presses the Enter key. To specify any of these arguments, you use the constants in the first three enumerations that are summarized in this figure.

Like the ShowDialog method, the Show method of the MessageBox class returns a value that indicates how the user responded to the dialog box. The value that's returned is one of the members of the DialogResult enumeration. These members represent the buttons that can be displayed in a dialog box, and the return value is automatically set to the appropriate member when the user clicks a button.

The first example in this figure shows how to code a Show method that specifies all five arguments. Notice that the third argument indicates that only Yes and No buttons should be included in the dialog box, and the fifth argument indicates that the second button, in this case, No, should be the default button. You can see the result of this statement in this figure.

The second example shows how you can use the DialogResult value that's returned by the Show method to determine which button the user clicked in the dialog box. Here, an if statement tests if the DialogResult value that was returned by the Show method is equal to DialogResult.Yes. If it is, it means that the user clicked the Yes button, and the code within the if statement is executed.

The syntax for the Show method of the MessageBox class

```
MessageBox.Show(text[, caption [, buttons[, icon[, defaultButton]]]]);
```

The enumerations that work with the MessageBox class

Enumeration	Members
`MessageBoxButtons`	OK, OKCancel, YesNo, YesNoCancel, AbortRetryIgnore
`MessageBoxIcon`	None, Information, Error, Warning, Exclamation, Question, Asterisk, Hand, Stop
`MessageBoxDefaultButton`	Button1, Button2, Button3
`DialogResult`	OK, Cancel, Yes, No, Abort, Retry, Ignore

A statement that displays a dialog box and gets the user response

```
DialogResult button =
    MessageBox.Show("Are you sure you want to save this data?", "Payment",
        MessageBoxButtons.YesNo,
        MessageBoxIcon.Question,
        MessageBoxDefaultButton.Button2);
```

The dialog box that's displayed

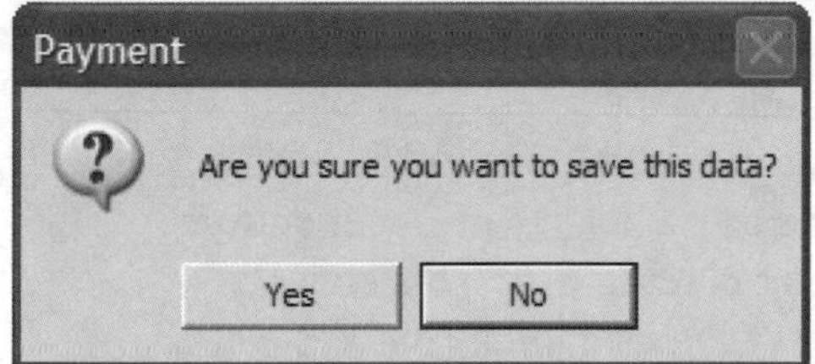

A statement that checks the user response

```
if (button == DialogResult.Yes)
    isDataSaved = true;
```

Description

- You can use the Show method of the MessageBox class to display a message to a user and accept a response from the user.
- You use the first three enumerations listed above to specify the buttons and icon that will appear in the dialog box and the button that's treated as the default.
- If you omit the *buttons* argument, the OK button is displayed by default. If you omit the *icon* argument, no icon is displayed by default. If you omit the *defaultButton* argument, the first button is the default.
- The Show method returns a DialogResult value that corresponds to one of the members of the DialogResult enumeration. You can use this value to determine which button the user clicked.

Figure 10-12 How to display a dialog box and get the user response

How to cancel the Closing event of a form

Figure 10-13 shows how you can use a dialog box to cancel the Closing event of a form. This technique is often used when a user attempts to close a form that contains unsaved data.

To start, it's important to understand that the Closing event is executed when the user attempts to close the form but before the form is actually closed. For example, this event occurs if the user clicks a button on the form that calls the Close method for the form. It also occurs if the user clicks the Close button in the upper right corner of the form.

This figure presents the event handler for the Closing event of a form. Notice that this event handler receives two parameters. You can use the Cancel property of the second parameter, *e*, to determine whether or not the form is closed. By default, this property is set to false, which means that the form will be closed. If you don't want to close the form, you can set this property to true.

The event handler shown here starts by checking a class variable named isDataSaved to determine if the form contains unsaved data. If it doesn't, no additional processing is performed and the form is closed. If the form contains unsaved data, however, a dialog box is displayed that asks the user if the data should be saved. As you can see, this dialog box contains Yes, No, and Cancel buttons as well as a warning icon. Since the code for this dialog box doesn't specify a default button, the first button is the default.

After the dialog box is displayed, if statements are used to check the user's response and perform the appropriate action. If the user clicks the Cancel button, for example, the Cancel property of the e parameter is set to true. This cancels the Closing event and returns the user to the form. If the user clicks the Yes button, the code checks if the form contains valid data. If it does, the SaveData method is called to save the data and the form is closed. If it doesn't, the Cancel property of the e parameter is set to true and the Closing event is cancelled. Notice that no code is executed if the user clicks the No button. That means that the form is closed without saving the data.

The code for a dialog box that cancels the Closing event

```
private void frmCustomer_Closing(object sender,
    System.ComponentModel.CancelEventArgs e)
{
    if (isDataSaved == false)
    {
        string message =
            "This form contains unsaved data.\n\n" +
            "Do you want to save it?";

        DialogResult button =
            MessageBox.Show(message, "Customer",
            MessageBoxButtons.YesNoCancel,
            MessageBoxIcon.Warning);

        if (button == DialogResult.Yes)
        {
            if (IsValidData())
                this.SaveData();
            else
                e.Cancel = true;
        }
        if (button == DialogResult.Cancel)
            e.Cancel = true;
    }
}
```

The dialog box that's displayed by the code shown above

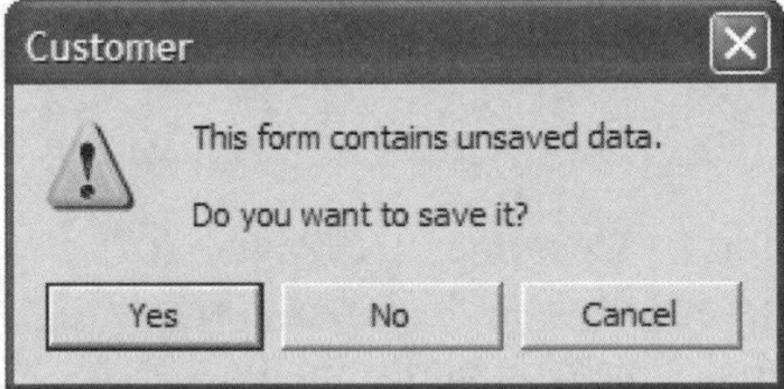

Description

- The event handler for the Closing event of a form receives a parameter named *e* that's created from the CancelEventArgs class. The Cancel property of this parameter lets you specify whether or not the event should be canceled. To cancel the event, set this property to true.

Figure 10-13 How to cancel the Closing event of a form

The Payment application

This chapter closes by presenting the operation, property settings, and code for a project that contains two forms that use the controls and coding techniques that were presented in this chapter. By studying the code for this application, you will get a better idea of how you can use these controls and techniques in your own applications.

The operation of the Payment application

Figure 10-14 shows how the Payment application works. To start, this application displays the Customer form. On this form, the user must select a customer from the Customer Name combo box. Then, the user must click the Select Payment button to display the Payment dialog box and specify payment information for the selected customer.

Within the Payment dialog box, the user can select to charge the customer's credit card and then enter the required information. Or, the user can select to bill the customer directly. To complete the form, the user clicks the OK button. Then, control is returned to the Customer form and the payment information is displayed on that form. To save the payment information, the user clicks the Save button.

The property settings for the Customer and Payment forms

Figure 10-15 presents the property settings for the Customer and Payment forms and their controls. As you can see, the properties for the Payment form have been set so this form looks and acts like a dialog box. In addition, the DropDownStyle properties for the two combo boxes have been set to DropDownList so the user must select an item from the list. Finally, the DialogResult property of the Cancel button has been set to Cancel, which happens automatically when the CancelButton property of the form is set to the Cancel button.

The code for the Customer form

Figure 10-16 presents the code for the Customer form. Notice that the Main method creates and displays an instance of this form when the application starts.

Immediately following the Main method, a Boolean variable named isDataSaved is declared and initialized to true. This variable determines whether the data that's currently displayed in the form has been saved. It's set to false any time the data in the Customer Name combo box or the Payment label changes. To accomplish that, both the SelectedIndexChanged event of the combo box and the TextChanged event of the label are wired to the DataChanged method.

The Customer form

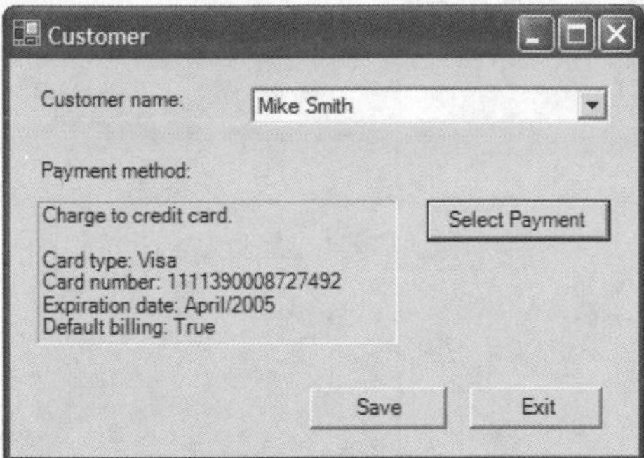

Two versions of the Payment dialog box

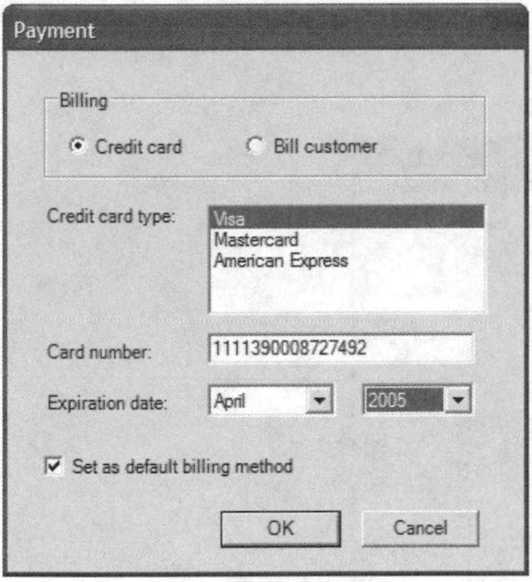

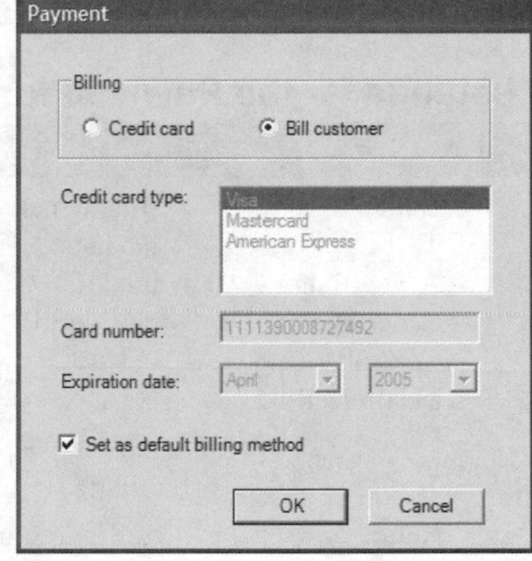

Description

- The Customer Name combo box in the Customer form lets the user select a customer.
- The Select Payment button in the Customer form displays the Payment dialog box, which lets the user specify payment information for the customer.
- If the Credit Card option is selected, the user must select a credit card type, enter a card number, and select an expiration month and year.
- If the Bill Customer option is selected, the Credit Card Type, Card Number, and Expiration Date controls are disabled.
- When the user clicks the OK button on the Payment form, control returns to the Customer form and the payment information is displayed in the Payment Method label.

Note

- This application doesn't actually save the data the user enters. In a production application, however, the data would be saved to a database or file.

Figure 10-14 The operation of the Payment application

The property settings for the Customer form

Default name	Property	Setting
Form1	Name Text AcceptButton CancelButton	frmCustomer Customer btnSave btnExit
ComboBox1	Name DropDownStyle	cboNames DropDownList
Label3	Name Text	lblPayment ""
Button1	Name	btnSave
Button2	Name	btnExit
Button3	Name	btnSelectPayment

The property settings for the Payment form

Default name	Property	Setting
Form2	Name Text AcceptButton CancelButton ControlBox MaximizeBox FormBorderStyle	frmPayment Payment btnOK btnCancel False False FixedDialog
GroupBox1	Text	Billing
RadioButton1	Name Checked	rdoCreditCard True
RadioButton2	Name	rdoBillCustomer
ListBox1	Name	lstCreditCardType
TextBox1	Name	txtCardNumber
ComboBox1	Name DropDownStyle	cboExpirationMonth DropDownList
ComboBox2	Name DropDownStyle	cboExpirationYear DropDownList
CheckBox1	Name Checked	chkDefault True
Button1	Name	btnOK
Button2	Name DialogResult	btnCancel Cancel

Description

- In addition to the properties shown above, you'll want to set the text and alignment properties so the forms look like the forms shown in figure 10-14.

Figure 10-15 The property settings for the Customer and Payment forms

The code for the Customer form **Page 1**

```
/// <summary>
/// The main entry point for the application.
/// </summary>
[STAThread]
static void Main()
{
    Application.Run(new frmCustomer());
}

bool isDataSaved = true;

private void frmCustomer_Load(object sender, System.EventArgs e)
{
    cboNames.Items.Add("Mike Smith");
    cboNames.Items.Add("Nancy Jones");
}

private void DataChanged(object sender, System.EventArgs e)
{
    // This event hander handles the SelectedIndexChanged event for the customer
    // name combo box and the TextChanged event for the Payment Method label.
    //
    isDataSaved = false;
}

private void btnSelectPayment_Click(object sender, System.EventArgs e)
{
    Form paymentForm = new frmPayment();
    DialogResult button = paymentForm.ShowDialog();
    if (button == DialogResult.OK)
        lblPayment.Text = paymentForm.Tag.ToString();
}

private void btnSave_Click(object sender, System.EventArgs e)
{
    if (IsValidData())
        SaveData();
}

private void SaveData()
{
    // The code for saving the data to a file or database goes here...
    //
    cboNames.SelectedIndex = -1;
    lblPayment.Text = "";
    isDataSaved = true;
    cboNames.Focus();
}
```

Figure 10-16 The code for the Customer form (part 1 of 2)

When the Customer form is loaded, the event handler for the Load event adds two names to the Customer Name combo box. In a production application, of course, the combo box would include many more names, and they would be loaded from a file or database. But for the purposes of this chapter, two names are sufficient.

When the user clicks the Select Payment button, the Click event handler for that button displays the Payment form as a dialog box. Then, if the user clicks the OK button in that dialog box, the payment data is displayed in the Payment Method label on the Customer form. As you can see, this data is stored in the Tag property of the Payment form.

If the user clicks the Save button, the Click event handler for that button calls the IsValidData method shown on page 2 of this listing. This method checks that the user has selected a customer and entered a payment. If so, the Click event handler calls the SaveData method. This method sets the SelectedIndex property of the Customer Name combo box to -1 so that no customer is selected, and it clears the Payment Method label. Then, it sets the isDataSaved variable to true and moves the focus to the combo box. In a production application, this data would be saved to a file or database.

The last method is executed when the user tries to close the Customer form. This is the same method you saw in figure 10-13, so you shouldn't have any trouble understanding how it works.

The code for the Payment form

Figurc 10-17 presents the code for the Payment form. To start, the event handler for the Load event of the form adds the appropriate items to the list box and the two combo boxes on the form. Then, it sets the SelectedIndex property for these controls so the first item is selected.

When the user clicks the OK button on this form, the Click event handler starts by calling the IsValidData method shown on page 2 of this listing. If the Credit Card radio button is selected, this method checks that the user entered a credit card number and selected an item other than the first one from the two combo boxes. That's necessary because the first item contains user instructions.

If the data is valid, the Click event handler for the OK button continues by creating a string that includes the payment information. Then, it stores that string in the Tag property of the Payment form. As you've already seen, the Customer form uses this property to display the payment information. Finally, the Click event handler sets the DialogResult property of the form to OK so that control is returned to the Customer form.

When the user selects one of the radio buttons on this form, the CheckedChanged event occurs. This event is wired to the Billing_CheckChanged event handler. If the Credit Card radio button is selected when this event handler is executed, it calls the EnableControls method to enable the other controls on the form so the user can enter the required information. If the Credit Card button isn't selected, however, it means that the Bill Customer button is selected. Then, this event handler calls the DisableControls method to disable the other controls.

The code for the Customer form **Page 2**

```
private bool IsValidData()
{
    if (cboNames.SelectedIndex == -1)
    {
        MessageBox.Show("You must select a customer.", "Entry Error");
        cboNames.Focus();
        return false;
    }
    if (lblPayment.Text == "")
    {
        MessageBox.Show("You must enter payment information.", "Entry Error");
        return false;
    }
    return true;
}

private void btnExit_Click(object sender, System.EventArgs e)
{
    this.Close();
}

private void frmCustomer_Closing(object sender,
    System.ComponentModel.CancelEventArgs e)
{
    if (isDataSaved == false)
    {
        string message =
            "This form contains unsaved data.\n\n" +
            "Do you want to save it?";

        DialogResult button =
            MessageBox.Show(message, "Customer",
            MessageBoxButtons.YesNoCancel,
            MessageBoxIcon.Warning);

        if (button == DialogResult.Yes)
        {
            if (IsValidData())
                this.SaveData();
            else
                e.Cancel = true;
        }
        if (button == DialogResult.Cancel)
            e.Cancel = true;
    }
}
```

Figure 10-16 The code for the Customer form (part 2 of 2)

The code for the Payment form

Page 1

```
private void frmPayment_Load(object sender, System.EventArgs e)
{
    lstCreditCardType.Items.Add("Visa");
    lstCreditCardType.Items.Add("Mastercard");
    lstCreditCardType.Items.Add("American Express");
    lstCreditCardType.SelectedIndex = 0;

    string[] months = {"Select a month...",
                       "January", "February", "March", "April",
                       "May", "June", "July", "August",
                       "September", "October", "November", "December"};
    foreach (string month in months)
        cboExpirationMonth.Items.Add(month);
    cboExpirationMonth.SelectedIndex = 0;

    int year = DateTime.Today.Year;
    int endYear = year + 8;
    cboExpirationYear.Items.Add("Select a year...");
    while (year < endYear)
    {
        cboExpirationYear.Items.Add(year);
        year++;
    }
    cboExpirationYear.SelectedIndex = 0;
}

private void btnOK_Click(object sender, System.EventArgs e)
{
    if (IsValidData())
    {
        string msg = null;
        if (rdoCreditCard.Checked == true)
        {
            msg += "Charge to credit card." + "\n";
            msg += "\n";
            msg += "Card type: " + lstCreditCardType.Text + "\n";
            msg += "Card number: " + txtCardNumber.Text + "\n";
            msg += "Expiration date: "
                + cboExpirationMonth.Text + "/"
                + cboExpirationYear.Text + "\n";
        }
        else
        {
            msg += "Send bill to customer." + "\n";
            msg += "\n";
        }
        bool isDefaultBilling = chkDefault.Checked;
        msg += "Default billing: " + isDefaultBilling;

        this.Tag = msg;
        this.DialogResult = DialogResult.OK;
    }
}
```

Figure 10-17 The code for the Payment form (part 1 of 2)

The code for the Payment form Page 2

```
private bool IsValidData()
{
    if (rdoCreditCard.Checked)
    {
        if (txtCardNumber.Text == "")
        {
            MessageBox.Show("You must enter a credit card number.",
                "Entry Error");
            txtCardNumber.Focus();
            return false;
        }
        if (cboExpirationMonth.SelectedIndex == 0)
        {
            MessageBox.Show("You must select a month.", "Entry Error");
            cboExpirationMonth.Focus();
            return false;
        }
        if (cboExpirationYear.SelectedIndex == 0)
        {
            MessageBox.Show("You must select a year.", "Entry Error");
            cboExpirationYear.Focus();
            return false;
        }
    }
    return true;
}

private void Billing_CheckedChanged(object sender, System.EventArgs e)
{
    // This event hander handles the CheckedChanged event of both radio buttons.
    //
    if (rdoCreditCard.Checked)
        EnableControls();
    else
        DisableControls();
}

private void EnableControls()
{
    lstCreditCardType.Enabled = true;
    txtCardNumber.Enabled = true;
    cboExpirationMonth.Enabled = true;
    cboExpirationYear.Enabled = true;
}

private void DisableControls()
{
    lstCreditCardType.Enabled = false;
    txtCardNumber.Enabled = false;
    cboExpirationMonth.Enabled = false;
    cboExpirationYear.Enabled = false;
}
```

Figure 10-17 The code for the Payment form (part 2 of 2)

Perspective

In this chapter, you learned how to use five new controls for building Windows applications. These controls are the ones you'll use most often. If you need to use any of the controls that weren't presented here, though, you should be able to figure out how to do that on your own. In most cases, it's just a matter of becoming familiar with the properties, methods, and events that are available, and you can usually do that by reviewing the documentation for the control and the class it's based on.

In addition, you learned how to work with a project that contains two or more forms. Specifically, you learned how to work with projects that use dialog boxes. For many projects, the skills presented in this chapter are the only ones you'll need when you're working with the forms of an application. In chapter 12, however, you'll learn another technique for passing data between forms. And in chapter 23, you'll learn some additional skills for working with the forms of an application.

Summary

- The *combo box* and *list box* controls display a list of items that the user can select from. To work with the items stored in these lists, you can use the properties and methods of the Items collection.
- The *radio button* and *check box* controls let the user select one or more items. All of the radio buttons in a group are mutually exclusive, but each check box is independent of the others.
- To group radio buttons or other controls, you place them in a *group box* control. Then, you can move all of the controls in the group in the Form Designer by moving the group box.
- You can use Tab Order view of a form to change the *tab order* of the controls on a form rather than changing the TabIndex properties of the controls directly.
- A project can contain two or more forms. You can use the Project menu to add new or existing forms to a project.
- The Main method defines the entry point for an application. This method is generated automatically for the first form of an application.
- You can use a *dialog box* to accept information from the user and return a result value. A dialog box is a *modal form* that must be closed before the application can continue.
- You can use the DialogResult enumeration and the Tag property to pass data between a form and a dialog box.

Terms

combo box
list box
radio button
group box
check box
tab order
constructor
documentation comment
modal form
modeless form

Objectives

- Given the specifications for a form that uses any of the controls presented in this chapter, design and code the form.
- Given a form with two or more controls, set the tab order of the controls using the Tab Order view of the form.
- Given the specifications for an application that displays custom or standard dialog boxes, design and code the application.
- Describe how you work with the items in a combo box list or a list box.
- Distinguish between radio button and check box controls.
- Describe how group boxes and radio buttons work together.
- Explain what you must do to rename a form.
- Explain how the first form of an application is displayed.
- Describe two ways you can pass data between forms.
- Describe how you can use a dialog box to cancel the Closing event of a form.

Exercise 10-1 Create the Payment application

This exercise will guide you through the process of creating the Payment application that's described in this chapter. To make that easier for you, you'll start from an application that contains the Customer form.

Open the project and prepare the two forms

1. Open the Payment application that's in the C:\C#.NET\Chapter 10\Payment directory. This application contains a single form named Form1.
2. Rename Form1 to frmCustomer. Make sure to change both the file name and the name that's used in the code. Then, modify the Main method so it displays this form when the application starts.
3. Add a second form named frmPayment to the project.

Design the Payment form

4. Add the controls to the Payment form and set the properties for this form and its controls as described in figures 10-14 and 10-15.
5. Use Tab Order view to set the tab order for the controls on the Payment form if necessary.

Add the code for the Customer form

6. Generate the event handlers for the Load event of the Customer form, for the Closing event of the form, and for the Click event of all three buttons. Then, add the global isDataSaved variable, and add the code for these events as shown in figure 10-16.
7. Generate an event handler named DataChanged for the SelectedIndexChanged event of the Customer Name combo box. Then, wire this event handler to the TextChanged event of the Payment Method label, and add the code to this event handler so it sets the isDataSaved variable to false.
8. Add the SaveData and IsValidData methods.
9. Test the Customer form to make sure that it works properly. At this point, you should be able to display the Payment form, but it won't work correctly since you haven't added any code to it.

Add the code for the Payment form

10. Generate the event handlers for the Load event of the Payment form and for the Click event of both buttons. Then, add the code for these events as shown in figure 10-17.
11. Generate an event handler named Billing_CheckChanged for the CheckChanged event of the Credit Card radio button. Then, wire this event handler to the CheckChanged event of the Bill Customer radio button, and add the code for this event handler.
12. Add the EnableControls, DisableControls, and IsValidData methods.
13. Test the program to be sure that it works as described in figure 10-14. When you're sure it does, close the project.

Exercise 10-2 Enhance the Future Value application

This exercise will guide you through the process of adding a combo box and a list box to the Future Value application.

Open the Future Value application and add two controls

1. Open the Future Value application that's in the C:\C#.NET\Chapter 10\FutureValue directory.
2. Delete the Number of Years text box and replace it with a Number of Years combo box. Then, delete the Future Value label and replace it with a Future Values list box.

Add the code that works with the controls

3. Generate the event handler for the Load event of the form. Then, add code that loads the numbers 1 through 20 in the Number of Years combo box, and add code that selects 3 as the default number of years.
4. Modify the event handler for the Click event of the Calculate button so it adds the year-end total for future value to the Future Values list box. For example, if you calculate the future value for three years, the Future Value form should return a result like this:

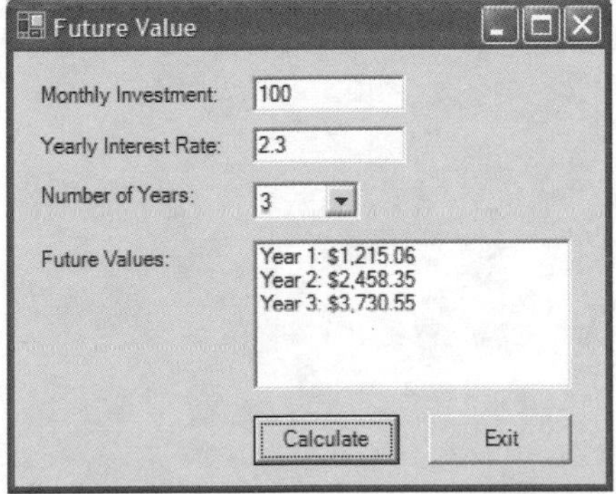

5. To get this to work correctly, you'll need to use the Clear method of the list box to clear the list box each time the Calculate button is clicked. In addition, you can use the modulus operator (%) to add the future value after every twelve months of the calculation. For example:

```
if (month % 12 == 0) // add the future value to the list box
```

6. Test this application to make sure it works correctly.

11

How to debug an application

In chapters 2 and 5, you learned how to enter break mode when a run-time error occurs, how to use data tips to find out what value a variable or property contains, how to use breakpoints to enter break mode before a specific statement is executed, and how to step through the statements in an application from a breakpoint. These are the basic debugging skills that you need for debugging simple applications.

As your applications get more complicated, though, debugging gets more complicated. In fact, if you've done much programming, you know that debugging is often the most difficult and time-consuming phase of programming. The good news is that Visual Studio offers many other tools for testing and debugging. In this chapter, you'll learn how to use the most useful ones, and you'll review the tools you've already been introduced to.

Basic debugging techniques

Before you begin debugging, you can set the options that control how Visual Studio handles exceptions. Then, you can use the basic debugging skills that you learned in previous chapters to find and fix most types of exceptions.

How to set the options for debugging

Figure 11-1 presents the dialog box you can use to set the options for debugging. Although you can set these options for individual exception classes or for the exception classes in individual namespaces, you're most likely to set them for all the exception classes in the Common Language Runtime. To do that, you highlight the Common Language Runtime Exceptions entry before you set the options.

The first set of options in this dialog box determines what happens when an exception occurs. By default, the Continue option is selected, so the application will continue instead of breaking into the debugger. This gives any exception-handling code a chance to be executed. In most cases, that's what you want. If you set this option to Break into the debugger, however, you can use the debugging features described in this chapter to set breakpoints and check variables *before* any exception-handling code is executed.

The second set of options determines what happens if an exception is thrown but isn't handled by the application. In most cases, you'll want to break into the debugger so you can determine the cause of the exception, and that's the default. If you set this option to Continue, though, the application will crash, just as it would for the end user of your application after it has been distributed. As a result, you can use this setting to simulate what will happen to the users of your application when they encounter exceptions.

By the way, the "Use parent setting" options are enabled when you select one of the categories or exceptions below the Common Language Runtime Exceptions entry. Then, if you specify the setting for that entry, the settings for the next higher level are applied to the selected category or exception.

The Exceptions dialog box

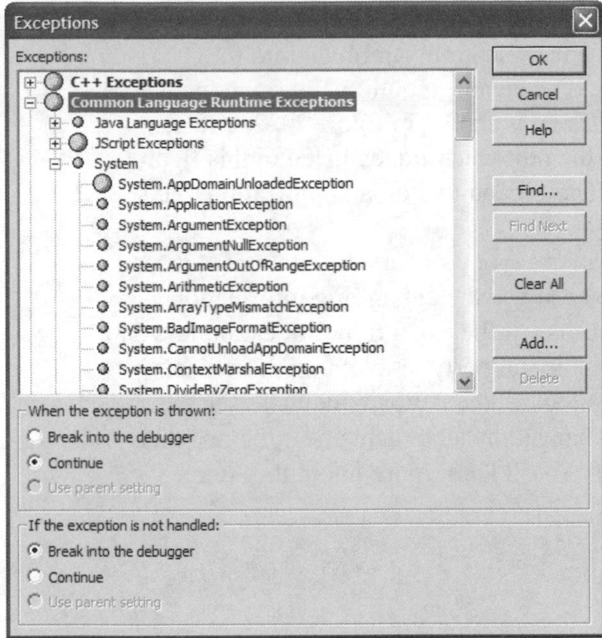

When the exception is thrown

Option	Description
Break into the debugger	Causes the application to enter break mode when an exception occurs, even if exception-handling code is available.
Continue	Causes the application to continue. If exception-handling code is available, it is executed.
Use parent setting	Uses the setting of the parent exception.

If the exception is not handled

Option	Description
Break into the debugger	Causes the application to enter break mode when exception-handling code isn't available.
Continue	Causes the application to end.
Use parent setting	Uses the setting of the parent exception.

Description

- To display the Exceptions dialog box, use the Debug→Exceptions command.
- To set the options for all exceptions in the CLR, select the Common Language Runtime Exceptions entry. To set the options for a category of exceptions or a specific exception, select that category or exception.

Figure 11-1 How to set the options for debugging

How to work in break mode

If the debugging options are set so an application can break into the debugger, the dialog box that's displayed when an exception is thrown includes a Break button that lets you enter *break mode* as shown in figure 11-2. You can also enter break mode by using one of the other techniques listed in this figure. In particular, you can use the Break All command to stop an application that's caught in an infinite loop.

When you enter break mode after an exception occurs, the statement that was executing is highlighted. Then, you can use the debugging information that's available to try to determine the cause of the exception. For example, you can place the mouse pointer over a variable, property, or expression to display its current value in a *data tip*. You can also look in the Autos window to see the values of the variables that have been changed by statements near the one that was executing when the break occurred. You'll learn more about the Autos window in a moment.

The Future Value application in break mode

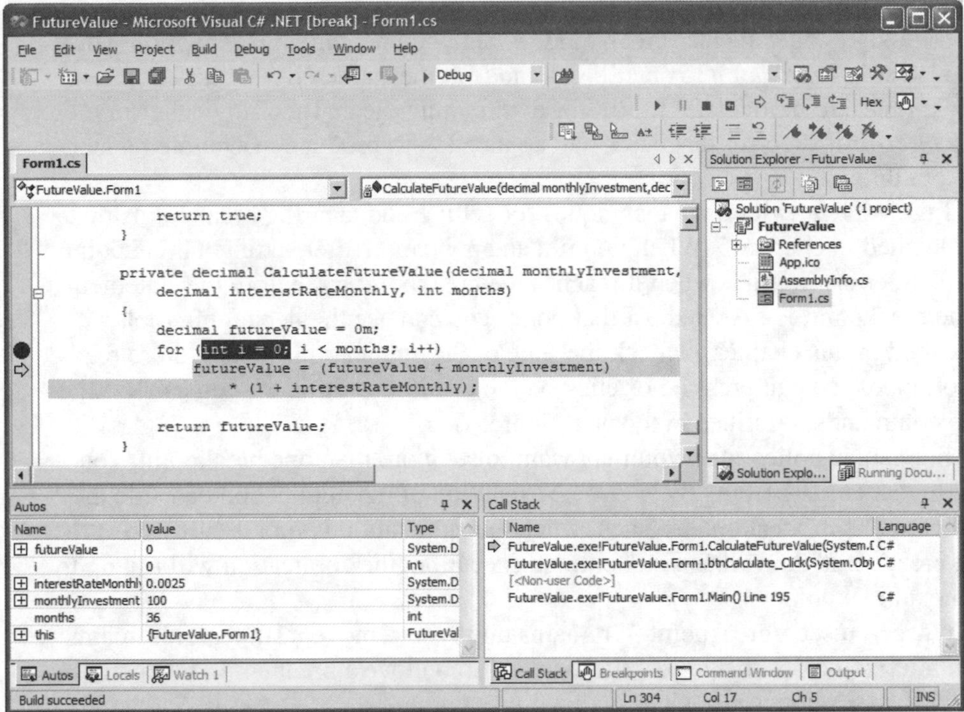

Three ways to enter break mode

- Click on the Break button in the dialog box that's displayed when an unhandled exception occurs.
- Set a breakpoint on a statement to enter break mode before that statement is executed.
- Choose the Debug→Break All command or press Ctrl+Alt+Break while the application is executing.

Description

- When you enter *break mode*, Visual Studio displays the Code Editor and highlights the next statement to be executed or the statement that was executing when the exception occurred.
- You can use the debugging windows and the Debug toolbar that's displayed in break mode to control the execution of the application and determine the cause of an exception.
- To display the value of a variable or property in a *data tip*, position the mouse pointer over it in the Code Editor. To display a data tip for an expression, select the expression and then point to it. The expression must not contain a method call.
- To exit break mode and end the application, click on the Stop Debugging button in the Debug toolbar. To continue application execution, press F5 or click on the Continue button in the Standard or Debug toolbar.

Figure 11-2 How to work in break mode

How to use breakpoints

Although you can enter break mode when you encounter an exception, you can also set a *breakpoint* to enter break mode at the statement of your choice. Breakpoints are particularly useful for determining the cause of logical errors. A *logical error* is an error that causes an application to produce inaccurate results without throwing an exception.

Figure 11-3 reviews the techniques for setting and clearing breakpoints that you learned in chapter 5. When you run an application after setting a breakpoint, it will enter break mode when it reaches the breakpoint but before the statement at the breakpoint is executed. At that point, you can use the debugging tools described in this chapter to check the state of the application. When you're ready to continue, you can press F5 or click on the Continue button, or you can use the Step commands described in the next figure.

For some applications, you may want to set more than one breakpoint. You can do that either before you begin the execution of the application or while the application is in break mode. Then, when the application is run, it will stop at the first breakpoint. And when you continue execution, the application will run up to the next breakpoint.

Once you set a breakpoint, it remains until you remove it. In fact, it remains even after you close the project. If you want to remove a breakpoint, you can use one of the techniques presented in this figure.

You can also work with breakpoints from the *Breakpoints window*. For example, you can disable a breakpoint by removing the check mark in front of the breakpoint. Then, the breakpoint remains in the Breakpoints window, but it is disabled until you enable it again. To disable or enable all breakpoints, you can use the buttons that are available from the Breakpoints window. Similarly, you can use the Clear All Breakpoints button to remove all breakpoints.

The Future Value application after a breakpoint is taken

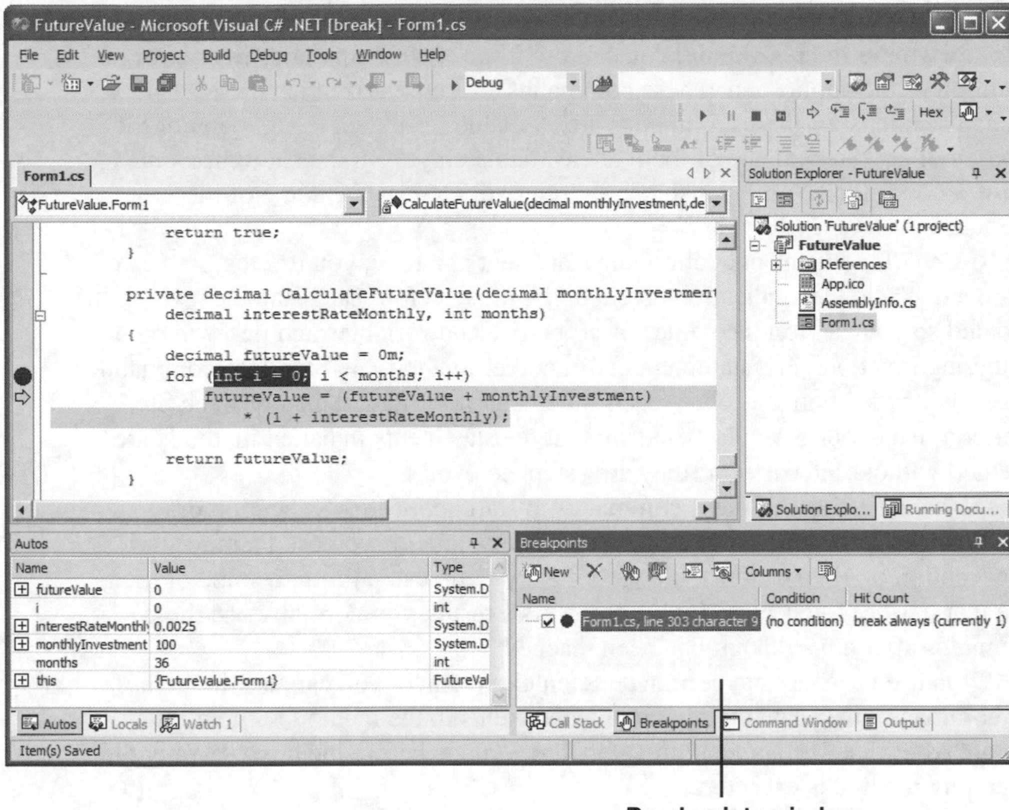

How to set and clear breakpoints

- To set a *breakpoint*, click in the margin indicator bar to the left of a statement. Or, press the F9 key to set a breakpoint at the insertion point. You can set a breakpoint before you run an application or while the application is in break mode.
- To remove a breakpoint, use either technique for setting a breakpoint. To remove all breakpoints at once, use the Debug→Clear All Breakpoints command.

Description

- You can set a breakpoint only on a line that contains an executable statement. You cannot set breakpoints on blank lines, comments, or declarations.
- When Visual Studio encounters a breakpoint, it enters break mode before it executes the statement that contains the breakpoint.
- The current breakpoints are displayed in the Breakpoints window. This window is most useful for enabling and disabling existing breakpoints, but you can also use it to add, modify, move, and delete breakpoints.

Figure 11-3 How to use breakpoints

How to control the execution of an application

Once you're in break mode, you can use a variety of commands to control the execution of the application. These commands are summarized in figure 11-4. As you can see, most of these commands are available from the Debug menu or the Debug toolbar, but a couple of them are available only from the shortcut menu for the Code Editor. You can also use shortcut keys to execute some of these commands.

To *step through* an application one statement at a time, you use the Step Into command. Then, the application enters break mode before each statement is executed so you can test the values of properties and variables and perform other debugging functions. If a statement calls another method, the Step Into command causes the application to execute each statement of the called method. The Step Over command works similarly except that the statements in called methods are executed without interruption (they are "stepped over").

You can use either of these commands to start application execution or to restart execution when an application is in break mode. If you use them to start the execution of a typical form class, though, you first step through some of the code that has been generated for the form. As a result, you normally use these commands after a breakpoint has been reached.

If you use the Step Into command to enter a method, you can use the Step Out command to execute the remaining statements in the method without interruption. After that, the application enters break mode before the next statement in the calling method is executed.

To skip code that you know is working properly, you can use the Run To Cursor or Set Next Statement command. You can also use the Set Next Statement command to rerun lines of code that were executed before an exception occurred. And if you've been working in the Code Editor and have forgotten where the next statement to be executed is, you can use the Show Next Statement command to move to it.

Commands in the Debug menu and toolbar

Command	Toolbar	Keyboard	Description
Start/Continue		F5	Start or continue execution of the application.
Break All		Ctrl+Alt+Break	Suspend execution of the application.
Stop Debugging			Stop debugging and end execution of the application.
Restart			Restart the entire application.
Show Next Statement			Display the next statement to be executed. Also available from the shortcut menu for the Code Editor.
Step Into		F11	Execute one statement at a time.
Step Over		F10	Execute one statement at a time except for called methods.
Step Out		Shift+F11	Execute the remaining lines in the current method.

Commands in the Code Editor's shortcut menu

Command	Description
Run to Cursor	Execute the application until it reaches the statement that contains the insertion point.
Set Next Statement	Set the statement that contains the insertion point as the next statement to be executed.

Description

- If you use the Step Into or Step Over command to start the execution of an application, Visual Studio will enter break mode before it executes the first statement in the application. If you use the Run to Cursor command, Visual Studio will enter break mode when it reaches the statement that contains the insertion point.
- Once the application enters break mode, you can use the Step Into, Step Over, Step Out, and Run To Cursor commands to execute one or more statements.
- To alter the normal execution sequence of the application, you can use the Set Next Statement command. Just place the insertion point in the statement you want to execute next, issue this command, and click on the Continue button.
- To enter break mode when you need to stop the execution of an application, you can use the Break All command.

Figure 11-4 How to control the execution of an application

How to use the debugging windows

Now that you know how to work with break mode, you're ready to learn how to use the primary debugging windows. These windows include the Autos window, the Locals window, the Watch windows, the Command window, and the Call Stack window.

How to use the Autos and Locals windows to monitor variables

If you need to see the values of several variables or properties used in the same area of an application, you can do that using the Autos or the Locals windows. By default, these windows are displayed in the group of windows in the lower left corner of Visual Studio when an application enters break mode. If they're not displayed, you can display them by selecting Autos or Locals from the Debug→Windows submenu.

The contents of the Autos and Locals windows are illustrated in figure 11-5. The difference between the two is in the amount of information they display and the scope of that information.

The *Autos window* displays information about the variables, properties, and constants used in the current statement and the previous statement. The *Locals window* displays information about the variables and controls within the scope of the current method. In this figure, both the Autos window and the Locals window display similar information. However, the information in the Autos window is usually more limited than it is in the Locals window. When you're debugging a form, both windows use the this keyword to include information about all of the controls on the form and that information can be extensive.

Besides displaying the values of variables and properties, you can use the Autos and Locals windows to change these values. To do that, you simply double-click on the value you want to change and enter a new value. Then, you can continue the execution of the application.

The Autos window

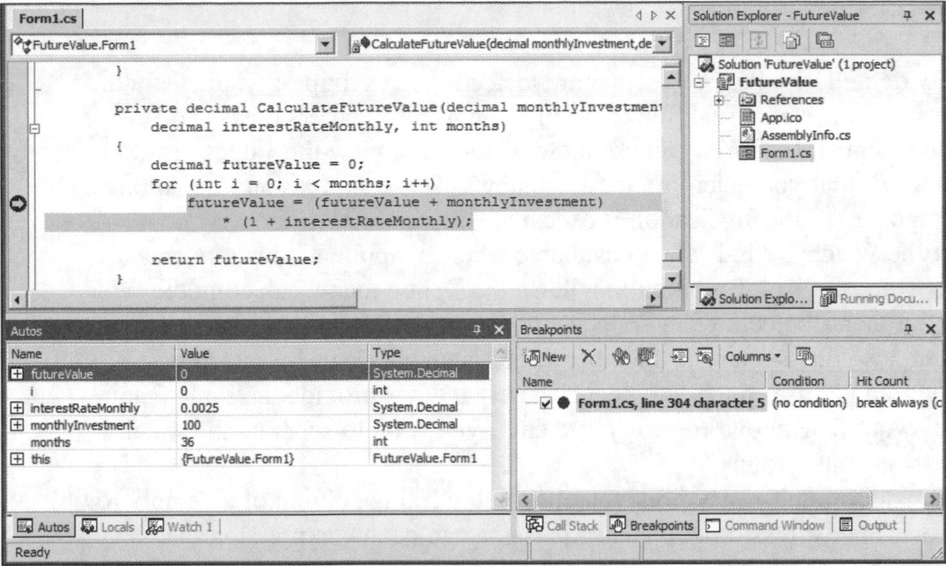

The Locals window

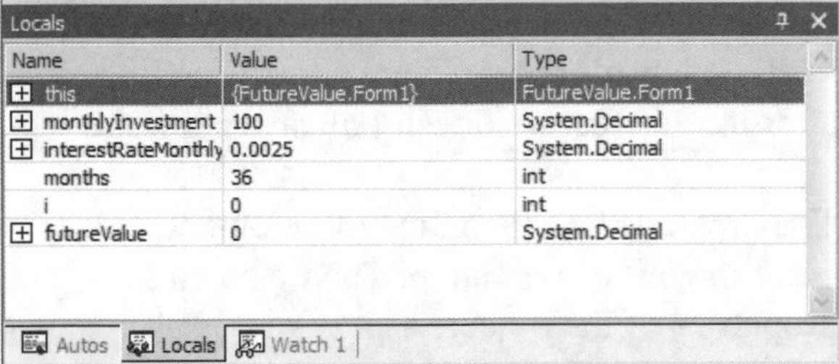

Description

- The *Autos window* displays information about variables, properties, and constants used by the current statement and the previous statement. To display the Autos window, click on the Autos window tab or use the Debug→Windows→Autos command.
- The *Locals window* displays information about the variables and controls within the scope of the current method. To display the Locals window, click on the Locals tab or use the Debug→Windows→Locals command.
- If you are debugging a form and you click on the plus sign to the left of the this keyword in either the Autos or Locals window, the properties and variables of the form are displayed.
- To change the value of a property or variable from either window, double-click on the value in the Value column, then type a new value and press the Enter key.

Figure 11-5 How to use the Autos and Locals windows to monitor variables

How to use Watch windows to monitor expressions

By default, the *Watch windows* are located in the group of windows in the lower left corner of Visual Studio when an application enters break mode, as shown in figure 11-6. You can use these windows to view the values of *watch expressions* that you enter into these windows. These expressions are automatically updated as the application is executed.

If the Watch 1 window isn't available when an application enters break mode, you can display it by pulling down the Debug menu, selecting the Windows submenu, selecting the Watch submenu, and selecting the Watch 1 item. You can also display any of the other three watch windows by selecting the appropriate item from this submenu. These windows provide the same features as the Watch 1 window. You can use them if you want to separate the watch expressions into groups.

To add a watch expression, you click in the Name column of an empty row and enter the expression. A watch expression can be any expression that's recognized by the debugger. If the expression exists in the application, you can select it in the Code Editor and drag it to the Watch window. The Watch window in this figure shows two expressions that are recognized by the debugger, the futureValue variable and the Text property of the Future Value label. Unfortunately, the debugger for Visual Studio 2003 doesn't recognize many expressions that are valid expressions in C#. As a result, this feature doesn't always work the way you would expect.

If the expression you add to the Watch window is the name of an object, the Watch window will display a plus sign to the left of the name. Then, you can click on the plus sign to display the properties of the object. A plus sign is also added to an expression if it's the name of an array. Then, you can click on the plus sign to display the elements in the array.

You can change the value of a watch expression by clicking on the value in the Value column and entering the new value. To delete a watch expression, you can use the Delete Watch command on the shortcut menu that's displayed when you right-click on an expression. To delete all watch expressions, you can use the Select All command on the shortcut menu followed by the Delete Watch command.

When and how to use the Quick Watch feature

You can use the Quick Watch feature to display the value of an expression that exists in your application code. To do that, you just highlight the expression and choose Quick Watch from the Debug menu. Remember, though, that you can also display the value of an expression by displaying a data tip, so you really don't need this feature.

A Watch window

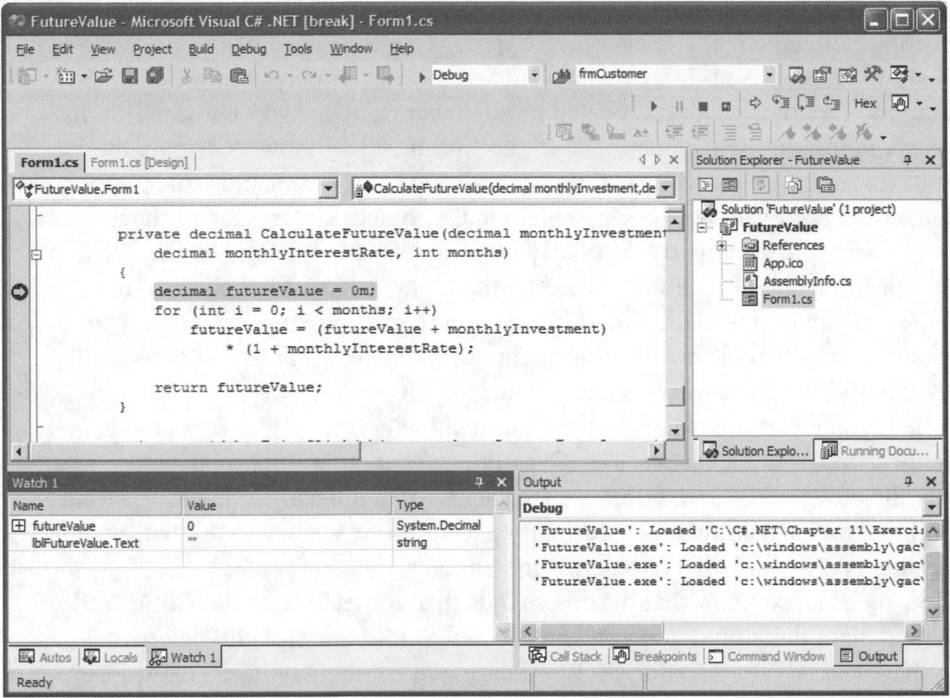

Description

- The *Watch windows* let you view the values of *watch expressions* while an application is in break mode. To display a Watch window, click on its Watch tab. Or, select Debug→Windows→Watch and choose the Watch 1, Watch 2, Watch 3, or Watch 4 command.
- To add an expression to a Watch window, click on an empty row in the Name column, then type the expression. You can also highlight an expression in the Code Editor and drag it into a Watch window.
- If an expression is out of scope, the Watch window will display a message instead of a value.
- If you enter the name of an object or an array in the Watch window, a tree control will appear next to its name. Then, you can use this control to expand or collapse this entry.
- To change the value of a watch expression, double-click on its value in the Value column, enter the new value, and press the Enter key.
- Any expressions you add to the Watch window remain in effect until they're deleted.
- To delete a watch expression, right-click on the expression and select the Delete Watch command from the shortcut menu. To delete all watch expressions, right-click on the Watch window, select the Select All command, and select the Delete Watch command.

Figure 11-6 How to use Watch windows to monitor expressions

How to use the Command window

Another window that you can use for debugging is the *Command window* that's shown in figure 11-7. By default, this window is displayed in Immediate mode in the group of windows located in the lower right corner of Visual Studio.

You can use the Immediate mode of the Command window to display the value of a variable or property, and you can also use the Command window to execute code. For example, you can enter an assignment statement to change the value of a variable or property. Similarly, you can use this window to execute a method or to display the value returned by the method. This can be useful for testing the result of a method with different arguments. When you do this, you can execute the available methods from classes in the .NET Framework as well as any methods that you have coded in your project.

When you enter commands in the Command window, they're executed in the same scope as the application that's running. That means that you can't display the value of a variable that's out of scope and you can't execute a private method that's in a class that isn't currently executing. If you try to do that, Visual Studio displays a blank line or an error message.

You should also know that the commands that you enter into the Command window remain there until you exit from Visual Studio or explicitly delete them using the Clear All command in the shortcut menu for the window. That way, you can use standard Windows techniques to edit and re-use the same commands from one execution of an application to another without having to re-enter them. Unlike expressions in the Watch window, though, the command results aren't updated as the application executes.

To execute a command that you've already entered in the Command window, just place the insertion point in the command and press the Enter key. This copies the command to the bottom of the window. Then, you can change it if necessary and press Enter to execute it.

The Command window in Immediate mode

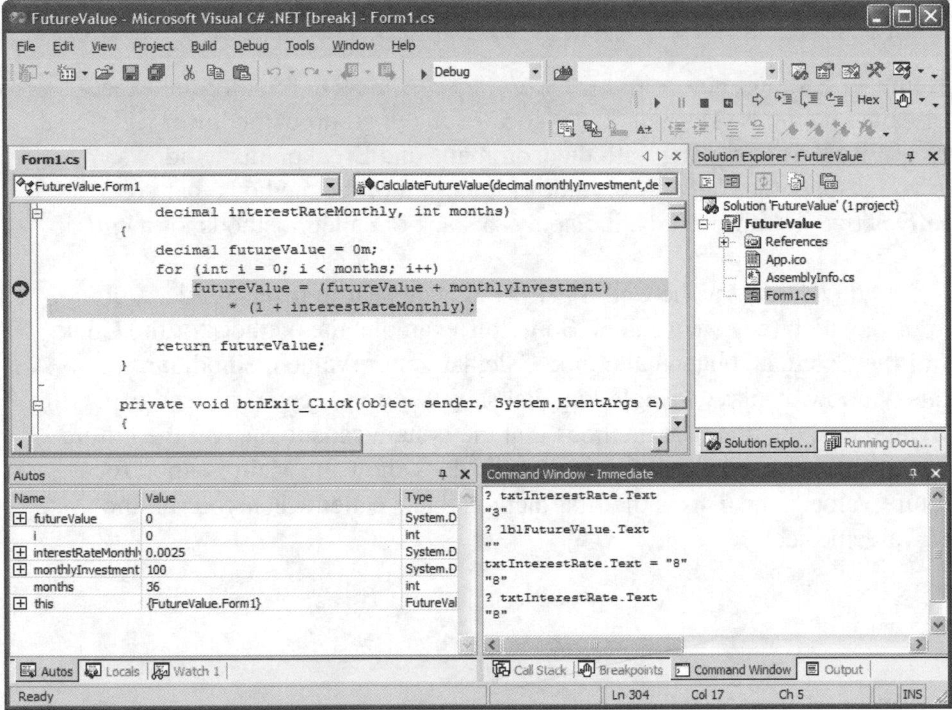

Description

- You can use Immediate mode of the *Command window* to display and assign values from an application during execution. To display this window, click on the Command Window tab or use the Debug→Windows→Immediate command.
- To display a value in the Command window, enter a question mark followed by the expression whose value you want to display. Then, press the Enter key.
- To assign a different value to a variable or property enter an assignment statement in the Command window. Then, press the Enter key.
- To execute a method from the Command window, enter its name and any arguments it requires. Then, press the Enter key. If you want to display the result of a method, precede the method call with a question mark.
- To reissue a command, use the Up and Down arrow keys to scroll through the commands until you find the one you want. Then, place the insertion point in the command and press the Enter key to add the command to the bottom of the Command window. Modify the command if necessary, then press the Enter key to execute it.
- To remove all commands and output from the Command window, use the Clear All command in the shortcut menu for the window.

Figure 11-7 How to use the Command window

How to use the Call Stack window to monitor called methods

Figure 11-8 shows how to use the *Call Stack window* to monitor the execution of called methods. This window is located in the group in the lower right corner of Visual Studio along with the Command and Breakpoints windows. When you display the Call Stack window, it lists all of the methods that are currently active. In other words, it displays a stack of called methods, or a *call stack*.

The methods listed in the Call Stack window appear in reverse order from the order in which they were called. So in this example, the method for the Click event of the Calculate button called the CalculateFutureValue method. Notice that this window displays a single line that says "Non-user code" instead of displaying all of the non-user methods that the system calls to display the Future Value form. However, the Call Stack window does show the Main method for the Future Value form. This is the first method that's called when you run the Future Value project.

The Call Stack window

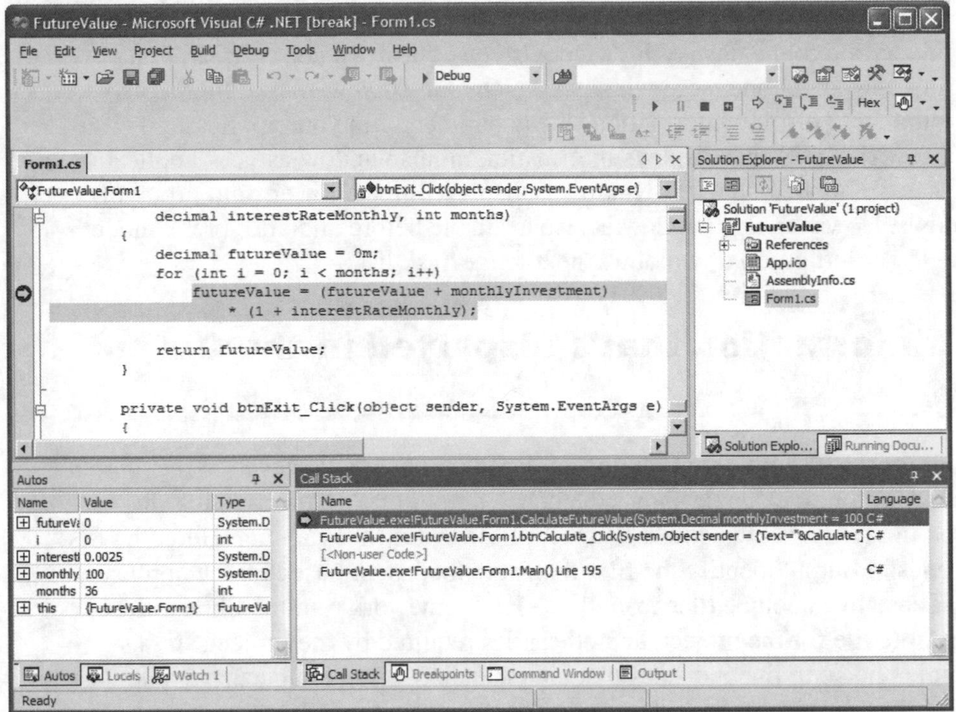

Description

- The *Call Stack window* lists all of the methods that are active when an application enters break mode. To display this window, click on the Call Stack tab or use the Debug→Windows→Call Stack command.
- In the Call Stack window, the current method is listed at the top of the window, followed by the method that called it (if any), and so on. This list of method names is referred to as a *call stack*.
- You can use the commands in the shortcut menu for the Call Stack window to control what's displayed in this window.

Figure 11-8 How to use the Call Stack window to monitor called methods

How to use the Output window

In addition to the debugging windows you've learned about so far, you should know about one more window: the *Output window*. Visual Studio uses this window to display information as you build and run your applications. You can also write code that displays information in this window as your application executes. In break mode, this window is displayed in the lower right group of windows. However, this window is also available before and after break mode, in the lower left group of windows, next to the Task list.

Project information that's displayed in the Output window

Figure 11-9 shows two types of information that are displayed in the Output window. The first example shows the debug output that's automatically displayed in the Output window after an application finishes running. Here, the first five lines of output identify the files that were loaded and used by the application. These files include files from the .NET Framework runtime library, the executable file for the project, and other files required by the project. In this example, the sixth line indicates that an unhandled exception occurred, and the seventh line provides a brief description of that exception. Then, the eighth line displays the completion code for the project.

In the second example, you can see the output that's displayed after a project has been built. This output indicates the progress and result of the build. In this case, a single project was built and the build was successful. If you run a project, it is automatically built before it is run. As a result, this output is available when you run a project. However, to display it, you must select the Build item from the combo box that's at the top of the Output window. On the other hand, if you build a solution by selecting one of the Build commands from the Build menu, the Output window will automatically select the Build option and show this information.

Most of the time, you won't need the information that's displayed in the Output window. If a build error occurs, for example, the error is displayed in the Task List window and you can use that window to locate and correct the error. And if an unhandled exception occurs, you can use the information in the dialog box that's displayed to identify the cause of the exception. Of course, once you close this dialog box, the information about the exception is only available in the Output window. As a result, if you need to look up information about the exception after you've closed the dialog box for the exception, you can get the information from this window.

An Output window that shows debug output

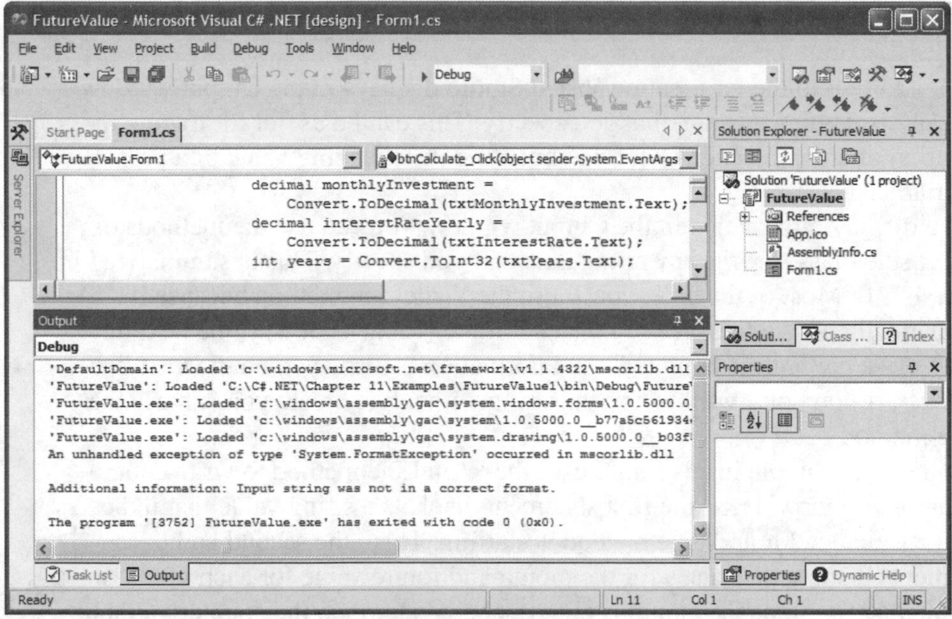

An Output window that shows build output

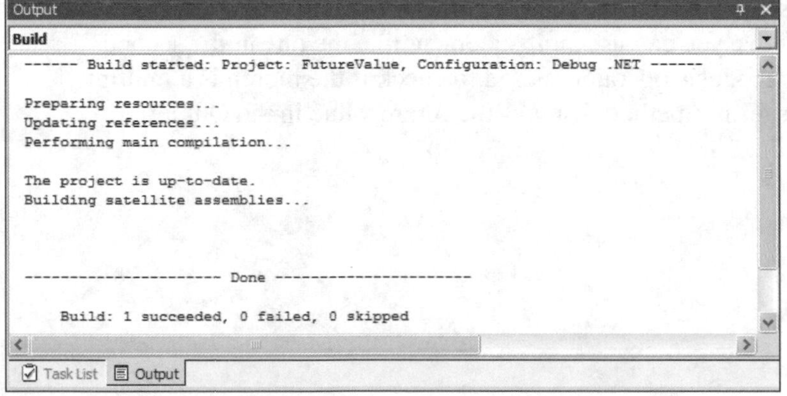

Description

- After a solution finishes running, the *Output window* automatically displays the debug output. This output lists the files that were loaded and used by the project, information about unhandled exceptions (if any), and a completion code.
- When you build a project or solution, the Output window automatically displays the build output. This output includes an indication of how many projects were built successfully, how many builds failed, and how many projects weren't built.
- You can use the combo box at the top of the Output window to select whether build or debug output is displayed.

Figure 11-9 Project information that's displayed in the Output window

How to use the Console class to display data in the Output window

In addition to the information Visual Studio displays in the Output window, you can display information that you specify. This can be useful for tracing the execution of an application or for documenting the changing value of a property or variable.

To display information in the Output window, you can use the methods of the Console class to write any string data that you specify. This is summarized in figure 11-10. Most of the time, you'll use the WriteLine method because it automatically adds a line break to the end of the string. That way, the next time one of these methods is executed, the information is displayed on the next line. However, if you don't want to end the string with a line break, you can use the Write method.

The first example in this figure uses the WriteLine method to write data to the Output window. Here, the first statement displays a string value that indicates that the CalculateFutureValue method is starting. Then, the second and third statements display the values for the month and future value for each month in the calculation. Since the month is always one greater than the counter variable for the loop, you can get the month by adding one to the counter variable.

Sometimes you may only want to display data in the Output window when a certain condition is true. If, for example, you only want to display the future value every 12 months, you can use an if statement like the one in the second example. Here, the modulus operator is used to check if the month is a multiple of 12. If so, the WriteLine method displays the future value in the Output window.

The result of the WriteLine method in the Output window

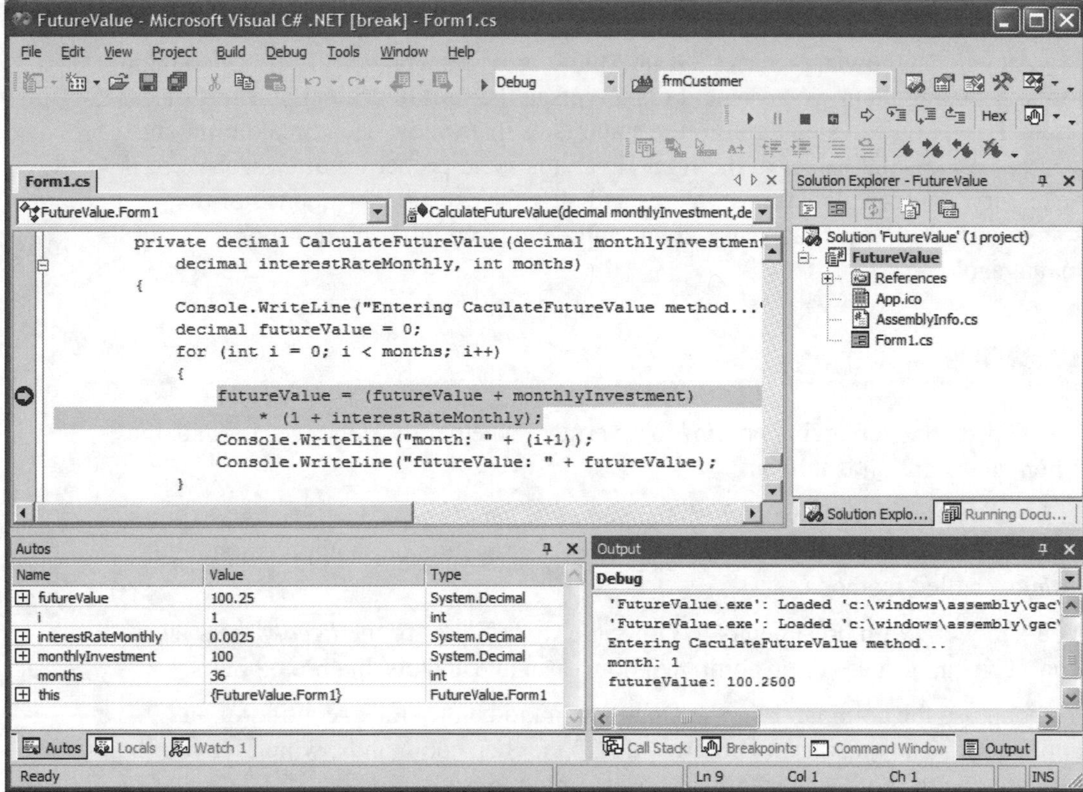

Methods of the Console class that display data in the Output window

Method	Description
Write(string)	Displays the value of the specified string.
WriteLine(string)	Displays the value of the specified string, followed by a line break.

Three statements that display data in the Output window

```
Console.WriteLine("Entering CalculateFutureValue method...");
Console.WriteLine("month: " + (i+1));
Console.WriteLine("futureValue: " + futureValue);
```

Code that uses an if statement to control when data is written

```
if ((i+1)%12 == 0) // every 12 months
    Console.WriteLine("futureValue: " + futureValue);
```

Description

- You can use the Write methods of the Console class to display data in the Output window. This can be useful for tracing application execution or for documenting changes in the values of variables.

Figure 11-10 How to use the Console class to display data in the Output window

Perspective

As you can now appreciate, Visual Studio provides a powerful set of debugging tools. By using them, you can set breakpoints at the start of critical portions of code. Then, you can step through the statements that follow each breakpoint, and you can review the values of the related variables and properties after each step. If necessary, you can also change values and alter the execution sequence of the statements. With tools like these, a difficult debugging job becomes more manageable.

Summary

- You can set the debugging options to determine whether the debugger is available when an exception is thrown.
- In *break mode*, you can work with the values of variables, properties, and expressions. You can also set *breakpoints*, control the execution of an application, and monitor called methods.
- You can work with breakpoints in either the Code Editor or the *Breakpoints window*. You can use the Breakpoints window to enable and disable breakpoints.
- You can use the commands in the Debug menu to control the execution of an application. The most useful commands are the Step commands, which let you execute one or more statements before returning to break mode.
- You can use the *Autos window* and *Locals window* to display and modify the values of properties and variables while debugging an application.
- You can use the *Watch window* to display the current values of *watch expressions* each time the application enters break mode.
- You can use Immediate mode of the *Command window* to display and modify variables during application execution and to execute methods.
- You can use the *Call Stack window* to review the *call stack* that lists the methods that are active when an application enters break mode.
- When you build or run a project, information about that operation is displayed in the *Output window*.
- You can use the Write and WriteLine methods of the Console class to display custom information in the Output window as an application executes.

Terms

break mode
data tip
breakpoint
logical error
step through an application
Breakpoints window
Autos window
Locals window
Watch window
watch expression
Command window
Call Stack window
call stack
Output window

Objectives

- Use the debugging techniques presented in this chapter to debug any unhandled exceptions or logical errors in the applications that you develop.
- Describe the differences between the three Step commands that you can use to control the execution of an application.
- Describe the primary differences between the Autos window, the Locals window, and the Watch window.
- Describe the use of the Immediate mode of the Command window.
- Describe the call stack that's displayed in the Call Stack window.
- Explain how you can use the Console class to display information in the Output window.

Exercise 11-1 Step through an application

If you did exercise 5-2 in chapter 5, you've already set breakpoints, used the Autos window, and stepped through an application. So in this exercise, you'll use some of the new skills that were presented in this chapter.

Open and run the Future Value application

1. Open the Future Value application that's in the C:\C#.NET\Chapter 11\FutureValue directory.
2. Set a breakpoint on the statement in the btnCalculate_Click method that calls the method that calculates future value. Then, run the project until it enters break mode.

Use the Locals windows

3. Click on the Locals tab to display the Locals window, click on the plus sign to the left of the this keyword, scroll down to txtMonthlyInvestment, and click on its plus sign. Then, scroll down to the Text property to see the string value that it stores.

4. Press F11 to step through the statements, and notice the parameters and variables that are displayed in the Locals window at each step. Then, set a second breakpoint on the last statement in the CalculateFutureValue method, and press F5 to run the application until it enters break mode again.
5. Locate the months variable, double-click in the Value column for this variable, enter 24, and press the Enter key to change its value. Then, press F5 to continue execution, and notice that the value you entered for the months variable is used to calculate the future value.

Use the Breakpoints window to disable both breakpoints

6. Display the Breakpoints window and click the Disable All Breakpoints button at the top of the Breakpoints window. Notice how this disables both break points without removing them. Then, press F5 to continue execution. Since no breakpoints are enabled, this should display the Future Value form.
7. Display the Breakpoints window and click the Enable All Breakpoints button at the top of the Breakpoints window. This should enable both breakpoints. Then, run the program until the application enters break mode again.

Use the Command window to work with a variable and method

8. In break mode, display the Command window and display the value of the years and months variables in this window. Then, display the percentage format of the monthly interest rate by calling the ToString method from the monthlyInterestRate variable like this:

```
? monthlyInterestRate.ToString("p")
```

9. Assign a value of 12 to the months variable by entering an assignment statement in the Command window.

Use a Watch window to monitor expressions

10. Display the Watch 1 window, highlight the futureValue variable, and drag it to that window. Then, click in the Name column of the first blank row in the Watch window and enter this expression:

```
i < months
```

11. Continue executing the application and check the values in the Watch window until the value of the second expression is False. Then, use the Breakpoints window to disable both breakpoints, and click on the Stop Debugging button in the Debug toolbar to end the application.

Use the Output window to display application information

12. In the btnCalculate_Click method, use the WriteLine method of the Console class to display the values of the monthly investment, yearly interest rate, years, and future value variables. Then, run the application and check the Output window to see how these values are displayed.
13. When you're through experimenting, close the project.

Section 3

Object-oriented programming with C#

In the first two sections of this book, you've learned how to use classes that are provided as part of the .NET Framework. For instance, you've learned how to use the properties, methods, and events of the form and control objects that are defined by the .NET classes, and you've learned how to use the ArrayList class to create collection objects that can hold other objects. Although that's one aspect of object-oriented programming, it's not the whole picture.

In addition to using the .NET classes, you can create your own classes. That's what the four chapters in this section teach you to do. Chapter 12 shows you the basics of creating classes. Then, chapter 13 expands on those basics to show you how to create classes that include more advanced features. Chapter 14 shows you how to use inheritance, one of the most important features of object-oriented programming. And chapter 15 shows you how to use three additional features of object-oriented programming: interfaces, structures, and class libraries.

You can read the chapters in this section any time after you complete the first 11 chapters of this book, and you should read them in sequence. However, only chapter 12 is a prerequisite for sections 4 and 5. So if you want to learn database programming before you learn more about object-oriented programming, you can skip to section 4 after you complete chapter 12. Or, if you want to learn how a database class is implemented for a text, binary, or XML file, you can skip to chapter 21 or 22 after you read chapter 12. Eventually, though, you need to master the object-oriented skills that are presented in chapters 13 through 15, so be sure to return to them.

12

How to create and use classes

This chapter presents the basics of creating and using classes in C# applications. Here, you'll learn how to create classes that include properties, methods, fields, and constructors, as well as classes that contain static members. In addition, you'll see a complete application that uses three user-defined classes.

When you complete this chapter, you'll start to see how creating your own classes can help simplify the development of an application. As a bonus, you'll have a better understanding of how the .NET classes work.

An introduction to classes

The topics that follow introduce you to the concepts you need before you create your own classes. First, you'll learn how classes are typically used in a business application to simplify the overall design of the application. Next, you'll learn about the variety of members you can add to a class. Then, you'll see a complete example of a simple class. Finally, you'll learn how classes are instantiated to create objects.

How classes can be used to structure an application

Figure 12-1 shows how you can use classes to simplify the design of a business application using a *multi-layered architecture*, also called a *multi-tiered architecture.* In a multi-layered application, the classes that perform different functions of the application are separated into two or more layers, or tiers.

A *three-tiered* application architecture like the one shown in this figure consists of a presentation layer, a middle layer, and a database layer. In practice, the middle layer is sometimes eliminated and its functions split between the database and presentation layers. On the other hand, the design of some applications further develops the middle layer into additional layers.

The classes in the *presentation layer* handle the details of the application's user interface. For a Windows application, this consists of the form classes that display the user interface. One class is required for each form displayed by the application.

The classes of the *database layer* are responsible for all database access required by the application. These classes typically include methods that connect to the database and retrieve, insert, add, and delete information from the database. Then, the other layers can call these methods to access the database, leaving the details of database access to the database classes. Although we refer to this layer as the database layer, it can also contain classes that work with data that's stored in files.

The *middle layer* provides an interface between the database layer and the presentation layer. This layer often includes classes that correspond to business entities (for example, products and customers). It may also include classes that implement business rules, such as discount or credit policies.

One key advantage of developing applications using a tiered architecture is that it allows application development to be spread among members of a development team. For example, one group of developers might work on the database layer, another group on the middle layer, and still another group on the presentation layer.

Another advantage is that it allows classes to be shared among applications. In particular, the classes that make up the database and middle layers can be placed in *class libraries* that can be used by more than one project. You'll learn how to work with class libraries in chapter 15.

The architecture of a three-tiered application

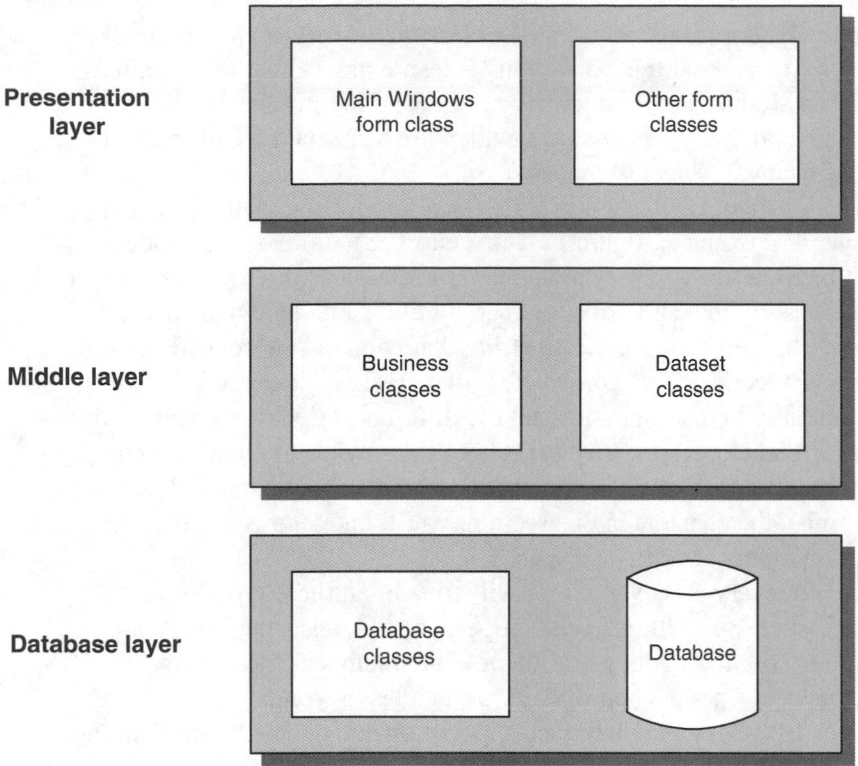

Description

- To simplify development and maintenance, many applications use a *three-tiered architecture* to separate the application's user interface, business rules, and database processing. Classes are used to implement the functions performed at each layer of the architecture.
- The classes in the *presentation layer* control the application's user interface. For a Windows Forms application, the user interface consists of the various forms that make up the application.
- The classes in the *database layer* handle all of the application's data processing.
- The classes in the *middle layer*, sometimes called the *business rules layer*, act as an interface between the classes in the presentation and database layers. In some cases, these classes correspond to business entities, such as customers or products. This layer may also include classes that implement business rules, such as discount or credit policies.
- In some cases, the classes that make up the database layer and the middle layer are implemented in class libraries that can be shared among applications. For more information, see chapter 15.

Figure 12-1 How classes can be used to structure an application

The members you can define within a class

As you already know, the *members* of a class include its *properties*, *methods*, and *events*. Throughout this book, you've seen many examples of applications that work with the .NET Framework classes and their members. You've also seen examples that use *constructors*, which are a special type of method that's executed when an object is created.

The classes you design yourself can also have properties, methods, constructors, and events. For example, figure 12-2 presents the members of a Product class that can be used to work with products. This class has three properties that store the code, description, and price for each product, a method named GetDisplayText that returns a formatted string that contains the code, description and price for a product, and two constructors that create instances of the class.

The second table in this figure lists all the different types of members a class can have. You already know how to code two of these types of members: constants and enumerations. You also know the basic skills for coding methods. By the time you finish the chapters in this section, you'll know how to create the other types of members as well.

Of course, not every class you create will contain all these types of members. In fact, most classes will have just properties, methods, and constructors. But it's important to know about all of the possible member types so you'll be able to decide which types are appropriate for the classes you create.

This figure also reviews the basic concepts of object-oriented programming that were first introduced in chapter 3. In addition, it presents a fundamental concept of object-oriented programming that you may not be familiar with. This is the concept of *encapsulation*.

Encapsulation lets the programmer hide, or encapsulate, some of the data and operations of a class while exposing others. For example, although a property or method of a class can be called from other classes, its implementation is hidden within the class. That way, users of the class can think of it as a black box that provides useful properties and methods. This also means that you can change the code within a class without affecting the other classes that use it. This makes it easier to enhance or change an application because you only need to change the classes that need changing. You'll get a better idea of how encapsulation works when you see the code for the Product class in the next figure.

The members of a Product class

Properties	Description
`Code`	A string that contains a code that uniquely identifies each product.
`Description`	A string that contains a description of the product.
`Price`	A decimal that contains the product's price.
Method	**Description**
`GetDisplayText(sep)`	Returns a string that contains the code, description, and price in a displayable format. The sep parameter is a string that's used to separate the elements. It's typically set to a tab or new line character.
Constructors	**Description**
`()`	Creates a product object with default values.
`(code, description, price)`	Creates a product object using the specified code, description, and price values.

Types of class members

Class member	Description
Property	Represents a data value associated with an object instance.
Method	An operation that can be performed by an object.
Constructor	A special type of method that's executed when an object is instantiated.
Event	A signal that notifies other objects that something noteworthy has occurred.
Field	A variable that's declared at the class level.
Constant	A constant.
Indexer	A special type of property that allows individual items within the class to be accessed by index values. Used for classes that represent collections of objects.
Operator	A special type of method that's performed for a C# operator such as + or ==.
Enumeration	An enumeration.
Class	A class that's defined within the class.

Class and object concepts

- An *object* is a self-contained unit that has *properties*, *methods*, and other *members*. A *class* contains the code that defines the members of an object.
- An object is an *instance* of a class, and the process of creating an object is called *instantiation.*
- *Encapsulation* is one of the fundamental concepts of object-oriented programming. It lets you control the data and operations within a class that are exposed to other classes.
- The data of a class is typically encapsulated within a class using *data hiding*. In addition, the code that performs operations within the class is encapsulated so it can be changed without changing the way other classes use it.
- Although a class can have many different types of members, most of the classes you create will have just properties, methods, and constructors.

Figure 12-2 The members you can define within a class

The code for the Product class

Figure 12-3 shows the complete code for the Product class whose members were described in figure 12-2. As you can see, it begins with a class statement that declares the Product class with the public access modifier. This access modifier lets other classes access the class.

The code within the class block defines the members of the Product class. In the rest of this chapter, you'll learn how to write code like the code shown here. For now, I'll just present a preview of this code so you have a general idea of how it works.

The first three statements in this class are declarations for three class variables, called *fields*. As you'll see in a minute, these fields are used to store the data for the Code, Description, and Price properties. Because these variables are defined with the private access modifier, they cannot be referred to from outside the class.

After the fields are declarations for the two constructors of the Product class. The first constructor, which accepts no arguments, creates an instance of the Product class and initializes its fields to default values. The second constructor creates an instance of the class and initializes it with values passed via the code, description, and price parameters.

Next are the declarations for the three properties of the Product class. These properties provide access to the values stored in the three fields. Within each of these property declarations are two blocks of code that get and set the value of the property.

Last is the declaration for the GetDisplayText method, which accepts a string parameter named *sep*. This method returns a string that concatenates the code, description, and price values, separated by the value passed via the sep parameter.

Notice that you always use the public access modifier to identify the properties and methods that can be accessed from other classes. In contrast, you use the private access modifier to declare fields that you don't want to be accessed from other classes. In this case, for example, the fields can only be accessed through the properties defined by the class. You can also use the private access modifier to code properties and methods that you don't want to be accessed from other classes.

The Product class

```
using System;
namespace ProductMaintenance
{
    public class Product
    {
        private string code;
        private string description;
        private decimal price;

        public Product()
        {
        }

        public Product(string code, string description, decimal price)
        {
            this.Code = code;
            this.Description = description;
            this.Price = price;
        }

        public string Code
        {
            get
            {
                return code;
            }
            set
            {
                code = value;
            }
        }

        public string Description
        {
            get
            {
                return description;
            }
            set
            {
                description = value;
            }
        }

        public decimal Price
        {
            get
            {
                return price;
            }
            set
            {
                price = value;
            }
        }

        public string GetDisplayText(string sep)
        {
            return code + sep + price.ToString("c") + sep + description;
        }
    }
}
```

Fields

Empty constructor

A custom contructor

The Code property

The Description property

The Price property

The GetDisplayText method

Figure 12-3 The code for the Product class

How instantiation works

The process of creating an object from a class is called *instantiation.* Figure 12-4 describes how instantiation works. Here, you can see two object *instances* that were created from the Product class. Each instance represents a different Product object. Because both instances were created from the same class, they both have the same properties. However, the instances have distinct values for each property. For example, the value of the Code property for the product1 object is JAVA, but the value of the Code property for the product2 object is VASP.

The code example in this figure shows how you can create these two object instances. Here, the first line of code declares two variables named product1 and product2 that have a type of Product. Then, the next two lines create Product objects. To do that, they use the new keyword, followed by the name of the constructor for the Product class and the values that will be used to initialize the objects.

At this point, it's important to realize that a class defines a *reference type*. That means that the variable that's used to access an object contains the address of the memory location where the object is stored, not the object itself. In other words, the product1 variable holds a *reference* to a Product object, not an actual Product object.

Two Product objects that have been instantiated from the Product class

product1	product2
Code=JAVA Description=Murach's Beginning JAVA 2 Price=49.50	Code=VASP Description=Murach's ASP.NET Web Programming with VB.NET Price=49.50

Code that creates these two object instances

```
Product product1, product2;
product1 = new Product("JAVA", "Murach's Beginning JAVA 2", 49.50m);
product2 = new Product("VASP",
    "Murach's ASP.NET Web Programming with VB.NET", 49.50m);
```

Description

- When an object is instantiated, a *constructor* is executed to initialize the data that makes up the object. If a class doesn't provide a constructor, a default constructor is executed. The default constructor simply initializes all the data to default values.
- The data that makes up an object is sometimes referred to as the object's *state*. Once an object has been instantiated, its state can change.
- The state of an object changes whenever you change thc value of one of the object's properties or public fields. The state can also change when you call a method that affects the data stored within an object.
- An application can create two or more instances of the same class. Each instance is a separate entity with its own state. If you change the state of one object, the state of other objects created from the same class is not affected.
- A class defines a *reference type*. That means that the variable that's used to access an object instantiated from a class contains the address of the object, not the actual object.

Figure 12-4 How instantiation works

How to create a class

Now that you've learned about the members that make up a class and you've seen the code for the Product class, you're ready to learn the basic skills for creating and using your own classes. The topics that follow present these skills.

How to add a class file to a project

To create a user-defined class, you start by adding a *class file* to your project. To do that, you use the dialog box shown in figure 12-5. When you complete this dialog box, the class file will appear in the Solution Explorer with the extension *cs*.

When you add a class to a project, Visual Studio automatically generates the class declaration and an empty constructor. Then, you can complete the class by adding fields, properties, methods, and whatever other members the class may require.

Before I go on, you should notice the three comment lines before the class declaration. These lines provide information that Visual Studio can use to create web-based documentation for the class. You'll learn more about how to provide documentation in chapter 13. For now, you can ignore these lines.

The dialog box for adding a class

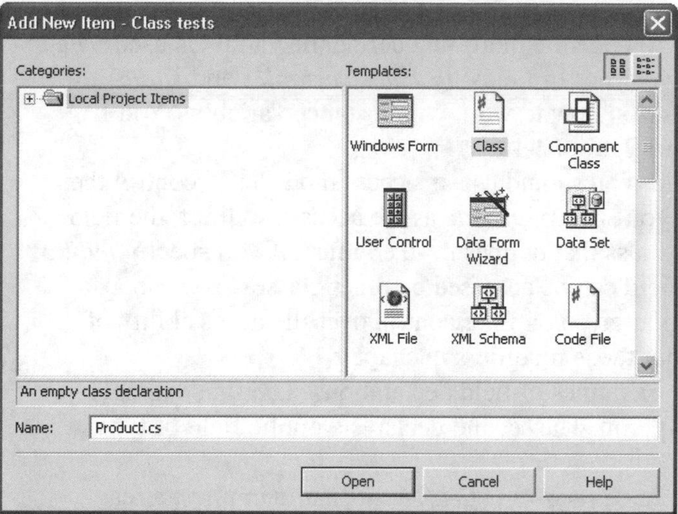

The starting code for the new class

```
using System;

namespace ProductMaintenance
{
    /// <summary>
    /// Summary description for Product.
    /// </summary>
    public class Product
    {
        public Product()
        {
            //
            // TODO: Add constructor logic here
            //
        }
    }
}
```

Description

- To add a new class to a project, use the Project→Add Class command to display the Add New Item dialog box. Then, enter the name you want to use for the new class and click the Open button.
- When you complete the Add New Item dialog box, a *class file* is added to the project. This class file will appear in the Solution Explorer window with the extension *cs*.
- The namespace and class blocks are automatically added to the class along with an empty constructor for the class. Then, you can enter the code for the class within the class block.

Figure 12-5 How to add a class file to a project

How to code fields

Figure 12-6 shows how to code the fields that define the variables used by a class. A class can contain two types of fields: *instance variables* and *static variables*. This figure shows you how to work with instance variables. You'll learn about static variables in figure 12-10.

When you declare a field, you should use an access modifier to control the accessibility of the field. If you specify *private* as the access modifier, the field can be used only within the class that defines it. In contrast, if you specify *public* as the access modifier, the field can be accessed by other classes. You can also use other access modifiers that give you finer control over the accessibility of your fields. You'll learn about those modifiers in chapter 14.

This figure shows three examples of field declarations. The first example declares a private field of type int. The second declares a public field of type decimal.

The third example declares a *read-only field*. As its name implies, a read-only field can be read but not modified. The only time you can assign a value to a read-only field is in the field declaration. In this respect, a read-only field is similar to a constant. The difference is that the value of a constant is set when the class is compiled. In contrast, the value of a read-only field is not set until runtime.

Note that although fields work like regular variables, they must be declared within the class body, not inside properties, methods, or constructors. That way, they're available throughout the entire class. In this book, all of the fields for a class are declared at the beginning of the class. However, when you read through code from other sources, you may find that the fields are declared at the end of the class or at other locations within the class.

This figure also presents another version of the Product class that uses public fields instead of properties. This works because the properties of the Product class that was presented in figure 12-3 didn't do anything except get and set the values of private fields. Because of that, you could just provide direct access to the fields by giving them public access as shown here. In some cases, though, a property will perform additional processing. Then, you'll need to use a property instead of a public field.

By the way, you may notice that the names of public fields in this class and in the second and third examples at the beginning of this figure begin with a capital letter. That's because these fields are used in place of properties, and the names of properties are always capitalized. In contrast, the name of the private field in the first example begins with a lowercase letter because it can only be accessed within the class.

Examples of field declarations

```
private int quantity;              // A private field.
public decimal Price;              // A public field.
public readonly int Limit = 90;    // A public read-only field.
```

A version of the Product class that uses public fields instead of properties

```
public class Product
{
    // Public fields
    public string Code;
    public string Description;
    public decimal Price;

    public Product()
    {
    }

    public Product(string code, string description, decimal price)
    {
        this.Code = code;
        this.Description = description;
        this.Price = price;
    }

    public string GetDisplayText(string sep)
    {
        return Code + sep + Price.ToString("c") + sep + Description;
    }
}
```

Description

- A variable that's defined at the class level within a class is called a *field*.
- A field can be a primitive data type, a class or structure from the .NET Framework, or a user-defined class or structure.
- You can use the *private* access modifier to prevent other classes from accessing a field. Then, the field can be accessed only from within the class.
- An *instance variable* is a field that's defined in a class and is allocated when an object is instantiated. Each object instance has a separate copy of each instance variable.
- If you initialize an instance variable, the initialization will occur before the constructor for the class is executed. As a result, the constructor may assign a new value to the variable.
- You can create a *read-only field* by specifying the *readonly* access modifier in the field's declaration. Then, you can retrieve the field's value, but you can't change it. Note that you provide the value for a read-only field when you declare it.
- A *public field* is a field that's declared with the *public* access modifier. Public fields can be accessed by other classes within the application, much like properties. However, properties have additional features that make them more useful than public fields.

Figure 12-6 How to code fields

How to code properties

Figure 12-7 presents the syntax for coding a property. As you can see, a property declaration specifies both the type and name of the property. In addition, a property is typically declared with the public access modifier so it can be accessed by other classes.

Within the block that defines a property, you can include two blocks called *accessors* because they provide access to the property values. The *get accessor* is executed when a request to retrieve the property value is made, and the *set accessor* is executed when a request to set the property value is made. If both get and set accessors are included, the property is called a *read/write property*. If only a get accessor is included, the property is called a *read-only property*. You can also create a *write-only property*, which has just a set accessor, but that's uncommon.

In most cases, each property has a corresponding private instance variable that holds the property's value. In that case, the property should be declared with the same data type as the instance variable. It's also common to use the same name for the property and the instance variable, but to use Camel notation for the instance variable name (first word starts with a lowercase character, all words after that start with uppercase characters) and to use Pascal notation for the property name (each word starts with an uppercase character). For example, the name of the instance variable for the Code property is code. And a property named UnitPrice would have a corresponding instance variable named unitPrice.

Because a get accessor returns the value of the property, it typically ends with a return statement that provides that value. In the first property in this figure, for example, the return statement simply returns the value of the instance variable that holds the property value. The second property, however, illustrates that the get accessor can be more complicated than that. Here, the get accessor performs a calculation to determine the value that's returned.

The set accessor uses an implicit parameter named value to access the value to be assigned to the property. Typically, the set accessor simply assigns this value to the instance variable that stores the property's value. However, the set accessor can perform more complicated processing if necessary. For example, it could perform data validation.

The syntax for coding a public property

```
public type PropertyName
{
    [get { get accessor code }]
    [set { set accessor code }]
}
```

A read/write property

```
public string Code
{
    get
    {
        return code;
    }
    set
    {
        code = value;
    }
}
```

A read-only property

```
public decimal DiscountAmount
{
    get
    {
        discountAmount = subtotal * discountPercent;
        return discountAmount;
    }
}
```

A statement that sets a property value

```
product.Code = txtProductCode.Text;
```

A statement that gets a property value

```
string code = product.Code;
```

Description

- You use a *property* to get and set data values associated with an object. Typically, each property has a corresponding private instance variable that stores the property's value.
- It's common to use the same name for the property and the related instance variable, but to begin the property name with an uppercase letter and the instance variable name with a lowercase letter.
- You can code a *get accessor* to retrieve the value of the property. Often, the get accessor simply returns the value of the instance variable that stores the property's value.
- You can code a *set accessor* to set the value of the property. Often, the set accessor simply assigns the value passed to it via the *value* keyword to the instance variable that stores the property's value.
- A property that has both a get and a set accessor is called a *read/write property*. A property that has just a get accessor is called a *read-only property*. And a property that has just a set accessor is called a *write-only property*.

Figure 12-7 How to code properties

How to code methods

Figure 12-8 shows you how to code the methods for a class. Because the basics of coding methods were presented in chapter 6, most of the information in this figure should review for you. In fact, this figure only introduces two new techniques. The first is the use of the public access modifier on a method declaration, which makes the method available to other classes.

The second is the concept of overloading. When you *overload* a method, you code two or more methods with the same name, but with unique combinations of parameters. In other words, you code methods with unique *signatures*.

For a method signature to be unique, the method must have a different number of parameters than the other methods with the same name, or at least one of the parameters must have a different data type. Note that the names of the parameters aren't part of the signature. So using different names isn't enough to make the signatures unique. Also, the return type isn't part of the signature. As a result, you can't create two methods with the same name and parameters but different return types.

The purpose of overloading is to provide more than one way to invoke a given method. For example, this figure shows two versions of the GetDisplayText method. The first one is the one you saw in figure 12-3 that accepts a parameter named sep. The second one doesn't accept this parameter. Instead, it uses a comma and a space to separate the code, price, and description.

When you refer to an overloaded method, the number of arguments you specify and their types determine which version of the method is executed. The two statements in this figure that call the GetDisplayText method illustrate how this works. Because the first statement specifies an argument, it will cause the version of the GetDisplayText method that accepts a parameter to be executed. In contrast, the second statement doesn't specify an argument, so it will cause the version of the GetDisplayText method that doesn't accept a parameter to be executed.

In chapter 3, you learned that if you type the name of a method followed by a left parenthesis into the Code Editor, Visual Studio's IntelliSense feature displays a list of the method's parameters. You may not have realized, though, that if up and down arrows appear to the left of the argument list, it indicates that the method is overloaded. Then, you can click the up and down arrows or press the up and down arrow keys to move from one overloaded method to another.

This works with overloaded methods in user-defined classes as well. For example, the illustration in this figure shows how the Intellisense feature displays the overloaded GetDisplayText methods. In this case, the first of the two methods is displayed.

The syntax for coding a public method

```
public returnType MethodName([parameterList])
{
    statements
}
```

A method that accepts parameters

```
public string GetDisplayText(string sep)
{
    return code + sep + price.ToString("c") + sep + description;
}
```

An overloaded version of the GetDisplayText method

```
public string GetDisplayText()
{
    return code + ", " + price.ToString("c") + ", " + description;
}
```

Two statements that call the GetDisplayText method

```
lblProduct.Text = product.GetDisplayText("\t");
lblProduct.Text = product.GetDisplayText();
```

How the IntelliSense feature lists overloaded methods

```
Product product = new Product(txtCode.Text);
lblProduct.Text = product.GetDisplayText(
                  ▲1 of 2▼ string Product.GetDisplayText (string sep)
```

Description

- To provide other classes with access to a method, you declare it using the public access modifier. To prevent other classes from accessing a method, you declare it using the private access modifier.
- The name of a method combined with its parameters form the method's *signature*. Although you can use the same name for more than one method, each method must have a unique signature.
- When you create two or more methods with the same name but with different parameter lists, the methods are *overloaded*. It's common to use overloaded methods to provide two or more versions of a method that work with different data types or that supply default values for omitted parameters.
- When you type a method name followed by a left parenthesis, the IntelliSense feature of Visual Studio displays the parameters expected by the method. If up and down arrows are displayed as shown above, you can click these arrows or press the up and down arrow keys to display each of the method's overloaded parameter lists.

Figure 12-8 How to code methods

How to code constructors

By default, when you use the new keyword to create an instance of a user-defined class, C# assigns default values to all of the instance variables in the new object. If that's not what you want, you can code a special method called a *constructor* that's executed when an object is created from the class. Figure 12-9 shows you how to do that.

To create a constructor, you declare a public method with the same name as the class name. For example, a constructor for the Product class must be named Product. Within the constructor, you initialize the instance variables, and you include any additional statements you want to be executed when an object is created from the class. Note that a constructor must not be declared with a return type.

The first example in this figure is the constructor that's generated automatically when you create a class using the Project→Add Class command. This constructor doesn't provide for any parameters, so it's called when you create an instance of the class without specifying any arguments. Because this constructor has no executable statements, it simply initializes all the instance variables to their default values (excluding read-only variables). The default values for the various data types are listed in this figure.

In some cases, a class might not be defined with any constructors. For example, you could delete the constructor that's generated automatically when you create a class. Or, you could code a class within another class (see chapter 13) and not declare a constructor for that class. In that case, C# provides a *default constructor* that's equivalent to the constructor shown in the first example.

The second constructor in this figure shows that you can overload constructors just like you can overload methods. Here, a constructor that accepts three parameters is defined. This constructor uses the values passed to the parameters to initialize the instance variables. This technique is often used to set initial property values when an object is created.

The third constructor shows how you might provide a constructor for the Product class that accepts just a product code as a parameter. Then, it calls a method named GetProduct in a database class named ProductDB to retrieve the data for the specified product. After the data is retrieved, the constructor uses it to initialize the instance variables.

Notice that both the second and third constructors use the this keyword to refer to the properties whose values are being initialized. Although this isn't required, it makes it clear that the property that's being referred to is defined in the current class and not in another class.

This figure also presents statements that execute the three constructors shown here. The first statement executes the constructor with no parameters. The second statement executes the constructor with three parameters. And the third statement executes the constructor with one parameter. Although you've seen statements like these before, you should now have a better understanding of how they work.

A constructor with no parameters

```
public Product()
{
    //
    // TODO: Add constructor logic here
    //
}
```

A constructor with three parameters

```
public Product(string code, string description, decimal price)
{
    this.Code = code;
    this.Description = description;
    this.Price = price;
}
```

A constructor with one parameter

```
public Product(string code)
{
    Product p = ProductDB.GetProduct(code);
    this.Code = p.Code;
    this.Description = p.Description;
    this.Price = p.Price;
}
```

Statements that call these constructors

```
Product product1 = new Product();
Product product2 = new Product("JAVA", "Murach's Beginning Java 2", 49.50m);
Product product3 = new Product(txtCode.Text);
```

Default values for instance variables

Data type	Default value
All numeric types	zero (0)
Boolean	false
Char	binary 0 (null)
Object	null (no value)
Date	12:00 a.m. on January 1, 0001

Description

- The name of a constructor must be the same as the name of the class. In addition, a constructor must always be declared with the public access modifier, and it can't specify a return type.
- To code a constructor that has parameters, code a data type and name for each parameter within the parentheses that follow the class name.
- The name of a class combined with its parameter list form the signature of the constructor. Each constructor must have a unique signature.
- If a constructor doesn't assign a value to an instance variable and the variable hasn't been initialized, the variable will be assigned a default value as shown above.

Figure 12-9 How to code constructors

How to code static members

As figure 12-10 shows, *static members* are members that can be accessed without creating an instance of a class. The idea of static members shouldn't be new to you because you've seen them used in several chapters in this book. In chapter 4, for example, you learned how to use static methods of the Math and Convert classes. And in chapter 9, you learned how to use static members of the DateTime structure and the String class. This figure shows how to create static members in your own classes.

To create a static member, you simply include the *static* keyword on the declaration for the member. The class shown in this figure, for example, provides static members that can be used to perform data validation. This class has a static field named title, a static property named Title, and a static method named IsPresent.

The static IsPresent method validates the Text property of a text box control to make sure the user entered a value. If the Text property is an empty string, the IsPresent method displays an error message, sets the focus to the text box, and returns false. Otherwise, it returns true. Note that this method uses the Tag property of the text box to get the name that's displayed in the dialog box.

The second example in this figure shows how you might call the static IsPresent method to validate three text boxes. Here, the return values from three calls to the IsPresent method are tested. If all three calls return true, a Boolean variable named isValidData is set to true. Otherwise, this variable is set to false.

Although the class shown in this figure contains only static members, a class that has static members can also include non-static members. Then, when you create an instance of that class, all of the instances share the static members. Because of that, you can't access a static member from an instance of the class. Instead, you can only access it only from the class itself.

Keep in mind, too, that a static property or method can only refer to other static members. For example, because the Title property shown in this figure is declared as static, the title field it refers to must be declared as static. Similarly, if a property or method refers to another method, that method must be declared as static.

A class that contains static members

```
public class Validator
{
    private static string title = "Entry Error";

    public static string Title
    {
        get
        {
            return title;
        }
        set
        {
            title = value;
        }
    }

    public static bool IsPresent(TextBox textBox)
    {
        if (textBox.Text == "")
        {
            MessageBox.Show(textBox.Tag + " is a required field.", Title);
            textBox.Focus();
            return false;
        }
        return true;
    }
```

Code that uses static members

```
if (  Validator.IsPresent(txtCode.Text) &&
      Validator.IsPresent(txtDescription.Text) &&
      Validator.IsPresent(txtPrice.Text) )
    isValidData = true;
else
    isValidData = false;
```

Description

- A *static member* is a field, property, or method that can be accessed without creating an instance of the class. To define a static member, you use the *static* keyword.
- If you create instances of a class that contains static members, all of those instances share the same copy of the class's static members. Because of that, you can't refer to a static member through an instance of the class. You can refer to a static member only through the class that defines it.
- Static properties and methods can refer only to other static members or to variables declared within the property or method.
- A constant that's declared with the public keyword is implicitly static. You can't code the static keyword on a constant declaration.

The Product Maintenance application

Now that you've learned the basic skills for creating classes, the topics that follow present a Product Maintenance application that maintains a simple file of products. As you'll see, this application uses three classes in addition to the two form classes it uses.

The operation of the Product Maintenance application

Figure 12-11 describes the operation of the Product Maintenance application. As you can see, this application uses two forms. The main form displays a list of the products that are stored in a file in a list box. The user can use this form to add or delete a product.

If the user clicks the Add Product button, the New Product form is displayed as a dialog box. Then, the user can enter the data for a new product and click the Save button to add the product to the file. After the product is saved, the list box in the Product Maintenance form is refreshed so it includes the new product. The user can also click the Cancel button on the New Product form to cancel the add operation.

To delete a product, the user selects the product in the list and clicks the Delete product button. Then, a dialog box is displayed to confirm the operation. If the operation is confirmed, the product is deleted and the list box is refreshed so it no longer includes the deleted product.

This figure also shows how the Tag properties of the three text boxes on the New Product form are set. As you'll see in a minute, the methods of the data validation class use the Tag property of these text boxes to display meaningful error messages if the user enters incorrect data.

The Product Maintenance form

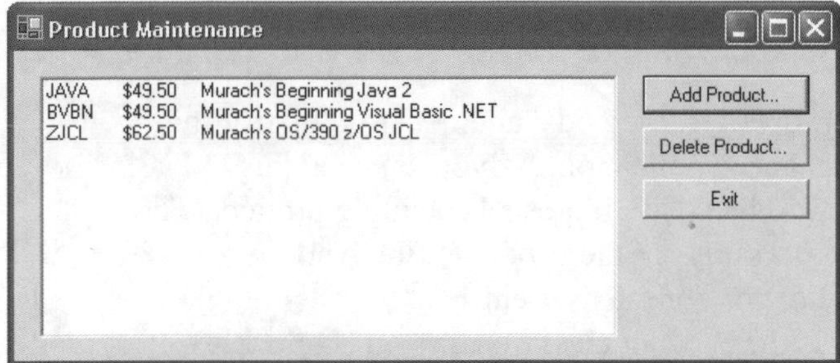

The New Product form

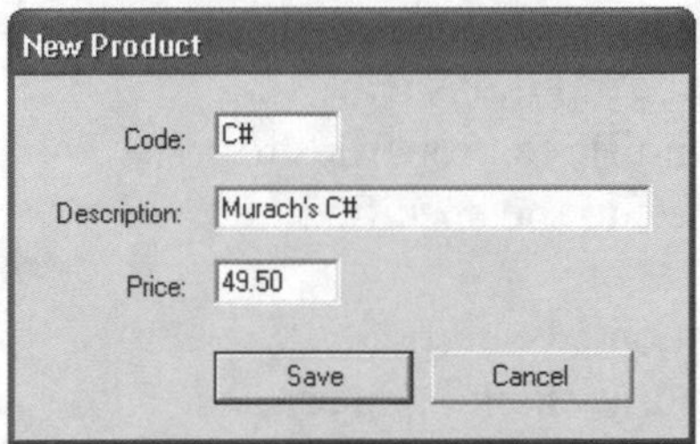

The Tag property settings for the text boxes on the New Product form

Control	Tag property setting
txtCode	Code
txtDescription	Description
txtPrice	Price

Description

- The Product Maintenance application retrieves product information from a file, displays it in a list box, and lets the user add or delete products.
- To add a product, the user clicks the Add Product button to display the New Product form. Then, the user can enter the data for the new product and click the Save button. Alternatively, the user can click the Cancel button to cancel the add operation. In either case, the user is returned to the Product Maintenance form.
- To delete a product, the user selects the product to be deleted and then clicks the Delete Product button. Before the product is deleted, the delete operation is confirmed.
- The Tag properties of the three text boxes on the New Product form are set so that the Validator class can display meaningful error messages if the user enters invalid data.

Figure 12-11 The operation of the Product Maintenance application

The classes used by the Product Maintenance application

Figure 12-12 summarizes the properties, methods, and constructors for the classes used by the Product Maintenance application. As you can see, this application uses three classes. The Product class represents a single product. The ProductDB class handles the I/O processing for the Products file. And the Validator class handles the data validation for the user entries.

The Product class is the same as the Product class you saw in figure 12-3. It has three properties named Code, Description, and Price that define the values for a Product object. It has a single method named GetDisplayText that returns a string that contains the code, description, and price in a format that can be displayed in the list box of the Product Maintenance form. And it has two constructors: one that initializes the Code, Description, and Price properties to their default values, and one that initializes these properties to the specified values.

The ProductDB class contains two methods. The first one, GetProducts, retrieves all of the products from the Products file and returns them in an array list. The second one, SaveProducts, accepts an array list of Product objects and writes the products in the array list to the Products file, overwriting the previous contents of the file.

Note that the specifications for these methods don't indicate the format of the Products file. That's because the details of how this class saves and retrieves product information are of no concern to the Product Maintenance application. That's one of the benefits of encapsulation: You don't have to know how the class works. You just have to know what members it contains and how you refer to them.

The Validator class contains four static members that provide for different types of data validation. For example, the IsPresent method checks if the user entered data into a text box, and the IsDecimal method checks if the data the user entered is a valid decimal value. If one of these methods determines that the data is invalid, it displays an error message using the Title property as the title for the dialog box, it moves the focus to the text box that's being validated, and it returns false. Otherwise, it returns true.

The Product class

Property	Description
`Code`	A string that contains a code that uniquely identifies the product.
`Description`	A string that contains a description of the product.
`Price`	A decimal that contains the product's price.
Method	**Description**
`GetDisplayText(sep)`	Returns a string that contains the code, description, and price separated by the sep string.
Constructor	**Description**
`()`	Creates a Product object with default values.
`(code, description, price)`	Creates a Product object using the specified values.

The ProductDB class

Method	Description
`GetProducts()`	A static method that returns an array list that contains a Product object for each product in the Products file.
`SaveProducts(arrayList)`	A static method that writes the products in the specified array list to the Products file.

The Validator class

Property	Description
`Title`	A static string that contains the text that's displayed in the title bar of a dialog box that's displayed for an error message.
Method	**Description**
`IsPresent(textBox)`	A static method that returns a Boolean value that indicates if data was entered into the specified text box.
`IsInt32(textBox)`	A static method that returns a Boolean value that indicates if an integer was entered into the specified text box.
`IsDecimal(textBox)`	A static method that returns a Boolean value that indicates if a decimal was entered into the specified text box.
`IsWithinRange(textBox, min, max)`	A static method that returns a Boolean value that indicates if the value entered into the specified text box is within the specified range.

Note: Each of these methods displays an error message in a dialog box and moves the focus to the text box if the data is invalid.

Note

- Because you don't need to know how the ProductDB class works, its code isn't shown in this chapter. Please refer to chapters 21 and 22 for three different versions of this class.

Figure 12-12 The classes used by the Product Maintenance application

The code for the Product Maintenance application

Figures 12-13 through 12-15 show the code for the Product Maintenance form, the New Product form, and the Validator class. You saw the code for the Product class in figure 12-3, so I won't repeat it here. And, because you don't need to know how the ProductDB class is implemented to understand how this application works, I won't present the code for that class here either. If you're interested, however, you'll find three different implementations of this class in chapters 21 and 22.

The code for the Product Maintenance form, shown in figure 12-13, begins by declaring a class variable named products of type ArrayList. Then, in the Load event handler for the form, the GetProducts method of the ProductsDB class is called to fill this array list with Product objects created from the data in the Products file. Then, the FillProductListBox method is called. This method uses a foreach loop to add the string returned by each product's GetDisplayText method to the list box. Notice that a tab character is passed to this method so that the products appear as shown in figure 12-11.

If the user clicks the Add Product button, an instance of the New Product form is created, and the GetNewProduct method of that form is called. If the Product object returned by this method isn't null, the product is added to the array list of products. Then, the SaveProducts method of the ProductDB class is called to update the Products file, and the FillProductListBox method is called to refresh the list box so the new product is included.

If the user selects a product in the list and clicks the Delete Product button, a confirmation dialog box is displayed. Then, if the user confirms the deletion, the product is removed from the array list, the Products file is updated, and the list box is refreshed.

The code for the New Product form is shown in figure 12-14. It declares a private Product object named product. Then, the GetNewProduct method that's called from the Product Maintenance form starts by displaying the New Product form as a dialog box. If the user clicks the Save button in this dialog box, the IsValidData method is called to validate the data. This method calls the IsPresent method of the Validator class for each text box on the form. In addition, it calls the IsDecimal method for the Price text box.

If all of the values are valid, a new Product object is created with the values entered by the user, the dialog box is closed, and the Product object is returned to the Product Maintenance form. In contrast, if the user clicks the Cancel button, the dialog box is closed and the product variable, which is initialized to null, is returned to the Product Maintenance form.

The code for the Validator class, shown in figure 12-15, should present no surprises. In fact, you saw code similar to this code back in figure 12-10. The only difference is that this version of the Validator class includes an IsDecimal method as well as an IsPresent method. Note that because the Product Maintenance application doesn't use the IsInt32 or IsWithinRange methods, I omitted those methods from this figure.

The code for the Product Maintenance form

```
public class frmProductMaintenance : System.Windows.Forms.Form
{
    private ArrayList products = null;

    private void frmProductMain_Load(object sender, System.EventArgs e)
    {
        products = ProductDB.GetProducts();
        FillProductListBox();
    }

    private void FillProductListBox()
    {
        lstProducts.Items.Clear();
        foreach (Product p in products)
        {
            lstProducts.Items.Add(p.GetDisplayText("\t"));
        }
    }

    private void btnAdd_Click(object sender, System.EventArgs e)
    {
        frmNewProduct newProductForm = new frmNewProduct();
        Product product = newProductForm.GetNewProduct();
        if (product != null)
        {
            products.Add(product);
            ProductDB.SaveProducts(products);
            FillProductListBox();
        }
    }

    private void btnDelete_Click(object sender, System.EventArgs e)
    {
        int i = lstProducts.SelectedIndex;
        if (i != -1)
        {
            Product product = (Product) products[i];
            string message = "Are you sure you want to delete "
                + product.Description + "?";
            DialogResult button =
                MessageBox.Show(message, "Confirm Delete",
                MessageBoxButtons.YesNo);
            if (button == DialogResult.Yes)
            {
                products.Remove(product);
                ProductDB.SaveProducts(products);
                FillProductListBox();
            }
        }
    }

    private void btnClose_Click(object sender, System.EventArgs e)
    {
        this.Close();
    }
}
```

Figure 12-13 The code for the Product Maintenance form

The code for the New Product form

```
public class frmNewProduct : System.Windows.Forms.Form
{
    private Product product = null;

    public Product GetNewProduct()
    {
        this.ShowDialog();
        return product;
    }

    private void btnSave_Click(object sender, System.EventArgs e)
    {
        if (IsValidData())
        {
            product = new Product(txtCode.Text,
                txtDescription.Text, Convert.ToDecimal(txtPrice.Text));
            this.Close();
        }
    }

    private bool IsValidData()
    {
        return Validator.IsPresent(txtCode) &&
               Validator.IsPresent(txtDescription) &&
               Validator.IsPresent(txtPrice) &&
               Validator.IsDecimal(txtPrice);
    }

    private void btnCancel_Click(object sender, System.EventArgs e)
    {
        this.Close();
    }

}
```

Figure 12-14 The code for the New Product form

The code for the Validator class

```
public class Validator
{
    private static string title = "Entry Error";

    public static string Title
    {
        get
        {
            return title;
        }
        set
        {
            title = value;
        }
    }

    public static bool IsPresent(TextBox textBox)
    {
        if (textBox.Text == "")
        {
            MessageBox.Show(textBox.Tag + " is a required field.", Title);
            textBox.Focus();
            return false;
        }
        return true;
    }

    public static bool IsDecimal(TextBox textBox)
    {
        try
        {
            Convert.ToDecimal(textBox.Text);
            return true;
        }
        catch (FormatException)
        {
            MessageBox.Show(textBox.Tag + " must be a decimal number.", Title);
            textBox.Focus();
            return false;
        }
    }

}
```

Note

- The code for the IsInt32 and IsWithinRange methods isn't shown here because these methods aren't used by the Product Maintenance application.

Figure 12-15 The code for the Validator class

How to work with classes in Visual Studio

Now that you've seen a complete application that uses classes, the last two topics of this chapter introduce some additional Visual Studio features that are designed for working with classes. Although you don't have to use these features, they can make classes easier to work with in some cases.

How to use the Class View window

The *Class View window* is a tabbed window that's displayed by default in the group with the Solution Explorer window. As figure 12-16 shows, this window contains a hierarchical view of the classes in your solution as well as the members of each class. In short, class view gives you an overall view of the structure of your application.

The solution shown here is for the Product Maintenance application that was presented in figures 12-11 through 12-15. Here, I've expanded the class list to show the individual members that make up the Product class. As you can see, the list of members for this class includes the GetDisplayText method, the two constructors for this class, the Code, Description, and Price properties, and the private fields named code, description, and price. Notice the padlock on the icons for the private fields. They indicate that these fields are not accessible from outside the class.

You can also use the Class View window to display the code for any item in the Code Editor window. To do that, just double-click the item in the Class View window. In this figure, for example, you can see the code that was displayed when I double-clicked the Price property.

The Class View window

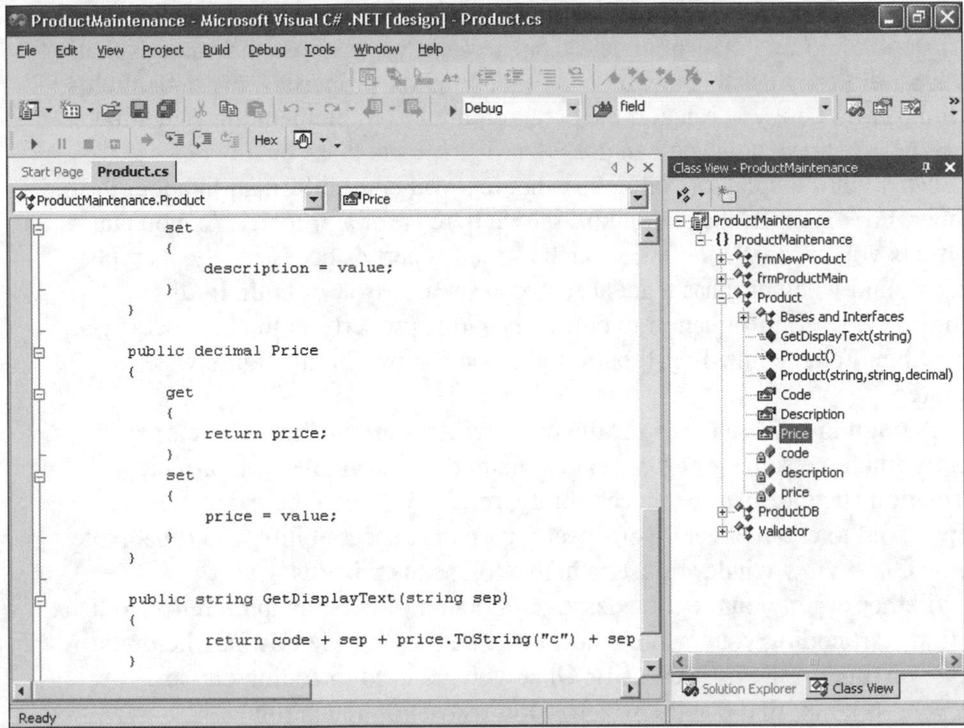

Description

- The *Class View window* lets you browse the classes in a solution.
- The Class View window displays each class and its members, including properties, methods, events, and fields, in a hierarchical tree view. You can expand or collapse the tree by clicking the plus and minus signs.
- To display the Class View window, click the Class View tab that's grouped with the Solution Explorer window, or use the View→Class View command.
- You can double-click an item in the Class View window to display the code that defines that item in the Code Editor window.

Figure 12-16 How to use the Class View window

How to use wizards to create class members

Instead of coding class members from scratch, you can use the wizards that Visual Studio provides to generate code skeletons for properties, methods, fields, and indexers. Then, you can add the code required to implement these members. Figure 12-17 shows how you can use wizards to create class members.

Each wizard displays a dialog box that lets you enter information about the member. For example, the dialog box shown here is for a property. As you can see, it lets you specify information such as the property's accessibility, its type, its name, and whether it has a get accessor, a set accessor, or both. In this example, I entered information to define the Code property of the Product class. Then, when I clicked the Finish button, the code shown in this figure was generated.

Although the dialog boxes for the other wizards aren't shown here, they work in much the same way. To create a method, for example, you provide information such as its name, accessibility, return type, and the parameters it accepts. And to create a field, you specify its name, accessibility, and type. Note that the Class View window must be active to use the wizards.

Whether or not you use the wizards is a matter of personal preference. When you first start coding your own classes, for example, the wizards may help you to code members quickly and easily. Once you get used to coding classes, however, you may find that the wizards don't save you much time.

The C# Add Property Wizard

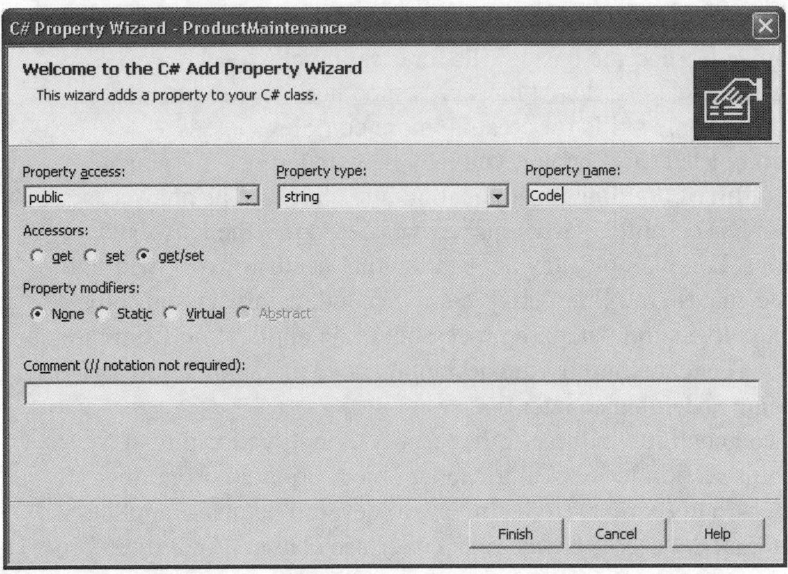

The code generated for the property shown above

```
public string Code
{
    get
    {
        return null;
    }
    set
    {
    }
}
```

Description

- Visual Studio provides several wizards that you can use to add properties, methods, fields, and indexers to C# classes.
- To use a wizard, open the Class View window and select the class you want to add a member to. Then, choose the appropriate command from the Project menu (Add Method, Add Property, Add Field, or Add Indexer), enter the appropriate information into the dialog box that's displayed, and click the Finish button.
- You can also access a wizard by right-clicking a class in the Class View window and then choosing the Add Method, Add Property, Add Field, or Add Indexer command from the shortcut menu that's displayed.
- The wizards automatically insert the starting code for a member into your class. Then, you can enter any additional code that's required.

Figure 12-17 How to use wizards to create class members

Perspective

In this chapter, you've learned the basic skills for creating classes. However, there's a lot more to creating classes than what's presented here. In the next three chapters, then, you'll learn some skills for creating more complex classes.

Now that you've completed this chapter, you may be wondering why you should go to the extra effort of dividing an application into classes. The answer is twofold. First, dividing the code into classes makes it easier to use the classes in two or more applications. For example, any application that needs to work with the data in the Products file can use the ProductDB class. Second, using classes helps you separate the business logic and database processing of an application from the user interface elements. That can simplify the development of the application and make it easier to maintain and enhance later on.

At this point, you can continue in three different ways. First, you can read the next three chapters in this section to learn more about object-oriented programming. Second, you can skip to section 4 to learn how to develop database applications both with and without the use of business and database classes. And third, you can skip to chapters 21 and 22 to learn how to implement database classes with text, binary, and XML files. If you skip to section 4 or 5 after chapter 12, though, be sure to return to chapters 13 through 15 later on because they present the rest of the object-oriented skills that every programmer should have.

Summary

- In a *three-tiered architecture*, an application is separated into three layers: The *presentation layer* consists of the user interface; the *database layer* consists of the database and the database classes that work with it; and the *middle layer* provides an interface between the presentation layer and the database layer.
- An *object* contains *members*, such as *properties*, *methods*, and *events*. An object is *instantiated* from a *class*, which contains the code that defines the members of an object.
- *Encapsulation* lets you control the data and operations within a class that are exposed to other classes. When data is encapsulated within a class, it's called *data hiding*.
- The data that is stored in an object can be referred to as its *state*. Each object is a separate entity with its own state.
- A *field* is a variable that's defined at the class level. A *public field* can be accessed by other classes. A private field cannot.
- An *instance variable* is a field that's allocated when an object is instantiated. Each object has a separate copy of each instance variable.
- You use properties to get and set the data associated with an object. Each property can have a *get accessor* that retrieves the value of a property and a *set accessor* that sets the value of the property.

- A method defines the operations that an object can perform. You can *overload* methods by declaring them with the same name but with different parameter lists.
- A *constructor* is a special type of method that creates an instance of a class. A constructor typically initializes the instance variables defined by the class.
- A *static member* is a field, property, or method that is accessed directly from the class rather than from an instance of a class. If you create instances of a class that contains static members, all of the instances share those members.
- You can use the *Class View window* to browse the classes in a solution.
- You can use the wizards provided by Visual Studio to add starting code for properties, methods, fields or indexers.

Terms

multi-layered architecture
multi-tiered architecture
three-tiered architecture
presentation layer
database layer
middle layer
business rules layer
object
property
method
member
class
instantiation
encapsulation
data hiding
constructor
state
reference type
class file
field
instance variable
read-only field
public field
get accessor
set accessor
read/write property
read-only property
write-only property
signature
overloaded method
static member
Class View window

Objectives

- Given the specifications for an application that uses classes with any of the members presented in this chapter, develop the application and its classes.
- List and describe the three layers of a three-tiered application.
- Explain what encapsulation is and describe its main benefit.
- Explain what instantiation is and how it works.
- Explain what a field is and describe the two types of variables they can define.
- Explain how the get and set accessors of a property work.
- Describe the concept of overloading a method.
- Describe the function of a constructor.

- Explain what a static member is and how it's used.
- Describe the features that Visual Studio provides for working with classes.

Exercise 12-1 Create a Customer Maintenance application that uses classes

In this exercise, you'll create a Customer Maintenance application that uses three classes. To make this application easier to develop, we'll give you the starting forms with all the controls you'll need, a complete Validator class that you'll use to validate the data the user enters, and a complete CustomerDB class that you'll use to work with the data in a file of customers.

Open the project and add a Customer class

1. Open the project named CustomerMaintenance in the C:\C#.NET\Chapter 12\CustomerMaintenance directory.
2. Add a class named Customer to this project, and add the following properties, method, and constructors to this class:

Property	Description
`FirstName`	Gets or sets a string that contains the customer's first name.
`LastName`	Gets or sets a string that contains the customer's last name.
`Email`	Gets or sets a string that contains the customer's email address.
Method	**Description**
`GetDisplayText()`	Returns a string that contains the customer's name and email address formatted like this: Joanne Smith, jsmith@armaco.com.
Constructor	**Description**
`()`	Creates a customer object with default values.
`(firstName, lastName, email)`	Creates a customer object using the specified values.

Add code to implement the Add Customer form

3. Display the code for the Add Customer form, and declare a class variable named customer of type Customer with an initial value of null.
4. Add a public method named GetNewCustomer that displays the form as a dialog box and returns a Customer object.

5. Add an event handler for the Click event of the Save button that validates the data on the form using the Validator class (all three fields are required), and then creates a new customer object and closes the form if the data is valid.
6. Add an event handler for the Click event of the Cancel button that simply closes the form.

Add code to implement the Customer Maintenance form

7. Display the code for the Customer Maintenance form, and declare a class variable named customers of type ArrayList with an initial value of null.
8. Add an event handler for the Load event of the form that uses the GetCustomers method of the CustomerDB class to load the customers array list and then adds the customers to the Customers list box. Use the GetDisplayText method of the Customer class to format the customer data.
9. Add an event handler for the Click event of the Add button that creates a new instance of the Add Customer form and executes the GetNewCustomer method of that form. If the customer object that's returned by this method is not null, this event handler should add the new customer to the array list, call the SaveCustomers method of the CustomerDB class to save the array list, and then refresh the Customers list box.
10. Add an event handler for the Click event of the Delete button that removes the selected customer from the array list, calls the SaveProducts method of the CustomerDB class to save the array list, and refreshes the Customers list box. Be sure to confirm the delete operation.
11. Add an event handler for the Click event of the Exit button that closes the form.

Run and test the application

12. Run the application and test it to be sure that it works properly. When you're done, end the application, but leave the solution open if you're going to continue with the next exercise.

Exercise 12-2 Add a static method to the Validator class

In this exercise, you'll add a static method to the Validator class of the Customer Maintenance application that validates email addresses. Then, you'll modify the code for the Add Customer form so it uses this new method.

1. If it's not already open, open the project named CustomerMaintenance in the C:\C#.NET\Chapter 12\CustomerMaintenance directory.
2. Add a static method named IsValidEmail to the Validator class. This method should accept a text box as a parameter and then check the Text property of that text box to be sure that the email address includes both an @ character and a period. If the email address is invalid, this method should display an error message, set the focus to the text box, and return false. Otherwise, it should return true.
3. Modify the code in the Add Customer form so it uses the IsValidEmail method to validate the email address.
4. Run the application, and test it to be sure it works properly.

More skills for working with classes

In the last chapter, you learned some basic skills for creating and working with classes. Now, this chapter will teach you some additional skills that you can use to create more complex classes. That includes creating indexers, throwing argument exceptions, raising events, and overloading operators. In addition, this chapter will show you how you can organize and document your classes so they're easy for other programmers to use.

More skills for implementing class members

In the topics that follow, you'll learn three new skills for implementing class members. Although you may not use the features presented here often, you should at least have a general idea how they work. Then, if you ever need to use them, you can return to these topics and study them in more detail.

The Product and ProductList classes

To demonstrate the techniques that are presented in this chapter, I'll use an enhanced version of the Product class you saw in chapter 12, along with a new class named ProductList. The designs of these two classes are presented in figure 13-1.

Like the Product class that was presented in chapter 12, the version shown here includes three properties named Code, Description, and Price, a method named GetDisplayText, and two constructors. In addition, this class provides two operators that let you compare the values in two Product objects.

As you may recall, the Product Maintenance application that was presented in chapter 12 used the ArrayList class to store Product objects. The application in this chapter will use the ProductList class instead. As you'll see, this class represents a collection of Product objects that are stored in an array list.

The ProductList class includes a Count property that indicates how many products are in the product list and indexers that let you access a product based on its index or product code. It also includes an overloaded Add method. The first version of this method accepts a single parameter: a Product object that's added to the product list. The second version accepts three parameters: code, description, and price. The ProductList class uses these parameters to create a Product object, which is then added to the list. The ProductList class also includes a Remove method that removes a specified product from the list, a Fill method that fills the product list with the data in a file, and a Save method that saves the product list to a file.

Besides these methods, the ProductList class includes a + operator that adds a product to the list and a – operator that removes an item from the list. And it includes an event named Changed. This event is raised whenever the contents of the product list changes due to a product being added to or removed from the list. As you'll see, the Product Maintenance application uses this event to determine when it should save the product list and refresh the list box that displays the products.

The Product class

Property	Description
Code	A string that contains a code that uniquely identifies each product.
Description	A string that provides a description of the product.
Price	A decimal that represents the product's price.
Method	**Description**
GetDisplayText(sep)	Returns a string that contains the code, description, and price in a displayable format. The sep parameter is a string that's used to separate the elements.
Constructor	**Description**
()	Creates a Product object with default values.
(code, description, price)	Creates a Product object using the specified code, description, and price values.
Operator	**Description**
==	Compares Product objects for equality by comparing their code, description, and price values.
!=	Compares Product objects for inequality by comparing their code, description, and price values.

The ProductList class

Property	Description
Count	An integer that indicates how many Product objects are in the list.
[index]	An indexer that provides access to the product at the specified position.
[code]	An indexer that provides access to the product with the specified code.
Method	**Description**
Add(product)	Adds the specified Product object to the list.
Add(code, description, price)	Creates a Product object with the specified code, description, and price values, and then adds the Product object to the list.
Remove(product)	Removes the specified Product object from the list.
Fill()	Fills the list with product data from a file.
Save()	Saves the products to a file.
Operator	**Description**
+	Adds a Product object to the list.
-	Removes a Product object from the list.
Event	**Description**
Changed	Raised whenever a Product object is added to or removed from the list.

Figure 13-1 The Product and ProductList classes

How to create an indexer

As figure 13-2 shows, an *indexer* is a special type of property that lets you create classes that represent collections of objects. An indexer lets other classes that use the class access a specific item in the collection by specifying an index value.

The first example in this figure shows an indexer for the ProductList class. Notice that this class starts by declaring a private field named products of type ArrayList. This array list will be used to store products within a ProductList object. Then, an indexer with the type Product is declared. Notice that this indexer is not given a name. Instead, it uses the this keyword to refer to the current object. This keyword is followed by a parameter that identifies the index used by the indexer. Unlike most parameters, which are coded within parentheses, the parameter for an indexer is coded with brackets.

Like any other property, an indexer can provide get and set accessors. For example, the get accessor in the first example uses an integer index to return a Product object from the products array list based on its position in the list. Notice that the object that's retrieved from the array list must be cast to a Product object. That's because an array list stores Object types, but the indexer must return a Product type. However, casting isn't required for the set accessor since an object of any type can be stored in an array list.

The second example in this figure shows another possible indexer for the ProductList class. This indexer varies from the first one in two ways. First, it doesn't include a set accessor, so it provides read-only access to the products list. Second, it uses a string index that provides for accessing the products by product code. To do that, this get accessor uses a foreach loop to search the products array list, and it returns the first product whose Code property matches the index value. If no match is found, null is returned.

The third example in this figure shows how you can use these indexers. The first two statements create a new ProductList object and add a product to it using the Add method. Then, the next statement uses the indexer that accepts an integer to retrieve the product by its position in the array list. Finally, the last statement uses the indexer that accepts a string to retrieve the product by its product code.

An indexer that uses an integer as an index

```
private ArrayList products;

public Product this[int i]
{
    get
    {
        return (Product) products[i];
    }
    set
    {
        products[i] = value;
    }
}
```

A read-only indexer that uses a string as an index

```
public Product this[string code]
{
    get
    {
        foreach (Product p in products)
            if (p.Code == code)
                return p;
        return null;
    }
}
```

Code that uses these indexers

```
ProductList products = new ProductList();
products.Add("JAVA", "Murach's Beginning JAVA 2", 49.50m);
Product p1 = products[0];
Product p2 = products["JAVA"];
```

Description

- An *indexer* is a special type of property that lets a user of the class access individual items within the class by specifying an index value. Indexers are used for classes that represent collections of objects.
- Before you add an indexer to a class, you should create an array or a collection as a private instance variable to hold the objects that will be accessed using the indexer.
- The declaration for an indexer includes the type of object it indexes, the this keyword, and a parameter that defines the index to be used, enclosed in brackets.
- The indexer's get accessor should return the object specified by the index value that's passed to it from the underlying collection. The indexer's set accessor should set the object of the underlying collection specified by the index value that's passed to it to the object passed via the value keyword.
- Although the index used by an indexer is typically an int, it doesn't have to be.

How to throw argument exceptions

When you create your own classes, you should make sure that they check for invalid data. In particular, a property set accessor should validate the arguments that are passed to it before it sets the associated property value. Then, if the data is invalid, an exception should be thrown to notify the user of the class that an error has occurred. A method should also validate arguments that are passed to it when appropriate.

Figure 13-3 shows how argument exceptions should be handled. Here, the set accessor for a property named Code uses the value keyword to check that the string argument that's passed to it is no more than four characters in length. If the length is greater than four, an exception is thrown. Otherwise, the instance variable named code is set to the passed value.

As you learned in chapter 7, the throw statement specifies an exception object for the exception to be thrown. The .NET Framework defines the three exception classes listed in this figure as standard exceptions you can use when validating arguments. If an argument is outside the range of values that are acceptable for a property, for example, you should throw an ArgumentOutOf-RangeException. If an attempt is made to set a property to a null value and the property requires a value, you should throw an ArgumentNullException. For any other argument errors, you should throw an ArgumentException.

Notice that all three of these exceptions accept a *message* parameter. You should use this parameter to provide an error message that indicates what is wrong with the data.

If you code a property or method that throws argument exceptions, you might think that you would code a statement that refers to that property or method within a try-catch statement so that you could catch the exception when it occurs. However, I don't recommend that. Instead, you should validate the data before passing it to the property or method. The if statement shown in this figure, for example, checks the length of the product code the user enters before it sets the Code property. That way, the exception should never occur.

So why include the validation code in the class at all? Because if you design your classes so they're reusable, you can't always count on other programmers validating the data they pass to the class. So including this validation code makes the class completely self-contained.

A property that validates data in its set procedure

```
public class ProductList
{
    private string code;

    public string Code
    {
        get
        {
            return code;
        }
        set
        {
            if (value.Length > 4)
                throw new ArgumentException(
                    "Maximum length of Code is 4 characters.");
            code = value;
        }
    }
...
```

Exceptions to throw when validating arguments

Exception	Description
ArgumentOutOfRangeException(message)	Use when the value is outside the acceptable range of values.
ArgumentNullException(message)	Use when the value is null and a null value is not allowed.
ArgumentException(message)	Use when the value is invalid for any other reason.

An if statement that validates data before setting a property value

```
if (txtCode.Text.Length <= 4)
    Product.Code = txtCode.Text;
```

Description

- A class should throw an exception whenever it encounters an error it can't recover from. The most common type of error a class should check for is an invalid argument that's passed to the set accessor of a property or to a method.
- If a class detects an invalid argument, it should throw one of the three argument exceptions listed above. The throw statement should pass a message that describes the error as an argument.
- When you refer to a property or method that throws an argument exception, you shouldn't use a try-catch statement to catch the exception. Instead, you should validate the data before you pass it to the property or method. That way, you can be sure that the exception won't be thrown.
- All of the argument exceptions are part of the System namespace.

Figure 13-3 How to throw argument exceptions

How to define and use class events

In addition to fields, properties, indexers, methods, and constructors, a class can also define *events*. An event is a signal that a particular action has occurred on an object that's created from the class. Then, any class that uses that object can respond to the event by wiring an event handler to it. Figure 13-4 illustrates how this works.

To define an event, you start by coding an event declaration as shown at the top of this figure. On this declaration, you provide the name of the event and a *delegate* that determines the parameters that will be passed to the event handler. The first statement in the ProductList class in this figure, for example, declares an event named Changed that will use the standard EventHandler delegate. This delegate is used with events that don't require any event data. It passes two arguments to the event handler: the object that raised the event and an EventArgs object that contains no event data.

Once you've declared an event, you can raise it by referring to it by name as shown in the Add method of the ProductList class. As you can see, this method raises the Changed event after it adds a product to the products array list. Notice that the this keyword is used as the first parameter, which causes the object that raised the event to be passed to the event handler. Then, the second parameter passes an empty EventArgs object to the event handler.

If you wanted to pass additional information to an event handler, you could define a new class that inherits the EventArgs class and that contains the additional information. Then, you could create a delegate that used the new class to pass this information. Finally, you could create an instance of this class and pass it as the second argument of the event. For more information on how to do that, see online help.

To respond to an event that's raised by a class, you use code like that shown in the second example. This code includes an event handler named ChangedHandler that will handle the event. Notice that this event handler accepts the two parameters that will be passed by the Changed event. Also notice that these parameters are named sender and e just as they are in the other event handlers you've seen in this book. Although that's not required, we recommend you use these names for consistency.

To use the event handler, you start by creating an instance of the class that raises the event. In this case, an instance of the ProductList class named products is created. Then, you wire the event handler to the event. Here, the ChangedHandler event handler is wired to the Changed event of the products object. As a result, the ChangedHandler method will be called whenever the Changed event is raised for this object.

In most cases, you'll code the statement that wires the event handler in the Load event of the form that uses it. However, you can also wire an event handler in the constructor of any class. The only restriction is that this statement must be executed before the event is raised. If the event is raised before you've wired the event handler to it, the event handler won't execute.

The syntax of an event declaration

```
public event Delegate EventName;
```

Code that declares and raises an event in the ProductList class

```
public class ProductList

    public event EventHandler Changed;

    public void Add(Product product)
    {
        products.Add(product);
        Changed(this, EventArgs.Empty);
    }
...
```

Code that uses a class event

```
// A class variable
ProductList products = new ProductList();

// Place this code in a constructor or in a form's Load event handler
products.Changed += new EventHandler(ChangedHandler);

// The event handler
private void ChangedHandler(object sender, EventArgs e)
{
    MessageBox.Show("The Changed event was raised.");
}
```

Description

- An *event* is a signal that an action has occurred on an object that was created from the class. To create an event that can be used by other classes, the event must be declared with public access at the class level. Then, the event can be called from any properties or methods that need to raise the event.
- An event declaration specifies a *delegate* that will handle the event along with an event name. The delegate determines what arguments are passed to the method that handles the event. In most cases, you'll use the EventHandler delegate, which passes two arguments: an object that represents the sender of the event, and an EventArgs object.
- To raise the event, you refer to it by its name, and you code the arguments required by the delegate. For the EventHandler delegate, you can specify *this* as the first argument to pass the current object to the event handler, and you can specify EventArgs.Empty as the second argument so that no additional information is passed to the event handler.
- If you want to pass additional information to an event handler, you can create a class that inherits the EventArgs class. For more information, see the C# documentation.
- To handle an event from another class, you create an instance of the class that raises the event and assign it to a class variable. Then, you declare an event handler with a signature that matches the event's signature. Finally, you wire the event to the event handler in the class constructor or, if the class is a form, in the Load event handler.

Figure 13-4 How to define and use class events

How to overload operators

Both the Product and the ProductList classed described in figure 13-1 use *overloaded operators*. The Product class overloads the == and != operators so you can compare product objects to one another. The ProductList class overloads the + and - operators so you can add products to and remove products from the product list using these operators rather than the Add and Remove methods. The following topics explain how you implement overloaded operators like these.

An introduction to operator overloading

Figure 13-5 presents some basic information about *operator overloading*. First, you should know that you can overload both unary and binary operators. The most common operators you can overload are listed in this figure.

C# defines the meanings of these operators for built-in types such as decimal, int, string, and DateTime. However, for user-defined types such as the Product or ProductList classes presented in this chapter, these operators are either undefined or are defined in ways that may not be appropriate for the class. For example, the + operator isn't defined for user-defined types, but the == operator is. By default, if you compare two object variables using the == operator, they're considered equal if they refer to the same object.

With operator overloading, you can create your own implementations of C# operators that are appropriate for your classes. For example, a more appropriate definition of the == operator for the Product class would be to consider two Product variables equal if they refer to objects with the same Code, Description, and Price properties.

As the syntax at the top of this figure shows, you use the *operator* keyword to declare an operator. In the operator declaration, you specify the result type, which indicates the type of object that's returned by the operation. In most cases, the result type is the same as the class that contains the declaration (for example, Product in the Product class). Then, you specify the operator you want to define, followed by one or two operands depending on whether the operator is a unary or a binary operator.

Notice that operators are always declared as static. That way, they can deal with null operands properly. That will make more sense when you see the code for the overloaded == operator.

Overloaded operators often depend on methods that are defined by the class. In the next figure, for example, you'll see that the + operator for the ProductList class uses the Add method of the class to add a product to the list. And in the figure after that, you'll see that the == and != operators for the Product class are implemented by calling the Equals method. Because this method is inherited from the System.Object class, you'll need to write your own version of this method so that it gives the same results as the == and != operators.

One complication that arises when you override the Equals method is that you must also override the GetHashCode method. Like Equals, GetHashCode is

The syntax for overloading unary operators

```
public static resultType operator unary-operator(type operand)
```

The syntax for overloading binary operators

```
public static resultType operator
    binary-operator(type-1 operand-1, type-2 operand-2)
```

Common operators you can overload

Unary operators

```
+ - ! ++ -- true false
```

Binary operators

```
+ - * / % & | == != > <  >= <=
```

The Equals method of the Object class

Method	Description
Equals(object)	Returns a Boolean value that indicates whether the current object refers to the same instance as the specified object. If that's not what you want, you can override this method as shown in figure 13-7.
Equals(object1, object2)	A static version of the Equals method that compares two objects to determine if they refer to the same instance.

The GetHashCode method of the Object class

Method	Description
GetHashCode()	Returns an integer value that's used to identify objects in a hash table. If you override the Equals method, you must also override the GetHashCode method.

Description

- You can use the *operator* keyword to overload a built-in operator within a class. For example, you might overload the + operator in the ProductList class so that it can be used to add products to the list. You might also overload the == and != operators in the Product class so you can compare Product objects to see if they contain identical data rather than whether they refer to the same instance.
- You can overload all of the unary and binary operators shown above, as well as some that aren't presented in this book. When you overload a binary operator, *operand-1* is the operand that appears to the left of the operator, and *operand-2* is the operand that appears to the right of the operator.
- Overloaded operators are always static so they can deal with null operands properly.
- When you overload relational operators like == and !=, you need to provide your own versions of the Equals and GetHashCode methods. See figure 13-7 for details.

Figure 13-5 An introduction to operator overloading

defined by the System.Object class, so all classes inherit it. Certain types of collections within the .NET Framework use the GetHashCode method to return a *hash code* that's used to store and locate objects in the collection. One of the rules of .NET class design is that any two objects that are considered equal by the Equals method must return the same value for the GetHashCode method. As a result, if you change the way the Equals method determines whether objects are equal, you must also change the GetHashCode method.

How to overload arithmetic operators

Figure 13-6 shows how to overload arithmetic operators such as + and -. For instance, the code at the top of this figure shows an implementation of the + operator for the ProductList class. This operator is used to add a Product object to the product list. As you can see, the declaration for the + operator specifies ProductList as the result type, which means that it will return a ProductList object. In addition, this operator accepts two parameters: a ProductList object named pl and a Product object named p. Then, the code for the + operator calls the Add method of the pl operand, passing the p object as the argument. This method adds the p object to the products array list that's stored in the p1 object. Then, the + operator returns the pl object.

The second code example shows how you might use the + operator in an application to add a Product object to a product list. First, a new ProductList object named products is created. Then, a new Product object named p is created. Finally, the + operator is used in an assignment statement to add the product to the product list.

The last statement in this figure shows another way that you can use the overloaded + operator of the ProductList class to add a Product object to a product list. As you can see, this statement uses the += shortcut assignment operator. You may remember from chapter 4 that you can use shortcut operators like these in place of the assignment operator when the expression that's being assigned involves an arithmetic operation. You can use these shortcut operators with overloaded operators as well. Note that you don't need to provide any special code to use a shortcut operator. That's because when you use a shortcut operator, the compiler automatically converts it to an equivalent assignment statement that uses the assignment operator (=) and an arithmetic operator.

How to overload comparison operators

Figure 13-7 on the next page shows that comparison operators are often more difficult to overload than arithmetic operators. Here, the first example shows how to implement the == operator for the Product class so you can compare products based on their values rather than on object references. The two objects that will be compared are passed as arguments to this operator.

The operator starts by using the Equals method of the Object class to check both objects to see if they're equal to null. This implementation of the Equals

Part of a ProductList class that overloads the + operator

```
public class ProductList
{
    private ArrayList products;

    public Add(Product p)
    {
        products.Add(p);
    }

    public static ProductList operator + (ProductList pl, Product p)
    {
        pl.Add(p);
        return pl;
    }
    .
    .
}
```

Code that uses the + operator of the ProductList class

```
ProductList products = new ProductList();
Product p = new Product("JAVA", "Murach's Beginning Java 2", 49.50m);
products = products + p;
```

Another way to use the + operator

```
products += p;
```

Description

- You can overload the built-in arithmetic operators so they perform customized functions on objects created from the class that defines them.
- You should overload only those arithmetic operators that make sense for a class. For example, it's reasonable to overload the + operator for the ProductList class as a way to add products to a product list. But it doesn't make sense to overload the * or / operators for this class.
- You don't overload the += or -= operators separately. Instead, these operators are handled automatically by the overloaded + and - operators.

Note

- Although C# uses the += operator to add event handlers to an event, this is not an example of overloading operators. Instead, the use of the += operator for wiring events is a language feature that's built in to the C# compiler.

Figure 13-6 How to overload arithmetic operators

method is based on reference, not value. As a result, it lets you test an object to see if it is null. This testing is necessary to prevent the overloaded == operator from throwing an exception if one of the operands is null.

If both operands are null, the == operator returns true. If the first operand is null but the second one isn't, it returns false. And if the first operand isn't null, the == operator calls the Equals method of the first operand to compare it with the second operand, and then returns the result of the comparison. Notice that the declaration for the Equals method includes the override keyword. That means that it overrides the Equals method defined by the Object class. You'll learn more about overriding methods in the next chapter.

The Equals method starts by testing the object that's passed to it, in this case, the second operand of the == operator, for a null. If this object is null, the Equals method returns false. That makes sense, because no object should be considered equal to a null.

If the object that's passed to the Equals method isn't null, this method casts the object to a Product object named p. Then, it compares its own Code, Description, and Price values with the Code, Description, and Price values of the p object. If all three properties are equal, it returns true. Otherwise, it returns false.

Before I go on, you might want to consider why it's necessary for the == operator to be static. If it weren't, you would have to call it from an instance of the Product class, for example, p1. But what if p1 was null? In other words, what if p1 didn't refer to an instance of the Product class? In that case, you couldn't use the == operator. In order to work with null operands, then, overloaded operators must be declared as static.

When you overload a comparison operator, you must also overload the operator that performs the opposite operation. If you overload the == operator, for example, you must also overload the != operator. Similarly, if you overload the < operator, you must also overload the > operator. The code that's used to implement the != operator in the Product class is also shown in this figure. As you can see, this operator defines itself in terms of the == operator. That way, you can be sure that these operators return consistent results.

The last method that's required to overload the == operator is the GetHashCode method. Like the Equals method, this method overrides the GetHashCode method that's defined by the Object class. The main requirement for the GetHashCode method is that it must always return the same value for any two objects that are considered equal by the Equals method. The easiest way to accomplish that is to combine the values that are used for comparison in the Equals method to create a string, and then return the hash code of that string as shown here.

The second example in this figure shows how you can use the == operator to compare two Product objects. First, two object variables named p1 and p2 are created from the Product class with identical values. Then, the products are compared in an if statement using the == operator. Because both products have the same Code, Description, and Price values, this comparison returns true. If the Product class didn't override the == operator, however, this comparison would return false because the p1 and p2 variables refer to different instances of the Product class, even though they both have the same values.

Code that overloads the == operator for a Product class

```
public static bool operator == (Product p1, Product p2)
{
    if (Object.Equals(p1, null))
        if (Object.Equals(p2, null))
            return true;
        else
            return false;
    else
        return p1.Equals(p2);
}

public static bool operator != (Product p1, Product p2)
{
    return !(p1 == p2);
}

public override bool Equals(Object obj)
{
    if (obj == null)
        return false;
    Product p = (Product)obj;
    if (this.Code == p.Code &&
        this.Description == p.Description &&
        this.Price == p.Price)
        return true;
    else
        return false;
}

public override int GetHashCode()
{
    string hashString = this.Code + this.Description + this.Price.ToString();
    return hashString.GetHashCode();
}
```

Code that uses the == operator of the Product class

```
Product p1 = new Product("JAVA", "Murach's Beginning Java 2", 49.50m);
Product p2 = new Product("JAVA", "Murach's Beginning Java 2", 49.50m);
if (p1 == p2)           // This evaluates to true. Without the overloaded
                        // == operator, it would evaluate to false.
```

Description

- If you overload the == operator, you must also override the non-static Equals method. Then, the == operator should use this Equals method for its equality test.
- Before it calls the Equals method, the overloaded == operator should test the operands for null values. If both operands are null, they should be considered equal. If only the first operand is null, the operands should be considered unequal.
- Relational operators must always be implemented in pairs. For example, if you overload the == operator, you must also overload the != operator. Similarly, if you overload the < operator, you must also overload the > operator.
- When you override the Equals method, you must also override the GetHashCode method. That's because the GetHashCode method must return the same hash code for any two instances that are considered equal by the Equals method.

Figure 13-7 How to overload the == operator

An enhanced version of the Product Maintenance application

Now that you've learned the techniques for enhancing your classes with features such as indexers, argument exceptions, events, and overloaded operators, the following topics present an enhanced version of the Product Maintenance application that uses those features. From the user's standpoint, this application operates exactly like the one that was presented in chapter 12. The only difference is that the classes in this version of the application are implemented differently. Specifically, the classes include most of the additional members that were shown in figure 13-1. (Because this application doesn't require testing products for equality, the Product class shown here doesn't implement the == or != operators.)

Because the code for the New Product form that's used in this version of the Product Maintenance application is identical to the code shown in chapter 12, I won't repeat it here. In addition, like the application in chapter 12, you should know that this application will work with any of the three versions of the ProductDB class that are presented in chapters 21 and 22.

The code for the Product Maintenance form

Figure 13-8 shows the code for the enhanced version of the Product Maintenance form. Because most of this code is the same as in chapter 12, I've highlighted the key differences here.

First, the products variable that's used by the class to store Product objects is a ProductList object, not an ArrayList object. As a result, this version of the application can use the features of the ProductList class, such as the indexer, the Fill and Save method, the overloaded + and - operators, and the Changed event.

In the Load event handler for the form, the ChangedHandler method (which appears at the end of the listing) is wired to the Changed event of the products object. As you'll see in a minute, this event is raised any time a product is added to, removed from, or changed in the product list. Then, the ChangedHandler method calls the Save method of the products object to save the new list, and it calls the FillProductListBox method to refresh the list box.

After it wires the Changed event, the Load event handler calls the Fill method of the products object to fill the product list. Then, it calls the FillProductListBox method to fill the list box. Notice that this method uses a for loop to retrieve each product in the products list by its index instead of using a foreach loop.

The Click event handler for the Add button calls the GetNewProduct method of the New Product form to get a new product. Then, if the Product object that's returned by this method isn't null, the += operator is used to add the product to the products list.

The Click event handler for the Delete button uses an indexer of the ProductList class to retrieve the selected product from the products list. Then,

The code for the Product Maintenance form

```
private ProductList products = new ProductList();

private void frmProductMain_Load(object sender, System.EventArgs e)
{
    products.Changed += new EventHandler(ChangedHandler);
    products.Fill();
    FillProductListBox();
}

private void FillProductListBox()
{
    Product p;
    lstProducts.Items.Clear();
    for (int i = 0; i < products.Count; i++)
    {
        p = products[i];
        lstProducts.Items.Add(p.GetDisplayText("\t"));
    }
}

private void btnAdd_Click(object sender, System.EventArgs e)
{
    frmNewProduct newForm = new frmNewProduct();
    Product product = newForm.GetNewProduct();
    if (product != null)
    {
        products += product;
    }
}

private void btnDelete_Click(object sender, System.EventArgs e)
{
    int i = lstProducts.SelectedIndex;
    if (i != -1)
    {
        Product product = products[i];
        string message = "Are you sure you want to delete "
            + product.Description + "?";
        DialogResult button = MessageBox.Show(message, "Confirm Delete",
            MessageBoxButtons.YesNo);
        if (button == DialogResult.Yes)
        {
            products -= product;
        }
    }
}

private void btnClose_Click(object sender, System.EventArgs e)
{
    this.Close();
}

private void ChangedHandler(object sender, EventArgs e)
{
    products.Save();
    FillProductListBox();
}
```

Figure 13-8 The code for the Product Maintenance form

assuming the user confirms that the product should be deleted, it uses the -= operator to remove the product from the list.

The code for the Product class

Figure 13-9 shows the code for the Product class. This version of the Product class is almost identical to the version you saw in chapter 12. In fact, the only difference is that the set accessor for the Code property includes a validation routine that throws an ArgumentException if the product code is more than four characters in length.

The New Product form (which isn't shown here) sets this property based on the value the user enters into the Code text box. Because the MaxLength property of this text box is set to 4, however, the user can't enter more than four characters. So the value that's passed to the Code property will always be valid.

The code for the ProductList class

Figure 13-10 shows the code for the ProductList class, which stores a collection of Product objects. As you can see, this class begins by declaring an ArrayList object named products. This instance variable is used internally to store the product list.

Next, the ProductList class declares an event named Changed that uses the standard EventHandler delegate. As you'll see in a minute, this event is raised whenever the contents of the products array list are changed.

The two indexers for this class let users of the class access a specific product in the list by specifying an integer value or a product code. These indexers are almost identical to the two indexers that were shown in figure 13-2, so you shouldn't have any trouble understanding how they work. The only difference is that the set accessor for the first indexer raises the Changed event to indicate that the contents of the products list have been changed.

The Fill method of the ProductList class, shown on page 2 of this listing, calls the GetProducts method of the ProductDB class to get the products from a file. Similarly, the Save method calls the SaveProducts method of this class to save the products to a file.

The ProductList class also provides two overloads for the Add method: one that accepts a Product object and one that accepts a code, description and price. It also includes a Remove method that removes the specified Product object. As you can see, all three of these methods raise the Changed event.

Finally, this class provides an overloaded + operator and an overloaded - operator. The overloaded + operator calls the first Add method to add the specified object to the product list and then returns the updated product list. Similarly, the – operator calls the Remove method to remove the specified product from the product list and then returns the updated product list.

The code for the Product class

```
public class Product
{
    private string code;
    private string description;
    private decimal price;

    public Product()
    {
    }

    public Product(string code, string description, decimal price)
    {
        this.Code = code;
        this.Description = description;
        this.Price = price;
    }

    public string Code
    {
        get
        {
            return code;
        }
        set
        {
            if (value.Length > 4)
                throw new ArgumentException("Maximum length of Code is 4 characters.");
            code = value;
        }
    }

    public string Description
    {
        get
        {
            return description;
        }
        set
        {
            description = value;
        }
    }

    public decimal Price
    {
        get
        {
            return price;
        }
        set
        {
            price = value;
        }
    }

    public string GetDisplayText(string sep)
    {
        return code + sep + price.ToString("c") + sep + description;
    }
}
```

Figure 13-9 The code for the Product class

The code for the ProductList class

Page 1

```
using System.Collections;

public class ProductList
{

    private ArrayList products;

    public event EventHandler Changed;

    public ProductList()
    {
        products = new ArrayList();
    }

    public int Count
    {
        get
        {
            return products.Count;
        }
    }

    public Product this[int i]
    {
        get
        {
            return (Product) products[i];
        }
        set
        {
            products[i] = value;
            Changed(this, EventArgs.Empty);
        }
    }

    public Product this[string code]
    {
        get
        {
            foreach (Product p in products)
                if (p.Code == code)
                    return p;
            return null;
        }
    }
```

Figure 13-10 The code for the ProductList class (part 1 of 2)

The code for the ProductList class Page 2

```
        public void Fill()
        {
            products = ProductDB.GetProducts();
        }

        public void Save()
        {
            ProductDB.SaveProducts(products);
        }

        public void Add(Product product)
        {
            products.Add(product);
            Changed(this, EventArgs.Empty);
        }

        public void Add(string code, string description, decimal price)
        {
            Product p = new Product(code, description, price);
            products.Add(p);
            Changed(this, EventArgs.Empty);
        }

        public void Remove(Product product)
        {
            products.Remove(product);
            Changed(this, EventArgs.Empty);
        }

        public static ProductList operator + (ProductList pl, Product p)
        {
            pl.Add(p);
            return pl;
        }

        public static ProductList operator - (ProductList pl, Product p)
        {
            pl.Remove(p);
            return pl;
        }
    }
```

Figure 13-10 The code for the ProductList class (part 2 of 2)

How to organize and document your classes

The following topics present some additional information that's useful for creating real-world classes. First, you'll learn how to organize applications that use two or more classes by coding more than one class per file and by working with namespaces. Then, you'll learn how to add XML documentation to your classes.

Two ways to code two or more classes in a single file

In most cases, you'll code each class that's required by an application in a separate file. If two or more classes are closely related, however, you might want to consider storing them in the same file. Figure 13-11 shows two ways you can do that.

First, you can simply code the class declarations one after the other as shown in the first example. The advantage of doing that is that it makes it easier to manage the files that make up the application. If the classes are large, however, you should place them in separate files even if they are closely related. Otherwise, it may be difficult to locate the code for a specific class.

You can also code two or more classes in a single file by nesting one class within another class. *Nested classes* are useful when one class only makes sense within the context of the other class. The second example in this figure illustrates how you nest two classes. Here, the class named InnerClass is nested within a class named OuterClass. Then, to refer to the inner class, you have to qualify it with the name of the outer class.

Although you won't need to use nested classes often, it sometimes makes sense to do so. You'll see an example of one such situation in chapter 15.

A file with two classes coded one after the other

```
public class Class1
{
   // Body of Class1
}

public class Class2
{
   // Body of Class2
}
```

A file with nested classes

```
public class OuterClass
{
    // Body of OuterClass

    public class InnerClass
    {
        // Body of InnerClass
    }
}
```

Description

- When two classes are closely related, it sometimes makes sense to code them in the same file, especially if the classes are relatively small. That way, the project consists of fewer files.
- One way to code two classes in a single file is to code them one after the other as shown in the first example above.
- Another way to code two classes in a single file is to nest one class within the other as shown in the second example above. This is useful when one class is used only within the context of another class.
- To refer to a nested class from another class, you must qualify it with the name of the class it's nested within like this:
  `OuterClass.InnerClass`

Figure 13-11 Two ways to code two or more classes in a single file

How to work with namespaces

As you know, a *namespace* is a container that is used to group related classes. For example, all of the .NET Framework classes that are used for creating Windows forms are grouped in the System.Windows.Forms namespace, and all of the classes for working with collections are grouped in the System.Collections namespace.

Every C# class must belong to a namespace. This namespace is identified by a namespace statement that appears near the beginning of the C# source file. This is illustrated in all three of the examples in figure 13-12.

When you create a C# application, Visual Studio creates a namespace that has the same name as the project. Then, it stores all of the classes you create for that project in that namespace. For example, the default form for the Product Maintenance application is stored in a namespace named ProductMaintenance as shown in the first example in this figure. In addition, any other class you create as part of this project is stored in the same namespace.

You can also nest namespaces. In fact, most of the .NET Framework namespaces are nested. For example, System.Collections is actually a namespace named Collections that's nested within a namespace named System. As this figure shows, you can create nested namespaces using one of two techniques. First, you can code a namespace statement within another namespace as shown in the second example. This example creates a namespace named Murach.Validation. The more common technique, however, is to simply name all of the namespaces on a single namespace statement as shown in the third example.

Although all of the classes of a project are typically stored in the same namespace, those classes use classes that are stored in other namespaces. For example, all C# applications use classes that are defined by the .NET Framework. To use a class in another namespace, you typically include a using statement for that namespace at the beginning of the class. Alternatively, you can qualify any reference to the class with the name of the namespace.

For simple C# projects, you don't need to worry about namespaces because Visual Studio takes care of them for you. However, namespaces may become an issue in two situations. The first situation occurs if you copy a class from one project into another project. When you do that, you may need to change the name of the namespace in the class file to the name of the namespace for the project you copied the class into.

The second situation occurs if you want to share a class among several projects by creating a class library. In that case, you should create a separate namespace for the classes in the library. You'll learn how to do that in chapter 15.

Code that declares a namespace

```
namespace ProductMaintenance
{
    public class Form1 : System.Windows.Forms.Form
    {
        // Body of Form1 class
    }

}
```

Code that declares nested namespaces

```
namespace Murach
{
    namespace Validation
    {
        // Body of Validation namespace
    }
}
```

Another way to nest namespaces

```
namespace Murach.Validation
{
    // Body of Validation namespace
}
```

Description

- A *namespace* is a container that can be used to group related classes. In most cases, all of the classes that make up a C# project are part of the same namespace.
- The namespace statement that appears near the beginning of a source file identifies the namespace that classes defined in that file belong to. By default, when you add a class to a project, it's added to a namespace with the same name as the project.
- Namespaces can be nested. One way to nest namespaces is to include a namespace statement within the body of another namespace. Another way is to code the fully-qualified name of the nested namespace in a namespace statement.
- To use a class in a namespace other than the current namespace, you must either provide a using statement that names the other namespace, or you must qualify the class with the name of the namespace.

Figure 13-12 How to work with namespaces

How to add XML documentation to a class

As you already know, you can add general comments to any C# program by using comment statements that begin with a pair of slashes. You can also use a documentation feature called *XML documentation* to create documentation for the classes and class members you create. XML documentation can make your classes easier for other programmers to use by providing information about the function of the class and its members. This information can then be used to create web pages that document the class. Some of this information also appears in screen tips that are displayed when you work with the class in Visual Studio.

Figure 13-13 shows how to add XML documentation to a class. Although XML documentation is based on XML syntax, you don't have to know much about XML to use it. As you can see, XML documentation lines begin with three slashes and appear immediately before the class or member they document.

The documentation for a class or member can contain one or more *documentation elements*. Each element begins with a *start tag*, such as <summary>, and ends with an *end tag*, such as </summary>. The contents of the element appear between the start and end tags. The table shown in this figure lists the most commonly used XML documentation elements.

The easiest way to create XML documentation is to type three slashes on the line that immediately precedes a class or class member. Then, Visual Studio automatically generates skeleton XML documentation for you. This includes whatever tags are appropriate for the class or member you're documenting. For example, if you type three slashes on the line before a member that lists parameters and has a return type, Visual Studio will generate a summary tag for the method, a param tag for each parameter passed to the method, and a returns tag for the method's return value. You can then type descriptive information between these tags to complete the documentation for the class.

Part of a Validator class that includes XML documentation

```
/// <summary>
/// Provides static methods for validating data.
/// </summary>
public class Validator
{
    public Validator()
    {
    }

    /// <summary>
    /// The title that will appear in dialog boxes.
    /// </summary>
    public static string Title = "Entry Error";

    /// <summary>
    /// Checks whether the user entered data into a text box.
    /// </summary>
    /// <param name="textBox">The text box control to be validated.</param>
    /// <returns>True if the user has entered data.</returns>
    public static bool IsPresent(TextBox textBox)
    {
        if (textBox.Text == "")
        {
            MessageBox.Show(textBox.Tag + " is a required field.", Title);
            textBox.Focus();
            return false;
        }
        return true;
    }
```

XML elements you can use for class documentation

Element	Description
`<summary>`	Provides a general description of a class, property, method, or other element.
`<value>`	Describes the value of a property.
`<returns>`	Describes the return value of a method.
`<param name="name">`	Describes a parameter of a method.

Description

- You can use special *XML tags* in C# source code to provide class documentation.
- An XML documentation line begins with three slashes. Each *documentation element* begins with a *start tag*, such as <summary>, and ends with an *end tag*, such as </summary>. You code the description of the element between these tags.
- A summary element is automatically added for a class when you add the class using the Project→Add Class command.
- If you type three slashes on the line immediately preceding a class or member declaration, Visual Studio automatically generates empty elements for you. Then, you just fill in the text that's appropriate for each element.

Figure 13-13 How to add XML documentation to a class

How to view XML documentation

Once you've added XML documentation to a class, you can use Visual Studio's Tools➔Build Comment Web Pages command to create web pages that display the class documentation as shown in figure 13-14. For example, the screen at the top of this figure shows a portion of the documentation I created for a Validator class. As you can see, the documentation includes a description of the class itself, as well as the name and description of each class member. Then, you can click the hyperlinks for the members to display additional information about each member. For example, if you click the IsPresent hyperlink, a page for the IsPresent method will be displayed that includes the documentation you provided for this method.

When you use the Tools➔Build Comment Web Pages command, the web pages are displayed in Visual Studio so you can examine them. In addition, the pages themselves are stored in a new directory that's created in the directory that holds the application's solution file. Then, you can use a web browser to display these pages outside of Visual Studio. Or, you can copy the files to a web server and make them available from the Internet or a local intranet.

The XML documentation you provide is also used in the screen tips that appear in the Visual Studio Code Editor window. In the example in this figure, I typed the Validator class and a period, so the IntelliSense feature displayed a list of the members of the Validator class. Then, I moved the mouse pointer to highlight the IsPresent method. When I did that, Visual Studio displayed a screen tip that includes the signature of the IsPresent method along with the summary I provided in the XML documentation.

A Code Comment Web Report generated by Visual Studio

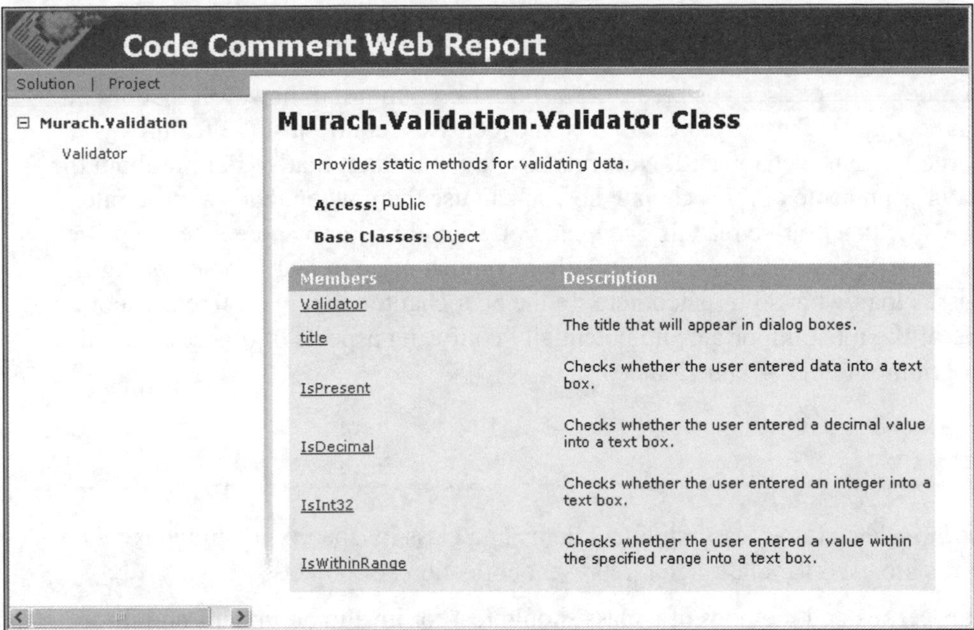

A screen tip that displays the documentation for a class member

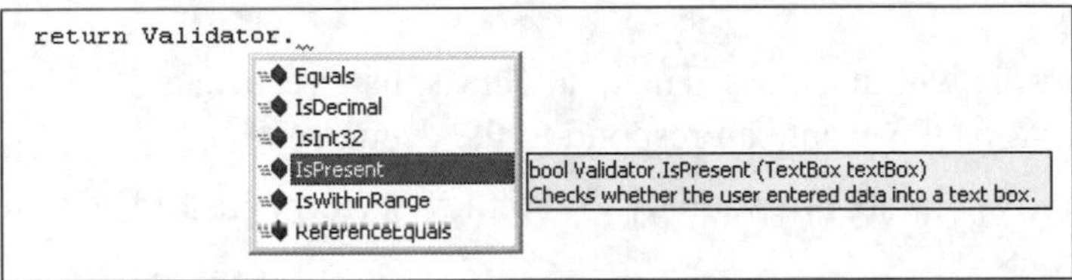

Description

- To create web pages that document the code in a C# project, choose the Tools➔Build Comment Web Pages command. The web pages that are created include information about each class and class member in the project, along with information from any XML documentation elements you've added.
- When you run the Build Comment Web Pages command, a Code Comment Web Report like the one shown above is displayed in Visual Studio. In addition, a folder is created in the same folder that contains the solution file to hold the HTML files for the report. That way, you can display the documentation in a browser outside of Visual Studio.
- The XML documentation that you add to a class is also visible in the screen tips that appear when IntelliSense features are activated.

Figure 13-14 How to view XML documentation

Perspective

In this chapter, you've learned about a variety of features that you can include in the classes you create. You should keep in mind, however, that not all classes require these features. In fact, most classes require just the features you learned about in chapter 12. Nevertheless, it's important that you know about the features presented in this chapter so you can use them when that's appropriate.

Now that you've read this chapter, you should begin to appreciate the power and complexity of C# classes. Still, there's much more to learn about coding C# classes than what's presented here. In the next chapter, then, you'll learn about one of the most important and potentially confusing aspects of object-oriented programming in C#: inheritance.

Summary

- An *indexer* lets you access individual items in a class by specifying an index value. Indexers are used for classes that represent collections of objects.
- The properties and methods of a class should test for invalid arguments and throw an argument exception if an argument is invalid. Even so, you should validate data before it's passed to a property or method so the property or method won't throw an exception.
- You can declare and raise *events* within a class. Then, any class that creates an instance of the class that contains the event can respond to the event.
- You can overload some of the operators provided by C# so they perform customized functions within your classes.
- If two or more classes are closely related, you can code them in the same file. You can do that by coding one class after the other or by nesting one class within another.
- Each class is part of a namespace, and all of the classes in a project are typically part of the same namespace. You can also nest namespaces so that one namespace contains other namespaces.
- You can use the *XML documentation feature* of C# to document a class and its members. Then, you can generate web pages that display that information.

Terms

indexer
event
delegate
overloaded operator
operator overloading
hash code
nested classes
namespace
XML documentation
documentation element
XML tag
start tag
end tag

Objectives

- Given the specifications for an application that uses classes with any of the features presented in this chapter, develop the application and its classes.
- Add the XML documentation required by any class.
- Explain what an indexer is and how it's used.
- Explain why you should include validation code in your classes.
- Explain the purpose of operator overloading.
- Describe two ways that you can code two or more classes in a single file, and explain when you might do that.
- Explain how namespaces are used, and describe two ways to nest namespaces.

Exercise 13-1 Create a Customer Maintenance application that uses classes

In this exercise, you'll create a Customer Maintenance application that uses classes with the features presented in this chapter. To make this application easier to develop, we'll give you the starting forms and classes.

Open the project and add validation code to the Customer class

1. Open the project named CustomerMaintenance in the C:\C#.NET\Chapter 13\CustomerMaintenance directory.
2. Add code to the set accessors for the FirstName, LastName, and Email properties that throws an exception if the value is longer than 50 characters.
3. Run the application, and add a new customer with an email address that's longer than 50 characters to see what happens. Then, end the application.
4. Set the MaxLength properties of the First Name, Last Name, and Email text boxes to 50. Then, run the application again and try to add a new customer with an email address that's longer than 50 characters to see what happens.

Add a CustomerList class

5. Add a class named CustomerList to the project, and add the following members to this class:

Property	Description
`Count`	An integer that indicates how many Customer objects are in the list.
`[index]`	An indexer that provides access to the Customer at the specified position.

Method	Description
`Add(customer)`	Adds the specified Customer object to the list.
`Remove(customer)`	Removes the specified Customer object from the list.
`Fill()`	Fills the list with customer data from a file using the GetCustomers method of the CustomerDB class.
`Save()`	Saves the customers to a file using the SaveCustomers method of the CustomerDB class.

6. Modify the Customer Maintenance form to use this class. Then, run the application and test it to be sure it works properly.

Add overloaded operators to the CustomerList class

7. Add overloaded + and - operators to the CustomerList class that add and remove a customer from the customer list.
8. Modify the Customer Maintenance form to use these operators instead of the Add and Remove methods. Then, run and test the application.

Add an event to the CustomerList class

9. Add an event named Changed to the CustomerList class. This event should use the EventHandler delegate and should be raised any time the customer list changes.
10. Modify the Customer Maintenance form to use the Changed event to save the customers and refresh the list box any time the list changes.
11. Run and test the application. If you're going to continue with the next exercise, leave the solution open. Otherwise, close it.

Exercise 13-2 Add XML documentation to the Customer Maintenance application

1. If it's not already open, open the CustomerMaintenance application that you modified in exercise 13-1.
2. Add XML documentation for each member of the Customer class.
3. Use the Tools→Build Comment Web Pages command to build the web documentation. If a message is displayed indicating that the report was created with minor errors, click OK.
4. Click the CustomerMaintenance link on the first page that's displayed, then expand the CustomerMaintenance project on the next page and click the link for the Customer class. Scroll through the documentation for this class, and click the link for any member to display its documentation.
5. Continue experimenting until you're comfortable with how the web report works. Then, close the solution.

14

How to work with inheritance

Inheritance is one of the key concepts of object-oriented programming. It lets you create a class that's based on another class. As you'll see in this chapter, inheritance is used throughout the classes of the .NET Framework. In addition, you can use it in the classes that you create.

An introduction to inheritance

Inheritance allows you to create a class that's based on another class. When used correctly, inheritance can simplify the overall design of an application. The following topics present an introduction to the basic concepts of inheritance. You need to understand these concepts before you learn how to write the code needed to implement classes that use inheritance.

How inheritance works

Figure 14-1 illustrates how inheritance works. When inheritance is used, a *derived class* inherits the properties, methods, and other members of a *base class*. Then, the objects that are created from the derived class can use these inherited members. The derived class can also provide its own members that extend the base class. In addition, the derived class can *override* properties and methods of the base class by providing replacement definitions for them.

The two classes shown in this figure illustrate how this works. Here, the base class is System.Windows.Forms.Form, the .NET Framework class that all Windows forms inherit. As this figure shows, this class has several public properties and methods, such as the Text property and the Close method. (This class has many more properties and methods. I included just a few representative ones here.)

The derived class in this figure is the class for the New Product form in the Product Maintenance application (ProductMaintenance.frmNewProduct). As you can see, two groups of members are listed for this class. The first group includes the properties and methods that the class inherits from its base class. The second group includes the members that have been added to the derived class. In this case, the derived class includes five new properties (the text box and button controls) and one new method (GetNewProduct).

Although this figure doesn't show it, a derived class can also replace an inherited property or method with its own version of the property or method. You'll learn how this works later in this chapter.

How inheritance works

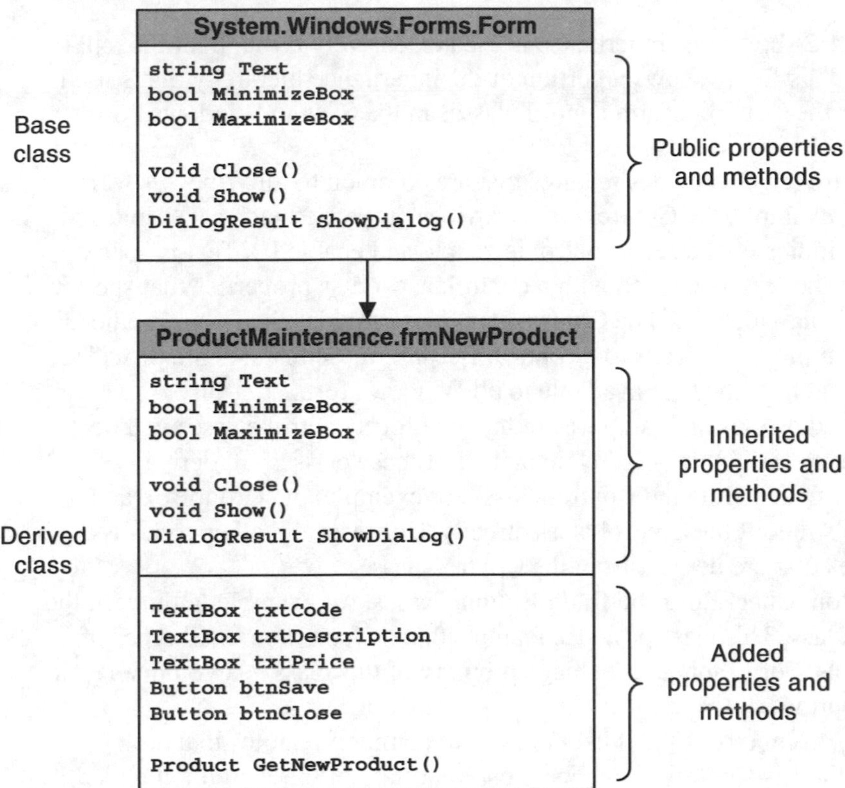

Description

- *Inheritance* lets you create a new class based on an existing class. Then, the new class *inherits* the properties, methods, and other members of the existing class.
- A class that inherits from an existing class is called a *derived class*, *child class*, or *subclass*. A class that another class inherits is called a *base class*, *parent class*, or *superclass*.
- A derived class can *extend* the base class by adding new properties, methods, or other members to the base class. It can also replace a member from the base class with its own version of the member. Depending on how that's done, this is called *hiding* or *overriding*.
- When you create a new form in C#, the form inherits the .NET Framework class named System.Windows.Forms.Form. As a result, all C# forms inherit the members defined by this base class. Then, as you add controls and code to the form, you extend the base class by creating new properties and methods.

Figure 14-1 How inheritance works

How the .NET Framework uses inheritance

Figure 14-2 shows that inheritance is used extensively throughout the .NET Framework. This figure shows a portion of the inheritance hierarchy that's used by several of the Windows form control classes in the System.Windows.Forms namespace.

The Control class provides features that are common to all Windows form controls. For example, the Control class provides properties such as Visible and Enabled that indicate whether a control is visible and enabled, a Text property that specifies the text associated with a control, as well as properties that specify a control's display location. The Control class also provides the Focus method, which lets you move the focus to a control. Because these features are provided by the Control class, they are available to all Windows form controls.

The shaded classes in this figure are the nine form control classes you've learned about so far in this book. Note that all of these classes are derived directly or indirectly from the Control class. For example, the GroupBox and Label controls inherit the Control class directly. However, the other controls inherit classes that are derived from the Control class.

The Button, CheckBox, and RadioButton classes, for example, all inherit the ButtonBase class. This class provides features that are common to all types of button controls. For example, the Image property of this class lets you display an image on a button control.

Similarly, combo boxes and list boxes have common features that are provided by the ListControl class. The most important of these are the Items property, which provides the list that's displayed by the control, and the SelectedIndex, SelectedValue, and SelectedItem properties, which let you access the item that's selected in the list.

Likewise, the TextBoxBase class provides some features that are common to text box controls. That includes the MultiLine property that lets you display multiple lines and the ReadOnly property that lets you create read-only text boxes. By the way, if you're wondering why an intermediate TextBoxBase class is used in the TextBox hierarchy, it's because the .NET Framework provides a second type of text box, called a RichTextBox, that also inherits TextBoxBase. Because the RichTextBox control isn't covered in this book, however, I didn't include it in this figure.

You may be surprised to learn that the Form class itself is also derived from the Control class by way of two other classes: ContainerControl and ScrollableControl. A form's ability to contain other controls is provided by the ContainerControl class. And a form's ability to display scroll bars if its controls can't all be displayed at once is provided by the ScrollableControl class.

Don't be dismayed by the amount of detail presented in this figure. In fact, the actual inheritance hierarchy for the classes in the System.Windows.Forms namespace is far more complicated than indicated here. The intent of this figure is simply to illustrate that inheritance is a feature that's used extensively within the .NET Framework.

The inheritance hierarchy for form control classes

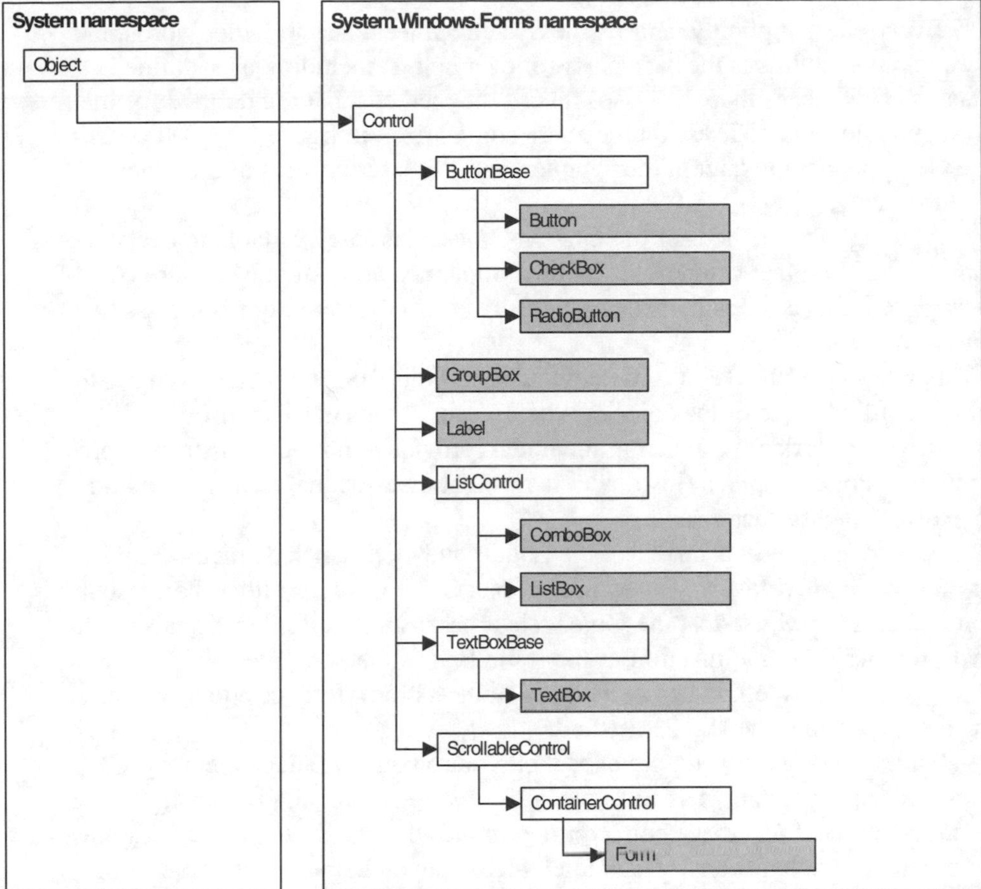

Description

- The .NET Framework uses inheritance extensively in its own classes. For example, inheritance is used throughout the System.Windows.Forms namespace.
- All of the control classes are derived from a base Control class. This class provides properties and methods that all controls have in common, such as Tag and Text. Like all classes, the Control class is ultimately derived from System.Object.
- Some controls have an additional layer of inheritance. For example, the ListControl class provides features common to ListBox and ComboBox controls, such as the SelectedValue property.
- The *fully qualified name* of a class includes the name of the namespace that the class belongs to. For example, the fully qualified name for the ComboBox control is System.Windows.Forms.ComboBox.

Figure 14-2 How the .NET Framework uses inheritance

Methods inherited from the System.Object class

Every class implicitly inherits the System.Object class. In other words, the System.Object class is the base class for every class, including user-defined classes. This means that all classes inherit the methods that are defined for the System.Object class. These methods are summarized in figure 14-3. I'll describe the GetType method later in this chapter, and I'll describe each of the other methods now.

Although the methods of the System.Object class are available to every class, a derived class can provide its own implementation of one or more of these methods. As a result, these methods may work differently from class to class.

For example, the default implementation of the ToString method returns the fully qualified name of the object's type. Because that's not very useful, it's common to override the ToString method to provide a more useful string representation. For example, a Customer class might override the ToString method so it returns the customer's name.

As you learned in chapter 13, the Equals and GetHashCode methods are often used to provide a way to compare objects using values rather than instance references. Notice also that the Object class has a static ReferenceEquals method that provides the same function as the static Equals method. The ReferenceEquals method lets you test two objects for reference equality even if the class overrides the Equals method.

Unlike C++ and other languages that require you to manage memory, C# uses a mechanism known as *garbage collection* to automatically manage memory. When the garbage collector determines that the system is running low on memory and that the system is idle, it frees the memory for any objects that don't have any more references to them. Before it does that, though, it calls the Finalize method for each of those objects, even though the default implementation of this method doesn't do anything. Although you can override the Finalize method to provide specific finalization code for an object, you rarely need do that.

The last method shown in this figure is MemberwiseClone. You can use this method to create a simple copy of an object that doesn't expose other objects as properties or fields. You'll learn more about cloning objects in the next chapter.

Methods of the System.Object class

Method	Description
`ToString()`	Returns a string that contains the fully qualified name of the object's type.
`Equals(object)`	Returns true if this object refers to the same instance as the specified object. Otherwise, it returns false, even if both objects contain the same data.
`Equals(object1, object2)`	A static version of the Equals method that compares two objects to determine if they refer to the same instance.
`ReferenceEquals(object1, object2)`	A static method that determines whether two object references refer to the same instance. This method is typically not overridden, so it can be used to test for instance equality in classes that override the Equals method.
`GetType()`	Returns a Type object that represents the type of an object.
`GetHashCode()`	Returns the integer hash code for an object.
`Finalize()`	Frees resources used by an object. This method is called by the garbage collector when it determines that there are no more references to the object.
`MemberwiseClone()`	Creates a shallow copy of an object. For more information, refer to chapter 15.

Description

- System.Object is the root base class for all classes. In other words, every class inherits either System.Object or some other class that ultimately inherits System.Object. As a result, the methods defined by System.Object are available to all classes.
- When creating classes, it's a common practice to override the ToString and Equals methods so they work appropriately for each class. For example, the ToString method might return a value that uniquely identifies an object. And the Equals method might compare two objects to see if their values are equal.
- The *hash code* for an object is an integer that uniquely identifies the object. Given the same data, each instance of an object should return the same hash code. A common way to implement the GetHashCode method is to return ToString().GetHashCode(). This returns the hash code of the object's ToString() result.
- In general, you don't need to override the Finalize method for an object, even though its default implementation doesn't do anything. That's because the .NET *garbage collector* automatically reclaims the memory of an object whenever it needs to. Before it does that, though, it calls the Finalize method of the object.

Figure 14-3 Methods inherited from the System.Object class

How to use inheritance in your applications

Figure 14-4 describes the two main ways inheritance is typically used in business applications. First, it can be used to simplify the task of creating classes that represent similar types of objects. For example, the first inheritance hierarchy in this figure shows how you might use inheritance to create classes for two types of products: books and software products. As you can see, the Product class is used as the base class for the Book and Software classes. These subclasses inherit the Code, Description, and Price properties as well as the GetDisplayText method from the Product class. In addition, each class adds a property that's unique to the class: The Book class adds an Author property, and the Software class adds a Version property.

The second inheritance hierarchy in this figure shows how you can use the classes of the .NET Framework as base classes for your own classes. Here, a ProductList class inherits the System.Collections.ArrayList class. That way, the ProductList class has all of the features of an array list, but is designed to work specifically with Product objects rather than with any type of object. For example, the ProductList class overrides the Add method so that it accepts only Product objects.

An important aspect of inheritance is that you can use a subclass as an argument or return value for any method that is designed to work with the base class. For example, the Add method of the ProductList class accepts a parameter of type Product. Because both the Book and Software classes are subclasses of the Product class, you can pass either a Book or a Software object to the Add method to add a book or software product to the product list. You'll learn more about how this works in figure 14-7.

Business classes for a Product Maintenance application

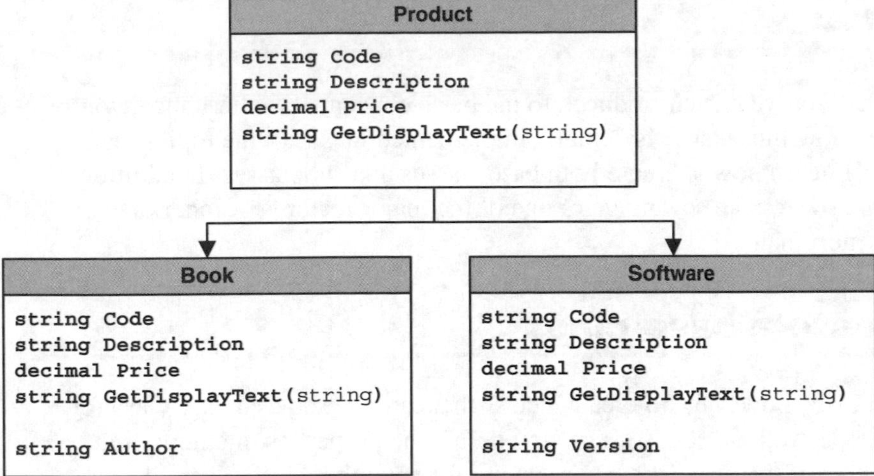

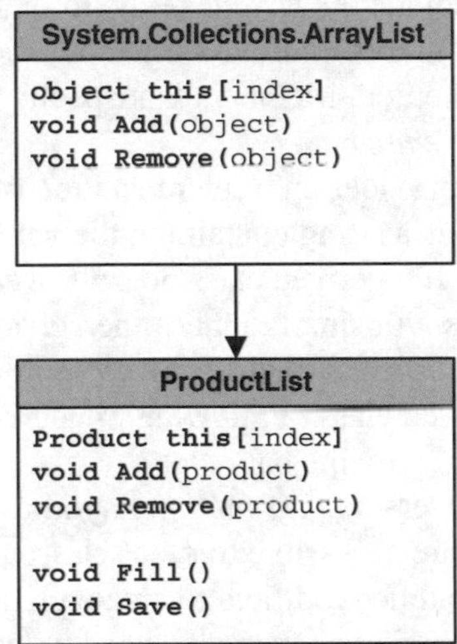

Description

- You can use inheritance in your applications to create generic base classes that implement common elements of related subclasses. For example, if you need separate classes to represent distinct types of products, you can create a Product base class, then use it to create a separate subclass for each type of product.
- It's also common to create classes that inherit from classes that are defined by the .NET Framework. For example, you might create a ProductList class that inherits the ArrayList class. Then, the ProductList class can be written so that it can hold only Product objects rather than any type of object.
- When you inherit a class, you can use the derived class whenever an instance of the base class is called for. For example, a ProductList object based on a class that inherits ArrayList can be used whenever an ArrayList object is called for.

Figure 14-4 How to use inheritance in your applications

Basic skills for working with inheritance

Now that you've been introduced to the basic concepts of inheritance, you're ready to see how inheritance is actually implemented in C#. In the topics that follow, you'll learn how to create both base classes and subclasses. In addition, you'll learn how to take advantage of one of the major features of inheritance, called polymorphism.

How to create a base class

Figure 14-5 shows how to create a class that can be used as a base class for one or more derived classes. To start, you define the properties, methods, and other members of the class just as you would for any other class. Then, if you want a class that's derived from this class to be able to override one of the members of the base class, you include the *virtual* keyword on the declaration for that member. The code shown in this figure, for example, uses the virtual keyword on the GetDisplayText method. Members that specify the virtual keyword are often called *virtual members*.

Notice that the Product class provides an implementation of the GetDisplayText method that returns a string containing the values for the Code, Description, and Price properties. If a derived class doesn't override the GetDisplayText method, that class will simply inherit the version implemented by this class. As a result, creating a virtual member gives you the option of overriding the member in the derived class or allowing the derived class to defer to the version of the member defined by the base class.

The table in this figure lists several *access modifiers* you can use to indicate whether members of a base class are accessible to other classes. You already know how to use the private and public modifiers to create private and public members. When you work with inheritance, you also need to know about the protected modifier. A *protected member* is a member that can be accessed within the defining class and within any class that's derived from the defining class, but not by any other class. Protected members let derived classes access certain parts of the base class without exposing those parts to other classes.

The internal and protected internal access modifiers are rarely used, but I included them here so you'll understand how they work in case you ever encounter them. These modifiers are sometimes useful when you work with class libraries or with solutions that have more than one project. To understand how they work, remember that when you build a project, all of the classes that make up the project are compiled into a single assembly. Members that use the internal keyword alone are accessible to all of the classes within that assembly, but not to classes in other assemblies. Similarly, members that specify protected internal are accessible to derived classes that are a part of the same assembly, but not to derived classes in other assemblies.

The code for a simplified version of the Product base class

```
public class Product
{
    public string Code;
    public string Description;
    public decimal Price;

    public virtual string GetDisplayText(string sep)
    {
        return Code + sep + Description + sep + Price.ToString("c");
    }
}
```

Access modifiers

Keyword	Description
`public`	Available to all classes.
`protected`	Available only to the current class or to derived classes.
`internal`	Available only to classes in the current assembly.
`protected internal`	Available only to the current class, derived classes, or classes in the current assembly.
`private`	Available only to the containing class.
`virtual`	Creates a virtual method or property that can be overridden by a subclass. For more information, refer to figure 14-7. This modifier can be used in combination with the other modifiers in this table.

Description

- You create a base class the same way you create any other class: by defining its properties, methods, events, and other members required to implement the class.
- *Access modifiers* specify the accessibility of the members declared by a class. Public members are accessible to other classes, while private members are accessible only to the class in which they're defined.
- *Protected members* are accessible within the class in which they're declared. They can also be used by any class that inherits the class in which they're declared.
- A derived class can access the public and protected members of its base class, but not the private members.
- *Internal members* are accessible by other classes in the same assembly, but not by classes in other assemblies. This can sometimes be useful to control access to members declared by classes in a class library. For more information about class libraries, see chapter 15.
- If you want to be able to override a member in a derived class, you must include the *virtual* keyword on the member declaration.
- If you don't code an access modifier, the default access is private.

Figure 14-5 How to create a base class

How to create a subclass

Figure 14-6 shows how to create a subclass. To indicate that a class is a subclass, you follow the class name on the class declaration with a colon and the name of the base class that the subclass inherits. For example, the code for the Book class shown in this figure specifies that the Book class is a subclass of the Product class.

After you identify the base class, you can extend its functionality by coding additional properties, methods, or other members. In this figure, for example, you can see that the Book class adds a new constructor and a new public field named Author. In addition, it overrides the GetDisplayText method defined by the Product class.

The constructor for the Book subclass accepts four parameters: code, description, author, and price. Coding a colon after the constructor name followed by the base keyword and a parameter list indicates that this constructor should call the constructor from the base class using the specified parameters. In this case, the base class constructor is called using the code, description, and price parameters that were passed to the constructor of the Book class. Then, the base class constructor initializes the Code, Description, and Price properties with these values. After the base class constructor is called, the code in the Book subclass constructor is executed. As you can see, this code initializes the Author field with the value passed to the author parameter.

To override the GetDisplayText method, the method declaration includes the override keyword. Note that when you override a method, the override must have the same signature as the method it's overriding. In this case, the method must have a single string parameter. This parameter receives the separator that's used to format the Code, Description, Author, and Price properties.

Notice that this GetDisplayText method provides its own complete implementation. In contrast, the GetDisplayText method shown in the second code example builds on to the implementation of this method in the Product class. To do that, it starts by calling the GetDisplayText method of the base class, which returns a formatted string that contains the Code, Description, and Price properties. Then, it adds the Author property to the end of this string.

This figure also introduces the concept of *hiding*. When you use the new keyword on a subclass member, the member *hides* the corresponding base class member. As a result, the subclass doesn't inherit the original version of the member, but uses the new version instead. Hiding is similar to overriding, but can be used only with non-virtual methods or properties. Because hiding doesn't provide for polymorphism as described in the next topic, you should avoid hiding in most cases. Instead, you should use virtual methods and properties whenever you expect to provide a different implementation of the method or property in a subclass.

The syntax for creating subclasses

To declare a subclass

```
public class subclass-name : base-class-name
```

To create a constructor that calls a base class constructor

```
public class-name(parameter-list) : base(parameter-list)
```

To call a base class method or property

```
base.method-name(parameter-list)
base.property-name
```

To hide a non-virtual method or property

```
public new type name
```

To override a virtual method or property

```
public override type name
```

The code for a Book class

```
public class Book : Product
{
    public string Author;          // A new public field

    public Book(string code, string description, string author,
        decimal price) : base(code, description, price)
    {
        this.Author = author;      // Initializes the Author field after
    }                              // the base class constructor is called.

    public override string GetDisplayText(string sep)
    {
        return this.Code + sep + this.Description
            + "( " + this.Author + ")" + sep + this.Price.ToString("c");
    }
}
```

Another way to override a method

```
public override string GetDisplayText(string sep)
{
    return base.GetDisplayText(sep) + "( " + this.Author + ")";
}
```

Description

- A constructor of a derived class automatically calls the default constructor of the base class before the derived class constructor executes. If you want to call a non-default base class constructor, you can specify the constructor to call when you declare the constructor of the derived class. Then, you can pass parameters to the base class constructor.
- You use the *base* keyword to refer to a member of the base class.
- You use the *override* keyword to override a virtual member of the base class.
- You can also use the *new* keyword to provide a new implementation for a non-virtual method or property of the base class. This is called *hiding*. In most cases, however, it's better to use virtual and overridden methods and properties so you can take advantage of polymorphism, as described in figure 14-7.

Figure 14-6 How to create a subclass

How polymorphism works

Polymorphism is one of the most important features of object-oriented programming and inheritance. As figure 14-7 shows, polymorphism lets you treat objects of different types as if they were the same type by referring to a base class that's common to both objects. For example, consider the Book and Software classes that were presented in figure 14-4. Because both of these classes inherit the Product class, objects created from these classes can be treated as if they were Product objects.

One benefit of polymorphism is that you can write generic code that's designed to work with a base class. Then, you can use that code with instances of any of class that's derived from the base class. For example, the Add method for the ProductList class that was described in figure 14-4 accepts a Product object as a parameter. Because the Book and Software classes are derived from the Product class, the Add method will also work with Book and Software objects.

The code examples in this figure illustrate a confusing but useful aspect of polymorphism. The first example shows a virtual method named GetDisplayText that's defined in the Product base class. This method returns a string that includes the Code, Description, and Price properties. The next two examples show overridden versions of the GetDisplayText method for the Book and Software classes. The Book version of this method calls the GetDisplayText method of the base class and then adds the author's name to the end of the string that's returned by that method. Similarly, the Software version calls the GetDisplayText method of the base class and then adds the software version to the end of the string that's returned.

The last code example in this figure shows how you can use polymorphism with these classes. This code begins by creating an instance of the Book class and assigning it to a variable named *b*. Then, it creates an instance of the Software class and assigns it to a variable named *s*.

Next, a variable named p of type Product is declared, and the Book object is assigned to it. Then, the GetDisplayText method of the Product class is called. When the .NET Framework sees that the GetDisplayText method of the Product class is a virtual method, however, it checks to see what type of object the p variable refers to. In this case, the p variable refers to a Book object, so it calls the overridden version of the GetDisplayText method that's defined by the Book class.

The example then does the same thing with the Software object. First, this object is assigned to the p variable. Then, the GetDisplayText method defined by the Product class is called. This time, .NET determines that the product is a Software object, so it calls the overridden version of the GetDisplayText method that's defined by the Software class.

Note that to use this type of polymorphism, you must code the virtual keyword on the base class member. Otherwise, you can't override the member in the derived classes. Then, any call to the base class member executes that member regardless of the object type.

Three versions of the GetDisplayText method

A virtual GetDisplayText method in the Product base class

```
public virtual string GetDisplayText(string sep)
{
    return code + sep + price.ToString("c") + sep + description;
}
```

An overridden GetDisplayText method in the Book class

```
public override string GetDisplayText(string sep)
{
    return base.GetDisplayText() + sep + author;
}
```

An overridden GetDisplayText method in the Software class

```
public override string GetDisplayText(string sep)
{
    return base.GetDisplayText() + sep + version;
}
```

Code that uses the overridden methods

```
Book b = new Book("JAVA", "Murach's Beginning Java 2",
                  "Steelman", 49.50m);
Software s = new Software("NPTK",".NET Programmer's Toolkit",
                          "2.1", 149.50m);
Product p;
p = b;
MessageBox.Show(p.GetDisplayText("\n"));  // Calls Book.GetDisplayText
p = s;
MessageBox.Show(p.GetDisplayText("\n"));  // Calls Software.GetDisplayText
```

Description

- *Polymorphism* is a feature of inheritance that lets you treat objects of different subclasses that are derived from the same base class as if they had the type of the base class. If, for example, Book is a subclass of Product, you can treat a Book object as if it were a Product object.
- If you access a virtual member of a base class object and the member is overridden in the subclasses of that class, polymorphism determines the member that's executed based on the object's type. For example, if you call the GetDisplayText method of a Product object, the GetDisplayText method of the Book class is executed if the object is a Book object.
- Polymorphism is most useful when you have two or more derived classes that use the same base class. It allows you to write generic code that targets the base class rather than having to write specific code for each object type.

Figure 14-7 How polymorphism works

An inheritance version of the Product Maintenance application

Now that you've learned how to create base classes and subclasses, the following topics present a version of the Product Maintenance application that uses inheritance. This version of the application uses the classes that were described in figure 14-4. It works with a Products file that can hold two distinct types of products: books and software.

Note that this version of the Product Maintenance application won't work with the ProductDB classes that are presented in chapters 21 and 22, since those classes are designed to work only with Product objects. Instead, this version of the application requires a ProductDB class that can save and retrieve data for both Book and Software objects. Although this class isn't presented here, you shouldn't have any trouble figuring out how to implement it after you read chapter 21 or 22.

The operation of the Product Maintenance application

Figure 14-8 shows the operation of this version of the Product Maintenance application. As you can see, the Product Maintenance form looks just like the one you saw in chapter 12. From this form, you can click the Add Product button to display the New Product form, or you can select a product in the list and then click the Delete Product button to delete a product.

The main difference between this application and the applications presented in chapters 12 and 13 is that the New Product form includes two radio buttons. These buttons let the user choose whether a book or a software product is added to the file. Note that the label that's displayed for the third text box changes depending on which of these buttons is selected. If the Book button is selected, this label is set to Author. If the Software button is selected, it's set to Version.

The Product Maintenance form

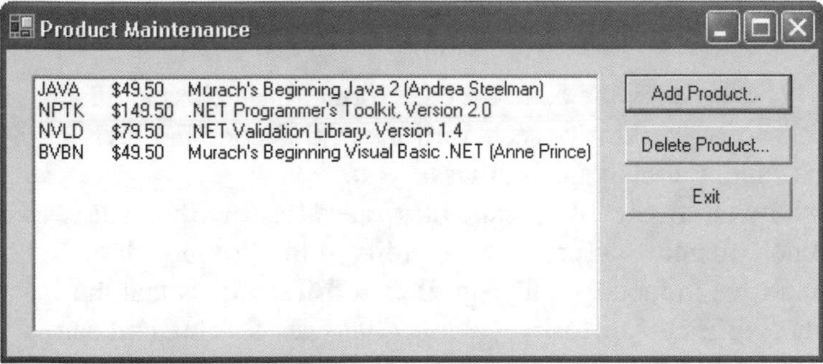

Two versions of the New Product form

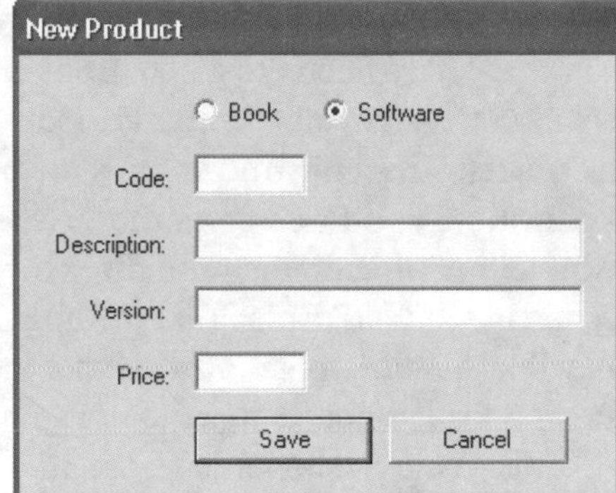

Description

- This version of the Product Maintenance application handles two types of products: books and software.
- The New Product form has a radio button that lets the user choose to create a book or a software product. The label for the third text box changes depending on which option is selected.

Figure 14-8 The operation of the Product Maintenance application

The code for the Product, Book, and Software classes

Figures 14-9 through 14-11 show the code for the Product base class and its two subclasses, Book and Software. You've seen portions of this code in previous figures, so most of it should already be familiar to you.

The Product class, shown in figure 14-9, is the base class for the Book and Software classes. It's almost identical to previous versions of the Product class you saw in chapters 12 and 13. In fact, the only significant difference is that the GetDisplayText method specifies the virtual keyword. That way, this method can be overridden by the Book and Software classes.

The Book class, shown in figure 14-10, specifies the Product class as its base class. Then, it declares a private instance variable to hold the value of the Author property. Next, it provides two constructors. The first is an empty constructor that lets you create a new Book object with default values. The second constructor lets you specify the code, description, author, and price for a new Book object. This constructor calls the base constructor to initialize the Code, Description, and Price properties. As a result, the body of this constructor is just a single line of code that initializes the Author property.

The overridden GetDisplayText method for the Book class calls the base GetDisplayText method to get a string that includes the code, price, and description. Then, it adds the author's name in parentheses to the end of this string.

The Software class, shown in figure 14-11, is similar to the Book class. It too provides a constructor that calls the base constructor to initialize the Code, Description, and Price properties before it initializes the Version property. It also overrides the GetDisplayText method by calling the base GetDisplayText method and then adding the version information to the end of the string that's returned.

The code for the Product class

```
public class Product
{
    private string code;
    private string description;
    private decimal price;

    public Product()
    {
    }

    public Product(string code, string description, decimal price)
    {
        this.Code = code;
        this.Description = description;
        this.Price = price;
    }

    public string Code
    {
        get
        {
            return code;
        }
        set
        {
            code = value;
        }
    }

    public string Description
    {
        get
        {
            return description;
        }
        set
        {
            description = value;
        }
    }

    public decimal Price
    {
        get
        {
            return price;
        }
        set
        {
            price = value;
        }
    }

    public virtual string  GetDisplayText(string sep)
    {
        return code + sep + price.ToString("c") + sep + description;
    }
}
```

Figure 14-9 The code for the Product class

The code for the Book class

```
public class Book : Product
{
    private string author;

    public Book()
    {
    }

    public Book(string code, string description, string author,
        decimal price) : base(code, description, price)
    {
        this.Author = author;
    }

    public string Author
    {
        get
        {
            return author;
        }
        set
        {
            author = value;
        }
    }

    public override string GetDisplayText(string sep)
    {
        return base.GetDisplayText(sep) + " (" + author + ")";
    }

}
```

Description

- The Book class inherits the Product class. It adds a property named Author and overrides the GetDisplayText method.

Figure 14-10 The code for the Book class

The code for the Software class

```
public class Software : Product
{
    private string version;

    public Software()
    {
    }

    public Software(string code, string description, string version,
        decimal price) : base(code, description, price)
    {
        this.Version = version;
    }

    public string Version
    {
        get
        {
            return version;
        }
        set
        {
            version = value;
        }
    }

    public override string GetDisplayText(string sep)
    {
        return base.GetDisplayText(sep) + ", Version " + version;
    }

}
```

Description

- The Software class inherits the Product class. It adds a property named Version and overrides the GetDisplayText method.

The code for the ProductList class

Figure 14-12 shows the code for the ProductList class, which is used to hold the Book and Software objects that are maintained by the Product Maintenance application. This class inherits the ArrayList class. As a result, the basic functions of the ProductList class, such as its ability to hold multiple Product objects, are provided by the base class.

Notice that this class doesn't include a Changed event like the ProductList class you saw in the last chapter. In addition, it doesn't include overloaded + and - operators. That way, it will be easier for you to focus on the basic differences that result from using ArrayList as the base class.

The ProductList class defines an indexer that provides read-only access to an individual Product object based on its index. As you can see, this indexer simply uses the base class indexer to retrieve an object from the base array list. Then, it casts this object to a Product object and returns it.

Next, the Add method adds a Product object to the product list by calling the Add method of the base class. Notice that this Add method accepts a Product object. Instead of doing that, I could have provided two versions of the Add method: one that accepts Book objects and another that accepts Software objects. But since the Book and Software classes are subclasses of the Product class, specifying a Product parameter for the Add method lets this single method be used to add both Book and Software objects. Similarly, the Remove method removes the specified Product object from the list by calling the Remove method of the base class.

The Fill method calls the GetProducts method of the ProductDB class to load the products in the Products file into an array list of products. It then uses a foreach loop to add each product in the array list to the base array list by calling the Add method of the base class.

The Save method is a little simpler. It calls the SaveProducts method of the ProductDB class to save the current instance of the ProductList class to the Products file. To do that, it specifies *this* as the argument of this method.

The code for the ProductList class

```
public class ProductList : System.Collections.ArrayList
{

    public new Product this[int i]
    {
        get
        {
            return (Product)base[i];
        }
    }

    public void Add(Product product)
    {
        base.Add(product);
    }

    public void Remove(Product product)
    {
        base.Remove(product);
    }

    public void Fill()
    {
        ArrayList products = ProductDB.GetProducts();
        foreach (Product product in products)
            base.Add(product);
    }

    public void Save()
    {
        ProductDB.SaveProducts(this);
    }

}
```

Description

- This version of the ProductList class inherits the System.Collections.ArrayList class of the .NET Framework. As a result, it doesn't need to define an ArrayList instance variable because the class is itself a type of array list.

Figure 14-12 The code for the ProductList class

The code for the Product Maintenance form

Figure 14-13 shows the code for this version of the Product Maintenance form. Since this code is similar to the code for the Product Maintenance form you saw chapter 13, I won't review every detail here. Note, however, that because the ProductList class doesn't provide a Changed event, this version of the Product Maintenance form doesn't include a ChangedHandler event hander or code that wires the Changed event to this event handler. In addition, because the ProductList class doesn't include overloaded + and - operators, this Product Maintenance form uses the Add and Remove methods of the ProductList class to work with the products in the list.

The only other significant difference between the code for this form and the one shown in chapter 13 is in the FillProductListBox method. Here, I was able to use a foreach loop to process the product list rather than a for loop that uses the indexer of the ProductList class. That's because the ProductList class in this version of the application inherits the ArrayList class, and the ArrayList class provides the features that are necessary for a collection to be processed this way. In fact, the ability to use a foreach statement like this is one of the main advantages of inheriting the ArrayList class. You'll learn more about the features that make this possible in the next chapter.

You can also see polymorphism at work in this foreach loop. Here, the statement that adds the text to the Items collection of the list box calls the GetDisplayText method for each product. Because GetDisplayText is a virtual method that's overridden by both the Book and Software classes, this code calls thc GctDisplayText method of the Book class for Book objects and the GetDisplayText method of the Software class for Software objects. To confirm that's what's happening, you can look back to figures 14-10 and 14-11 to see the differences between these two methods, and you can look back to figure 14-8 to see the differences in the resulting display.

The code for the Product Maintenance form

```
public class frmProductMain : System.Windows.Forms.Form
{
    private ProductList products = new ProductList();

    private void frmProductMain_Load(object sender, System.EventArgs e)
    {
        products.Fill();
        FillProductListBox();
    }

    private void FillProductListBox()
    {
        lstProducts.Items.Clear();
        foreach (Product p in products)
            lstProducts.Items.Add(p.GetDisplayText("\t"));
    }

    private void btnAdd_Click(object sender, System.EventArgs e)
    {
        frmNewProduct newForm = new frmNewProduct();
        Product product = newForm.GetNewProduct();
        if (product != null)
        {
            products.Add(product);
            products.Save();
            FillProductListBox();
        }
    }

    private void btnDelete_Click(object sender, System.EventArgs e)
    {
        int i = lstProducts.SelectedIndex;
        if (i != -1)
        {
            Product product = (Product) products[i];
            string message = "Are you sure you want to delete "
                + product.Description + "?";
            DialogResult button =
                MessageBox.Show(message, "Confirm Delete",
                MessageBoxButtons.YesNo);
            if (button == DialogResult.Yes)
            {
                products.Remove(product);
                products.Save();
                FillProductListBox();
            }
        }
    }

    private void btnClose_Click(object sender, System.EventArgs e)
    {
        this.Close();
    }

}
```

Figure 14-13 The code for the Product Maintenance form

The code for the New Product form

Figure 14-14 shows the code for the New Product form. Here, you can see that event handlers for the CheckedChanged events of the two radio buttons are used to set the Text and Tag properties of the third label control to reflect the radio button that's selected. In addition, the event handler for the Click event of the Save button tests the Checked property of the Book radio button to determine whether it should create a Book or Product object. The only other difference between the code for this form and the forms presented in chapters 12 and 13 is that the IsValidData method in this form uses the IsPresent method of the Validator class to validate the author or version that the user enters.

The code for the New Product form

```
public class frmNewProduct : System.Windows.Forms.Form
{
    private Product product = null;

    public Product GetNewProduct()
    {
        this.ShowDialog();
        return product;
    }

    private void rbBook_CheckedChanged(object sender, System.EventArgs e)
    {
        lblAuthorOrVersion.Text = "Author: ";
        txtAuthorOrVersion.Tag = "Author";
    }

    private void rbSoftware_CheckedChanged(object sender, System.EventArgs e)
    {
        lblAuthorOrVersion.Text = "Version: ";
        txtAuthorOrVersion.Tag = "Version";
    }

    private void btnSave_Click(object sender, System.EventArgs e)
    {
        if (IsValidData())
        {
            if (rbBook.Checked)
                product = new Book(txtCode.Text, txtDescription.Text,
                    txtAuthorOrVersion.Text, Convert.ToDecimal(txtPrice.Text));
            else
                product = new Software(txtCode.Text, txtDescription.Text,
                    txtAuthorOrVersion.Text, Convert.ToDecimal(txtPrice.Text));
            this.Close();
        }
    }

    private bool IsValidData()
    {
        return Validator.IsPresent(txtCode) &&
               Validator.IsPresent(txtDescription) &&
               Validator.IsPresent(txtAuthorOrVersion) &&
               Validator.IsPresent(txtPrice) &&
               Validator.IsDecimal(txtPrice);
    }

    private void btnCancel_Click(object sender, System.EventArgs e)
    {
        this.Close();
    }

}
```

Figure 14-14 The code for the New Product form

Object types and casting

Now that you've learned the basics of inheritance and you've seen an example of an application that uses it, you're ready to learn some additional techniques that are often required when you work with inheritance. That includes casting objects and getting information about an object's type.

How to use the Type class to get information about an object's type

As you know, the System.Object class includes a GetType method that you can use to get a Type object that represents the type of a .NET object. Figure 14-15 lists some of the members of the Type class that you can use to get information about an object. For example, you can use the Name property to get the name of a type, such as "Product or "Book;" you can use the Namespace property to get the name of the namespace that contains a type, such as "ProductMaintenance;" and you can use the FullName property to get the fully qualified name of a type, such as "ProductMaintenance.Book." In addition, you can use the BaseType property to get a Type object that represents the type of the class that a type inherits.

The first code example in this figure shows how you can use these properties to display information about an object. Here, the GetType method is used to get information about a Book object that's accessed through a variable of type Product. Notice that even though the variable has a type of Product, the Type object that's returned by the GetType method represents a Book object.

The second code example in this figure shows how you can code an if statement to test an object's type. Here, I simply called the Product object's GetType method to get a Type object. Then, I compared the Name property of that object with a string to determine if the object is of type Book.

The third code example shows another way to test an object's type. Here, I used the static GetType method of the Type class to get a Type object for the Book class of the ProductMaintenance namespace. Then, I compared this type object to the Type object that's returned by the GetType method of the Product. Notice that when you use the GetType method of the Type class, you must supply the fully qualified name of the class you want to get a Type object for.

The Type class

Property	Description
`Name`	Returns a string that contains the name of a type.
`FullName`	Returns a string that contains the fully qualified name of a type, which includes the namespace name and the type name.
`BaseType`	Returns a Type object that represents the class that a type inherits.
`Namespace`	Returns a string that contains the name of the namespace that contains a type.
Method	**Description**
`GetType(fullname)`	A static method that returns a Type object for the specified name.

Code that uses the Type class to get information about an object

```
string msg;
Product p;
p = new Book("JAVA", "Murach's Beginning Java 2",
        "Andrea Steelman", 49.50m);
Type t = p.GetType();
msg = "Name: " + t.Name + "\n";
msg += "Namespace: " + t.Namespace + "\n";
msg += "FullName: " + t.FullName + "\n";
msg += "BaseType: " + t.BaseType.Name + "\n";
MessageBox.Show(msg, "Type Examples");
```

The resulting dialog box

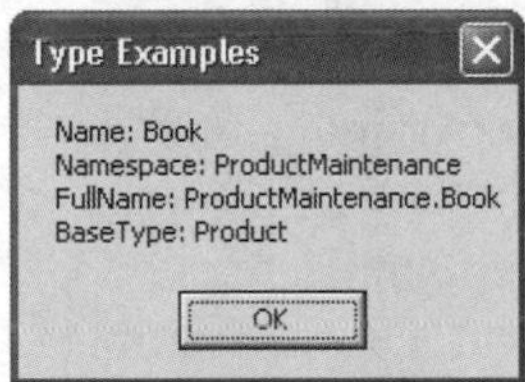

How to test an object's type

```
if (p.GetType().Name == "Book")
```

Another way to test an object's type

```
if (p.GetType() == Type.GetType("ProductMaintenance.Book"))
```

Description

- Every object has a GetType method that returns a Type object that corresponds to the object's type.
- You can use the properties of the Type class to obtain information about the type of any object, such as the type's name and the name of its base class.
- The properties and methods shown above are only some of the more than 90 properties and methods of the Type class.
- You can use the static GetType method to get a Type object for any class. This is useful when you want to check to see if an object is of a particular type.

Figure 14-15 How to use the Type class to get information about an object's type

How to use casting with inheritance

Another potentially confusing aspect of using inheritance is knowing when to cast inherited objects explicitly. The basic rule is that C# can implicitly cast a subclass to its base class, but you must use explicit casting if you want to treat a base class object as one of its subclasses. Figure 14-16 illustrates how this works.

The two methods at the top of this figure both call the GetDisplayText method to get data in a displayable format. The first method, named DisplayProduct, accepts a Product object and executes the GetDisplayText method of the Product class, so it can be used with either a Book or a Software object. In contrast, the second method, named DisplayBook, accepts a Book object and calls the GetDisplayText method of the Book class, so it can only be used with Book objects.

The second code example shows code that doesn't require casting. Here, the first statement creates a new Book object and assigns it to a variable of type Book. Then, the DisplayProduct method is called to format the Book object that this variable refers to. Although the DisplayProduct method expects a Product object, it can cast the Book object to a Product object since Book is a subclass of the Product class.

The third example is similar, but it assigns the new Book object to a variable of type Product. Then, it calls the DisplayBook method. Because this method expects a Book object, however, the Product object must be explicitly cast to a Book object. If it isn't, the C# compiler will display a compiler error indicating that it can't convert a Product object to a Book object.

The fourth example shows code that results in a casting exception. Here, a Software object is assigned to a variable of type Product. Then, the DisplayBook method is called to format the object that this variable refers to. Notice that this variable is explicitly cast to a Book object since that's what the DisplayBook method expects. Because the p variable holds a Software object rather than a Book object, however, this cast results in a casting exception.

The last example shows how you can use the as operator to avoid throwing an exception if a cast is invalid. The as operator is similar to a cast, but returns null if the object can't be converted to the specified type. In the example, a null value will be passed to the DisplaySoftware method because the object referenced by the p variable is a Book object, which can't be cast to a Software object.

Two methods that display product information

```
public void DisplayProduct(Product p)
{
    MessageBox.Show(p.GetDisplayText());
}

public void DisplayBook(Book b)
{
    MessageBox.Show(b.GetDisplayText());
}
```

Code that doesn't require casting

```
Book b = new Book("JAVA", "Murach's Beginning Java 2", "Steelman", 49.50m);
DisplayProduct(b);          // Casting is not required because Book
                            // is a subclass of Product.
```

Code that requires casting

```
Product p = new Book("JAVA", "Murach's Beginning Java 2",
                     "Steelman", 49.50m);
DisplayBook((Book)p);       // Casting is required because DisplayBook
                            // accepts a Book object.
```

Code that throws a casting exception

```
Product p = new Software("NPTK", ".NET Programmer's Toolkit",
                         "2.5", 149.50m);
DisplayBook((Book)p);       // Will throw a casting exception because p is a
                            // Software object, not a Book object.
```

Code that uses the as operator

```
Product p = new Book("JAVA", "Murach's Beginning Java 2", "Steelman", 49.50m);
DisplaySoftware(p as Software);   // Passes null because p is not a Software object
```

Description

- C# can implicitly cast a subclass to its base class. As a result, you can use a subclass whenever a reference to its base class is called for. For example, you can specify a Book object whenever a Product object is expected because Book is a subclass of Product.
- You must explicitly cast a base class object when a reference to one of its subclasses is required. For example, you must explicitly cast a Product object to Book if a Book object is expected.
- If you attempt to cast a base class object to a subclass, InvalidCastException will be thrown if the object is not of the correct type. For example, if you store a Software object in a variable of type Product and then try to cast the Product variable to a Book, a casting exception will be thrown.
- You can use the as operator to cast an object to another type without throwing a casting exception if the cast is invalid. The as operator simply returns null if the cast is invalid.

Figure 14-16 How to use casting with inheritance

How to work with abstract and sealed classes

The last two topics of this chapter show how you can require or restrict the use of inheritance in the classes you create by using abstract and sealed classes.

How to work with abstract classes

An *abstract class* is a class that can't be instantiated. In other words, it can be used only as a base class that other classes can inherit. Figure 14-17 shows how to work with abstract classes.

To declare an abstract class, you include the *abstract* keyword in the class declaration as shown in the Product class at the top of this figure. Then, you can code any members you want within this class. In addition, you can code *abstract methods* and *abstract properties*. For example, the Product class shown here includes an abstract method named GetDisplayText. As you can see, the declaration for this method includes the abstract keyword, and no method body is coded. You code an abstract property using a similar technique, as illustrated by the second example.

When you include abstract properties and methods in an abstract class, you must override them in any class that inherits the abstract class. This is illustrated in the third example in this figure. Here, you can see that a class named Book that inherits the Product class overrides the abstract GetDisplayText method that's defined by that class. Although you must override abstract properties and methods, you should notice that they're not declared with the virtual keyword. That's because abstract properties and methods are implicitly virtual.

At this point, you may be wondering why you would use abstract classes. To help you understand, consider the Product Maintenance application that's presented in this chapter. This application uses two types of product objects: Book objects and Software objects. However, there's nothing to stop you from creating instances of the Product class as well. As a result, the Product class hierarchy actually allows for three types of objects: Book objects, Software objects, and Product objects.

If that's not what you want, you can declare the Product class as an abstract class. Then, you can't create instances of the Product class itself. Instead, the Product class can only be used as the base class for other classes.

Note that this doesn't mean that you can't declare variables of an abstract type. It simply means that you can't use the new keyword with an abstract type to create an instance of the type. For example, if you declared the Product class as an abstract class, you could still declare a Product variable that could hold Book or Software objects. But you wouldn't be able to use the new keyword with the Product class to create a Product object.

An abstract Product class

```
public abstract class Product
{
    public string Code;
    public string Description;
    public decimal Price;

    public abstract string GetDisplayText(string sep);
    // No method body is coded.
}
```

An abstract read-only property

```
public abstract bool IsValid
{
    get;          // No body is coded for the get accessor.
}
```

A class that inherits the abstract Product class

```
public class Book : Product
{
    public string Author;

    public override string GetDisplayText(string sep)
    {
        return this.Code & sep + this.Description
            + "( " + this.Author + ")" + sep + this.Price.ToString("c");
    }

}
```

Description

- An *abstract class* is a class that can be inherited by other classes but that you can't use to create an object. To declare an abstract class, code the *abstract* keyword in the class declaration.
- An abstract class can contain properties, methods, and other members just like other base classes. In addition, an abstract class can contain abstract methods and properties.
- To create an *abstract method*, you code the *abstract* keyword in the method declaration and you omit the method body.
- To create an *abstract property*, you code the abstract keyword in the property declaration. Then, you code a get accessor, a set accessor, or both get and set accessors with no bodies.
- Abstract methods and properties are implicitly virtual, and you can't code the *virtual* keyword on an abstract method or property.
- When a subclass inherits an abstract class, all abstract methods and properties in the abstract class must be overridden in the subclass.
- An abstract class doesn't have to contain abstract methods or properties. However, any class that contains an abstract method or property must be declared as abstract.

Figure 14-17 How to work with abstract classes

How to work with sealed classes

In contrast to an abstract class that must be inherited, a *sealed class* is a class that can't be inherited. Because C# doesn't have to generate code that provides for inheritance and polymorphism when it compiles sealed classed, using them can result in a minor performance benefit. If you know that a class won't be used as a base class, then, you should consider creating a sealed class.

Figure 14-18 shows how to create and work with sealed classes, as well as sealed properties and methods. To create a sealed class, you include the sealed keyword in the class declaration as shown in the example at the top of this figure. Then, you add the members that are required by the class just as you do for any other class.

You can also seal selected properties and methods of a class by omitting the sealed keyword from the class declaration and coding it on just the properties and methods you want to seal. Then, you can use the class as a base class for other classes, but you can't override the sealed members. This is illustrated in the group of examples in this figure.

This example uses three classes named A, B, and C. Class A is a base class that declares a virtual method named ShowMessage. Class B inherits class A and overrides the ShowMessage method. In addition, class B seals this method. Then, class C inherits class B and attempts to override the ShowMessage method. Because class B sealed the ShowMessage method, however, this results in a compiler error.

In most cases, an entire class will be sealed rather than specific methods or properties. Because of that, you won't have to worry about whether individual properties and methods of a class are sealed. If you ever encounter sealed properties or methods, however, you should now understand how they work.

Keep in mind too that it's often hard to know when someone else might want to inherit a class that you create. So you shouldn't seal a class unless you're certain that no one else will benefit by extending it.

The class declaration for a sealed Book class

```
public sealed class Book : Product
```

How sealed methods work

A base class named A that declares a virtual method

```
public class A
{
    public virtual void ShowMessage()
    {
        MessageBox.Show("Hello from class A");
    }
}
```

A class named B that inherits class A and overrides and seals its method

```
public class B : A
{
    public sealed override void ShowMessage()
    {
        MessageBox.Show("Hello from class B");
    }
}
```

A class named C that inherits class B and tries to override its sealed method

```
public class C : B
{
    public override void ShowMessage()    // Causes compiler error
    {
        MessageBox.Show("Hello from class C");
    }
}
```

Description

- A *sealed class* is a class that can't be inherited. To create a sealed class, you code the *sealed* keyword in the class declaration.
- Sealing a class can result in a minor performance improvement for your application because the C# compiler doesn't have to allow for inheritance and polymorphism. As a result, it can generate more efficient code.
- You can also seal individual properties and methods. To create a *sealed property* or a *sealed method*, code the sealed keyword in the property or method declaration.
- You can only seal a property or method if the property or method overrides a member of the base class. This allows you to create a virtual member in a base class, then seal it in a derived class so that any subclasses derived from that class can't override the member. This feature is rarely used in business applications.

Figure 14-18 How to work with sealed classes

Perspective

Conceptually, this is probably the most difficult chapter in this book. Although the basic idea of inheritance isn't that difficult to understand, the complications of virtual members, overridden members, casting, and abstract and sealed classes are enough to make inheritance a difficult topic. So if you find yourself a bit confused right now, don't be disheartened. It will become clearer as you actually use the techniques you've learned here.

The good news is that you don't have to understand every nuance of how inheritance works to use it. In fact, you've used inheritance in every C# application you've written without even knowing it. Now that you've completed this chapter, though, you should have a better understanding of how the .NET Framework works, and you should have a greater appreciation for how much the Framework does on your behalf. In addition, you should have a better idea of how you can use inheritance to improve the design of your own classes.

Summary

- *Inheritance* lets you create a new class based on an existing class. The existing class is called the *base class*, *parent class*, or *superclass*, and the new class is called the *derived class*, *child class*, or *subclass*.
- A derived class inherits all of the members of its base class. The derived class can *extend* the base class by adding its own members.
- All classes inherit the System.Object class, which provides methods such as ToString, Equals, and GetType.
- You can use inheritance in your own applications by creating your own base classes or by inheriting classes defined by the .NET Framework.
- You can use *access modifiers* to limit the accessibility of members declared by a class. Public members can be accessed by other classes. Private members can be accessed only within the defining class. And *protected members* can be accessed only within the defining class or within a class that inherits the defining class.
- *Virtual members* can be *overridden* by derived classes. This is how C# implements *polymorphism*, which is a feature of inheritance that lets you treat subclasses as though they were their base class.
- You use the GetType method to get a Type object for any object. Then, you can use the properties of the Type object to get information about the type of the original object.
- C# can implicitly cast a subclass type to its base class type, but you must use explicit casting to cast a base class type to a subclass type.
- An *abstract class* is a class that can be inherited, but can't be used to create an object. A *sealed class* is one that can't be inherited.

Terms

inheritance
derived class
child class
subclass
base class
parent class
superclass
hiding
overriding
fully qualified name
hash code
garbage collector
access modifier
virtual member
protected member
internal member
polymorphism
abstract class
abstract method
abstract property
sealed class
sealed property
sealed method

Objectives

- Given the specifications for an application that uses any of the inheritance features presented in this chapter, develop the application.
- Explain how inheritance is used within the .NET Framework classes.
- Explain why methods such as ToString, Equals, and GetHashCode are available to all objects and when you might override these methods.
- Explain the purpose of protected access.
- Explain what polymorphism is and how it is implemented in C#.
- Describe the use of the Type class.
- Explain when it's necessary to use explicit casting when working with objects created from derived classes.
- Explain what abstract and sealed classes and members are.

Exercise 14-1 Create a Customer Maintenance application that uses inheritance

In this exercise, you'll create a Customer Maintenance application that uses classes with the inheritance features presented in this chapter. This application works with two types of customers: retail customers and wholesale customers. Both customer types are derived from a Customer base class, both extend the Customer class by adding a property, and separate forms are used to add the two types of customers. To make this application easier to develop, we'll give you the starting forms and classes.

The design of the Customer Maintenance form

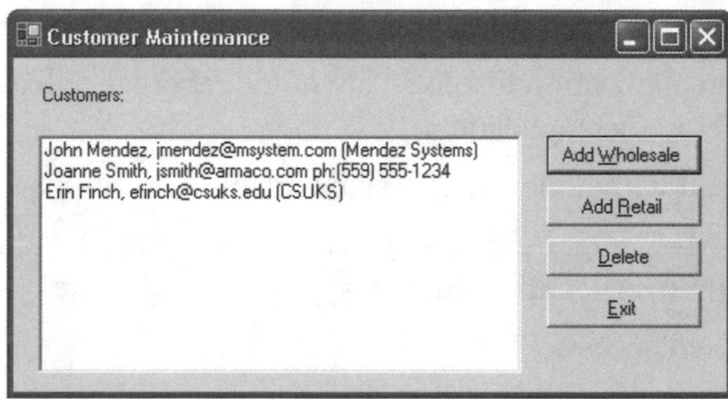

The design of the Add Customer forms

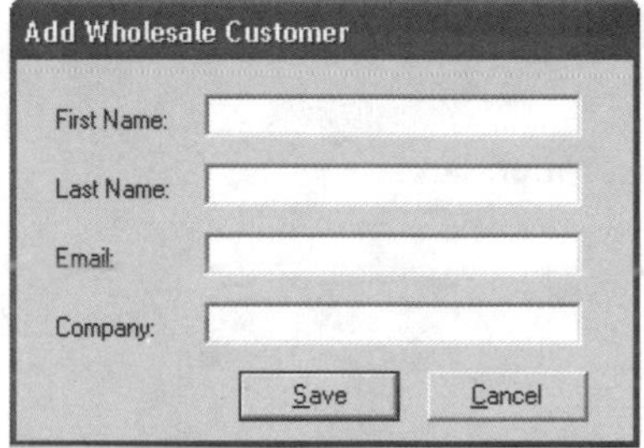

Open the project and create the derived classes

1. Open the project named CustomerMaintenance in the C:\C#.NET\Chapter 14\CustomerMaintenance directory.
2. Add a class named WholesaleCustomer that inherits the Customer class. This new class should add a string property named Company. It should also provide a constructor that accepts four parameters (first name, last name, email, and company) to initialize the class properties. This constructor should call the base class constructor to initialize the properties defined by that class. Finally, this class should override the GetDisplayText method to add the company name in parentheses to the end of the display string, as in this example:

   John Mendez, jmendez@msystem.com (Mendez Systems)

3. Add another class named RetailCustomer that inherits the Customer class and adds a string property named HomePhone. Like the WholesaleCustomer class, the RetailCustomer class should provide a constructor that accepts four parameters, and it should override the GetDisplayText method so the phone number is added to the end of the string like this:

    Joanne Smith, jsmith@armaco.com ph: (559) 555-1234

Complete the code for the forms

4. Complete the event handlers for the Click events of the Save buttons on the Add Wholesale Customer and Add Retail Customer forms so they create a new customer of the appropriate type using the data entered by the user.
5. Complete the event handlers for the Click events of the Add Wholesale and Add Retail buttons on the Customer Maintenance form. These methods should create an instance of the appropriate Add Customer form and then call its GetNewCustomer method. The Customer object that's returned should be saved in a local variable of type Customer. Then, if the returned value isn't null, the customer should be added to the customer array list, the data should be saved to disk, and the list box should be updated.
6. Run the application to make sure it works. If you're going to continue with the next exercise, leave the solution open. Otherwise, close it.

Exercise 14-2 Modify the CustomerList class to inherit the ArrayList class

This exercise builds on the Customer Maintenance application you created in exercise 14-1 by modifying the CustomerList class so it inherits the .NET Framework's ArrayList class.

1. If it isn't already opened, open the CustomerMaintenance application in the C:\C#.NET\Chapter 14\CustomerMaintenace directory.
2. Modify the CustomerList class so it inherits the System.Collections.ArrayList class instead of using a private array list variable to hold the customer list.
3. Modify the FillCustomerListBox method of the Customer Maintenance form so it fills the list box using a foreach statement instead of a for statement.
4. Run the application and test it to be sure it works properly.

15

How to work with interfaces, structures, and class libraries

This chapter presents three additional features for developing object-oriented programs in C#. First, you'll learn how to use interfaces. Interfaces are similar to abstract classes, but they have several advantages that make them easier to create and more flexible to use. Next, you'll learn how to use structures. Structures are similar to classes, but they represent value types rather than reference types. Finally, you'll learn how to make classes easier to reuse by storing them in class libraries.

How to work with interfaces

In some object-oriented programming languages, such as C++ and Pearl, a class can inherit more than one class. This is known as *multiple inheritance*. In C#, however, a class can inherit only one other class.

Although C# doesn't support multiple inheritance, it does support a special type of coding element known as an *interface*. An interface provides many of the advantages of multiple inheritance without some of the problems that are associated with it. In the topics that follow, you'll learn how to work with interfaces. In particular, you'll learn how to implement three interfaces that are defined by the .NET Framework.

An introduction to interfaces

In some ways, an interface is similar to an abstract class. That's why figure 15-1 compares interfaces to abstract classes. To start, abstract classes and interfaces can both include one or more members that aren't implemented. In the case of an abstract class, the implementation for these members must be provided by any subclass that inherits the abstract class. Similarly, the implementation for the members of an interface must be included in any class that *implements* the interface. The difference is that an interface can't include the implementation for any of its members, but an abstract class can.

An important difference between abstract classes and interfaces is that a C# class can inherit only one class (abstract or not), but it can implement more than one interface. This is how C# interfaces can be used to provide some of the features of multiple inheritance.

The examples in this figure show how a simple interface is declared and implemented by a class. The first example shows the declaration for the ICloneable interface, one of the interfaces defined by the .NET Framework. This interface includes a single method named Clone that allows an object to create a copy of itself. Any class that implements the ICloneable interface must provide an implementation of the Clone method.

The second example shows a simplified version of a Product class that implements the ICloneable interface. Here, you can see that the class statement for the Product class lists ICloneable as an interface that's implemented by the class. Then, the class provides an implementation of the Clone method that creates a new Product object, assigns values to it, and returns it.

Note in these examples that the interface name begins with the capital letter I. This is true of all the interfaces defined by the .NET Framework. Although that's not a requirement, it helps you distinguish between interfaces and classes. So if you create your own interfaces, we recommend that you give them names that begin with the letter I.

The ICloneable interface

```
public interface ICloneable          // ICloneable is one of the interfaces defined
{                                    // by the .NET Framework.
    object Clone();
}
```

A Product class that implements the ICloneable interface

```
public class Product : ICloneable
{
    public string Code;
    public string Description;
    public decimal Price;

    public object Clone()            // An implementation of the Clone method
    {
        Product p = new Product();
        p.Code = this.Code;
        p.Description = this.Description;
        p.Price = this.Price;
        return p;
    }
}
```

A comparison of interfaces and abstract classes

- Both interfaces and abstract classes provide signatures for members that a class must implement.
- All of the members of an interface are abstract. In contrast, an abstract class can implement some or all of its members.
- A class can inherit only one class (including abstract classes), but a class can implement more than one interface.
- Interfaces can't declare static members, but abstract classes can.

Description

- An *interface* consists of a set of signatures for one or more methods, properties, indexers, or events. An interface doesn't provide an implementation for any of its members. Instead, it indicates what members must be defined by any class that *implements* the interface.
- The most common use for interfaces is to provide a standardized way of implementing a commonly used function or feature.
- By convention, interface names begin with the letter I to distinguish them from classes.
- To implement an interface, a class must name the interface on the class declaration, and it must provide an implementation for every member of the interface.
- An interface can inherit other interfaces. Then, any class that implements the interface must also implement the inherited interfaces.

Figure 15-1 An introduction to interfaces

Some of the interfaces defined by the .NET Framework

The .NET Framework defines hundreds of interfaces. Fortunately, most of them are intended for use by other Framework classes. As a result, you don't need to learn them all. To give you an idea of what some of these interfaces do, however, figure 15-2 lists a few of them.

The first table in this figure lists four general purpose .NET interfaces: ICloneable, IComparable, IConvertible, and IDisposeable. Of these four, the one you're most likely to implement is ICloneable. This interface lets you create objects that can produce copies of themselves. It consists of a single method, Clone, that returns a copy of the object. You saw an example of a class that implements ICloneable in figure 15-1, and you'll see a more complete example of this class and how it's used in figure 15-5.

The IComparable interface provides a standard way for an object to compare itself with another object. However, most business classes don't have any real basis for determining whether one instance of the class is greater than, equal to, or less than another. For example, how would you determine whether one product object is greater than, equal to, or less than another product object? By comparing the product codes? The price? The amount of inventory on hand? Because it doesn't usually make sense to compare any of these types of values, you aren't likely to implement this interface for business objects.

The IConvertible interface lets you define type conversions that convert a custom type to one of the standard .NET types. Again, there isn't a natural way to convert most business classes to a standard .NET type. For example, how would you convert a Product object to an integer or a decimal? As a result, you aren't likely to implement this interface for most business classes.

The IDisposeable interface provides a single method, Dispose, that's used to free resources that aren't automatically freed by the .NET garbage collector, such as open files. In most cases, you can design your classes so its methods automatically free these resources before they finish. For example, a method might open a file, read its contents, and then close the file. Because of that, the IDisposeable interface isn't typically used by business classes.

The second table in this figure lists several interfaces that are used by collection classes. The most important of these are IEnumerable and IEnumerator, which provide a standard mechanism for iterating through the items of a collection. If you implement these interfaces in a class, you can then use the class in a foreach statement. In fact, this is the main benefit of implementing the IEnumerable and IEnumerator interfaces. You'll learn how to implement these two interfaces in figures 15-7 and 15-8.

The other three interfaces listed in the second table provide standard ways to implement collection features. The ICollection interface defines a basic collection that maintains a count of items, can be synchronized, and can copy the collection items to an array. The IList interface adds an indexer and methods to add, clear, and remove items. And the IDictionary interface implements a dictionary, which can be used to maintain key/value pairs.

Commonly used .NET interfaces

Interface	Members	Description
ICloneable	object Clone()	Creates a duplicate copy of an object.
IComparable	int CompareTo(object)	Compares objects.
IConvertible	TypeCode GetTypeCode() decimal ToDecimal() int ToInt32() ...	Converts an object to one of the common language runtime types, such as Int32, Decimal, or Bool.
IDisposeable	void Dispose()	Frees unmanaged resources.

Commonly used .NET interfaces for collections

Interface	Members	Description
IEnumerable	IEnumerator GetEnumerator()	Gets an enumerator for the collection.
IEnumerator	object Current bool MoveNext() void Reset()	Defines an enumerator that provides read-only, forward-only access to a collection.
ICollection	int Count bool IsSynchronized object SyncRoot void CopyTo(array, int)	Provides basic properties for an enumerable collection. This interface inherits IEnumerable.
IList	[int indexer] int Add(object) void Clear() void Remove(object) void RemoveAt(int)	Manages a basic list of objects. This interface inherits ICollection and IEnumerable.
IDictionary	[int indexer] ICollection Keys ICollection Values int Add(object) void Remove(object) void Clear()	Manages a collection of key/value pairs. This interface inherits ICollection and IEnumerable.

Description

- The .NET Framework defines many interfaces that you can implement in your classes. In this chapter, you'll see examples of classes that implement ICloneable, IEnumerable, and IEnumerator.
- The ICollection interface inherits the IEnumerable interface, which means that any class that implements ICollection must also implement IEnumerable. Similarly, the IList and IDictionary interfaces inherit ICollection and IEnumerable.
- This table only lists the most important members of each interface. For a complete description of these interfaces and a list of their members, see the online documentation.

Figure 15-2 Some of the interfaces defined by the .NET Framework

How to create an interface

Figure 15-3 shows how to create an interface. As you can see in the syntax diagrams at the top of this figure, you declare an interface using the *interface* keyword. This keyword is followed by the interface name. Then, if the interface inherits other interfaces, the interface name is followed by a colon and a list of the inherited interfaces.

Within the body of an interface, you can declare one or more methods, properties, and events. Although these declarations are similar to the declarations for a class, there are three important differences. First, because an interface doesn't provide the implementation for its members, method declarations and the get and set accessors within a property always end in a semi-colon. Second, you can't code access modifiers on a member declaration for an interface. Instead, all members are considered to be public and abstract. If you inadvertently code the public or abstract keyword on a member declaration, the compiler will generate an error message. Third, interfaces can't define static members, so you can't use the static keyword.

The two code examples in this figure show the definitions of two interfaces. The first is for the ICloneable interface, which includes a single method named Clone. The second is for the IDictionary interface, which inherits the ICollection and IEnumerable interfaces. Notice in this example that the get and set accessors for the indexer (this) are coded on a single line. This is a common coding convention for defining interfaces.

Both of the interfaces shown in this figure are defined by the .NET Framework. Although you can create your own interfaces, that isn't commonly done in business applications. Instead, you're more likely to create classes that implement interfaces that are defined by the .NET Framework, such as the ones shown here.

If you find that you need to create your own interface, however, you can do that by adding a new class to your project using the Project→Add Class command. Then, you can delete the class declaration from this file and add the interface declaration using the syntax shown in this figure.

The syntax for creating an interface

```
public interface InterfaceName
{
    type methodName(parameters);        // Declares a method

    type propertyName                   // Declares a property
    {
        [get;]                          // Declares a get accessor
        [set;]                          // Declares a set accessor
    }
    ...
}
```

The syntax for creating an interface that inherits other interfaces

```
public interface InterfaceName : interface-name-1[, interface-name-2...]
{
    interface members...
}
```

An interface that defines one method

```
public interface ICloneable
{
    object Clone();
}
```

An interface that inherits two interfaces

```
public interface IDictionary : ICollection, IEnumerable
{
    // Properties
    bool IsFixedSize {get;}
    bool IsReadOnly {get;}
    object this[object key] {get; set;}
    ICollection Keys {get;}
    ICollection Values {get;}

    // Methods
    void Add(object key, object value);
    void Clear();
    bool Contains(object key);
    IEnumerator GetEnumerator();
    void Remove(object key);
}
```

Description

- The declaration for an interface is similar to the declaration for a class. The only difference is that you use the *interface* keyword instead of the class keyword.
- Methods and properties that are declared within an interface can't include implementation. As a result, method declarations and get and set accessors always end with a semi-colon.
- You shouldn't include any access modifiers on interface members. All members are considered to be public and abstract, and static members aren't allowed.
- Although you can declare your own interfaces, you're more likely to implement the interfaces provided by the .NET Framework.

Figure 15-3 How to create an interface

How to implement an interface

Figure 15-4 shows how to code a class that implements one or more interfaces. To do that, you code the class name, followed by a colon and a list of the interfaces on the class declaration. Note that if the class also inherits another class, you must list the class before the interfaces.

The three class declarations in this figure illustrate how this works. The first class declaration is for a Product class that implements the ICloneable interface. The second class declaration is for a ProductList class that implements two interfaces: IEnumerable and IEnumerator. And the third class declaration is for a ProductList class that inherits the System.Collections.ArrayList class and implements the ICloneable interface.

When you enter the name of an interface on a class declaration, you'll notice that Visual Studio displays a tip like the one shown in this figure. This tip indicates that you can press the Tab key to generate stubs for the interface. If you do that, code similar to the code in the last example in this figure is inserted into the class. Then, you can enter the code that's needed to implement each stub that was generated.

Notice in this example that the generated code is bracketed by #region and #endregion directives. Regions like this are typically collapsed in the Code Editor window so you can't see the code they contain. To expand the code region, however, you can just click the + symbol that appears next to the collapsed region.

The syntax for implementing an interface

```
public class-name : [base-class-name,] interface-name-1
                    [, interface-name-2]...
```

A Product class that implements ICloneable

```
public class Product : ICloneable
```

A ProductList class that implements two interfaces

```
public class ProductList : IEnumerable, IEnumerator
```

A ProductList class that inherits ArrayList and implements ICloneable

```
public class ProductList : System.Collections.ArrayList, ICloneable
```

The prompt that's displayed when you enter an interface name

```
/// <summary>
/// Summary description for Product.
/// </summary>
public class Product : ICloneable
{                    Press TAB to implement stubs for interface 'System.ICloneable'
    public Product()
    {
        //
        // TODO: Add constructor logic here
        //
    }
```

The code that's generated when you implement the ICloneable interface

```
#region ICloneable Members

public object Clone()
{
    // TODO:  Add Product.Clone implementation
    return null;
}

#endregion
```

Description

- To declare a class that implements one or more interfaces, type a colon after the class name, then list the interfaces that the class implements.
- If a class inherits another class, you must include the name of the inherited class before the names of any interfaces the class implements.
- After you type the name of an interface on a class declaration, Visual Studio will prompt you to press the Tab key to generate stubs for the members of the interface. These stubs will appear in a hidden region of the class code. Then, you can display this region and add the code required to implement the members.

Figure 15-4 How to implement an interface

A Product class that implements the ICloneable interface

Now that you've seen the basic skills for creating and implementing interfaces, figure 15-5 presents an example of a Product class that implements the ICloneable interface. This example is similar to the example that was shown in figure 15-1, but it includes additional features to make the example more complete.

The Product class begins by declaring three public fields named Code, Description, and Price. Then, the implementation for the Clone method is provided in the region that's generated by Visual Studio. In this case, the Clone method creates a new product, copies the Code, Description, and Price values from the current product to the new product, and returns the new product. The rest of the Product class defines the two constructors for this class along with the GetDisplayText method.

The second code example in this figure illustrates how you can use the Clone method of the Product class. First, a Product variable named p1 is declared and a new product is created and assigned to it. Then, a second Product variable named p2 is declared, and the Clone method of the p1 product is used to create a copy that's assigned to this variable. Notice that because the Clone method returns an object type, the return value must be cast to the Product type so it can be assigned to the p2 variable. Finally, a dialog box is used to display the string that's returned by the GetDisplayText method for both products. As you can see, both products contain the same data.

In this example, the data of a Product object is stored in three fields with built-in value types. But what if you wanted to clone a more complicated object with fields that represent other objects? For example, consider an Invoice class with a Customer property that returns a Customer object that's stored in a private field. In that case, you can clone the Invoice object using either a shallow copy or a deep copy.

If you use a *shallow copy*, the Customer field of the cloned Invoice object would refer to the same Customer object as the original Invoice object. In contrast, if you use a *deep copy*, the Customer field of the cloned Invoice object would refer to a clone of the Customer object. The easiest way to accomplish that would be to implement the ICloneable interface in the Customer class and then call the Clone method of this class from the Invoice object. However, you could also clone the Customer object within the Clone method of the Invoice class.

As defined by the ICloneable interface, the Clone method doesn't specify whether the returned value should be a deep copy or a shallow copy. So you can implement whichever type of copy you think is most appropriate for a class. Just be sure to specify whether the Clone method returns a deep copy or a shallow copy in the class documentation so users of the class will know what to expect when they use the Clone method.

The code for the cloneable Product class

```
public class Product : ICloneable
{
    public string Code;
    public string Description;
    public decimal Price;

    #region ICloneable Members

    public object Clone()
    {
        Product p = new Product();
        p.Code = this.Code;
        p.Description = this.Description;
        p.Price = this.Price;
        return p;
    }
    #endregion

    public Product()
    {
    }

    public Product(string code, string description, decimal price)
    {
        this.Code = code;
        this.Description = description;
        this.Price = price;
    }

    public string GetDisplayText(string sep)
    {
        return this.Code + sep + this.Description
            +sep + this.Price.ToString("c");
    }

}
```

Code that creates and clones a Product object

```
Product p1 = new Product("JAVA", "Murach's Beginning Java 2", 49.50m);
Product p2 = (Product)p1.Clone();
string msg = p1.GetDisplayText("\n") + "\n\n" + p2.GetDisplayText("\n");
MessageBox.Show(msg, "A cloned product");
```

The dialog box that's displayed by the code shown above

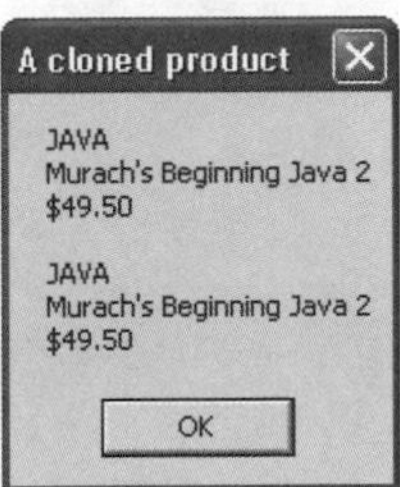

Figure 15-5 A Product class that implements the ICloneable interface

How to use an interface as a parameter

Figure 15-6 shows how to use an interface as a parameter of a method. To do that, you code the name of the interface as the parameter type as shown in the first example. Here, a method named MakeArrayList accepts two parameters: an object that implements ICloneable and an integer. This method returns an array list that is filled with copies of the object specified by the first parameter. The number of copies to be included in the array list is specified by the second parameter. To generate the copies, the MakeArrayList method uses the Clone method of the object that's passed to it.

When you declare a method that accepts an interface as a parameter, you can pass any object that implements that interface to the method. This is illustrated in the second code example in this figure. Here, a new Product object is created and stored in a variable named product. Then, the MakeArrayList method is used to create three copies of the Product object. You can see the result in the dialog box that's shown in this figure.

The key point here is that the MakeArrayList method doesn't know what type of object it's cloning. All it knows is that the object implements the ICloneable interface, which means that it has a Clone method.

A MakeArrayList method that uses an interface as a parameter

```
public ArrayList MakeArrayList(ICloneable obj, int count)
{
    ArrayList objects = new System.Collections.ArrayList();
    for (int i = 0; i < count; i++)
        objects.Add(obj.Clone());
    return objects;
}
```

Code that calls the MakeArrayList method

```
Product product = new Product("JAVA", "Murach's Beginning Java 2", 49.50m);
ArrayList products = this.MakeArrayList(product, 3);
string msg = "";
foreach (Product p in products)
  msg += p.GetDisplayText("\n") + "\n\n";
MessageBox.Show(msg, "Cloned Products");
```

The dialog box that's displayed by the code shown above

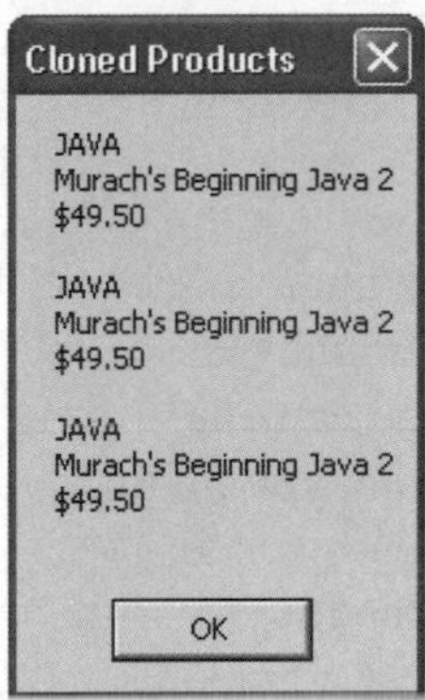

Description

- You can declare a parameter that's used by a method as an interface type. Then, you can pass any object that implements the interface to the parameter.
- In the example shown above, the MakeArrayList method accepts a parameter with a type of ICloneable and then creates an array list with the number of objects specified by the second parameter. Since the Product class implements the ICloneable interface, it can be passed as an argument to the MakeArrayList method.

Figure 15-6 How to use an interface as a parameter

An example that implements the enumerator interfaces

Now that you've learned how to create and implement a simple interface, I'll present a more complicated example. Specifically, I'll present an example that implements the two interfaces required to iterate through, or *enumerate*, a collection: IEnumerable and IEnumerator. First, you'll learn how these interfaces work. Then, you'll see a version of the ProductList class that implements these interfaces instead of inheriting the ArrayList class.

The IEnumerable interface

The IEnumerable interface indicates that a class represents a collection that can be enumerated. As you can see in figure 15-7, it provides just one method, named GetEnumerator. This method returns an *enumerator*, which is simply an object that implements the IEnumerator interface. The enumerator is then used to iterate through the items in the collection.

A question that often comes up when you're learning how to use these interfaces is why a separate enumerator object is required to enumerate a collection. In other words, why can't you just define the enumerator within the class that uses it? The answer is that if you use a separate enumerator, you can enumerate the collection two or more times simultaneously. For example, you might want to let a user open two windows, each of which enumerates the objects in the same collection. Then, the user can browse the items in the collection independently in each of these windows. Because each window must maintain its own position within the collection, a separate enumerator must be used for each.

The IEnumerator interface

The GetEnumerator method returns an object that implements the IEnumerator interface. The second table in figure 15-7 describes the property and methods of this interface. The Current property simply returns the current object in the collection that's being enumerated. The MoveNext method advances the enumerator to the next object in the collection, and the Reset method resets the enumerator to its initial position. Note that the enumerator is initially positioned before the first element in the collection. As a result, MoveNext must be called before the Current property can be accessed.

The most common way to implement an enumerator is for the enumerator to store its own copy of the collection to be enumerated and to use a private index field to keep track of its position within the collection. When the enumerator is first created, this index is set to -1 to position the enumerator before the first object in the collection. If the Current property is accessed when the index is -1, InvalidOperationException should be thrown. This exception should also be thrown if the position is beyond the last object in the collection.

The IEnumerable and IEnumerator interfaces

```
public interface IEnumerable
{
    IEnumerator GetEnumerator();
}

public interface IEnumerator
{
    object Current {get;}
    bool MoveNext();
    void Reset();
}
```

The IEnumerable interface

Method	Description
GetEnumerator	Returns an enumerator for the collection. The enumerator must implement the IEnumerator interface.

The IEnumerator interface

Property	Description
Current	A read-only property that returns the current object. Throws InvalidOperationException if the MoveNext method has not yet been called or if MoveNext has already moved past the last object in the collection.
Method	**Description**
MoveNext	Advances to the next object in the collection. Returns false when it reaches the last object in the collection.
Reset	Resets the enumerator to the beginning of the collection. This invalidates the Current property; the MoveNext method must be called to access the first object in the collection.

Description

- The IEnumerable and IEnumerator interfaces provide a generalized way to iterate through, or *enumerate*, the items in a collection. Any class that implements these interfaces can be used with the foreach statement.
- An *enumerator* is an object that implements the IEnumerator interface. The enumerator usually works by maintaining an internal index that keeps track of the current position within the collection. When the enumerator is initialized, the index is set to -1. The MoveNext method increments the internal index by 1, and the Reset method resets it to -1. The Current property returns the object indicated by the internal index.
- The enumerator is usually implemented as a separate class. However, this class is often nested within the class that implements IEnumerable.

Figure 15-7 The IEnumerable and IEnumerator interfaces

To move to the next object in a collection, you use the MoveNext method. This method should increment the index by 1 and return true if the last item in the collection has not yet been reached. If the MoveNext method advances to the last item in the collection, it should return false.

The Reset method resets an enumerator to its initial state. In other words, it resets the index to -1 so the enumerator is positioned before the first object in the collection. The MoveNext method must then be called before the Current property can be used to retrieve an object.

The code for the ProductList class

Figure 15-8 shows the code for a version of the ProductList class that implements an enumerator. This enumerator allows a ProductList object to be processed by the foreach statement. Before I describe the details of how this class works, I want to point out that ProductList class in chapter 14 provided this same capability by inheriting the ArrayList class. Although inheriting ArrayList (or any other class that provides an enumerator) is much easier than implementing an enumerator yourself, there are two reasons you might want to do that.

First, because C# doesn't support multiple inheritance, you'll need to implement your own enumerator if the collection class needs to inherit a class other than the ArrayList class. Second, you may want to implement a more advanced or efficient enumerator than the one that's provided by the ArrayList class. For example, an enumerator might retrieve data from a file or database rather than from an array list.

The first thing you should notice about the ProductList class in this figure is that the class that implements the enumerator is nested within it (see page 2 of this listing). Although you don't have to nest the enumerator class within the ProductList class, it makes sense to do that because the enumerator is only used within the ProductList class.

As you can see, the class declaration for the ProductList class specifies that this class implements the IEnumerable interface. The code for the GetEnumerator method that's declared by this interface is shown at the bottom of page 1 of this listing. This method simply returns an instance of the ProductEnumerator class. As you'll see in a minute, the constructor for the ProductEnumerator class accepts an array list as a parameter. When the GetEnumerator method calls this constructor, then, it passes the array of Product objects that are stored in the products variable. The ProductEnumerator object can then be used to iterate through this collection.

The code for the ProductEnumerator class

The ProductEnumerator class is shown on page 2 of this listing. It begins by declaring two private instance variables. The first one is an array list named products that will hold the data to be enumerated. The second one is an integer named index that will be used to maintain the enumerator's position in the collection.

A ProductList class that implements IEnumerable and IEnumerator Page 1

```
public class ProductList : IEnumerable
{
    private ArrayList products = new ArrayList();

    public ProductList()
    {
    }

    public Product this[int i]
    {
        get
        {
            return (Product)this.products[i];
        }
    }

    public int Count
    {
        get
        {
            return this.products.Count;
        }
    }

    public void Add(Product p)
    {
        this.products.Add(p);
    }

    public void Add(string code, string description, decimal price)
    {
        Product p = new Product(code, description, price);
        this.products.Add(p);
    }

    public void Remove(Product product)
    {
        this.products.Remove(product);
    }

    public void Fill()
    {
       products = ProductDB.GetProducts();
    }

    public void Save()
    {
        ProductDB.SaveProducts(this);
    }

    public System.Collections.IEnumerator GetEnumerator()
    {
        return new ProductEnumerator(this.products);
    }
```

Figure 15-8 A ProductList class that implements an enumerator (part 1 of 2)

The constructor for this class accepts an array list as a parameter. It sets the products variable to the array list that's passed via this parameter. Then, it sets the index variable to -1 so the enumerator is initially positioned before the first object in the collection.

The Current property returns the object at the position specified by the index variable. Before it does that, though, it checks that the index value is valid. If it's equal to -1, it means that the enumerator is positioned before the first object in the array list. If it's greater than or equal to the number of objects in the array list, it means that it's positioned after the last object in the array list. In either case, InvalidOperationException is thrown.

The MoveNext property increments the index by 1. Then, it checks the new index value to see if it's less than the Count property of the array list and returns the resulting Boolean value. That means that if the index value is less than the number of items in the array list, MoveNext returns true. Otherwise, it returns false. Notice that nothing prevents you from calling MoveNext repeatedly even after the last object has been retrieved. However, if you try to use the Current property to retrieve the current object after the last object has already been retrieved, an exception will be thrown.

The last method in the ProductEnumerator class is the Reset method. This method repositions the enumerator to immediately before the first object in the array list by setting the index variable to -1.

Code that uses the ProductList enumerator

Figure 15-8 also shows two code examples that use the enumerator for the ProductList class. The first example starts by creating a ProductList object named products and then calling the Fill method to fill it with products from a file. Then, it declares a string variable that will be used to hold a message that's displayed in a dialog box.

Next, an enumerator variable named pEnum is declared, and the GetEnumerator method of the products object is called to get an enumerator for the product list. Notice that the type for the enumerator variable is IEnumerator.

Once the enumerator is obtained, a while loop is used to retrieve each product from the product list. As you can see, the MoveNext method is used to advance to the next product, and the Current property is used to retrieve that product. The GetDisplayText method is called for each product to format it for display. The while loop ends when MoveNext returns false.

The second code example shows that most of the code in the first example can be replaced by a foreach loop. The foreach statement automatically handles the details of getting the enumerator and using the MoveNext method and the Current property to retrieve each product. Because of that, there's usually no reason to use the enumerator directly as shown in the first example. I included it here to help you understand how enumerators and the foreach statement work.

A ProductList class that implements IEnumerable and IEnumerator Page 2

```
    public class ProductEnumerator : IEnumerator
    {
        private ArrayList products;
        private int index;

        public ProductEnumerator(ArrayList products)
        {
            this.products = products;
            index = -1;
        }

        public object Current
        {
            get
            {
                if (this.index == -1)
                    throw new InvalidOperationException(
                        "You must call MoveNext before you use Current.");
                if (this.index >= products.Count)
                    throw new InvalidOperationException(
                        "You have moved past the end of the collection.");
                return this.products[index];
            }
        }

        public bool MoveNext()
        {
            index++;
            return (index < products.Count);
        }

        public void Reset()
        {
            this.index = -1;
        }
    }
}
```

Code that uses the ProductList enumerator

```
ProductList products = new ProductList();
products.Fill();
string msg = "";

IEnumerator pEnum;
pEnum = products.GetEnumerator();
Product p;
while (pEnum.MoveNext());
{
    p = pEnum.Current();
    msg += p.GetDisplayText("\n") + "\n\n";
}
```

An easier way to use the enumerator

```
foreach (Product p in products)
    msg += p.GetDisplayText("\n") + "\n\n";
```

Figure 15-8 A ProductList class that implements an enumerator (part 2 of 2)

How to work with structures

A *structure* is similar to a class, but it defines a value type rather than a reference type. Although structures require less memory overhead and instantiate faster than classes, it's generally considered a good programming practice to use them only for objects that contain a small amount of data and for objects that you want to work like the .NET values types, such as the int, decimal, and DateTime types. Figure 15-9 shows how to create and use structures.

How to create a structure

To create a structure, you code a *struct* statement that names the structure. Then, in the body of the structure, you can create members just as you can for classes. In fact, a structure can have all of the same types of members that a class can have, including fields, properties, methods, events, and operators. Structures can also have static members as well as instance members.

To illustrate, consider the Product structure shown in this figure. It includes three public fields, a constructor that sets the values of those fields, and a public method named GetDisplayText that formats the fields for display. Except for the struct keyword in the structure declaration, this code is identical to code you would find in a class.

However, structures don't support all of the features that are supported by classes. For example, while structures implicitly inherit the Object class, they are implicitly sealed and don't support any further inheritance. In addition, a structure can't contain a parameterless constructor. And if you provide a constructor that includes parameters, this constructor must initialize all instance variables in the structure as shown in this figure.

How to use a structure

To use a structure, you start by declaring a variable with the structure type just as you would any other data type. For example, the first statement in the first code example declares a variable named p of type Product.

When you declare a variable with a structure type, an instance of that structure is created but values aren't assigned to its instance variables. Then, you must assign values to those variables before you can call any properties or methods of the structure. That's why the three assignment statements that follow the structure declaration in this figure set the values of the Code, Description, and Price fields before the last statement calls the GetDisplayText method.

Because an instance is automatically created when you declare a structure, you don't need to use the new keyword to create an instance. If the structure defines a constructor that accepts parameters, however, you can use the new keyword just as you would for a class as shown in the last example in this figure.

The syntax for creating a structure

```
public struct StructureName
{
    structure members...
}
```

A Product structure

```
public struct Product
{
    public string Code;
    public string Description;
    public decimal Price;

    public Product(string code, string description, decimal price)
    {
        this.Code = code;                       // If you code a constructor
        this.Description = description;         // you must initialize
        this.Price = price;                     // all instance variables
    }

    public string GetDisplayText(string sep)
    {
        return Code + sep + Price.ToString("c") + sep + Description;
    }

}
```

Code that declares a variable as a structure type and assigns values to it

```
Product p;              // Create an instance of the Product structure
p.Code = "JAVA";        // Assign values to each instance variable
p.Description = "Murach's Beginning Java 2";
p.Price = 49.50m;
string msg = p.GetDisplayText("\n"); // Call a method
```

Code that uses the structure's constructor

```
Product p = new Product("JAVA", "Murach's Beginning Java 2", 49.50m);
```

Description

- A *structure* is similar to a class, but it represents a value type rather than a reference type.
- A structure can contain the same types of members as a class, including fields, properties, methods, constructors, and events.
- When you code a structure, you can't code a parameterless constructor. As a result, you only need to use the new keyword to create an instance of a structure when you're passing values to a constructor that accepts parameters.
- You can't call any of the properties or methods of a structure until you initialize all of the instance variables of the structure.
- Although structures implicitly inherit the Object class, they are implicitly sealed. As a result, they don't support any further inheritance.

Figure 15-9 How to work with structures

How to create and use class libraries

So far, the classes you've seen have been created as part of a Windows Application project. If you want to be able to use the classes you create in two or more projects, however, you'll want to store them in class libraries. Simply put, a *class library* consists of a collection of related classes. When you use a class library, you can use any of the classes in the library without copying them into the project.

How class libraries work

Figure 15-10 illustrates the difference between using classes created within a Windows Application project and classes created within a class library project. As you can see, classes that are created in a Windows project must be included in every project that uses them. In contrast, classes that are created in a class library project exist separately from any project that uses them. Because of that, they are available to any project that has access to the class library.

One of the benefits of using class libraries is that the size of each project that uses them is reduced. That's because each project includes only a reference to the class library rather than the code for each class that it needs. Also, because the classes in a class library are already compiled, Visual Studio does not have to compile them every time you build the application. This results in faster compile times.

Another benefit of using class libraries is that they simplify maintenance. If you must make a change to a class that's in a class library, you can change the class without changing any of the applications that use the library. When you're done, the modified library is immediately available to the projects that use it.

But probably the main benefit of using class libraries is that they let you create reusable code. If you design your classes carefully and place them in a library, you can reuse them in other projects that require similar functions. In most cases, you'll use the classes directly. However, you can also use them as base classes for new classes you add to your projects.

Two projects that use the Validator class

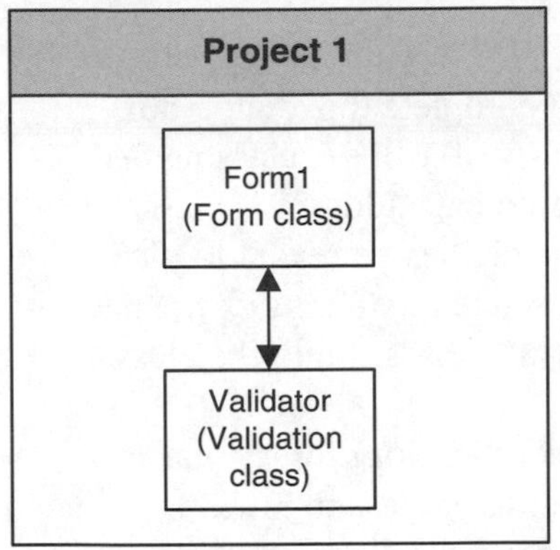

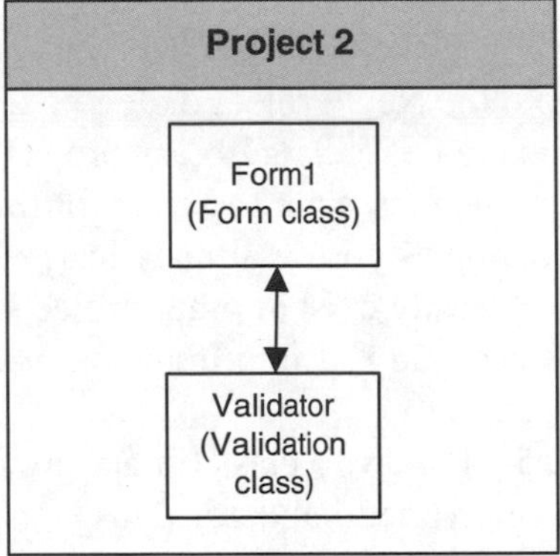

Two projects that access the Validator class via a class library

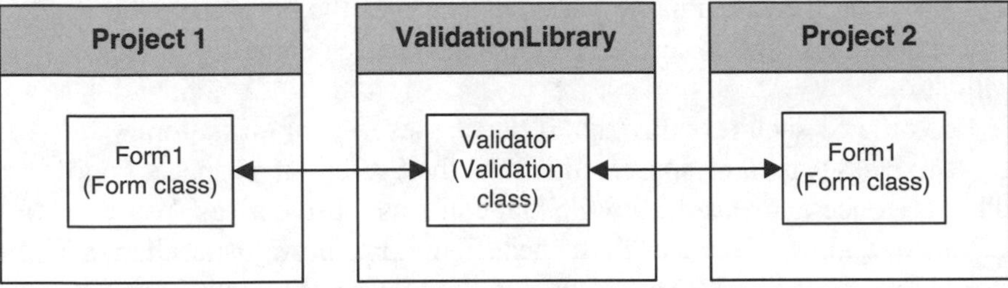

Description

- *Class libraries* provide a central location for storing classes that are used by two or more applications.
- When you store a class in a class library, you don't have to include the class in each application that uses it. Instead, you include a reference to the class in those applications.
- When you modify a class in a class library, the changes are immediately available to all applications that use the library.
- To create a class library, you develop a class library project. Then, when you build the project, Visual Studio creates a *DLL file* for the class library. It's this *DLL* that you refer to from any application that needs to use the class library.

Figure 15-10 How class libraries work

How to create a class library project

To create a class library project, you use the Class Library template that's available from the New Project dialog box. After you complete this dialog box, Visual Studio creates a class library project that consists of a single class named Class1. Then, you can enter the code for this class and create additional classes using the techniques you've already learned. Or, if the classes you want to place in the library already exist in other projects, you can delete the Class1.cs file and use the Project➔Add Existing Item command to copy the classes into the class library project.

Figure 15-11 shows a class library project named ValidationLibrary that includes a class named Validator. This is the same Validator class that was presented in chapter 12. In this case, though, the class is stored in a class library project instead of in the Windows project that uses it.

Notice the name of the namespace for this class. When you place classes in a class library, you should create a namespace that indicates the purpose of the classes in the namespace. In this case, I created a namespace named Murach.Validation.

Before I go on, you should realize that if the classes in your class library require access to classes in namespaces other than the System namespace, you'll need to add a reference to the assembly file that contains those classes. You'll learn the details of adding references in the next figure. For now, just realize that the Validator class uses the MessageBox class in the System.Windows.Forms namespace. Because of that, a reference to this namespace was added to the ValidationLibrary class library.

When you're done designing a class library, you build it to create an assembly. The assembly for a class library is a *DLL file*, or just *DLL*. This is a file with the *dll* extension that contains the executable code for the class library. This file is stored in the Bin\Debug folder beneath the project folder for the project. Then, you can include a reference to this file in other projects as described in the next topic.

As you're developing a class library, it's often useful to create the class library as a project in a solution that also has a Windows form project. That way, you can use the Windows form project to test the class library. To add a new class library project to an existing solution, right-click the solution in the Solution Explorer, then choose Add➔New Project. You can also add an existing class library project to a solution by choosing Add➔Existing Project.

A class library project

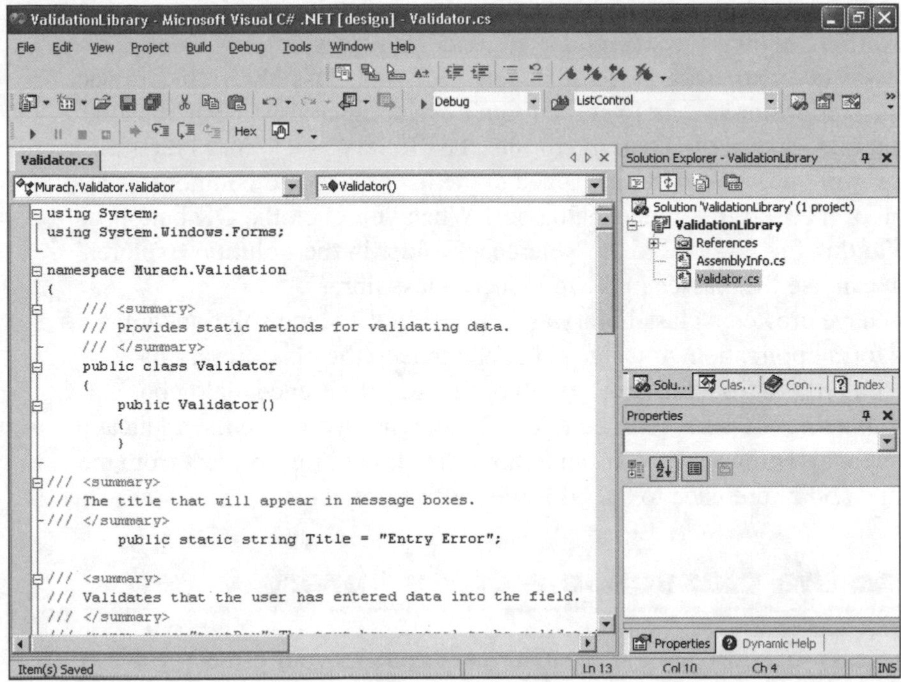

Description

- To create a class library project, display the New Project dialog box. Then, select the Class Library template and enter a name and location for the project.
- By default, a class library project includes a single class named Class1. You can modify this class any way you want or delete it from the project. You can also add new classes using the Project→Add Class command or add classes from another project using the Project→Add Existing Item command.
- You should create a namespace for your class library that indicates the purpose of the classes contained in the library. In this example, the namespace is Murach.Validation.
- To compile a class library project, select the Build→Build Solution command. Then, the class library is compiled into a DLL file that's stored in the Bin\Debug folder for the project.

Note

- The Validator class shown above requires the System.Windows.Forms namespace so it can use the MessageBox class to display error messages. Because class libraries don't have access to this namespace by default, a reference to this namespace has been added to the project. See figure 15-12 for information on how to add a reference to a project.

Figure 15-11 How to create a class library project

How to add a reference to a class library

Figure 15-12 shows how you add a reference to a class library so you can use its classes in an application. To add a reference to a class library in a project, you use the Add Reference dialog box. From this dialog box, you can click the Browse button to locate the DLL file for the class library you want to refer to. Then, when you select that file, it's added to the list of selected components at the bottom of the Add Reference dialog box. When you click the OK button, a reference to this file is added to the References folder in the Solution Explorer. Then, you can use the classes in the referenced class library.

If you have created a class library as a project in the same solution with a Windows form application, you can add a reference to the class library by selecting the project from the Projects tab of the Add Reference dialog box instead of locating the DLL for the project. Then, when you have the application working the way you want it, you can remove the class library project from the solution and add a reference to the DLL file for this project.

How to use the classes in a class library

Once you have added a reference to a class library to your project, you can use the classes in the class library the same way you use the .NET Framework classes. First, you can add a using statement at the beginning of a C# class that specifies the namespace used by the class library to make it easier to refer to the classes it contains. The code example in figure 15-12, for example, shows a using statement for the Murach.Validation namespace.

After you add the using statement, you can use the classes in the library as if they were part of the same project. A complication arises, however, if the class you want to refer to in the class library has the same name as a class in another namespace in the project or has the same name as the namespace that contains the project (which is usually the same as the project name). In that case, you have to qualify the name of the class so C# knows where to look for it.

A project that includes a reference to a class library

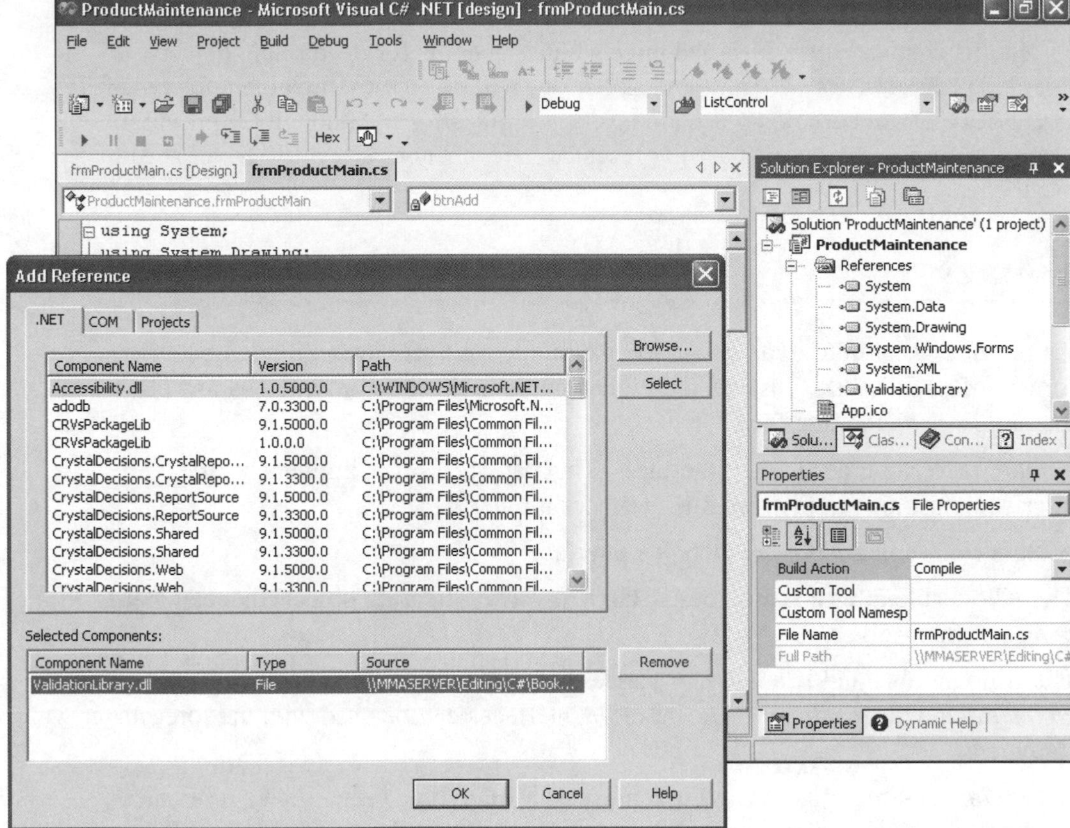

A using statement that simplifies access to the validation class library

```
using Murach.Validation;
```

How to use a class library

- Add a reference to the class library to your project by right-clicking the References folder in the Solution Explorer and selecting the Add Reference command from the shortcut menu that's displayed. In the Add Reference dialog box, click the Browse button in the .NET tab, then locate the DLL for the class library and double-click it to add it to the Selected Components list at the bottom of the Add Reference dialog box.
- If the class library project is included in the same solution as the client project, that project will appear in the list at the top of the Projects tab. Then, you can add a reference for the class library by double-clicking the project name.
- Once you have created a reference to the class library, you can include a using statement that names the class library in any class that uses it. You can then use the classes in the class library without qualification. Alternatively, you can qualify the class names with the namespace name you assigned to the library.

Figure 15-12 How to use a class library

Perspective

In this chapter, you've learned three additional skills for developing object-oriented programs in C#. With these skills, you will be able to implement the types of classes that are commonly used in business applications. Although C# provides some additional features that aren't presented here, chances are you'll never need to use them.

Summary

- An *interface* is similar to an abstract class, but doesn't provide an implementation for any of its members. Instead, the implementation must be provided by any class that *implements* the interface.
- An interface can inherit other interfaces. Then, any class that implements the interface must also implement the interfaces it inherits.
- A class can implement more than one interface.
- The ICloneable interface provides a standard way of creating objects that can make copies of themselves.
- The IEnumerable and IEnumerator classes let you create collections that can be *enumerated*. Classes that implement these interfaces can be used with the foreach statement.
- A *structure* is similar to a class but represents a value type rather than a reference type. Structures have limitations that make them useful only in certain situations.
- A *class library* lets you store one or more classes in a central location that can be shared by multiple applications.

Terms

interface
implement an interface
multiple inheritance
shallow copy
deep copy
enumerate
enumerator
structure
class library
DLL file

Objectives

- Given the specifications for an application that uses an interface, a structure, or a class library, develop the application.
- Describe the difference between an interface and an abstract class, and describe the advantages and disadvantages of each.
- Describe the difference between a structure and a class.
- Describe the benefits of placing classes in a class library.

Exercise 15-1 Implement the ICloneable interface

In this exercise, you'll create an application that includes a Customer class that implements the ICloneable interface. This application creates an ArrayList that contains clones of a pre-defined Customer object and displays the cloned customers in a list box as shown below. To make this application easier to develop, we'll give you the starting form and classes.

The design of the Clone Customer form

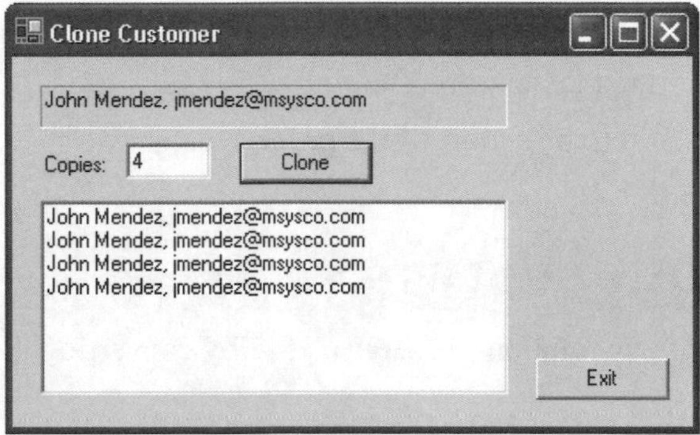

Development procedure

1. Open the project named CloneCustomer in the C:\C#.NET\Chapter 15\ CloneCustomer directory.
2. Display the code for the form, and notice that the Load event handler creates a Customer object, stores it in a variable named customer, and displays the customer in the label at the top of the form.
3. Modify the Customer class so it implements the ICloneable interface.
4. Add an event handler for the Click event of the Clone button. This event handler should check the value the user enters into the Copies text box to be sure it's an integer. Then, it should create an ArrayList that contains clones of the Customer object. Finally, it should display the cloned customers in the list box.
5. Run the application and test it to make sure it works properly.

Exercise 15-2 Implement an enumerator

In this exercise, you'll modify your solution to exercise 15-1 so the clones are stored in a CustomerList object that implements an enumerator.

1. If it isn't already open, open the CloneCustomer application in the C:\C#.NET\Chapter 15\CloneCustomer directory.
2. Modify the CustomerList class so it implements the IEnumerable interface. (This class wasn't used by the previous exercise.) To do that, the GetEnumerator method should return an enumerator defined by a nested class named CustomerEnumerator.
3. Modify the code in the form class so it stores the cloned Customer objects in a CustomerList object rather than in an array list.
4. Run the application and test it to be sure it works properly.

Exercise 15-3 Use a structure

In this exercise, you'll modify your solution to exercise 15-2 by converting the Customer class to a structure.

1. If it isn't open already, open the CloneCustomer application in the C:\C#.NET\Chapter 15\CloneCustomer directory.
2. Modify the Customer class so it defines a structure. Be sure to omit the parameterless constructor since they're not allowed in structures.
3. Run the application, and notice that you don't have to modify the form class for it to work with the structure.

Exercise 15-4 Create and use a class library

In this exercise, you'll create a class library that contains the Validator class. Then, you'll use that class library with the CloneCustomer application.

1. Create a new Class Library project named ValidationLib. Then, delete the empty Class1.cs file, and add the Validator.cs file from the CloneCustomer project that you worked on in the previous exercises.
2. Change the namespace in the Validator class to Murach.Validation. Then, add a reference to the System.Windows.Forms.dll assembly.
3. Use the Build→Build Solution command to build the class library, then close the solution.
4. Open the CloneCustomer project and delete the Validator.cs file. Then, add a reference to the ValidationLib assembly you created in step 3, and add a using statement for the Murach.Validation namespace to the Form1 class.
5. Run the project and test it to make sure the validation works correctly. When you're sure it does, close the solution.

Section 4

Database programming with C#

Most real-world applications store their data in databases. As a result, this section is devoted to teaching you the essentials of database programming in C#. When you complete it, you should be able to develop complete database applications using the latest data access method, called ADO.NET.

To start this section, chapter 16 introduces you to the concepts and terms you need to know when you develop database applications with ADO.NET. Then, chapter 17 shows you how to develop a simple database application with ADO.NET and a data grid control. Next, chapters 18 and 19 show you how to develop applications that use bound and unbound controls to work with the data in a dataset. Finally, chapter 20 shows you how to use data commands to access the underlying database directly.

When you complete these chapters, you'll be able to develop serious, real-world, database applications. You will also have a solid foundation for learning additional ADO.NET programming techniques on your own.

16

An introduction to database programming

Before you can develop a database application, you need to be familiar with the concepts and terms that apply to database applications. In particular, you need to understand what a relational database is and how you work with it using SQL and ADO.NET. So that's what you'll learn in this chapter.

To illustrate these concepts and terms, this chapter presents examples that use the *Microsoft SQL Server Desktop Engine* (*MSDE*). This is a scaled-back version of Microsoft *SQL Server* that you can run on your own PC. Because MSDE is based on SQL Server, though, the applications you develop with MSDE will also run on SQL Server.

An introduction to client/server systems

In case you aren't familiar with client/server systems, this topic introduces you to their essential hardware and software components. Then, the rest of this chapter presents additional information on these components and on how you can use them in database applications.

The hardware components of a client/server system

Figure 16-1 presents the three hardware components of a client/server system: the clients, the network, and the server. The *clients* are usually the PCs that are already available on the desktops throughout a company. And the *network* is made up of the cabling, communication lines, network interface cards, hubs, routers, and other components that connect the clients and the server.

The *server*, commonly referred to as a *database server*, is a computer that has enough processor speed, internal memory (RAM), and disk storage to store the files and databases of the system and provide services to the clients of the system. This computer is usually a high-powered PC, but it can also be a midrange system like an AS/400 or Unix system, or even a mainframe system. When a system consists of networks, midrange systems, and mainframe systems, often spread throughout the country or world, it is commonly referred to as an *enterprise system*.

To back up the files of a client/server system, a server usually has a tape drive or some other form of offline storage. It often has one or more printers or specialized devices that can be shared by the users of the system. And it can provide programs or services like email that can be accessed by all the users of the system. In larger networks, however, features such as backup, printing, and email are provided by separate servers. That way, the database server can be dedicated to the task of handling database requests.

In a simple client/server system, the clients and the server are part of a *local area network* (*LAN*). However, two or more LANs that reside at separate geographical locations can be connected as part of a larger network such as a *wide area network* (*WAN*). In addition, individual systems or networks can be connected over the Internet.

A simple client/server system

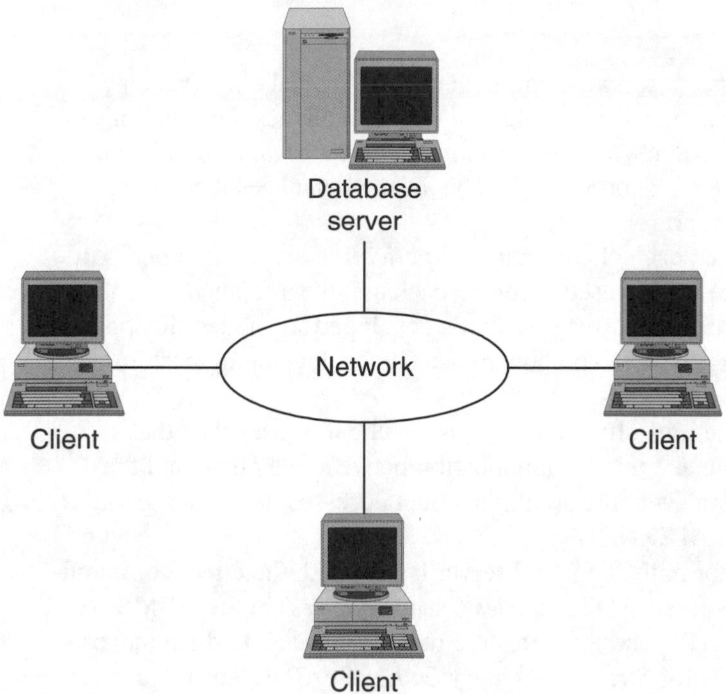

The three hardware components of a client/server system

- The *clients* are the PCs, Macintoshes, or workstations of the system.
- The *server* is a computer that stores the files and databases of the system and provides services to the clients. When it stores databases, it's often referred to as a *database server*.
- The *network* consists of the cabling, communication lines, and other components that connect the clients and the servers of the system.

Client/server system implementations

- In a simple *client/server system* like the one shown above, the server is typically a high-powered PC that communicates with the clients over a *local area network* (*LAN*).
- The server can also be a midrange system, like an AS/400 or a Unix system, or it can be a mainframe system. Then, special hardware and software components are required to make it possible for the clients to communicate with the midrange and mainframe systems.
- A client/server system can also consist of one or more PC-based systems, one or more midrange systems, and a mainframe system in dispersed geographical locations. This type of system is commonly referred to as an *enterprise system*.
- Individual systems and LANs can be connected and share data over larger private networks, such as a *wide area network* (*WAN*), or a public network like the Internet.

Figure 16-1 The hardware components of a client/server system

The software components of a client/server system

Figure 16-2 presents the software components of a typical client/server system. In addition to a *network operating system* that manages the functions of the network, the server requires a *database management system* (*DBMS*) like Microsoft SQL Server, Oracle, or MySQL. This DBMS manages the databases that are stored on the server.

In contrast to a server, each client requires *application software* to perform useful work. This can be a purchased software package like a financial accounting package, or it can be custom software that's developed for a specific application. This book, of course, shows you how to use C# for developing custom software for database applications.

Although the application software is run on the client, it uses data that's stored on the server. To make this communication between the client and the *data source* possible for a C# application, the client accesses the database via a *data access API* such as ADO.NET.

Once the software for both client and server is installed, the client communicates with the server by passing *SQL queries* (or just *queries*) to the DBMS through the data access API. These queries are written in a standard language called *SQL*, which stands for *Structured Query Language*. SQL lets any application communicate with any DBMS. After the client sends a query to the DBMS, the DBMS interprets the query and sends the results back to the client. (In conversation, SQL is pronounced as either *S-Q-L* or *sequel*.)

As you can see in this figure, the processing done by a client/server system is divided between the clients and the server. In this case, the DBMS on the server is processing requests made by the application running on the client. Theoretically, at least, this balances the workload between the clients and the server so the system works more efficiently. In contrast, in a file-handling system, the clients do all of the work because the server is used only to store the files that are used by the clients.

Client software, server software, and the SQL interface

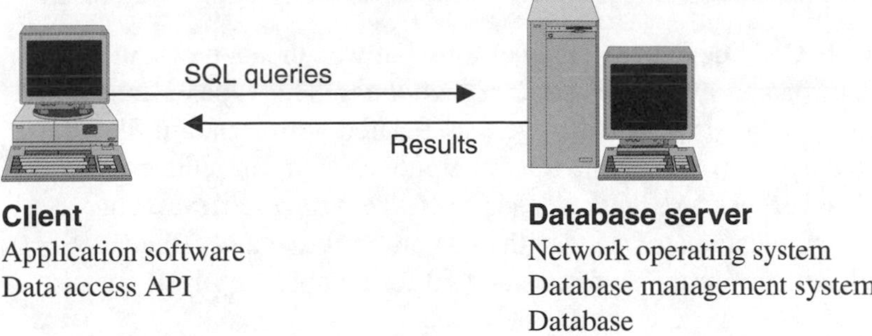

Client
Application software
Data access API

Database server
Network operating system
Database management system
Database

Server software

- To manage the network, the server runs a *network operating system* such as Windows Server 2003.
- To store and manage the databases of the client/server system, each server requires a *database management system* (*DBMS*) such as Microsoft SQL Server.
- The processing that's done by the DBMS is typically referred to as *back-end processing*, and the database server is referred to as the *back end*.

Client software

- The *application software* does the work that the user wants to do. This type of software can be purchased or developed.
- The *data access API* (*application programming interface*) provides the interface between the application and the DBMS. The newest data access API is ADO.NET, which is a part of Microsoft's .NET Framework.
- The processing that's done by the client software is typically referred to as *front-end processing*, and the client is typically referred to as the *front end*.

The SQL interface

- The application software communicates with the DBMS by sending *SQL queries* through the data access API. When the DBMS receives a query, it provides a service like returning the requested data (the *query results*) to the client.
- *SQL,* which stands for *Structured Query Language*, is the standard language for working with a relational database.

Client/server versus file-handling systems

- In a client/server system, the processing done by an application is typically divided between the client and the server.
- In a file-handling system, all of the processing is done on the clients. Although the clients may access data that's stored in files on the server, none of the processing is done by the server. As a result, a file-handling system isn't a client/server system.

Figure 16-2 The software components of a client/server system

An introduction to relational databases

In 1970, Dr. E. F. Codd developed a model for what was then a new and revolutionary type of database called a *relational database*. This type of database eliminated some of the problems that were associated with standard files and other database designs. By using the relational model, you can reduce data redundancy, which saves disk storage and leads to efficient data retrieval. You can also view and manipulate data in a way that is both intuitive and efficient. Today, relational databases are the de facto standard for database applications.

How a table is organized

The model for a relational database states that data is stored in one or more *tables*. It also states that each table can be viewed as a two-dimensional matrix consisting of *rows* and *columns*. This is illustrated by the relational table in figure 16-3. Each row in this table contains information about a single product.

In practice, the rows and columns of a relational database table are sometimes referred to by the more traditional terms, *records* and *fields*. In fact, some software packages use one set of terms, some use the other, and some use a combination. In this book, we've used the terms *rows* and *columns*.

If a table contains one or more columns that uniquely identify each row in the table, you can define these columns as the *primary key* of the table. For instance, the primary key of the Product table in this figure is the ProductCode column.

In this example, the primary key consists of a single column. However, a primary key can also consist of two or more columns, in which case it's called a *composite primary key*.

In addition to primary keys, some database management systems let you define additional keys that uniquely identify each row in a table, called *non-primary keys*. In SQL Server, these keys are also called *unique keys*, and they're implemented by defining *unique key constraints* (also known simply as *unique constraints*). The only difference between a unique key and a primary key is that a unique key can be null and a primary key can't.

Indexes provide an efficient way to access the rows in a table based on the values in one or more columns. Because applications typically access the rows in a table by referring to their key values, an index is automatically created for each key you define. However, you can define indexes for other columns as well. If, for example, you frequently need to sort the rows in the Products table by the Description column, you can set up an index for that column. Like a key, an index can include one or more columns.

The Products table in the MMABooks database

Primary key **Columns**

ProductCode	Description	UnitPrice	OnHandQuantity
ADON	Murach's VB.NET Database Programming with ADO.NET	49.55	4781
ASPN	Murach's ASP.NET Web Programming with VB.NET	49.5	5960
BVBN	Murach's Beginning Visual Basic .NET	49.5	4727
CRFC	Murach's CICS Desk Reference	50	1865
DB1R	DB2 for the COBOL Programmer, Part 1 (2nd Edition)	45	4825
DB2R	DB2 for the COBOL Programmer, Part 2 (2nd Edition)	45	621
JAVA	Murach's Beginning Java 2	45	1294
MCBL	Murach's Structured COBOL	62.5	2386
MCCP	Murach's CICS for the COBOL Programmer	54	2368
MJSP	Murach's JAVA Servlets and JSP	49.5	4999
MSQL	Murach's SQL for SQL Server	49.5	3142
VB60	Murach's Visual Basic 6	45	1878
ZJLR	Murach's OS/390 and z/os JCL	62.5	677

Rows

Concepts

- A *relational database* uses *tables* to store and manipulate data. Each table consists of one or more *records*, or *rows*, that contain the data for a single entry. Each row contains one or more *fields*, or *columns*, with each column representing a single item of data.
- Most tables contain a *primary key* that uniquely identifies each row in the table. The primary key often consists of a single column, but it can also consist of two or more columns. If a primary key uses two or more columns, it's called a *composite primary key*.
- In addition to primary keys, some database management systems let you define one or more *non-primary keys*. In SQL Server, these keys are called *unique keys*, and they're implemented using *unique key constraints*. Like a primary key, a non-primary key uniquely identifies each row in the table.
- A table can also be defined with one or more *indexes*. An index provides an efficient way to access data from a table based on the values in specific columns. An index is automatically created for a table's primary and non-primary keys.

Figure 16-3 How a table is organized

How the tables in a database are related

The tables in a relational database can be related to other tables by values in specific columns. The two tables shown in figure 16-4 illustrate this concept. Here, each row in an Invoices table is related to one or more rows in a InvoiceLineItems table. This is called a *one-to-many relationship*.

Typically, relationships exist between the primary key in one table and the *foreign key* in another table. The foreign key is simply one or more columns in a table that refer to a primary key in another table. In SQL Server, relationships can also exist between a unique key in one table and a foreign key in another table. For simplicity, though, I'll assume relationships are based on primary keys.

Although it isn't apparent in this figure, the InvoiceLineItems table has a composite primary key that consists of two columns: InvoiceID and ProductCode. As a result, any row in the InvoiceLineItems table can be uniquely identified by a combination of its invoice ID and product code. However, the InvoiceLineItems table can have more than one row for a given invoice ID and more than one row for a given product code.

One-to-many relationships are the most common type of database relationships. However, two tables can also have a one-to-one or many-to-many relationship. If a table has a *one-to-one relationship* with another table, the data in the two tables could be stored in a single table. Because of that, one-to-one relationships are used infrequently.

In contrast, a *many-to-many relationship* is usually implemented by using an intermediate table, called a *linking table*, that has a one-to-many relationship with the two tables in the many-to-many relationship. In other words, a many-to-many relationship can usually be broken down into two one-to-many relationships.

The relationship between the Invoices and InvoiceLineItems tables

Primary key

InvoiceID	CustomerID	InvoiceDate	ProductTotal	SalesTax	ShippingAndHandlir	InvoiceTotal
75	10	11/21/2003	49.5	3.71	3.75	56.96
76	701	11/21/2003	148.5	11.14	6.25	165.89
77	10	11/21/2003	49.5	3.71	3.75	56.96
78	10	11/21/2003	139.5	10.46	6.25	156.21
79	10	11/21/2003	49.5	3.71	3.75	56.96
80	11	11/21/2003	99	7.42	5	111.42

Foreign key

InvoiceID	ProductCode	UnitPrice	Quantity	ItemTotal
75	ADON	49.5	1	49.5
76	ADON	49.5	2	99
76	ASPN	49.5	1	49.5
77	ADON	49.5	1	49.5
78	ADON	49.5	1	49.5
78	DB2R	45	2	90
79	ADON	49.5	1	49.5
80	ADON	49.5	2	99

Concepts

- The tables in a relational database are related to each other through their key columns. For example, the InvoiceID column is used to relate the Invoices and InvoiceLineItems tables above. The InvoiceID column in the InvoiceLineItems table is called a *foreign key* because it identifies a related row in the Invoices table.
- Usually, a foreign key corresponds to the primary key in the related table. In SQL Server, however, a foreign key can also correspond to a unique key in the related table.
- When two tables are related via a foreign key, the table with the foreign key is referred to as the *foreign key table* and the table with the primary key is referred to as the *primary key table*.
- The relationships between the tables in a database correspond to the relationships between the entities they represent. The most common type of relationship is a *one-to-many relationship* as illustrated by the Invoices and InvoiceLineItems table. A table can also have a *one-to-one relationship* or a *many-to-many relationship* with another table.

Figure 16-4 How the tables in a database are related

How the columns in a table are defined

When you define a column in a table, you assign properties to it as indicated by the design of the Products table in figure 16-5. The two most important properties for a column are Column Name, which provides an identifying name for the column, and Data Type, which specifies the type of information that can be stored in the column. With SQL Server, you can choose from *system data types* like the ones in this figure, and you can define your own data types that are based on the system data types. As you define each column in a table, you generally try to assign the data type that will minimize the use of disk storage because that will improve the performance of the queries later.

In addition to a data type, you must identify whether the column can be *null*. Null represents a value that's unknown, unavailable, or not applicable. It isn't the same as an empty string or a zero numeric value. Columns that allow nulls often require additional programming, so many database designers avoid columns that allow nulls unless they're absolutely necessary.

You can also assign a *default value* to each column. Then, that value is assigned to the column if another value isn't provided. If a column doesn't allow nulls and doesn't have a default value, you must supply a value for the column when you add a new row to the table. Otherwise, an error will occur.

Each table can also contain a numeric column whose value is generated automatically by the DBMS. In SQL Server, a column like this is called an *identity column*, and you establish it using the Identity, Identity Seed, and Identity Increment properties. Identity columns are often used as the primary key for a table.

A *check constraint* defines the acceptable values for a column. For example, you can define a check constraint for the Products table in this figure to make sure that the UnitPrice column is greater than zero. A check constraint like this can be defined at the column level because it refers only to the column it constrains. If the check constraint for a column needs to refer to other columns in the table, however, it can be defined at the table level.

After you define the constraints for a database, they're managed by the DBMS. If, for example, a user tries to add a row with data that violates a constraint, the DBMS sends an appropriate error code back to the application without adding the row to the database. The application can then respond to the error code.

An alternative to constraints is to validate the data that is going to be added to a database before the program tries to add it. That way, the constraints shouldn't be needed and the program should run more efficiently. In many cases, both data validation and constraints are used. That way, the programs run more efficiently if the data validation routines work, but the constraints are there in case the data validation routines don't work or aren't coded.

The Server Explorer design view window for the Products table

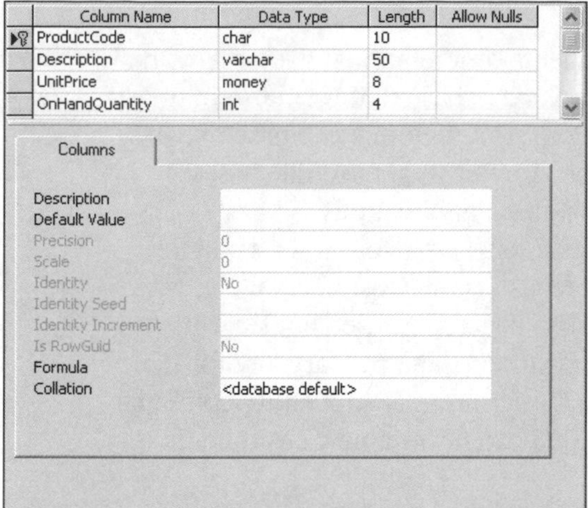

Common SQL Server data types

Type	Description
bit	A value of 1 or 0 that represents a True or False value.
char, varchar, text	Any combination of letters, symbols, and numbers.
datetime, smalldatetime	Alphanumeric data that represents a date and time. Various formats are acceptable.
decimal, numeric	Numeric data that is accurate to the least significant digit. The data can contain an integer and a fractional portion.
float, real	Floating-point values that contain an approximation of a decimal value.
bigint, int, smallint, tinyint	Numeric data that contains only an integer portion.
money, smallmoney	Monetary values that are accurate to four decimal places.

Description

- The *data type* that's assigned to a column determines the type of information that can be stored in the column. Depending on the data type, the column definition can also include its length, precision, and scale.
- Each column definition also indicates whether or not the column can contain *null values*. A null value indicates that the value of the column is not known.
- A column can be defined with a *default value*. Then, that value is used for the column if another value isn't provided when a row is added to the table.
- A column can also be defined as an *identity column*. An identity column is a numeric column whose value is generated automatically when a row is added to the table.
- To restrict the values that a column can hold, you define *check constraints*. Check constraints can be defined at either the column level or the table level.

Figure 16-5 How the columns in a table are defined

The design of the MMABooks database

Now that you've seen how the basic elements of a relational database work, figure 16-6 shows the design of the MMABooks database that we'll use in the programming examples throughout this section. Although this database may seem complicated, its design is actually much simpler than most databases you'll encounter when you work on actual database applications.

The purpose of the MMABooks database is to track invoices for a small book publisher. The top-level table in this database is the Customers table, which contains one row for each of the customers who have purchased books. This table records the name and address for each customer. The primary key for the Customers table is the CustomerID column. This column is an identity column, so SQL Server automatically generates its value whenever a new customer is created.

Information for each invoice is stored in the Invoices table. Like the Customers table, the primary key for this table, InvoiceID, is an identity column. To relate each invoice to a customer, the Invoices table includes a CustomerID column. A foreign key constraint is used to enforce this relationship. That way, an invoice can't be added for a customer that doesn't exist, and customers with invoices can't be deleted.

The InvoiceLineItems table contains the line item details for each invoice. The primary key for this table is a combination of the InvoiceID and ProductCode columns. The InvoiceID column relates each line item to an invoice, and a foreign key constraint that cascades updates and deletes from the Invoices table is defined to enforce this relationship. The ProductCode column gives each line item a unique primary key value.

The Products table records information about the company's products. The primary key for this table is the ProductCode column, which can contain a 10-character code. In addition to the product code, each product row contains a description of the product, the unit price, and the number of units currently on hand.

The Customers table is also related to the States table through its State column. The States table contains the state name and the 2-letter state code for each state. Its primary key is the StateCode column.

The final table in the MMABooks database, OrderOptions, contains information that's used to calculate the sales tax and shipping charges that are applied to each invoice. Because this table consists of a single row, it doesn't have a primary key.

The tables that make up the MMABooks database

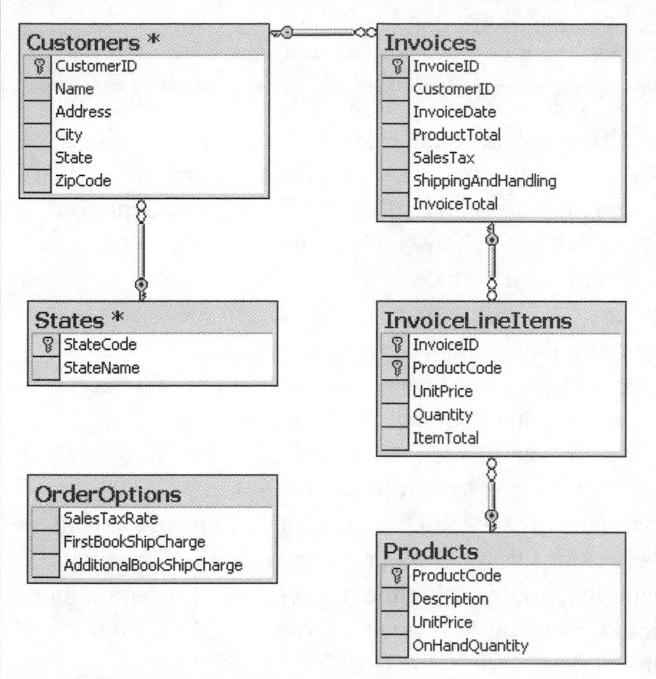

Description

- The Customers table contains a row for each customer. Its primary key is CustomerID, an identity column that's generated automatically when a new customer is created. State is a foreign key that relates each customer to a row in the States table.
- The Invoices table contains a row for each invoice. Its primary key is InvoiceID, an identity column that's generated automatically when a new invoice is created. CustomerID is a foreign key that relates each invoice to a customer.
- The InvoiceLineItems table contains one row for each line item of each invoice. Its primary key is a combination of InvoiceID and ProductCode. InvoiceID is a foreign key that relates each line item to an invoice, and ProductCode is a foreign key that relates each line item to a product.
- The Products table contains a row for each product. Its primary key is ProductCode, a 10-character code that identifies each product.
- The States table contains a row for each state. Its primary key is StateCode.
- The OrderOptions table contains a single row that stores the sales tax and shipping charges used by the application.
- The relationships between the tables in this diagram appear as links, where the endpoints indicate the type of relationship. A key indicates the "one" side of a relationship, and the infinity symbol (∞) indicates the "many" side.

Figure 16-6 The design of the MMABooks database

How to use SQL to work with the data in a relational database

In the topics that follow, you'll learn about the four SQL statements that you can use to manipulate the data in a database: Select, Insert, Update, and Delete. As you'll learn later in this book, you can often let Visual Studio generate the Insert, Update, and Delete statements for you based on the Select statement you specify. To master the material in this book, however, you need to understand what these statements do and how they're coded.

Although you'll learn the basics of coding these statements in the topics that follow, you may want to know more than what's presented here. In that case, we recommend our book, *Murach's SQL for SQL Server*. In addition to the Select, Insert, Update, and Delete statements, this book teaches you how to code the statements that you use to define the data in a database, and it teaches you how to use other features of SQL Server that the top professionals use.

Although SQL is a standard language, each DBMS is likely to have its own *SQL dialect*, which includes extensions to the standard language. So when you use SQL, you need to make sure that you're using the dialect that's supported by your DBMS. In this chapter and throughout this book, all of the SQL examples are for Microsoft SQL Server's dialect, which is called *Transact-SQL*.

How to query a single table

Figure 16-7 shows how to use a Select statement to query a single table in a database. In the syntax summary at the top of this figure, you can see that the Select clause names the columns to be retrieved and the From clause names the table that contains the columns. You can also code a Where clause that gives criteria for the rows to be selected. And you can code an Order By clause that names one or more columns that the results should be sorted by and indicates whether each column should be sorted in ascending or descending sequence.

If you study the Select statement below the syntax summary, you can see how this works. Here, the Select statement retrieves three columns from the Customers table for all customers who live in the state of Washington. It sorts the returned rows by the Last Name column.

This figure also shows the *result table*, or *result set*, that's returned by the Select statement. A result set is a logical table that's created temporarily within the database. When an application requests data from a database, it receives a result set.

Simplified syntax of the Select statement

```
 Select column-1 [, column-2]...
 From table-1
[Where selection-criteria]
[Order By column-1 [Asc|Desc] [, column-2 [Asc|Desc]]...]
```

A Select statement that retrieves and sorts selected columns and rows from the Customers table

```
Select LastName, FirstName, City
From Customers
Where State = 'WA'
Order By LastName
```

The result set defined by the Select statement

	LastName	FirstName	City
1	Allen	Craig	Pullman
2	Antalocy	S.	Seattle
3	Cassara	Glenn	Van
4	Giraka	Eric	Seatle
5	Hester	Maurice	Kennewickm
6	Howell	Kim	Renton
7	Mcmillen	G	Kirkland
8	Millard	Dwayne	Seattle
9	Oneil	Ri	Olympia
10	Seaver	Glenda	Mountlake Terrace
11	Smith	Lloyd	Pullman
12	Sundaram	Kelly	Oregon

Concepts

- The result of a Select statement is a *result table*, or *result set*, like the one shown above. A result set is a logical set of rows that consists of all of the columns and rows requested by the Select statement.
- The Select clause lists the columns to be included in the result set. This list can include *calculated columns* that are calculated from other columns.
- The From clause names the table the data will be retrieved from.
- The Where clause provides a condition that specifies which rows should be retrieved. To retrieve all rows from a table, omit the Where clause.
- The Order By clause lists the columns that the results are sorted by and indicates whether each column is sorted in ascending or descending sequence.
- To select all of the columns in a table, you can code an asterisk (*) in place of the column names. For example, this statement will select all of the columns from the Customers table:

  ```
  Select * From Customers
  ```

Figure 16-7 How to query a single table

How to join data from two or more tables

Figure 16-8 presents the syntax of the Select statement for retrieving data from two tables. This type of operation is called a *join* because the data from the two tables is joined together into a single result set. For example, the Select statement in this figure joins data from the InvoiceLineItems and Products table into a single result set.

An *inner join* is the most common type of join. When you use an inner join, rows from the two tables in the join are included in the result set only if their related columns match. These matching columns are specified in the From clause of the Select statement. In the Select statement in this figure, for example, rows from the InvoiceLineItems and Products tables are included only if the value of the ProductCode column in the Products table matches the value of the ProductCode column in one or more rows in the InvoiceLineItems table.

Notice that each column in the From clause is qualified to indicate which table the column is to be retrieved from. For example, the InvoiceID, ProductCode, UnitPrice, and Quantity columns are retrieved from the InvoiceLineItems table, but the Description column comes from the Products table. Qualification is only required for columns that exist in both tables. In this case, only the ProductCode column requires qualification because both the InvoiceLineItems and the Products tables have a column named ProductCode. However, I recommend you qualify all of the columns just to make it clear which table each column is being retrieved from.

Although this figure shows how to join data from two tables, you should know that you can extend this syntax to join data from additional tables. If, for example, you want to include data from the Invoice table along with the InvoiceLineItems and Products data, you could code a From clause like this:

```
From Invoices
    Inner Join InvoiceLineItems
        On Invoices.InvoiceID = InvoiceLineItems.InvoiceID
    Inner Join Products
        On InvoiceLineItems.ProductCode =
Products.ProductCode
```

Then, in the column list of the Select statement, you can include any of the columns in the Invoices, InvoiceLineItems, and Products tables.

The syntax of the Select statement for joining two tables

```
Select column-list
From table-1
    [Inner] Join table-2
    On table-1.column-1 {=|<|>|<=|>=|<>} table-2.column-2
[Where selection-criteria]
[Order By column-list]
```

A Select statement that joins data from the InvoiceLineItems and Products tables

```
Select InvoiceLineItems.InvoiceID, InvoiceLineItems.ProductCode,
       Products.Description, InvoiceLineItems.UnitPrice,
       InvoiceLineItems.Quantity
From InvoiceLineItems
    Inner Join Products
        On Products.ProductCode = InvoiceLineItems.ProductCode
Where InvoiceID = 78
```

The result set defined by the Select statement

	InvoiceID	ProductCode	Description	UnitPrice	Quantity
1	78	ADON	Murach's VB.NET Database Programming with ADO.NET	49.5000	1
2	78 .	DB2R	DB2 for the COBOL Programmer, Part 2 (2nd Edition)	45.0000	2

Concepts

- A *join* lets you combine data from two or more tables into a single result set.
- The most common type of join is an *inner join*. This type of join returns rows from both tables only if their related columns match.

Figure 16-8 How to join data from two or more tables

How to add, update, and delete data in a table

Figure 16-9 presents the basic syntax of the SQL Insert, Update, and Delete statements. You use these statements to add new rows to a table, to update the data in existing rows, and to delete existing rows.

To add a single row to a table, you specify the name of the table you want to add the row to, the names of the columns you're supplying data for, and the values for those columns. The statement in this figure, for example, adds a row to the Products table. If you're going to supply values for all the columns in a table, you can omit the column names. If you do that, though, you must be sure to specify the values in the same order as the columns appear in the table. To avoid errors, I recommend you always code the column list.

Note that if a table includes an identity column, you shouldn't provide a value for that column in an Insert statement. Instead, SQL Server will generate a value for the identity column when it inserts the row.

To change the values of one or more columns in a table, you use the Update statement. On this statement, you specify the name of the table you want to update, expressions that indicate the columns you want to change and how you want to change them, and a condition that identifies the rows you want to change. In the example in this figure, the Update statement changes the UnitPrice column for the product identified by product code MCCP to 54.00.

To delete rows from a table, you use the Delete statement. On this statement, you specify the table you want to delete rows from and a condition that indicates the rows you want to delete. The Delete statement in this figure deletes all the rows from the Invoices table for customer 1558.

How to add a single row

The syntax of the Insert statement for adding a single row

```
Insert [Into] table-name [(column-list)]
    Values (value-list)
```

A statement that adds a single row to the Products table

```
Insert Into Product (ProductCode, Description, UnitPrice, OnHandQuantity)
    Values ("MC#", "Murach's C#", 49.50, 3000)
```

How to update rows

The syntax of the Update statement

```
Update table-name
    Set expression-1 [, expression-2]...
    [Where selection-criteria]
```

A statement that updates the UnitPrice column for a specified product

```
Update Products
    Set UnitPrice = 54.00
    Where ProductCode = "MCCP"
```

How to delete rows

The syntax of the Delete statement

```
Delete [From] table-name
    [Where selection-criteria]
```

A statement that deletes a specified customer

```
Delete From Customers
    Where CustomerID = 1558
```

Description

- You use the Insert, Update, and Delete statements to maintain the data in a database table.
- The Insert statement can be used to add one or more rows to a table. Although the syntax shown above is for adding just one row, there is another syntax for adding more than one row.
- The Update and Delete statements can be used to update or delete one or more rows in a table using the syntax shown above.

Figure 16-9 How to add, update, and delete data in a table

An introduction to ADO.NET and the .NET data providers

ADO.NET (ActiveX Data Objects .NET) is the primary data access API for the .NET Framework. It provides the classes that you use as you develop database applications with C# as well as other .NET languages. These classes can be divided into two categories: the .NET data providers, which provide the classes that you use to access the data in a database, and datasets, which provide the classes that you use to store and work with data in your applications. In the topics that follow, you'll learn how ADO.NET uses these classes to provide access to the data in a database. You'll also learn about two ways you can create ADO.NET objects in your C# programs.

The .NET data providers

A *.NET data provider* is a set of classes that enable you to access data that's managed by a particular database server. All .NET data providers must include core classes for creating the four types of objects listed in the first table in figure 16-10. You'll learn more about how these objects work in the topics that follow.

The second table in this figure lists the four data providers that come with the .NET Framework. The SqlClient data provider is designed to provide efficient access to a Microsoft SQL Server database. The OleDb data provider is a generic data provider that can access any database that supports the industry standard OLE DB interface. Although you can use the OleDb data provider to access a SQL Server database, you shouldn't do that unless you plan on migrating the data to another database since the SQL Server data provider is optimized for accessing SQL Server data. The OracleClient provider lets you access data stored in Oracle databases. The Odbc provider lets you access any database that can work with ODBC, another industry standard database interface.

In addition to the .NET data providers, you should also know that several database vendors have developed .NET data providers that are optimized for use with their databases. For example, .NET data providers are available for the popular MySQL database and for SQL Anywhere. Before you develop an application using the OleDb or Odbc providers, then, you should check with your database vendor to see if a specialized .NET data provider is available.

The third table in this figure lists the names of the classes you use to create objects using the SqlClient, OleDb, OracleClient, or Odbc providers. Notice that these classes use prefixes ("Sql," "OleDb," "Oracle," and "Odbc") to indicate which provider each class belongs to.

When you develop a C# application that uses ADO.NET, you'll want to add a using statement for the namespace that contains the data provider classes at the beginning of each source file that uses those classes. These namespaces are listed in the second table in this figure.

.NET data provider core objects

Object	Description
Connection	Establishes a connection to a database.
Command	Represents an individual SQL statement that can be executed against the database.
Data reader	Provides read-only, forward-only access to the data in a database.
Data adapter	Provides the link between the command and connection objects and a dataset object.

Data providers included with the .NET framework

Provider	Namespace	Description
SqlClient	System.Data.SqlClient	Lets you access SQL Server databases.
OleDb	System.Data.OleDb	Lets you access any database that supports OLE DB.
Odbc	System.Data.Odbc	Lets you access any database that supports ODBC.
OracleClient	System.Data.OracleClient	Lets you access Oracle databases.

Class names for the data providers

Object	SqlClient	OleDb	OracleClient	Odbc
Connection	SqlConnection	OleDbConnection	OracleConnection	OdbcConnection
Command	SqlCommand	OleDbCommand	OracleCommand	OdbcCommand
Data reader	SqlDataReader	OleDbDataReader	OracleDataReader	OdbcDataReader
Data adapter	SqlDataAdapter	OleDbDataAdapter	OracleDataAdapter	OdbcDataAdapter

A using statement for the SQL Server data provider namespace

```
using System.Data.SqlClient;
```

Description

- The *.NET data providers* provide the ADO.NET classes that are responsible for working directly with a database. In addition to the core classes shown above, classes are provided for other functions such as passing parameters to commands or working with transactions.
- To use a .NET data provider in a program, you should add a using statement for the appropriate namespace at the beginning of the source file. Otherwise, you'll have to qualify each class you refer to with the SqlClient, OleDb, Odbc, or OracleClient namespace since these namespaces aren't included as references by default.
- The Odbc and OracleClient data providers became available with version 1.1 of the .NET Framework, which is included with Visual Studio .NET 2003.
- Other .NET data providers are available to provide efficient access to non-Microsoft databases, such as MySQL and SQL Anywhere.

Figure 16-10 The .NET data providers

How the basic ADO.NET components work

Figure 16-11 shows the primary ADO.NET components you use to work with data in a Windows application. To start, the data used by an application is stored in a *dataset* that contains one or more *data tables*. To retrieve data from the database and load it into a data table, you use a *data adapter*.

The main function of the data adapter is to manage the flow of data between a dataset and a database. To do that, it uses *commands* that define the SQL statements to be issued. The command for retrieving data, for example, typically defines a Select statement. Then, the command connects to the database using a *connection* and passes the Select statement to the database. After the Select statement is executed, the result set it produces is sent back to the data adapter, which stores the results in the data table.

To update the data in a database, the data adapter determines which rows in the data table have been inserted, updated, or deleted. Then, it uses commands that define Insert, Update, and Delete statements for the data table to update the associated rows in the database. Like the command that retrieves data from the database, the commands that update the database use a connection to connect to the database and perform the requested operation.

Although it's not apparent in this figure, the data in a dataset is independent of the database that the data was retrieved from. In fact, the connection to the database is typically closed after the data is retrieved from the database. Then, the connection is opened again when it's needed. Because of that, the application must work with the copy of the data that's stored in the dataset. The architecture that's used to implement this type of data processing is referred to as a *disconnected data architecture*. Although this is more complicated than a connected architecture, the advantages offset the complexity.

One of the advantages of using a disconnected data architecture is improved system performance due to the use of fewer system resources for maintaining connections. Another advantage is that it makes ADO.NET compatible with ASP.NET web applications, which are inherently disconnected.

Basic ADO.NET components

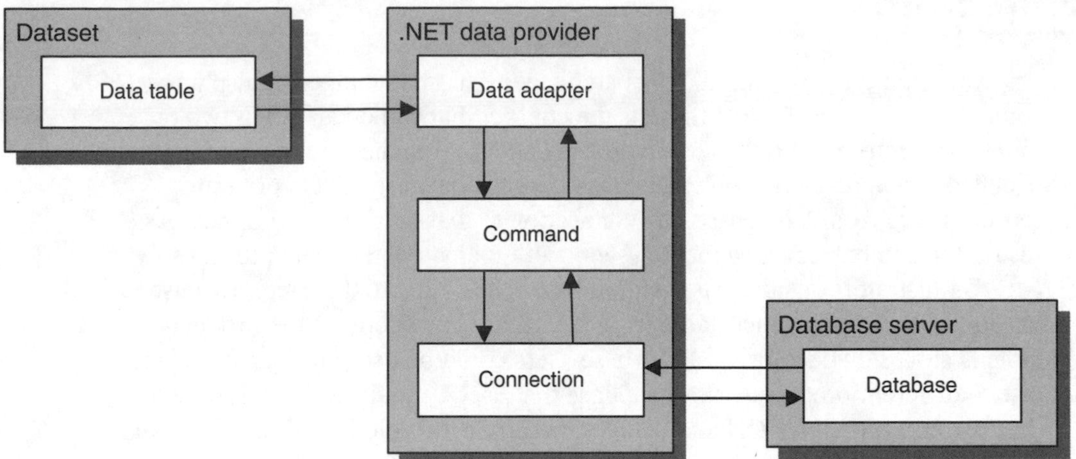

Description

- When you use the .NET data provider objects to retrieve data from a database, you can store the data in an object called a *dataset*.
- A dataset contains one or more *data tables* that store the data from the database. Then, the application can retrieve and work with the data in the data tables, and it can insert, update, and delete rows in the data tables.
- To retrieve data from a database and store it in a data table, a *data adapter* object issues a Select statement that's stored in a *command* object. Next, the command object uses a *connection* object to connect to the database and retrieve the data. Then, the data is passed back to the data adapter, which stores the data in the dataset.
- To update the data in a database based on the data in a data table, the data adapter object issues an Insert, Update, or Delete statement that's stored in a command object. Then, the command object uses a connection to connect to the database and update the data.
- The data provider remains connected to the database only long enough to retrieve or update the specified data. Then, it disconnects from the database and the application works with the data via the dataset object. This is referred to as a *disconnected data architecture*.
- The disconnected data architecture offers improved system performance due to the use of fewer system resources for maintaining connections.

Figure 16-11 How the disconnected data architecture works

Concurrency and the disconnected data architecture

Although the disconnected data architecture has advantages, it also has some disadvantages. One of those is the conflict that can occur when two or more users retrieve and then try to update data in the same row of a table. This is called a *concurrency* problem. This is possible because once a program retrieves data from a database, the connection to that database is dropped. As a result, the database management system can't manage the update process.

To illustrate, consider the situation shown in figure 16-12. Here, two users have retrieved the Products table from a database, so a copy of the Products table is stored on each user's PC. These users could be using the same program or two different programs. Now, suppose that user 1 modifies the unit price in the row for product ADON and updates the Products table in the database. And suppose that user 2 modifies the description in the row for the same product, then tries to update the Products table in the database. What will happen? That will depend on the *concurrency control* that's used by the programs.

When you use ADO.NET, you have two choices for concurrency control. By default, a program uses *optimistic concurrency*, which checks whether a row has been changed since it was retrieved. If it has, the update or deletion will be refused and a *concurrency exception* will be thrown. Then, the program should handle the error. For example, it could display an error message that tells the user that the row could not be updated and then retrieve the updated row so the user can make the change again.

In contrast, the *"last in wins"* technique works the way its name implies. Since no checking is done with this technique, the row that's updated by the last user overwrites any changes made to the row by a previous user. For the example above, the row updated by user 2 will overwrite changes made by user 1, which means that the description will be right but the unit price will be wrong. Since errors like this corrupt the data in a database, optimistic concurrency is used by most programs, which means that your programs have to handle the concurrency exceptions that are thrown.

If you know that concurrency will be a problem, you can use a couple of programming techniques to limit concurrency exceptions. If a program uses a dataset, one technique is to update the database frequently so other users can retrieve the current data. The program should also refresh its dataset frequently so it contains the recent changes made by other users.

Another way to avoid concurrency exceptions is to retrieve and work with just one row at a time. That way, it's less likely that two users will update the same row at the same time. In contrast, if two users retrieve the same table, they will of course retrieve the same rows. Then, if they both update the same row in the table, even though it may not be at the same time, a concurrency exception will occur when they try to update the database.

Of course, you will understand and appreciate this more as you learn how to develop your own database applications. As you develop them, though, keep in mind that most applications are multi-user applications. That's why you have to be aware of concurrency problems.

Two users who are working with copies of the same data

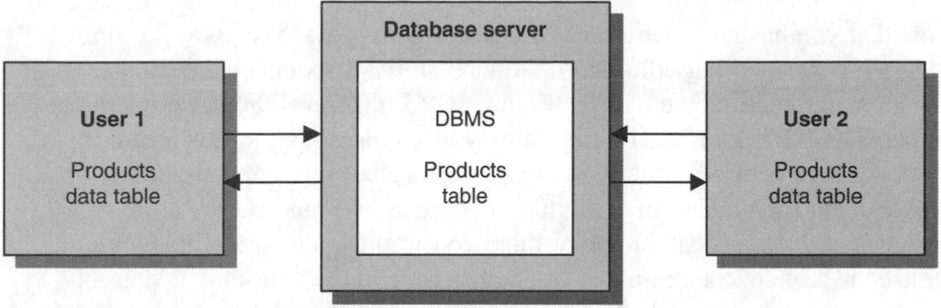

What happens when two users try to update the same row

- When two or more users retrieve the data in the same row of a database table at the same time, it is called *concurrency*. Because ADO.NET uses a disconnected data architecture, the database management system can't prevent this from happening.
- If two users try to update the same row in a database table at the same time, the second user's changes could overwrite the changes made by the first user. Whether or not that happens, though, depends on the *concurrency control* that the programs use.
- By default, ADO.NET uses *optimistic concurrency*. This means that the program checks to see whether the database row that's going to be updated or deleted has been changed since it was retrieved. If it has, a *concurrency exception* occurs and the update or deletion is refused. Then, the program should handle the exception.
- If optimistic concurrency isn't in effect, the program doesn't check to see whether a row has been changed before an update or deletion takes place. Instead, the operation proceeds without throwing an exception. This is referred to as "*last in wins*" because the last update overwrites any previous update. And this can lead to errors in the database.

How to avoid concurrency errors

- For many applications, concurrency errors rarely occur. As a result, optimistic concurrency is adequate because the users will rarely have to resubmit an update or deletion that is refused.
- If concurrency is likely to be a problem, a program that uses a dataset can be designed so it updates the database and refreshes the dataset frequently. That way, concurrency errors are less likely to occur.
- Another way to avoid concurrency errors is to design a program so it retrieves and updates just one row at a time. That way, there's less chance that two users will retrieve and update the same row at the same time.

Figure 16-12 Concurrency and the disconnected data architecture

How a dataset is organized

Now that you have a general idea of how the data provider classes provide access to a database, you need to learn more about the disconnected part of ADO.NET's architecture: the dataset. Figure 16-13 illustrates the basic organization of an ADO.NET dataset. The first thing you should notice in this figure is that a dataset is structured much like a relational database. It can contain one or more tables, and each table can contain one or more columns and rows. In addition, each table can contain one or more constraints that can define a unique key within the table or a foreign key of another table in the dataset. If a dataset contains two or more tables, the dataset can also define the relationships between those tables.

Although a dataset is structured much like a relational database, it's important to realize that each table in a dataset corresponds to the result set that's returned from a Select statement, not necessarily to an actual table in a database. For example, a Select statement may join data from several tables in a database to produce a single result set. In this case, the table in the dataset would represent data from each of the tables involved in the join.

You should also know that each group of objects in the diagram in this figure is stored in a collection. All of the columns in a table, for example, are stored in a collection of columns, and all of the rows are stored in a collection of rows. You'll learn more about these collections in the next figure and in chapter 20.

The basic dataset object hierarchy

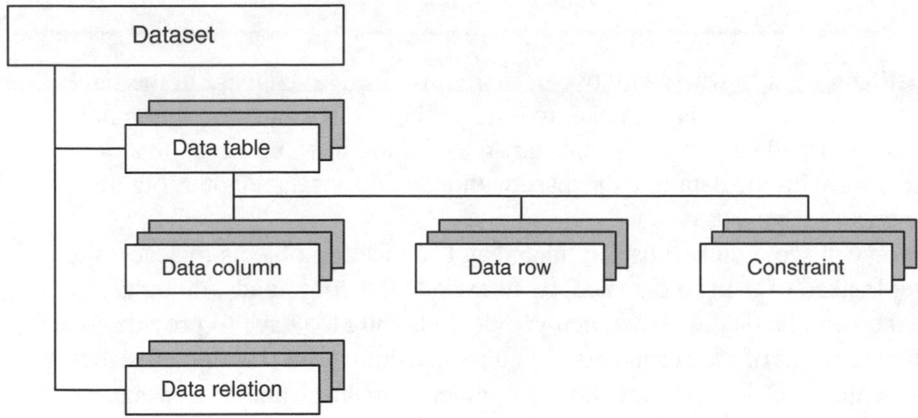

Description

- A dataset object consists of a hierarchy of one or more data table and *data relation* objects.
- A data table object consists of one or more *data column* objects and one or more *data row* objects. The data column objects define the data in each column of the table, including its name, data type, and so on, and the data row objects contain the data for each row in the table.
- A data table can also contain one or more *constraint* objects that are used to maintain the integrity of the data in the table. A unique key constraint ensures that the values in a column, such as the primary key column, are unique. And a foreign key constraint determines how the rows in one table are affected when corresponding rows in a related table are updated or deleted.
- The data relation objects define how the tables in the dataset are related. They are used to manage constraints and to simplify the navigation between related tables.
- All of the objects in a dataset are stored in collections. For example, the data table objects are stored in a data table collection, and the data row objects are stored in a data row collection. You can refer to these collections through properties of the containing objects.

Figure 16-13 How a dataset is organized

How to work with data without using a data adapter

When you want to work with two or more rows from a database at the same time, you typically use a data adapter to retrieve those rows and store them in a dataset as described earlier in this chapter. You should know, however, that you can also work with the data in a database without using a data adapter. Figure 16-14 shows you how.

As you can see, you still use command and connection objects to access the database. Instead of using a data adapter to execute the commands, though, you execute the commands directly. When you do that, you also have to provide code to handle the result of the command. If you issue a command that contains an Insert, Update, or Delete statement, for example, the result is an integer that indicates the number of rows that were affected by the operation. You can use that information to determine if the operation was successful.

If you execute a command that contains a Select statement, the result is a result set that contains the rows you requested. To read through the rows in the result set, you use a *data reader* object. Although a data reader provides an efficient way of reading the rows in a result set, you can't use it to modify those rows. In addition, it only lets you read rows in a forward direction. Once you read the next row, the previous row is unavailable. Because of that, you typically use a data reader to retrieve and work with a single database row at a time.

ADO.NET components for accessing a database directly

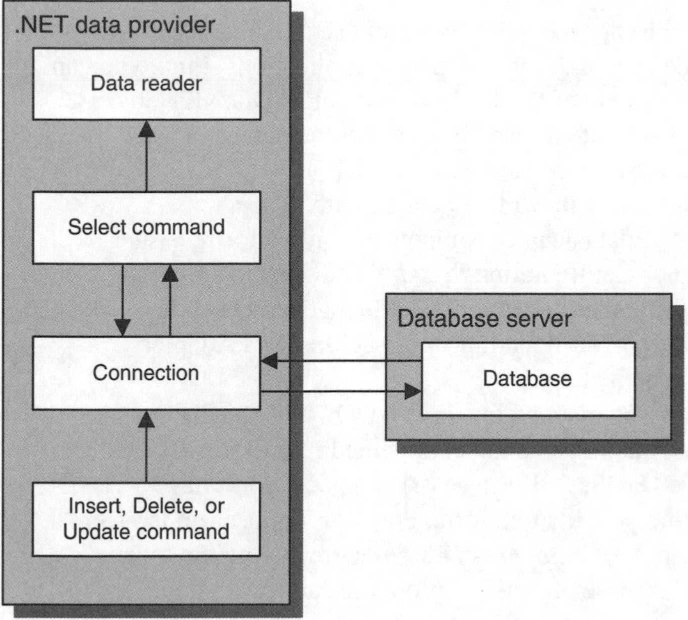

Description

- Instead of using a data adapter to execute commands to retrieve, insert, update, and delete data from a database, you can execute those commands directly.
- To retrieve data from a database, you execute a command object that contains a Select statement. Then, the command object uses a connection to connect to the database and retrieve the data. You can then read the results one row at a time using a *data reader* object.
- To insert, update, or delete data in a database, you execute a command object that contains an Insert, Update, or Delete statement. Then, the command object uses a connection to connect to the database and update the data. You can then check the value that's returned to determine if the operation was successful.
- If you use this technique in an application that maintains the data in a database, you typically work with a single row at a time. Because of that, the chance of a concurrency error occurring is reduced.

Figure 16-14 How to work with data without using a data adapter

Two ways to create ADO.NET objects

Figure 16-15 shows two basic techniques you can use to create the ADO.NET objects you need as you develop database applications. First, you can use the components in the Data tab of the Toolbox to create ADO.NET objects by dragging and dropping them onto a form. Notice that the names of most of the components in the Data tab are prefixed with "OleDb," "Sql," "Odbc," or "Oracle" just like the data provider they're associated with.

When you drag one of the data adapter components onto a form, Visual Studio starts the Data Adapter Configuration Wizard. This wizard gathers information about the data you want to retrieve and then generates code to create the required ADO.NET objects. You'll learn how to use the Data Adapter Configuration Wizard in the next chapter.

The project shown in this figure contains three ADO.NET objects: a data adapter named productDataAdapter, a connection named mmaBooksConnection, and a dataset named productDataSet1. Because these objects don't have a visual interface like the controls that you add to a form, they don't appear on the form itself. Instead, they appear in the *Component Designer tray* below the form. Then, when you select one of these objects, its properties appear in the Properties window and you can work with them from there.

The second technique for creating ADO.NET objects is to write the code yourself. The code shown in this figure, for example, creates three objects: a connection named mmaBooksConnection, a data adapter named productDataAdapter, and a dataset named productDataSet. It also uses the Fill method of the data adapter to retrieve data from the database identified by the connection and load it into the dataset. (Don't worry if you don't understand this code yet. You'll learn how it works in chapter 20.)

Although creating ADO.NET objects through code is more time-consuming than using the components and wizards, it can result in more compact and efficient code. In addition, creating ADO.NET objects through code lets you encapsulate an application's database processing in specialized database access classes. You'll see an example of that in chapter 20.

ADO.NET objects created using components in the Toolbox

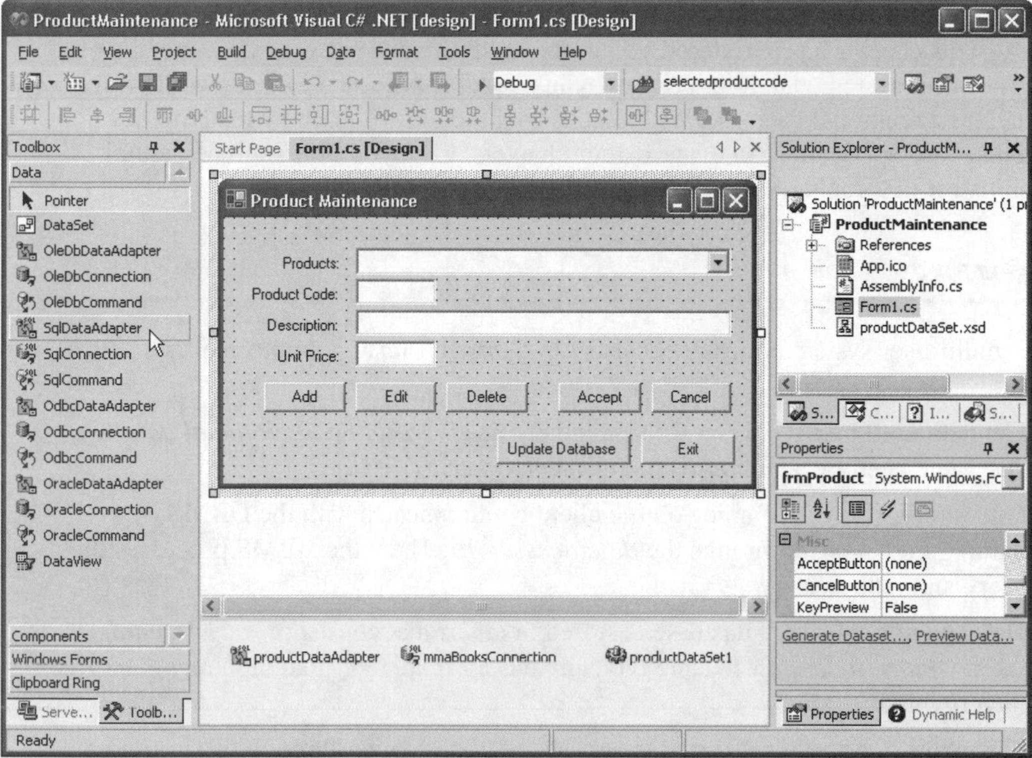

ADO.NET objects created using code

```
string connectionString = "data source=DOUG\VSdotNET;"
    + "initial catalog=MMABooks;integrated security=SSPI";
SqlConnection mmaBooksConnection = new SqlConnection(connectionString);

string productSelect = "Select * From Products";
SqlDataAdapter productDataAdapter;
productDataAdapter = new SqlDataAdapter(productSelect, mmaBooksConnection);

DataSet productDataSet = new DataSet();
productDataAdapter.Fill(productDataSet, "Products");
```

Description

- You can use the ADO.NET components in the Data tab of the Toolbox to add ADO.NET objects to a form. Then, you can set the properties of the objects using the Properties window.
- If you add a data adapter from the Toolbox, the Data Adapter Configuration Wizard is started. This wizard helps you create the data adapter and the related connection and command objects. See chapter 17 for details.
- To create ADO.NET objects in code, you write a declaration that identifies the class each object is created from. You'll learn how to write code like this in chapter 20.

Figure 16-15 Two ways to create ADO.NET objects

Perspective

This chapter has introduced you to the hardware and software components of a multi-user system and described how you use ADO.NET and SQL to work with the data in a relational database. With that as background, you're now ready to develop a database application. In the next four chapters, then, you'll learn the essential skills for developing Windows applications that use ADO.NET.

Summary

- A multi-user system typically consists of *clients* and *servers* connected by a *network*.
- The data used by a *client/server system* is typically stored in a *relational database* that's managed by a *database management system* (*DBMS*).
- *Application software* running on the client communicates with the DBMS by sending *SQL queries* through the *data access API*. Then, the DBMS processes the query and returns any *query results*.
- The data in a relational database is stored in *tables* that consist of *rows* (*records*) and *columns* (*fields*). Each table typically has a *primary key* that uniquely identifies each row in the table.
- The tables in a relational database are related to each other through their *primary keys* and *foreign keys*. Most relationships are *one-to-many* relationships.
- To retrieve data from a table, you use a SQL Select statement that stores the rows and columns you request in a *result table*, or *result set*. You can also use a Select statement to *join* the data from two or more tables.
- To add records to a table, you use the SQL Insert statement. To update records in a table, you use the SQL Update statement. And to delete records from a table, you use the SQL Delete statement.
- The .NET Framework provides two types of ADO.NET objects: *data provider* objects and *dataset* objects.
- Data provider objects provide access to a database. A *data adapter* object executes SQL statements stored in *command* objects. A command object connects to a database using a *connection* object.
- A dataset object contains the data that's retrieved from a database. Because this is a copy of the data in the database, changes you make to it aren't reflected in the database. This is referred to as a *disconnected data architecture* because you can work with the data without maintaining a connection to the database.
- A *concurrency* problem occurs when two users retrieve the same row in a database table and try to update it. Then, if *optimistic concurrency* is used for *concurrency control*, the second update will be refused and a *concurrency exception* will be thrown. Otherwise, the second update will overwrite the first, which is referred to as "*last in wins.*"

- A dataset contains one or more *data table* objects. Each data table object contains one or more *data column* objects that define the columns in the table and one or more *data row* objects that contain the data of the table.
- You can also execute command objects directly instead of executing them through a data adapter. If the command returns a result set, you can use a *data reader* to read through the rows in the result set one row at a time.
- You can create ADO.NET objects by dragging components from the Data tab of the Toolbox to a form or by declaring the objects in code.

Terms

Microsoft SQL Desktop Engine (MSDE)
SQL Server
client
server
database server
network
client/server system
enterprise system
local area network (LAN)
wide area network (WAN)
network operating system
database management system (DBMS)
back-end processing
back end
application software
data source
data access API
application programming interface
front-end processing
front end
SQL query
query
Structured Query Language (SQL)
query results
relational database
table
record
row
field
column
primary key
composite primary key
non-primary key
unique key
unique key constraint
index
foreign key
foreign key table
primary key table
one-to-many relationship
one-to-one relationship
many-to-many relationship
linking table
data type
system data type
null value
default value
identity column
check constraint
SQL dialect
Transact-SQL
result table
result set
calculated column
join
inner join
ADO.NET
ActiveX Data Objects .NET
.NET data provider
dataset
data table
data adapter
command
connection
disconnected data architecture
concurrency
concurrency control
optimistic concurrency

concurrency exception
"last in wins"
data relation
data column
data row
constraint
data reader
Component Designer tray

Objectives

- Describe the hardware components of a typical multi-user system.
- Describe the software components of a typical multi-user database application.
- Explain how a table in a relational database is organized.
- Explain how the tables in a relational database are related.
- Describe the use of these SQL statements: Select, Insert, Update, Delete.
- Describe the use of these ADO.NET components: data adapter, data command, data connection, data reader, dataset, data table.
- Compare the structure of a dataset with the structure of a relational database.
- Describe concurrency, optimistic concurrency control, and "last in wins."
- Describe two ways that you can create ADO.NET components.

17

How to develop a simple database application

Now that you know the concepts and terms that you need for developing database applications with ADO.NET, this chapter shows you how to develop simple database applications of your own. First, you'll learn how to use the Data Adapter Configuration Wizard to create the data adapter, command, and connection objects. Then, you'll learn how to create and work with a dataset and how to use a data grid control to work with the data in the dataset.

How to use the Data Adapter Configuration Wizard

The easiest way to create the components you need to work with a database is to use the Data Adapter Configuration Wizard. The topics that follow lead you step-by-step through the process of using this wizard. When you're done, you'll have the data adapter, command, and connection objects you need for developing a database application.

How to start the wizard

To start the Data Adapter Configuration Wizard, display the Toolbox, click the Data tab to display the data components, and then double-click the data adapter component you want to use. When you do that, the first dialog box of the wizard is displayed as shown in figure 17-1. This dialog box describes the function of the wizard.

This also adds a data adapter to the Component Designer tray at the bottom of the designer window. Then, as you proceed through the wizard's dialog boxes, the data adapter is configured according to the information you provide. To proceed with the configuration, you can click on the Next button.

If you want to define the data adapter and the other data components without using the wizard, you can click the Cancel button from this dialog box. Then, you can use the Properties window to set the properties for the data adapter, and you can use the Data tab of the Toolbox to create the other ADO.NET components. Because the wizard quickly and easily creates all the components you need, however, I recommend that you use it whenever possible.

The dialog box that's displayed when you start the Data Adapter Configuration Wizard

Description

- The Data Adapter Configuration Wizard helps you create the data adapter, connection, and command objects for working with a database.
- To start the wizard, simply double-click on a data adapter component in the Data tab of the Toolbox. The data adapter is then added to the Component Designer tray at the bottom of the designer window, and the first dialog box of the wizard is displayed.
- The first dialog box displays a welcome message and describes the function of the wizard. To continue with the wizard, click on the Next button.
- If you click on the Cancel button from the wizard's Welcome dialog box, the wizard is canceled. Then, you can set the properties of the data adapter from the Properties window, and you can create the other ADO.NET objects using the components in the Data tab of the Toolbox.

Figure 17-1 How to start the wizard

How to define the connection

The next dialog box helps you define the connection object as illustrated in figure 17-2. From this dialog box, you can select an existing connection (one you've used previously), or you can click the New Connection button to display the Data Link Properties dialog box shown here. This dialog box helps you identify the database that you want to access and provides the information you need to access it.

When the Data Link Properties dialog box is first displayed, the Connection tab is visible. In this tab, you select the name of the server that contains the database you want to access; enter the information that's required to log on to the server; and select the name of the database you want to access. How you do that, though, varies depending on whether you're using MSDE on your own PC or whether you're using a database on your company's or school's computer.

If you're using MSDE on your own PC and you've downloaded and installed MSDE from Microsoft's web site as described in appendix A, the server name should be VSDOTNET. Next, for the logon information, you should select the Use Windows NT Integrated Security option. Then, MSDE will use the login name and password that you use for your computer as the name and password for the database too. As a result, you won't need to provide a separate user name and password in this dialog box. Last, you select the name of the database that you want to connect to. When you're done, you can click the Test Connection button to be sure that the connection works.

In contrast, if you're using a database that's on your company's or school's server, you need to get the connection information from the network administrator, the database administrator, or your instructor. That will include the server name, logon information, and database name. Once you establish a connection to a database, you can use that connection for all of the other applications that use that database.

If you use the Data Adapter Configuration Wizard to configure a SQL data adapter, the wizard configures the data adapter to use the SQL Server provider. Likewise, if you use the wizard to create an Oracle data adapter, the wizard configures the data adapter to use the Oracle provider. However, if you use the wizard to configure an OLE DB data adapter, you'll need to click the Provider tab of the Data Link Properties dialog box to select which OleDb provider you want to use. The default provider is the OleDb provider for SQL Server.

The dialog boxes for defining a connection

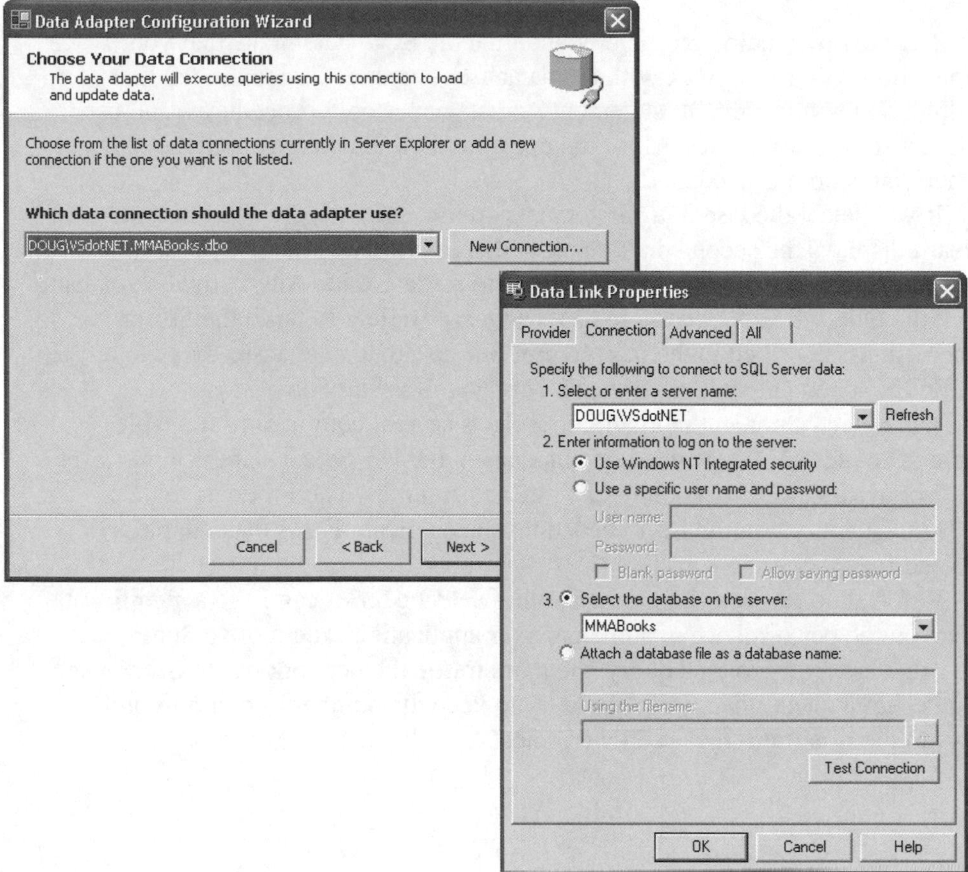

Description

- The Choose Your Data Connection dialog box asks you to identify the data connection you want to use. If you've already defined a data connection, you can select it from the drop-down list. Otherwise, you can click the New Connection button to create a connection.
- When you click the New Connection button, the Connection tab of the Data Link Properties dialog box is displayed. You use this dialog box to provide the information that's needed to connect to the database.
- If you're creating an OleDbDataAdapter, the default is to use the OLE DB provider for SQL Server. If that's not what you want, you can select a different OLE DB provider from the Provider tab. The information that's required on the Connection tab will vary depending on the provider you choose.
- To be sure that the connection is configured properly, you can click the Test Connection button.

Figure 17-2 How to define the connection

How to define the SQL statements

The next two dialog boxes let you define the SQL statements that your application will use to work with the database. The three options in the first dialog box let you use SQL statements, create new stored procedures, and use existing stored procedures. All of the examples in this book use SQL statements rather than stored procedures.

If you select the Use SQL Statements option and click the Next button, the wizard displays the second dialog box in this figure. This dialog box lets you enter the Select statement you want to use to retrieve data. Alternatively, you can click the Query Builder button to use the Query Builder to build the Select statement as described in the next figure. Because that's the easiest way to create the Select statements you need, that's what you'll usually do.

The Select statement in this figure selects several columns from a table named Products. You saw this table in chapter 16. The Select statement retrieves the ProductCode, Description, and UnitPrice columns. The Products table's OnHandQuantity column isn't needed for the application this data adapter will be used for.

Before I go on, you should realize that Select queries can have a significant effect on the performance of a client/server application. The more columns and rows that are returned by a query, the more traffic the network has to bear. When you design a query, then, you should try to keep the number of columns and rows to the minimum required by a project.

The dialog boxes for defining the SQL statements

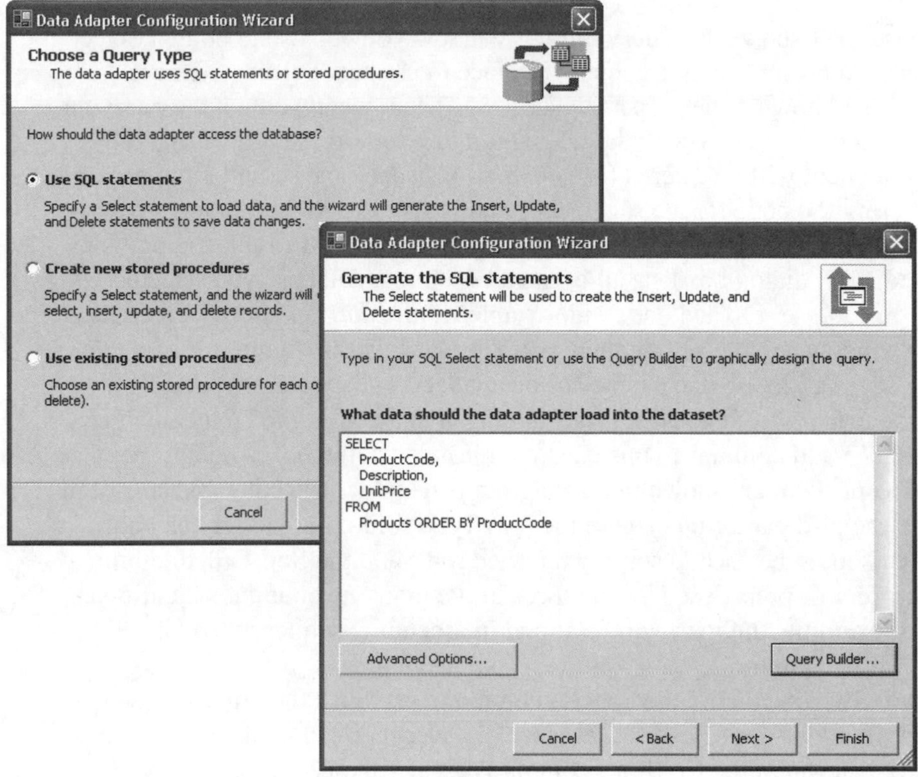

Description

- You use the Choose a Query Type dialog box to specify whether the database will be accessed using SQL statements, new stored procedures, or existing stored procedures.
- If you choose to use SQL statements, the Generate the SQL Statements dialog box is displayed when you click the Next button. This dialog box lets you enter the Select statement that will be used to retrieve the data. You can also click the Query Builder button from this dialog box to build the Select statement interactively (see figure 17-4).
- By default, the wizard attempts to generate Insert, Update, and Delete statements based on the Select statement. To do that, the Select statement must include the table's primary key. If you don't want to generate Insert, Update, and Delete statements, you can change the advanced options as described in figure 17-5.
- If you choose to create new stored procedures, a dialog box is displayed that lets you enter a Select statement. Then, after you enter the names you want to use for the stored procedures, the wizard generates those stored procedures with the appropriate Select, Insert, Update, and Delete statements.
- If you choose to use existing stored procedures, the wizard displays a dialog box that lets you select the stored procedures to use for select, insert, update, and delete operations.

Figure 17-3 How to define the SQL statements

How to use the Query Builder

Figure 17-4 shows the *Query Builder* window you can use to build a Select statement. You can use this graphical interface to create a Select statement without even knowing the proper syntax for it. Then, when you get the query the way you want it, you can click the OK button to return to the wizard and the Select statement will be entered for you. This is usually easier and more accurate than entering the code for the statement directly into the wizard dialog box.

When the Query Builder window first opens up, the Add Table dialog box is displayed. This dialog box lists all of the tables in the database you selected. Then, you can use it to add one or more tables to the *diagram pane* of the Query Builder window so you can use them in your query. In this figure, for example, you can see that the Products table has been added to the diagram pane.

In the *grid pane*, you can see the columns that are going to be included in the query. To add columns to this pane, you just check the boxes before the column names that are shown in the diagram pane. Once the columns have been added to the grid pane, you can use the Sort Type column to identify any columns that should be used to sort the returned rows and the Sort Order column to give the order of precedence for the sort if more than one column is identified. Here, for example, the rows will be sorted in ascending sequence by the ProductCode column.

Similarly, you can use the Criteria column to establish the criteria to be used to select the rows that will be retrieved by the query. For example, to retrieve only the rows where the UnitPrice column is greater than $10.00, you could specify "> 10.00" in the Criteria column for the UnitPrice column. Since no criteria are specified in this query, all of the rows will be retrieved.

As you create the query, the *SQL pane* shows the current version of the resulting Select statement. You can also run this query at any time to display the selected rows in the *results pane*. That way, you can be sure that the query works the way you want it to. To run the query, right-click anywhere in the Query Builder window, then choose Run from the menu that appears.

The Query Builder window

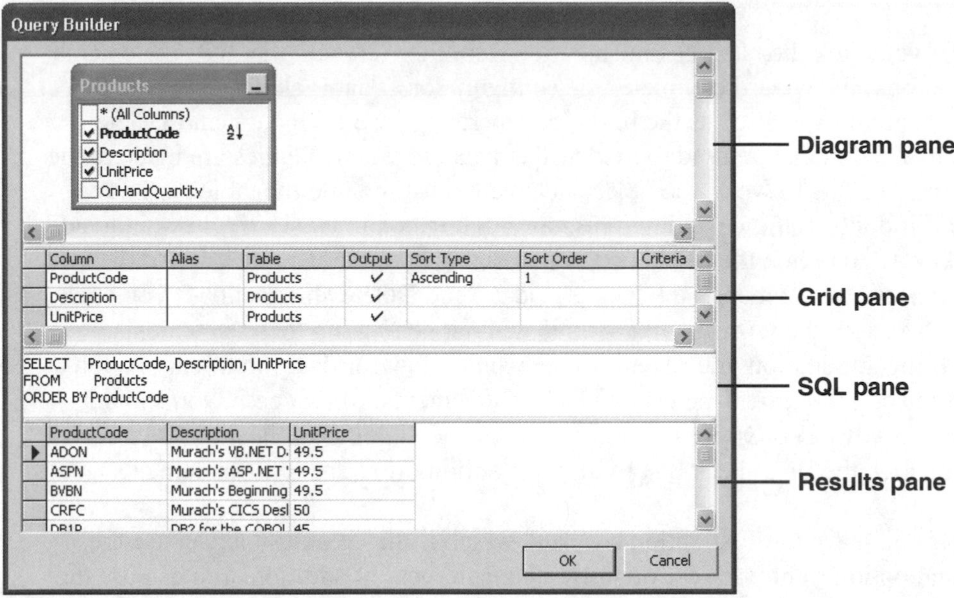

Description

- When you first start the *Query Builder*, the Add Table dialog box is displayed. You can use this dialog box to select the tables you want to include in the query. Then, those tables are displayed in the *diagram pane*.
- To include a column from a table in the query, click on the box to its left. Then, that column is added to the *grid pane*. You can also select all the columns at once by checking the * (All Columns) item.
- To create a calculated column, enter an expression in the Column column and then enter the name you want to use for the column in the Alias column.
- To sort the returned rows by one or more columns, select the Ascending or Descending option from the Sort Type column for those columns in the sequence you want them sorted. You can also use the Sort Order column to set the sort sequence.
- To specify selection criteria (like a specific value that the column must contain to be selected), enter the criteria in the Criteria column.
- To use a column for sorting or for specifying criteria without including it in the query results, remove the check mark from the Output column.
- As you select columns and specify sort and selection criteria, the Query Builder builds the Select statement and displays it in the *SQL pane*.
- You can also use the Query Builder shortcut menu to work with a query. To display the results of a query, for example, select the Run command from this menu. The results are displayed in the *results pane*.

Figure 17-4 How to use the Query Builder

How to set advanced SQL generation options

If you click the Next or Finish button from the Generate the SQL Statements dialog box, the wizard completes the configuration. That includes using the Select statement you specified as the basis for generating Insert, Update, and Delete statements that can be used to modify the database when changes are made to the dataset. For this to work, the Select statement must include the table's primary key. If it doesn't, the wizard will display a dialog box that asks if you want to add the key. If you click the Yes button in this dialog box, the wizard will add the key column and then generate the Insert, Update, and Delete statements. If you click the No button, the wizard will continue without generating these statements.

If the application you're developing won't allow for data modification, you won't need the Insert, Update, and Delete statements. In that case, you should click the Advanced Options button to display the dialog box shown in figure 17-5. Then, click the first check box to turn this option off so the extra statements aren't generated.

If you leave the first option checked, which is the default, you can use the second option to provide for optimistic concurrency. In addition, you can use the third option to determine if the dataset will be refreshed after each insert or update operation. These options are also on by default, which is appropriate in most situations.

As you should remember from the last chapter, optimistic concurrency applies to updates and deletions. If this option is on, the wizard adds code to the Update and Delete statements that checks the data in the database rows that are going to be updated or deleted against the original values in these rows. Then, if the data has changed, the update or deletion is refused and a concurrency exception is thrown. That prevents one user from making changes to rows that have been changed by another user. For that reason, you almost always use optimistic concurrency for multi-user applications that update and delete rows.

When you choose the Refresh the Dataset option, the wizard generates two additional Select statements. One comes after the Insert statement that's used to add a new row to the database, and it retrieves the new row into the dataset. This is useful if you add rows to a table that contains an identity column, columns with default values, or columns whose values are calculated from other columns. That way, the information that's generated for these columns by the database is available from the dataset. The other is a Select statement that's added after the Update statement used to modify a row. This ensures that the dataset has current information following an update.

Of course, if the values that are generated by the database aren't used by your application, it isn't necessary to refresh the dataset with this information. In fact, it would be inefficient to do that. In some cases, though, you need to refresh the dataset for your application if you want it to work properly.

The dialog box for setting advanced SQL generation options

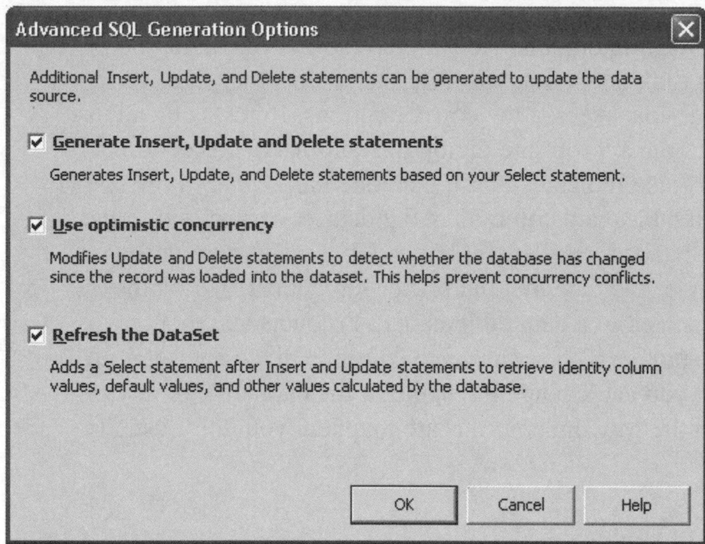

Description

- If you click the Advanced Options button from the Generate the SQL statements dialog box, the Advanced SQL Generation Options dialog box is displayed. This dialog box lets you set the options related to the generation of the Insert, Update, and Delete statements that will be used to update the database.
- If your application doesn't need to add, change, or delete rows in the database, you should remove the check mark from the Generate option. Then, the other options become unavailable.
- The Use Optimistic Concurrency option determines whether or not the application checks to be sure that the rows that are updated or deleted haven't been changed by another user since they were retrieved. If this option is checked, the wizard adds code to the Update and Delete statements to provide for this checking.
- If you remove the check mark from the Use Optimistic Concurrency option, rows are updated and deleted whether or not they've been changed by another user since they were retrieved.
- The Refresh the DataSet option determines whether or not the dataset is refreshed after an insert or update operation. If this option is selected, a Select statement that retrieves the affected row is executed after each Insert and Update statement.

Figure 17-5 How to set advanced SQL generation options

How to complete the configuration

After it generates the SQL statements, the wizard displays the dialog box shown in figure 17-6. This dialog box lists the SQL statements that were generated so you can be sure that you selected the correct options. If not, you can use the Back button to return to the appropriate dialog box and make corrections.

The Results dialog box also indicates that it generated *table mappings*. Table mappings determine which tables and columns in the dataset correspond to the tables and columns of the database. For example, the table mappings for the data adapter created in this chapter indicate that the source table identified by the Select statement will be mapped to a data table named Products and that the columns within the source table will be mapped to columns in the dataset with the same names. Although you can change the name of the data table or any of the data columns and even the way the columns are mapped, you don't usually need to do that.

The dialog box that displays the configuration results

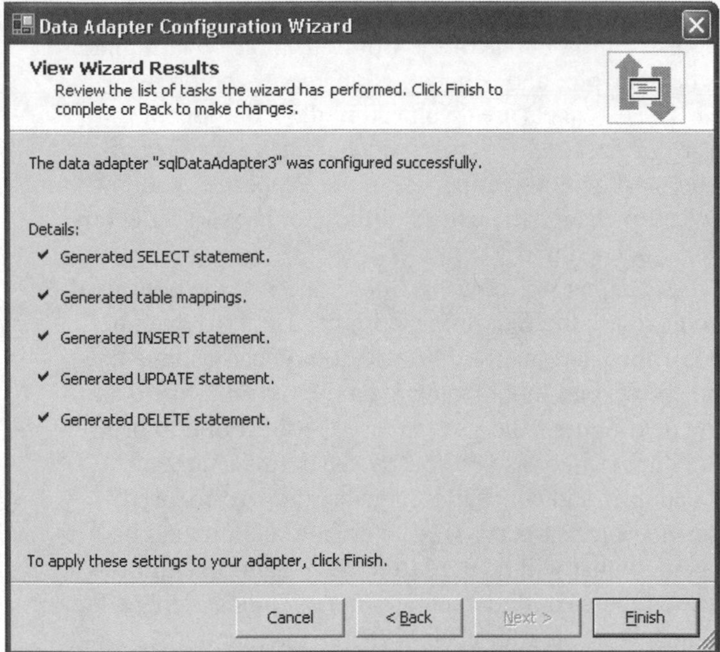

Description

- When you click the Next button from the Generate the SQL statements dialog box, the wizard completes the configuration and displays the results in the View Wizard Results dialog box. To create the adapter with this configuration, click the Finish button.
- In addition to Select, Insert, Update, and Delete statements, the wizard generates *table mappings*. The table mappings map the columns in the source table with columns in the data table that's created when you generate a dataset from the data adapter (see figure 17-8).
- Although you can use the TableMappings property of the data adapter to change the table mappings, you shouldn't need to do that.

Figure 17-6 How to complete the configuration

The objects created by the Configuration Wizard

When you click the Finish button in one of the Configuration Wizard dialog boxes, the wizard creates data adapter and connection objects based on the information you specified. These objects are displayed in the Component Designer tray as you can see in figure 17-7. Then, you can click on either of these objects to display and work with its properties in the Properties window. For example, you might want to change the names of these objects to reflect the table and database they're associated with.

When you select the data adapter object, three links appear at the bottom of the Properties window. You can use the first link, Configure Data Adapter, to redisplay the dialog boxes of the Configuration Wizard so you can change the configuration. You can use the second link to generate a dataset from the data adapter as you'll see in the next figure. And you can use the third link to preview the data that's defined by a data adapter as you'll see later in this chapter.

In addition to the data adapter and connection objects, the wizard also creates one or more command objects. At the least, it creates a command object that defines the Select statement that will be used to retrieve data. In addition, if you indicated that you wanted the wizard to generate Insert, Update, and Delete statements, a command object is created for each of these statements.

Even though the command objects don't appear in the Component Designer tray, you can still review their properties by selecting them from the list of objects at the top of the Properties window. You can also access these objects through the data adapter object. In the Properties window in this figure, for example, you can see the property of the data adapter that refers to the Select command: SelectCommand. If you scroll down this window, you can see the properties for the Insert, Update, and Delete commands too. You'll learn more about working with these properties later in this chapter. For now, just realize that if you expand the property for one of these commands, you can work with the properties of that command.

The objects created by the Data Adapter Configuration Wizard

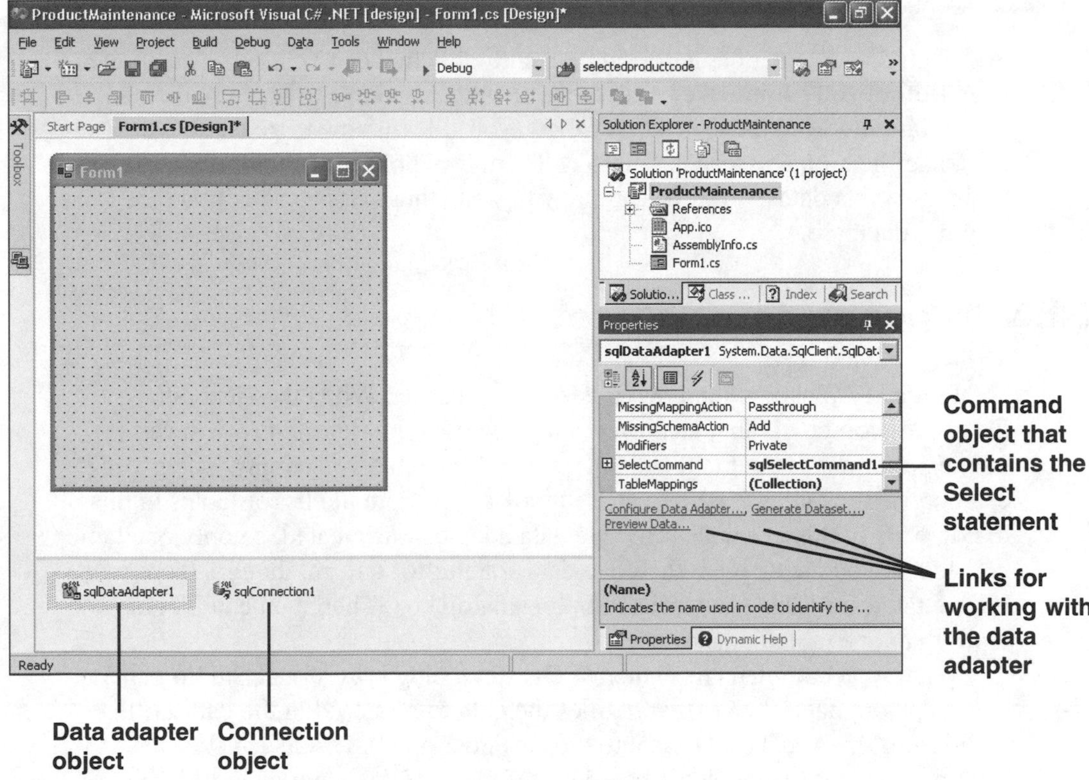

Description

- When the configuration is complete, the data adapter and connection objects created by the wizard are displayed in the Component Designer tray. To display the properties for either object, just click on it.
- The wizard also creates the command objects that will be used to execute the Select, Insert, Update, and Delete statements against the database. You can access these objects through properties of the data adapter as shown above. Or, you can select the object from the drop-down list at the top of the Properties window.
- You can use the links that are displayed in the Properties window or the commands in the Data menu to work with the data adapter.

Figure 17-7 The objects created by the Configuration Wizard

How to work with a dataset

Each data adapter defines a single result table that can be used in an application. Before you can use the result table, though, you have to load the data for it into a dataset. So in the topics that follow, you'll learn how to generate a dataset for an application and load data into it. Then, for applications that make changes to the data in a dataset, you'll learn how to write those changes back to the original database.

How to generate a dataset

Figure 17-8 shows you how to generate a dataset. When the Generate Dataset dialog box is first displayed, the New option is selected so you can create a new dataset with the default name or the name you supply. Then, you can choose the tables to be included in the dataset from the list of tables in this dialog box. In this example, only one data adapter was created, so only one table is listed. If you create more than one data adapter for a form, though, there will be one table for each adapter listed in this dialog box. Then, you can include more than one table in the dataset.

When you complete the Generate Dataset dialog box, Visual Studio generates a custom dataset class that defines the data to be stored in the dataset. In addition, if the Add This Dataset to the Designer option is selected, Visual Studio creates a dataset object based on the class. If that's not what you want, you can remove the check mark from this option so only the class is generated. If you do that, though, you have to create a dataset object through code. In most cases, you'll leave this option checked so the dataset object is created for you.

You can also use this dialog box to modify an existing dataset. To do that, select the dataset you want to modify from the Existing combo box. Then, you can add or remove tables from the dataset by checking or unchecking the appropriate tables. If you do that, though, keep in mind that this changes the original dataset class, but not the dataset object that was created from it. Because of that, you'll need to create a new dataset object as well.

The dialog box for generating a dataset

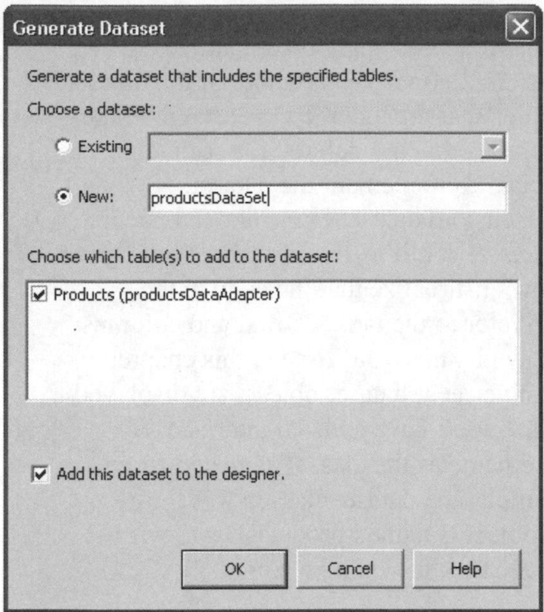

Description

- A dataset lets you work with the data defined by the Select statements in one or more data adapters. To generate a dataset, select the data adapter or the form it's associated with, and then choose the Data→Generate Dataset command from the menu bar or click on the Generate Dataset link that's displayed in the Properties window.
- In the Generate Dataset dialog box that's displayed, select the New option and enter the name you want to use for the dataset class that will be created. Then, select the tables you want to include in the dataset from the list that's provided.
- The list of tables that's displayed in this dialog box includes the result tables defined by the data adapters in the project (each data adapter defines a single result table). A dataset can include any or all of the tables in the list.
- The name for each table in the list is taken from the name of the source table in the Select statement for the data adapter. If the Select statement defines a join, the name of the first source table in the statement is used.
- To add an instance of the dataset class that's created to the application, select the Add This Dataset to the Designer option (this is the default). If you don't select this option, you can create an instance of the dataset class in the code for the application or by using the Dataset component in the Toolbox.
- You can also use the Generate Dataset dialog box to change an existing dataset. If you've already defined one or more datasets, the Existing option will be selected when you display this dialog box and you can select the dataset you want to change from the drop-down list. Then, you can add or delete tables from the dataset.

Figure 17-8 How to generate a dataset

The dataset schema file, class, and object

Figure 17-9 shows the dataset schema file, class, and object that are created when you generate a dataset. The *schema file* defines the structure of the dataset, including the tables it contains, the columns that are included in each table, the data types of each column, and the constraints that are defined for each table. The schema is then used by the dataset class to implement the dataset.

A dataset object that's created from a custom dataset class, like the one shown in this figure, is called a *typed dataset*. You'll learn more about how typed datasets work in the next chapter. For now, just realize that the code in the dataset class makes it possible for you to refer to the tables, rows, and columns in the typed dataset using the simplified syntax that you'll see in this chapter.

Like the other ADO.NET objects you've seen, dataset objects are displayed in the Component Designer tray since they don't have a visual interface. By default, a dataset object is given the same name as the class it's created from with a number added to the end. For example, the dataset class in this figure is named productsDataSet and the dataset object is named productsDataSet1. If you created another dataset from the same class, it would be named productsDataSet2. And so on.

A dataset schema file, class, and object

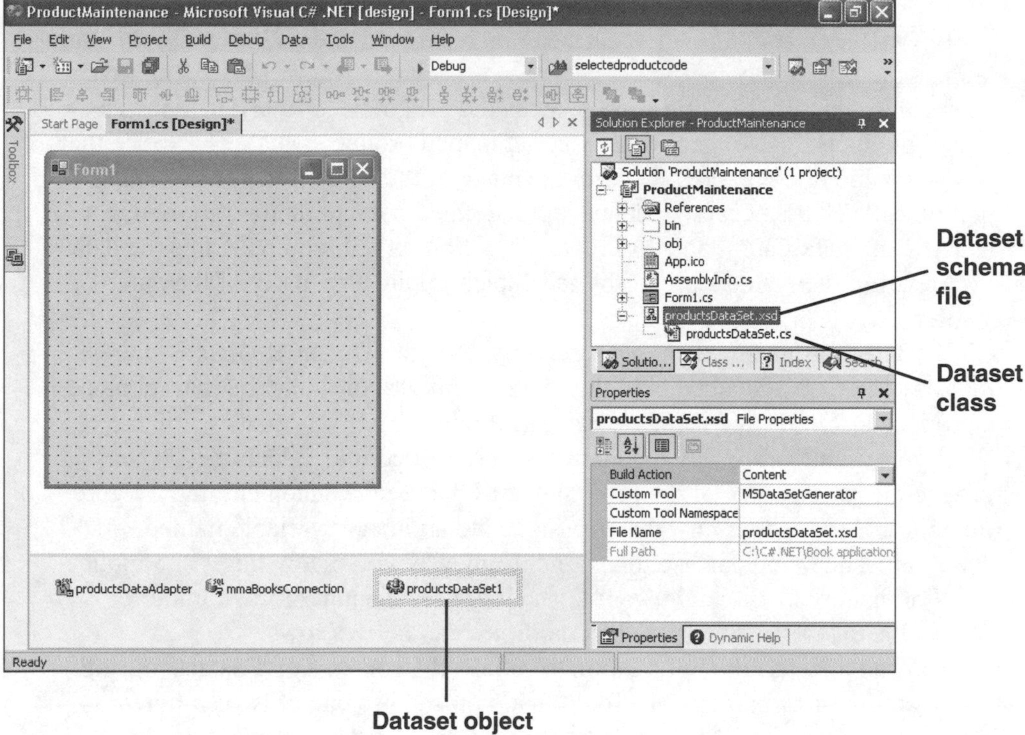

Description

- When you generate a dataset, Visual Studio creates a dataset *schema file* that defines the structure of the dataset. This file is listed in the Solution Explorer and is given the name you specify in the Generate Dataset dialog box with a file extension of *xsd*.
- The dataset generator also creates a custom dataset class. By default, this class isn't displayed in the Solution Explorer. To display it, click the Show All Files button at the top of the Solution Explorer and then expand the schema file for the dataset. The dataset class will appear below the schema file.
- If you selected the option in the Generate Dataset dialog box to add the dataset to the designer, a dataset object is created from the dataset class and added to the Component Designer tray. This object is given the same name as the dataset class, but with a numeric suffix.

Figure 17-9 The dataset schema file, class, and object

How to fill and clear a dataset

Before you can work with a dataset, you have to load data into it. To do that, you use the Fill method of the data adapter as shown in figure 17-10. The first statement in this figure, for example, loads the data defined by a data adapter named productsDataAdapter into a dataset named productsDataSet1. Notice that only the name of the dataset, and not the name of the data table, is used in this method call. That's because a data adapter defines a single table even though a dataset can contain more than one data table. So this Fill method stores the data it retrieves in the table identified by the TableMappings property of the data adapter.

If you want to name the table for clarity, though, you can do that as illustrated by the second statement in this figure. This assumes that the dataset name is productsDataSet1 and the table name is Products.

If you want to know how many rows were loaded into a dataset, you can retrieve the return value of the Fill method as the second statement in the figure illustrates. Here, the return value is assigned to an integer variable named rowCount. Then, you can use this variable any way you like within your application. For example, you might want to use it to keep a count of the number of rows in the dataset as the user adds, modifies, and deletes rows.

You can also use the Fill method to refresh the contents of a dataset during the execution of an application. To do that, you can use one of two techniques. First, you can use the Clear method of the dataset or a data table within the dataset to remove all the rows from that dataset or data table as illustrated in the last two statements in this figure. Then, you can use the Fill method to load the table with new data. This is the preferred method, and it's usually the most efficient.

Second, you can use the Fill method without clearing the dataset or data table. Then, if the table being refreshed is defined with a primary key, the rows in the existing table are updated by the rows in the database table. That, however, can be a time-consuming process if the table contains a large number of rows. That's why we recommend that you clear the table first. If the table isn't defined with a primary key, the newly retrieved rows are appended to the existing rows, which isn't usually what you want. In that case, you'll want to be sure to clear the dataset or data table before executing the Fill method.

Another way to refresh a dataset is to refresh each row as it's added or updated within the application. You already learned how to use the Data Adapter Configuration Wizard to provide for that, and you'll learn more about how that works later in this chapter. This technique is usually more efficient than refreshing the entire data table or dataset because only new or modified rows are refreshed. On the other hand, if other users will be modifying the same database data at the same time, you may want to refresh the entire data table periodically so it reflects the changes made by other users.

How to fill a data table

Two forms of the Fill method

```
dataAdapter.Fill(dataSet)
dataAdapter.Fill(dataSet.dataTable)
```

Code that that fills a dataset

```
productsDataAdapter.Fill(productsDataSet1);
```

Code that retrieves the return value and names the table to be filled

```
rowCount = productsDataAdapter.Fill(productsDataSet1.Products);
```

How to clear a dataset or data table

The syntax of the Clear method for a dataset or data table

```
dataset.Clear()
dataset.datatable.Clear()
```

Code that clears all the tables in a dataset

```
productsDataSet1.Clear();
```

Code that that clears a single data table

```
productsDataSet1.Products.Clear();
```

Description

- The Fill method retrieves rows from the database using the Select statement specified by the SelectCommand property of the data adapter. The rows are stored in a data table within the dataset you specify.
- In most cases, you don't need to specify the name of the table where you want the results stored. Instead, the table is identified by the data adapter. However, you may want to code the table name for clarity.
- When the Fill method is executed, the connection object that's associated with the SelectCommand object is opened automatically. After the dataset is loaded, the connection object is closed.
- If you use the Fill method to refresh a table that already contains data, it will merge the rows retrieved from the database with the existing rows in the dataset based on the table's primary key. If the table isn't defined with a primary key, the Fill method appends the rows to the end of the table.
- The Fill method returns an integer value with the number of rows that were added or refreshed.
- The Clear method removes all the data from the data table or dataset you specify. You can use this method to clear the data from a table that isn't defined with a primary key before you refresh that table. You can also use it to improve the efficiency of a retrieval operation for a table with a primary key.
- An exception will be raised by the data provider if a database error occurs while retrieving the data.

Figure 17-10 How to fill and clear a dataset

How to update the database with changes made to a dataset

Figure 17-11 shows how to use the Update method of a data adapter to update a database with the changes made to a dataset. Notice in the syntax of this method that, just like the Fill method, you can specify the name of a dataset or a data table within a dataset. In most cases, though, you'll just name the dataset as shown in the first statement in this figure. Then, the table identified by the data adapter is used to update the database.

The Update method checks the RowState property of each row in the table to determine if it's a new row, a modified row, or a row that should be deleted. If it's a new row, the Insert statement identified by the InsertCommand property of the data adapter is used to add the row to the table in the database. Similarly, the Update statement identified by the UpdateCommand property is used to update a modified row, and the Delete statement identified by the DeleteCommand property is used to delete a row. After each Insert or Update statement is executed, the RowState property of the affected row is updated to reflect that it has not changed. After a Delete statement is executed, the row is simply deleted from the dataset.

If you want to know how many rows were updated, you can retrieve the return value of the Update method as illustrated by the second example in this figure. You might want to use this value to display a message to the user that indicates the number or rows that were updated. Or, you might want to use it to determine if the update completed successfully. In the next figure, though, you'll learn other ways to test for the successful completion of an update operation.

To be sure that changes have been made to a dataset before executing the Update method, you can use the HasChanges method of the dataset. This method returns true if the dataset has been updated and false if it hasn't. You can see how this method is used in the third example in this figure.

Two forms of the Update method

```
dataAdapter.Update(dataSet)
dataAdapter.Update(dataSet.dataTable)
```

Code that updates a database with the data in a dataset

```
productsDataAdapter.Update(productsDataSet1);
```

Code that retrieves the return value from an Update method

```
rowsUpdated = productsDataAdapter.Update(productsDataSet1);
```

Code that checks for changes to the dataset before updating the database

```
if (productsDataSet1.HasChanges)
    productsDataAdapter.Update(productsDataSet1);
```

The DataRowState enumeration

Constant	Description
Added	The row has been added to the dataset.
Deleted	The row has been deleted from the dataset.
Modified	The row has been changed.
Unchanged	The row has not changed.

Description

- The Update method saves changes made in the data table to the database that the data was retrieved from. To do that, it checks the RowState property of each row in the data table to determine if the row has changed. This property contains one of the constants in the DataRowState enumeration shown above.
- If the RowState property of a row indicates that the row has been deleted, the SQL Delete statement for the data adapter is executed for the row. If it indicates that the row has been modified, the SQL Update statement is executed. And if it indicates that the row has been added, the SQL Insert statement is executed.
- Before you execute the Update method, you should check if any changes have been made to the dataset. To do that, you can use the HasChanges method of the dataset. This method checks the RowState property of each row in the dataset to determine if changes have been made and returns a Boolean value.
- When the Update method is executed, a connection to the database is opened automatically. The connection is closed when the update is complete.
- The Update method returns an integer value that indicates the number of rows that were updated.

Figure 17-11 How to update the database with changes made to a dataset

How to handle data provider errors

When you access a database using ADO.NET, there is always the possibility that an unrecoverable error might occur. Some errors result from mistakes in your code, such as misspelled column or table names. Other errors have nothing to do with your code. For example, the database server might be shut down when you try to access it, or the network connection to the database server might be broken. Either way, your applications should always anticipate such problems by catching any database exceptions that might occur.

Figure 17-12 shows the exceptions thrown by the .NET data providers when an unrecoverable error occurs. As you can see, each data provider has its own exception class. So, if you're using the SQL Server data provider, you should catch exceptions of the SqlException class. If you're using the OleDb provider, you should catch OleDbException exceptions. And so on.

The code example in this figure shows how you can catch a SqlException that might occur when attempting to fill a dataset using a SQL data adapter. Here, an error message is displayed if a SqlException occurs. The error message uses the Number and Message properties of the SqlException class to display details about the exception.

Although it's uncommon, more than one server error can occur as the result of a single database operation. In that case, an error object is created for each error. These objects are stored an a collection that you can access through the Errors property of the exception object. Each error object contains a Number and Message property just like the exception object. However, because the Number and Message properties of the exception object are set to the Number and Message properties of the first error in the Errors collection, you don't usually need to work with the individual error objects.

.NET data provider exception classes

Name	Description
SqlException	Thrown if a server error occurs when accessing a SQL Server database
OleDbException	Thrown if a server error occurs when accessing an OLE DB database.
OracleException	Thrown if a server error occurs when accessing an Oracle database.
OdbcException	Thrown if a server error occurs when accessing an ODBC database.

Properties of the .NET data provider exception classes

Property	Description
Number	An error number that identifies the type of error.
Message	A message that describes the error.
Source	The name of the provider that generated the error.
Errors	A collection of error objects that contain information about the errors that occurred during a database operation.

Code that catches a SQL exception

```
try
{
    productsDataAdapter.Fill(productsDataSet1);
}
catch (SqlException ex)
{
    string errorMessage = "Database error #" + ex.Number + ": " + ex.Message;
    MessageBox.Show(errorMessage, "SQL Server error");
}
```

Description

- Whenever the data provider (SQL Server, OLE DB, Oracle, or ODBC) encounters a situation it can't handle, a data provider exception is thrown.
- The Number and Message properties pinpoint the specific server error that caused the data provider exception to be thrown.
- Because more than one server error can occur when you update a database, the data provider exception classes include an Errors property that holds a collection of error objects. The Number and Message properties of the data provider exception identify the first error in the Errors collection. Although you can use the Errors property to display the number and message for each individual error, displaying the number and message for the first error is sufficient in most cases.

Figure 17-12 How to handle data provider errors

How to handle update errors

In addition to data provider errors, errors can occur on ADO.NET components when you update a database. The most common cause of an ADO.NET error is a concurrency exception. Although you might think that this error would be generated by the database rather than ADO.NET, it's not. To understand why, you need to remember that the SQL statements that are executed for an update or delete operation contain code that checks that a row hasn't changed since it was retrieved. But if the row has changed, the row with the specified criteria won't be found and the SQL statement won't be executed. When the data adapter discovers that the row wasn't updated or deleted, however, it realizes that there was a concurrency error and throws an exception.

To provide for this situation, you can use a technique like the one shown in figure 17-13. To use this technique, you must set the ContinueUpdateOnError property of the data adapter to True. Then, if an error occurs during the update, the data adapter won't throw an exception. Instead, it will flag the row to indicate that it has an error, and it will continue the update operation until all of the rows in the data table have been processed.

To flag an error, the data adapter sets the HasErrors property of the row to True, and it sets the RowError property of the row to a description of the error. It also sets the HasErrors property of the table and dataset to True. That way, you can use these properties to check for errors before checking each individual row.

The example in this figure shows one way you can use this update technique. After the Update method is executed, an if statement checks the HasErrors property of the dataset to determine if any errors were encountered. If so, a foreach statement processes each of the rows in the Products table to locate the ones that have errors. If it finds an error, it appends the product code and the description of the error that's stored in the RowError property to an error message string. After all of the rows have been processed, the Show method of the MessageBox class is called to display the error message.

In a production application, of course, you would want to include some additional processing for each error. For example, you might want to retrieve the rows in error and let the user modify and update them again. However, because the processing that's performed will vary from one application to another, I haven't included it here. You'd also want to include the Update method in a try block to catch any data provider errors that might occur.

Common properties for working with update errors

Object	Property	Description
DataAdapter	ContinueUpdateOnError	Determines whether an Update should continue when an error occurs. The default is False, which causes an exception to be thrown and the update to end.
DataSet DataTable DataRow	HasErrors	Indicates whether errors were encountered during the update of the dataset, table, or row. These properties are automatically set to True if an error is encountered and the ContinueUpdateOnError property of the data adapter is set to True.
DataRow	RowError	Contains a description of the error that occurred.

Code that handles update errors

```
productsDataAdapter.Update(productsDataSet1);
if (productsDataSet1.HasErrors)
{
    string errorMessage = "The following rows were not updated: \n\n";
    foreach (productsDataSet.ProductsRow productRow
             in productsDataSet1.Products.Rows)
    {
        if (productRow.HasErrors)
           errorMessage += productRow.ProductCode + ": " +
                           productRow.RowError + "\n";
    }
    MessageBox.Show(errorMessage, "Update errors");
}
```

Description

- When you perform a multi-row update, an exception will be thrown and the update operation will end if a concurrency error (or any other error) occurs on a row. To avoid that, you can set the ContinueUpdateOnError property of the data adapter to True. Then, no exception is thrown and the update operation will process the remaining rows.
- If the ContinueUpdateOnError property is set to True and an error occurs on the update of a row, the HasErrors properties of the row, table, and dataset are set to True. In addition, the RowError property of the row is set to a description of the error. You can use these properties to identify the rows in error and process them appropriately.

Figure 17-13 How to handle update errors

How to use a data grid control with a dataset

Now that you've learned how to create and work with a dataset, you're ready to learn how to display the data it contains on a form so the user can work with it. In this topic, you'll learn how to use a data grid control to display all of the rows and columns in a dataset at once. In the next chapter, you'll learn how to use text boxes and combo boxes to display the data in individual columns of a single row.

A Product Maintenance form that uses a bound data grid control

Figure 17-14 presents a Product Maintenance form that displays the contents of the Products dataset that was created from the Select statement shown in figure 17-3. The *data grid control* on this form lets the user add, modify, and delete rows from the dataset. To do that, the control is *bound* to the dataset. You'll learn how to bind a data grid to a dataset in just a moment.

For now, just realize that when a data grid is bound to a dataset, it automatically displays the data in that dataset. Likewise, it automatically updates the dataset when the user adds, modifies, or deletes a row. That means that the only code that's required is the code that loads the dataset and updates the database. Because of that, using a data grid control is the quickest and easiest way to provide access to a dataset.

Keep in mind that the data grid control is bound to the dataset, not to the database. So nothing will appear in the data grid until you fill the dataset. And although any changes the user makes to the data in the data grid will be immediately reflected in the dataset, those changes won't be written back to the database until the application calls the data adapter's Update method.

The design of the Product Maintenance form

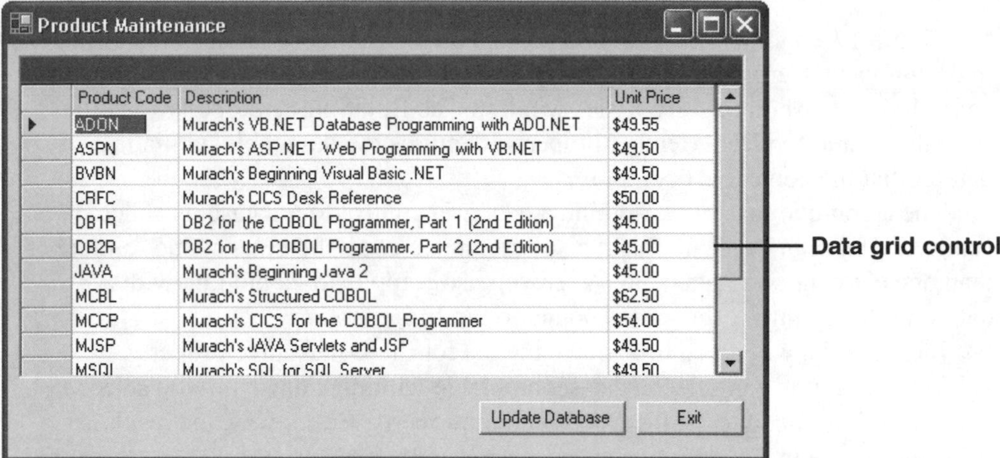

Description

- The Product Maintenance application lets the user view, add, modify, and delete rows in the Products table. To do that, it uses a *data grid control*, which displays data in a row and column format.
- The data grid control provides built-in functionality for maintaining the data in a data table. Because of that, no code is required to display the data or to implement the add, modify, and delete operations.
- When this application is first loaded, it retrieves data from the database and stores it in the data table used by the data grid.
- When the user clicks the Update Database button, the database is updated with changes made to the dataset. The user can click this button after one row or a group of rows have been added, changed, or deleted.
- To use the built-in functionality of a data grid control, you must *bind* it to a data table as described in figure 17-15. Then, you can work with the data as described in figure 17-18.
- The ContinueUpdateOnError property is set to True so an exception won't be thrown if a concurrency error occurs.

Figure 17-14 A Product Maintenance application that uses a bound data grid control

How to bind a data grid control to a dataset

Figure 17-15 shows the data grid control on the Product Maintenance form in design view. Here, you can see the two properties for binding a data grid control to a dataset in the Properties window. The DataSource property identifies the dataset, and the DataMember property identifies the data table within the dataset that the control is bound to.

The technique that's used to bind a data grid control to a dataset is called *complex data binding*. With this type of binding, a control can be bound to more than one element of a data table. When you use complex data binding with a data grid, for example, the grid is bound to the entire table.

Incidentally, when you drop down the list for the DataSource property, you'll see that you can select a dataset or a table within a dataset. If you select a table, you don't need to set the DataMember property. Either way, the result is the same, so the technique you use is a matter of preference.

A data grid control bound to the Products table

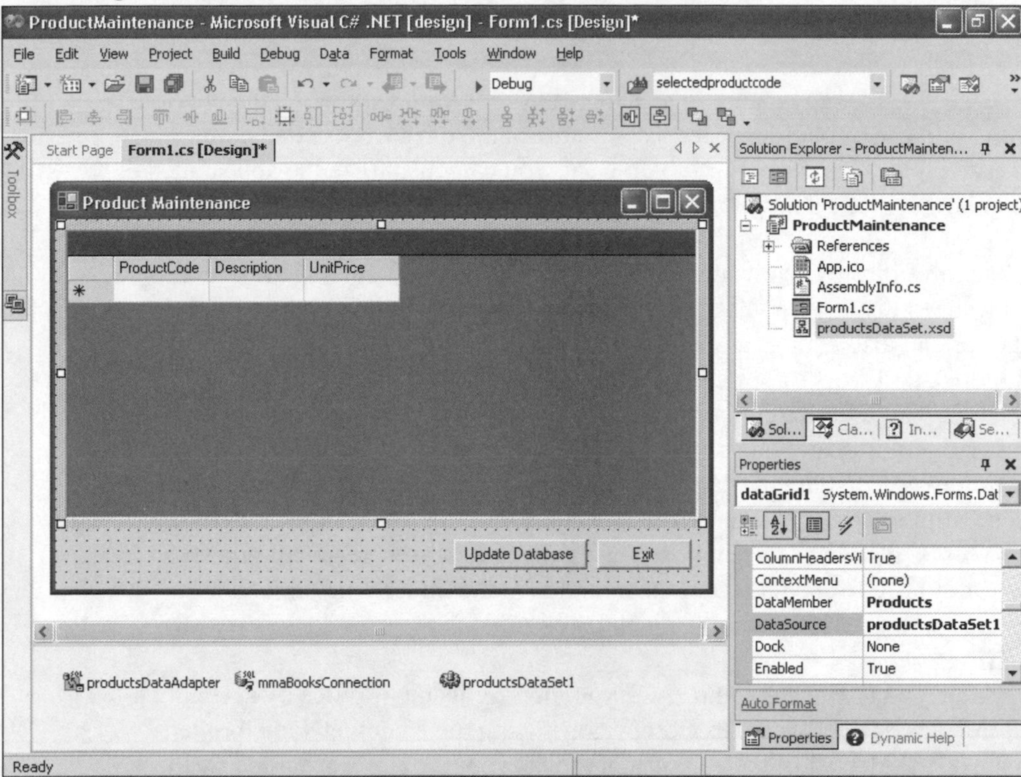

The properties for binding a data grid control to a dataset

Property	Description
DataSource	A data source, such as a dataset.
DataMember	The name of a data table associated with the data source.

Description

- You bind a data grid control to a dataset using a technique called *complex data binding*. This just means that the control is bound to more than one data element. A data grid control, for example, is bound to an entire table.
- To bind a data grid control, you set its DataSource and DataMember properties as indicated above. Then, all of the rows and columns in the table you specify are displayed in the data grid.

Note

- You can also set the DataSource property so it points to a specific data table. In that case, you set the DataMember property to (none).

Figure 17-15 How to bind a data grid control to a dataset

How to customize the column layout for a data grid control

By default, each column in a data grid has the width shown in the previous figure, and each column header displays the name of the associated column in the data table. If that's not what you want, you can customize the appearance of the columns in the data grid as described in figure 17-16.

To start, you create a *table style* for the grid using the DataGridTableStyle Collection Editor. Then, you identify the data table that contains the columns you want to display by selecting it from the MappingName property drop-down list. You can also change any of the other table style properties so that the data grid looks and works the way you want it to.

Next, you create a column style for each column you want to display in the data grid. To do that, you use the DataGridColumnStyle Collection Editor. This editor lets you display the data in each column of the data table in a text box or, if a column contains Boolean data, in a check box. In this example, all of the data will be displayed in text boxes. Note that when you create column styles, you don't have to include all of the columns in the underlying table. For example, you may want to omit an identity column so the user doesn't try to modify it.

After you create a column style, you identify its data source by selecting a column name from the list that drops down from the MappingName property. This list includes all of the columns in the data source that's specified by the MappingName property of the table style. In this case, it's all of the columns in the Products table.

Some of the other properties you'll use frequently are Alignment, which specifies the alignment of the data within a column; HeaderText, which specifies the text that's displayed in the column header; and Width, which determines the width of the column. Finally, you can use the Format property to specify how the data in the column should be formatted when it's displayed. When you format columns, you can use any of the standard formatting codes provided by the .NET Framework.

The Collection Editor Dialog Boxes

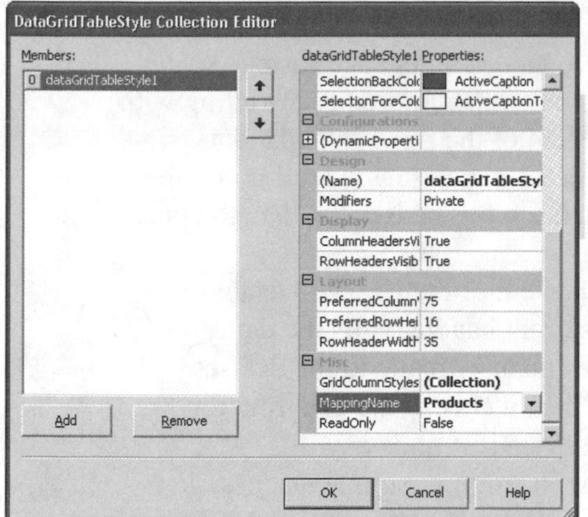

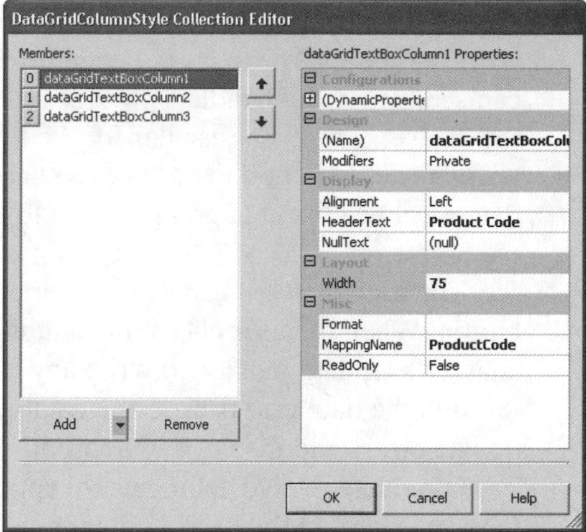

Column styles used for the Product Maintenance application

Column style name	MappingName	Width	HeaderText	Format
dataGridTextBoxColumn1	ProductCode	75	Product Code	
dataGridTextBoxColumn2	Description	300	Description	
dataGridTextBoxColumn3	UnitPrice	75	Unit Price	c

Description

- To customize the column layout for a data grid control, you create a *table style* for the data table that's displayed by the grid and a *column style* for each column that's displayed.
- To create a table style, click the TableStyles property for the data grid control in the Properties window, then click on the ellipsis (…) that appears for that property. Click the Add button to create a new table style, then set the properties the way you want them. At the least, you should set the MappingName property to the data table to be displayed.
- To create column styles, click the GridColumnStyles property in the DataGridTableStyle Collection Editor dialog box, then click the ellipsis that appears for that property.
- To create a column style, click Add, then set the properties for the column style. At the minimum, you should set the MappingName property to the column to be displayed. You may also want to set the Width, HeaderText, and Format properties.

Figure 17-16 How to customize the column layout for a data grid control

The code for the Product Maintenance application

Figure 17-17 presents the code for the Product Maintenance form. As you can see, two event handlers provide all the code that's required for working with the dataset. The event handler for the Load event of the form calls the data adapter's Fill method to retrieve the data from the database and load it into the dataset. Since the data grid is bound to the dataset, this causes the data to appear on the form.

The second event handler is for the Click event of the Update Database button. When the user clicks this button, this event handler calls the data adapter's Update method to write any updates the user made to the dataset through the data grid back to the database. Then, it checks the data row for update errors and displays an appropriate message if it finds any.

Of course, we've deliberately kept this application as simple as possible so you can focus on the basic skills for creating and working with ADO.NET objects. In practice, you usually won't use a data grid control to manage the maintenance functions of a dataset. In addition, you'll usually have to handle any concurrency exceptions that are thrown by an application.

The event handlers for the Product Maintenance application

```
private void frmProductMaintenance_Load(object sender, System.EventArgs e)
{
    try
    {
        productsDataAdapter.Fill(productsDataSet1);
    }
    catch (SqlException)
    {
        MessageBox.Show("A database error has occurred.", "Database Error",
            MessageBoxButtons.OK, MessageBoxIcon.Exclamation);
    }
}

private void btnUpdateDatabase_Click(object sender, System.EventArgs e)
{
    if (productsDataSet1.HasChanges())
    {
        try
        {
            productsDataAdapter.Update(productsDataSet1);
        }
        catch (SqlException ex)
        {
            string errorMessage = "Database error #" + ex.Number +
                ": " + ex.Message;
            MessageBox.Show(errorMessage, "SQL Server error");
        }
        if (productsDataSet1.HasErrors)
        {
            string errorMessage = "The following rows were not updated: \n\n";
            foreach (productsDataSet.ProductsRow productRow
                    in productsDataSet1.Products.Rows)
            {
                if (productRow.HasErrors)
                    errorMessage += productRow.ProductCode.Trim() + ": " +
                    productRow.RowError + "\n";
            }
            MessageBox.Show(errorMessage, "Update errors");
        }
    }
}

private void btnClose_Click(object sender, System.EventArgs e)
{
    this.Close();
}
```

Figure 17-17 The code for the Product Maintenance form's event handlers

How to work with the data in a data grid control

If you haven't used a data grid control before, you may be wondering how to work with the data it displays. So figure 17-18 summarizes the techniques for doing that. In addition, it shows how the data grid automatically displays update errors.

To modify an existing row, you simply click in the column whose value you want to change and enter the change. Then, the change is saved to the dataset when you press the Tab key to move to the next column or the Enter key to move to the next row. The change is also saved if you click anywhere else in the data grid. Of course, the data you enter must be valid for the data type of the data column that the column of the data grid is bound to. If it's not, the data grid will reject the change and redisplay the original value.

To delete a row, you start by clicking on the row header to the left of the row to select it. Then, you press the Delete key to delete it. Note that the row is deleted immediately without any confirmation.

To add a new row, you scroll to the last row in the data grid. This row has an asterisk in the row header. Then, you can enter the appropriate value in each column as shown in the form at the top of this figure. Note that as soon as you begin entering a new row, another blank row is added at the bottom of the control.

If you realize that you've made a mistake as you enter a value in a column, you can press the Esc key to cancel the change. Then, the column returns to its original value. You can also return the values in all of the columns in a row to their original values by pressing the Esc key twice. Note, however, that this works only if you don't have the CancelButton property of the form set to a button control. If you do, the Click event of that button is executed the second time you press the Esc key.

If update errors occur when you update the database with changes you make to a dataset, the data grid automatically displays an error icon for the rows that have errors. Then, if you place the mouse pointer over this icon, a data tip that describes the error is displayed. In the second form in this figure, for example, you can see that a concurrency error occurred. Note, however, that the add operation that was started in the first form was completed successfully. That's because the ContinueUpdateOnError property of the data adapter was set to True so that an error wouldn't cause the update operation to end.

The Product Maintenance program with a row being added to the data grid

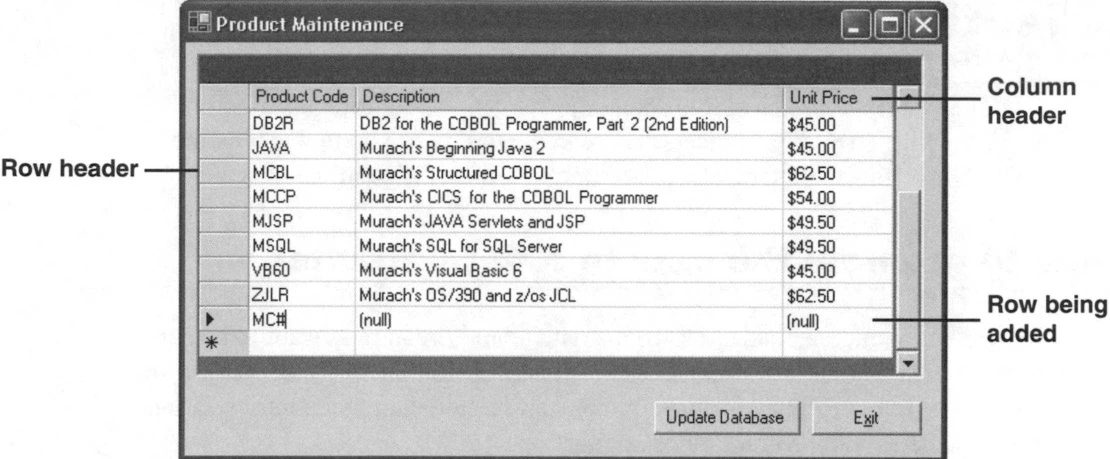

The Product Maintenance application showing a concurrency error

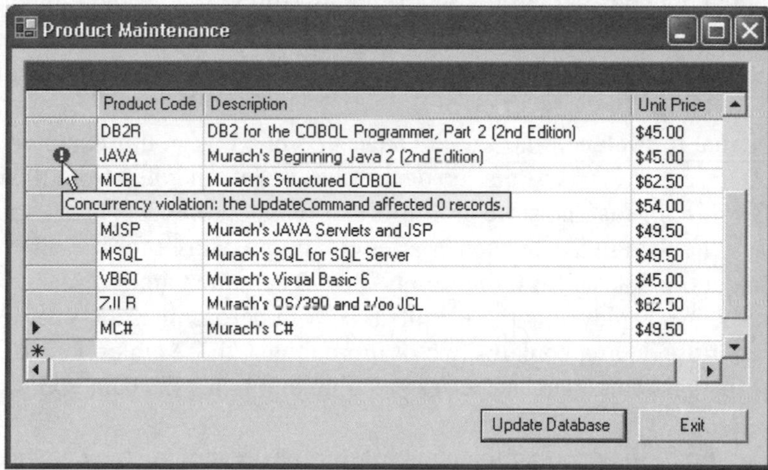

Basic techniques for working with the data in a data grid

- The data grid control works much like a spreadsheet. You can change the value in any column by typing a new value. To delete a row, click the row header and press Delete. To add a row, scroll to the bottom of the dataset, click in the row that has an asterisk (*) in the row header, and enter the data for each column of the new row.
- To cancel a change, press the Esc key. To cancel all the changes made to a row, press the Esc key twice.
- If a concurrency error or other type of error occurs, the data grid control marks the row in error with an exclamation mark. You can point the mouse at the exclamation mark to see a description of the error.

Figure 17-18 How to work with the data in a data grid control

Other skills for working with ADO.NET objects

The last three topics of this chapter present some additional skills for working with ADO.NET objects. These skills will help you understand the ADO.NET objects better and work with them more efficiently.

How to preview the data in a data adapter

Before you create a dataset from a data adapter, you may want to be sure that the data adapter retrieves the correct data. To do that, you can preview the data as shown in figure 17-19. Here, you can see the data that's retrieved and used by the Product Maintenance application.

When you first display the Data Adapter Preview dialog box, the Results box will be empty. Then, you can click the Fill Dataset button to retrieve the data defined by the data adapter in the Data Adapters combo box. If more than one data adapter is defined, you can select the one you want to use from this combo box. When you make a selection and click the Fill Dataset button, the results are displayed in the Results box.

Notice that the value of the Target Dataset combo box in this example is Untyped Dataset. That means that no dataset has been generated from the data adapter. Because of that, no structural information about the data is available. If you preview the data in a data adapter after creating a dataset for it, however, you can select the dataset from this combo box. Then, the names of the columns in the dataset are displayed in the Results box even before the data is retrieved. In addition, if the dataset contains two or more tables, those tables are listed in the Data Tables list, and you can select the table that holds the data you want to display.

Keep in mind, though, that the main reason for previewing the data in a data adapter is to be sure it's what you want *before* you generate a dataset for it. Because of that, you'll typically work with an *untyped dataset* as shown in this figure.

The dialog box for previewing the data in a data adapter

Data Adapter Preview

Data adapters: productsDataAdapter

Fill Dataset

Parameters:

Adapter	Name	Data Type	Value

Target dataset: ProductMaintenance.prod

Data tables: Products

Results: Dataset Size: 2526 bytes (2.4 Kb)

Products: 14 Row(s)

ProductCode	Description	UnitPrice
ADON	Murach's VB.	49.5500
ASPN	Murach's ASP	49.5000
BVBN	Murach's Begi	49.5000
CRFC	Murach's CIC	50.0000
DB1R	DB2 for the C	45.0000
DB2R	DB2 for the C	45.0000
JAVA	Murach's Begi	45.0000
MC#	Murach's C#	49.5000
MCBL	Murach's Stru	62.5000
MCCP	Murach's CIC	54.0000
MJSP	Murach's JAV	49.5000
MSQL	Murach's SQL	49.5000
VB60	Murach's Visu	45.0000
ZJLR	Murach's OS/	62.5000

Clear Results Close Help

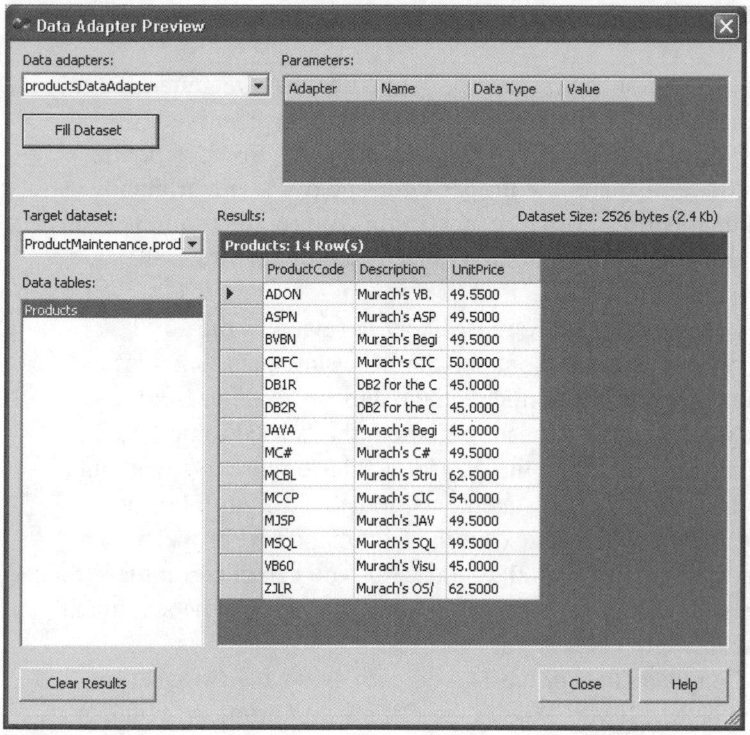

Description

- To preview the data in a data adapter, select the Data→Preview Data command or click on the Preview Data link that's displayed in the Properties window for the data adapter. This displays the Data Adapter Preview dialog box.
- To display the data specified by a data adapter, select the data adapter from the combo box at the top of the dialog box and then click the Fill Dataset button. The results are displayed in the Results box.
- You can sort the results by clicking on the header for the column you want to sort by. Click once to sort in ascending sequence. Click again to sort in descending sequence.
- You can change the width of a column by dragging the line to the right of its column header or by double-clicking on this line to change the column width so it accommodates the values in all the rows.
- If you've already created a dataset from a data adapter, you can select the dataset from the Target dataset list. Then, the column headers for the columns in that dataset are displayed in the Results box before the results are retrieved. Otherwise, the results are saved in an *untyped dataset* whose structure is unknown until the data is retrieved.
- If the dataset you select contains two or more tables, you can select the table you want to display by highlighting it in the Data Tables list.

Figure 17-19 How to preview the data in a data adapter

How to review the properties for generated ADO.NET objects

Figure 17-20 shows how you can review the properties that are generated for the data adapter, command, and connection objects. As you have learned, the data adapter includes properties that refer to the related Select, Insert, Update, and Delete commands. If you expand the property for one of these command objects, you can see the properties of that object. In this figure, for example, you can see the properties of the Update command object used by the Product Maintenance form.

The command object property you're most likely to review is the CommandText property. This property contains the SQL statement that's issued when the Update method is executed to update the database. In this case, the CommandText property contains the Update statement that's used to update the database with changes made to a row in the dataset. I'll have more to say about this statement and the Insert and Delete statements in the next figure. For now, just realize that you can display the full text of the CommandText property in a ToolTip by pointing to the property with the mouse. Or you can click on the ellipsis button that appears when you select the property to display the statement in the Query Builder window.

In addition to the CommandText property, you can review the Connection property of a command object. If you expand the Connection property, you can see the properties of the connection object as shown in this figure. Specifically, you can see the value of the ConnectionString property, which provides the information that the command object will use to connect to the database. The connection string in this example can be used to connect to a database named MMABooks in a data source named DOUG\VSdotNET. Although this string contains other information, you don't need to worry about it when you use the Configuration Wizard since it's generated for you based on the information you supply.

Each ADO.NET object also has a Name property. When the Configuration Wizard creates an object, it gives it a generic name like sqlDataAdapter1, sqlConnection1, or sqlSelectCommand1. In most cases, you'll want to change the names of these objects to reflect their contents and make them easier to work with.

If you change the name of one of these objects, you should know that the properties in related objects are changed automatically. If you change the name of the connection object, for example, the Connection properties in all of the related command objects are changed. And if you change the name of a command object, the related property in the data adapter object is changed.

The UpdateCommand property for a data adapter

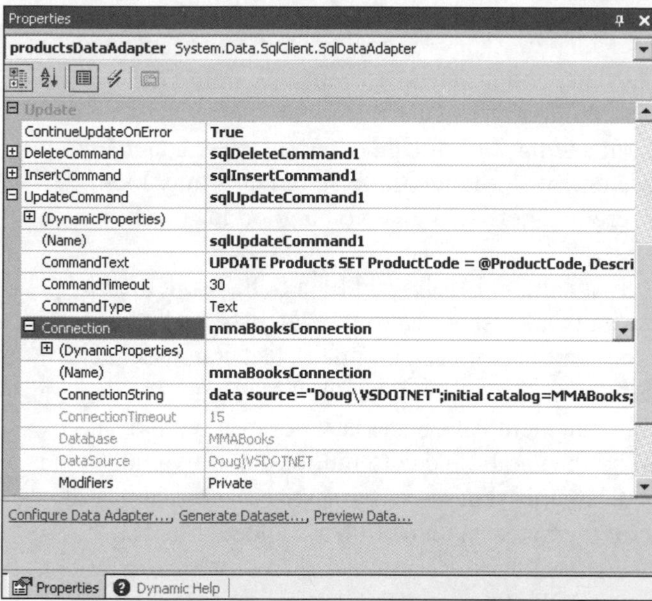

Description

- You can use the Properties window to review the properties that are generated by the Configuration Wizard for the data adapter, command, and connection objects.
- The properties in the Update group for a data adapter include the insert, update, and delete command objects. You can expand these objects to see their properties, and you can expand the connection object within each command object to see its properties.
- To work with the SQL statement in a CommandText property, you can click on the ellipsis button that appears when that property is selected. This displays the statement in the Query Builder window.

Figure 17-20 How to review the properties for generated ADO.NET objects

How to interpret the generated SQL statements

The Update method of a data adapter issues the SQL statements associated with the data adapter's Insert, Update, and Delete statements. To help you understand what these statements do, figure 17-21 presents the Select statement for the Product Maintenance form and the Insert, Update, and Delete statements that were generated from this statement. Although these statements may look complicated, the information presented here will give you a good idea of how they work.

To start, notice that the Insert statement is followed by a Select statement. This statement retrieves the row that was just added to the database and uses it to update the row in the dataset. You may remember that this Select statement is added if you select the Refresh the DataSet option when you configure the data adapter. In this case, though, this statement isn't necessary because none of the data for a new row is generated by the database due to null or default value settings. As a result, you could delete this statement to improve the efficiency of the operation. The same is true of the Select statement that's added after the Update statement.

Another option that affects the SQL statements that are generated is the Use Optimistic Concurrency option. If you select this option, code is added to the Where clauses of the Update and Delete statements to check whether any of the columns have changed since they were retrieved from the database. This code compares the current value of each column in the database against the original value of the column, which is stored in the dataset. If none of the values have changed, the operation is performed. Otherwise, it's not.

Most of the statements in this figure use one or more *parameters*, variables whose names start with an at sign (@). For example, parameters are used in the Values clause of the Insert statement and the Set clause of the Update statement to refer to the current values of the columns in the dataset. They're used in the Where clauses of the Update and Delete statements to refer to the original values of the columns in the dataset. And they're used in the Where clauses of the Select statements after the Insert and Update statements to refer to the current row. The wizard inserts parameters when it creates the command objects for a data adapter. Then, before each statement is executed, the database server substitutes the appropriate value for each variable.

This should give you more perspective on how the dataset is refreshed and how optimistic concurrency is provided when you use ADO.NET. Because of the disconnected data architecture, these features can't be provided by the database management system or by ADO.NET. Instead, they are provided by the SQL statements that are generated by the Configuration Wizard.

SQL that retrieves product rows

```
SELECT
  ProductCode,
  Description,
  UnitPrice
FROM
  Products ORDER BY ProductCode
```

SQL that inserts a product row and refreshes the dataset

```
INSERT INTO Products(ProductCode, Description, UnitPrice)
     VALUES (@ProductCode, @Description, @UnitPrice);
SELECT ProductCode, Description, UnitPrice FROM Products
    WHERE (ProductCode = @ProductCode)
```

SQL that updates a vendor row and refreshes the dataset

```
UPDATE Products
    SET ProductCode = @ProductCode,
        Description = @Description,
        UnitPrice = @UnitPrice
    WHERE (ProductCode = @Original_ProductCode)
      AND (Description = @Original_Description)
      AND (UnitPrice = @Original_UnitPrice);
SELECT ProductCode, Description, UnitPrice FROM Products
    WHERE (ProductCode = @ProductCode)
```

A SQL Delete statement that deletes a vendor row

```
DELETE FROM Products
    WHERE (ProductCode = @Original_ProductCode)
      AND (Description = @Original_Description)
      AND (UnitPrice = @Original_UnitPrice)
```

Description

- If you select the Use Optimistic Concurrency option when you create a data adapter, the wizard adds code to the Update and Delete statements that checks that the data hasn't changed since it was retrieved.
- If you select the Refresh the DataSet option, the wizard adds a Select statement after the Insert and Update statements that refreshes the new or modified row in the dataset.
- The SQL statements use *parameters* to identify the new values for an insert or update operation. Parameters are also used for the original column values, which are used to check that a row hasn't changed for an update or delete operation. The values for these parameters are stored in and retrieved from the dataset.
- If a table contains an identity column, the *system function* named @@IDENTITY is used to get the value that's generated for a new row so the row in the dataset can be refreshed.

Figure 17-21 How to interpret the generated SQL statements

Perspective

In this chapter, you learned the basic skills for creating and working with ADO.NET objects. But there's a lot more to learn about ADO.NET. So in the next three chapters, you'll learn how to use ADO.NET with bound controls like text boxes, you'll learn how to use ADO.NET with unbound controls, and you'll learn how to use data commands without using a data adapter.

Summary

- You can use the Data Adapter Configuration Wizard to create a data adapter and the connection and command objects it uses to work with a database.
- The Wizard can generate the Insert, Update, and Delete statements that will be used to update the database from the Select statement you specify.
- The *Query Builder* provides a visual interface you can use to generate a Select statement based on the selections you make.
- After you create a data adapter, you can generate a dataset *schema file* that defines the structure of the dataset in which the data adapter will store the data it retrieves. You can also generate and instantiate a dataset class.
- To load data into a data table, you use the Fill method of the data adapter. To remove all the data from a dataset or data table, you use the Clear method of the dataset or data table. And to update the database with changes made to a data table, you use the Update method of the data adapter.
- When you perform a multi-row update, you'll want the data adapter to process all the rows without throwing an error. Then, you can use the properties of the row, table, and dataset to handle any errors that occurred.
- You can use *complex data binding* to bind a *data grid control* to a data table. Then, the data grid control displays the data in the data table automatically. It also provides for adding, updating, and deleting rows in the table.
- You can use *table styles* and *column styles* to customize the column layout for a data grid control.

Terms

Query Builder
diagram pane
grid pane
SQL pane
results pane
table mappings
schema file
typed dataset
data grid control
bound control
complex data binding
table style
column style
untyped dataset
parameter

Objectives

- Given the data requirements for a form, use the Data Adapter Configuration Wizard to define a data adapter that provides access to that data.
- Given the specifications for an application that uses a data grid control to work with the data in a dataset, design and code the application.
- Describe the objects that the Data Adapter Configuration Wizard generates and explain how they're related.
- Explain how you use a data adapter and dataset to work with database data.
- Explain how you typically handle concurrency errors for a multi-row update.
- Define complex data binding and explain how you use it with a data grid.

Exercise 17-1 Create a data adapter and preview the data

In this exercise, you'll create a data adapter using the Data Adapter Configuration Wizard. Then, you'll preview the data defined by that adapter.

Before you start these exercises...

If you're going to use MSDE on your own PC to do the database exercises for this book, you need to install MSDE and attach the MMABooks database to it. If you haven't already done that, please refer to appendix A. If the MMABooks database is going to be on the server at your company or school, you need to find out what information you need for establishing a connection to the database.

Start a new project and create the data adapter

1. Start Visual Studio, and then start a new project named ProductMaintenance in the C:\C#.NET\Chapter 17 directory.
2. Open the Toolbox, click on the Data tab, and then double-click on the SqlDataAdapter component to start the Data Adapter Configuration Wizard.
3. Click the Next button in the Welcome dialog box to display the dialog box for selecting the connection. Then, click the New Connection button to display the Data Link Properties dialog box.
4. Enter the information for connecting to the MMABooks database into the Connection tab of this dialog box. Then, click the Test button to make sure the connection works. If it doesn't, fix the entries and test it again. Once you have it working, click the OK button to return to the previous dialog box.
5. Click the Next button to display the Choose a Query Type dialog box. Make sure the Use SQL Statements option is selected, and then click the Next button to display the Generate the SQL Statements dialog box.

6. Click the Query Builder button to display the Query Builder window. Add the Products table to the diagram pane of the Query builder using the Add Table dialog box, then close this dialog box.
7. Check the ProductCode, Description, and UnitPrice fields in the Products table. Then, select the Ascending option from the Sort Type column of the ProductCode field in the grid pane. A Select statement like the one shown in the SQL pane in figure 17-4 should be generated.
8. Right-click in the diagram pane and select the Run command from the shortcut menu. The results of the query will be displayed in the results pane as shown in figure 17-4. Click the OK button to return to the Wizard.
9. Click the Advanced Options button in the Generate the SQL Statements dialog box. Remove the check mark from the Refresh the DataSet option and then click the OK button.
10. Click the Next button in the Generate the SQL Statements dialog box to display the View Wizard Results dialog box. This dialog box should indicate that Select, Insert, Update, and Delete statements were generated along with table mappings. Click the Finish button to create the data adapter, command, and connection objects.

Review the properties of the ADO.NET objects and preview the data

11. Click on the data adapter object in the Component Designer tray to display its properties in the Properties window. Then, click on the plus sign to the left of the SelectCommand group to display and review the properties for the command object that contains the Select statement. Next, click on the plus sign to the left of the Connection group to display and review the properties for this object.
12. Expand the InsertCommand group for the data adapter, click on the CommandText property, and then click on the ellipsis button that's displayed. The Insert statement that's executed when a row is added to the database will be displayed in the Query Builder window. Notice that a Select statement isn't included after this statement since you deselected the Refresh the DataSet option. Review the Insert statement, and then close this window. Repeat this procedure for the UpdateCommand and DeleteCommand groups.
13. With the data adapter still selected, click the Preview Data link at the bottom of the Properties window to display the Data Adapter Preview dialog box. Click the Fill Dataset button to display the results of the Select statement.
14. To widen the DescriptionName column so you can see all the data in each row, double-click on the line to the right of the column header. When the mouse pointer is in the right position, a double-headed arrow will appear. Review the results and close the dialog box.
15. Save the project and keep the solution open if you're going to continue with the next exercise. Otherwise, close the solution.

Exercise 17-2 Create the Product Maintenance form

In this exercise, you'll create a Product Maintenance form like the one shown in figure 17-14 that uses a data grid control to work with the data in a dataset.

Open the project and generate the dataset

1. If it's not already open, open the project you created in exercise 17-1.
2. Select the data adapter object in the Component Designer tray, and then click the Generate Dataset link at the bottom of the Properties window to display the Generate Dataset dialog box.
3. With the New option selected, enter productsDataSet for the name of the dataset. Then, make sure that the Products table and the Add This Dataset to the Designer option are selected, and click the OK button. A dataset schema file named productsDataSet.xsd should appear in the Solution Explorer, and a dataset object named productsDataSet1 should appear in the Component Designer tray.

Design and code the form

4. Add two button controls to the default form, name them btnUpdateDatabase and btnExit, and change their Text properties so they look like the buttons shown in figure 17-15. Then, change the properties of the form so it looks like the one in this figure.
5. Double-click on the form to open the Code Editor window and start an event handler for the Load event. Then, enter a statement to fill the dataset.
6. Start an event handler for the Click event of the Update Database button, and then enter a statement to update the database. This statement should be executed only if changes have been madc to thc dataset.
7. Start an event handler for the Click event of the Exit button, and then enter a statement to close the form.
8. Add a data grid control to the form, and then size and position the form and its controls so it looks like the one shown in figure 17-15. Then, select the data grid control and set the DataSource and DataMember properties so they refer to the Products table in the dataset you created.
9. Add a table style and column styles to the data grid so that it will appear as shown in figure 17-14.

Build and test the form

10. Run the project and change the data in any row and column of the data grid. (You can widen the Description column first if you want to so you can see all of the data.) Notice the pencil icon that appears in the row header of the changed row to indicate that it's being changed. Now, press the Tab key to move to the next column and update the row in the dataset.

11. Scroll to the bottom of the data in the data grid, and click in the first column of the last row (the one with an asterisk in its row header). The word (null) will appear in each column to indicate that no data has been entered. Enter a product code, description, and unit price for the new row, pressing the Tab key to move from one column to the next. When you press the Tab key from the last column, the new row is added to the dataset.
12. Click the Update Database button to apply the changes to the database. Then, click on the column header for the Product Code column to sort the products by product code. This will move the product you just added to the appropriate position in the data grid. Click on the Product Code column header again to see that the products are now sorted in descending sequence by product code.
13. Locate the row you just added and click on its row header. Then, press the Delete key to delete it from the dataset, and click the Update Database button to delete it from the database. When you're through experimenting, close the form.

Add exception handling

14. Add code to the Load event handler that will catch any SQL exceptions that occur when the dataset is filled. If an error occurs, this code should display a dialog box with a generic error message.
15. Add code to the event handler for the Click event of the Update Database button that catches any SQL exceptions that occur when the database is updated. If an error occurs, this code should display a dialog box with a message that includes the Number and Message properties of the exception object.
16. Add code to the Click event handler that checks for errors in the dataset following the update. If any errors occur, this code should display the product code and RowError property of each row in error.
17. Set the ContinueUpdateOnError property of the data adapter to True.
18. Run the application and change the data for one of the products, but don't click the Update Database button.
19. Use the Windows Explorer to locate the executable file for this application in the C:\C#.NET\Chapter 17\ProductMaintenance\bin\Debug directory. Double-click on this file to start another copy of the application. Make a change to same product as in step 18, and click the Update Database button. Close the application.
20. Return to the first copy of the application, and click the Update Database button. When you do, a dialog box should be displayed indicating that a concurrency error occurred, and an exclamation mark should appear in the row header for the product.
21. If this worked correctly, close the dialog box, the application, and the solution. Otherwise, make the necessary corrections.

18

How to work with datasets using bound controls

In the last chapter, you learned how to use the Data Adapter Configuration Wizard to generate a typed dataset. You also learned how to use a data grid control that's bound to that dataset to work with its data. In this chapter, you'll learn more about how typed datasets work and how you can bind other controls like text boxes and combo boxes to them.

How to work with typed datasets

A typed dataset class includes definitions for several classes. In addition to the dataset class itself, three classes are generated for each table in the dataset. Figure 18-1 lists two of these classes and some of the properties and methods they provide. For example, the dataset class includes a property that lets you retrieve a table from the dataset, the data table class includes a property that lets you retrieve a row from the table, and the data row class includes a property that lets you retrieve a column value from a row.

Notice that the names of some of the classes, properties, and methods depend on the name of the table or a column in the table. For example, the name of the class that defines a row in the Products table is named ProductsRow. Similarly, the name of the property that lets you retrieve the Products table from the dataset is Products, and the name of the property that lets you retrieve the value of the ProductCode column from a row in the Products table is ProductCode.

The code example in this figure illustrates how this works. Here, the first statement declares a variable named productRow as a ProductsRow. Then, the next statement retrieves the first row in the Products table and assigns it to that variable. To do that, it uses the Products property of the productsDataSet1 dataset to retrieve the Products table. Then, it uses the Item property of the Products table to retrieve the first row in the table, which has an index value of 0. Finally, the last statement in this example uses the Description property of the row to retrieve the value of the Description column and assign it to the Text property of a text box.

Although it's not necessary for you to understand the details of how a typed dataset is implemented, you do need to be aware of the properties and methods that are provided by a typed dataset so that you can use them when necessary. As you'll see in this chapter, you'll use basic properties like the ones shown in the example in this figure when you work with bound controls. When you work with unbound controls, however, you'll use some of the other properties and methods listed in this figure. You'll learn more about these in the next chapter.

In addition to the properties and methods shown in this figure, you should know that each class that's defined by a typed dataset inherits properties and methods from another class. Specifically, the dataset class inherits the DataSet class, the data table class inherits the DataTable class, and the data row class inherits the DataRow class. Because of that, you can use the properties and methods defined by those classes in addition to the ones defined by the typed dataset. You'll see how some of these properties and methods are used in chapter 20.

Classes defined by a typed dataset

Class	Description	Example
Dataset	The dataset itself.	productsDataSet
Data table	A table in the dataset.	ProductsDataTable
Data row	A row in the data table.	ProductsRow

The dataset class

Property	Description	Example
`tablename`	Gets a table.	Products

The data table class

Property	Description	
`Count`	Gets the number of rows in the table.	
`Item`	Gets the row with the specified index.	
Method	**Description**	**Example**
`Add``tablename`**`Row()`**	Adds the specified data row to the table, or adds a row with the specified values to the table.	AddProductsRow
`FindBy``columnname`**`()`**	Finds a row based on the specified key value.	FindByProductCode
`New``tablename`**`Row()`**	Creates a new row based on the table definition.	NewProductsRow
`Remove``tablename`**`Row()`**	Removes the specified data row from the table.	RemoveProductsRow

The data row class

Property	Description	Example
`columnname`	Gets or sets the value of a column.	ProductCode

Code that retrieves a data row and the value of a column in that row

```
productsDataSet.ProductsRow productRow;
productRow = productsDataSet1.Products.Item[0];
txtDescription.Text = productRow.Description;
```

Description

- When you create a typed dataset, you can use the classes, properties, and methods it defines to work with the dataset.
- The names of some of the classes, properties, and methods depend on the names of the tables and columns.
- The dataset, data table, and data row classes of a typed dataset inherit the DataSet, DataTable, and DataRow classes respectively. That means that they can use the properties and methods defined by those classes.

Figure 18-1 How to work with typed datasets

How to bind controls to individual data columns

In the topics that follow, you'll learn how use bound text box controls to display the data in the individual columns of a data table. When you bind controls to individual data columns, the data in the current row of the table is displayed in those controls. Then, you can navigate through the other rows to display the data they contain.

A Product Display form that uses bound controls

To illustrate the basic skills for working with bound controls, I'll use the Product Display form shown in figure 18-2. This form lets the user display the data in the Products table. To do that, each text box on this form is bound to an individual column in the Products table. Then, the user can click the navigation buttons that are provided to move from one row in this table to another.

Notice that the number of the current row and the total number of rows in the table are displayed in a label between the navigation buttons. That helps give the users a feel for where they are in the table. Keep in mind, though, that if the table is large, you'll want to provide a way for users to access a row directly rather than having to scroll through hundreds of rows to get to a specific one. You'll learn one way to do that later in this chapter.

The Product Display form

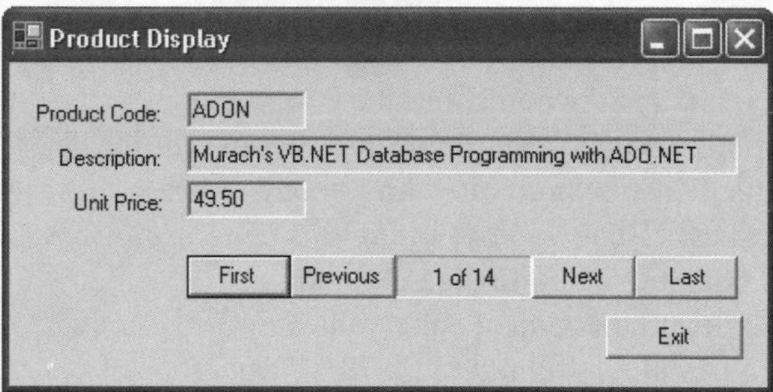

Description

- The Product Display form lets you display the data in a single row of the Products data table. To do that, each of the text boxes on this form is bound to an individual column in the table.
- When this form is first displayed, it contains the data from the first row in the Products table. To navigate to another row, the user can click the First, Previous, Next, or Last button.
- To give users an idea of where they are in the table, this form includes a label control that indicates the position of the row that's currently displayed and the total number of rows in the table.
- Although the navigation provided by this form is acceptable for a dataset that contains a small number of rows, it may be unwieldy for datasets that contain more than a few dozen rows.

The data adapter used by this form

- This form uses a data adapter to retrieve data from the Products table in the database. See figure 18-6 for details.

Figure 18-2 A Product Display form that uses bound controls

How to bind text box controls

Figure 18-3 shows how to bind a text box control to a data column. To do that, you expand the DataBindings group for the control in the Properties window and then select the appropriate column from the drop-down list for the Text property. In this case, the Product Code text box is being bound to the ProductCode column of the Products table. This type of binding is called *simple data binding* because the control is bound to a single data element.

When you run a form with bound text box controls, the values in the bound columns of the current row are automatically assigned to the Text properties of the controls. That causes the values to be displayed in the text boxes. Then, as you move from one row to another, the data in the controls changes to reflect the data in the current row. In addition, if you change the data in one or more of the bound controls, those changes are saved to the row when you move to another row. (Although the Product Display form doesn't provide for modifications, it could easily be changed to do so.) You'll learn how to move from one row to another in figure 18-5.

A text box that's bound to a column in the Products data table

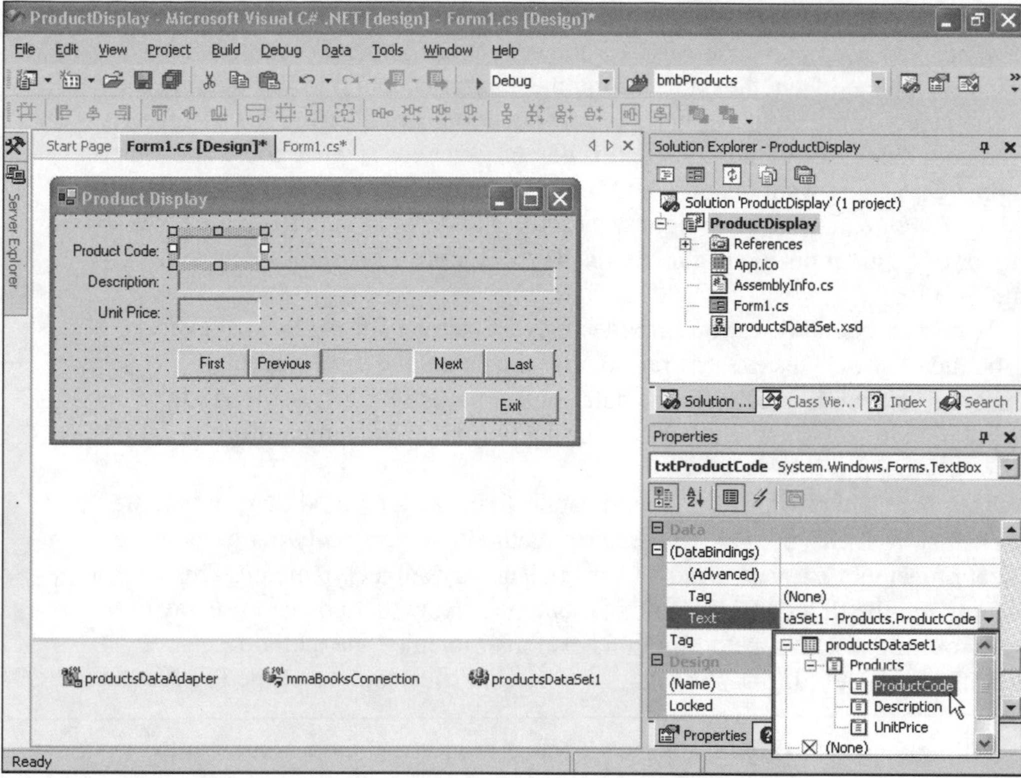

How to bind a text box control to a data column

- To bind a text box control to a data column, set the Text property in the DataBindings group to the name of the data column. This type of binding is called *simple data binding* because the control is bound to a single data element, in this case, a single column value.
- When a text box is bound to a data column, the value of that column in the current row is displayed in the control as the program executes. In addition, if the value of the control changes, that value is saved in the data table.
- The drop-down list that's available for the Text property lists all of the datasets, data tables, and data columns that are available to the project, so you can navigate through this list to locate the column you want.

Figure 18-3 How to bind text box controls

How to format bound data

When you use bound controls, the contents of each bound control is automatically obtained from the data column the control is bound to. By default, the data obtained from the data column is converted to a string before it's assigned to the bound control. In most cases, this default behavior is what you want. But in some cases, you want to apply additional formatting to the data before it's displayed. For example, you might want to format decimal data to control the number of decimal positions that are displayed. Figure 18-4 shows how to do that.

To format bound data, you provide an event handler for the Format event of the bound control. This event is raised after the data to be displayed by the control has been retrieved from the data source, but before it's assigned to the control. As a result, the event handler for the Format event can modify the data before it's displayed.

The first step to formatting bound data is to create a method that can handle the Format event. To do that, you create a method that accepts two arguments: an Object object named *sender* and a ConvertEventArgs object named *e*. This is illustrated in the first code example in this figure. Note that you can use any name you want for this method. In this example, I named the method FormatPrice since it formats the value of the UnitPrice column of the Products table.

Within this method, you can use the Value property of the e argument to work with the column value. Because this property returns an object, the method starts by using the GetType property to verify that the value of the object is a decimal. If so, it casts the object to a decimal. Finally, it converts the decimal to a string with two decimal places and assigns the result to the Value property.

Once you've created a method to serve as the event handler for the Format event of the control, the next step is to wire the method to that event. To understand how this wiring works, you need to realize that the Format event is not raised directly by a control. Instead, this event is raised by the binding object that's created for each bound property of the control. To wire an event handler to the Format event, then, you must first retrieve the binding object for the bound property. Then, you can add your event handler as a delegate to the binding object's Format event.

The second code example in this figure shows the two lines of code needed to do that. The first line declares a Binding variable and assigns the binding object for the Text property of the txtUnitPrice text box to it. As you can see, you can access the binding object through the control's DataBindings property. This property returns a collection of all the data bindings for the control, indexed by the name of the property each binding refers to.

The second line in this example shows how to create a delegate for the binding object's Format event. Here, the ConvertEventHandler class creates a new delegate that refers to the FormatPrice method. Then, the += operator adds this new delegate to the handlers for the binding object's Format event.

The Value property of the ConvertEventArgs class

Property	Description
`Value`	An object that contains the value that's bound to the control. The Format event should set this property to the string to be displayed by the control.

A method that formats a decimal value

```
private void FormatPrice(object sender, ConvertEventArgs e)
{
    if (e.Value.GetType().ToString() == "System.Decimal")
    {
        decimal unitPrice = (decimal) e.Value;
        e.Value = unitPrice.ToString("f2");
    }
}
```

Code that wires an event handler to the Format event of a text box

```
Binding b = txtUnitPrice.DataBindings["Text"];
b.Format += new ConvertEventHandler(FormatPrice);
```

Description

- Before it sets the value of a control's bound property, the binding manager causes the Format event of the control to be raised. You can wire an event handler to this event, and the event handler can change the format of the data before it's assigned to the bound property.
- The Format event handler is passed a ConvertEventArgs argument. The Value property of this argument contains the data to be bound to the control. The event handler should assign the formatted data to the Value property before returning.
- To avoid casting errors, the Format event handler should check the type of the Value property before attempting any data conversion or casting.
- To wire the Format event handler, first get the Binding object for the control. You can do that using the control's DataBindings property, specifying the name of the bound property as an index. Then, create a new instance of the ConvertEventHandler delegate that points to the event handler, and add this delegate to the Format event of the Binding object.

Figure 18-4 How to format bound data

How to navigate through the rows in a data table

Controls that are bound to a data source display information for the current row of the data source. As figure 18-5 shows, the *binding manager* is responsible for keeping track of the current row for each data source that's bound to a form. When the form first loads, the binding manager displays the first row of the data source. However, you can use the binding manager to navigate to other rows in the data source.

The syntax at the top of this figure shows how to create a variable of type BindingManagerBase to access the binding manager for a given data source. As you can see, you use the BindingContext property of the form to refer to its bindings. The BindingContext property is indexed by the dataset and table name because each bound data source has its own binding manager.

The first code example in this figure shows how you can access the binding manager for the Products table. Here, the first statement declares a variable that will refer to the binding manager, and the second statement uses the BindingContext property of the form to access the binding manager. Notice that you must specify both the dataset and the data table name as indexers to the BindingContext property even if the dataset contains only one table.

The second code example shows how to use the binding manager to navigate through the rows in the data table. Although it isn't apparent from the figure, this method is wired to the Click event of four buttons that let the user move to the first row, the next row, the previous row, and the last row in the data table. To determine which button was clicked, this method uses a switch statement that checks the Name property of thc sender parameter that's passed to the method. This property contains the name of the button that was clicked. If, for example, the Name property contains the value "btnFirst," you know that the user clicked the First button. Then, the code should move to the first row in the data table so its data is displayed. Note that to access the Name property, the sender parameter must first be cast to a Button object.

To move to a specific row in a data table, you set the Position property of the binding manager. To move to the first row, for example, you set the Position property to 0 since the collection of rows in a table is zero-based. To move to the next row in a table, you add 1 to the Position property. To move to the previous row, you subtract 1 from the Position property. And to move to the last row, you set the Position property to the value of the Count property minus 1. (Since the Count property indicates the number of rows in the table, you must subtract 1 to convert this number to the index value of the last row.)

Notice that the code for moving to the previous row works even if the first row is already displayed. That's because the binding manager won't let you set the Position property to a value less than 1. So if the value of this property is 0, subtracting 1 from it has no effect. Similarly, the binding manager won't let you set the Position property to a value greater than the Count property minus 1. So you don't need to check whether the last row is displayed before adding 1 to the Position property.

The syntax for accessing a binding manager

```
bindingManagerBase = this.BindingContext[dataSet, tableName]
```

Common BindingManagerBase properties

Property	Description
Position	A zero-based index that indicates the current position in the data table.
Count	The number of rows in the data table.

Code that creates a BindingManagerBase object

```
private BindingManagerBase productsBindingManager;
productsBindingManager = this.BindingContext[productsDataSet1, "Products"];
```

Code that navigates through the rows in a data table

```
private void NavigateProducts(object sender, System.EventArgs e)
{
    Button btn = (Button) sender;
    switch (btn.Name)
    {
        case "btnFirst":
            productsBindingManager.Position = 0;
            break;
        case "btnPrevious":
            productsBindingManager.Position--;
            break;
        case "btnNext":
            productsBindingManager.Position++;
            break;
        case "btnLast":
            productsBindingManager.Position
                = productsBindingManager.Count - 1;
            break;
    }
}
```

Description

- You use a *binding manager* to manage all of the controls on a form that are bound to the same data table.
- To create a binding manager, you use the BindingContext property of the form to get a BindingManagerBase object. This object is created automatically when controls on the form are bound to the columns in a data table.
- The binding manager ensures that all controls that are bound to the same data table are synchronized. That way, when you move to another row, the data-bound controls will display the values in that row.
- If the form provides for updating the rows in a data table, moving from one row to another causes any changes made to the current row to be saved to the data table.

Figure 18-5 How to navigate through the rows in a data table

The property settings for the Product Display form

Figure 18-6 presents some of the property settings for the Product Display form. As you can see, the Text property of each text box control is bound to the appropriate data column of the Products table in the dataset named productsDataSet1. The product code text box, for example, is bound to the ProductCode column.

The other property settings shown here are for the label that displays the number of the current row and the total number of rows in the table. It's displayed with a fixed, three-dimensional border, and the text it contains will be centered in the control. In a moment, you'll see how the contents of this control change as the program executes.

Because this form doesn't provide for data modification, the ReadOnly properties of all of the text boxes have been set to True and the TabStop properties have been set to False. In addition, no Insert, Update, or Delete statements were generated when the data adapter was created.

This figure also shows the Select statement used to retrieve data from the Products table. This Select statement retrieves the ProductCode, Description, and UnitPrice columns and sorts the results based on the ProductCode column.

Property settings for the data-bound text boxes

Name	Text (DataBindings) as shown in the Properties window
txtProductCode	productsDataSet1 – Products.ProductCode
txtDescription	productsDataSet1 – Products.Description
txtUnitPrice	productsDataSet1 – Products.UnitPrice

Property settings for the lblPosition label

Property	Setting
Name	lblPosition
BorderStyle	Fixed3D
TextAlign	MiddleCenter

The Select statement for the data adapter

```
SELECT ProductCode, Description, UnitPrice
FROM Products
ORDER BY ProductCode
```

Description

- Because this form doesn't provide for updating data, Insert, Update, and Delete statements aren't generated.
- The ReadOnly property of each text box is set to True so the data in the controls can't be modified, and the TabStop property of each text box is set to False so the focus doesn't move to those controls when the user presses the Tab key.
- The dataset class is given the name productsDataSet, and the dataset object is generated with the name productsDataSet1.
- The data adapter uses a simple Select statement to retrieve all of the rows from the Products table.

Figure 18-6 The property settings and data adapter for the Product Display form

The code for the Product Display application

Figure 18-7 presents the C# code for the Product Display application. To start, this code declares a variable of type BindingManagerBase to hold a reference to the binding manager for the bound controls on the form. Then, the Load event handler for the form begins by setting this variable to the binding manager. Next, it wires the event handler for the Format event of the Unit Price text box to the FormatPrice method. Then, it calls the data adapter's Fill method to load the dataset. Finally, it calls the DisplayPosition method to format the label that indicates the current position in the table.

The FormatPrice method is identical to the one you saw in figure 18-4, so I won't discuss it further here. The DisplayPosition method uses both the Position and Count properties of the binding manager to display the number of the current row and the total number of rows. Because the Position property hasn't been set explicitly at this point, it defaults to 0. Because of that, the first row in the table is displayed on the form after the Load event has been processed.

When the user clicks one of the navigation buttons to display another row, the NavigateProducts method sets the Position property so the requested row is displayed on the form. This is the key to this program, and you already saw how this code works in figure 18-5. After the new position is established, the DisplayPosition method is called to format the position label so it reflects the new position.

The code for the Product Display application

```
private BindingManagerBase productsBindingManager;

private void frmProductDisplay_Load(object sender, System.EventArgs e)
{
    productsBindingManager
        = this.BindingContext[productsDataSet1, "Products"];

    Binding b = txtUnitPrice.DataBindings["Text"];
    b.Format += new ConvertEventHandler(FormatPrice);

    productsDataAdapter.Fill(productsDataSet1);
    DisplayPosition();
}

private void FormatPrice(object sender, ConvertEventArgs e)
{
    if (e.Value.GetType().ToString() == "System.Decimal")
    {
        decimal unitPrice = (decimal) e.Value;
        e.Value = unitPrice.ToString("f2");
    }
}

private void DisplayPosition()
{
    lblPosition.Text = Convert.ToString(productsBindingManager.Position + 1)
        + " of " + productsBindingManager.Count.ToString();
}

private void NavigateProducts(object sender, System.EventArgs e)
{
    Button btn = (Button)sender;
    switch (btn.Name)
    {
        case "btnFirst":
            productsBindingManager.Position = 0;
            break;
        case "btnPrevious":
            productsBindingManager.Position--;
            break;
        case "btnNext":
            productsBindingManager.Position++;
            break;
        case "btnLast":
            productsBindingManager.Position
                = productsBindingManager.Count - 1;
            break;
    }
    DisplayPosition();
}

private void btnExit_Click(object sender, System.EventArgs e)
{
    this.Close();
}
```

Figure 18-7 The code for the Product Display application

How to use bound controls to add, update, and delete data rows

Once you understand how the binding manager works, you shouldn't have any trouble using it to navigate through the rows in a data table as illustrated by the Product Display application. But you can use the binding manager for more than just navigation. You can also use it to add, update, and delete rows from a table. You'll learn how to do that in the topics that follow.

A Product Maintenance application that uses bound controls

Figure 18-8 presents a Product Maintenance application that lets the user add, modify, and delete rows from the Products table. When this application first starts, the data for the first product in the table is displayed just as it is on the Product Display form. Instead of providing navigation buttons that let the user move to another product, though, the Product Maintenance application lists all of the existing products in a combo box at the top of the form. Then, the user can select a product to display its data, which is clearly more efficient than using the controls shown in figure 18-2.

Once the data for a product is displayed, the user can click the Edit button to enable the text box controls for the product code, description, and unit price for input. Then, the user can modify the data and click the Accept button to accept the changes. Alternatively, the user can click the Cancel button to restore the text boxes to their original values.

The user can also click the Delete button after selecting a product to delete that product. In that case, a message box is displayed to confirm the operation.

To add a new product, the user clicks the Add button. This clears and enables the text boxes so the user can enter data for the new product. Then, the user can click the Accept or Cancel button to accept or reject the new product.

One of the most difficult aspects of this application is managing the Enabled and ReadOnly properties of the text boxes and the Enabled properties of the buttons. For example, when the user selects a product from the drop-down list, the text boxes should be read-only, the Add, Edit, and Delete buttons should be enabled, and the Accept and Cancel buttons should be disabled. If the user clicks the Add or Edit button, the text box controls should be enabled for input, the Add, Edit, and Delete buttons should disabled, and the Accept and Cancel buttons should be enabled. Then, when the user clicks the Accept or Cancel button, the controls should be returned to their original state.

Note also that the Update Database button is initially disabled. This button should be enabled only when the user has made a change by adding, editing, or deleting a product. Then, the user can click this button to save all the changes to the database.

The Product Maintenance form

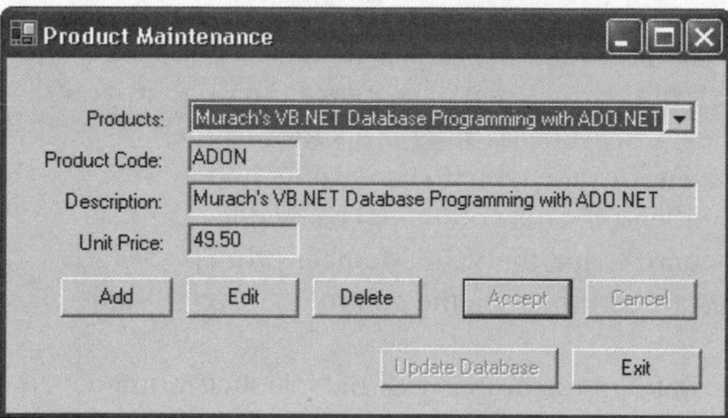

Description

- The Products combo box at the top of this form lists the description for each product in the Products table.
- To add a new product, the user clicks the Add button. This clears the text boxes, enables input so the user can enter the data for the new product, and enables the Accept and Cancel buttons so the user can accept or reject the new product.
- To modify an existing product, the user selects the product from the combo box and then clicks the Edit button. This enables input so the user can change the data for the product and enables the Accept and Cancel buttons so the user can accept or reject the modification.
- To delete a product, the user selects the product from the combo box and clicks the Delete button. Before the row is deleted, a confirmation message is displayed.
- To update the database with the changes made to the dataset, the user clicks the Update Database button. This button is enabled only when a product has been added, changed, or deleted.

Figure 18-8 A Product Maintenance application that uses bound controls

How to bind combo box and list box controls

Figure 18-9 shows how to use *complex data binding* to bind a combo box or list box control so that it displays all of the rows in a data source. To do that, you use the DataSource, DisplayMember, and ValueMember properties of the control. The DataSource property identifies the table the control is bound to. Then, the DisplayMember property identifies the column whose values are displayed in the list portion of the control, and the ValueMember property identifies that column whose values are returned via the control's SelectedValue property.

In this figure, for example, the DataSource property of the Products combo box is set to productsDataSet1.Products (the Products table), the DisplayMember property is set to the Description column, and the ValueMember property is set to the ProductCode column. That way, this combo box will list the description for each product in the Products table. Then, when the user selects a product, the application can retrieve the product code of the selected product by using the SelectedValue property.

Although it's not illustrated in this figure, you can also simple-bind a combo box or list box. To do that, you bind the SelectedValue property to a column of a data source, much as you would bind the Text property of a text box or label control. Then, when the current row of the binding manager changes, the selected item of the combo or list box is automatically changed based on the value of the column that the SelectedValue property is bound to. In addition, if the user selects a different item from the list, the column in the data source is changed to the value selected by the user.

A combo box or list box can also be both complex bound and simple bound. For example, you might use complex binding in an order entry application to display all of the rows in the Products table in a combo box. In addition, you might use simple binding to bind the SelectedValue property of the combo box to the ProductCode property of the InvoiceLineItems table. That way, the user can select the product code for an invoice line item by selecting the product from the combo box.

A combo box that's bound to a dataset

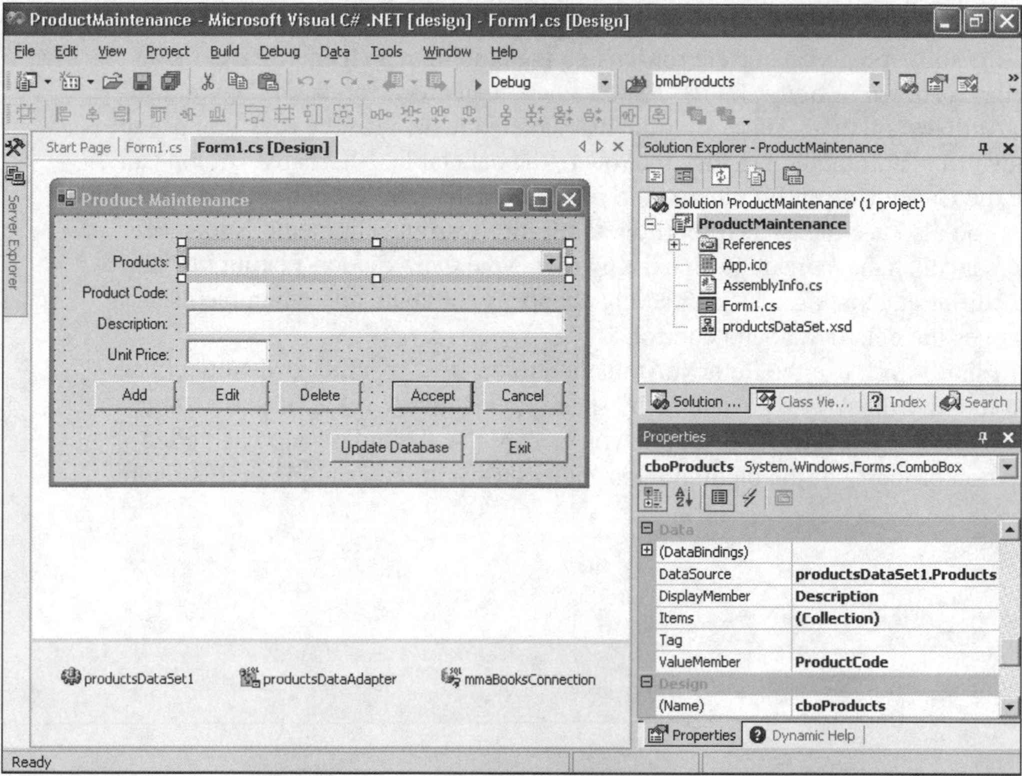

Combo box and list box properties for binding

Property	Description
`DataSource`	The name of the data table that contains the data displayed in the list.
`DisplayMember`	The name of the data column whose data is displayed in the list.
`ValueMember`	The name of the data column whose value is stored in the list. This value is returned by the SelectedValue property of the control.
`SelectedValue`	Gets the value of the currently selected item. You can also simple-bind this property to a column in a data source.

Description

- To complex-bind a combo box or list box to a data table so all the values in a column of a data table are included in the list, use the DataSource, DisplayMember, and ValueMember properties.
- You can also simple-bind a combo box or list box by setting the SelectedValue property to the name of the data column in a data table. Then, when another row in the data source specified by the DataSource property is displayed, the appropriate value in the list is displayed. In addition, when another item is selected from the list, the data column that's bound to the SelectedValue property is updated.

Figure 18-9 How to bind combo box and list box controls

How to add, update, and delete data rows

To add, update, and delete rows using the binding manager, you use the methods shown in figure 18-10. To add a new blank row, for example, you use the AddNew method. Then, after the user enters the data for the row, you use the EndCurrentEdit method to save the row to the data table. Alternatively, you can use the CancelCurrentEdit method to remove the new row from the table.

You also use the EndCurrentEdit and CancelCurrentEdit methods to save and cancel changes made to an existing row. Note that you don't explicitly start the edit of an existing row. Instead, that happens automatically when the user changes the data in a bound control.

Finally, you use the RemoveAt method to delete a specific row. Notice that you identify the row to be deleted by specifying its index value. If you want to delete the current row, for example, you can specify the index value using the Position property of the binding manager as shown in the example in this figure.

Common BindingManagerBase methods

Method	Description
`AddNew()`	Adds a new blank row to a data table.
`RemoveAt(index)`	Deletes the row with the specified index from a data table.
`EndCurrentEdit()`	Ends the edit by saving the changes to the current row.
`CancelCurrentEdit()`	Reverses the changes made to the current row.

A statement that adds a new row to a dataset

```
productsBindingManager.AddNew();
```

A statement that removes the current row from a dataset

```
producstBindingManager.RemoveAt(productsBindingManager.Position);
```

A statement that saves the changes to the current row and ends the edit operation

```
productsBindingManager.EndCurrentEdit();
```

A statement that cancels the changes to the current row

```
productsBindingManager.CancelCurrentEdit();
```

Code that catches a ConstraintException if an attempt is made to add a row with a duplicate primary key

```
try
{
    productsBindingManager.EndCurrentEdit();
}
catch (ConstraintException)
{
    MessageBox.Show("There is already a product with that code.",
                    "Entry Error");
    txtProductCode.Focus();
}
```

Description

- When you add a new row using the AddNew method, the Position property of the binding manager is set to one more than the position of the last row in the data table.
- You can use the EndCurrentEdit and CancelCurrentEdit methods to cancel or save the changes to an existing row or a new row that was added using the AddNew method.
- When you call the EndCurrentEdit method, a ConstraintException will be raised if you have attempted to add a row with a primary key that already exists in the table or if you have attempted to change an existing row's primary key to a key that already exists.

Figure 18-10 How to add, update, and delete data rows

The property settings for the Product Maintenance form

Figure 18-11 presents some of the property settings for the Product Maintenance form. The first thing you should notice is that the Select statement for this application is identical to the Select statement for the Product Display application presented earlier in this chapter. However, because this application updates the Products table, Insert, Update, and Delete statements are generated for it.

Like the text boxes on the Product Display form, the Text property of each text box on the Product Maintenance form is bound to a column in the Products table. In addition, the Products combo box is complex-bound to the Products table. Notice that the DisplayMember property specifies the Description column so that the combo box displays a list of product descriptions, but the ValueMember property isn't set. Since this application won't use the SelectedValue property to retrieve the value that's stored in the list, it's not necessary to set the ValueMember property.

Before I go on, you should notice that the MaxLength property for two of the text boxes have been changed from the default. When you use the data in a text box to update a column in a table, you'll want to be sure that the user doesn't enter more characters than are allowed by the column definition. In this case, you want to be sure that the user doesn't enter more than 10 characters for the product code and 50 characters for the description. The easiest way to do that is to set the MaxLength property, which specifies the maximum number of characters the user can enter into the control.

The Select statement for the data adapter

```
SELECT ProductCode, Description, UnitPrice
FROM Products
ORDER BY ProductCode
```

Property settings for the data-bound text boxes

Name	Text (DataBindings) as shown in the Properties window	MaxLength
txtProductCode	productsDataSet1 - Products.ProductCode	10
txtDescription	productsDataSet1 - Products.Description	50
txtUnitPrice	productsDataSet1 - Products.UnitPrice	

Property settings for the data-bound combo box

Property	Value
Name	cboProducts
DropDownStyle	DropDownList
DataSource	productsDataSet.Products
DisplayMember	Description

Notes

- Because the data in the Products table will be updated, Insert, Update, and Delete statements are generated for it.
- The dataset class is given the name productsDataSet, and the dataset object is generated with the name productsDataSet1.
- The MaxLength properties of the text boxes are set so that the user can't enter more characters than are allowed by the columns they're bound to.

Figure 18-11 The property settings for the Product Maintenance form

The code for the Product Maintenance application

Figure 18-12 presents the code for the Product Maintenance application. It starts by defining two variables used throughout the form. The first is a Boolean variable that indicates whether or not the user is currently adding a new product. The second variable holds a reference to the binding manager.

The Load event handler for the form begins by setting the binding manager variable to the binding manager for the Products table and wiring the Format event handler for the Unit Price text box to the FormatPrice method. Then, it calls the data adapter's Fill method to fill the dataset. Finally, it calls a method named DisableAddEditMode to set the initial state of the form controls.

The DisableAddEditMode method sets the form controls so the user can select a product from the combo box or click the Add, Edit, or Delete button but can't enter data into the text boxes or click the Accept or Cancel buttons. In addition, this method sets the Enabled property of the Update Database button based on the dataset's HasChanges property. As a result, if any changes have been made to the dataset, the Update Database button will be enabled. Otherwise, this button will be disabled. The last statement in this method moves the focus to the Products combo box so the user can select a product.

The EnableAddEditMode method does the opposite of the DisableAddEditMode method. It sets the form controls so the user can enter data into the text boxes and click the Accept or Cancel buttons but can't select a product from the combo box or click the Add, Edit, or Delete buttons. In addition, it sets the Enabled property of the Update Database button to false so the user can't click this button until the current operation is accepted or canceled. Finally, it moves the focus to the Product Code text box so the user can enter or edit the product code.

The code for the Product Maintenance application — Page 1

```
private bool isAddMode;
private BindingManagerBase productsBindingManager;

private void frmProductMaintenance_Load(object sender, System.EventArgs e)
{
    productsBindingManager
        = this.BindingContext[productsDataSet1, "Products"];
    Binding b = txtUnitPrice.DataBindings["Text"];
    b.Format += new ConvertEventHandler(FormatPrice);
    productsDataAdapter.Fill(productsDataSet1);
    DisableAddEditMode();
}

private void FormatPrice(object sender, ConvertEventArgs e)
{
    if (e.Value.GetType().ToString() == "System.Decimal")
    {
        decimal unitPrice = (decimal) e.Value;
        e.Value = unitPrice.ToString("f2");
    }
}

private void DisableAddEditMode()
{
    cboProducts.Enabled = true;
    txtProductCode.ReadOnly = true;
    txtDescription.ReadOnly = true;
    txtUnitPrice.ReadOnly = true;
    btnAdd.Enabled = true;
    btnEdit.Enabled = true;
    btnDelete.Enabled = true;
    btnAccept.Enabled = false;
    btnCancel.Enabled = false;
    btnUpdateDatabase.Enabled = productsDataSet1.HasChanges();
    cboProducts.Focus();
}

private void EnableAddEditMode()
{
    cboProducts.Enabled = false;
    txtProductCode.ReadOnly = false;
    txtDescription.ReadOnly = false;
    txtUnitPrice.ReadOnly = false;
    btnAdd.Enabled = false;
    btnEdit.Enabled = false;
    btnDelete.Enabled = false;
    btnAccept.Enabled = true;
    btnCancel.Enabled = true;
    btnUpdateDatabase.Enabled = false;
    txtProductCode.Focus();
}
```

Figure 18-12 The code for the Product Maintenance application (part 1 of 3)

When the user selects a product from the Products combo box, the event handler for the SelectedIndexChanged event is executed. This event handler simply sets the Position property of the binding manager to the SelectedIndex property of the combo box. In other words, it positions the binding manager to the selected row. This works because the items in the combo box are in the same sequence as the rows in the Products table, and both use a zero-based index.

If the user clicks the Add button, that button's Click event handler starts by calling the AddNew method to add a new row to the Products table. Then, it calls the EnableAddEditMode method so the user can enter the data for the new product. Finally, it sets the isAddMode variable to true to indicate that the user is currently adding a new product.

If the user clicks the Edit button, that button's Click event handler calls the EnableAddEditMode method so the user can modify the data for the current product. Then, it sets isAddMode to false to indicate that the user is not adding a new product.

If the user clicks the Accept button, that button's Click event handler is executed. This method starts by calling the IsValidData method. The IsValidData method, in turn, calls the IsPresent method to check that the user entered data into all three fields. Notice that it doesn't check whether a decimal value was entered into the Unit Price field. That's because when you bind a control to a data column, the data is automatically checked to be sure that it's valid for the data type of the column. If it's not, the field is cleared. Then, because the IsValidData method checks that a value is entered in the Unit Price field, a message is displayed indicating that an entry is required.

If the data is valid, the Click event handler continues by calling the binding manager's EndCurrentEdit method to save the changes to the current row. In addition, if the user was adding a new row, it sets the combo box to the new row and sets isAddMode to false. Finally, it calls the DisableAddEditMode method to reset the form.

Notice that these statements are coded within the try block of a try-catch statement. That's because when the EndCurrentEdit method is executed, a constraint exception will occur if the user added a product using an existing product code or changed the product code of an existing row to a product code that already exists. In that case, the catch block catches the exception and displays an error message.

The code for the Product Maintenance application Page 2

```
private void cboProducts_SelectedIndexChanged(object sender,
    System.EventArgs e)
{
    productsBindingManager.Position = cboProducts.SelectedIndex;
}

private void btnAdd_Click(object sender, System.EventArgs e)
{
    productsBindingManager.AddNew();
    EnableAddEditMode();
    isAddMode = true;
}

private void btnEdit_Click(object sender, System.EventArgs e)
{
    EnableAddEditMode();
    isAddMode = false;
}

private void btnAccept_Click(object sender, System.EventArgs e)
{
    if (IsValidData())
    {
        try
        {
            productsBindingManager.EndCurrentEdit();
            if (isAddMode)
            {
                cboProducts.SelectedIndex = productsBindingManager.Count - 1;
                isAddMode = false;
            }
            DisableAddEditMode();
        }
        catch (ConstraintException)
        {
            MessageBox.Show("There is already a product with that code.",
                "Entry Error");
            txtProductCode.Focus();
        }
    }
}

private bool IsValidData()
{
    if (!IsPresent(txtProductCode, "Product Code"))
        return false;
    if (!IsPresent(txtDescription, "Description"))
        return false;
    if (!IsPresent(txtUnitPrice, "Unit Price"))
        return false;

    return true;
}
```

Figure 18-12 The code for the Product Maintenance application (part 2 of 3)

If the user clicks the Cancel button instead of the Accept button, the Click event handler for that button starts by calling the CancelCurrentEdit method to cancel the changes made to the current row. Then, if a row was being added, it positions the binding manager to the row that's currently selected in the combo box so that the data for that row is redisplayed, and it sets isAddMode to false. Finally, it calls the DisableAddEditMode method to reset the form.

The event handler for the Click event of the Delete button is called when the user clicks the Delete button. This method starts by displaying a message box to confirm that the user wants to delete the row. If the user responds by clicking the Yes button, the binding manager's RemoveAt method is called to remove the current row. Then, the DisableAddEditMode method is called to reset the display.

The next method is the Click event handler for the Update Database button. It starts by calling the data adapter's Update method to update the database with changes the user has made to the dataset. Then, it clears the dataset and reloads it. That way, the user will see any changes that have been made by other users. Finally, the DisableAddEditMode method is called to reset the form.

Notice that this method doesn't check if changes have been made to the dataset before updating the database. That's because this method can be executed only if the Update Database button is enabled, and that button is enabled only if changes have been made to the dataset.

The next to last method is the Click event handler for the Exit button. This method simply closes the form, which causes the Closing event of the form to fire. The last method shown in this listing handles this event. Note that this method also fires if the user clicks the close button in the upper right corner of the form.

The Closing method starts by checking if any changes have been made to the dataset that haven't been saved to the database. If so, a dialog box is displayed to ask the user if the form should be closed without saving the changes. If the user responds by clicking the No button, the Cancel property of the e parameter that's passed to this method is set to true so that the form remains open. Otherwise, it's closed. If no changes have been made to the dataset, the form is closed without displaying a message box.

The code for the Product Maintenance application Page 3

```
private bool IsPresent(TextBox textBox, string name)
{
    if (textBox.Text == "")
    {
        MessageBox.Show(name + " is a required field.", "Entry Error");
        textBox.Focus();
        return false;
    }
    return true;
}

private void btnCancel_Click(object sender, System.EventArgs e)
{
    productsBindingManager.CancelCurrentEdit();
    if (isAddMode)
    {
        productsBindingManager.Position = cboProducts.SelectedIndex;
        isAddMode = false;
    }
    DisableAddEditMode();
}
private void btnDelete_Click(object sender, System.EventArgs e)
{
    if (MessageBox.Show("Delete " + cboProducts.Text + "?",
        "Confirm Delete", MessageBoxButtons.YesNo,
        MessageBoxIcon.Question) == DialogResult.Yes)
    {
        productsBindingManager.RemoveAt(productsBindingManager.Position);
        DisableAddEditMode();
    }
}

private void btnUpdateDatabase_Click(object sender, System.EventArgs e)
{
    productsDataAdapter.Update(productsDataSet1);
    productsDataSet1.Clear();
    productsDataAdapter.Fill(productsDataSet1);
    DisableAddEditMode();
}

private void btnExit_Click(object sender, System.EventArgs e)
{
    this.Close();
}

private void frmProductMaintenance_Closing(object sender,
    System.ComponentModel.CancelEventArgs e)
{
    if (productsDataSet1.HasChanges())
        if (MessageBox.Show("You have made changes that have not " +
            "been saved to the database.\n" +
            "If you continue, these changes will be lost.\n" +
            "Continue?", "Confirm Exit", MessageBoxButtons.YesNo,
            MessageBoxIcon.Warning) == DialogResult.No)
            e.Cancel = true;
}
```

Figure 18-12 The code for the Product Maintenance application (part 3 of 3)

Perspective

One goal of this chapter has been to teach you the skills you need for developing database applications with bound controls. The other goal has been to introduce you to the complexity of this type of programming. Although the two applications in this chapter are far simpler than most real-world applications, they do illustrate the skills that you'll need on the job.

Summary

- You can use the classes, properties, and methods defined by a typed dataset to work with the dataset.
- You can use *simple data binding* to bind a text box control to a column in a data table. Then, the value of the column in the current row is displayed in the control, and any changes to that value are saved to the data table.
- You can use the Format event of a bound control to format the data that's displayed in the control.
- You can use a form's *binding manager* to manage the bound controls on the form. This object lets you specify the current position within the rows of a data table and makes sure that all controls are synchronized.
- You can use *complex-data binding* to bind a combo box or list box to a column in a data table so the values in that column are displayed in the list. You can also simple-bind a combo box or list box to a data column so the value in the current row can be displayed and updated using the control.
- You can use the methods of a binding manager to add a new row to a data table, delete an existing row from a data table, save changes to the current row in a data table, and cancel changes to the current row.

Terms

complex data binding
simple data binding
binding manager

Objectives

- Given the specifications for an application that displays, adds, modifies, and deletes the rows in a data table, develop the application with bound controls.
- Write the code that formats the data that's displayed in bound controls.
- List and describe the three main classes defined by a typed dataset.
- Describe the use of a binding manager.

Exercise 18-1 Display the invoice data

In this exercise, you'll create an Invoice Display form that uses text box controls to work with the data in a dataset. To make that easier for you to do, we'll give you a starting form that contains all the controls that you'll need.

The design of the Invoice Display form

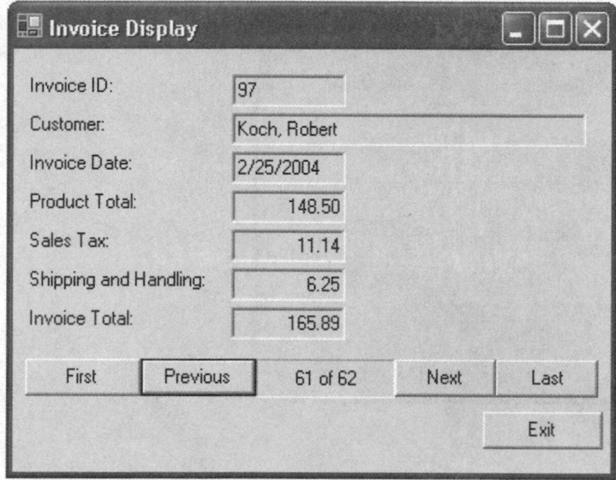

Development procedure

1. Open the project named InvoiceDisplay in the C:\C#.NET\Chapter 18 directory.
2. Use the Data Adapter Configuration Wizard to create a data adapter that will retrieve the data required by the Invoice Display form. This data adapter will need to retrieve data from both the Invoices and the Customers table, and the invoices should be sorted by invoice ID. Be sure not to generate Insert, Update, and Delete statements since this program won't use them.
3. Preview the data to be sure the Select statement associated with the data adapter retrieves the correct data. Then, generate a dataset from the data adapter.
4. Bind the text boxes on the form to the appropriate columns in the dataset.
5. Add the code for creating the binding manager, filling the data adapter, and displaying the current position when the form is loaded. Add the code for navigating through the rows and for displaying the data in each row. And add the code for closing the form when the Exit button is clicked. Then, test the application to make sure it works correctly, but notice that the data isn't formatted.
6. Add a method to format the invoice date so that it's displayed in short date format. Add another method to format the numeric data on the form so that it's displayed with two decimal places. And add the code to the Load event of the form to apply this formatting to the bound data. Then, test this enhancement.

Exercise 18-2 Maintain the Customers table

In this exercise, you'll create a Customer Maintenance form like the one shown below that lets you add, modify, and delete rows in the Customers table using a typed dataset and bound controls. To make this form easier to develop, we'll give you a starting form that contains all the controls you'll need.

The design of the Customer Maintenance form

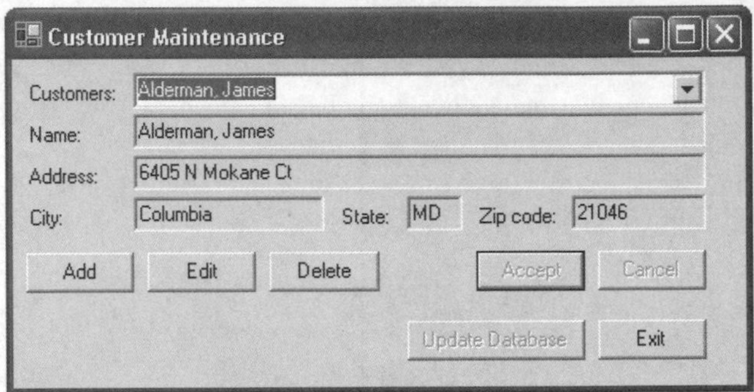

Development procedure

1. Open the project named CustomerMaintenance in the C:\C#.NET\Chapter 18 directory. Then, use the Configuration Wizard to create a data adapter that can be used to add, update, and delete rows in the Customers table. The customers should be sorted by name. Generate a dataset from the data adapter.
2. Bind the combo box and text boxes to the appropriate columns of the Customers table in the dataset.
3. Add the code required to create the binding manager for the form, fill the dataset, display the customer data when the user selects a customer from the combo box, and close the form when the user clicks the Exit button. Test the application to make sure this works correctly.
4. Add the code required to implement the Add, Edit, and Delete functions. Be sure that the ReadOnly properties of the text boxes and the Enabled properties of the combo box and button controls are set as appropriate, that the data is validated before being accepted, and that the dataset is checked for changes before the form is closed. Note that you do not need to check for a constraint exception when you add or update a row since the primary key for the table is an identity column that's automatically generated by the DBMS.
5. Test the application to be sure that these functions work properly. Notice that when you enter a state code, it's always converted to uppercase. That's because the Case property of this text box has been set to Upper.
6. Add the code required to update the database and refresh the dataset. Then, test the application one more time and make any necessary corrections.

19

How to work with datasets using unbound controls

When you use bound controls as described in the last chapter, you can display and update data quickly and easily. In many cases, though, you won't have as much control over how the data is processed as you would like. Because of that, professional programmers frequently use unbound controls in their applications. So in this chapter, you'll learn how to use unbound controls with datasets. In effect, you'll learn how to manually perform the processing that's automatically done by the binding manager when you use bound controls.

How to work with unbound controls

In the Product Maintenance program you saw in the last chapter, the controls were bound to the Products data table. Because of that, you worked with this table using a binding manager. When you work with unbound controls, however, you work directly with the dataset. You'll learn how to do that in the topics that follow.

How to process unbound data

Figure 19-1 summarizes the functions of the binding manager that you must provide for when you work with unbound controls. As you can see, some of these functions are provided by properties and methods of the binding manager that you learned about in the last chapter. Others, such as moving data from a data column to a form control and vice versa, are provided automatically by the binding manager.

When you use unbound controls, you must provide for all of these functions explicitly using the methods, properties, and statements indicated in this figure. You'll learn how to implement these functions in the figures that follow. You'll also see how to use many of them in a complete application when I present an unbound version of the Product Maintenance application.

This figure also indicates when each of the methods, properties, and statements should be performed. For the most part, you shouldn't have any trouble understanding this information. Notice, however, that a new row isn't added to a data table until the user accepts the data for the new row. Although you might think that you would add a row as soon as the user indicates that he wants to add a new row, that's not necessary since the controls on the form aren't bound to the underlying data table. If you don't understand this now, it'll make more sense when you see the complete code for the Product Maintenance application.

Binding manager functions that must be provided through code

Function	Method, property, or statement	When it should be executed
Retrieve a row and move values from columns in the data row to input controls	Indexer of data table to retrieve a row by position; FindBy*columnname* method of the data table to retrieve a row by key. Assignment statements using data row properties to access individual columns.	When the form is first loaded, when the user selects another row to be displayed, when a row is deleted, when the addition of a new row or changes to an existing row are canceled, and when the data table is refreshed.
Clear input controls	Assign empty strings to Text property of input controls	When the user indicates that he or she wants to add a new row.
Create a new data row	New*tablename*Row method of the data table	When the user indicates that the dataset should be updated with the data for a new row.
Move values from controls to the selected row or a new row	Assign the Text properties of input controls to data row properties	When the user indicates that the dataset should be updated with the data for a new row or the changes to an existing row.
Add a row to the table	Add*tablename*Row method of the data table	When the user indicates that the dataset should be updated with the data for a new row. This is done after the new row object is created and values are assigned to its columns.
Delete a row from the table	Delete method of a data row	When the user indicates that a row should be deleted from the dataset.
Keep track of the current row	Assignment statements	When the form is first loaded, when the user selects another row to be displayed, when the user indicates that the dataset should be updated with the data for a new row, when a row is deleted, and when the data table is refreshed.

Description

- When you process data that's not bound to controls on a form, you must provide the same functions that are provided by the binding manager for the form. That includes displaying the rows in the data table, adding new rows to the data table, and updating and deleting existing rows.

Figure 19-1 How to process unbound data

How to retrieve and work with a data row

One of the basic skills for working with data in a typed dataset is retrieving a specific row from one of the dataset's data tables so you can work with the data in the row. Figure 19-2 shows you how to do that. To start, you should declare a variable that will hold the row as illustrated by all four examples in this figure. The typed dataset includes a class you can use for this purpose. For the products dataset, the data row class is productsDataSet.ProductsRow.

After you declare a variable to hold a row, you can retrieve a row and assign it to that variable. This figure shows two ways to do that. First, you can retrieve a row using its index as illustrated in the first example. Here, I've declared an integer variable named *i* to indicate the row I want to retrieve. Then, I used *i* as an indexer for the data table (productsDataSet1.Products) to retrieve the indicated row.

The rest of the code in this example retrieves values from individual columns of the row and assigns them to the Text property of the form's input controls. Here, you can see that the value of each column is retrieved using a property of the row. To retrieve the value of the Description column, for example, productRow.Description is used.

If a table has a primary key, you can use the technique illustrated in the second example to retrieve a row from the table. This example uses the data table's FindBy*columnname* method to retrieve a row by its key value. In this case, the table is the Products table and the primary key is the ProductCode column. Notice that the name of the method includes the name of this column. To retrieve a row from this table based on its key value, you pass the key value as an argument to the FindByProductCode method. In this example, a variable named productCode is used to identify the key value.

The third example is similar, but it uses a value selected from a combo box to retrieve a row. For this to work, the combo box must be complex-bound to a data source using the DataSource, DisplayMember, and ValueMember properties. In addition, the ValueMember property must be set to the data column that contains the key value. Then, when an item is selected from the list, the SelectedValue property can be used to get the value of the column specified by the ValueMember property. Although this is the easiest way to get the value of an item that's selected from a combo box, you can also implement this function without binding the combo box to a data source. You'll see how to do that later in this chapter.

You can also use the FindBy*columnname* method with a primary key that consists of two or more columns. In that case, the name of the method includes the names of all the key columns in sequence, as you can see in the fourth example in this figure. Then, the arguments that contain the values for these columns are coded in the same sequence.

Code that retrieves a row by its index and assigns column values to form controls

```
productsDataSet.ProductsRow productRow;
int i;
// code that sets i to the appropriate index value
.
productRow = productsDataSet1.Products[i];
txtProductCode.Text = productRow.ProductCode;
txtDescription.Text = productRow.Description;
txtUnitPrice.Text = productRow.UnitPrice.ToString("f2");
```

Code that uses the FindBy*columnname* method to retrieve a row with a specified key value

```
productsDataSet.ProductsRow productRow;
string productCode;
// code that sets productCode to the appropriate key value
.
productRow = productsDataSet1.Products.FindByProductCode(productCode);
```

Code that uses the FindBy*columnname* method to retrieve a row with the value selected from a combo box

```
productsDataSet.ProductsRow productRow;
productRow = productsDataSet1.Products.FindByProductCode(
        cboProducts.SelectedValue);
```

Code that uses the FindBy*columnname* method to retrieve a row with a composite key

```
productsDataSet.InvoiceLineItemsRow lineItemRow;
int invoiceID;
string productCode;
// code that sets invoiceID and productCode to appropriate values
.
lineItemRow = productsDataSet1.InvoiceLineItems.FindByInvoiceIDProductCode(
              invoiceID, productCode);
```

Description

- To declare a variable for a row in a data table, you use the class for the data row that's defined by the typed dataset.
- To retrieve a specific row from a data table, you can use an index to specify the row you want to retrieve. Or, you can use the FindBy*columnname* method to retrieve the row with the specified key value. If the row doesn't exist, this method returns null.
- The FindBy*columnname* method is defined for the primary key of a table. The name of this method includes the name of the key column.
- You can also use the FindBy*columnname* method with a combo box or a list box that's complex-bound to a data table. To do that, you must set the ValueMember property of the control to the column that contains the key value. That way, you can use the SelectedValue property to retrieve the value of a selected item.
- To get the values of the columns in a row, use the properties of the row that have the same names as the columns in the data table.

Figure 19-2 How to retrieve and work with a data row

How to modify or delete an existing data row

Figure 19-3 illustrates how you modify or delete an existing data row. Note that the examples in this figure assume that you have already retrieved a row using a variable named productRow as described in the previous figure. Then, you can modify the data in the row using code like that shown in the first example. The statements in this example simply use the Text properties of the text box controls used for input to set the column properties of the data row. Notice that the last statement converts the Text property of the Unit Price text box to a decimal so it can be stored in the UnitPrice column.

Before I go on, you should realize that because the DataRow class is a reference type, a data row variable holds a reference to a data row within the dataset, not a copy of the data row. As a result, you don't have to explicitly save the changes made to the data row back to the dataset. Instead, any changes you make to the data row immediately affect the data in the dataset.

You can use two different techniques to delete a row from a data table. First, you can use the Delete method of the data row to mark the row as deleted, as shown in the second example in this figure. Then, the row isn't deleted permanently until you issue the Update method of the data adapter. Second, you can use the Remove*tablename*Row method of the table to permanently remove the row from the table as illustrated in the third example. Since the row is removed permanently when you use this method, issuing an Update method later will have no effect on the database. Because of that, you should use the Delete method if you want to delete the row from the database, and you should use the Remove*tablename*Row method only if you want to delete the row from the dataset but not from the database.

Code that modifies the values in the data row

```
productRow.ProductCode = txtProductCode.Text;
productRow.Description = txtDescription.Text;
productRow.UnitPrice = Convert.ToDecimal(txtUnitPrice.Text);
```

A statement that uses the Delete method to mark the row as deleted

```
productRow.Delete()
```

A statement that uses the Remove method to delete the row

```
productsDataSet.Products.RemoveProductsRow(productRow);
```

Description

- To set the values of the columns in a row, you use the properties of the data row.
- The Delete method of a row marks the row for deletion. The row isn't actually removed from the data table (or the database) until the Update method of the data adapter is executed.
- The Remove*tablename*Row method permanently removes a row from the table. To identify the row to be removed, you code it as an argument on this method. You should use this method only if you want to delete the related row in the dataset but not in the database.
- If you issue the Update method of a data adapter and the row is updated successfully in the database, the changes are committed to the dataset. That means that any rows that are marked as deleted are removed from the data table.

Figure 19-3 How to modify or delete an existing data row

How to add a data row

Figure 19-4 shows how you add new rows to a data table. To do that, you use the New*tablename*Row method of the table, and you assign the result to a data row variable as shown in the first example in this figure. Then, you assign values to the columns in the row just as you do for an existing row. When you're done, you use the Add*tablename*Row method of the table to add the new row to the table.

When you add new rows to a data table, they're added to the end of the table. If you add a new row to the Products table using the Product Maintenance program, for example, you'll notice that the Product appears at the end of the list in the Products combo box. If that's not what you want, you can update the database and then refresh the dataset as shown in the second example in this figure. Then, the rows will be displayed in the sequence that's specified by the Select statement that retrieves them.

Code that creates a new row, assigns values to it, and adds it to the dataset

```
ProductsDataSet.ProductsRow productRow;
productRow = productsDataSet1.Products.NewProductsRow();
productRow.ProductCode = txtProductCode.Text;
productRow.Description = txtDescription.Text;
productRow.UnitPrice = Convert.ToDecimal(txtUnitPrice.Text);
productsDataSet1.Products.AddProductsRow(productRow);
```

Code that updates the database and refreshes the dataset

```
productsDataAdapter.Update(productsDataSet1.Products);
productsDataSet1.Clear();
productsDataAdapter.Fill(productsDataSet1.Products);
```

Description

- To create a new row based on the schema of a table, you use the New*tablename*Row method of the table and assign the result to a data row variable.
- To set the values of the columns in a new row, you use the properties of the data row just as you do when you're working with an existing row.
- After you assign values to the columns in the row, you use the Add*tablename*Row method of the table to add the row to the table.
- When you add new rows to a data table, they're added to the end of the data table. Then, after you update the database with the new rows, you can refresh the data table using the Clear and Fill methods so that the new rows are in the correct sequence.

Figure 19-4 How to add a data row

How to work with row states

Earlier in this chapter, I mentioned that when you use the Delete method to delete a data row, the row isn't actually removed from the data table. Instead, the row is simply marked for deletion so that the corresponding row in the database will be deleted when the Update method of the data adapter is called. As figure 19-5 shows, ADO.NET uses the RowState property of a row to keep track of the state of the row.

Initially, the RowState of every row in a table is set to Unchanged. If you add a row, the row's RowState property is set to Added. And if you update or delete an existing row, the RowState property of the affected row is changed to Modified or Deleted. Note that if you delete a row, you can no longer access any of the data in the row even though the row still exists in the table. In addition, because RowState is a read-only property, you can't undelete a deleted row by changing its RowState property back to Unchanged.

The last row state listed in this figure, Detached, requires some additional explanation. This row state indicates that the row is not a part of any Rows collection. This can happen in two ways. First, when you create a new instance of a data row using the New*tablename*Row method, the row is given Detached state until you use the Add*tablename*Row method to add the row to the table. Then, the row's state is changed to Added. Second, if you use the Remove*tablename*Row method to remove a row from the table, the row is given Detached state.

To refer to a row state, you use the members of the DataRowState enumeration. The two examples in this figure show you how this works. The first example simply checks the RowState property of a row to determine if the row is unchanged. As a result, whatever statements you code within the braces will be executed only if the row has not been modified.

The second example shows how you can load all the rows of a table except for those that have been marked for deletion into a combo box. Here, each row in the Products table is checked to make sure it hasn't been deleted. If it hasn't, the DictionaryEntry structure is used to create a DictionaryEntry that contains the product code and description for the product. Then, the DictionaryEntry is added to the collection of items in the combo box.

You may remember from chapter 8 that the DictionaryEntry structure has two properties: Key and Value. In this example, the product code is assigned to the Key property and the description is assigned to the Value property. Then, to display the value of one of these properties in the combo box list, you must set the DisplayMember property of the combo box. If you want to display the description in the combo box, for example, you would set the DisplayMember property to Value since the description is stored in the Value property.

Before I go on, you should realize that when you issue the Update method, the row state of any inserted or modified row that was updated is changed to Unchanged. In addition, any rows that were marked for deletion are permanently removed from the table. In other words, the changes are committed to the data table and can't be reversed.

DataRowState enumeration members

Member	Description
Unchanged	No changes have been made to the row.
Added	The row has been added to the table.
Modified	One or more column values in the row have been changed.
Deleted	The row has been marked for deletion.
Detached	The row has been deleted or removed from the collection of rows, or a new row has been created using the New*tablename*Row method but not added to the table.

Code that checks the current state of a row

```
if (productRow.RowState == DataRowState.Unchanged)
{
    ...
}
```

Code that excludes deleted rows from a combo box

```
cboProducts.Items.Clear();
DictionaryEntry productEntry;
foreach (productsDataSet.ProductsRow pr in productsDataSet1.Products.Rows)
{
    if (pr.RowState != DataRowState.Deleted)
    {
        productEntry = new DictionaryEntry(pr.ProductCode, pr.Description);
        cboProducts.Items.Add(productEntry);
    }
}
```

Description

- The state of a data row depends on the operations that have been performed on the row and whether or not the operations have been committed.
- To determine if a row has a given state, use the RowState property of the row. To refer to a row state, use the members of the DataRowState enumeration.
- When you execute the Update method of a data adapter, all of the rows with a state of Deleted are removed from the data table. All other rows are given a row state of Unchanged.

Note

- If you use the DictionaryEntry structure to load entries into a combo box or list box, you must set the DisplayMember property of the control to Key or Value to display the Key or Value property of each DictionaryEntry object.

Figure 19-5 How to work with row states

A Product Maintenance application that uses unbound controls

Now that you've seen the basic techniques for working with unbound data, you're ready to see a program that uses unbound controls. The application I'll present here is an unbound version of the Product Maintenance application you saw in chapter 18.

The design and operation of the Product Maintenance form

Figure 19-6 presents the Product Maintenance form. If you review its operation, you'll see that it works just like the form that was presented in the last chapter. In this case, however, all of the controls are unbound.

Although it's not shown here, the data adapter for this application uses the same Select statement as the one in the last chapter, and Insert, Update, and Delete statements are generated from this statement. In addition, the MaxLength properties of the Product Code and Description text boxes are set so that the user can't enter more characters than are allowed by the associated data columns. The DisplayMember property of the Products combo box is also set so that it displays the Value property of the DictionaryEntry objects that are loaded into it.

The Product Maintenance form

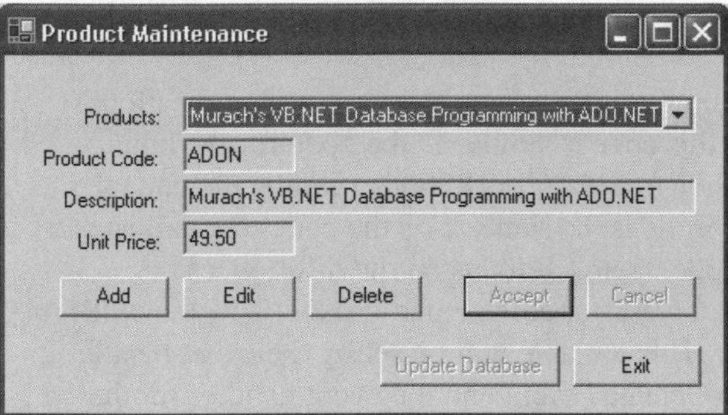

Description

- The Products combo box at the top of this form lists the description for each product in the Products table.
- To add a new product, the user clicks the Add button. This clears the text boxes, enables input so the user can enter the data for the new product, and enables the Accept and Cancel buttons so the user can accept or reject the new product.
- To modify an existing product, the user selects the product from the combo box and then clicks the Edit button. This enables input so the user can change the data for the product and enables the Accept and Cancel buttons so the user can accept or reject the modification.
- To delete a product, the user selects the product from the combo box and clicks the Delete button. Before the row is deleted, a confirmation message is displayed.
- To update the database with the changes made to the dataset, the user clicks the Update Database button. This button is enabled only when a product has been added, changed, or deleted.

Note

- The DisplayMember property of the Products combo box is set to Value so that the Value properties of the DictionaryEntry objects that are loaded into the combo box are displayed in the list.

Figure 19-6 The design and operation of the Product Maintenance form

The code for the Product Maintenance application

The code for the unbound version of the Product Maintenance application is presented in figure 19-7. Much of this code is similar to the code for the bound version of this program that was shown in chapter 18. For example, the code that manages the status of the input controls is the same, as is the code that validates the input data. As I describe this code, then, I'll focus on the differences.

To start, this program declares a class variable named productRow that will hold a reference to the current row. This variable will be set by the event handler for the combo box's SelectedIndexChanged event and the event handler for the Add button's Click event. It will also be accessed by various methods throughout the application.

The Load event handler for the form begins by calling the data adapter's Fill method to retrieve the product data from the database. Then, it calls a method named FillProductsComboBox to load the product codes and descriptions into the Products combo box. This method contains code like the code you saw in figure 19-5, so you shouldn't have any trouble understanding how it works. After the combo box is loaded, the Load event handler sets its SelectedIndex property to 0 so that the first product in the list is displayed. Finally, it calls the DisableAddEditMode method to initialize the form controls.

The code for the Product Maintenance application **Page 1**

```
private bool isAddMode;
private productsDataSet.ProductsRow productRow;

private void frmProduct_Load(object sender, System.EventArgs e)
{
    productsDataAdapter.Fill(productsDataSet1);
    FillProductsComboBox();
    cboProducts.SelectedIndex = 0;
    DisableAddEditMode();
}

private void FillProductsComboBox()
{
    cboProducts.Items.Clear();
    DictionaryEntry productEntry;
    foreach (productsDataSet.ProductsRow pr in productsDataSet1.Products.Rows)
    {
        if (pr.RowState != DataRowState.Deleted)
        {
            productEntry = new DictionaryEntry(pr.ProductCode,
                pr.Description);
            cboProducts.Items.Add(productEntry);
        }
    }
}

private void DisableAddEditMode()
{
    cboProducts.Enabled = true;
    txtProductCode.ReadOnly = true;
    txtDescription.ReadOnly = true;
    txtUnitPrice.ReadOnly = true;
    btnAdd.Enabled = true;
    btnEdit.Enabled = true;
    btnDelete.Enabled = true;
    btnAccept.Enabled = false;
    btnCancel.Enabled = false;
    btnUpdateDatabase.Enabled = productsDataSet1.HasChanges();
    cboProducts.Focus();
}
```

Figure 19-7 The code for the Product Maintenance application (part 1 of 5)

The event handler for the SelectedIndexChanged event of the Products combo box displays the data for the selected product. To get the selected row, it uses the FindByProductCode method of the Products table. To get the product code for the selected product, it calls a method named SelectedProductCode. This method retrieves the DictionaryEntry for the selected item and returns its Key property as a string.

Once the selected product has been retrieved, the ShowProductData method is called. This method assigns the values in the product row to the Text properties of the appropriate text boxes. Notice that, like the code you saw in figure 19-2, the UnitPrice column is converted to a string and then formatted so it's displayed with two decimal places.

If the user clicks the Add button, the Click event handler for this button is executed. This event handler calls the ClearProductFields method to clear the three input fields. Then, it calls the EnableAddEditMode method to enable the input controls, and it sets the isAddMode variable to true. Notice that this method doesn't create a data row. That's not necessary until the user clicks the Accept button and the data has been validated.

The code for the Product Maintenance application Page 2

```
private void EnableAddEditMode()
{
    cboProducts.Enabled = false;
    txtProductCode.ReadOnly = false;
    txtDescription.ReadOnly = false;
    txtUnitPrice.ReadOnly = false;
    btnAdd.Enabled = false;
    btnEdit.Enabled = false;
    btnDelete.Enabled = false;
    btnAccept.Enabled = true;
    btnCancel.Enabled = true;
    btnUpdateDatabase.Enabled = false;
    txtProductCode.Focus();
}

private void cboProducts_SelectedIndexChanged(object sender,
    System.EventArgs e)
{
    productRow =
       productsDataSet1.Products.FindByProductCode(SelectedProductCode());
    ShowProductData();
}

private string SelectedProductCode()
{
    DictionaryEntry dictEntry =
        (DictionaryEntry)cboProducts.SelectedItem;
    return dictEntry.Key.ToString();
}

private void ShowProductData()
{
    txtProductCode.Text = productRow.ProductCode;
    txtDescription.Text = productRow.Description;
    txtUnitPrice.Text = productRow.UnitPrice.ToString("f2");
}

private void btnAdd_Click(object sender, System.EventArgs e)
{
    ClearProductFields();
    EnableAddEditMode();
    isAddMode = true;
}

private void ClearProductFields()
{
    txtProductCode.Text = "";
    txtDescription.Text = "";
    txtUnitPrice.Text = "";
}

private void btnEdit_Click(object sender, System.EventArgs e)
{
    EnableAddEditMode();
    isAddMode = false;
}
```

Figure 19-7 The code for the Product Maintenance application (part 2 of 5)

The Click event handler for the Accept button on page 3 of this listing begins by calling the IsValidData method to validate the data. This method works just like the one in chapter 18 except that it calls a method named IsDecimal to check that the unit price is a decimal value. That's necessary because the Unit Price text box isn't bound to the UnitPrice column, so the data type checking isn't done automatically.

If the data is valid, the processing that follows depends on whether the isAddMode variable is true or false. If it's true, a new product row is created. Then, the FillProductRow method is called to set the new row's column values to the values entered by the user. Next, the new row is added to the data table. Finally, the combo box is updated so it shows the new product and isAddMode is set to false.

If isAddMode is false when the user clicks the Accept button, the FillProductRow method is called to set the row's column values to the values entered by the user. Then, the FillProductsComboBox method is called to refresh the combo box so that it reflects the changes made to the product. Notice that an integer variable is used to save the value of the SelectedIndex property before the FillProductsComboBox method is called. That way, the same product can be selected again after the combo box has been updated.

Like the bound version of this application, most of the code in the Accept event handler is coded within a try block that will catch a constraint exception. You may recall that a constraint exception will be raised if the user tries to add a product using a product code that already exists or if the user tries to change the product code for an existing row to a product code that already exists. In that case, an error message is displayed and the operation is not performed.

If the user clicks the Cancel button to cancel out of an operation, the event handler for the Click event of this button, shown on page 4, starts by checking if a row was being added. If so, the FindByProductCode method is used to get the row for the product that was previously displayed. This works because that product is still selected in the Products combo box. Then, the ShowProductData method is called to redisplay the data for that product. This method is also called if a product was bcing modified. That way, the original values for the row are redisplayed.

The Click event handler for the Delete button, shown on page 5, starts by displaying a dialog box to confirm the delete operation. If it's confirmed, the Delete method of the product row is called to mark the row for deletion. Then, the FillProductsComboBox method is called to update the products combo box so that the deleted row is no longer included. In addition, the SelectedIndex property of the combo box is set to 0 so that the first product is displayed.

The Click event handler for the Update Database button updates the database and then clears and refills the dataset just like the unbound version of this application. In addition, it refills the Products combo box and sets its SelectedIndex property to 0 so that the first product is displayed.

The last two procedures work just like the ones you saw in the last chapter. They handle the processing for closing the form when the user clicks the Exit button or the close button of the form.

The code for the Product Maintenance application Page 3

```
private void btnAccept_Click(object sender, System.EventArgs e)
{
    if (IsValidData())
    {
        try
        {
            if (isAddMode)
            {
                productRow = productsDataSet1.Products.NewProductsRow();
                FillProductRow();
                productsDataSet1.Products.AddProductsRow(productRow);
                FillProductsComboBox();
                cboProducts.SelectedIndex = cboProducts.Items.Count - 1;
                isAddMode = false;
            }
            else
            {
                FillProductRow();
                int i = cboProducts.SelectedIndex;
                FillProductsComboBox();
                cboProducts.SelectedIndex = i;
            }
            DisableAddEditMode();
        }
        catch (ConstraintException)
        {
            MessageBox.Show("There is already a product with that code.",
                "Entry Error");
            txtProductCode.Focus();
        }
    }
}

private bool IsValidData()
{
    if (!IsPresent(txtProductCode, "Product Code"))
        return false;
    if (!IsPresent(txtDescription, "Description"))
        return false;
    if (!IsPresent(txtUnitPrice, "Unit Price"))
        return false;
    if (!IsDecimal(txtUnitPrice, "Unit Price"))
        return false;

    return true;
}
```

Figure 19-7 The code for the Product Maintenance application (part 3 of 5)

The code for the Product Maintenance application Page 4

```
private bool IsPresent(TextBox textBox, string name)
{
    if (textBox.Text == "")
    {
        MessageBox.Show(name + " is a required field.", "Entry Error");
        textBox.Focus();
        return false;
    }
    return true;
}

private bool IsDecimal(TextBox textBox, string name)
{
    try
    {
        Convert.ToDecimal(textBox.Text);
        return true;
    }
    catch(FormatException)
    {
        MessageBox.Show(name + " must be a decimal value.", "Entry
Error");
        textBox.Focus();
        return false;
    }
}

private void FillProductRow()
{
    productRow.ProductCode = txtProductCode.Text;
    productRow.Description = txtDescription.Text;
    productRow.UnitPrice = Convert.ToDecimal(txtUnitPrice.Text);
}

private void btnCancel_Click(object sender, System.EventArgs e)
{
    if (isAddMode)
    {
        productRow =
           productsDataSet1.Products.FindByProductCode(SelectedProductCode());
        isAddMode = false;
    }
    ShowProductData();
    DisableAddEditMode();
}
```

Figure 19-7 The code for the Product Maintenance application (part 4 of 5)

The code for the Product Maintenance application Page 5

```
private void btnDelete_Click(object sender, System.EventArgs e)
{
    if (MessageBox.Show("Delete " + cboProducts.Text + "?",
        "Confirm Delete", MessageBoxButtons.YesNo,
        MessageBoxIcon.Question) == DialogResult.Yes)
    {
        productRow.Delete();
        FillProductsComboBox();
        cboProducts.SelectedIndex = 0;
        DisableAddEditMode();
    }
}

private void btnUpdateDatabase_Click(object sender, System.EventArgs e)
{
    productsDataAdapter.Update(productsDataSet1);
    productsDataSet1.Clear();
    productsDataAdapter.Fill(productsDataSet1);
    FillProductsComboBox();
    cboProducts.SelectedIndex = 0;
    DisableAddEditMode();
}

private void btnExit_Click(object sender, System.EventArgs e)
{
    this.Close();
}

private void frmProduct_Closing(object sender,
    System.ComponentModel.CancelEventArgs e)
{
    if (productsDataSet1.HasChanges())
        if (MessageBox.Show("You have made changes that have not " +
            "been saved to the database.\n" +
            "If you continue, these changes will be lost.\n" +
            "Continue?", "Confirm Exit", MessageBoxButtons.YesNo,
            MessageBoxIcon.Warning) == DialogResult.No)
            e.Cancel = true;
}
```

Figure 19-7 The code for the Product Maintenance application (part 5 of 5)

Perspective

Although the unbound application in this chapter requires a few more lines of code than the bound application in the last chapter, it shouldn't be any more difficult for you to understand. In general, when you don't bind controls to a dataset, you just work directly with the dataset instead of working with it through the binding manager. This technique is preferred for many applications because it gives you more control over how the data is processed.

Now that you know how to use both bound and unbound controls with typed datasets, you may want to look at how a typed dataset is defined. To do that, you can double-click on the productsDataSet.cs class file in the Solution Explorer. (You may need to click the plus sign next to the productsDataSet.xsd file to see it.) Then, the C# code that defines the dataset is displayed in the Code Editor window. Although you may not understand all of the code, you should understand enough to get a good feel for how a typed dataset lets you work with data. Then, you can compare that to the techniques you'll learn in the next chapter for working directly with data commands.

Summary

- If you don't bind form controls to a dataset, you have to provide for the functions of the binding manager through code. In addition, you have to use the properties and methods of the data objects to work with the data instead of using the properties and methods of the binding manager.
- You can use the properties and methods provided by a typed dataset to retrieve, modify, and delete an existing row and to add a new row. Some of these properties and methods are defined by the typed dataset and some are inherited from other classes.
- Each row in a data table has a state that depends on the operations that have been performed on the row and whether or not the operations have been committed.

Objectives

- Given the specifications for an application that uses a typed dataset and unbound controls, design and code the application.
- Add the code necessary to work with row states to any application.
- List and describe the properties and methods you use to (1) retrieve a row from a typed dataset, (2) modify or delete a row, and (3) add a new row.
- List and describe the five possible states of a data row.

Exercise 19-1 Maintain Customers table

In this exercise, you'll create a Customer Maintenance form like the one shown below that lets you add, modify, and delete rows in the Customers table using a typed dataset and unbound controls. To make this form easier to develop, we'll give you a starting form that contains all the controls you'll need.

The design of the Customer Maintenance form

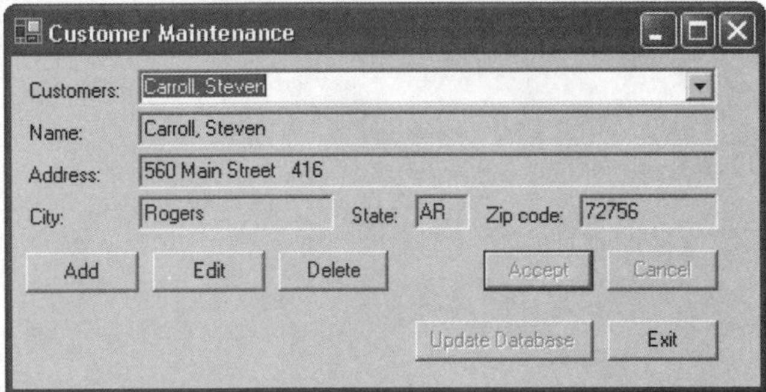

Development procedure

1. Open the project named CustomerMaintenance in the C:\C#.NET\Chapter 19 directory. Then, use the Configuration Wizard to create a data adapter that can be used to add, update, and delete rows in the Customers table. The customers should be sorted by name. Generate a dataset from the data adapter.
2. Add the code required to fill the dataset, fill the combo box with DictionaryEntry objects, display the customer data when the user selects a customer from the combo box, and close the form when the user clicks the Exit button. Be sure to set the DisplayMember property of the combo box to Value so that the Value properties of the DictionaryEntry objects are displayed in the list. Then, test the application to make sure that this works properly.
3. Add the code required to implement the Add, Edit, and Delete functions. Be sure that the ReadOnly properties of the text boxes and the Enabled properties of the combo box and button controls are set as appropriate, that the data is validated before being accepted, and that the dataset is checked for changes before the form is closed. Note that you do not need to check for a constraint exception when you add or update a row since the primary key for the table is an identity column that's automatically maintained by the database. Test the application to be sure that these functions work properly.
4. Add the code required to update the database and refresh the dataset. Test the application one more time and make any necessary corrections. When it works the way you want it to, close the solution.

20

How to work with ADO.NET classes through code

In the preceding chapters, you've seen how to use the Data Adapter Configuration Wizard to create data adapter, connection, and command objects. But you can also create and work with these objects through code. In addition, you can execute data commands directly without using a data adapter. Then, you can process the results without using a dataset. These are the skills that you'll learn in this chapter.

One advantage of creating ADO.NET objects through code is that you can separate that code from the code for the user interface. To do that, you place the ADO.NET code in separate databases classes like the ones you saw in chapter 12. Then, your applications will be easier to read and maintain.

How to work with connections and commands

Before you can access the data in a database, you must create a connection object. Then, you must create one or more command objects that contain the SQL statements you want to execute against the database. You'll learn how to create and work with connection and command objects in the topics that follow.

How to create and work with connections

Figure 20-1 shows how you create and use a connection to access a SQL Server database. As you can see from the syntax at the top of this figure, you can specify a connection string when you create the connection. If you do, this string is assigned to the ConnectionString property. That's the case in the code example shown in this figure. If you don't specify a connection string when you create the connection, you have to assign a value to the ConnectionString property after you create the connection object.

The SqlConnection class provides Open and Close methods you can use to open and close the database connection. If you use a data adapter to retrieve and update database data, you don't need to use these methods because the data adapter automatically opens and closes the connection when it needs to access the database. If you'll be using data commands to access the database, however, you'll need to open and close the connection explicitly.

This figure also shows some of the common values that you specify in a connection string for a SQL Server database. The SQL Server connection string, for example, specifies the name of the server where the database resides, the name of the database, and the type of security to be used.

Because the requirements for each provider differ, you may need to consult the documentation for that provider to determine what values to specify. The second connection string shown in this figure, for example, is for the Jet OLE DB provider. As you can see, this connection string includes the name of the provider and the location of the database.

Notice in both the SQL Server and the Jet OLE DB connection strings that you must code two backslash characters (\\) for each backslash you want to include. As you may recall from chapter 4, the backslash identifies an escape sequence when coded within a string. Because of that, you have to code the \\ escape sequence to include a single backslash character.

Before I go on, you should realize that the connection strings for production applications are frequently stored in configuration files outside the application. That way, they can be accessed by any application that needs them, and they can be modified without having to modify and recompile each application. How an application actually retrieves the connection string depends on how it's stored. If it's stored in a text file, for example, the application can use a text reader as shown in chapter 21; if it's stored in an XML file, the application can use an XML reader as shown in chapter 22.

Two constructors for the SqlConnection class

```
sqlConnection = new SqlConnection();
sqlConnection = new SqlConnection(connectionString);
```

Common properties and methods of a connection

Property	Description
`ConnectionString`	Provides information for accessing a SQL Server database.
Method	**Description**
`Open()`	Opens the connection using the specified connection string.
`Close()`	Closes the connection.

Common values used in the ConnectionString property

Name	Description
Data source/Server	The name of the instance of SQL Server you want to connect to.
Database/Initial catalog	The name of the database you want to access.
Integrated security	Determines whether the connection is secure. Valid values are True, False, and SSPI. SSPI uses Windows integrated security and is equivalent to True.
Persist security info	Determines whether sensitive information, such as the password, is returned as part of the connection. The default is False.
Packet size	The number of bytes in the packets used to communicate with SQL Server. The default is 8192, but the Configuration Wizard sets this value to 4096.
User id	The user id that's used to log in to SQL Server.
Password/Pwd	The password that's used to log in to SQL Server.
Workstation ID	The name of the workstation that's connecting to SQL Server.

A connection string for the SQL Server provider

```
server=DOUG\\VSdotNET;database=MMABooks;integrated security=SSPI
```

A connection string for the Jet OLE DB provider

```
Provider=Microsoft.Jet.OLEDB.4.0;Data Source=C:\\Databases\\MMABooks.mdb
```

Code that creates, opens, and closes a SQL connection

```
string conString = "server=DOUG\\VSdotNET;database=MMABooks;"
                 + "integrated security=SSPI";
SqlConnection mmaBooksConnection = new SqlConnection(conString);
mmaBooksConnection.Open();
...
mmaBooksConnection.Close();
```

Description

- You can set the ConnectionString property after you create a connection or as you create it by passing the string to the constructor of the connection class.
- The values you specify for the ConnectionString property depend on the type of database you're connecting to.

Figure 20-1 How to create and work with connections

How to create and work with commands

After you define the connection to the database, you create the command objects that contain the SQL statements you want to execute against the database. Figure 20-2 shows three constructors for the SqlCommand class. The first one doesn't require arguments. When you use this constructor, you must set the Connection property to the connection to be used by the command and the CommandText property to the text of the SQL statement before you execute the command.

The second constructor accepts the SQL command text as an argument. Then, you just have to set the Connection property before you can execute the command. The third constructor accepts both the connection and the command text as arguments. The code example in the figure uses this constructor.

Another property you may need to set is the CommandType property. This property determines how the value of the CommandText property is interpreted. The values you can specify for this property are members of the CommandType enumeration that's shown in this figure. The default value is Text, which causes the value of the CommandText property to be interpreted as a SQL statement. If the CommandText property contains the name of a stored procedure, however, you'll need to set this property to StoredProcedure. And if the CommandText property contains the name of a table, you'll need to set this property to TableDirect. Then, all the rows and columns will be retrieved from the table. Note that this setting is only available for the OLE DB data provider.

The last property that's shown in this figure, Parameters, lets you work with the collection of parameters for a command. As you'll see in the next topic, you can use parameters to restrict the data that's retrieved by a Select statement, to specify the row to be deleted by a Delete statement, or to provide column values for an Insert or Update statement.

In addition to the properties shown in this figure, you can also use the three Execute methods of a command object to execute the statement it contains. You'll learn how to use these methods later in this chapter.

Three constructors for the SqlCommand class

```
sqlCommand = new SqlCommand();
sqlCommand = new SqlCommand(cmdText);
sqlCommand = new SqlCommand(cmdText, connection);
```

Common properties and methods of a command

Property	Description
Connection	The connection used to connect to the database.
CommandText	A SQL statement, the name of a stored procedure, or the name of a table.
CommandType	A member of the CommandType enumeration that determines how the value in the CommandText property is interpreted.
Parameters	The collection of parameters for the command.
Method	**Description**
ExecuteReader()	Executes a query and returns the result as a data reader object.
ExecuteNonQuery()	Executes the command and returns an integer representing the number of rows affected.
ExecuteScalar()	Executes a query and returns the first column of the first row returned by the query.

CommandType enumeration members

Member	Description
Text	The CommandText property contains a SQL statement. This is the default.
StoredProcedure	The CommandText property contains the name of a stored procedure.
TableDirect	The CommandText property contains the name of a table (OLE DB provider only).

Code that creates a SqlCommand object that executes a Select statement

```
string selectStatement = "SELECT ProductCode, Description, UnitPrice "
                       + "FROM Products "
                       + "ORDER BY ProductCode";
SqlCommand selectCommand
    = new SqlCommand(selectStatement, mmaBooksConnection);
```

Description

- The CommandText and Connection properties are set to the values you pass to the constructor of the command class. If you don't pass these values to the constructor, you must set the CommandText and Connection properties after you create the command object.
- If you set the CommandText property to the name of a stored procedure or table, you must also set the CommandType property.

Figure 20-2 How to create and work with commands

How to use parameters in SQL statements

A *parameter* is a variable that's used in a SQL statement. Parameters let you create statements that retrieve or update database data based on variable information. For example, an application that maintains the Products table can use a parameter in the Where clause of a Select statement to retrieve a specific row from the Products table based on the value of the ProductCode column. A Select statement that uses parameters in the Where clause is called a *parameterized query*. You can also use parameters in other types of SQL statements, including Insert, Update, and Delete statements.

To use parameters in a SQL statement, you use placeholders as shown in figure 20-3. These placeholders indicate where the parameters should be inserted when the statement is executed. Unfortunately, database management systems don't use a standard syntax for coding placeholders.

For example, the first select statement in this figure is for SQL Server. As you can see, you use a *named variable* to identify a parameter. Note that the name of the variable must begin with an at sign (@) and is usually given the same name as the column it's associated with. Oracle also uses named variables, but the names must begin with a colon (:) as illustrated in the second Select statement. In contrast, the placeholder for an OLE DB or ODBC parameter is a question mark, as shown in the third Select statement.

After you define the SQL statement, you create the parameter objects and set their values. The next figure shows you how to do that.

A SQL Server Select statement that uses a parameter

```
SELECT ProductCode, Description, UnitPrice
FROM Products
WHERE ProductCode = @ProductCode
```

An Oracle Select statement that uses a parameter

```
SELECT ProductCode, Description, UnitPrice
FROM Products
WHERE ProductCode = :ProductCode
```

An OLE DB or ODBC Select statement that uses a parameter

```
SELECT ProductCode, Description, UnitPrice
FROM Products
WHERE ProductCode = ?
```

A SQL Server Insert statement that uses parameters

```
INSERT INTO Products
(ProductCode, Description, UnitPrice)
VALUES (@ProductCode, @Description, @UnitPrice)
```

Description

- A *parameter* lets you place variable information into a SQL statement.
- When you use a parameter in the Where clause of a Select statement, the resulting query is often called a *parameterized query* because the results of the query depend on the value of the parameters.
- Parameters are also often used in Insert or Update statements to provide the values for the database row or rows to be inserted or updated. Likewise, you can use parameters in a Delete statement to indicate which row or rows should be deleted.
- To use parameters, you code a SQL statement with placeholders for the parameters. Then, you create a parameter object that defines each parameter, and you add it to the Parameters collection of the command object that contains the SQL statement.
- The placeholder for a parameter in a SQL Server command is a *named variable* whose name begins with an at sign (@). For Oracle, the name of a variable begins with a colon (:). In most cases, you'll give the variable the same name as the column it's associated with.
- If you're using the OLE DB or ODBC provider, you code the placeholder for a parameter as a question mark. The question mark simply indicates the position of the parameter.

Figure 20-3 How to use parameters in SQL statements

How to create and work with parameters

Figure 20-4 shows you how to create and work with SQL parameters. Here, you can see three constructors for the SqlParameter class. Although there are others, these are the three you're most likely to use. You create a parameter for an OLE DB, ODBC, or Oracle command using similar techniques.

Before you can use a parameter, you must assign a name, a data type, and a value to it. If you don't pass these values as arguments to the constructor when you create the object, you can do that using some of the properties shown in this figure. Notice that you can specify the data type using either the DbType or SqlDbType property for a SQL Server parameter. (Similarly, you can use either the DbType property or the OleDbType, OdbcType, or OracleType property for an OLE DB, ODBC, or Oracle parameter.)

The first example in this figure shows how to create a parameter and add it to the collection of parameters for a command using a single statement. This statement uses the second constructor for the SqlParameter class to create a parameter named @ProductCode. This is the parameter that's used by the first Select statement in figure 20-3. Then, this statement uses the Add method of the Parameters collection to add the parameter to the collection of parameters for a command named selectCommand. This is the command that contains the Select statement.

The second example creates a parameter and adds it to the Parameters collection without using the constructor for the SqlParameter class. This works because the Add method accepts either an SqlParameter object or the property values for that object. Note that when you use this technique, you must specify a parameter name and a value or type.

Note that in both of these examples, a variable is not created to refer to the parameter object. To access the parameter object after you've created it, then, you can use the parameter name as an indexer to the Parameters collection of the command object. This is illustrated in the third code example in this figure, which shows how to set the Value property of the @ProductCode parameter.

The fourth example shows another technique for working with parameters. This example starts by creating a parameter object and assigning it to a variable named unitPriceParm. Then, it uses this variable to set the parameter's properties. Notice that the DbType property is set to DbType.Currency since the UnitPrice column in the Products table has a data type of Currency. Finally, this code adds the parameter to the command's Parameters collection.

When you assign a name to a SQL Server or Oracle parameter, you should realize that it must be the same name that's specified in the SQL statement. That's because ADO.NET associates the parameters with the placeholders by name. Because of that, if a statement uses two or more parameters, you can add them to the Parameters collection in any sequence. In contrast, OLE DB and ODBC parameters must be added to the collection in the same order that they appear in the SQL statement. In that case, ADO.NET associates the parameters with the placeholders in the SQL statement by sequence since the placeholders aren't named.

Three constructors for the SqlParameter class

```
sqlParameter = new SqlParameter();
sqlParameter = new SqlParameter(parameterName, value);
sqlParameter = new SqlParameter(parameterName, type);
```

Common properties of a SQL Server parameter

Property	Description
`DbType`	A member of the DbType enumeration that determines the type of data that the parameter can hold. The default value is DbType.String.
`ParameterName`	The name of the parameter.
`Size`	The maximum size of the value that the parameter can hold.
`SqlDbType`	A member of the SqlDbType enumeration that determines the type of data that the parameter can hold. This property is synchronized with the DbType property.
`Value`	The value of the parameter.

A statement that adds a new parameter to a Parameters collection

```
selectCommand.Parameters.Add(
    new SqlParameter("@ProductCode", product.ProductCode);
```

Another way to create a parameter and add it to a Parameters collection

```
selectCommand.Parameters.Add("@ProductCode", product.ProductCode);
```

Code that changes the value of an existing parameter

```
selectCommand.Parameters["@ProductCode"].Value = product.ProductCode;
```

Code that creates a parameter variable and adds it to the parameters collection

```
SqlParameter unitPriceParm = new SqlParameter();
unitPriceParm.ParameterName = "@UnitPrice";
unitPriceParm.DbType = DbType.Currency;
unitPriceParm.Value = product.UnitPrice;
insertCommand.Parameters.Add(unitPriceParm);
```

Description

- When you create a parameter, you can specify the parameter name along with a value or a data type. If you don't specify these values, you can set the values of the associated properties after you create the parameter.
- When you create parameters for a SQL Server or Oracle command, you must give them the same names you used in the SQL statement, including the at sign (@) or colon (:). Then, you can add the parameters to the parameters collection in any order you want since ADO.NET refers to them by name.
- Because the parameters for an OLE DB or ODBC command aren't named in the SQL statement, the parameters can be given any name you want. However, they must be added to the Parameters collection in the same order that they appear in the statement.
- You can refer to a parameter by using the parameter name as an indexer to the parameters collection of the command or by assigning the parameter to a variable.

Figure 20-4 How to create and work with parameters

How to execute data commands

The method you use to execute the SQL statement associated with a command object depends on the operation the SQL statement performs. The three methods you're most likely to use are ExecuteReader, which lets you retrieve and work with a result set created by a Select statement; ExecuteScalar, which lets you retrieve a single value using a Select statement; and ExecuteNonQuery, which lets you execute an Insert, Update, or Delete statement. You'll learn how to use all three of these methods in the topics that follow.

How to create and work with a data reader

To execute a command that contains a Select statement that returns a result set, you use the ExecuteReader method as shown in figure 20-5. This method executes the Select statement and creates a data reader object. Then, you can use the properties and methods of the data reader to work with the result set.

Notice that when you execute the ExecuteReader method, you can specify a behavior. The behavior you specify must be a member of the CommandBehavior enumeration. The most commonly used members of this enumeration are listed in this figure. You can use these members to simplify your code or to improve the efficiency of your application.

After you create a data reader, you use the Read method to retrieve the next row of data in the result set. Note that you must also execute the Read method to retrieve the first row of data because it isn't retrieved automatically when the data reader is created.

To access a column from the most recently retrieved row, you use the column name as an indexer. For example, productReader["ProductCode"] retrieves the value of the ProductCode column for the most recently retrieved row for a data reader named productReader. You can also specify a column by its position in the row by using an integer indexer. For example, productReader[0] retrieves the value of the first column.

The code example in this figure illustrates how you use a data reader. First, a SqlCommand object is created to read data from the Products table. Then, the connection is opened and the ExecuteReader method is used to retrieve the product data and create a data reader that can process the product rows. Because the CloseConnection behavior is included on this method, the connection will be closed automatically when the data reader is closed. The ExecuteReader method also opens the data reader and positions it before the first row in the result set.

Next, a while loop is used to loop through the rows in the result set. The condition on this statement executes the Read method of the data reader. This works because the Read method returns a Boolean value that indicates whether the result set contains additional rows. As long as this condition is true, the program processes the row that was retrieved. In this case, the program adds the value of the ProductCode column to a combo box list. After all of the rows have been processed, the data reader is closed.

Two ways to create a SqlDataReader object

```
sqlDataReader = sqlCommand.ExecuteReader();
sqlDataReader = sqlCommand.ExecuteReader(behavior);
```

Common CommandBehavior enumeration members

Member	Description
CloseConnection	Closes the connection when the data reader is closed.
Default	Equivalent to specifying no command behavior.
SingleRow	Only a single row is returned.

Common properties and methods of a SqlDataReader object

Property	Description
IsClosed	Gets a value that indicates if the data reader is closed.
[columnname]	Gets the value of the column with the specified name.
[index]	Gets the value of the column at the specified position.
Method	**Description**
Close()	Closes the data reader.
Read()	Retrieves the next row and returns a Boolean value that indicates whether there are additional rows.

Code that uses a data reader to populate a list box with product codes

```
string selectStatement = "SELECT ProductCode, Description FROM Products";
SqlCommand selectCommand
    = new SqlCommand(selectStatement, mmaBooksConnection);
mmaBooksConnection.Open();
SqlDataReader productReader;
productReader
    = selectCommand.ExecuteReader(CommandBehavior.CloseConnection);
while (productReader.Read())
    cboProducts.Items.Add(productReader["ProductCode"]);
productReader.Close();
```

Description

- A data reader lets you read rows from the result set defined by a command object. To create a data reader object, you use the ExecuteReader method of the command. Before you execute this method, you must open the connection that's used by the data reader.
- The data reader is opened automatically when it's created. While it's open, no other data readers can be opened on the same connection. The exception is if you're using an Oracle data reader, in which case other Oracle data readers can be open at the same time.
- When you first create a data reader, it's positioned before the first row in the result set. To retrieve the first row, you have to execute the Read method.
- You can specify two or more command behavior members by combining them using the And operator.
- You can use either a column name or its index to refer to a column in a data reader.

Figure 20-5 How to create and work with a data reader

How to execute queries that return a single value

The first example in figure 20-6 shows you how to execute a command that returns a single value, called a *scalar value*. To do that, you execute the ExecuteScalar method of the command. In this case, the command contains a Select statement that retrieves a count of the number of products in the Products table. This type of summary value is often called an *aggregate value*. A scalar value can also be the value of a single column, a calculated value, or any other value that can be retrieved from the database.

Note that the ExecuteScalar method returns an Object type. Because of that, you must cast that object to an appropriate data type to get its value. In this example, the object is cast to an integer.

Before I go on, you should realize that you can use the ExecuteScalar method with a Select statement that retrieves more than one value. In that case, though, the ExecuteScalar method returns only the first value and the others are discarded.

How to execute action queries

As you know, you can use an Insert, Update, or Delete statement to perform actions against a database. For that reason, these statements are often referred to as *action queries*. To execute an action query, you use the ExecuteNonQuery method of a data command as shown in the second example in figure 20-6.

This example executes a command that contains an Insert statement that adds a row to the Products table. Notice that the ExecuteNonQuery method returns an integer that indicates the number of rows in the database that were affected by the operation. You can use this value to check that the operation was successful.

Code that creates and executes a command that returns an aggregate value

```
string selectStatement = "SELECT Count(*) FROM Products";
SqlCommand selectCommand
    = new SqlCommand(selectStatement, mmaBooksConnection);
mmaBooksConnection.Open();
int productCount = (int) selectCommand.ExecuteScalar();
mmaBooksConnection.Close();
lblProductCount.Text = productCount.ToString();
```

Code that creates and executes a command that inserts a row

```
string insertStatement = "INSERT INTO Products "
                       + "(ProductCode, Description, UnitPrice) "
                       + "VALUES (@ProductCode, @Description, @UnitPrice)";
SqlCommand insertCommand
    = new SqlCommand(insertStatement, mmaBooksConnection);
insertCommand.Parameters.Add("@ProductCode", product.ProductCode);
insertCommand.Parameters.Add("@Description", product.Description);
insertCommand.Parameters.Add("@UnitPrice", product.UnitPrice);
mmaBooksConnection.Open();
try
{
    int productCount = insertCommand.ExecuteNonQuery();
}
catch (SqlException ex)
{
    MessageBox.Show(ex.Message);
}
finally
{
    mmaBooksConnection.Close();
}
```

Description

- You use the ExecuteScalar method of a command object to retrieve a single value, called a *scalar value*.
- The value that's returned can be the value of a single column and row in the database, a calculated value, an *aggregate value* that summarizes data in the database, or any other value that can be retrieved from the database.
- If the Select statement returns more than one column or row, only the value in the first column and row is retrieved by the ExecuteScalar method.
- You use the ExecuteNonQuery method of a command object to execute an Insert, Update, or Delete statement, called an *action query*. This method returns an integer that indicates the number of rows that were affected by the query.

Figure 20-6 How to execute queries that don't return a result set

How to work with untyped datasets and data adapters

An *untyped dataset* is one that isn't based on a custom dataset class. Instead, it's based on the generic ADO.NET DataSet class. In the two topics that follow, you'll learn the basic skills for creating and working with untyped datasets.

How to create and work with untyped datasets

Figure 20-7 presents the basic skills for creating and working with an untyped dataset. To create an untyped dataset, you can use one of the constructors shown in this figure. The first statement in this figure, for example, creates an untyped dataset and assigns it to a variable named productsDataSet. You can also assign a name to the dataset when you create it. In most cases, though, you won't need to do that.

To work with an untyped dataset, you use the properties and methods of the DataSet class. These properties let you access the various collections that make up a dataset. To access the collection of tables in a dataset, for example, you use the Tables property of the dataset. To access the collection of rows in a table, you use the Rows property of the table.

The second and third statements in this figure help illustrate how this works. Both statements access a table in the productsDataSet dataset. The second statement accesses a table using the name as an indexer for the Tables collection. The third statement accesses a table by position. In this case, an index value of 0 is specified, so the first table is retrieved. You use similar techniques to refer to items in other collections.

Two constructors for the DataSet class

```
dataset = New DataSet();
dataset = New DataSet(dataSetName);
```

Common properties used to access data collections

Class	Property	Description
DataSet	Tables	A collection of the tables in the dataset.
DataTable	Rows	A collection of the rows in a data table.
	Columns	A collection of the columns in a data table.

A statement that creates an untyped dataset

```
DataSet productsDataSet = new DataSet();
```

A statement that refers to a table in the dataset by name

```
cboProducts.DataSource = productsDataSet.Tables["Products"];
```

A statement that refers to a table in the dataset by index

```
cboProducts.DataSource = productsDataSet.Tables[0];
```

Description

- An *untyped dataset* is one that's created from the generic ADO.NET DataSet class. You use the properties and methods of this class to work with an untyped dataset and the objects it contains.
- The information within a dataset is stored in collections. To refer to a collection, you can use a property of the parent object. To refer to the collection of tables in a dataset, for example, you use the Tables property of the dataset as shown above.
- You can use either an object's name or its index to refer to an object in a collection.

Figure 20-7 How to create and work with untyped datasets

How to create and work with data adapters

Figure 20-8 presents two constructors you can use to create a SQL Server data adapter. If you use the first constructor, you don't pass an argument to the constructor. In that case, you have to set the value of the SelectCommand property after you create the data adapter. This property identifies the SqlCommand object that will be used to retrieve data when the Fill method of the data adapter is executed. If you use the second constructor, you can associate a SqlCommand object with the data adapter when you create the adapter.

If you will be updating the data that's retrieved by a data adapter, you'll also need to create command objects that contain Insert, Update, and Delete statements and assign them to the InsertCommand, UpdateCommand, and DeleteCommand properties of the data adapter. You'll see an example that does that later in this chapter.

This figure also presents the two methods of a data adapter that you're most likely to use: Fill and Update. As you already know, you use the Fill method to load a data table with data from a database, and you use the Update method to update a database with changes made to a data table. Notice in the code example in this figure that the name of the table to be created is coded as the second argument of the Fill method. That's because, unlike a data adapter that you create with the Configuration Wizard, the table mappings aren't generated automatically. So if you omit the table name argument, the data is placed in a table named "Table," which usually isn't what you want. By the way, if the table you specify already exists, its data is refreshed when you execute the Fill method. Otherwise, the table is created.

When you call the Fill method, the data adapter automatically creates schema information in the dataset to indicate which columns are contained in the table. However, the data adapter doesn't automatically create a primary key for the table, so you won't be able to retrieve data rows based on their key values. If you want the data adapter to create a primary key for the table, you set the data adapter's MissingSchemaAction property to the AddWithKey member of the MissingSchemaAction enumeration before you fill the dataset.

Two constructors for the SqlDataAdapter class

```
sqlDataAdapter = new SqlDataAdapter();
sqlDataAdapter = new SqlDataAdapter(selectCommand);
```

Common properties and methods of the SqlDataAdapter class

Property	Description
SelectCommand	The command object used to retrieve data from the database.
InsertCommand	The command object used to insert new rows into the database.
UpdateCommand	The command object used to update rows in the database.
DeleteCommand	The command object used to delete rows from the database.
MissingSchemaAction	A member of the MissingSchemaAction enumeration that determines the action that's taken when the data retrieved by a Fill method doesn't match the schema of a table in the dataset.
Method	**Description**
Fill(dataSet, tableName)	Retrieves rows from the database using the command specified by the SelectCommand property and stores them in a data table.
Update(dataSet, tableName)	Saves changes made in the data table to the database using the commands specified by the InsertCommand, UpdateCommand, and DeleteCommand properties.

MissingSchemaAction enumeration members

Member	Description
Add	Adds the columns in the source table to the schema. This is the default.
AddWithKey	Adds the columns and primary key in the source table to the schema.
Error	A SystemException is generated.
Ignore	The columns that don't match the schema are ignored.

Code that creates a SqlDataAdapter object and then loads the dataset

```
SqlDataAdapter productsDataAdapter = new SqlDataAdapter();
productsDataAdapter.SelectCommand = selectCommand;
productsDataAdapter.MissingSchemaAction = MissingSchemaAction.AddWithKey;
productsDataAdapter.Fill(productsDataSet, "Products");
```

Description

- The SelectCommand property is set to the value you pass to the constructor of the data adapter. If you don't pass a Select command to the constructor, you must set this property after you create the data adapter.
- By default, the Fill method maps the data in the source table to a data table named "Table." Since that's usually not what you want, you should include the name of the data table as the second argument of the Fill method.

Figure 20-8 How to create and work with data adapters

A Product Maintenance application that uses data commands

The following topics present another version of the Product Maintenance application that you saw in the last two chapters. This version uses data commands to retrieve, insert, update, and delete rows from the Products table. Although this application is relatively simple, it illustrates the basic skills you'll need to develop more complex database applications.

The design of the Product Maintenance application

Figure 20-9 shows the form for the Product Maintenance application. This form is almost identical to the form used by the previous versions of this application. The only difference is that this form doesn't include an Update Database button. Instead, any time the user adds, modifies, or deletes a product, the change is immediately applied to the database.

This figure also summarizes the class design for this version of the Product Maintenance application. As you can see, this version uses two classes in addition to the form class: a Product class, which represents a single product row, and a ProductDB class, which provides static methods that handle all of the database processing for the application.

The ProductDB class has five public methods. The GetProducts method returns a DataTable object that holds the product codes and descriptions for all of the rows in the Products table. The application binds the Products combo box to this table. This shows that you can use a data table outside of a dataset.

The GetProduct method returns a Product object based on the product code that's passed to it. If no product is found with the specified product code, this method returns null.

The AddProduct, UpdateProduct, and DeleteProduct methods let you add, update, or delete a single product. These methods all return a Boolean value that indicates whether the operation was successful. As you can see, the AddProduct method accepts a Product object that supplies the data for the product to be added as an argument. The UpdateProduct method accepts an old Product object that contains the original data for the row and a new Product object that contains the updated product data. And the DeleteProduct method accepts the Product object that should be deleted. As you'll see in a minute, the UpdateProduct and DeleteProduct methods use the original product data to check for concurrency errors.

The Product Maintenance form

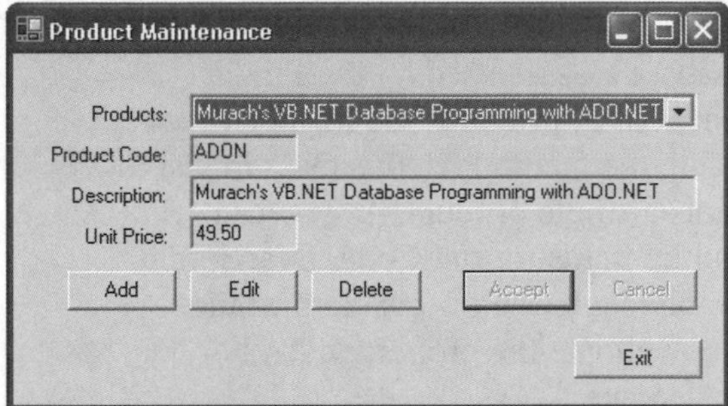

Properties of the Product class

Property	Description
ProductCode	A code that uniquely identifies the product.
Description	A text description of the product.
UnitPrice	The sales price of the product.

Methods of the ProductDB class

Method	Description
GetProducts()	Returns a DataTable object containing all the products in the Products table.
GetProduct(productCode)	Retrieves the specified product from the Products table. Returns null if the product doesn't exist.
AddProduct(product)	Adds a product to the Products table. Returns true if the product was successfully added. Otherwise, returns false.
UpdateProduct(oldProduct, newProduct)	Updates the specified product. Returns true if the product was successfully updated. Otherwise, returns false.
DeleteProduct(product)	Deletes the specified product. Returns true if the product was successfully deleted. Otherwise, returns false.

Description

- The operation of the Product Maintenance application is similar to the versions that were presented in chapters 18 and 19. The only difference is that the database is updated automatically whenever the user clicks the Accept or Delete button.
- This version of the Product Maintenance application uses two classes in addition to the form class. The Product class represents a single product in the Products table. The ProductDB class is responsible for performing the database operations required by the application.

Figure 20-9 The design of the Product Maintenance application

The code for the database classes

Figure 20-10 shows the code for the database classes used by the Product Maintenance application. The first class, ProductDB, provides the methods used to access the MMABooks database. I'll explain the methods in this class in just a moment. The second class, Product, represents a single product. As you can see on page 3 of this listing, it simply defines public fields for the Code, Description, and UnitPrice properties. A more realistic implementation of this class would probably use property get and set accessors to validate the property data. For this example, however, simple public fields are adequate.

The first method in the ProductDB class, GetProducts, returns a DataTable that contains the product codes and descriptions for all of the products in the Products table, sorted by product code. To do that, it creates a SqlCommand object with a Select statement that retrieves the appropriate data. Next, it creates a data adapter using this command and the connection returned by a method named GetConnection (see page 3 of this class). Then, it creates an untyped dataset and uses the data adapter to fill it with a table named Products. Finally, it returns the Products table.

The GetProduct method returns a Product object that contains the data for the product row specified by the product code that's passed to it. This method creates a SqlCommand object with a parameterized query that contains a placeholder for the product code. Then, it creates the parameter and sets its value to the product code that was passed to the method. Notice that because the default data type for a parameter is string, it's not necessary to set the data type of the product code parameter explicitly.

After the command and parameter are created, the connection is opened and the ExecuteReader method is used to execute the command and create a data reader object. Notice that the ExecuteReader method specifies the SingleRow command behavior because the query will return just one row. Then, the Read method of the data reader is used to retrieve that row, the values of that row are assigned to a new Product object, the connection object is closed, and the Product object is returned to the calling method. Notice that if the Select statement doesn't return a row, null is returned to the calling method. That could happen if another user deleted the requested product after it was retrieved.

The code for the ProductDB class **Page 1**

```
using System.Data;
using System.Data.SqlClient;

public class ProductDB
{
    public static DataTable GetProducts()
    {
        string selectStatement = "SELECT ProductCode, Description "
                               + "FROM Products "
                               + "ORDER BY ProductCode";
        SqlCommand selectCommand =
            new SqlCommand(selectStatement, GetConnection());
        SqlDataAdapter productsDataAdapter =
            new SqlDataAdapter(selectCommand);
        DataSet productsDataSet = new DataSet();
        productsDataAdapter.Fill(productsDataSet, "Products");
        return productsDataSet.Tables["Products"];
    }

    public static Product GetProduct(string productCode)
    {
        SqlConnection mmaBooksConnection = GetConnection();
        string selectStatement = "SELECT ProductCode, Description, UnitPrice "
                               + "FROM Products "
                               + "WHERE ProductCode = @ProductCode";
        SqlCommand selectCommand =
            new SqlCommand(selectStatement, mmaBooksConnection);
        selectCommand.Parameters.Add("@ProductCode", productCode);
        SqlDataReader productReader;
        mmaBooksConnection.Open();
        productReader = selectCommand.ExecuteReader(CommandBehavior.SingleRow);
        if (productReader.Read())
        {
            Product product = new Product();
            product.Code = (string) productReader["ProductCode"];
            product.Description = (string) productReader["Description"];
            product.Price = (decimal) productReader["UnitPrice"];
            mmaBooksConnection.Close();
            return product;
        }
        else
        {
            mmaBooksConnection.Close();
            return null;
        }
    }
```

Figure 20-10 The code for the database classes (part 1 of 3)

The AddProduct method adds a new row to the Products table. This method receives a Product object that contains the data for the new row. Then, a command object that contains an Insert statement with a parameter for each column in the row is created, and the properties of the Product object are assigned to these parameters. Next, the ExecuteNonQuery method of the command object is executed within a try-catch statement that catches SQL Server exceptions. That way, if a product with the specified code already exists, this method will return false to the calling method to indicate that the operation was unsuccessful. (Although other SQL Server exceptions can occur, this is the most likely one.) Otherwise, this method returns true.

Notice that the value returned by the ExecuteNonQuery method isn't assigned to a variable, since this value isn't used by the program. In that case, the return value is discarded.

The UpdateProduct method receives two arguments: a Product object named oldProduct that contains the original data for the product row to be updated and another Product object named newProduct that supplies the new values for the product. The properties of these objects are used to set the values of the parameters defined by the Update statement associated with the command object. Notice that the properties of the oldProduct object are assigned to parameters in the Where clause of the Update statement. That way, the Update statement will update the row only if none of the product columns have been changed since the product row was retrieved.

After the parameter values are set, this method uses the ExecuteNonQuery method to execute the Update statement. This method is executed within a try-catch statement that catches any SQL Server errors that occur. The most likely error is that the product code was changed to a code that already exists in the table.

If no errors occurred, the value that's returned by the ExecuteNonQuery method is then tested to determine whether the update was successful. If it wasn't, it probably means that the product has been modified or deleted by another user. In that case, false is returned to the calling method. Otherwise, true is returned.

The code for the ProductDB class Page 2

```
public static bool AddProduct(Product product)
{
    SqlConnection mmaBooksConnection = GetConnection();
    string insertStatement
        = "INSERT Products "
        + "(ProductCode, Description, UnitPrice) "
        + "VALUES (@ProductCode, @Description, @UnitPrice)";
    SqlCommand insertCommand =
        new SqlCommand(insertStatement, mmaBooksConnection);
    insertCommand.Parameters.Add("@ProductCode", product.Code);
    insertCommand.Parameters.Add("@Description", product.Description);
    insertCommand.Parameters.Add("@UnitPrice", product.Price);
    insertCommand.Parameters["@UnitPrice"].SqlDbType = SqlDbType.Decimal;
    try
    {
        mmaBooksConnection.Open();
        insertCommand.ExecuteNonQuery();
        mmaBooksConnection.Close();
        return true;
    }
    catch (SqlException)
    {
        mmaBooksConnection.Close();
        return false;
    }
}

public static bool UpdateProduct(Product oldProduct, Product newProduct)
{
    SqlConnection mmaBooksConnection = GetConnection();
    string updateStatement = "UPDATE Products SET "
                           + "ProductCode = @NewProductCode, "
                           + "Description = @Description, "
                           + "UnitPrice = @UnitPrice "
                           + "WHERE ProductCode = @OldProductCode "
                           + "AND Description = @OldDescription "
                           + "AND UnitPrice = @OldUnitPrice";
    SqlCommand updateCommand =
        new SqlCommand(updateStatement, mmaBooksConnection);
    updateCommand.Parameters.Add("@NewProductCode", newProduct.Code);
    updateCommand.Parameters.Add("@Description", newProduct.Description);
    updateCommand.Parameters.Add("@UnitPrice", newProduct.Price);
    updateCommand.Parameters["@UnitPrice"].SqlDbType = SqlDbType.Decimal;
    updateCommand.Parameters.Add("@OldProductCode", oldProduct.Code);
    updateCommand.Parameters.Add("@OldDescription", oldProduct.Description);
    updateCommand.Parameters.Add("@OldUnitPrice", oldProduct.Price);
    updateCommand.Parameters["@OldUnitPrice"].SqlDbType = SqlDbType.Decimal;
    try
    {
        mmaBooksConnection.Open();
        int count = updateCommand.ExecuteNonQuery();
        mmaBooksConnection.Close();
        if (count > 0)
            return true;
        else
            return false;
    }
```

Figure 20-10 The code for the database classes (part 2 of 3)

The DeleteProduct method receives a Product object as an argument. This method implements concurrency checking using the same technique as the Update method. That is, it specifies the value of each of the product columns in the Where clause of the Delete statement. The return value is set to false if the delete operation is unsuccessful due to a concurrency error or any SQL Server error. Otherwise, it's set to true.

The last method in the ProductDB class is a private method named GetConnection that returns a SqlConnection object. As you've already seen, the other methods of this class call this method to establish a connection to the database. Note that the connection string is hard coded into this method. In a production application, you'd probably store the connection string in an external configuration file. Then, the GetConnection method would read the connection string from this file. That way, you could change the location of the database without recompiling the program.

The code for the ProductDB class — Page 3

```
        catch (SqlException)
        {
            mmaBooksConnection.Close();
            return false;
        }
    }

    public static bool DeleteProduct(Product product)
    {
        SqlConnection mmaBooksConnection = GetConnection();
        string deleteStatement
            = "DELETE FROM Products "
            + "WHERE ProductCode = @ProductCode "
            + "AND Description = @Description "
            + "AND UnitPrice = @UnitPrice";
        SqlCommand deleteCommand =
            new SqlCommand(deleteStatement, mmaBooksConnection);
        deleteCommand.Parameters.Add("@ProductCode", product.Code);
        deleteCommand.Parameters.Add("@Description", product.Description);
        deleteCommand.Parameters.Add("@UnitPrice", product.Price);
        deleteCommand.Parameters["@UnitPrice"].SqlDbType = SqlDbType.Decimal;
        try
        {
            mmaBooksConnection.Open();
            int count = deleteCommand.ExecuteNonQuery();
            mmaBooksConnection.Close();
            if (count > 0)
                return true;
            else
                return false;
        }
        catch (SqlException)
        {
            return false;
        }
    }

    private static SqlConnection GetConnection()
    {
        string connectionString =
            "server=DOUG\\VSdotNET;database=MMABooks;Integrated Security=SSPI";
        return new SqlConnection(connectionString);
    }

}
```

The code for the Product class

```
class Product
{
    public string Code;
    public string Description;
    public decimal Price;
}
```

Figure 20-10 The code for the database classes (part 3 of 3)

The code for the form class

Figure 20-11 presents the code for the Product Maintenance form. Much of the code for this form is the same as the code for the unbound version that was presented in chapter 19. As a result, I'll just describe the code that varies significantly from the unbound version.

To start, notice that this form uses a class variable named product that will hold the product that's currently displayed on the form. This Product object is retrieved by the GetProduct method of the ProductDB class and is used throughout the application.

The Load event handler for the form begins by calling the BindProductsComboBox method. This method calls the GetProducts method of the ProductDB class to get a data table containing the products data. Then, it binds the Products combo box to the data table. Notice that the first line of this method removes the event handler for the combo box's SelectedIndexChanged event. Then, the last line of this method restores the event handler. This is necessary because the SelectedIndexChanged event will be fired when the data binding properties are set.

The event handler for the SelectedIndexChanged event, shown on page 2 of this listing, calls the GetProduct method of the ProductDB class to get a Product object for the product that's selected by the user. If the product that's returned is null, the program assumes that another user has deleted the product. In that case, an appropriate error message is displayed and the BindProductsComboBox method is called again so that the deleted product is no longer included in the list.

The event handler for the Accept button's Click event, shown on page 3, validates the user's input by calling the IsValidData method. Then, its processing depends on whether isAddMode is true or false. If it's true, a new Product object is created and the SetProductData method is called to set the Product object's properties. This method, shown on page 4, simply assigns the values the user entered into the text boxes on the form to the Product object's properties. Next, the AddProduct method of the ProductDB class is called to add the new product to the database. If this method returns false, an error message is displayed to indicate that the product could not be added. Finally, the Products combo box is bound again so that the new product is included in the list, and isAddMode is set to false.

If isAddMode was false when the user clicked the Accept button, a new Product object named oldProduct is created, and the values of the product variable are assigned to its properties. Then, the SetProductData method is called to set the properties of the product variable to the values entered by the user. Next, the UpdateProduct method of the ProductDB class is called to update the product row. If the update fails, an error message is displayed. Finally, the BindProductsComboBox method is called to refresh the combo box in case the product code or description was changed.

The code for the Product Maintenance form Page 1

```
private bool isAddMode;
private Product product;

private void frmProductMaintenance_Load(object sender, System.EventArgs e)
{
    BindProductsComboBox();
    cboProducts.SelectedIndex = 0;
    product = ProductDB.GetProduct(cboProducts.SelectedValue.ToString());
    ShowProductData();
    DisableAddEditMode();
}

private void BindProductsComboBox()
{
    cboProducts.SelectedIndexChanged -=
        new System.EventHandler(cboProducts_SelectedIndexChanged);
    DataTable productsTable = ProductDB.GetProducts();
    cboProducts.DataSource = productsTable;
    cboProducts.DisplayMember = "Description";
    cboProducts.ValueMember = "ProductCode";
    cboProducts.SelectedIndexChanged +=
        new System.EventHandler(cboProducts_SelectedIndexChanged);
}

private void DisableAddEditMode()
{
    cboProducts.Enabled = true;
    txtProductCode.ReadOnly = true;
    txtDescription.ReadOnly = true;
    txtUnitPrice.ReadOnly = true;
    btnAdd.Enabled = true;
    btnEdit.Enabled = true;
    btnDelete.Enabled = true;
    btnAccept.Enabled = false;
    btnCancel.Enabled = false;
    cboProducts.Focus();
}

private void EnableAddEditMode()
{
    cboProducts.Enabled = false;
    txtProductCode.ReadOnly = false;
    txtDescription.ReadOnly = false;
    txtUnitPrice.ReadOnly = false;
    btnAdd.Enabled = false;
    btnEdit.Enabled = false;
    btnDelete.Enabled = false;
    btnAccept.Enabled = true;
    btnCancel.Enabled = true;
    txtProductCode.Focus();
}
```

Figure 20-11 The code for the Product Maintenance form (part 1 of 4)

The code for the Product Maintenance form — Page 2

```
private void cboProducts_SelectedIndexChanged(object sender, System.EventArgs e)
{
    product = ProductDB.GetProduct(cboProducts.SelectedValue.ToString());
    if (product == null)
    {
        MessageBox.Show("Another user has deleted that product.", "Error");
        BindProductsComboBox();
        cboProducts.SelectedIndex = 0;
        product = ProductDB.GetProduct(cboProducts.SelectedValue.ToString());
    }
    ShowProductData();
}

private void ShowProductData()
{
    txtProductCode.Text = product.Code;
    txtDescription.Text = product.Description;
    txtUnitPrice.Text = product.Price.ToString("f2");
}

private void btnAdd_Click(object sender, System.EventArgs e)
{
    ClearProductFields();
    EnableAddEditMode();
    isAddMode = true;
}

private void ClearProductFields()
{
    txtProductCode.Text = "";
    txtDescription.Text = "";
    txtUnitPrice.Text = "";
}

private void btnEdit_Click(object sender, System.EventArgs e)
{
    EnableAddEditMode();
    isAddMode = false;
}
```

Figure 20-11 The code for the Product Maintenance form (part 2 of 4)

The code for the Product Maintenance form — Page 3

```
private void btnAccept_Click(object sender, System.EventArgs e)
{
    if (IsValidData())
    {
        if (isAddMode)
        {
            product = new Product();
            SetProductData();
            if (!ProductDB.AddProduct(product))
                MessageBox.Show("Could not add product. A product " +
                    "with that code may already exist.", "Database Error");
            BindProductsComboBox();
            cboProducts.SelectedValue = product.Code;
            isAddMode = false;
        }
        else
        {
            Product oldProduct = new Product();
            oldProduct.Code = product.Code;
            oldProduct.Description = product.Description;
            oldProduct.Price = product.Price;
            SetProductData();
            if (!ProductDB.UpdateProduct(oldProduct, product))
                MessageBox.Show("Could not update product. A product " +
                    "with that code may already exist or another user " +
                    "may have deleted or modified the product.",
                    "Database Error");
            BindProductsComboBox();
        }
        DisableAddEditMode();
    }
}

private bool IsValidData ()
{
    if (!IsPresent(txtProductCode, "Product Code"))
        return false;
    if (!IsPresent(txtDescription, "Description"))
        return false;
    if (!IsPresent(txtUnitPrice, "Unit Price"))
        return false;
    if (!IsDecimal(txtUnitPrice, "Unit Price"))
        return false;
    return true;
}

private bool IsPresent(TextBox textBox, string name)
{
    if (textBox.Text == "")
    {
        MessageBox.Show(name + " is a required field.", "Entry Error");
        textBox.Focus();
        return false;
    }
    return true;
}
```

Figure 20-11 The code for the Product Maintenance form (part 3 of 4)

The Click event handler for the Delete button starts by displaying a dialog box to confirm the delete operation. If the operation is confirmed, it then calls the DeleteProduct method of the ProductDB class to delete the product. If this method returns false, a message is displayed indicating that the product couldn't be deleted. Then, the BindProductsComboBox method is called to refresh the combo box so that the deleted product is no longer included in the list, and the data for the first product is displayed.

Now that you've seen the complete code for this application, you should have a good feel for what's involved in working with ADO.NET components that you create through code. At this point, you might want to compare this application with the one in chapter 19. If you do, you'll see that one of the biggest differences is that the application in this chapter requires considerably more code. Although at first you may think of this as a drawback to using the techniques presented here, most professional programmers consider it an advantage. That's because you can see exactly how each component is defined, and you have complete control over how the data is processed. In addition, you can place the code in separate database classes.

The code for the Product Maintenance form Page 4

```
private bool IsDecimal(TextBox textBox, string name)
{
    try
    {
        Convert.ToDecimal(textBox.Text);
        return true;
    }
    catch(FormatException)
    {
        MessageBox.Show(name + " must be a decimal value.", "Entry Error");
        textBox.Focus();
        return false;
    }
}

private void SetProductData()
{
    product.Code = txtProductCode.Text;
    product.Description = txtDescription.Text;
    product.Price = Convert.ToDecimal(txtUnitPrice.Text);
}

private void btnCancel_Click(object sender, System.EventArgs e)
{
    if (isAddMode)
    {
        product = ProductDB.GetProduct(cboProducts.SelectedValue.ToString());
        isAddMode = false;
    }
    ShowProductData();
    DisableAddEditMode();
}

private void btnDelete_Click(object sender, System.EventArgs e)
{
    if (MessageBox.Show("Delete " + cboProducts.Text + "?",
        "Confirm Delete", MessageBoxButtons.YesNo,
        MessageBoxIcon.Question) == DialogResult.Yes)
    {
        if (!ProductDB.DeleteProduct(product))
            MessageBox.Show("Could not delete product. " +
                "Another user may have deleted or modified the product.",
                "Database Error");
        BindProductsComboBox();
        cboProducts.SelectedIndex = 0;
        product = ProductDB.GetProduct(cboProducts.SelectedValue.ToString());
        ShowProductData();
        DisableAddEditMode();
    }
}

private void btnExit_Click(object sender, System.EventArgs e)
{
    this.Close();
}
```

Figure 20-11 The code for the Product Maintenance form (part 4 of 4)

How to use transactions

So far, all of the database programming examples you've seen in this book have updated a single table. In the real world, however, database applications often update two or more tables. If those tables are related, you'll need to coordinate the update operations so that the integrity of the data in the tables is maintained. To do that, you can use transactions.

How to create and work with transactions

A *transaction* is a group of related database commands that you combine into a single logical unit. Figure 20-12 presents the methods you use to create and work with transactions.

To start a transaction, you use the BeginTransaction method of a connection object. This creates a transaction object that you can then use to work with the transaction. Note that before you execute the BeginTransaction method, you must open the connection. Also note that the SqlTransaction class doesn't have a public constructor. As a result, the only way to create a SqlTransaction object is to use the BeginTransaction method.

To use a transaction, you associate it with one or more data commands. To do that, you assign the transaction object to the Transaction property of each command. Note that each of the commands must be associated with the same connection object on which the transaction was started.

After you associate a transaction with a command, any SQL statement you execute using that command becomes part of the transaction. Then, if all of the commands in the transaction execute without error, you can *commit* the transaction. That means that all of the changes that have been made to the database since the beginning of the transaction are made permanent. To commit a transaction, you use the Commit method of the transaction.

In contrast, if any of the commands cause an error, all of the changes made to the database since the beginning of the transaction can be reversed, or *rolled back*. To rollback a transaction, you use the Rollback method of the transaction.

The syntax for creating a transaction object

```
sqlTransaction = sqlConnection.BeginTransaction();
```

Methods of the SqlTransaction class

Method	Description
`Commit()`	Commits the changes to the database, making them permanent.
`Rollback()`	Reverses the changes made to the database to the beginning of the transaction.

Code that begins a transaction on a connection

```
SqlTransaction orderTran;
mmaBooksConnection.Open();
orderTran = mmaBooksConnection.BeginTransaction();
```

Code that associates the transaction with a command

```
orderCmd = new SqlCommand();
orderCmd.Connection = mmaBooksConnection;
orderCmd.Transaction = orderTran;
```

Code that commits the transaction

```
orderTran.Commit();
```

Code that rolls back the transaction

```
orderTran.Rollback();
```

Description

- A *transaction* is a group of SQL statements that are combined into a logical unit. By default, each SQL statement is treated as a separate transaction.
- When you *commit* a transaction, the changes made to the database become permanent. Until it's committed, you can undo all of the changes since the beginning of the transaction by *rolling back* the transaction.
- The BeginTransaction method of a connection begins a transaction on an open connection and returns a transaction object. To associate a transaction with a command, you set the Transaction property of the command to the transaction object.
- If you close a connection while a transaction is pending, the changes are rolled back.

Figure 20-12 How to create and work with transactions

An Order Entry application that uses a transaction

To help you understand when you might use a transaction, figure 20-13 presents the main form and classes used by an Order Entry application that works with the MMABooks database. To enter an order, the user first selects the customer who is placing the order from the Order Entry form. The user can do that in one of two ways: by entering the customer's ID number in the Customer ID text box and clicking the Get Customer button, or by clicking the Find Customer button to display the Find Customer dialog box. This dialog box lets the user search for customers by name or state.

To specify which products should be ordered, the user selects a product from the combo box, enters the quantity in the Quantity text box, and clicks the Add button. Then, a line item appears in the data grid for that product. To delete a line item, the user selects the line item in the data grid and clicks the Delete button.

When the order is complete, the user can accept the order by clicking the Accept Order button. This writes the data for the order to the Invoice and InvoiceLineItems tables in the MMABooks database. The user can also click the Cancel Order button to clear all of the input fields and start a new order.

The Order class that's used by this application represents a single order. It contains a CustomerID property that identifies the customer who placed the order, along with a LineItems property that contains a collection of the line items for the order. In addition, it includes several properties that provide totals for the order.

The LineItemList class is a collection class that inherits the ArrayList class. The indexer for this class lets you access the individual LineItem objects in the collection. In addition to the indexer, this class includes two properties that get the sum of the total and quantity of the line items. It also includes methods that let you add and delete line items from the collection. These properties and methods aren't shown here since they aren't used by the OrderDB class, which is the class that uses the transaction.

The LineItem class represents an individual line item. It includes properties for each of the five columns that are displayed in the data grid on the Order Entry form.

The last class shown in this figure is the OrderDB class. This class provides a single static method named WriteOrder. This method is called when the user clicks the Accept Order button on the Order Entry form. It accepts an Order object as a parameter. As you'll see in a minute, it uses a transaction to insert the appropriate rows into the Invoices and InvoiceLineItems tables. This method's return value is the value that's generated for the invoice's InvoiceID column, which is an identity column.

In addition to the classes shown, the Order Entry application uses several other classes. Two of them are the form classes for the Order Entry and Find Customer forms. The others define the other objects used by the application and provide for accessing other tables in the MMABooks database. If you'd like to see the code for these classes, you can download the Order Entry application from our web site. For information on how to do that, see appendix A.

The Order Entry form

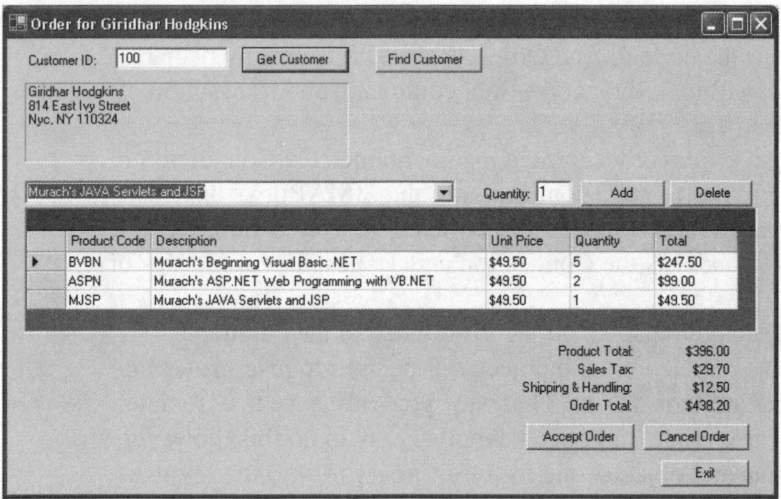

The Order class

Property	Type	Description
`CustomerID`	int	The ID for the customer who placed the order.
`LineItems`	LineItemList	A collection of LineItem objects for the order.
`ProductTotal`	decimal	The total for all the line items.
`SalesTax`	decimal	The sales tax for the order.
`ShippingAndHandling`	decimal	The shipping and handling charges for the order.
`OrderTotal`	decimal	The grand total for the order.

The LineItemList class

Property	Type	Description
`[index]`	LineItem	A line item.

The LineItem class

Property	Type	Description
`ProductCode`	string	The product code for the product ordered.
`Description`	string	The description for the product ordered.
`UnitPrice`	decimal	The unit price for the product ordered.
`Quantity`	int	The quantity ordered.
`ItemTotal`	decimal	The unit price multiplied by the quantity.

The OrderDB class

Method	Type	Description
`WriteOrder(order)`	int	Writes the specified order to the database. The return value is the invoice number created for the order.

Figure 20-13 The design of the Order Entry application

The code for the OrderDB class

Figure 20-14 presents the code for the OrderDB class. It begins by declaring three class variables that will hold the connection, command, and transaction objects used by this class.

The WriteOrder method starts by calling a method named GetConnection in a class named MMABooksDB to get a connection to the MMABooks database. Then, it opens the connection and starts a transaction on the connection. Next, it creates a command object and sets the Connection and Transaction properties of that object.

At this point, an SQL statement has not been assigned to the command object. That's because the same command object will be used to insert rows into the Invoices and InvoiceLineItems tables. That way, you only have to associate the transaction with a single command object. Another way to do this, however, would be to use two command objects: one for inserting a row into the Invoices table and one for inserting a row into the InvoiceLineItems table. Then, you would have to associate the transaction with both command objects if you wanted them to be executed as part of the same transaction.

After the connection and command objects are established, the WriteOrder method writes the invoice data to the database. To do that, it starts by calling the InsertInvoice method to insert the invoice into the Invoices table. Because this method uses properties of the order object, that object is passed to it. Then, this method returns the invoice ID that was assigned to the new invoice. This value is saved in a local variable named invoiceID.

If the InsertInvoice method is successful, the WriteOrder method continues by calling the InsertLineItem method for each line item in the order object's LineItems collection. Notice that the invoiceID variable is passed to this method along with the line item. That way, this value can be assigned to the InvoiceID column of each line item.

If all of the line items are written successfully, the WriteOrder method commits the transaction, closes the connection, and returns the generated invoice ID to the calling method. However, if an error occurs while inserting a row into the Invoices or InvoiceLineItems table, the code in the catch block rolls back the transaction and displays an error message to indicate that the order wasn't posted. In that case, a return value of 0 is passed back to the calling method.

The InsertInvoice method starts by setting the CommandText property of the command object to the Insert statement that will be used to insert the invoice. As you can see, this statement will use parameters to specify the values that are assigned to the columns in the invoice row.

The code for the OrderDB class Page 1

```
using System;
using System.Data;
using System.Data.SqlClient;
using System.Windows.Forms;

public class OrderDB
{
    private static SqlConnection mmaBooksConnection;
    private static SqlCommand orderCmd;
    private static SqlTransaction orderTran;

    public static int WriteOrder(Order order)
    {
        mmaBooksConnection = MMABooksDB.GetConnection();
        mmaBooksConnection.Open();
        orderTran = mmaBooksConnection.BeginTransaction();
        orderCmd = new SqlCommand();
        orderCmd.Connection = mmaBooksConnection;
        orderCmd.Transaction = orderTran;
        try
        {
            int invoiceID = InsertInvoice(order);
            foreach (LineItem li in order.LineItems)
                InsertLineItem(li, invoiceID);
            orderTran.Commit();
            mmaBooksConnection.Close();
            return invoiceID;
        }
        catch (SqlException ex)
        {
            orderTran.Rollback();
            string msg;
            msg = "A database error has occurred. The order was not posted.\n"
                + "Error number: " + ex.Number + "\n"
                + ex.Message;
            MessageBox.Show(msg, "Database Error",
                MessageBoxButtons.OK, MessageBoxIcon.Exclamation);
            return 0;
        }
    }

    private static int InsertInvoice(Order order)
    {
        orderCmd.CommandText = "INSERT INTO Invoices "
                             + "(CustomerID, InvoiceDate, ProductTotal, "
                             + "SalesTax, ShippingAndHandling, InvoiceTotal) "
                             + "VALUES (@CustomerID, @InvoiceDate, "
                             + "@ProductTotal, @SalesTax, "
                             + "@ShippingAndHandling, @InvoiceTotal)";
```

Figure 20-14 The code for the OrderDB class (part 1 of 2)

The next statement clears the Parameters collection of the command object. That's necessary because this command is used to insert rows into both the Invoices and InvoiceLineItems tables. So different parameters will need to be created for each Insert statement.

The statements that follow create the parameters used by the Insert statement and set their values to the properties of the order object. Notice that to simplify the job of creating each parameter, I coded a method named AddParm. This method accepts the command object, the name of the parameter, the parameter's value, and the parameter's data type as arguments. Then, it creates a new parameter object, sets its properties using the values that are passed to it, and adds the parameter to the command object. By using this method, you can create each parameter with a single line of code.

After the parameters have been created, the InsertInvoice method calls the command's ExecuteNonQuery method to execute the Insert statement. Then, it changes the command's CommandText property to "SELECT @@IDENTITY" and executes this statement using the ExecuteScalar method. This SQL statement returns the identity value that was generated for the invoice. This value is then returned to the WriteOrder method.

The InsertLineItem method works similarly. It sets the CommandText property of the command object to an Insert statement that can be used to insert a line item. Then, it clears the Parameters collection of the command and uses the AddParm method to create the required parameters. Finally, it calls the ExecuteNonQuery method to insert the row.

Notice that neither the InsertInvoice nor the InsertLineItem method uses a try-catch statement to catch SQL Server exceptions. That's because each of these methods is called within the scope of the try-catch statement in the WriteOrder method. As a result, if a SQL Server exception occurs within either of these methods, the catch block in the WriteOrder method will be executed.

The code for the OrderDB class — Page 2

```
        orderCmd.Parameters.Clear();
        AddParm(orderCmd, "@CustomerID", order.CustomerID.ToString(),
            SqlDbType.Int);
        AddParm(orderCmd, "@InvoiceDate", DateTime.Now.Date.ToString(),
            SqlDbType.DateTime);
        AddParm(orderCmd, "@ProductTotal", order.ProductTotal.ToString(),
            SqlDbType.Money);
        AddParm(orderCmd, "@SalesTax", order.SalesTax.ToString(),
            SqlDbType.Money);
        AddParm(orderCmd, "@ShippingAndHandling",
            order.ShippingAndHandling.ToString(), SqlDbType.Money);
        AddParm(orderCmd, "@InvoiceTotal", order.OrderTotal.ToString(),
            SqlDbType.Money);
        orderCmd.ExecuteNonQuery();
        orderCmd.CommandText = "SELECT @@IDENTITY";
        int invoiceID = Convert.ToInt32(orderCmd.ExecuteScalar());
        return invoiceID;
    }

    private static void AddParm(SqlCommand cmd, string name, string value,
        SqlDbType type)
    {
        SqlParameter parm = new SqlParameter();
        parm.ParameterName = name;
        parm.Value = value;
        parm.SqlDbType = type;
        cmd.Parameters.Add(parm);
    }

    private static void InsertLineItem(LineItem li, int invoiceID)
    {
        orderCmd.CommandText = "INSERT INTO InvoiceLineItems "
                             + "(InvoiceID, ProductCode, "
                             + "UnitPrice, Quantity, ItemTotal) "
                             + "VALUES (@InvoiceID, @ProductCode, "
                             + "@UnitPrice, @Quantity, @ItemTotal)";
        orderCmd.Parameters.Clear();
        AddParm(orderCmd,"@InvoiceID", invoiceID.ToString(), SqlDbType.Money);
        AddParm(orderCmd,"@ProductCode", li.ProductCode.ToString(),
            SqlDbType.Char);
        AddParm(orderCmd,"@UnitPrice", li.UnitPrice.ToString(),
            SqlDbType.Money);
        AddParm(orderCmd,"@Quantity", li.Quantity.ToString(), SqlDbType.Int);
        AddParm(orderCmd,"@ItemTotal", li.ItemTotal.ToString(),
            SqlDbType.Money);
        orderCmd.ExecuteNonQuery();
    }

}
```

Figure 20-14 The code for the OrderDB class (part 2 of 2)

Perspective

In this chapter, you've learned how to create connection, command, and data adapter objects without using the Data Adapter Configuration Wizard. In addition, you've learned how to create and work with untyped datasets, how to execute data commands, and how to process two or more SQL statements as a single transaction. Now, you might want to consider when it makes sense to use these techniques.

To start, the Configuration Wizard typically generates more code for the data provider components than you actually need for an application. One reason to create data provider objects in code, then, is so that you can include just the features you need. This also gives you more precise control over how these objects work. And it makes it easier to separate the database code from the rest of the application by placing it in database classes.

As for untyped datasets, you'll need to use them if you encounter a situation where you don't know at design time what tables and columns the dataset will need to have. For example, an untyped dataset may be best in an application that includes an ad hoc query feature that lets the user select the columns to be displayed.

Of course, you'll also need to consider whether it makes sense to use a dataset at all. If an application accesses one row of a database table at a time, for example, it doesn't usually make sense to store that row in a dataset. If an application must have access to all the rows, or selected rows, from a table at once, however, it usually makes sense to store the data in a dataset.

Summary

- A *parameter* lets you include variable information in a SQL statement. A Select statement that includes parameters is sometimes called a *parameterized query*.
- To identify where the variable information will be inserted into a SQL statement, you code placeholders for the parameters. Before you execute the query, you must set the values of the parameters.
- You can use the methods of a data command object to execute Select queries that return result sets, Select queries that return a single value (called a *scalar value*), and Insert, Update, and Delete queries (called *action queries*).
- When you execute a query that returns a result set, you can access the rows and columns in the result set using a data reader.
- A scalar value can be the value of a single row and column, a calculated value, an *aggregate value* that summarizes data in the database, or any other value that can be retrieved from the database.
- When you execute an action query, the return value indicates the number of rows that were affected in the database.
- A *transaction* is a group of SQL statements that are combined into a logical unit. If all of the statements in the transaction succeed, the changes made to the database by those statements can be *committed*. Otherwise, the changes can be *rolled back*.

Terms

parameter
parameterized query
named variable
scalar value
aggregate value
action query
untyped dataset
transaction
commit a transaction
roll back a transaction

Objectives

- Given the specifications for an application that uses a data reader to retrieve data from a database, design and code the application.
- Given the specifications for an application that uses data commands to execute action queries or queries that return a scalar value, design and code the application.
- Given the specifications for an application that uses transactions, design and code the application.
- Use a parameter to limit the data that's processed by a data command.
- Explain what parameters are and how you use them in a SQL statement.
- Describe the basic techniques for creating a data reader and using it to retrieve rows and columns.
- Describe the two types of queries that don't return result sets, and explain how you use them.
- Explain what transactions are and why you might want to use them.

Exercise 20-1 Display customer invoices

In this exercise, you'll create a form like the one below that lets you display the invoices for a selected customer. To make this form easier to develop, we'll give you a starting form that contains all the controls you'll need.

The design of the Display Customer Invoices form

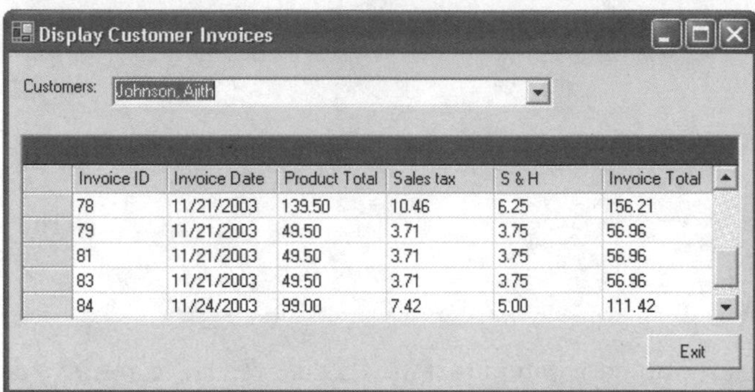

Open the project and add code to display the list of customers

1. Open the project named DisplayInvoicesByCustomer in the C:\C#.NET\Chapter 20 directory.
2. Add a class named MMABooksDB to this project. Add a public static method to this class named GetConnection that returns an SQL connection to the MMABooks database. Be sure to add a using statement for the System.Data.SqlClient namespace to this class.
3. Add another class named CustomerDB, and add using statements for both the System.Data and System.Data.SqlClient namespaces to this class. Add a public static method to this class named GetCustomerList that returns a table of customer IDs and names sorted by name. Use the GetConnection method in the MMABooksDB class to connect to the database.
4. Start an event handler for the Load event of the form. This event handler should call a method named BindCustomersComboBox that binds the Customers combo box to the table that's returned by the GetCustomerList method of the CustomerDB class. The combo box should display the customer name and store the customer ID.
5. Add an event handler for the Click event of the Exit button that closes the form. Then, run the application to be sure that the customers are retrieved and displayed properly.

Add code to display the invoices for the selected customer

6. Add another class named InvoiceDB, and add using statements for the System.Data and System.Data.SqlClient namespaces to this class. Add a public static method named GetCustomerInvoices. This method should accept a customer ID and return a table that contains all the invoices for that customer sorted by invoice ID.

7. Add an event handler for the SelectedIndexChanged event of the Customers combo box. This event handler should call a method named DisplayInvoices that binds the Invoices data grid to the table that's returned by the GetCustomerInvoices method of the InvoiceDB class. (To bind the data grid, just set its DataSource property to the data table.) Be sure to cast the customer ID to an int before you pass it to the GetCustomerInvoices method.
8. Add code to the beginning of the BindCustomersComboBox method to remove the SelectedIndexChanged event handler from the SelectedIndexChanged event of that control. Add this event handler back to the event at the end of that method.
9. Add code to display the invoices for the first customer when the form is loaded.
10. Run the application. Select a customer that has invoices to see if the Invoices are listed in the data grid. Select a customer that doesn't have invoices to see if the data grid is cleared. Continue testing until you're sure that this works correctly. Then, close the solution.

Exercise 20-2 Update shipping and handling

In this exercise, you'll create a form like the one below that lets the user update the shipping and handling amount for an invoice. To make this form easier to develop, we'll give you a starting form that contains all the controls you'll need.

The design of the Update Shipping and Handling form

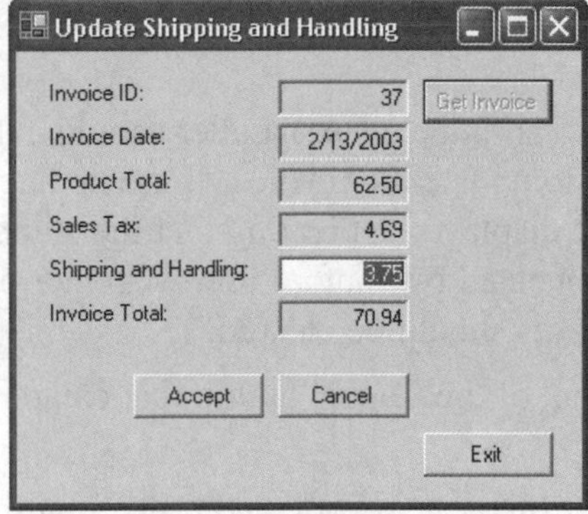

Open the project and add code to get an invoice and display its data

1. Open the project named UpdateShippingAndHandling in the C:\C#.NET\Chapter 20 directory.
2. Add a class named Invoice that defines a field for each of the columns in the Invoices table.
3. Add another class named InvoiceDB to this project, and add using statements for the System.Data and System.Data.SqlClient namespaces. Add a private static method to this class named GetConnection that returns an SQL connection to the MMABooks database.

4. Add a public static method named GetInvoice to the InvoiceDB class. This method should accept an invoice ID and return an Invoice object for that invoice. If an invoice isn't found with the specified ID, this method should return null. Use the GetConnection method to connect to the database.
5. Start an event handler for the Click event of the Get Invoice button. This event handler should call a method that validates the invoice ID the user enters to be sure that a value was entered and that the value is an integer.
6. If the invoice ID is valid, the Click event handler for the Get Invoice button should call the GetInvoice method to get the specified invoice and then store it in a class variable. If the invoice is found, its data should be displayed on the form. Otherwise, an error message should be displayed.
7. Add an event handler for the Click event of the Exit button that closes the form. Then, run the application and test it to be sure that it retrieves and displays invoices properly and that the invoice ID is validated properly.

Add code to update the shipping and handling

8. Add a method named UpdateShippingAndHandling to the InvoiceDB class that updates the shipping and handling amount for an invoice. This method should accept an Invoice object and the new shipping and handling amount and return a Boolean value that indicates if the update was successful. Assume that the shipping and handling is the only value that can be changed for an invoice and that an invoice can't be deleted. Be sure to update the invoice total to reflect the new shipping and handling amount.
9. Start an event handler for the Click event of the Accept button. This event handler should check that the shipping and handling the user entered is a valid decimal. If the user deletes the shipping and handling amount, it should be set to zero.
10. If the shipping and handling amount is valid, the event handler should call the UpdateShippingAndHandling method to update the invoice. If the update is not successful, an error message should be displayed indicating that the shipping and handling amount may have been changed by another user. Whether or not the update is successful, the form controls should be cleared.
11. Add an event handler for the Click event of the Cancel button that clears the form controls.
12. Add code to enable and disable the Get Invoice, Accept, and Cancel buttons, to change the ReadOnly properties of the Invoice ID and Shipping And Handling text boxes, and to move the focus to these text boxes as necessary.
13. Run the application and test it thoroughly to be sure it works properly. When you're done, close the solution.

Section 5

Specialized skills for C# developers

This section contains three chapters that present some specialized skills that you may need as you develop Windows applications in C#. Since you won't need them for all your applications, though, you can give these chapters a quick first reading just to find out what skills they offer. Then, you can return to these chapters for reference whenever you need the skills that they present.

In chapter 21, you'll learn how to read and write the data in two of the file types that are supported by .NET: text files and binary files. In chapter 22, you'll learn how to read and write the data in XML files, which will also prepare you for using XML in other contexts. And in chapter 23, you'll learn how to enhance a Windows application by using the multi-document interface and by adding features like menus, toolbars, and help to your forms.

21

How to work with text and binary files

In section 4, you learned how to develop applications that store and retrieve data from a database. Because databases provide powerful features for working with data, databases are typically used for the data in most business applications. For some applications, though, you may need to save data in a file on disk and then read that data whenever it's needed. In this chapter, you'll learn how to do that with two different types of files: text and binary.

An introduction to the System.IO classes

The System.IO namespace provides a variety of classes for working with files and for managing directories, files, and paths. You'll be introduced to those classes in the topics that follow. In addition, you'll learn about the types of files and streams supported by the System.IO classes and how they're used to perform file I/O.

The classes for managing directories, files, and paths

Figure 21-1 summarizes the classes in the System.IO namespace that you can use to manage directories, files, and paths. As you can see, you can use the methods of the Directory class to create or delete a directory or determine if a directory exists. And you can use the methods of the File class to copy, delete, or move a file, or to determine if a file exists. Since the methods for both of these classes are static methods, you call them directly from the class.

Before you begin working with any of the classes in the System.IO namespace, you typically code a using statement like the one shown in the first example. Then, you can refer to the classes in this namespace without qualifying each reference with the namespace. If you don't code a using statement for the System.IO namespace, you can still access classes within the namespace by qualifying the class reference with the namespace. For example, you can refer to the Directory class like this:

```
System.IO.Directory
```

That's a lot of extra typing, though.

The second example shows how to use some of the methods of the Directory class. This code starts by declaring a string that holds the path to a directory that contains a file to be processed. Then, an if statement uses the Exists method of the Directory class to determine if this directory exists. If it doesn't, it uses the CreateDirectory method to create it.

The third example shows how to use some of the methods of the File class. This code declares a string that will hold the path to a file named Products.txt. Then, the if statement that follows uses the Exists method of the File class to determine if this file exists. If it does, it uses the Delete method to delete it.

System.IO classes used to work with drives and directories

Class	Description
`Directory`	Used to create, edit, delete, or get information on directories (folders).
`File`	Used to create, edit, delete, or get information on files.
`Path`	Used to get path information from a variety of platforms.

Common methods of the Directory class

Method	Description
`Exists(path)`	Returns a Boolean value indicating whether a directory exists.
`CreateDirectory(path)`	Creates the directories in a specified path.
`Delete(path)`	Deletes a directory and its contents.

Common methods of the File class

Method	Description
`Exists(path)`	Returns a Boolean value indicating whether a file exists.
`Delete(path)`	Deletes a file.
`Copy(source, dest)`	Copies a file from a source path to a destination path.
`Move(source, dest)`	Moves a file from a source path to a destination path.

A statement that simplifies references to the System.IO classes

```
using System.IO;
```

Code that uses some of the Directory methods

```
string dir = @"C:\C#.NET\Files\";
if (!Directory.Exists(dir))
    Directory.CreateDirectory(dir);
```

Code that uses some of the File methods

```
string path = dir + "Products.txt";
if (File.Exists(path))
    File.Delete(path);
```

Description

- The classes for managing directories, files, and paths are stored in the System.IO namespace.
- To use the classes in the System.IO namespace, you should include a using statement. Otherwise, you have to qualify the references to its classes with System.IO.
- All of the methods of the Directory, File, and Path classes are static methods.

Figure 21-1 The classes for managing directories, files, and paths

How files and streams work

When you use the System.IO classes to do *I/O operations* (or *file I/O*), you can use two different kinds of files: *text files* or *binary files*. To illustrate, figure 21-2 shows the contents of a text file and a binary file as they look when displayed in a text editor. Although both of these files contain the same data, they look quite different.

In a *text file*, all of the data is stored as text characters (or strings). Often, the *fields* in this type of file are separated by delimiters like tabs or pipe characters, and the *records* are separated by end of line characters. Although you can't see the end of line characters in this figure, you know they're there because each record starts at the beginning of a new line.

In contrast, the data in a *binary file* can include text characters as well as data types. Because of that, the data isn't always displayed properly within a text editor. For example, you can't tell what the value of the Price field is in each of these records because this field had a decimal data type. Also, since the records in a binary file don't end with end of line characters, one record isn't displayed on each line in a text editor.

To handle I/O operations with text and binary files, the .NET Framework uses *streams*. You can think of a stream as the flow of data from one location to another. For instance, an *output stream* can flow from the internal memory of an application to a disk file, and an *input stream* can flow from a disk file to internal memory. When you work with a text file, you use a *text stream*. When you work with a binary file, you use a *binary stream*.

To work with streams and files using the System.IO namespace, you use the classes summarized in this figure. To create a stream that connects to a file, for example, you use the FileStream class. Then, to read data from a text stream, you use the StreamReader class. And to read data from a binary stream, you use the BinaryReader class. You'll learn how to use all of these classes later in this chapter.

Since you can store all of the built-in numeric data types in a binary file, this type of file is more efficient for applications that work with numeric data. In contrast, the numeric data in a text file is stored as characters so each field must be converted to a numeric data type before it can be used in arithmetic operations.

When you save a text or binary file, you can use any extension you want for the file name. In this book, though, *txt* is used as the extension for all text files, and *dat* is used for all binary files. For instance, the text file in this figure is named Products.txt, and the binary file is named Products.dat.

A text file displayed in a text editor

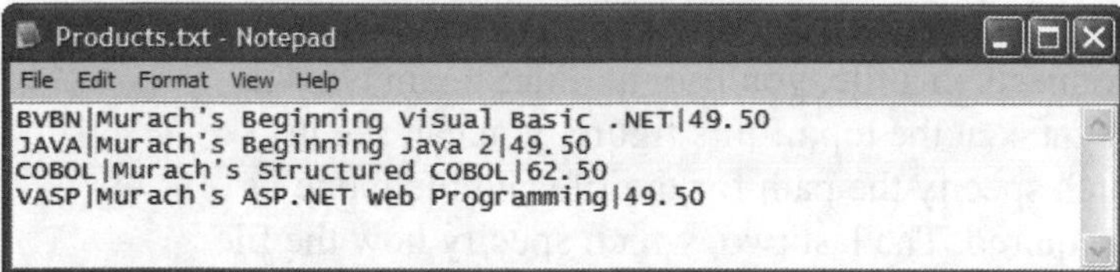

A binary file displayed in a text editor

Two types of files

Type	Description
Text	A file that contains text (string) characters. The *fields* in each record are typically delimited by special characters like tab or pipe characters, and the *records* are typically delimited by new line characters.
Binary	A file that can contain a variety of data types.

Two types of streams

Stream	Description
Text	Used to transfer text data.
Binary	Used to transfer binary data.

System.IO classes used to work with files and streams

Class	Description
FileStream	Provides access to input and output files.
StreamReader	Used to read a stream of characters.
StreamWriter	Used to write a stream of characters.
BinaryReader	Used to read a stream of binary data.
BinaryWriter	Used to write a stream of binary data.

Description

- An *input file* is a file that is read by a program; an *output file* is a file that is written by a program. Input and output operations are often referred to as *I/O operations* or *file I/O*.
- A *stream* is the flow of data from one location to another. To write data, you use an *output stream*. To read data, you use an *input stream*. A single stream can also be used for both input and output.
- To read and write text files, you use *text streams*. To read and write binary files, you use *binary streams*.

Figure 21-2 How files and streams work

How to use the FileStream class

To create a stream that connects to a file, you use the FileStream class as shown in figure 21-3. In the syntax at the top of this figure, you can see its arguments. The first two, which specify the path for the file and the mode in which it will be opened, are required. The last two, which specify how the file can be accessed and shared, are optional.

To code the mode, access, and share arguments, you use the FileMode, FileAccess, and FileShare enumerations. If, for example, you want to create a file stream for a file that doesn't exist, you can code the FileMode.Create member for the mode argument and a new file will be created. However, this member causes the file to be overwritten if it already exists. As a result, if you don't want an existing file to be overwritten, you can code the FileMode.CreateNew member for this argument. Then, if the file already exists, an exception is thrown as explained in the next figure.

For the access argument, you can code members that let you read records from the file, write records to the file, or both read and write records. If you omit this argument, the default is to allow both reading and writing of records.

For the share argument, you can code members that let other users read records, write records, or both read and write records at the same time that the first user is accessing the file. Or, you can code the None member to prevent sharing of the file. What you're trying to avoid is two users writing to a file at the same time, which could lead to errors. So if you code the access argument as ReadWrite or Write, you can code the share argument as Read or None. On the other hand, if you code the access argument as Read, you may want to code the share argument as Read or ReadWrite. Then, other applications may be able to write new data to the file while you're using it. However, when you set the share argument, additional permissions may be needed to be able to share this file while it's being used by the current process. In that case, you can use the Close method to close the file when you're done with it to allow other processes to access to the file.

The first example shows how to open a file stream for writing. Since this example uses the Write member to specify file access, this file stream can only be used to write the file, not to read it. And since this example uses the Create member for the mode argument, this code will create a new file if the file doesn't exist, or it will overwrite the existing file if the file already does exist. However, if the directory for this file doesn't exist, a directory not found exception will be thrown as described in the next figure.

The second example shows how to open a file stream for reading. This works similarly to opening a file stream for writing. However, the Open member is used to specify the mode argument. As a result, if the file doesn't exist, a file not found exception will be thrown as described in the next figure.

The syntax for creating a FileStream object

```
new FileStream(path, mode[, access[, share]])
```

Members in the FileMode enumeration

Member	Description
Append	Opens the file if it exists and seeks to the end of the file. If the file doesn't exist, it's created. This member can only be used with Write file access.
Create	Creates a new file. If the file already exists, it's overwritten.
CreateNew	Creates a new file. If the file already exists, an exception is thrown.
Open	Opens an existing file. If the file doesn't exist, an exception is thrown.
OpenOrCreate	Opens a file if it exists, or creates a new file if it doesn't exist.
Truncate	Opens an existing file and truncates it so its size is zero bytes.

Members in the FileAccess enumeration

Member	Description
Read	Data can be read from the file, but not written to it.
ReadWrite	Data can be read from and written to the file. This is the default.
Write	Data can be written to the file but not read from it.

Members in the FileShare enumeration

Member	Description
None	The file cannot be opened by other applications.
Read	Allows other applications to open the file for reading only. This is the default.
ReadWrite	Allows other applications to open the file for both reading and writing.
Write	Allows other applications to open the file for writing only.

Common method of the FileStream class

Method	Description
`Close()`	Closes the file stream and releases any resources associated with it.

Code that creates a FileStream object for writing

```
string path = @"C:\C#.NET\Files\Products.txt";
FileStream fs = new FileStream(path, FileMode.Create, FileAccess.Write);
```

Code that creates a new FileStream object for reading

```
string path = @"C:\C#.NET\Files\Products.txt";
FileStream fs = new FileStream(path, FileMode.Open, FileAccess.Read);
```

Note

- Operating system level permissions may limit which file access and file share options you can use.

Figure 21-3 How to use the FileStream class

How to use the exception classes for file I/O

In chapter 7, you learned the basic skills for handling exceptions. Now, figure 21-4 summarizes the exceptions that can occur when you perform I/O operations. Most of the time, you can write code so these exceptions are avoided. For example, you can avoid a directory not found exception by using the Exists method of the Directory class to be sure that the directory exists before you try to use it in the file path for a new file stream. Similarly, you can avoid a file not found exception by using the Exists method of the File class.

However, I/O exceptions are often serious problems like hardware problems that an application can't do anything about. For example, if an application needs to open a file that's on a network drive that isn't available, an exception will be thrown. In that case, it's common to handle the exception by displaying an error message as illustrated by the last catch block.

When handling I/O exceptions, it's common to use a finally block. In this block, it's common to use the stream's Close method to close all streams that are open. This frees the resources that are used to access the stream.

The code example shows how to handle some of the most common I/O exceptions. To start, the statement just before the try block declares a variable for the stream. That way, this variable is available to the catch blocks and the finally block. In this case, the stream is a FileStream object, but you'll learn how to work with other types of streams later in this chapter.

Within the try block, the first statement creates an instance of the stream. After this statement, the try block will contain more code that uses the stream to read and write data. Later in this chapter, you'll learn how to write this type of code. For now, you can assume that there is more code in the try block that uses the stream, and you can assume that this code may throw I/O exceptions, such as the exception that occurs when an application attempts to read beyond the end of the stream.

After the try block, the catch blocks are coded starting with the most specific type of exception and moving up the inheritance hierarchy towards the most general type of exception. In this case, both the directory not found and file not found exceptions inherit the IOException class. As a result, they must be coded before the IOException class. All three of these catch blocks display a dialog box that describes the type of exception to the user. This is a common way to handle I/O exceptions. However, in some cases, you may want to create a directory or file, or allow the user to search for a directory or file.

Within the finally block, an if statement is used to determine whether the exception was thrown before or after the stream was opened. If the exception was thrown before the stream was opened, the variable for the stream is equal to a null value. As a result, calling the Close method isn't necessary and would throw a null pointer exception. However, if the exception was thrown after the stream was opened, the variable is not equal to null. In that case, the Close method frees the resources used by the stream.

The exception classes for file I/O

Class	Description
IOException	The base class for exceptions that are thrown during the processing of a stream, file, or directory.
DirectoryNotFoundException	Occurs when part of a directory or file path can't be found.
FileNotFoundException	Occurs when a file can't be found.
EndOfStreamException	Occurs when an application attempts to read beyond the end of a stream.

Code that uses exception classes

```
string dirPath = @"C:\C#.NET\Files\";
string filePath = dirPath + "Products.txt";
FileStream fs = null;
try
{
    fs = new FileStream(filePath, FileMode.Open);
    // code that uses the file stream
    // to read and write data from the file
}
catch(FileNotFoundException)
{
    MessageBox.Show(filePath + " not found.", "File Not Found");
}
catch(DirectoryNotFoundException)
{
    MessageBox.Show(dirPath + " not found.", "Directory Not Found");
}
catch(IOException ioe)
{
    MessageBox.Show(ioe.Message, "IOException");
}
finally
{
    if (fs != null)
        fs.Close();
}
```

Description

- To catch any I/O exception, you can use the IOException class.
- To catch specific I/O exceptions, you can use the other exception classes that inherit from the IOException class such as the three shown in this figure.

Figure 21-4 How to use the exception classes for file I/O

How to work with text files

To read and write characters in a text file, you use the StreamReader and StreamWriter classes. When working with text files, you often need to use the techniques you learned in chapters 4 and 9 to build and parse strings.

How to write a text file

Figure 21-5 shows how to use the StreamWriter class to write data to a text file. This class lets you write any data to a text file by using the Write and WriteLine methods. When you use the WriteLine method, a line terminator is automatically added. Typically, a line terminator is used to end each record. However, the fields in a record are typically separated by special characters, such as tab characters or pipe characters, and you have to add those characters through code.

The example shows how this works. This code creates a file stream object for a file with write-only access and it creates a stream writer object for that file stream. Next, it uses a foreach loop to write the three properties for each Product object in an array list to the file with pipe characters as separators. For the last property, the WriteLine method is used to end the record with a line terminator. That way, each record will start on a new line. Finally, after all of the records have been written to the file by the foreach loop, the stream writer and file stream are closed.

The basic syntax for creating a StreamWriter object

```
new StreamWriter(stream)
```

Common methods of the StreamWriter class

Method	Description
`Write(data)`	Writes the data to the output stream.
`WriteLine(data)`	Writes the data to the output stream and appends a line terminator (usually a carriage return and a line feed).
`Close()`	Closes the StreamWriter object and the associated FileStream object.

Code that writes data from an array list to a text file

```
StreamWriter textOut =
    new StreamWriter(
    new FileStream(path, FileMode.Create, FileAccess.Write));

foreach (Product product in products)
{
    textOut.Write(product.Code + "|");
    textOut.Write(product.Description + "|");
    textOut.WriteLine(product.Price);
}
textOut.Close();
```

Description

- You can use the Write and WriteLine methods of a StreamWriter object to write data to a text file.
- If the fields that make up a record are stored in individual variables, you need to concatenate these variables to construct each record and you need to add special characters to delimit each field. However, since the WriteLine method adds the line terminator automatically, you can use it to end each record.

How to read a text file

Figure 21-6 shows how to use the StreamReader class to read data from a text file. To create a StreamReader object, you can use a FileStream object as the argument. Then, you can use the methods shown in this figure to work with the stream reader object.

The three Read methods let you read a single character, a single line of data (a record), or all of the data from the current position to the end of the file. In most cases, though, you'll use the ReadLine method to read one record at a time. You can also use the Peek method to see if there is additional data in the file before you read from it, and you can use the Close method to close the stream reader and file stream when you're done with them.

The example shows how you can use a stream reader to read the data in a file one record at a time. After the file stream and stream reader are created, a while loop is used to read the records in the file. The condition on this loop uses the Peek method to check that there is at least one more character. If there is, the ReadLine method reads the next record in the file into a string and that string is parsed into the individual fields. Then, each field is stored in one of the properties of a Product object, and each product is stored in an array list. When all of the records have been read, the Close method of the stream reader is used to close the stream reader and the file stream.

Note in this example that the FileStream object is instantiated in OpenOrCreate mode. Then, if the file exists, it is opened. Otherwise, a new file is created with no records in it. In either case, the code that follows works because it peeks into the file before it tries to read the data. If the file is empty, no records are read.

The basic syntax for creating a StreamReader object

```
new StreamReader(stream)
```

Common methods of the StreamReader class

Method	Description
`Peek()`	Returns the next available character in the input stream without advancing to the next position. If no more characters are available, this method returns –1.
`Read()`	Reads the next character from the input stream.
`ReadLine()`	Reads the next line of characters from the input stream and returns it as a string.
`ReadToEnd()`	Reads the data from the current position in the input stream to the end of the stream and returns it as a string. This is typically used to read the contents of an entire file.
`Close()`	Closes both the StreamReader object and the associated FileStream object.

Code that reads data from a text file and stores it in an array list

```
StreamReader textIn =
    new StreamReader(
    new FileStream(path, FileMode.OpenOrCreate, FileAccess.Read));

ArrayList products = new ArrayList();
while (textIn.Peek() != -1)
{
    string row = textIn.ReadLine();
    string[] columns = row.Split('|');
    Product product = new Product();
    product.Code = columns[0];
    product.Description = columns[1];
    product.Price = Convert.ToDecimal(columns[2]);
    products.Add(product);
}
textIn.Close();
```

Description

- You use a StreamReader object to read data from a text file. Because the records in most text files end with a line terminator (usually a carriage return and a line feed), you'll typically use the ReadLine method to read one record at a time.
- If the fields in a record are delimited by special characters, you need to parse the fields using the techniques of chapter 9.
- You can use the Peek method to determine if the input stream is positioned at the end of the stream.

Figure 21-6 How to read a text file

A class that works with a text file

In chapter 12, you learned how to develop an application that used a business class named Product. You also learned how to use two static methods in a database class named ProductDB to get the data for product objects and to save the data for product objects. However, you didn't learn how to code those database methods.

Now, in figure 21-7, you can see a ProductDB class that implements those methods using a text file. To start, the using statements specify the System.Collections and System.IO namespaces. That makes it easier to write the code that works with an array list of product objects and the input and output streams in this class. Then, this class provides two constants that specify the path for the directory and the path for the text file. This makes those constants available to all of the methods in the class.

The GetProducts method reads the product data from the file, stores that data in an array list of product objects, and returns the array list. After the StreamReader object and the array list are created, the foreach loop reads the data in the file and stores the product objects in an array list as described in the previous figure. When the loop ends, the stream reader and file stream are closed, and the method returns the array list. At least that's the way this method works if the file already exists.

Note, however, that the GetProducts method also works if the directory or file doesn't exist when the method is executed. This situation could occur the first time an application is run. In that case, the method creates the directory if the directory doesn't exist and an empty file if the file doesn't exist. Then, the code that follows will still work, but it won't read any records.

In contrast, the SaveProducts method writes the data in the product objects that are stored in an array list to the file. To start, this method accepts an array list of Product objects. Then, this method writes each product object to the file. Because the FileStream object is instantiated in Create mode, the product objects will be written to a new file if the file doesn't already exist and they will overwrite the old file if it does exist.

To keep the emphasis on the code for file I/O, this class doesn't include exception handling. In a production application, though, you would probably add exception handling to a class like this. That way, the exception can be caught and handled close to its source, which often helps to reduce the amount of exception handling code that's necessary for an application.

A class that works with a text file

```
using System;
using System.IO;
using System.Collections;

namespace ProductMaintenance
{
    public class ProductDB
    {
        private const string dir = @"C:\C#.NET\Files\";
        private const string path = dir + "Products.txt";

        public static ArrayList GetProducts()
        {
            if (!Directory.Exists(dir))
                Directory.CreateDirectory(dir);

            StreamReader textIn =
                new StreamReader(
                new FileStream(path, FileMode.OpenOrCreate, FileAccess.Read));

            ArrayList products = new ArrayList();
            while (textIn.Peek() != -1)
            {
                string row = textIn.ReadLine();
                string[] columns = row.Split('|');
                Product product = new Product();
                product.Code = columns[0];
                product.Description = columns[1];
                product.Price = Convert.ToDecimal(columns[2]);
                products.Add(product);
            }
            textIn.Close();

            return products;
        }

        public static void SaveProducts(ArrayList products)
        {
            StreamWriter textOut =
                new StreamWriter(
                new FileStream(path, FileMode.Create, FileAccess.Write));

            foreach (Product product in products)
            {
                textOut.Write(product.Code + "|");
                textOut.Write(product.Description + "|");
                textOut.WriteLine(product.Price);
            }
            textOut.Close();
        }
    }
}
```

Figure 21-7 A class that works with a text file

How to work with binary files

To read and write data in a binary file, you use the BinaryReader and BinaryWriter classes. You'll learn how to use these classes in the figures that follow, and you'll see a class that can be used to read and write a binary file.

How to write a binary file

Figure 21-8 shows how to use the BinaryWriter class to write data to a binary file. To start, you create a BinaryWriter object using the syntax at the top of this figure. To do that, you must supply a FileStream object as the argument for the constructor of the BinaryWriter class. This links the stream to the BinaryWriter object so it can be used to write to the file.

Once you create a BinaryWriter object, you can use its Write method to write all types of data. This method begins by figuring out what type of data has been passed to it. Then, it writes that type of data to the file. For example, if you pass a variable that contains a decimal value to the Write method, this method won't convert the decimal value to a string, it will write the decimal value to the file.

The example shows how this works. Here, a binary writer is created for a file stream that specifies a file that has write-only access. Since the mode argument has been set to Create, this will overwrite the file if it exists, and it will create the file if it doesn't exist. Then, a foreach loop is used to write the elements in an array list named products to the file. Since each element in the array list is an object of the Product class, each field in the object is written to the file separately using the Write method. After all of the elements in the array list have been written to the file, the Close method is used to close both the binary writer and the file stream.

The basic syntax for creating a BinaryWriter object

```
new BinaryWriter(stream)
```

Common methods of the BinaryWriter class

Method	Description
`Write(data)`	Writes the specified data to the output stream.
`Close()`	Closes the BinaryWriter object and the associated FileStream object.

Code that writes data from an array list to a binary file

```
BinaryWriter binaryOut =
    new BinaryWriter(
    new FileStream(path, FileMode.Create, FileAccess.Write));

foreach (Product product in products)
{
    binaryOut.Write(product.Code);
    binaryOut.Write(product.Description);
    binaryOut.Write(product.Price);
}

binaryOut.Close();
```

Description

- You use a BinaryWriter object to write data to a binary file. In most cases, you'll write one field at a time in a prescribed sequence.
- Unlike the BinaryReader class, which provides several methods for reading fields that contain different types of data (see figure 21-9), the BinaryWriter class provides a single Write method for writing data to a file. This method determines the type of data being written based on the data types of the variables.

Figure 21-8 How to write a binary file

How to read a binary file

Figure 21-9 shows you how to use the BinaryReader class to read data from a binary file. Like the BinaryWriter class, the argument that you pass to the BinaryReader is the name of the FileStream object that connects the stream to a file.

In a binary file, there's no termination character to indicate where one record ends and another begins. Because of that, you can't read an entire record at once. Instead, you have to read one character or one field at a time. To do that, you use the Read methods of the BinaryReader class that are shown in this figure. When you do, you must use the appropriate method for the data type of the field that you want to read. To read a Boolean field, for example, you use the ReadBoolean method. To read a Decimal field, you use the ReadDecimal method.

The BinaryReader class provides methods to read most of the data types provided by the .NET Framework. However, this figure only shows the most common of these methods. For a complete list of methods, see the online help information for the BinaryReader class.

Before you read the next character or field, you want to be sure that you aren't at the end of the file. To do that, you use the PeekChar method. Then, if there's at least one more character to be read, this method returns that character without advancing the cursor to the next position in the file. If there isn't another character, the PeekChar method returns a value of –1. Then, you can use the Close method to close the binary reader and the associated file stream.

The example shows how you can use some of these methods. Here, a FileStream object is created for a file that will have read-only access. Since the mode argument for the file stream specifies OpenOrCreate, this opens an existing file if one exists or creates a new file that's empty and opens it. Then, a new BinaryReader object is created for that file stream. Finally, the while loop that follows is executed until the PeekChar method returns a value of –1, which means the end of the file has been reached.

Within the while loop, the three fields in each record are read into the Product object. Because the first two fields in each record contain string data, the ReadString method is used to retrieve their contents. Because the third field contains decimal data, the ReadDecimal method is used to retrieve its contents. Then, the Product object is added to the array list. When the while loop ends, the Close method of the BinaryReader object is used to close both the binary reader and the file stream.

The basic syntax for creating a BinaryReader object

```
new BinaryReader(stream)
```

Common methods of the BinaryReader class

Method	Description
`PeekChar()`	Returns the next available character in the input stream without advancing to the next position. If no more characters are available, this method returns -1.
`Read()`	Returns the next available character from the input stream and advances to the next position in the file.
`ReadBoolean()`	Returns a Boolean value from the input stream and advances the current position of the stream by one byte.
`ReadByte()`	Returns a byte from the input stream and advances the current position of the stream accordingly.
`ReadChar()`	Returns a character from the input stream and advances the current position of the stream accordingly.
`ReadDecimal()`	Returns a decimal value from the input stream and advances the current position of the stream by 16 bytes.
`ReadInt32()`	Returns a 4-byte signed integer from the input stream and advances the current position of the stream by 4 bytes.
`ReadString()`	Returns a string from the input stream and advances the current position of the stream by the number of characters in the string.
`Close()`	Closes the BinaryReader object and the associated FileStream object.

Code that reads data from a binary file and stores it in an array list

```
BinaryReader binaryIn =
    new BinaryReader(
    new FileStream(path, FileMode.OpenOrCreate, FileAccess.Read));

ArrayList products = new ArrayList();
while (binaryIn.PeekChar() != -1)
{
    Product product = new Product();
    product.Code = binaryIn.ReadString();
    product.Description = binaryIn.ReadString();
    product.Price = binaryIn.ReadDecimal();
    products.Add(product);
}

binaryIn.Close();
```

Description

- You use a BinaryReader object to read a single character or an entire field from a binary file. To read a single character, you use the Read method. And to read a field, you use the method that indicates the type of data the field contains.
- You can use the PeekChar method to determine if the input stream is positioned at the end of the stream.

Figure 21-9 How to read a binary file

A class that works with a binary file

Figure 21-10 presents the code for the ProductDB class that you saw in figure 21-7, but this time it uses a binary file instead of a text file. Because the methods in this class are similar to the ones for the text file, you shouldn't have any trouble understanding how they work.

Note, however, that the signatures for the two methods in this class are the same as the signatures for the methods in the ProductDB class in figure 21-7. As a result, either of these classes can be used with the Product Maintenance application presented in chapter 12. This clearly illustrates the benefit of encapsulation: the calling method doesn't know or care how the method is implemented. As a result, the programmer can change the way these methods are implemented without changing the rest of the application.

A class that works with a binary file

```
using System;
using System.IO;
using System.Collections;

namespace ProductMaintenance
{
    public class ProductDB
    {
        private const string dir = @"C:\C#.NET\Files\";
        private const string path = dir + "Products.dat";

        public static ArrayList GetProducts()
        {
            if (!Directory.Exists(dir))
                Directory.CreateDirectory(dir);

            BinaryReader binaryIn =
                new BinaryReader(
                new FileStream(path, FileMode.OpenOrCreate, FileAccess.Read));

            ArrayList products = new ArrayList();
            while (binaryIn.PeekChar() != -1)
            {
                Product product = new Product();
                product.Code = binaryIn.ReadString();
                product.Description = binaryIn.ReadString();
                product.Price = binaryIn.ReadDecimal();
                products.Add(product);
            }

            binaryIn.Close();

            return products;
        }

        public static void SaveProducts(ArrayList products)
        {
            BinaryWriter binaryOut =
                new BinaryWriter(
                new FileStream(path, FileMode.Create, FileAccess.Write));

            foreach (Product product in products)
            {
                binaryOut.Write(product.Code);
                binaryOut.Write(product.Description);
                binaryOut.Write(product.Price);
            }

            binaryOut.Close();
        }
    }
}
```

Figure 21-10 A class that works with a binary file

Perspective

In this chapter, you learned how to read and write the data in text and binary files. These files can be used when you need a relatively easy way to store a limited number of records with a limited number of fields. They are not normally used for the critical data of an application because that's what a database is designed for.

Summary

- The Directory, File, and Path classes in the System.IO namespace can be used for managing directories, files, and paths.
- A *text file* contains text characters. A *binary file* can contain text characters as well as C# data types.
- I/O exceptions can occur as an application works with files, and these exceptions can be caught with try-catch statements.
- FileStream objects are used to open and close files. StreamReader and StreamWriter objects are used to read and write the data in text files. And BinaryReader and BinaryWriter objects are used to read and write the data in binary files.

Terms

input file
output file
I/O operations
file I/O
text file
field
record
binary file
stream
output stream
input stream
text stream
binary stream

Objectives

- Given the specifications for I/O operations that involve text or binary files, write the code for the operations.
- Distinguish between a text file and a binary file.
- Describe the use of a FileStream object.
- Name and describe two common types of I/O exceptions.
- Describe the use of StreamReader and StreamWriter objects.
- Describe the use of BinaryReader and BinaryWriter objects.

Exercise 21-1 Work with a text file

In this exercise, you'll write the data for Customer objects to a text file, and you'll read the data for Customer objects from a text file.

1. Open the Customer project in the C:\C#.NET\Chapter 21\CustomerText directory. This project contains the code for two forms, a Validator class, a Customer class, and the beginning of a CustomerDB class. Read the code for these classes and run the application to see how it works. This application should work, but it doesn't save the data or update the customer number.
2. Add code to the GetCustomers and SaveCustomers methods in the CustomerDB class so they read and write an array list of Customer objects from a text file. The path for the text file should be C:\C#.NET\Files\Customers.txt.
3. Add code to the methods in the two forms so they use the CustomerDB class to read and write the text file when appropriate.
4. Test the application by adding and deleting customers. To verify that the data is being saved to disk and is therefore available for the each new session, you can stop the application and run it again. When you're done, make sure to leave at least three customer records in the file.

Exercise 21-2 Work with a binary file

This exercise shows how to convert the application that you created in the previous exercise so it uses a binary file instead of a text file.

1. Use the Windows Explorer to copy the folder named C:\C#.NET\Chapter 21\CustomerText. Then, rename that folder C:\C#.NET\Chapter 21\CustomerBinary.
2. Open the Customer project in the C:\C#.NET\Chapter 21\CustomerBinary directory. Modify the CustomerDB class so it uses a binary file instead of a text file. Make sure to modify the path that's stored in this file so the data is saved in a file named C:\C#.NET\Files\Customers.dat, and make sure to leave the signatures of the GetCustomers and SaveCustomers methods as they are. That way, you won't need to modify the code in the form class that calls these methods.
3. Test the application by adding and deleting customers. When you're done, make sure to leave at least three customer records in the binary file.
4. Use a text editor to open the text file created in the previous exercise and the binary file created in this exercise. Note that it's easier to read the data that's stored in the text file.

22

How to work with XML

XML is a standard way of storing data. Although XML is often used to exchange data between applications, particularly web-based applications, it can also be used to store structured data in a file. In this chapter, you'll learn the basics of creating XML documents, and you'll learn how to store those documents in a file.

An introduction to XML

This topic introduces you to the basics of XML. Here, you'll learn what XML is, how it is used, and the rules you must follow to create a simple XML document.

An XML document

XML (*Extensible Markup Language*) is a standard way to structure data by using *tags* that identify each data element. In some ways, XML is similar to HTML, the markup language that's used to format HTML documents on the World Wide Web. As a result, if you're familiar with HTML, you'll have no trouble learning how to create *XML documents*.

Figure 22-1 shows a simple XML document that contains data for three products. Each product has a code, description, and price. In the next two figures, you'll learn how the tags in this XML document work. But even without knowing those details, you can pick out the code, description, and price for each of the three products represented by this XML document.

XML was designed as a way to structure data that's sent over the World Wide Web. When you use .NET to develop web applications, though, you don't have to deal directly with XML. Instead, the .NET Framework classes handle the XML details for you.

Besides its use for web applications, XML is used internally throughout the .NET Framework to store data and to exchange data between various components of the Framework. In particular, the database features described in section 4 rely on XML. When you retrieve data from a database, for example, the .NET Framework converts the data to XML. However, since this is done automatically, the programmer doesn't have to deal with XML directly.

You can also use XML files as an alternative to the text and binary files described in chapter 21. Later in this chapter, for example, you'll learn how to create a ProductDB class for the Product Maintenance application that uses an XML file.

Data for three products

Code	Description	Price
BVBN	Murach's Beginning Visual Basic .NET	49.50
JAVA	Murach's Beginning Java 2	49.50
ZJCL	Murach's OS/390 and z/OS JCL	62.50

The products.xml document

```
<?xml version="1.0" encoding="utf-8" ?>
<!--Product data-->
<Products>
  <Product Code="BVBN">
    <Description>Murach's Beginning Visual Basic .NET</Description>
    <Price>49.50</Price>
  </Product>
  <Product Code="JAVA">
    <Description>Murach's Beginning Java 2</Description>
    <Price>49.50</Price>
  </Product>
  <Product Code="ZJCL">
    <Description>Murach's OS/390 and z/OS JCL</Description>
    <Price>62.50</Price>
  </Product>
</Products>
```

Description

- *XML*, which stands for *Extensible Markup Language*, is a method of structuring data using special *tags*.
- The *XML document* in this figure contains data for three products. Each product has an *attribute* named Code and *elements* named Description and Price, which you'll learn more about in the next two figures.
- XML can be used to exchange data between different systems, especially via the Internet.
- Many .NET classes, particularly the database and web classes, use XML internally to store or exchange data.
- XML documents that are stored in a file can be used as an alternative to binary files, text files, or even database systems for storing data.
- When XML is stored in a file, the file name usually has an extension of xml.
- The .NET Framework includes several classes that let you read and write XML data. These classes are in the System.Xml namespace.

Figure 22-1 An XML document

XML tags, declarations, and comments

Figure 22-2 shows how XML uses tags to structure the data in an XML document. Here, each XML tag begins with the < character and ends with the > character. As a result, the first line in the XML document in this figure contains a complete XML tag. Similarly, the next three lines also contain complete tags. In contrast, the fifth line contains two tags, <Description> and </Description>, with a text value in between.

The first tag in any XML document is an *XML declaration*. This declaration identifies the document as an XML document and indicates which XML version the document conforms to. In this example, the document conforms to XML version 1.0. In addition, the declaration usually identifies the character set that's being used for the document. In this example, the character set is UTF-8, the most common one used for XML documents in English-speaking countries.

An XML document can also contain comments. These are tags that begin with <!-- and end with-->. Between the tags, you can type anything you want. For instance, the second line in this figure is a comment that indicates what type of data is contained in the XML document. It's often a good idea to include similar comments in your own XML documents.

XML elements

Elements are the building blocks of XML. Each element in an XML document represents a single data item and is identified by two tags: a *start tag* and an *end tag*. The start tag marks the beginning of the element and provides the element's name. The end tag marks the end of the element and repeats the name, prefixed by a slash. For example, <Description> is the start tag for an element named Description, and </Description> is the corresponding end tag.

It's important to realize that XML does not provide a pre-defined set of element names the way HTML does. Instead, you create your own element names to describe the contents of each element. Since XML names are case-sensitive, <Product> and <product> are not the same.

A complete element consists of the element's start tag, its end tag, and the *content* between the tags. For example, <Price>49.50</Price> indicates that the content of the Price element is 49.50. And <Description>Murach's Beginning Java 2</Description> indicates that the content of the Description element is *Murach's Beginning Java 2*.

Besides content, elements can contain other elements, known as *child elements*. This lets you add structure to a *parent element*. For example, a parent product element can have child elements that provide details about each product, such as the product's description and price. In this figure, for example, you can see that the start tag, end tag, and values for the Description and Price elements are contained between the start and end tags for the Product element. As a result, Description and Price are children of the Product element, and the Product element is the parent of both the Description and Price elements.

An XML document

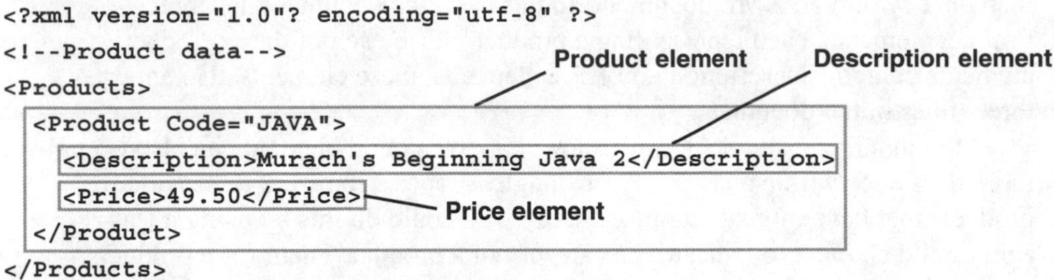
<?xml version="1.0"? encoding="utf-8" ?>
<!--Product data-->
<Products>
<Product Code="JAVA">
<Description>Murach's Beginning Java 2</Description>
<Price>49.50</Price>
</Product>
</Products>
Product element
Description element
Price element

Tags, XML declarations, and comments

- Each XML tag begins with < and ends with >.
- The first line in an XML document is an *XML declaration* that indicates which version of the XML standard is being used for the document. In addition, the declaration usually identifies the standard character set that's being used. For documents in English-speaking countries, UTF-8 is the character set that's commonly used.
- You can use the <!-- and --> tags to include comments in an XML document.

Elements

- An *element* is a unit of XML data that begins with a *start tag* and ends with an *end tag*. The start tag provides the name of the element and contains any attributes assigned to the element (see figure 22-3 for details on attributes). The end tag repeats the name, prefixed with a slash (/). You can use any name you want for an XML element.
- The text between an element's start and end tags is called the element's *content*. For example, <Description>Murach's Beginning Java 2</Description> indicates that the content of the Description element is the string *Murach's Beginning Java 2*.
- Elements can contain other elements. An element that's contained within another element is known as a *child element*. The element that contains a child element is known as the child's *parent element*.
- Child elements can repeat within a parent element. For instance, in the example above, the Products element can contain more than one Product element. Similarly, each Product element could contain repeating child elements. For instance, in the example above, each Product element could contain zero or more Category elements.
- The highest-level parent element in an XML document is known as the *root element*. An XML document can have only one root element.

Figure 22-2 XML tags, declarations, comments, and elements

As the XML document in figure 22-1 shows, an element can occur more than once within an XML document. In this case, the document has three Product elements, each representing a product. Since each of these Product elements contains Description and Price elements, these elements also appear three times in the document.

Although this example doesn't show it, a given child element can also occur more than once within a parent. For example, suppose you want to provide for products that have more than one category. You could do this by using a Category child element to indicate the category of a product. Then, for a product that belongs to multiple categories, you simply include multiple Category child elements within the Product element for that product.

The highest-level parent element in an XML document is known as the *root element*, and an XML document can have only one root element. In the examples in figures 22-1 and 22-2, the root element is Products. For XML documents that contain repeating data, it is common to use a plural name for the root element to indicate that it contains multiple child elements.

XML attributes

As shown in figure 22-3, *attributes* are a concise way to provide data for XML elements. In the products XML document, for example, each Product element has a Code attribute that provides an identifying code for the product. Thus, <Product Code="JAVA"> contains an attribute named Code whose value is JAVA.

Here again, XML doesn't provide a set of pre-defined attributes. Instead, you create attributes as you need them, using names that describe the content of the attributes. If an element has more than one attribute, you can list the attributes in any order you wish. However, you must separate the attributes from each other with one or more spaces. In addition, each attribute can appear only once within an element.

When you plan the layout of an XML document, you will often need to decide whether to use elements or attributes to represent each data item. In many cases, either one will work. In the products document, for example, I could have used a child element named Code rather than an attribute to represent each product's code. Likewise, I could have used an attribute named Description rather than a child element for the product's description.

Because attributes are more concise than child elements, it's often tempting to use attributes rather than child elements. Keep in mind, though, that an element with more than a few attributes soon becomes unwieldy. As a result, most designers limit their use of attributes to certain types of data, such as identifiers like product codes or customer numbers.

An XML document

```
<?xml version="1.0" encoding="utf-8" ?>
<!--Product data-->
<Products>
  <Product Code="JAVA">
    <Description>Murach's Beginning Java 2</Description>
    <Price>49.50</Price>
  </Product>
</Products>
```

Code attribute

Description

- You can include one or more *attributes* in the start tag for an element. An attribute consists of an attribute name, an equal sign, and a string value in quotes.
- If an element has more than one attribute, the order in which the attributes appear doesn't matter, but the attributes must be separated by one or more spaces.

When to use attributes instead of child elements

- When you design an XML document, you can use either child elements or attributes to represent the data for an element. The choice of whether to implement a data item as an attribute or as a separate child element is often a matter of preference.
- Two advantages of attributes are that they can appear in any order and they are more concise because they do not require end tags.
- Two advantages of child elements are that they are easier for people to read and they are more convenient for long string values.

Figure 22-3 XML attributes

How to work with the XML Designer

You can use the *XML Designer* that comes with Visual Studio to create or edit an XML document. To start, you can enter an XML document and save it in a file. Then, you can view the data that's stored in the XML document.

How to work with XML view

To create a new XML file and add it to your project, you can use the Project→Add New Item command as shown in figure 22-4. To open an existing XML document without adding the file to your project, you can use the File→Open command. Either way, the document is opened in the XML Designer window in its XML view.

When you use Visual Studio to create a new XML document, the XML declaration is added to the start of the document automatically. As you can see, the declaration in this example includes both the XML version attribute and the encoding attribute that indicates which character set the document uses. Unless you're working in a language other than English, you'll want to leave this attribute set to UTF-8.

When you work in the XML Designer window, the task of editing XML documents is simplified. For example, tags, content, attributes, values, and comments are color-coded so you can easily tell them apart. When you type a start tag, the XML editor automatically adds the end tag and positions the cursor between the start and end tags. In addition, the XML Designer makes it easy to work with the indentation of the child elements. If you work with the XML Designer for a while, you'll quickly see how easy it is to use.

An XML document in the XML Designer window

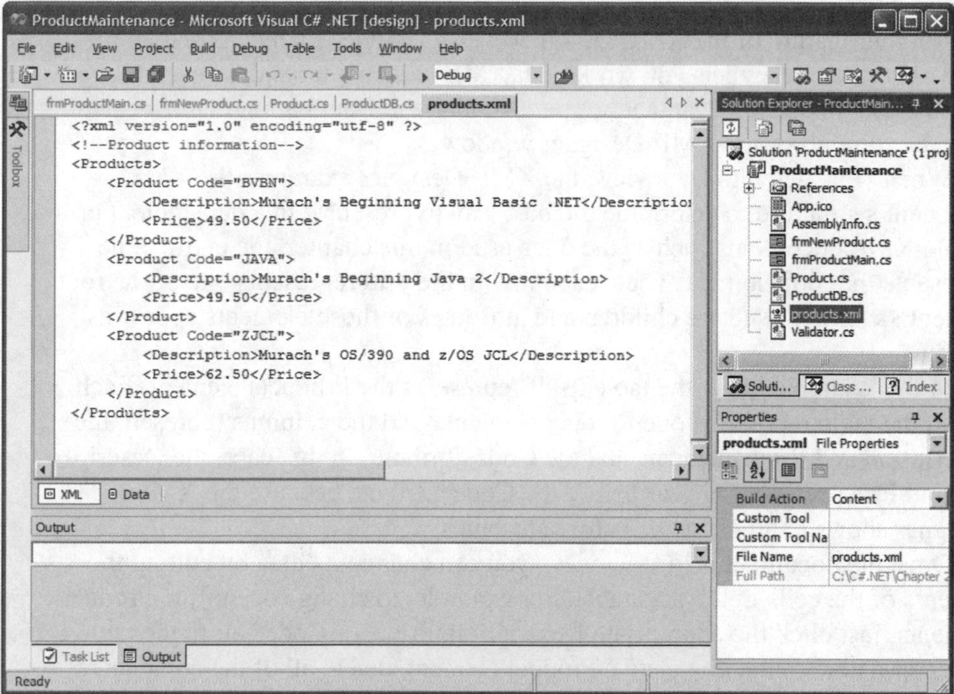

How to add an XML document to a project

- Choose the Project→Add New Item command. In the Add New Item dialog box, select XML document in the Templates box; type a name for the XML document in the Name text box; and click Open. This adds an XML document to your project, opens the document in the XML Designer window, and adds the XML declaration for the document.

How to open an existing XML document

- Use the File→Open command to open an existing XML document without adding the document to your project.

How to edit an XML document in Visual Studio

- When you type a start tag, Visual Studio automatically adds an end tag for the element and positions the insertion point between the start and end tags so you can type the element's content.
- When you type an attribute, Visual Studio automatically adds a pair of quotation marks and positions the insertion point between them so you can type the attribute value.

Figure 22-4 How to work with the XML Designer in XML view

How to work with Data view

Another feature of the XML Designer is its Data view, which is shown in figure 22-5. This view lets you work with XML data in a table that resembles a spreadsheet. To activate Data view, you just click the Data button that's located at the bottom left of the XML Designer window.

When you switch to Data view, the XML Designer examines the XML document's structure to determine the best way to present it in a data table. For simple XML documents such as the ones used in this chapter, the entire table represents the root element. Then, each row in the grid represents one of the root element's children, and the children and attributes of those elements appear as columns.

In this example, then, the table itself represents the Products element. Each row in the table represents one Product element. And the columns represent the Description and Price elements and the Code attribute. In this case, the Description and Price columns appear before the Code attribute because the XML Designer shows child elements before attributes.

Once the document is in Data view, you can change its data by editing the contents of the cells in the data table. For example, to change one of the Product elements, just click the appropriate Description, Price, or Code cell in the table and enter a new value. To delete a Product element, delete all of the contents of the row, select the row by clicking the box to the left of the row, and press the Delete key. And to add a new Product element, just enter the new values for the columns in the last row of the table.

When you switch back to XML view by clicking the XML button at the bottom of the Designer window, you'll see that the XML has been automatically updated to reflect any changes you made to the data. If you deleted a row, that row's Product element is deleted from the XML. And if you added a new row, a new Product element is added to the XML.

The real benefit of the Data view is that it lets you create an XML document by typing a minimum of XML. If, for example, you need to create an XML document that contains 50 Product elements, you start by typing the XML for just one Product element. Then, you switch to Data view and use the data table to enter the data for the rest of the Product elements. It's that easy.

An XML document in Data view

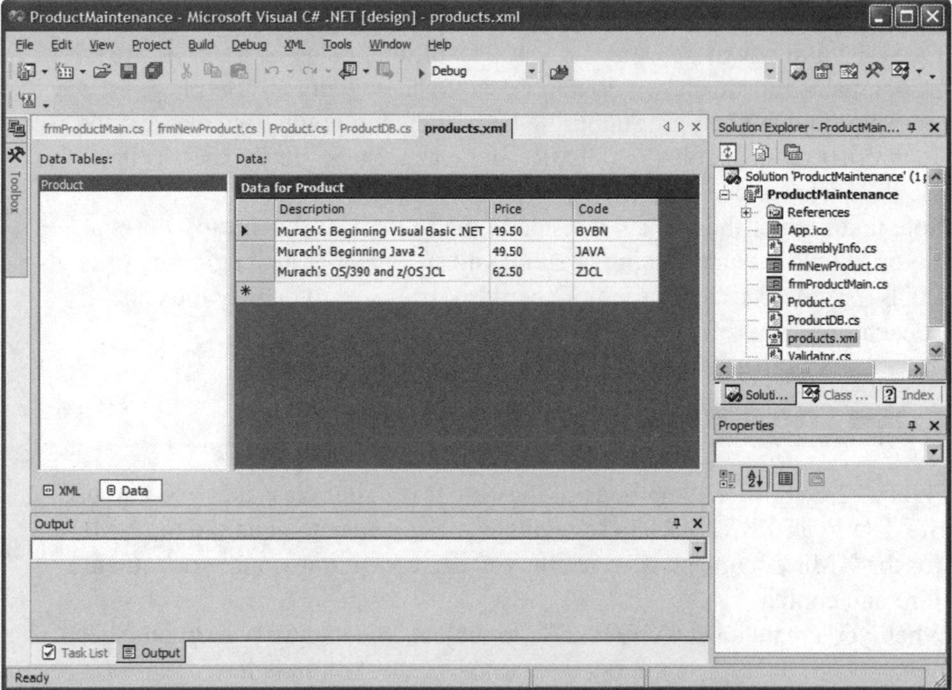

Description

- When you click the Data button at the bottom of an XML Designer window, Visual Studio displays the contents of the XML document as a data table.
- In this example, the entire table represents the Products element. Each Product element is presented as a row. The Description and Price elements and the Code attribute appear as columns.
- To modify any of the elements in the XML document, enter new values in the appropriate columns.
- To add a new row to the XML document, enter values for the columns in the bottom row of the table.
- To delete a row from the XML document, you must first delete the contents of the row. Then, you can select the row by clicking the box to the left of it and delete it by pressing the Delete key.
- You can return to XML view by clicking the XML button at the bottom left of the XML Designer window. When you do, you'll see that the document's XML has been updated to reflect any changes you made.

Figure 22-5 How to work with the XML Designer in Data view

How to work with XML

The .NET Framework provides nearly 150 different classes for working with XML documents. Fortunately, you don't need to know them all. In this topic, I'll get you started with XML programming by introducing you to two classes: the XmlTextWriter class and the XmlTextReader class. These are the classes that provide the basic services you need to write and read XML files.

Note that both of these classes reside in the System.Xml namespace. As a result, you should include a using System.Xml statement at the beginning of any .NET class that uses either of them. Otherwise, you have to qualify the class names each time you refer to them.

How to use the XmlTextWriter class

Figure 22-6 shows the methods of the XmlTextWriter class that you can use to write data to an XML file. These methods make it easy to generate the XML tags for the XML document. As a result, you can concentrate on the document's structure and content.

When you create a new XmlTextWriter object, you supply two arguments: the filename and the type of encoding to use. Usually, you pass the filename as a string variable that includes the path, and you set the encoding argument to UTF-8. Note that if the file you specify already exists, it's deleted and recreated. So you can't use this technique to add XML to an existing file.

Before you code any statements that write XML, I recommend that you set the XmlTextWriter's Formatting property to Formatting.Indented. That way, the XmlTextWriter will use spaces to indent child elements. This will make your XML files easier to read if they're opened in the XML Designer.

To write XML data, you use one of the Write methods of the XmlTextWriter class. Although this class actually has 27 Write methods, you can create basic XML documents using just the six Write methods in this figure.

When you use these methods, you need to use the WriteStartElement and WriteEndElement methods for elements that have children, such as the Products element. However, you don't need to use a WriteStartElement or WriteEndElement method to create an element that only contains content, such as the Description and Price elements. In this case, you can use the WriteElementString method to automatically write the start tag, the content, and the end tag.

The syntax for creating a new XmlTextWriter object

```
new XmlTextWriter(filePath, encoding)
```

Common properties and methods of the XmlTextWriter class

Property	Description
`Formatting`	Specifies whether the XmlTextWriter should use indentation to format the XML output. If you want indentation, you can specify Formatting.Indented.
Method	**Description**
`WriteStartDocument()`	Writes an XML declaration line at the beginning of a document.
`WriteComment(comment)`	Writes a comment to the XML document.
`WriteStartElement(elementName)`	Writes a start tag using the element name you provide.
`WriteAttributeString(attributeName, value)`	Adds an attribute to the current element.
`WriteEndElement()`	Writes an end tag for the current element.
`WriteElementString(elementName, content)`	Writes a complete element including a start tag, content, and end tag.
`Close()`	Closes the XmlTextWriter object.

Description

- The XmlTextWriter class lets you write XML data to a text file. If the Formatting property is set to Formatting.Indented, the XmlTextWriter will use indentation to indicate the structure of the data.
- When you create a new instance of the XmlTextWriter class, you specify the name or path of the file where you want to write the XML. If the file already exists, it's deleted and then recreated.
- You also specify the encoding scheme that the document will use when you create an XmlTextWriter object. In most cases, you can specify UTF-8 encoding.
- To write a start tag or end tag, use the WriteStartElement or WriteEndElement method. To write a start tag, value, and end tag in a single operation, use the WriteElementString method.
- To write an attribute, first use the WriteStartElement method to write the start tag. Then, use the WriteAttributeString method to write the attribute value.
- The XmlTextWriter class is part of the System.Xml namespace, so your code should include a using statement to refer to this namespace.
- If you attempt to create an invalid XML document, an XmlException will be thrown. For example, an XmlException will be thrown if you try to write two XML declarations or if you try to write an end tag before you've written a start tag.

Figure 22-6 How to use the XmlTextWriter class

Code that writes an XML document

Figure 22-7 shows the code that creates an XML document like the one that's in figure 22-1. This code gets its data from an array list of Product objects where each product has three properties: Code, Description, and Price.

To start, this code creates an XmlTextWriter object. This object uses the Products.xml file that's stored in the C:\C#.NET\Files\ directory, it uses UTF-8 encoding, and it uses indentation. Then, the WriteStartDocument method is used to write the XML declaration for the document.

The heart of this code is the foreach loop that writes a Product element for each Product object in the products array list. To write a Product element, the method uses the WriteStartElement method to write the start tag for the Product element, and then uses the WriteAttributeString method to add the Code attribute. Next, two WriteElementString methods are used to write the Description and Price elements. Finally, the WriteEndElement method is used to write the end tag for the Product element.

The foreach loop is preceded by a WriteStartElement method that writes the start tag for the document's root element. As a result, the foreach loop must be followed by a WriteEndElement method that writes the end tag for the root element. After that, the Close method is used to close the XmlTextWriter object.

In this code, the path of the XML document is coded as an absolute path like this:

```
string path = @"C:\C#.NET\Files\Products.xml";
```

In this case, the XML file isn't stored in the same directory as the rest of the files for the ProductMaintenance project. However, if you want to use an XML file that's part of the project, you can specify a relative path like this:

```
string path = @"..\..\Products.xml";
```

This works because the exe for the application runs in the bin\debug subdirectory of the project directory. As a result, you need to navigate back two directories to get to the directory that stores the files for the project.

Code that writes an XML document

```
string path = @"C:\C#.NET\Files\Products.xml";

XmlTextWriter xmlOut = new XmlTextWriter(path, System.Text.Encoding.UTF8);
xmlOut.Formatting = Formatting.Indented;

xmlOut.WriteStartDocument();
xmlOut.WriteStartElement("Products");

Product product = null;
for (int i = 0; i < products.Count; i++)
{
    product = (Product) products[i];
    xmlOut.WriteStartElement("Product");
    xmlOut.WriteAttributeString("Code", product.Code);
    xmlOut.WriteElementString("Description", product.Description);
    xmlOut.WriteElementString("Price", Convert.ToString(product.Price));
    xmlOut.WriteEndElement();
}

xmlOut.WriteEndElement();

xmlOut.Close();
```

Description

- This example saves an array list of Product objects as an XML document. The resulting XML document will be like the one in figure 22-1.
- To set the path for an XML file in the current project, you can use two dots to refer to the parent directory as in:

  `"..\..\Products.xml"`

  This works because the current project is run from the Bin\Debug subdirectory of the project directory.

Figure 22-7 Code that writes an XML document

How to use the XmlTextReader class

To read an XML document, you can use the XmlTextReader class that's summarized in figure 22-8. You can create a new XmlTextReader object by supplying the path of the XML file as a string to the constructor of the class.

Before you code the statements that read XML data, you should set the WhitespaceHandling property of the XmlTextReader object to indicate how you want white space handled. *White space* refers to spaces, tabs, and return characters that affect the appearance but not the meaning of an XML document. To simplify the task of processing XML data, you can set this property to WhitespaceHandling.None. This tells the XmlTextReader class to automatically skip white space in the XML document. That way, you don't have to write code to handle it.

Then, to read data from an XML document, you can use the various Read methods of the XmlTextReader class. This class treats an XML document as a series of *nodes*, and you can use the basic Read method to read the next node from the file. Because the concept of nodes is so important to reading XML data, the next figure describes them in detail and walks you through the process of reading a simple XML document node by node. For now, you just need to know that every tag in an XML document is treated as a separate node, and each element's content is also treated as a separate node. Attributes, however, are not treated as nodes. Instead, an attribute is a part of the node that represents the start tag that contains it.

When you invoke the Read method, the XmlTextReader gets the next node from the XML document and makes that node the *current node*. Then, you can use the XmlTextReader's NodeType, Name, or Value property to retrieve the node's type, name, or value. If you read past the last node in the document, the EOF property is set to True. As a result, you can use this property to tell when you have reached the end of the file.

In fact, you can process an entire XML document by using just the Read method to read the document's nodes one at a time, by using the NodeType property to determine what type of node has just been read, and by taking appropriate action based on the node type. However, the XmlTextReader has several other methods that simplify the task of dealing with common node types.

The ReadStartElement method starts by confirming that the current node is a start tag. If it is, the method checks to make sure that the name of the start tag matches the name you supply as an argument. If both of these conditions are met, the method then reads the next element. Otherwise, an XmlException is thrown.

The ReadEndElement method is similar, but it checks to make sure the current node is an end tag rather than a start tag, and it doesn't check the element name. If the current node is an end tag, the ReadEndElement method reads the next node. Otherwise, it throws an XmlException.

The ReadElementString method reads content from a simple content element (that is, an element that has content but no child elements). It skips forward over as many nodes as necessary until it reaches a start tag. Then, this method

The syntax for creating a new XmlTextReader object

```
new XmlTextReader(filePath)
```

Common properties and methods of the XmlTextReader class

Property	Description
WhitespaceHandling	Specifies how the XmlTextReader should handle white space in the XML input. To automatically ignore all white space, specify WhitespaceHandling.None.
NodeType	Returns a member of the XmlNodeType enumeration that indicates the type of the current node.
Name	Gets the name of the current node, if the node has a name.
Value	Gets the value of the current node, if the node has a value.
EOF	True if the XmlTextReader has reached the end of the input.
[name]	Gets the value of the specified attribute. If the current element does not have the attribute, this property returns an empty string.

Method	Description
Close()	Closes the XML input file.
Read()	Reads the next node.
ReadStartElement(name)	Checks that the current node is a start tag with the specified name, then advances to the next node. An XmlException is thrown if the current node is not a start tag with the specified name.
ReadEndElement()	Checks that the current node is an end tag, then advances to the next node. An XmlException is thrown if the current node is not an end tag.
ReadElementString(name)	Reads to the next start tag, checks that the name of the element matches the name specified, then reads the element content and returns it as a string value. An XmlException is thrown if the next element does not match the specified name or if the element does not have simple content.

Description

- The XmlTextReader class lets you read the contents of an XML document one *node* at a time.
- Spaces, tabs, and return characters (known as *white space*) are treated as nodes unless you specify that white space should be ignored by setting the WhitespaceHandling property to WhitespaceHandling.None.
- When you create a new instance of the XmlTextReader class, you can pass the name of the file that contains the XML.
- The various Read methods retrieve input data or verify that the current node is a particular type and then advance the cursor to the next node.
- The XmlTextReader class is part of the System.Xml namespace, so your code should include a using statement to refer to this namespace.

Figure 22-8 How to use the XmlTextReader class

confirms that the name of the tag matches the name you supply. If it does, this method reads the element's content node and returns it as a string value. But if the element name doesn't match the name you supply or if the element contains child elements rather than simple content, an XmlException is thrown.

To read attributes, you don't use a Read method. Instead, whenever the current node has attributes, you can access those attributes via the indexer. To do that, you code brackets ([]) immediately after the XmlTextReader variable, and you code the name of the attribute as a string argument within those brackets. To retrieve the Code attribute, for example, use ["Code"].

How the XmlTextReader class reads nodes

To use the XmlTextReader class properly, you need to understand exactly how it reads nodes. To help you with that, figure 22-9 presents a simple XML document and lists all of the nodes contained in that document. Even though this document contains just one Product element with two child elements, there are 12 nodes.

By studying this figure, you can see how the methods of the XmlTextReader class read the nodes. The first node is the XML declaration tag. The second node is the comment. The third node is the start tag for the Products element. And so on.

Notice that when the start tag for the Product element is reached, the Code attribute is available via the indexer. Also notice that the Description and Price child elements each use three nodes: one for the start tag, one for the content, and one for the end tag.

An XML document

```
<?xml version="1.0">
<!--Product data-->
<Products>
  <Product Code="JAVA">
    <Description>Murach's Beginning Java 2</Description>
    <Price>49.50</Price>
  </Product>
</Products>
```

The XML nodes in this document

NodeType	Name	Other properties
XmlDeclaration	xml	
Comment		Value = "Product data"
Element	Products	
Element	Product	["Code"] = "JAVA"
Element	Description	
Text		Value = "Murach's Beginning Java 2"
EndElement	Description	
Element	Price	
Text		Value = "49.50"
EndElement	Price	
EndElement	Product	
EndElement	Products	

Description

- For the XML declaration and each comment, the XmlTextReader class parses one node.
- For each element without content (usually, a parent element), the XmlTextReader class parses two modes: an Element node for the start tag and an EndElement node for the end tag.
- For each element with content, the XmlTextReader class parses three nodes: an Element node for the element's start tag, a Text node for the element's text value, and an EndElement node for the element's end tag.
- If an element contains an attribute, the attribute is available via the indexer when the Element node for the element is read.

Notes

- This example assumes that the WhitespaceHandling.None property has been set, so white space is ignored.
- The NodeType, Name, Value, and indexer values shown in the table above correspond to the XmlTextReader NodeType, Name, Value, and indexer properties.

Figure 22-9 How the XmlTextReader class reads nodes

Code that reads an XML document

Figure 22-10 shows code that loads the contents of the products.xml file into an array list of Product objects. The first statement specifies the path for the Products.xml file. The second statement creates a new array list to store the Product objects. The third statement uses this path to create a new instance of the XmlTextReader class to read the Products.xml file, which is in the C:\C#.NET\Files directory. And the fourth statement says that the methods for this XML reader should ignore white space.

After these statements, a while loop reads past any nodes in the XML file that occur before the first Product element. When this while loop finishes, the current node will be the first node in the file whose name is Product. In other words, the current node will be the start tag for the first Product element.

Next, a while loop reads and processes the data for each Product element in the file. This loop begins by using the indexer to retrieve the value of the Code attribute. This works because the while loop always begins with the reader positioned at the start tag for the Product element.

After the Code attribute has been retrieved and stored in the Product object, the loop uses the ReadStartElement method to read the next node, which is the Description element's start tag. Although it's also possible to use a Read method here, the ReadStartElement ensures that the reader is on the Product element.

After the start tag for the Product element has been read, the next two statements use the ReadElementString method to retrieve the contents of the Description element and the Price element. Then, this code uses the ReadEndElement method to read past the end tag for the Product element. And finally, since all the data has been stored in the Product object, the last line adds the Product object to the Products array list.

If the XML document contains another Product element, the current node will be the start tag for the next Product element, so the Name property will be Product and the loop will repeat. However, if the last Product element has been read, the current node will be the end tag for the Products element, so the loop will end because the Name property will be Products, not Product. In that case, the Close method is called to close the reader.

If the Products.xml file doesn't contain an XML document like the one shown in figure 22-1, one of the Read methods will throw an exception of the XmlException type. To catch this type of exception, you can code a try-catch statement just as you would for any other type of exception.

A class that works with an XML file

Figure 22-11 presents the code for a ProductDB class that works with the data in an XML file. This shows how the code presented in this chapter can be used to implement the database class that's used by ProductMaintenance application that has been presented in chapters 12 and 21. If you understood the earlier versions of this application, you shouldn't have any trouble understanding how this class works.

Code that reads an XML document

```
string path = @"C:\C#.NET\Files\Products.xml";

ArrayList products = new ArrayList();

XmlTextReader xmlIn = new XmlTextReader(path);
xmlIn.WhitespaceHandling = WhitespaceHandling.None;

while (xmlIn.Name != "Product")
    xmlIn.Read();

while (xmlIn.Name == "Product")
{
    Product product = new Product();
    product.Code = xmlIn["Code"];
    xmlIn.ReadStartElement("Product");
    product.Description =
        xmlIn.ReadElementString("Description");
    product.Price = Convert.ToDecimal(
        xmlIn.ReadElementString("Price"));
    xmlIn.ReadEndElement();
    products.Add(product);
}

xmlIn.Close();
```

Description

- This example loads the XML document in figure 22-1 into an array list of Product objects.
- To focus on the code that's used to read an XML file, this code doesn't include any exception handling. However, it's common to code a try-catch block that catches and handles any exceptions that this code might throw. In addition, it's common to include a finally block that frees the resources being used by this code.
- The first while loop reads nodes from the XML document until the first Product element is reached. This code skips over the XML declaration, the comment, and the root Products node.
- The second while loop processes each Product element. For each Product element, the values for the Code attribute and the Description and Price elements are retrieved. Then, the product is added to the products array list.

Figure 22-10 Code that reads an XML document

A class that works with an XML document **Page 1**

```
using System;
using System.Xml;
using System.Collections;

namespace ProductMaintenance
{
    public class ProductDB
    {
        private const string path = @"C:\C#.NET\Files\Products.xml";

        public static ArrayList GetProducts()
        {
            // create the array list
            ArrayList products = new ArrayList();

            // create the xml reader
            XmlTextReader xmlIn = new XmlTextReader(path);
            xmlIn.WhitespaceHandling = WhitespaceHandling.None;

            // read past all nodes to the first Product element
            while (xmlIn.Name != "Product")
                xmlIn.Read();

            // create one Product object for each Product element
            while (xmlIn.Name == "Product")
            {
                Product product = new Product();
                product.Code = xmlIn["Code"];
                xmlIn.ReadStartElement("Product");
                product.Description =
                    xmlIn.ReadElementString("Description");
                product.Price = Convert.ToDecimal(
                    xmlIn.ReadElementString("Price"));
                xmlIn.ReadEndElement();
                products.Add(product);
            }

            // close the xml reader
            xmlIn.Close();

            return products;
        }
```

Figure 22-11 The code for the ProductDB class (part 1 of 2)

A class that works with an XML document Page 2

```
        public static void SaveProducts(ArrayList products)
        {
            // create the xml writer
            XmlTextWriter xmlOut = new XmlTextWriter(
                path, System.Text.Encoding.UTF8);
            xmlOut.Formatting = Formatting.Indented;

            // write the start of the document
            xmlOut.WriteStartDocument();
            xmlOut.WriteStartElement("Products");

            // write each Product object to the xml file
            Product product = null;
            for (int i = 0; i < products.Count; i++)
            {
                product = (Product) products[i];
                xmlOut.WriteStartElement("Product");
                xmlOut.WriteAttributeString("Code",
                    product.Code);
                xmlOut.WriteElementString("Description",
                    product.Description);
                xmlOut.WriteElementString("Price",
                    Convert.ToString(product.Price));
                xmlOut.WriteEndElement();
            }

            // write the end tag for the root element
            xmlOut.WriteEndElement();

            // close the xml writer
            xmlOut.Close();
        }
    }
}
```

Figure 22-11 The code for the ProductDB class (part 2 of 2)

Perspective

In this chapter, you learned the basics of reading and writing XML documents using the XmlTextReader and XmlTextWriter classes. With these skills, you should be able to incorporate simple XML documents into your applications. You'll also have a better appreciation for the way XML is used internally by the database applications that you learned about in section 4.

However, this chapter is only an introduction to XML. There are many other XML features that I haven't presented here. For example, you can use *XML schemas* to define the layout for an XML document. Then, you can use .NET classes to make sure an XML document conforms to its schema. Another important XML feature is *DOM,* which stands for *Document Object Model.* When you use DOM, an entire XML document is represented as a single XmlDocument object with property collections that represent the XML document's nodes. In short, if you want to master XML, there's a lot more to learn.

Summary

- *XML* provides a standard way to structure data by using *tags* that identify data items.
- An *element* begins with a *start tag* and ends with an *end tag*. An element can contain data in the form of *content* that appears between the tags. It can also contain *child elements*.
- An *attribute* is a name and value that appears within an element's start tag.
- You can use Visual Studio's XML Designer to edit XML data.
- You can use the XmlTextWriter and XmlTextReader classes to write and read XML data. These classes are found in the System.Xml namespace.

Terms

XML (Extensible Markup Language)
tag
XML document
XML declaration
element
start tag
end tag
content
child element
parent element
root element
attribute
XML Designer
white space
node
current node

Objectives

- Use the XmlTextWriter class to write an XML document.
- Use the XmlTextReader class to read an XML document.
- Use the XML Designer to create and edit a new XML document in a project.
- In simple XML documents like the ones in this chapter, identify the following: tags, XML declarations, start tags, end tags, element content, root elements, parent elements, child elements, attributes, and comments.

Exercise 22-1 Work with an XML file

In this exercise, you'll modify the Customer application that you developed for chapter 12 so it works with an XML file.

1. Open the Customer project in the C:\C#.NET\Chapter 22\CustomerXML folder. This project contains the code for two forms, a Validator class, a Customer class, and the beginning of a CustomerDB class. Read the code for these classes and run the application to see how it works. This application should work, but it doesn't save the data or update the customer number.
2. Open the Customer.xml file that's stored in the C:\C#.NET\Files directory. This should open this file in the XML Designer in XML view so you can see how this data is structured. Then, switch to Data view and note the data that's stored in this file.
3. Add code to the CustomerDB class so the GetCustomers method reads the data from the XML file into an array list of Customer objects and so the SaveCustomers method writes the data from an array list of Customer objects to the XML file.
4. Test the application by adding and deleting customers. To verify that the data is being saved to disk and is therefore available for each new session, you can stop the application and run it again. You can also view the XML file in the XML Designer to make sure that it contains the correct data. When you're done, make sure to leave at least three customer records in the file.
5. Add exception handling to the ProductDB class that catches any exceptions that might be thrown and displays an appropriate dialog box.

23

How to enhance the user interface

In this chapter, you'll learn how to modify your applications so they can take advantage of two types of user interfaces. In addition, you'll learn how to add menus, toolbars, and help to your forms. When you're done with this chapter, you should be able to create a professional user interface that allows users to easily and intuitively interact with your application.

Two types of user interfaces

Figure 23-1 shows two versions of the Financial Calculations application that will be presented in this chapter. These applications let the user calculate the future value of an investment or the depreciation of an asset. These applications use the Future Value form that you learned about earlier in this book, and they use a Depreciation form that's new to this chapter. In addition, both of these applications include a third form that provides a way for the user to access these forms.

A single-document interface (SDI)

The first version of the Financial Calculations application uses a *single-document interface*, or *SDI*. In an SDI application, each form runs in its own application window, and this window is usually shown in the Windows taskbar. Then, you can click on the buttons in the taskbar to switch between the open forms.

When you use this interface, each form can have its own menus and toolbars. In addition, you can include a main form called a *startup form* that provides access to the other forms of the application. In this figure, for example, the startup form includes two buttons that the user can click on to display the Future Value and Depreciation forms.

A multiple-document interface (MDI)

The second version of this application uses a *multiple-document interface*, or *MDI*. In an MDI application, a container form called a *parent form* contains one or more *child forms*. Then, the menus and toolbars on the parent form contain the commands that let you open and view forms. The main advantage of a multiple-document interface is that the parent form can make it easier to organize and manage multiple instances of the child forms.

Single-document interface (SDI)

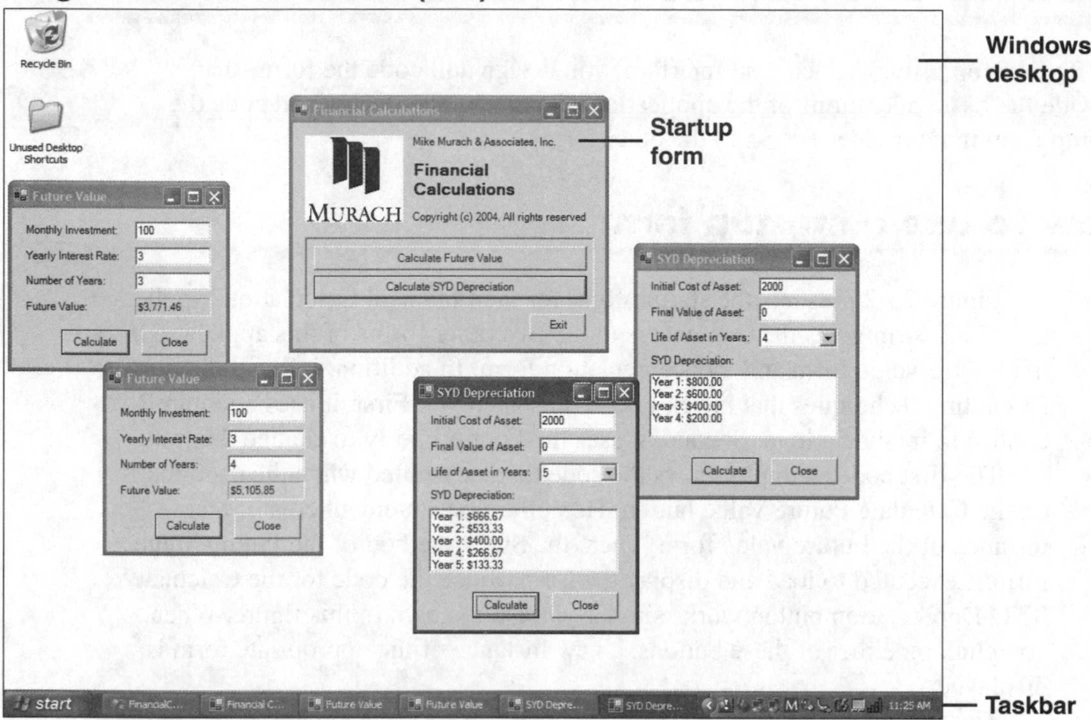

Multiple-document interface (MDI)

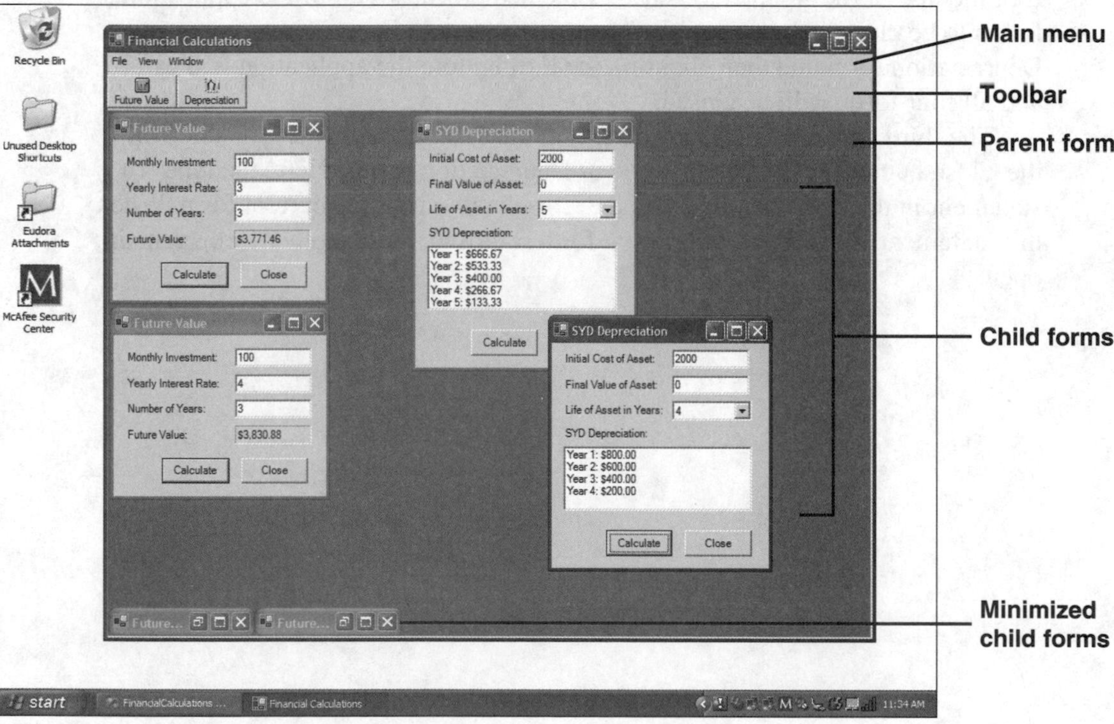

Figure 23-1 Single-document and multiple-document interfaces

How to develop SDI applications

To develop a single-document interface, you design and code the forms that provide the basic operations of the application. Then, you can design and code the startup form that provides access to the other forms.

How to use a startup form

Figure 23-2 presents the startup form for the Financial Calculations application. This form gives the user access to the two other forms of this application: the Future Value form and the Depreciation form. In addition, it illustrates some formatting techniques that haven't been presented yet. First, it uses a PictureBox control to include a logo. Second, it uses the Font property to change the font.

The first code example shows the code that's executed when the user clicks on the Calculate Future Value button. Here, the first statement creates a new instance of the Future Value form. Then, the Show method of the Future Value form is executed to load and display the form. Since the code for the Calculate SYD Depreciation button works similarly, it isn't shown in this figure. When you click on either of these buttons, a new instance of the appropriate form is displayed.

The second code example shows the code that's executed when the user clicks on the Exit button. Here, the lone statement in the event handler calls the Exit method of the Application class. This method causes all of the application's forms to be closed. For example, if the user opens two Future Value forms and a Depreciation form and then clicks on the Exit button, the application will exit and all four forms will be closed.

The third code example shows the code that's executed when you click on the Close button for the Future Value or Depreciation forms. Here, the lone statement in the event handler calls the Close method for the current form. When this statement is executed, the current form is closed, but the other forms remain open.

A startup form for the Financial Calculations application

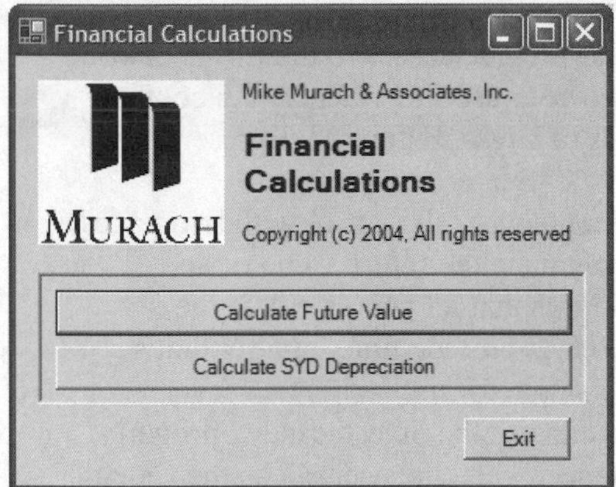

Code that displays a new instance of a form

```
private void btnFutureValue_Click(object sender, System.EventArgs e)
{
    Form newForm = new frmFutureValue();
    newForm.Show();
}
```

Code that exits the application and closes all forms

```
private void btnExit_Click(object sender, System.EventArgs e)
{
    Application.Exit();
}
```

Code that closes the current instance of a form

```
private void btnClose_Click(object sender, System.EventArgs e)
{
    this.Close();
}
```

Description

- An SDI application that consists of more than one form can begin with a *startup form* that directs the user to the other forms of the application.
- You can use the Font property of a control to change the font for the Text property of the control.
- You can use the Image property for a PictureBox control to display an image on a form. To do that, you click on the property setting, which opens an Open dialog box. Then, you open the file for the image, which stores the file in the property.
- A form that's displayed from a startup form should contain a Close button rather than an Exit button to indicate that the button will close the form and not exit the application and close all open forms.

Figure 23-2 How to use a startup form

How to use tabs to organize forms

One alternative to using a startup form to provide access to the forms of your application is to use a tab control to organize your user interface. A tab control allows you to create *tabs* that provide access to *pages*. Figure 23-3 presents the basic skills for working with tab controls.

As you can see, the form in this figure contains a tab control with two pages. The first tab provides controls that let you calculate the future value of an investment, and the second tab provides controls that let you calculate the depreciation of an asset. Together, these two tabs provide functionality that's similar to the forms in figures 23-1, but in a single form.

When you work with a tab control, you can use the SelectedIndex property to determine which tab is selected. For instance, when the user clicks the Calculate button, this code uses an if-else statement that checks this property to determine which tab is selected. Then, it executes the appropriate code as shown in the first code example.

The event you'll use most often with a tab control is the SelectedIndexChanged event. This event occurs when the SelectedIndex property of the control changes, which typically happens when a user clicks on another tab. For example, the event handler in this figure moves the focus to the appropriate control on a tab when that tab becomes the current tab. This method uses the SelectedIndex property to determine which tab is current.

A form that uses a tab control with two tabs

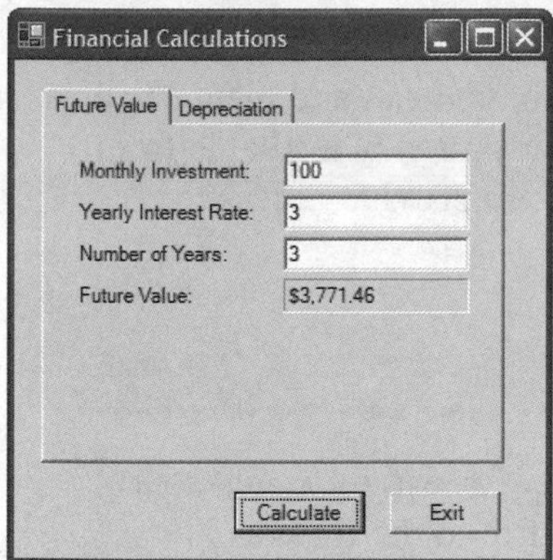

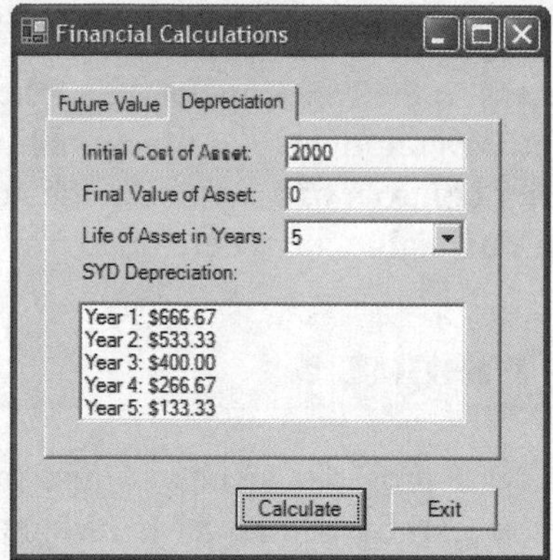

Code that uses the SelectedIndex property of the tab control

```
private void btnCalculate_Click(object sender, System.EventArgs e)
{
    if (tabCalculations.SelectedIndex == 0)
        DisplayFutureValue();
    else if (tabCalculations.SelectedIndex == 1)
        DisplayDepreciation();
}
```

Code that uses the SelectedIndexChanged event of the tab control

```
private void tabCalculations_SelectedIndexChanged(object sender,
    System.EventArgs e)
{
    if (tabCalculations.SelectedIndex == 0)
        txtMonthlyInvestment.Focus();
    else if (tabCalculations.SelectedIndex == 1)
        txtInitialCost.Focus();
}
```

Description

- Each tab control can contain two or more *tabs*. Each tab in a tab control contains a *page* where you add the controls for the tab.
- To add tabs, right-click on the tab control and select the Add Tab command from the shortcut menu.
- To set the text that's displayed in its associated tab, select the page and set the Text property.
- To remove a tab, right-click on the tab's page and select the Delete command from the shortcut menu.
- You can also add and remove tabs by selecting the tab control and using the TabPages property to display the TabPages Collection Editor.
- You can use the SelectedIndex property of the tab control to determine which tab is currently selected.
- The SelectedIndexChanged event occurs when another tab is selected.

Figure 23-3 How to work with tab controls

How to add menus to a form

To provide access to the functions of an application, you can add menus to a form. Menus sometimes duplicate the functionality that's already available from the buttons and other controls of a form, but they can also provide access to functions that aren't available anywhere else.

How to create menus

Visual Studio .NET provides an easy-to-use facility for adding *menus* to a form. To do that, you start by adding a MainMenu control to the form as illustrated in figure 23-4. When you add the MainMenu control, the Menu property of the form is automatically set to the name of that control but the control isn't displayed on the form. Instead, it's displayed in the Component Designer tray at the bottom of the Form Designer window.

Once you add the MainMenu control to the form, the Menu Designer is displayed at the top of the form. Then, you can add menus and *menu items* by typing the text you want to appear in the Menu Designer anywhere it says "Type Here." When you type the text for the first menu, additional areas open up below and to the right of that menu. As a result, it's easy to enter new menus, submenus, and menu items. As with other controls, you can use the ampersand character (&) to provide an access key when you enter the text for the menu item.

Once you've entered the menus and menu items for your application, you can easily set the Name property for each menu item. To do that, right-click anywhere on the menu system to display the shortcut menu and select the Edit Names command. This displays the names for each menu item so you can easily edit them. When setting the names for each menu item, it's a common coding convention to use mnu as the prefix for each name. For example, you might use mnuActionClear as the name for the Clear item of the Action menu.

If you need to insert a new item in a menu, you can right-click on the menu and select the Insert New command from the shortcut menu. Similarly, you can insert a separator bar by right-clicking on the menu and selecting the Insert Separator command. Or, you can type a dash (-) for the menu item's text. In addition, the shortcut menu for a menu item provides Cut, Copy, Paste, and Delete commands that you can use to work with menu items.

The beginning of the menu for the Future Value application

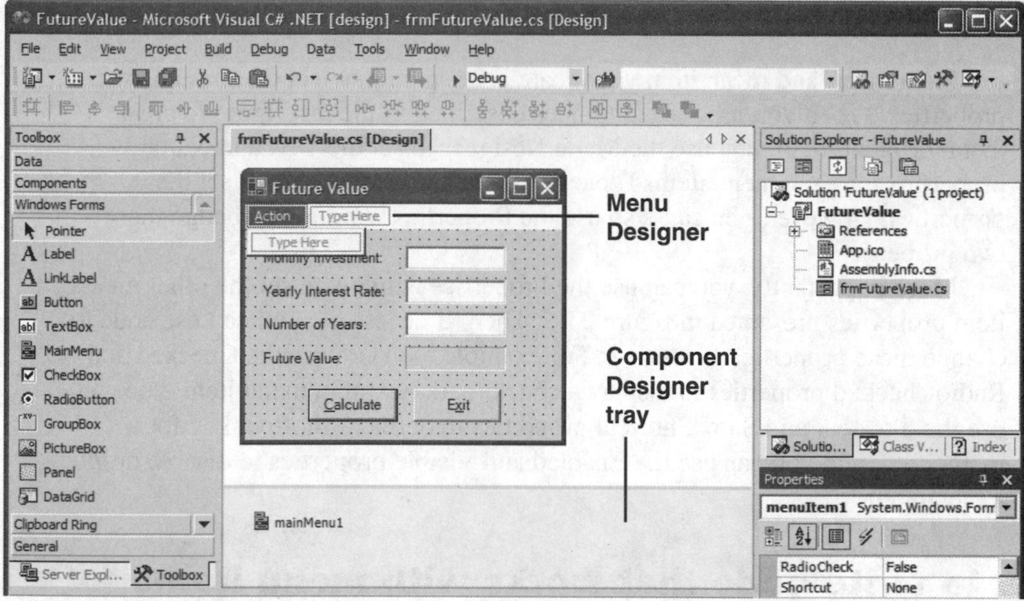

The complete menu with names displayed

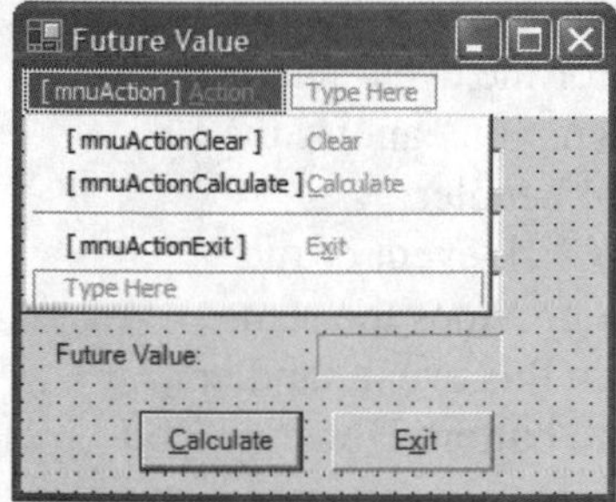

Description

- To add *menus* to a form, add a MainMenu control to a form. The control will appear in the Component Designer tray at the bottom of the Form Designer window, and the Menu property of the form will be set to the name of that control.
- To add items to the menu, click wherever it says "Type Here" in the Menu Designer. Then, type the text of the menu item and press the Enter key. Additional entry areas appear below and to the right of the entry.
- To edit the Name property for each menu item, right-click the menu to display its shortcut menu and select the Edit Names command from the resulting context menu. This will display the names for each menu item so you can easily edit them.
- The shortcut menu for a menu item also includes Insert New, Insert Separator, Cut, Copy, Paste, and Delete commands that you can use to insert new menu items, to insert separator lines, and to work with menu items.

Figure 23-4 How to create menus

How to set the properties that work with menu items

Each menu and menu item you create is a separate object that has its own properties. When you use the techniques described in the last figure to create a menu or menu item, you use the Menu Designer to set the Text and Name properties for each menu item. Typically, that's the easiest way to set these properties. However, you can also use the Properties window to change these two properties.

More importantly, you can use the Properties window to set the other menu item properties presented in figure 23-5. Then, if necessary, you can use code to change these properties at runtime. For example, you can use the Checked and RadioChecked properties to display a check mark next to a menu item, you can use the Shortcut and ShowShortcut properties to define a shortcut key for a menu item, and you can use the Enabled and Visible properties to disable or hide a menu item.

How to write code that works with menu items

The first code example in figure 23-5 shows the event handler for the Click event of the Clear item of the Action menu. Since the Click event is the default event for a menu item, you can generate the declaration for the event handler by double clicking the menu item in the Form Designer. Then, you can use the Code Editor to enter the code that's executed by the event handler.

The second code example shows the handler for the Click event of the Calculate item of the Action menu. Since this menu item provides the same functionality as the Calculate button, the lone statement in this event handler calls the event handler for the Click event of the Calculate button. However, you can handle this situation more elegantly by wiring both events to the same event handler as described in chapter 6.

Common menu item properties

Property	Description
Text	The text that will appear in the menu for the item. To provide an access key for a menu item, include an ampersand (&) in this property.
Name	The name that's used to refer to the menu item in code.
Checked	Determines if a check mark appears to the left of the menu item when it's selected.
RadioChecked	Determines if a radio button appears to the left of the menu item when it's selected.
Shortcut	Specifies the shortcut key associated with the menu item.
ShowShortcut	Determines if the shortcut key is displayed to the right of the menu item.
Enabled	Determines if the menu item is available or grayed out. If a menu item is disabled or enabled, all items subordinate to it are disabled or enabled.
Visible	Determines if the menu item is displayed or hidden. If a menu item is hidden or displayed, all items subordinate to it are hidden or displayed.

Code for a menu item that clears four controls

```
private void mnuActionClear_Click(object sender, System.EventArgs e)
{
    txtMonthlyInvestment.Text = "";
    txtInterestRate.Text = "";
    txtYears.Text = "";
    lblFutureValue.Text = "";
}
```

Code for a menu item that calls another event handler

```
private void mnuActionCalculate_Click(object sender, System.EventArgs e)
{
    btnCalculate_Click(sender, e);
}
```

Notes

- The Click event is the default event for a menu item. You can code a handler for this event just as you would for any other event. For example, you can generate an event handler for the Click event by double-clicking on the menu item.
- If a menu item executes the same code as another event handler, you can call that event handler as shown in the second example above. Or, you can use the Events tab of the Properties window to wire the Click event to an existing event handler.

Figure 23-5 How to work with menu items

How to develop MDI applications

If the application you're developing requires multiple instances of one or more forms, you may want to use a multiple-document interface. That way, you can create a parent form that acts as a container for all of the child forms. Then, you can provide standard Windows menus to make it easier to display and manage the child forms.

How to create parent and child forms

Figure 23-6 shows the design of a parent form for the Financial Calculations application that provides File and Window menus to access its child forms. To create parent and child forms, you begin by adding standard Windows forms to your project. Then, you set the IsMdiContainer property of the parent form to True to identify it as the parent form, and you set the MdiParent property of the child forms to the name of the parent form.

To do that, you can use the Form Designer to set the IsMdiContainer property at design-time, and you can use the Code Editor to write code that sets the MdiParent property at runtime. In the next figure, you'll learn how to write this code, and you'll learn how to write code that uses the ActiveMdiChild property and the LayoutMdi method.

An application with one parent form and two child forms

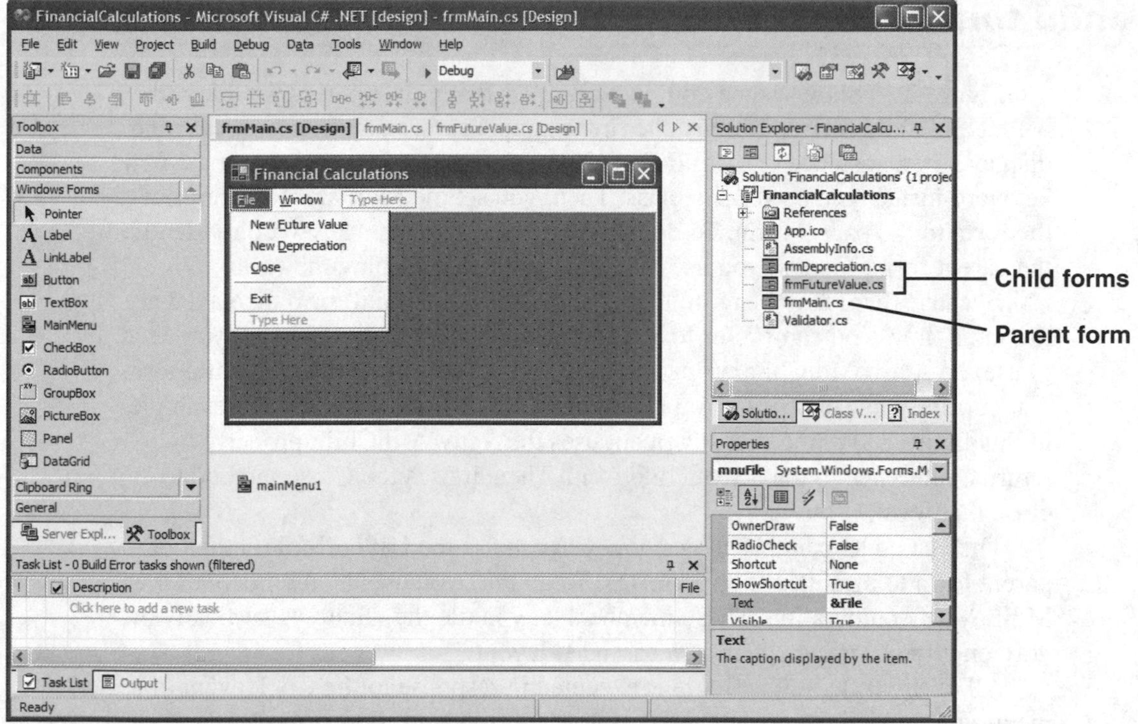

Properties and methods for a parent form

Property/Method	Description
IsMdiContainer	At design-time, you set this property to True to indicate that the form is a parent form.
ActiveMdiChild	At runtime, you can use this property to retrieve a reference to the active child form.
LayoutMdi(mdiLayout)	At runtime, you can use this method to arrange all child forms. To do that, you can specify one of the members of the MdiLayout enumeration: Cascade, TileVertical, TileHorizontal, and so on.

Typical property settings for a child form

Property	Description
MdiParent	At runtime, you can set this property to specify the parent form for a child form.

Note

- An MDI application can also include forms that aren't parent or child forms. These forms are typically modal forms like the ones that you learned about in chapter 10.

Figure 23-6 How to create parent and child forms

How to write code that works with parent and child forms

Figure 23-7 shows some coding techniques that you can use to work with parent and child forms. To start, the first example shows you how to create and display a new instance of a child form. You create a new instance using the new keyword just as you do for any class. Then, you set the MdiParent property of the form to the parent form. To do that, you can use the this keyword to identify the parent form. Finally, you use the Show method to display the form.

Because there may be more than one instance of a child form displayed at the same time, you can't refer to an individual form by name. Instead, you need to use the ActiveMdiChild property of the parent form to refer to the child form that currently has the focus. You can see how this works in the second example in this figure. Here, the first statement uses the ActiveMdiChild property to return a reference to the active child form. Then, it uses the Close method to close that form.

The last code example shows how you can use the LayoutMdi method of the parent form to arrange the child forms. To do that, you use the members of the MdiLayout enumeration. These members let you tile the windows vertically or horizontally or arrange them in a cascaded layout.

All of the code in this figure is executed in response to the Click event of a menu item, which occurs when the user selects the item. For example, the code that creates and displays a new instance of a child form is executed in response to the user selecting the New Future Value menu item from the File menu. And the code that closes the active child form is executed in response to the user selecting the Close menu item from the File menu.

When you need to display and organize the child forms of an MDI application, you can use menus that do that to the parent form. For example, it's common for a parent form to contain a File menu that allows you to display child forms, close the active child form, and exit the application, which closes all open child forms. Similarly, it's common for a parent form to contain a Window menu that allows the user to cascade or tile all child forms.

However, when you want to use menus that work directly with a child form, you can add the menus to that child form. If, for example, you want to add a Clear menu item that clears all the text boxes on a child form, you can add that item to a menu on the child form. Then, the menus for the child form will be displayed to the right of the menus for the parent form. For example, the Action menu that's displayed to the right of the Window menu in this figure is actually coded in the active child form, the Future Value form. As a result, when you run the Financial Calculations application and select the Future Value child form, this Action menu is automatically appended to the parent form's menus.

An MDI application with three child forms arranged vertically

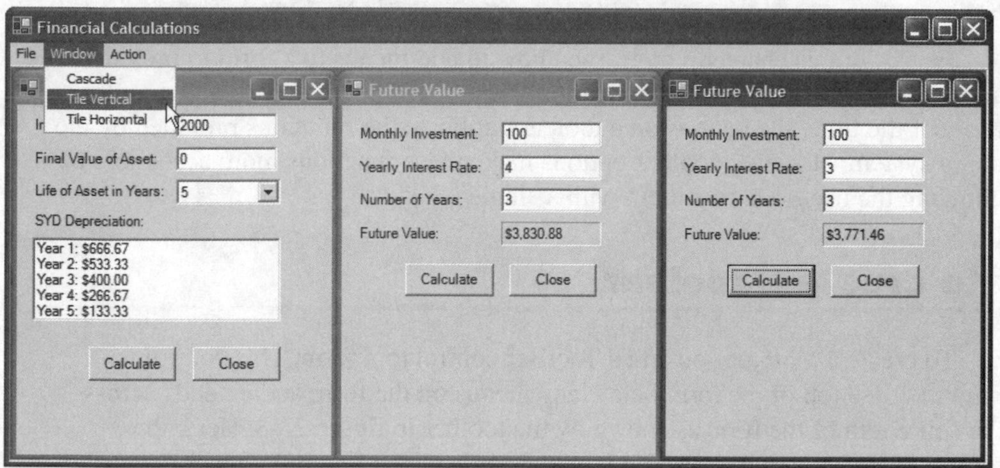

Code that creates and displays a new instance of a child form

```
private void mnuNewFutureValue_Click(object sender, System.EventArgs e)
{
    Form newForm = new frmFutureValue();
    newForm.MdiParent = this;
    newForm.Show();
}
```

Code that refers to the active child form

```
private void mnuClose_Click(object sender, System.EventArgs e)
{
    Form activeForm = this.ActiveMdiChild;
    if (activeForm != null)
        activeForm.Close();
}
```

Code that exits the application and closes all child forms

```
private void mnuExit_Click(object sender, System.EventArgs e)
{
    Application.Exit();
}
```

Code that arranges the child forms vertically

```
private void mnuTileVertical_Click(object sender, System.EventArgs e)
{
    this.LayoutMdi(MdiLayout.TileVertical);
}
```

Description

- In this example, the File and Window menus are stored in the parent form, and the Action menu is stored in the child form. As a result, the Action menu appears only when a child form that contains an Action menu is the active child form.

Figure 23-7 How to write code that works with parent and child forms

How to add toolbars to a form

Earlier in this chapter, you learned how to add menus to a form to provide access to the functions of an application. Now, you'll learn how to add a toolbar. Most of the time, the buttons on a toolbar duplicate the functions provided by the menu system. However, toolbar buttons make these functions more accessible by allowing the user to access them with a single click.

How to create a toolbar

To create a *toolbar*, you add a ToolBar control to a form. This control is *docked* at the top of the form below any menus on the form and extends across the full width of the form as shown by the toolbar in figure 23-8. Here, the toolbar includes two buttons that let the user display a Future Value or Depreciation form. To add buttons like these to a toolbar, you use the ToolBarButton Collection Editor shown in this figure.

Each button you add to a toolbar can display text, a graphic image, or both. To display text, you can set the Text property for that button. To display a graphic image, you first need to create an image list by adding an ImageList control to the form. When you add this control, it's displayed in the Component Designer tray.

After you add an ImageList control to the form, you add the images you want to use on the toolbar buttons to the image list using the Image Collection Editor that's available through the Images property of the control. Each image you add is assigned an index number that you can then use to refer to the image from the ToolBarButton collection editor. To do that, you set the ImageIndex property of the toolbar button to the index number of the image. But first, you have to set the ImageList property of the ToolBar control to the name of the ImageList control that contains the images.

By default, the buttons you add to a toolbar are displayed as standard push buttons. However, you can create other types of buttons by changing the Style property of the button. For example, you can create a button that displays a drop-down list by changing this property to DropDownButton. Then, you use the DropDownMenu property to identify a context menu that you want to display when the user clicks on this button. You can also create a toggle button by changing the Style property to ToggleButton. And you can add a separator between two buttons by changing the Style property to Separator.

Another toolbar button property you should notice is the ToolTipText property. This property lets you specify the text that's displayed when the user places the mouse pointer over the button, called a *tool tip*. This is particularly useful if the button contains only a graphic image. Then, the tool tip can contain text that describes the function of the button.

A toolbar with two toolbar buttons

The ToolBarButton Collection Editor dialog box

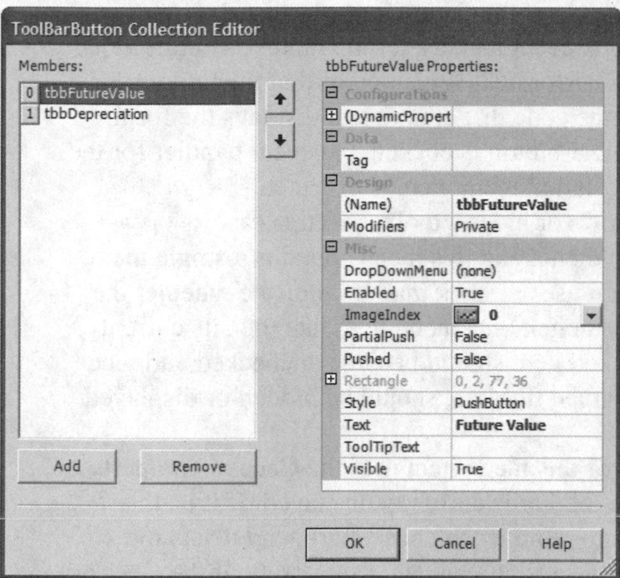

Description

- To create a *toolbar*, add a ToolBar control to a form. By default, the toolbar is *docked* at the top of the form below the menus and reaches across the width of the form.
- To add buttons to the toolbar, select the toolbar, select the Buttons property, click on the ellipsis that appears to display the ToolBarButton Collection Editor, and click on the Add button. Then, use this dialog box to set the properties for the button.
- To include text on a button, enter the text in the Text property. By default, the text appears below any image that's displayed on the button.
- To include an image on a button, create an image list as described in the next bullet, set the ImageList property of the toolbar to the name of an ImageList control that includes the image. Then, select the image from the drop-down list for the ImageIndex property of the toolbar button.
- To create an image list, add an ImageList control to the form. Then, select the Images property in the Properties window and click on the ellipsis that appears to display the Image Collection Editor. Use the Add button in this dialog box to add the images you want to use.
- The ToolTipText property lets you specify the text that's displayed when the user points to the button with the mouse (called a *tool tip*).

Figure 23-8 How to create a toolbar

How to write code that works with toolbars

After you create the toolbars for a form, you need to add the code that makes them work. To do that, you can code event handlers like the ones shown in figure 23-9.

The first code example handles the ButtonClick event of the toolbar. This event handler uses the Button property of the second parameter to determine which button was clicked. In this case, if the Future Value toolbar button was clicked, the code executes the Click event handler for the mnuNewFutureValue menu item. To do that, it uses the PerformClick method of that menu item. That way, you don't have to duplicate the code that creates and displays the form. Similarly, if the Depreciation toolbar button is clicked, the event handler for the Click event of the mnuNewDepreciation menu item is executed.

The second code example shows or hides a toolbar. In this case, a View menu has been added to the main menu, and this menu contains a single menu item named mnuToolbar. This item uses a check mark to indicate whether the toolbar is displayed. Each time you click on a menu item like this, its current status should be changed. A checked item should become unchecked and vice versa, and the toolbar, which is named tlbMain, should be hidden or displayed accordingly.

The code for the Click event of this menu item uses the Checked property of the menu item to determine if the toolbar is currently displayed. If it is, this method sets this property to false to remove the check mark, and it sets the Visible property of the toolbar to false so it's hidden. Conversely, if the Checked property of the menu item is false, it's set to true so a check mark is displayed, and the Visible property of the toolbar is set to true. Another way to code this handler is like this:

```
mnuToolbar.Checked = !mnuToolbar.Checked;
tlbMain.Visible = !tlbMain.Visible;
```

Here, the Not operator (!) is used to reverse the values of the menu item's Checked property and the toolbar's Visible property.

Code for the ButtonClick event of a toolbar

```
private void tlbMain_ButtonClick(object sender,
    System.Windows.Forms.ToolBarButtonClickEventArgs e)
{
    if (e.Button == tbbFutureValue)
        mnuNewFutureValue.PerformClick();
    else if (e.Button == tbbDepreciation)
        mnuNewDepreciation.PerformClick();
}
```

A View menu that shows or hides the toolbar

Code that shows or hides a toolbar depending on a menu selection

```
private void mnuToolbar_Click(object sender, System.EventArgs e)
{
    if (mnuToolbar.Checked == true)
    {
        mnuToolbar.Checked = false;
        tlbMain.Visible = false;
    }
    else if (mnuToolbar.Checked == false)
    {
        mnuToolbar.Checked = true;
        tlbMain.Visible = true;
    }
}
```

Description

- You use the ButtonClick event of a toolbar to respond to the user clicking on one of the buttons in that toolbar. A reference to the button that was clicked is passed to that event in the Button property of the e parameter. You can use an if statement to compare this property with the buttons in the toolbar to determine which one was clicked.
- You can use the PerformClick method of a button or menu item to cause the Click event to occur on that object. This is useful if a toolbar button or menu item duplicates code that's available from a button or another menu item.
- You can use the Checked method of a menu item to work with the check mark that's displayed to the left of the item.
- You can use the Visible property of a control to show or hide the control.

Figure 23-9 How to write code that works with toolbars

How to add help information

Because Windows Forms applications use the standard Windows interface, users who are already familiar with other Windows applications should quickly adapt to these applications. In addition, you should try to design and develop each application so it is as easy to use as is practical. Nevertheless, almost all applications can benefit from the addition of at least a minimum amount of help information.

One way to add help information to a form is to add a Help menu. Then, you can add items to that menu for various topics. When the user selects one of these items, you can display a dialog box with the appropriate information. You can also add help information to a form by using tool tips and context-sensitive help.

How to add tool tips

Earlier in this chapter, you learned how to add tool tips to toolbar buttons. In addition, you can add tool tips to each control on a form and to the form itself. Figure 23-10 shows how.

To add tool tips, you add a ToolTip control to the form. Then, a ToolTip property becomes available for the form and each of its controls. This property is listed in the Properties window along with the other properties of the form or control. You can set this property to the text you want displayed when the user places the mouse pointer over the form or control. The illustration in this figure, for example, shows the tool tip for the Initial Cost text box on the Depreciation form.

How to add context-sensitive help

If you want to display help information that's more extensive than what you would normally display in a tool tip, you can use the HelpProvider control. This control lets you provide *context-sensitive help* for a form or control. Then, the user can display the help for the control that has the focus by pressing the F1 key. If help text isn't provided for that control, the help text for the form is displayed if it's provided.

To specify the help text for a form or control, you use the HelpString property that becomes available when you add a HelpProvider control to the form. The illustration in this figure, for example, shows the help text for the Depreciation form.

A tool tip

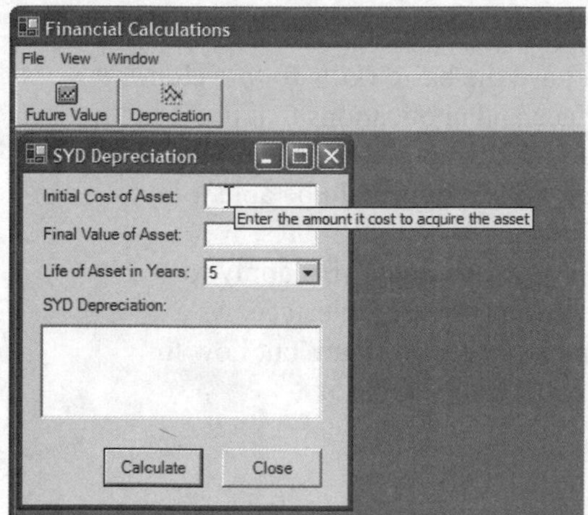

Context-sensitive help

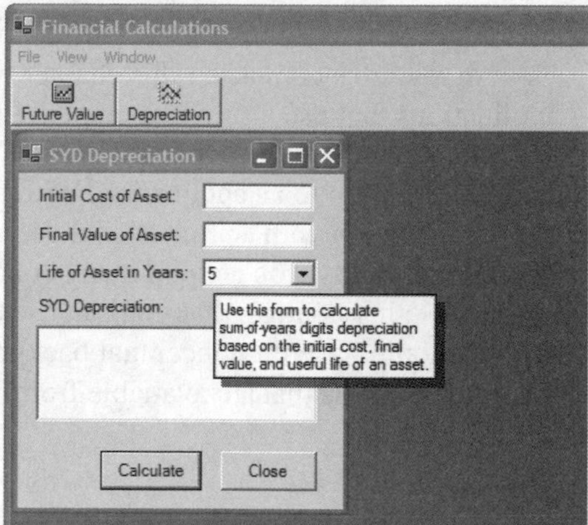

How to work with a tool tip

- A *tool tip* is a brief description of a control that's displayed automatically when you place the mouse pointer over that control.
- To create tool tips for a form, add a ToolTip control to the form. A control named toolTip1 will appear in the Component Designer tray at the bottom of the window.
- The ToolTip control makes a property named ToolTip on toolTip1 available for each control on the form and for the form itself. You can enter the text of the ToolTip for this property in the Properties window.

How to work with context-sensitive help

- To provide *context-sensitive help* for a form or control, add a HelpProvider control to the form. A control named helpProvider1 will appear in the Component Designer tray at the bottom of the window. This control makes several additional properties available for the form and each control it contains.
- To display a text string when the user presses the F1 key for the control that has the focus, enter the text for the HelpString on helpProvider1 property of the control.
- You can also enter help text for the HelpString property of the form. Then, that text is displayed at the location of the mouse pointer if a help string isn't specified for the control that has the focus.
- When you enter text for the HelpString on helpProvider1 property, the ShowHelp on helpProvider1 property automatically changes from False to True.

Figure 23-10 How work with tool tips and context-sensitive help

Perspective

Now that you've completed this chapter, you have the basic skills for developing applications that use a single-document interface and applications that use a multiple-document interface. In addition, you learned how to add menus, toolbars, and help information to an application. With those skills, you should be able to create an application with a professional user interface.

More importantly, you learned many concepts and techniques that apply to working with other controls that you can use to enhance the user interface. As a result, you should have the conceptual background you need to figure out how to use the other controls that are available from Visual Studio's Toolbox.

Summary

- In a *single-document interface (SDI)*, each form runs in its own application window. An application with this type of interface can include a *startup form* that provides access to the other forms of the application.
- The tab control lets you group controls into two or more *tabs* rather than creating separate forms for each group. Each tab provides access to a *page*.
- A form can include *menus* that provide access to basic Windows operations as well as operations specific to an application. When used on a parent form, a menu typically provides access to the child forms.
- To create menus, you add a MainMenu control to a form. Then, the Menu Designer lets you enter *menu items*.
- You can modify a menu item by changing its properties in the Properties window. You can also work with menu items by using the commands in the shortcut menu.
- In a *multiple-document interface (MDI)*, a *parent form* contains one or more *child forms* and provides a central location for working with those forms. An MDI application makes it easy to display and manage multiple instances of its child forms.
- A *toolbar* can include one or more buttons that provide access to commonly used functions of an application.
- You can add *tool tips* to the controls on a form to provide the user with a brief description of what they do. You can also provide *context-sensitive help* for a form or control that's displayed when the user presses F1.

Terms

single-document interface (SDI)
startup form
multiple-document interface (MDI)
parent form
child form
tab
page
menu
menu item
Menu Designer
Component Designer tray
toolbar
tool tip
context-sensitive help

Objectives

- Given the specifications for an application that uses a single-document interface, design and develop the application.
- Given the specifications for an application that uses a multiple-document interface, design and develop the application.
- Use the tab control to organize your application.
- Given an existing application, add menus, toolbars, and help information.
- Distinguish between a single-document and a multiple-document interface.

Exercise 23-1 Create the SDI application

In this exercise, you'll create the SDI version of the Financial Calculations application that's presented in this chapter.

Open the project and adjust the startup form

1. Open the FinancialCalculations project in the C:\C#.NET\Chapter 23\FinancialCalculationsSDI folder. This project contains the beginning of a startup form named frmMain.
2. Open the Designer window for the startup form, and note the use of a PictureBox control. Select this control and note how the Image property in the Properties window is set. Then, delete this setting and note that the image in the picture box is gone. To restore this image, click on the button for the Image setting to open the Open dialog box, find the file named Murach logo in the Chapter 23\FinancialCalculationsSDI folder, and click on the Open button.
3. Select the text box that contains "Financial Calculations" in a larger than normal font size. Then, click on the plus sign before the Font property in the Properties window. This lets you set font characteristic like font name, font size, bold, and italics. To see how this works, change the font name to Times New Roman, the font size to 15, and turn italics on.

Add existing forms and classes from other projects

4. Use the Add Existing Item dialog box to add the frmFutureValue.cs file in the C:\C#.NET\Chapter 23\FutureValue folder to your project.
5. Use the Add Existing Item dialog box to add the class file for the Validator class from the C:\C#.NET\Chapter 23\FutureValue folder to your project.
6. Use the Add Existing Item dialog box to add the frmDepreciation.cs file in the C:\C#.NET\Chapter 23\Depreciation folder to your project.

Add the code for the startup form and fix other coding issues

7. Add code to the startup form that creates instances of the Future Value and Depreciation forms and responds to the Click events of the three buttons. (See figure 23-2 if you need help.)
8. Change the Exit button on the Future Value form to a Close button, and change the handler for the Click event of this button so it closes the form instead of exiting the application.
9. If you were to run the application at this point, you would have build errors because the three forms are in different namespaces. One way to fix this problem is to add using statements at the beginning of the startup form that import the FutureValue and Depreciation namespaces. Do that now.
10. Run and test the application. When the startup form is displayed, use it to display multiple versions of the Future Value and Depreciation forms. Make sure the Close button on each form works properly, and make sure the Exit button on the startup form closes all open forms, even if several forms are open.
11. Another way to fix the namespace problem is to change the namespaces for the FutureValue and Depreciation forms to FinancialCalculations so all three forms are in the same namespace. To test that, delete the using statements you added in step 9, change the namespaces, and run the application again.
12. Close this version of the Financial Calculations project.

Exercise 23-2 Create the MDI application

In this exercise, you'll create the MDI version of the Financial Calculations application.

Convert the SDI application to an MDI

1. Create a copy of the FinancialCalculationsSDI folder. Rename this folder FinancialCalculationsMDI and store it in the C:\C#.NET\Chapter 23 folder.
2. Display the form named frmMain in Design view and delete all controls from this form.

3. Set the IsMdiContainer property of the Financial Calculations form to True to identify it as the parent form, and resize the form so it's large enough to hold several child forms.

Add the File menu to the parent form

4. Add a MainMenu control to the form, and notice that it's displayed in the Component Designer tray at the bottom of the Form Designer. Also notice that a box with the words "Type Here" appears at the top of the form where the menu will be displayed.
5. Use the Menu Designer to add the File menu with four menu items that will display a new Future Value form, display a new Depreciation form, close the active child form, and exit from the application. Include access keys if you'd like. Use the Menu Designer to name these menu items mnuNewFutureValue, mnuNewDepreciation, mnuClose, and mnuExit. And include a separator bar between the Close and Exit items.
6. Add an event handler for the Click event of each menu item as shown in figure 23-7.
7. Delete any code that's left over from the SDI version of the application.
8. Run and test the application. You should be able to display and use multiple versions of either form, you should be able to close the active child form, and you should be able to exit the application, closing all child forms.

Add the Window menu to the parent form

9. Use the Menu Designer to add a Window menu to the right of the File menu. Then, add three items to this menu that will let the user arrange the forms in a cascaded, vertical, or horizontal layout.
10. Right-click in the Window menu and select the Edit Names command. Click on each menu item in this menu and enter an appropriate name for it.
11. Code an event handler for the Click event of each of the items in the Window menu. Each event handler should use the LayoutMdi method of the form to arrange the child forms using one of the members of the MdiLayout enumeration as shown in figure 23-7.
12. Run the application and display two or more instances of each form. Then, use the items in the Window menu to arrange the open forms.

Add the Action menu to one child form

13. Use the Menu Designer to add an Action menu to the Future Value form. Then, add the Clear and Calculate items to this menu.
14. Code the event handlers for these items as described in figure 23-5.
15. Run the application and display two or more instances of each form. Note that the Action menu is only displayed when a Future Value form is the active child form, not when a Depreciation form is the active child form.

Add a toolbar and help

16. Add a toolbar to the main form and add the Future Value and Depreciation buttons as described in figure 23-8. The two icons for the buttons are stored in the C:\C#.NET\Chapter 23 folder.
17. Add a View menu that has a checked Toolbar item. Then, write the code that uses this menu item to display and hide the toolbar as described in figure 23-9, and add the code that handles the ButtonClick event of the toolbar.
18. Add tool tips and context-sensitive help information for both the Future Value form and the Depreciation form as described in figure 23-10.
19. Run the application and test it to make sure the toolbar and the help are working properly.

Appendix A

How to install and use the software and downloadable files for this book

To develop the applications presented in this book, you need to have Visual Studio .NET or the Standard Edition of Visual C# .NET installed on your system. In addition, if you're going to develop database applications that use databases stored on your own PC rather than on a remote server, you need to install MSDE (Microsoft SQL Server Desktop Engine). This appendix describes how to install these products. It also describes the files for this book that are available for download from our web site and tells you how you can use them.

How to use the downloadable files

Throughout this book, you'll see complete applications that illustrate the material presented in each chapter. To help you understand how they work, you can download the source code and data for some of these applications from our web site. Then, you can open and run them in Visual Studio.

These files come in a single download that also includes the source code and data you'll need for the exercises at the end of each chapter. Figure A-1 describes how you download, install, and use these files.

When you download the single install file and execute it, it will install all of the files for this book in the Murach\C#.NET directory on your C drive. Within this directory, you'll find a directory named Exercise starts that contains a single directory named C#.NET that contains all of the files and directories you'll need for the exercises presented in this book. Before you use these files and directories, though, you'll want to copy (not move) the C#.NET directory that contains them to the root directory of your C drive. That way, it will be easy to locate the files and directories you need as you're working on the exercises. In addition, if you make a mistake and want to restore a file to its original state, you can do that by copying it from the directory where it was originally installed.

You'll also find a directory named Book applications within the C:\Murach\C#.NET directory. This directory contains the source code for some of the Windows applications in this book. Within this directory, you'll find chapter directories, and within the chapter directories you'll find a directory that contains the source files for each application we provide. You can use Visual Studio to open and run these applications.

You may also need to prepare your system for using the database that comes with this book. That's the case if you want to use this database on your own PC rather than using a database that has been installed on a remote server. Then, you'll need to install MSDE on your system, and you'll need to attach the database for this book to MSDE. You can learn how to do that in figure A-3.

If you're using Visual Studio .NET 2002 or Visual C# .NET 2002, please be aware that you won't be able to open applications that were developed with the 2003 versions of these products. So be sure to download the 2002 versions of our applications and exercise starts. (If you're using C# 2003, you can open either the 2002 or 2003 versions of our applications, but you're better off with the 2003 versions.)

What the downloadable files for this book contain

- The source code and data for selected applications presented in the book
- The starting source code and data for all of the exercises included in the book

How to download and install the files for this book

- Go to www.murach.com, and go to the page for *Murach's C#*.
- Click the link for "FREE download of the book applications." Then, download "All book files 2003" if you're using C# 2003 or "All book files 2002" if you're using C# 2002. This will download one file named either cshp_allfiles2003.exe or cshp_allfiles2002.exe to the root directory of your C drive.
- Use the Windows Explorer to find the install file. Then, double-click this file and respond to the dialog boxes that follow. This installs the files in directories that start with C:\Murach\C#.NET.

How to prepare your system for doing the exercises

- Some of the exercises have you start from existing projects. The source code for these projects is in the C:\Murach\C#.NET\Exercise starts directory. Before you use these projects, you'll want to copy (not move) this directory and all of its subdirectories to the root directory of the C drive. From that point on, you can find the programs and files that you need in directories like C:\C#.NET\Chapter 01, C:\ C#.NET \Chapter 02, C:\ C#.NET \Files, and C:\ C#.NET \Database.

How to use the source code for the applications presented in this book

- The source code for selected applications presented in this book can be found in chapter directories in the C:\Murach\ C#.NET \Book applications directory. You can view this source code by opening the project or solution in the appropriate directory.
- Before you can run the applications for the programs that process a data file, you'll need to prepare your system for doing the exercises as described above. That way, the files used by these programs will be in the correct directories.

How to prepare your system for using the database

- If you're going to use the database that comes with this book on your own PC, you'll need to install MSDE and then attach the database to MSDE as described in figure A-3.

Notes for Visual Studio .NET 2002 users

- If you're using Visual Studio .NET 2002 or Visual C# .NET 2002, you won't be able to open applications that have been developed with the 2003 versions. As a result, you must be sure to download the 2002 files for this book.

Figure A-1 How to use the downloadable files for this book

How to install the .NET Framework and Visual Studio .NET

If you've installed Windows applications before, you shouldn't have any trouble installing Visual Studio .NET. You simply insert the first Visual Studio CD, and the setup program starts automatically. This setup program will lead you through the steps for installing Visual Studio as summarized in figure A-2.

The first step of the installation procedure for Visual Studio .NET (or the Standard Edition of Visual C# .NET) is to install the .NET Framework and other prerequisites for Visual Studio. The second step is to install Visual Studio itself. Although you will have a variety of options for what's actually installed, it's safest to just accept the defaults unless you're familiar with the various components and know exactly what you need. The final step is to apply any updates that have become available since the product was released. Note that you can also check for updates after you exit from the setup program by using the Help→Check for Updates command in the Visual Studio menu.

The Visual Studio .NET setup program

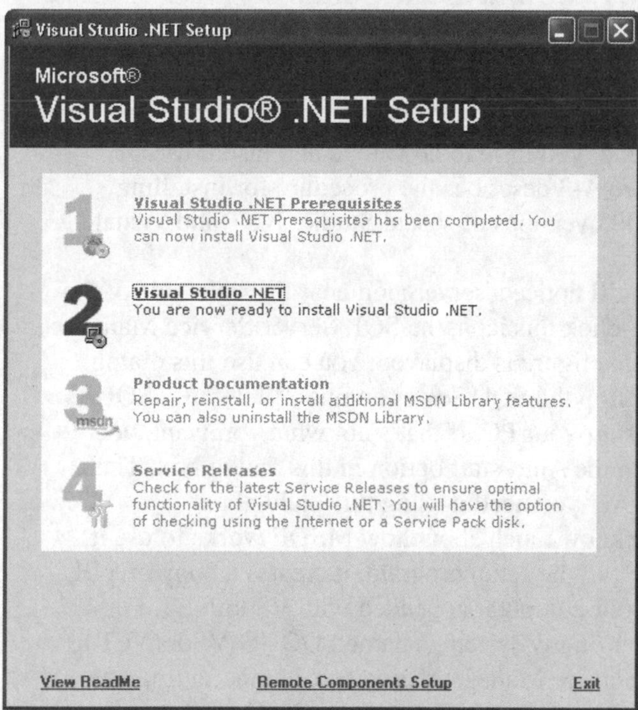

How to install Visual Studio .NET

- Insert Disc 1 of the Visual Studio .NET CDs and the setup program will start automatically.
- If the .NET Framework has not been installed on your system, you will need to install it before installing Visual Studio .NET. To do that, click the Visual Studio .NET Prerequisites link in the Setup dialog box.
- After the .NET Framework is installed, click the Visual Studio .NET link and follow the instructions to install Visual Studio .NET. When the Options page is displayed, you can usually just accept the default options unless you have special requirements.
- After you install Visual Studio .NET, click the Service Releases link to check for and install any updates that are available.

What if you're using the Standard Edition of Visual C# .NET?

- The setup program for the Standard Edition of Visual C# .NET is similar to the setup program for Visual Studio .NET, but fewer options are available on the Options page.

Figure A-2 How to install the .NET Framework and Visual Studio .NET

How to install MSDE and use it with our database

MSDE is a desktop version of Microsoft SQL Server that can be used to test database applications. MSDE came with Visual Studio .NET 2002 (and Visual C# .NET 2002), but it doesn't come with the 2003 versions of Visual Studio .NET and Visual C# .NET. Instead, you have to download and install MSDE from Microsoft's web site. Figure A-3 describes the procedure for installing MSDE for both the 2002 and 2003 versions of Visual Studio .NET and Visual C# .NET.

After you install MSDE, you'll notice a server icon near the right side of the Windows taskbar. If you double-click this icon, the SQL Server Service Manager dialog box shown at the top of this figure is displayed. You can use this dialog box to start, continue, pause, or stop the SQL Server engine. By default, SQL Server is started each time you start your PC. If that's not what you want, you can remove the check mark from the Auto-start option in this dialog box. Then, you can start SQL Server whenever you need it using this dialog box.

Although you don't need to know much about how MSDE works to use it, you should know that when you run the setup program, it creates a copy of SQL Server with the same name as your computer appended with VSdotNET. For example, the copy of SQL Server on my system is named DOUG\VSdotNET as you can see in the SQL Server Service Manager dialog box in this figure. After this server is installed and started, you can add databases to it. Then, you can create connections to those databases that you can use in your C# programs.

If you want to use the database that's available with the download for this book, you can do that without much trouble. First, you'll need to download and install the book files and then copy the C#.NET directory that's created to the root directory of your C drive as described in figure A-1. Then, you can run the batch file named DB_Attach.bat in the C:\C#.NET directory. This batch file runs a SQL Server script named DB_Attach.sql that attaches the database to the copy of SQL Server running on your computer.

Note, however, that if the copy of SQL Server on your system has a name other than the computer name appended with VSdotNET, the batch file we provide won't work. But you can easily change it so it will work. To do that, just open the file in a text editor, such as NotePad. When you do, you'll see a single command with this server specification:

```
%COMPUTERNAME%\VSdotNET
```

Then, you can just change this specification to the name of your server.

The SQL Server Service Manager

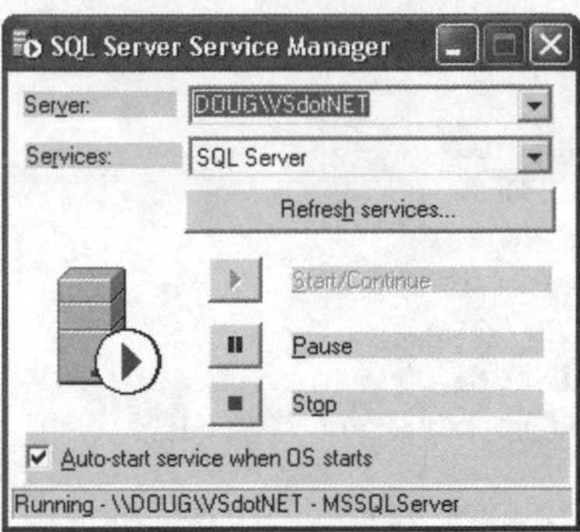

How to install and use MSDE

- If you're using Visual Studio .NET 2003, use Windows Explorer to navigate to this folder: C:\Program Files\Microsoft Visual Studio .NET 2003\Setup\MSDE. Then, double-click the msde_readme.htm document to display it in your browser. Click the link in that document to go to the Microsoft web site, and follow the directions on the page that's displayed to download and install MSDE. When you're done, restart your PC.
- If you're using Visual Studio .NET 2002, use Windows Explorer to navigate to this folder: C:\Program Files\Microsoft Visual Studio .NET\Setup\MSDE. Then, double-click the Setup.exe file to run it and install MSDE. When you're done, restart your PC. (If you didn't select the option to install MSDE when you installed Visual Studio .NET 2002, you can install it directly from Disk 3 of the distribution CDs. You'll find the setup program for MSDE in the Program Files\Microsoft Visual Studio .NET\Setup\MSDE folder.)
- After you install MSDE, SQL Server will start automatically each time you start your PC. An icon will appear near the right side of the Windows taskbar to indicate that this service is running. To manage this service, double-click the icon or select the Start→Programs→MSDE→Service Manager command to display the dialog box shown above.
- The setup program creates a copy of SQL Server with a name that consists of your computer name followed by \VSdotNET. You can use this name to define connections to the databases that you use with this server.

How to attach the database for this book to MSDE

- If you're going to use the MMABooks database used by the programs in Section 4 of this book on your own PC, you need to attach it to MSDE. To do that, you can use the batch file and SQL script that are downloaded and installed along with the other files for this book.
- To attach the database to MSDE, use the Windows Explorer to navigate to the C:\Murach\C#.NET\Database folder, and double-click the DB_Attach.bat file. That will run the batch file and attach the database.

Figure A-3 How to install MSDE and use it with our database

Index

A

D

E

F

G

H

I

Q

R

S

U

V

W

What software you need for this book

- Any version of Microsoft Visual Studio .NET or the Standard Edition of Microsoft Visual C# .NET.
- If you're going to use databases on your own PC, you need to install MSDE (Microsoft SQL Server Desktop Engine), which comes with both Visual Studio and Visual Basic 2002. For Visual Studio or Visual Basic 2003, you'll need to download the files for installing MSDE from the Microsoft web site.
- If you haven't installed these products yet, please read appendix A in this book.

The downloadable files for this book

- Complete source code and data for selected applications presented in this book
- Starting source code for many of the exercises in the book so you can get more practice in less time
- Data for the practice exercises
- Files that make it easy for you to set up the database if you're going to use your own PC as a database server

How to download the files for this book

- Go to www.murach.com, and go to the page for ***Murach's C#.***
- Click the link for "FREE download of the book applications." Then, download "All book files 2003" or "All book files 2002" based on the version of C# that you're using. This will download one file named either cshp_allfiles2003.exe or cshp_allfiles2002.exe to your C drive.
- Use the Windows Explorer to find the downloaded file. Then, double-click it and respond to the dialog boxes that follow. This installs the application files and database in folders that start with C:\Murach\C#.NET.
- From that point on, you can find the applications and data in folders like C:\Murach\C#.NET\Book applications\Chapter 03 and C:\Murach\C#.NET\Database.
- Go to appendix A for instructions on how to set up the database if it's going to reside on your own PC.